SCALING THE CORPORATE WALL

READINGS IN SOCIAL ISSUES OF THE NINETIES

S. Prakash Sethi
Baruch College
The City University of New York
and
Rochester Institute of Technology

Paul Steidlmeier
State University of New York
at Binghamton

Cecilia M. Falbe
State University of New York
at Albany

Prentice Hall, Englewood Cliffs, New Jersey 07632

Library of Congress Cataloging-in-Publication Data

Scaling the corporate wall: readings in social issues of the nineties
/[compiled by] S. Prakash Sethi, Paul Steidlmeier, Cecilia M.
Falbe.
    p. cm.
  Includes bibliographical references.
    ISBN 0-13-793340-1
    1. Industry—Social aspects—United States. 2. Business ethics—
-United States. I. Sethi, S. Prakash. II. Steidlmeier, Paul.
  III. Falbe, Cecilia M.
  HD60.5.U5S33 1990
  302.3'5'0973—dc20   90-14254
                                                          CIP

Front Cover Photo Credit: The Hennepin County Center, Minneapolis
    John Warnecke and Associates
Photo Courtesy of the Hennepin County Public Affairs Department

Editorial/production supervision and
    interior design: Fred Dahl and Rose Kernan
Cover design: Marianne Frasco
Prepress buyer: Trudy Pisciotti
Manufacturing buyer: Bob Anderson

©1991 by Prentice-Hall, Inc.
A Division of Simon & Schuster
Englewood Cliffs, New Jersey 07632

Printed in the United States of America

10 9 8 7 6 5 4 3 2 1

ISBN 0-13-793340-1

Prentice-Hall International (UK) limited, *London*
Prentice-Hall of Australia Pty. Limited, *Sydney*
Prentice-Hall Canada Inc., *Toronto*
Prentice-Hall Hispanoamericana, S.A., *Mexico*
Prentice-Hall of India Private Limited, *New Delhi*
Prentice-Hall of Japan, Inc., *Tokyo*
Simon & Schuster Asia Pte. Ltd., *Singapore*
Editora Prentice-Hall do Brasil, Ltda., *Rio de Janeiro*

Contents

Preface

Scaling the Corporate Wall brings to the reader, first, a set of analytical frameworks with which to analyze social issues and, second, a broad-based collection of current writings on issues of special concern to the field of business and society. This book of readings is designed to stand alone but it also fills the request for materials that provide background and depth for cases. As such, it also serves as a companion book of readings to a case book such as *Up against the Corporate Wall.* The readings are drawn from leaders in the field in the knowledge that they will provide insights to students as they grapple with the complexity of business society interactions.

Business and society draws from a number of fields including management, economics, political science, sociology, philosophy, ethics, and law. The section on analytical frameworks reflects this diversity. The lead-off article by Paul Steidlmeier discusses the components of an ethical approach to business and society issues. It provides a survey of the business ethics literature and outlines

the tasks of an explicitly ethical analysis of business.

Robert Harris and James Carman follow with two articles on the political economy of regulation in which they discuss the failure of the market and the subsequent failure of regulation designed to correct market failures. An article by David Silverstein describes the changing legal environment in which business/society issues are framed. Silverstein approaches the legal environment from a clear managerial perspective.

Prakash Sethi develops the concept of a "legitimacy gap" to describe a range of possible relations between business and society. He then presents a framework for classifying dimensions of corporate behavior as it evolves over stages of conflict in an industry.

The articles by Silverstein, Steidlmeier, and Sethi are moved to a different level when Bruce and Eileen Drake take the ethical and legal arguments a step further by integrating them into the management of corporate cultures.

The article by Charles Perrow traces new developments in the use of economic models in organizational analysis and then provides a critique and suggestions for extending this useful approach.

Finally, there are two pieces related to corporate performance. The first, by Jean McGuire, Alison Sundgren, and Thomas Schneeweis, takes an empirical approach to the relation of corporate social responsibility to firm financial performance. The second of these articles by John Aker, CEO of the IBM Corporation is a more qualitative discussion of the association between ethics and competitiveness.

In the special issues section, we provide readings on subjects of traditional concern in business and society relationships including the workplace, discrimination, corporate and executive liability, and the changing role of the multinational. The collection also includes works on a more recent focus of attention, the restructuring of corporate America. The themes of these articles are not specific to any particular case but rather cut across a number of cases.

A set of articles deals with the recent controversies over the restructuring of U.S. corporations. Iman Anabtawi provides the reader with a clear path through the legal maze of what constitutes insider trading, generally an important issue in mergers and acquisition. A selection from Congressional Hearings on Mergers and Acquisitions. The piece features testimony from prominent actors in the arena. Robert Mercer, CEO of Goodyear takes a negative view of hostile takeovers. Sir James Goldsmith and T. Boone Pickens candidly argue the opposite point of view. Finally, Feliz Rohatyn suggests that matters be judged on a case by case basis in the contest of certain reforms. The final article on mergers and acquisitions is an ethical reflection by Patricia Werhane. The article by Michael Jenson argues that the economic form, the public corporation, may have outlived its

usefulness. In explaining the number of corporations that have been taken private, Jensen explains that this form of organization in which there are no public shareholders resolves the traditional struggle between owners and managers.

Two articles examine the role of transnational corporations. Raymond Vernon reviews the ten years of corporate activity since the publication of his landmark article, "Sovereignty at Bay." Tom Donaldson goes on to provide a cogent ethical framework for analyzing the activities of global corporations.

Special matters of legal interest are covered in two articles. Sethi and Chopra discuss the issues involved in the corporate criminal liability and review trends in executive liability that have emerged recently. The article by Peter Shuck focuses on the ideological aspects of tort law.

Oliver Williams' article reviews the non-market forces that affect business, using examples of recent church activism in the cases of the Nestle company and U.S. firms in South Africa.

A group of articles deal with discrimination. We selected the Supreme Court decision regarding sex discrimination at Price Waterhouse. John Nalbandian reviews a number of recent decisions on affirmative action by the U.S. Supreme Court and concludes that affirmative action is not dead as some may presume. Nathan Glaser argues that there is public support for ending discrimination but public opposition to quotas and statistical goals.

Two articles deal with issues in the workplace. In an empirical article, Barbara Lawrence examines socially generated age effects, looking at the effect of age norms and age distributions on performance ratings. Robert Sass argues that employees have the right to be informed of the hazards of the work they are doing and the right to refuse hazardous work.

The collection closes with an article by

Prakash Sethi who presents a set of arguments and guidelines for participation by corporations in the political process.

This overveiw indicates the wide variety of sources from which the material in *Scaling the Corporate Wall* is drawn. We feel that bringing so many disparate sources together in one volume is a benefit in itself. We would like to thank all our various contributors for their generosity in making their work available. We recognize that there are many works of high quality that are not represented here. Authors always are forced to make difficult choices. These choices were guided by considerations of diversity, representativeness as well as "fit" with popular case material, especially as represented in *Up against the Corporate Wall.*

S. Prakash Sethi
Paul Steidlmeier
Cecilia M. Falbe

I

Analytical Framework

1

An Ethical Framework for Management

Paul Steidlmeier

SUNY — Binghamton

Some 2,400 years ago, the Greek philosopher Socrates was forced to commit suicide by drinking hemlock. His story told in *The Apology* by Plato, has inspired Western ethical thought ever since. In the view of his fellow Athenians Socrates's crime was that he undermined the established values of the day. For his part, Socrates protested that he was simply searching for the truth and a morally good life. Socrates maintained that the "unexamined life is not worth living." His examination took the form of questioning the difference between peoples' opinions (doxa) about what was humanly fulfilling and correct understanding (episteme) of that reality. He exposed the leaders of the day for acting out of mere expediency rather than out of commitment to the truth. According to Socrates, they were sophists or purveyors of false "wisdom." Three things about Socrates' legacy are worth noting. First, ethics for him was essentially a positive search for the good life (where one strives to act in accord with the truth). Second, he was neither a dogmatist nor content with what he already knew. Rather, he was a relentless questioner and searcher for

wisdom; (hence the term "philosopher"—a lover of wisdom). Third, he was committed to dialogue and talking matters through with those who saw things differently. These three points are relevant to management ethics today.

Socrates' spirit of critical inquiry provides my starting point for discussing business ethics. Ethics in my view is essentially positive and creative, searching out the truth of what human fulfillment means and then embracing it in action. For Socrates, such was the essence of the good moral life; his orientation was furthered by Plato and Aristotle. Following Aristotle (*Nichomachean Ethics*, Book VI), moral concerns are essentially practical and seek to realize the full flowering of the human person, excellence in the actualization of human capacity. In this context the discussion of moral virtues and vices takes place. The former represent life-giving patterns of behavior while the latter are essentially destructive of the person and community. Unfortunately, most discussions of business ethics today have concentrated on the latter. Business ethics is often negative and guilt-ridden, focusing on vices, rather than positively attempting to delineate paths of virtue. In concentrating on what should not be, no clear positive and creative vision has emerged of what should be.

Why has business ethics taken such a negative turn? How might the state of the question be fruitfully transformed? How might the social activity of business ethics be structured in a positive ethical framework? Why is it that a good deal of business ethics discussions are needlessly defensive and dogmatic?

Such questions provide the focus of this essay. I approach them by considering

1. the historical background to the contemporary business ethics question;

2. the search for an ethical framework;

3. an analysis of business activities in terms of economic values;

4. a probing of these same activities in terms of values of human development; and

5. processes of business ethics defined as precisely a social activity.

1. HISTORICAL BACKGROUND TO THE CONTEMPORARY "BUSINESS ETHICS" QUESTION

At the very time business ethics is becoming more established in academic circles and in management training seminars, a crisis is emerging regarding its foundations. There are several reasons for this.

First, business is dynamic and rapidly changing and it is often unclear what exactly we are talking about when we use the term business ethics. The problem is that a good deal of business ethics discourse is cast in static terms. We talk of labor, stockholders, consumers, and so forth without adequately considering how dynamically these stakeholder configurations are changing over the years. In Western civilization, there is a long

tradition of questioning business activities. Ethical treatises on private property, just prices, just wages, usury, and so forth are well known. These themes obviously touch the same stakeholder issues of owners, consumers and workers which we discuss today. However, the thrust of contemporary business ethics has special characteristics of its own. For example, discussions of the rights of property owners are not primarily focused on small businesses and shopkeepers. Rather the emphasis falls on the large corporation (big business). For its part, the corporation, especially since 1945, is a new type of social agent, quite distinct from any form of property that preceded it.

The term "business" does not mean the same thing in 1990 as it did in the times of Smith (1800s), Calvin (1600s), Aquinas (1200s), Augustine (400s), the beginnings of Christianity (100s), or the period of Socrates (500 B.C.). Likewise, the structural institutionalization of property, prices, interest, and markets and stakeholders have all changed dramatically. While much is to be learned from philosophical tradition, the ethical account of property in 990, for example, cannot be directly applied to the ethics of property in 1990. Nonhistorical approaches to such issues characterize many orthodox capitalists as well as socialists. We speak of "stockholders" as if the word has consistently meant the same thing for the past two hundred years. Such approaches are necessarily wide of the mark.

Second, modern business, as a new type of *large complex organization* (LCO), has had a hard time gaining social moral approval. It has never overcome the public's lurking suspicion of selfish profiteering and dirty tricks. Other large, complex organizations (for example, churches) have by no means been free of social injustices. Churches have mounted many a holy war and imposed inquisitorial discipline. Nation states have committed every imaginable excess in the name of patriotism, manifest destiny, and so forth. Strange

to say, these LCOs have found social legitimation an easier task than businesses have,
for they ennoble their causes in terms of self-
transcendence and a manifestly greater good.
They have saints and heroes; business has not
been so fortunate.

The issue here is the ultimate philosophical basis of legitimate authority and economic
power in society. Robert Nisbet (1977) put the
matter clearly from the business point of
view:

"One of the persistent mysteries of Western intellectual history has been the question of why capitalism, with its unique record in the production of goods and
services and its utterly vital role in making
possible the liberal democracies of the
West, has been almost from its beginning
the object of continuing attack. Why from
the outset was it faced with the radical
question of whether it could continue to
justify itself by spreading the employment
of goods it was able to produce to the great
mass of mankind? ... There are
exceptions—Adam Smith preeminent—
but ... down to the present the prevailing
attitude of intellectuals toward businessmen and what they do has been negative.
It has ranged from contempt and carica-
ture to outright hostility and attack. With
today's big and growing government effectively in the hands of the intellectuals who
dominate congressional, judicial, and presidential staffs, we may expect this attitude
to become more rather than less evident.
(p. 28)"

Nisbet's statement points out the notable
success of the capitalist system. However, he
does not give equal time to some of the negative social relations that accompanied its development (colonialism, the slave trade, the
exploitation of workers). For all the good
points of capitalism, there are also problems:
power abuse, persistent losers in the system,

pollution and so forth. I would add the historical problems of capitalism to Nisbet's statement while at the same time stating that the
problems of capitalism are not exclusive to
this system while other systems occupy the
high moral ground. That is clearly not the
case. However, if the contributions of the
system are to be taken seriously, so are its
defects. Capitalism is not well served by
crude propaganda; value questions are best
faced head on. Some businessmen would
maintain that market values and ethical
values are mutually exclusive realms. Other
recognize only the positive aspect of a market
system and ignore the negative. Such approaches are necessarily incomplete. They
contribute to the result that the modern corporation lacks social legitimization.

This raises a third historical point. With
the evolution of the modern corporation in
the 1800s, business ethics has been very
much historically intertwined with the law.
The avalanche of business related legislation
from the end of the Civil War to the present
clearly attests to this fact. There are two problems with associating business ethics too
closely with the law:

1. the law is taken as a proxy for ethics so that
   whatever is legal is thought to be all right;
   and
2. the legal approach reinforces an approach
   to ethics which is essentially negative:
   ethics is about what is forbidden.

While the law is an important aspect of business ethics, it does not represent an adequate
guide to moral behavior.

Fourth, business ethics today is rooted in
an analytical apparatus which is inadequate
to understand human motivation. It is dominated by a rational model of a person's economic motivation: the economic person is a
rational, self-interested, isolated individual,
who first computes prospective economic

benefits and costs, and then chooses freely and rationally between alternative courses of action. Hirschman (1985) and Hosmer (1984) have rightly criticized this model of human behavior as too reductive. Much of business activity is rooted in parable and symbol rather than critical and rational thought and it seeks more than simple economic gain. The dreams and stories of the hardworking, thrifty workers, entrepreneurs, frontier people, and other heroes of the marketplace are well known. More than calculating individual economic self-interest is at stake. Many non-economic motives of community, status and commitment must also be considered. This is important, for socially responsible business policy must be based on a broader view of human motivation if it is ever to be implemented.

Fifth, together with the rational model and the myths of the economic person, one finds the analogy of business activities to individual behavior. Drucker (1981) maintains that there is no ethics but individual ethics. Coye (1986) takes a similar approach but gives more attention to the corporation as an environment that is conducive or not conducive to individual morality. Others have recourse to legal tradition. Goodpastor and Matthews (1982) explore the analogy of the corporation and the moral person and succeed in clarifying its logical meaning. However helpful these thinkers are in clarifying the terms, their approaches remain too individualistic. In the nineteenth century there was, perhaps, more logic to the analogy of the corporation as a moral person, but less so today. While it may be legally useful, it obscures the nature of responsibility in cooperative human actions. In the end, the reduction of business ethics to a framework modeled on individual choice leads to hopeless confusion and loses any significant sense of social ethics. Social ethics is not mere individual concern about social issues (individual actions that affect others), but socially structured reflection, dialogue,

and action. As will be discussed later, many moral agents are involved in an interactive social process. Unless the social rather than individual nature of business ethics is addressed, the true meaning of economic freedom and competition in a social sense will be missed.

Sixth, there is a tendency to view business as off by itself. In such an analytical apparatus a narrow vision of the social contract is operative. The world of owners, managers, suppliers and customers is hypothetically imagined as if it could exist in a state hermetically sealed off from the rest of society. Society is then viewed as an "environment" in which business operates and something it must manage, rather than as part of the business' and business peoples' core personal identity. This issue is very important when one considers the problem of whether people are to be committed to improving the quality of society. If society is a "they" rather than a "we," such commitment will not materialize.

Finally, among discussions of "business ethics" there is no consensus on what the term means. In interviewing many business people and academics as well as surveying over 150 textbooks, Lewis (1985) has demonstrated that there is little agreement on either precise norms or delineation of responsibilities.

II. THE SEARCH FOR AN ETHICAL FRAMEWORK

The last point mentioned above essentially summarizes the breakdown of communication which afflicts contemporary business ethics. The focus of this section is to attempt to put together an analytical framework which addresses that issue. As I see it the basic tasks of ethics are straightforward: to see what is happening, to make a moral judgment and to act. These general tasks are summarized in Table One.

TABLE 1. The Ethical Tasks.

Ethical Processes	Points of Reflection
SEE	the system's rules of the game a business' policies an individual's actions
JUDGE	the end sought the means taken the consequences
ACT	who does what when and where how: process, oversight

"Seeing" in this context is essentially empirical and historical. The point is to arrive at a conclusion regarding what is happening. This can be the rules of the game in the system called *apartheid,* the labor policies of a company such as Iowa Beef Processors, or the action of an individual such as Ivan Boesky. Frequently, the systems, institutional and individual levels of "seeing" are combined in any particular moral social event such as insider trading.

"Juding" in an ethical sense reflects upon the moral acceptability of the ends sought, the means used, and the consequences of a system's rules, an institution's policies or an individual's actions. The judgment spans the moral agent(s) as well as all who are affected (that is, have a stake) in their decisions. Judgment reaches a conclusion: "X" is good or bad.

"Action" expresses the practical nature of ethics. It reflects the free choice of people, whether individually or collectively, to do what is good an avoid what is evil. Selecting the appropriate moral action is not at all easy. Presuppose that people agree that apartheid is wrong. How to overcome it is not clear. Those against apartheid are precisely divided between those who want the business community to withdraw investment and trade from South Africa and those who see it as one of the more progressive forces in that society and want it to remain to exercise leverage (Hennessey 1985; Williams 1985). Ethics is a creative and practical art. Great care must be

exercised to that proposed solutions are not worse than the evil they are trying to eliminate—the aftermath of many modern revolutions clearly attests to this. To conclude, moral actions should be grounded in solid methods of reasoning. In addition, they should be technologically feasible and systems-manageable. Those are difficult qualities to assure. For, on the practical level, ethical action only can be approached in terms of probabilities and in an experimental fashion.

Who is it who is doing the seeing, judging and acting is of vital importance. The most obvious answer to who performs these activities is any stakeholder—that is, any person or group whose actions or policies form part of the whole. In the case of *apartheid,* the participants and process became clearly global; the GM plant closing in Norwood, Ohio, on the other hand was more local. In either case, however, the ethical process is decidedly *social* and is open to anyone who is either a direct or indirect stakeholder in the event under consideration. Furthermore, it is also open to men and women of conscience, who may begin as outside observers but who, in the end, are not content to remain bystanders. Finally, it is clearly relevant to the whole process whether those involved in this ethical process are biased or not—that will be discussed in the next section for it is relevant to why different observers fail to agree when ostensibly analyzing the same facts.

III. THE CONFUSION OF CONTEMPORARY PHILOSOPHY: ARE THERE ANY NORMS?

Most business ethics tests present a buffet of ethical theories that are not harmonious with each other. The analytical tasks in business ethics are straightforward: to see what is happening, to make a moral judgment and to act. These activities presuppose clear norms.

The "scandal of philosophy," as nineteenth century thinkers put it, is that philosophers, over a span of thousands of years, have been unable to reach any uncontestable conclusions regarding norms of ethical behavior. That is, there is no sure guide to seeing, judging, and acting. Such a state of affairs has only hastened the appeal of businesspeople to legal norms, on the one hand, and introduced a sort of intuitive relativism in moral judgment, on the other (Donaldson and Werhane 1983, pp. 19–21).

Academic philsophy provides no sure guide. In many ways, it is in a sort of crisis of its own. It has more and more become an academie discipline in its own right, focusing on textual and historical studies, logic, and methodology. The result, more often than not, is learned footnotes about philosophers rather than philosophy. There is merit to such scholarly endeavors, of course, but in the meantime philsophy as a social activity where people reflectively search out the meaning of human experience—specifically in areas such as business, medicine, law, and so forth—has suffered.

The confusion generated by competing contemporary schools of philosophy is somewhat derived from false premises: that philosophy is primarily an academic discipline and that it should, in fact, provide fixed principles or a blueprint for human behavior. Those scandalized by the lack of a blueprint or consensus suffer from false expectations. They treat life (and being) more as a problem to be solved by techniques rather than as a mystery whose meaning is to be searched out, and creatively, as well as continually, reshaped in freedom. In my view the essence of philosophy is precisely to challenge the legitimacy of consensus rather than to provide it. Such an approach to philosophy is dynamic, as the root meaning of the word ("love of wisdom") suggests. Philosophy comprises a human search for meaning and, therefore, will always inherently be unfinished. This means that business ethics is not cut and dry. It is as much searching as it is finding.

Ethical reflection represents a dynamic human activity that is moored to floating reference points. These reference points (Table Two) provide the general reasons why ethicians perenially reach different conclusions regarding ethical values and obligations.

The empirical and historical assessment of what is happening is often at the root of differing ethical perceptions. In the case of smoking much of the subsequent moral argument hinges on the scientific evidence regarding the consequences of smoking on health and productivity. Similarly, in South Africa the different protagonists give distinctly differing historical accounts of their settlement of the land and their "rights."

Such assessment of "fact" is clearly linked to possible loyalties or biases of observers. The sources of such bias are manifold, ranging from individual to collective, from ratio-

TABLE 2. Sources of Differing Ethical Perceptions Among Observers.

Frame of Reference	Example
EMPIRICAL AND HISTORICAL	in the cases of comparable worth does the market discriminate?
LOYALTIES	perceptions of Afrikaaners vs. those of Zulus in evaluating apartheid
WORLDVIEW	Marxist vs. Islamic fundamentalism
METHODS OF REASONING	opinion-poll ethics vs. Kantian "transcendental" ethics of universal principles

Paul Steidlmeier

nal to non-verbal and symbolic. Moral analysis must explicitly confront the possibility of bias. One way of resolving such issues may be to invite the participation of independent and non-aligned third parties who might then arbitrate disputes.

The worldview of the participants is a matter of major importance. By worldview I mean one's perception of ultimate reality and meaning. This perception provides the rationale for moral goals guiding the inquiry of people. Worldview would help explain the differences in moral perception between the Ayotollah Khomeini and Ronald Reagan. Worldview points to the philosophical or religious quest for so-called "first principles" to which philosophers from Aristotle, to Augustine, Aquinas, Descartes, Kant, and Hegel, and contemporary thinkers have devoted themselves.

The point is that ethical inquiry is itself rooted in a grounding vision of human flourishing. The traditions of Western civilization (rooted as they are in Greco-Roman and Judaeo—Christian thought) present a grounding vision of personal excellence within community (emphasizing friendship, fellowship, justice, and the common good). The ethical quest for "first principles" in ethics is part of what is called ontology or metaphysics, the study of ultimate reality and meaning. It is more than a curiosity that in contemporary United States society these terms are popularly associated with magic and the occult. The neglect of grounding worldview in much of business ethics today means that it is characterized by what Heidegger called "the forgetfulness of being." Ethical discourse is reduced to opinion polls and behavioral surveys. It is unmoored from any sense of ultimate reality and fulfillment. These issues are not easy: the issue is the justification of one's ethical position (Goodpastor, 1985).

At this point I wish to emphasize that worldview is a reference point of pivotal importance in business ethics. In business ethics all ethical statements have an implicit worldview. Different worldviews lead to different moral imperatives for human behavior. For moral behavior is precisely seen as achieving some sort of excellence and actualization of ultimate reality. For example, caste discrimination in India is only intolerable if one believes in the fundamental dignity of all persons, either because all are children of God (a theological reason), or members of the same species (a philsophical reason). If one believes in reincarnation and an ontology that yields a caste structure of human interaction, then there is no moral imperative to give everyone equal social consideration. The issue will only be resolved by changing the foundations of worldview. Changing the country's constitution is not sufficient to effect change.

A final pivotal reference point of business ethics is found in accepted methods of reasoning. How does one figure out what sort of activities are good and bad (with reference to worldview?) Here theological and philosophical methodologies are often in sharp contrast, as are historical and behaviorist social science approaches. Many religious groups as well as utopian movements and political parties have solved the issue for the masses through the imposition of authority and discipline. Critical ethicians, however, want to know the logic of decision making. They want to know the reasons why. Concretely, in stating the facts and proposing moral solutions, they want to know what attention is paid to:

1. empirical analysis of behavior;
2. historical analysis and symbolic modes of expression; and
3. rational critical analysis.

For example, in the South African example of apartheid, the behaviorist-empirical approach will yield a model of behavior between the races and ethnic groups as well as a statistical profile of those observed. It can yield a profile of attitudes regarding acceptable behavior. But there is much more to the "fact" of apartheid. Narrative-historical method changes the picture. Afrikaaners tell their history of settling the land before others. Their stories and heroes, their symbolizations of themselves (as bearers of a certain civilization) and others, are an intrinsic part of the facts. While Zulus may agree with them on an empirical study, on narrative-historical levels they will present a widely different set of facts. The contrast is precisely over the genesis and meaning of the "facts."

Meaning is also gone over from a critical-rational point of view. This approach mediates the concrete reality with ultimate reality and worldview. Hence, for Christian Afrikaaners apartheid is grounded in a particular theology of creation that justifies the separation of the races. Those who object to apartheid cite precisely contradictions in principle between Christian ideals of equality and fellowship, on the one hand, and systematic discrimination, on the other. The position of foes of apartheid can be put in syllogistic form:

All persons posses equal dignity in community as children of God. Apartheid treats people as things and denies their dignity. Therefore, apartheid should be abolished.

By contrast, those who favor apartheid precisely understand the dignity of people(s) in a radically different way; thus, they can argue for its legitimacy.

Ethics in general, and business ethics in particular are dynamic and practical in the sense just discussed. What follows about the nature of business ethics? First, it deals with probabilities. Dealing with probabilities does not mean that people are not knowledgeable. Rather, their knowledge is not exhaustive and is subject to a certain range of variability as unknown factors became known. Second,

business ethics is primarily a social process of communal reflection on the adequacy of worldviews, methods of reasoning, and proposed courses of action. It continually focuses on all these reference points in processes of public dialogue. Third, the task of ethics is not merely eliminating evil (liberation) but creatively imagining alternatives and bringing them to be. Ethicians cannot remain content with denunciation of evil—that is the easiest part. They must become artisans of a new order. Fourth, as a form of communal action, the primary object of business ethics is to change the rules of the game by which society is ordered and the policies by which institutions are guided. In doing so, business ethics is really a process of social change, which entails a wide variety of agents and related responsibilities, actions, and outcomes. With apartheid, the change affects not only business, but all of politics and culture. The agents are international, national, and grass roots. They range from politicians and business leaders to church leaders, the press, and ethnic leaders, each with their own responsibilities. The actions engaged include legal reforms, boycotts, protest, and intellectual studies. There are multiple outcomes, ranging from a new geopolitical situation to changing economic structures.

IV. BUSINESS ACTIVITIES AND ECONOMIC VALUES

Business and economics have firm (but often unacknowledged) roots in philosophy. These roots become clear in the discussion of values. Both capitalist and socialist economic theories clearly relate economic values and human well-being. In this section, I clarify the corporation's social role with respect to economic values.

As Samuelson (1978) points out in his introduction to economics, any economic system addresses itself to three fundamental questions: what to produce, how to produce it, and for whom. The basic functions of a corporation in society directly affect the way these questions are answered in an economic system. A corporation, after all, does not operate in a vacuum but in the social context of government, interest groups, and consumer demands. Responsibility is accordingly shared for how the fundamental questions are answered. The individual enterprise is to be held accountable according to the measure of its actual participation in society and share in power and authority.

In determining its market line and deciding what to produce, a corporation performs the economic function of allocating scarce resources for a particular purpose in view of perceived demand. Thus, an enterprise may allocate resources for luxury cars rather than buses. Clearly, demand is not the same as needs. Demand represents the goods and services consumers seek, are willing to pay for, and do pay for.

Two principal issues are involved in the production of required goods and services in an economic system. First is the macroeconomic issue of how the economic system itself is organized. What are the *rules of the game* which govern resource accumulation, allocation and exchange? We generally characterize a system by whether it is socialist or predominantly private enterprise. The other principal issue is the microecnomic aspect of the problem: what are the *policies* which guide the firm? For example: what commodity shall the firm produce?, with what technology?, how are customers, workers and so forth to be treated? As a stream of goods and services is generated in an economic system, it is appropriate to ask for whose benefit they are generated and to examine the general distribution of economic benefits and costs in the corresponding society. This leads to an examination of stakeholders from two points of view: 1) as stakeholders in the system and 2) as stakeholders in the business enterprise.

The important issue with respect to the business enterprise, therefore, is to determine appropriate criteria for analyzing a corporation's social responsibility as the corporation addresses the three questions of what to produce, how to produce it, and for whom.

What is it fair to ask of a corporation? Business has traditionally responded by pointing to its economic efficiency, a concept that encompasses both technical and price/cost aspects (Friedman 1962, p. 133). The (physical) technical aspect of efficiency demands that the production process of any business get the most out of a fixed set of resources. Thus it measures output per unit of input: tons of wheat produced per hectare, per labor hour, per dollar of capital investment. But it also refers to the way the product itself generates goods and services. For example, one corporation may produce a car that goes 40 miles per gallon of gas, while another produces a similar car that goes 15 miles per gallon of gas. Obviously, the first car is more efficient in the way it uses fuel. It is fair and reasonable to ask corporations in both the private and the public sector to allocate scarce resources in the most efficient manner—a manner that optimizes the input-output relation both in the production process itself and in the performance of the product. This is an important aspect of business social responsibility.

The price/cost aspect of efficiency calls for making the most profit out of a given fixed output or spending the least possible amount of money to produce it. Profit maximization and cost minimization are related but not identical goals. At any rate, in price/cost efficiencies the amount of output remains fixed, and one then compares cost or profit per unit with other possible ways of producing the product. An example of this sort of efficiency is found in the international steel industry. Whereas some U.S. interests claim that the Japanese are "dumping" steel, the Japanese claim that it is not simply a matter of marketing strategy, but rather they are more price-efficient; that is, they can produce a ton of steel at less cost because their plants are technologically superior to U.S. plants. The notion of price/cost efficiencies means that one cannot simply focus on increasing gross output. Neglecting such efficiencies would mean higher costs for consumers, reduced investment for jobs, and less tax revenue. Likewise, this is an important aspect of business social responsibility.

To summarize the above one of the most important aspects of business social responsibility is precisely to run an efficient enterprise that meets consumer demands and treats people fairly in the process. The latter point needs more discussion.

V. BUSINESS ACTIVITIES AND VALUES OF HUMAN DEVELOPMENT

Given a view of social relations in which market values and ethical values coexist, one can discern a wide variety of problems that surface in the marketplace (Blostrom 1975; Donaldson and Werhane 1983; Luthans and Hodgetts 1976; Sethi 1982; Sturdivant 1985). The problems are categorized as follows. First, is consumerism, which deals with such matters as deceptive advertising, pricing policy, product quality, safety, service, and issues of fraud. Second, is the issue of resource use and the environment, where the focus is on pollution and waste of scarce resources through inefficient or frivolous use. Third, are issues affecting labor, such as job safety, wages, worker welfare and pensions, job security, meaningfulness of work, and the export of jobs abroad. Fourth, is the issue of responsibility of shareholders regarding such issues as investment in South Africa. Fifth, there are problems related to poverty and social inequality: in the cities the issues are the obsolescence of urban capital, urban poverty, the corporations' relations to local govern-

ments; in the regional scene the issues are plant location and abandonment, profiteering, transfer pricing, technology transfer, and job creation. Sixth, is the perversion of the public purpose through bribery, fraud, tax evasion, misallocation of resources, and exploitative development. Seventh, there is the issue of industrial democracy or codetermination of economic structures by workers and management. Finally, there are problems of equal opportunity and compensation as related to social discrimination based on race, sex, or creed.

In all these problems in the marketplace, two general groupings emerge:

1. business actions that cause social-ethical problems (for example, pollution); and
2. problems caused by society (for example, poverty and discrimination) in which business is a significant social agent. It is one thing to identify problem areas and another to come up with solutions.

Both tasks can be quite formidable.

Ethicians must be precise about what social ends and goals are being sought, and what are fair expectations of business in achieving them. I make an approach to these issues by first reviewing the business literature and then setting forth my own position. Traditional market economics is not devoid of an ethical position. The content of liberal ethics is frequently cast in terms of a business creed (Cavanagh 1972, Chapter 2). Several values lie at the heart of the traditional approach. The ethical rules that developed from them tended to focus on seven issues:

1. protecting the interests of property owners by promoting efficiency, reducing costs, and thereby increasing profits;
2. encouraging respect for the rights of private property;
3. refraining from anti-competitive practices;

4. guarding the freedom of labor, owners, and consumers, and discouraging government interference;

5. honoring contracts and refraining from fraud or coercion;

6. developing personal honesty, responsibility, and industriousness;

7. encouraging private contributions to charity.

This ethic was and is enormously appealing to the dominant North American cultural view of reality for a simple reason: the historical forces that created the ethic were the same forces that molded American traditions (Bellah et al. 1985, Chapter 2). The stress on the importance of profit and competition, for example, goes back to the social Darwinists and to the eighteenth-century economist Adam Smith. The values of individual freedom and minimal government interference can be traced to Mill and Bentham in the eighteenth century and to Locke and Hobbes in the seventeenth. The virtues of the work ethic have their sources in the early New England Puritan settlers, a group that in turn sprang out of the Protestant Reformation. The importance of charitable contributions derives from Judaeo—Christian scriptures, which urge a concern for the poor, the orphaned, the widowed, and the oppressed. The emphasis on honoring contracts is deeply rooted in the common law and Roman law traditions out of which North American legal institutions grew.

The private enterprise system has profound roots in narrative traditions that serve to legitimate the system. The great hero in North America is the self-made person who by hard work and thrift improves his/her life prospects. The moral integrity of the market system manifests itself in the story of the frontier and the land of opportunity, in consumer sovereignty and dollar votes, in the myth of progress and the American way of life, in the legend of God's blessing of America. There are stories, however, of questionable morals that never entered the mainstream: the Indians' stories of their homeland was drowned out by the white story of the frontier and development, the stories of the slaves by the claims of manifest destiny, the stories of the sufferings of the coal miners by the myth of progress.

Even granting historical ambiguities and inconsistencies, the traditional business creed has profound historical, religious, and philosophical roots. Because this view is so deeply ingrained in American thought, it has an almost irresistible appeal. Why, then, is it being questioned even within business circles? Quite simply, a new generation of businesspeople are admitting openly that their private decisions have some profound public effects, and they realize that it is not in their long-term political and economic interests to ignore them (O'Toole 1979; Bower 1983).

The main problem with the traditional creed is found in assumptions made about social power. Even if one turns to classical economic theory, one does not find any significant account of power in social relations. In classical economic thought the very theory of the marketplace assumed that power was not a problem; it assumed that competition was perfect and that power (over prices, market access, information, and so forth) was, therefore, fairly equally distributed. Should problems have arisen due to dysfunctions, then it was assumed that power abuses would have been held in check by the countervailing system of civil authority or by the particular Christian social conscience that characterized nineteenth-century western social values.

In neoclassical economic thought, power in the marketplace is circumscribed by very much the same assumptions. Yet the social conscience permeating the fabric of society has changed and become, behaviorally at least, more pragmatic, individualistic, and utilitarian. The traditional values of nineteenth-century Western Christianity have become more eroded in a pluralistic and increasingly secular society. That is, worldview has changed. Traditional sociocultural constraints on economic power abuse have become ineffective. Other restraints have increasingly come into existence. If one examines the history of business in the United States in the last one hundred years, it is clear that the checks on power and the redressing of social injustices have resided in legal force rather than in voluntary restraints.

Contemporary business circles are correctly preoccupied with their legal environment. Business circles understand power better than economic theorists, who assume power is no problem. Indeed, Mintzberg (1983) makes the case for corporate social responsibility in terms of self-interest, sound investment policy, and, more important, the likelihood of future government interference.

The issue is the moral quality of the market system. As George Lodge has pointed out, among business people there is an increasing recognition that a new business ideology must evolve to match the social power of business (Lodge 1975; Goodpaster 1985; Chamberlain 1977). The market is not hermetically sealed off from society; in terms of its power business is seen as having an even wider social contract with the public regarding overall social priorities. Accordingly, business tries to be a "good citizen" on the basis of what it sees as the mutual self-interest it shares with larger segments of society. This new business ideology, variously called the managerial model and corporatism (O'Toole 1979), profoundly believes in private enterprise and in the institutions of market and corporation. Furthermore, it sees the corporation as both the most efficient manager possible of economic resources and as a good citizen in helping to resolve broader social problems. The corporation's primary responsibility, however, remains economic effi-

ciency in attending to its business, its primary mission. Its execution of broader social responsibilities is understood by analogy to a system of taxation. Within a framework of social benefits and costs that accrue to all, members of society are all to do their part with social burdens distributed fairly. It is tacitly assumed that those with more abilities (managers) might do more with appropriate compensation.

However, in contemporary society there is a chorus of dissent even to this model of corporate social responsibility. It is difficult to generalize about protests, because they range from socialism to religious communitarian ethics, but two major configurations have emerged: ecohumanism and egalitarianism.

Those of a socialist persuasion, exemplified in North America by people such as Michael Harrington, have never accepted the logic of business in either the traditional or corporatist form. For them the issue turns to equality—equality of opportunity and equality in distribution. What they suggest is a refashioned notion of social justice based on new patterns of social participation and resource distribution. This call has been taken up by various groups, although not all have the same agendas. Under the label of humanism one sees the "green movement" of ecology and environment that puts emphasis on the physical quality of life and the benefits of appropriate technology and small-scale participation by all in society, as opposed to vast bureaucratic forms of management. Under this label there are also forms of humanist-communitarian ethics based on more explicit notions of social justice and the overall development of the person. Whereas all of these various groups express quite different viewpoints, they all pose the fundamental problem of social justice and emphasize new distributions of power in society.

Social justice (in distinction from mere economic efficiency) deals with much more than a firm and its technical economic performance. Social justice takes a broad view of the entire exchange system and judges the interrelations among the goals, structures, and functions of a firm and the goals, structures, and functions of other groups and persons in society as a whole. Herein lies a difficulty. The general definitions of technical and price/costs efficiencies have gained wide acceptance in our society. However, in the world today, with its many views of ultimate reality, personal meaning, and cultural values, the concept of justice remains decidedly pluralistic. In the business literature one does not find a general explanation of social justice and responsibility on which all agree.

Communitarian approaches to social justice in modern times have generally regarded strict economic efficiency as a necessary but not sufficient condition of general economic justice. The task is to creatively think through problems in terms of the ethical values people seek to realize.

The question of social justice is very complex. The language of moral analysis is by no means standard. Values underpinning the criteria of justice in contemporary society are quite pluralistic. My worldview is rooted in Judaeo-Christian traditions as well as Aristotelian traditions and contractarian thought. As an illustrative example of an ethical framework, I sketch some of its principal elements in Table Three.

In this ethical framework, there is a movement of thought out of commitment to a worldview to:

1. a general orientation, and then to
2. more precise principles (such as those of justice), and finally to
3. very specific prescriptions of right moral action, such as the imperative to defeat apartheid in South Africa and to do so by withdrawing investment.

TABLE 3. Elements of a Communitarian Ethical Framework.

I. The Grounding Worldview	
GENERAL ORIENTATION:	individual flourishing in community
GROUNDING NOTIONS:	individual dignity common good sharing of the goods of the earth
II. Moral Norms	
GENERAL MORAL NORMS	do no harm do good
PRESCRIPTIVE MORAL NORMS:	specific human rights and duties, expressed in principles of justice
	Generally:
	self-determination opportunity due process in conflict resolution fair distribution duties to contribute
	Specifically:
	keeping one's word in contracts honesty
FROM NORMS TO ACTION:	Examples:
	get out of South Africa new rules of disclosure to prevent insider trading

My approach embodies a communitarian ethic (in contrast to individualism, emotivism, or utilitarianism). The guiding worldview expresses general norms such as not to harm others and to do good to others. The reasons for not doing harm as well as doing good when able to are grounded in an ideal of community. Malfeasance destroys community. At the same time the building up of a community characterized by love, justice, and peace calls for beneficent actions. Related to this general worldview are three other considerations. These are that the goods of the earth belong to all, that there is an inalienable dignity of the person, and that the flourishing of people is expressed in a common good. Each of these notions has sparked the development of a considerable body of philosophical and theological literature too extensive to explore adequately here. I state my position as a conclusion of a long reflective process.

The above orientation is made more concrete when one turns to focus to prescriptive ethics. This sort of discourse is specific and delineates human rights and duties which must be respected. I summarize this thrust under the rubric of justice. In speaking of justice what concrete questions are to be faced? In justice discourse there is, first of all, an underlying question of general social equality and the legitimacy of social differences: do all persons and peoples deserve the same social consideration and treatment? The question is whether all persons and peoples are truly subjects of their political and economic structures and institutions or merely subject to them. My position is decidedly anti-discriminatory: that all persons and peoples do deserve the same social consideration and treatment. The reasons are based on the worldview just discussed. The point to underline is this: those of different worldviews will arrive at differing prescriptive stances of ethics. If consensus is to be built all of these issues must be thrashed out.

Equal social treatment of all raises themes that one finds recurrent in contemporary literature: liberty versus dependency; participation versus emargination; meeting needs versus deprivation; the duty to contribute to the common good versus apathy or unconcern; and due legal process versus arbitrary processes of sanctions and rewards. Each point poses a different question of general social equality. The positive content of the notion of justice can be made more specific in terms of these themes.

Liberty versus Dependence

Are all persons and peoples to enjoy the same degree of liberty and self-determination? My approach to community affirms the rights of peoples, and of individuals and groups within peoples, to self-determination. The argument is based on the fundamental dignity of the person. In this way the freedom of the oppressed and dependent takes priority over the licentious liberty of the powerful.

Participation versus Emargination

Are all persons and peoples to enjoy the same opportunities to participate in social structures? Emargination denies individuals and groups equal opportunity and the right to participate fully in political, economic, and social life. Pushed to the edges of these social structures and institutions, the emarginated must endure all the duties and strictures of society without receiving a fair share of the benefits. My approach affirms the right of poor and emarginated individuals and groups to participate in social structures in the face of their exclusion from these benefits by the powerful. Again, the argument is based on the dignity of the person. Also, emargination destroys community.

Deprivation versus Equality of Distribution

Should all persons and peoples receive the same amount of resources, goods and services, and power attached to social offices? Deprivation underscores the case of those who live in indigence and cannot meet their needs on either an individual or national level, while others enjoy enormous wealth. Regarding distribution of resources, and goods and services, my position affirms the priority of the needs of the poor over the mere wants of the rich. But a fair formula of distribution takes account of other factors as well. There are four criteria. The priority is given to needs and then to effort within a context of equal opportunity. Those who make a greater effort deserve more. Claims based on meritocracy (the best and the brightest) and even historical privilege (nobility) and recognized but are conditioned by the common good and the moral obligation to do good. The priorities in this approach are needs, effort, merit, and privilege, in that order. This does not preclude differences, but conditions them. The reasoning for this is based on the dignity of the person, the universal destiny of the goods of creation, and the prerequisites for a flourishing community. I realize this aspect of my position is very controversial. I have set forth my position in greater detail elsewhere (Steidlmeier 1984, pp. 88ff.) It is an articulation of a communitarian ethic.

Apathy and Egoism versus Contribution and Duty

Should all persons and peoples be required to make the same effort to contribute to society's wellbeing? The plight of the poor is often met with apathy and unconcern on the part of those who are wealthy. A communitarian approach stresses the duty of all to make a contribution to society according to abilities and finds the refusal to do so, whether deriving from egoism or apathy, an unacceptable position. There is a social duty to be responsive to the overall common good and to contribute according to one's ability. More is asked of those who have more. Such a golden-rule ethic derives from the prerequisites of community.

Dissent and Due Process versus Coercion

Should all persons and peoples enjoy the same degree of due process regarding sanctions, retribution, incentives, and compensation in social structures? Economic and political sanctions against those who break the social rules of the game can only be considered unjust if the rules of the game are themselves just. Coercive sanctions and unfair schemes of incentives that threat individuals, groups, and people as things, or as instruments for either individual, group, or national self-interest, are unacceptable. In the face of unjust rules of the game, dissent is a duty. Again the reasoning is based on human dignity in community.

How one answers these five questions directly depends on worldview. Based on a communitarian worldview they yield concrete (as well as controversial) criteria for evaluating ethical problems in business in terms of a series of specific rights and duties as applied to consumers, labor, shareholders and other stakeholders. It is notoriously difficult to establish such principles as legitimate moral goals. It is even more difficult to figure out how to achieve them.

The ethical realities of justice only come clear in a concrete situation. Abstract principles are like a skeleton in comparison with the realities of life. They do serve a purpose, however, in that they provide some good questions to be raised in the analysis of a particular case. Ethics is a practical and painstaking analysis of concrete experience. It is an art that can only be carried out through case analysis, where principles are applied to various concrete situations. There is a long history of case analysis in Western philosophical, Christian, and rabbinical traditions. The object is to figure out what sort of behavior would be moral or the best in a concrete situation, given the types of questions that ethical principles based on one's worldview suggest. The case tradition has not been all positive. Indeed the word casuistry (derived from the Latin *casus* meaning case) has come to denote the fudging of ethical principles through self-interested rationalizations and deceit. Case analysis is obviously subject to such twists and turns. Socrates himself focused on the bias of the Sophists. Bias is a real problem especially when one is intimately involved with a case. Nonetheless, case studies remain the only adequate grounds for the concrete task of ethical decision making. The object of case analysis is to sort out values, to judge ends, means and consequences, to assign responsibilities in terms of correlative rights and duties, and to decide upon a fair distribution of benefits and costs. Such tasks may be guided by principles, but they are in the end very unique.

VI. PROCESSES OF BUSINESS ETHICS

Business ethics represents a very complex process of social reflection and choice, which encompasses changing the social rules of the game as well as business policies and individual actions. It is profoundly social, for the elements of an ethical position outlined in table one, two and three are only worked through 1) with others in 2) a long historical process. As evidence, no leading business issue—whether the environment, workers rights, or consumerism—has been historically susceptible to a quick solution.

I reject individualist approaches to business ethics, which either claim that all ethics is individual or that business is morally analogous to an individual moral person. My position is that business ethics is social; hence, it not only concentrates on the social consequences of actions and policies, it is itself a social process. In clarifying this process I refer to two cases: apartheid, a social problem in which business is involved; and environmental pollution, a social problem that a business can cause.

Process 1: From Problem Identification to Consensus

The first sweep of the business ethics process is to go from the everyday facts to the identification of certain aspects of them as a problem. This is no easy step as the work of Rachel Carson on the environment or Ralph Nader on consumerism suggest. Neither the economic analysis nor the moral analysis come easy. Problem identification is generally followed by protracted years of dispute (20–25 years is not unusual) before majority consensus is arrived at. Complete consensus is practically impossible. This process is what was generally described as "see" and "judge" in Table One. On this point historical studies prove invaluable as a source of discovering the social dynamics involved.

The result of scrutinizing the consequences of business policies and underlying rules of the game will be a clear identification of the ethical problem. A complex process of social dialogue is involved. In the end, the problem will be identified as primarily a socially caused problem (such as apartheid) or a business-caused social problem (such as pollution). Once the problem is identified, people must figure out what to do about it. This calls for a further period of dialogue focused on building consensus and galvanizing political will.

Process 2: From Consensus to Action

The second part of the process is equally as formidable and historically time-consuming as the first. Actually overcoming racial and sexual discrimination is a matter of centuries rather than decades. Many good causes die from fatigue. Furthermore, great creative imagination is called for in identifying social change mechanisms and in weaving together the fruitful interaction of multiple social agents. Business ethics involves the simultaneous exercise of multiple responsibilities by a panoply of social agents. Nowhere is freedom completely unbounded: every person, institution and system is hemmed in by a variety of constraints upon choice, ranging from the lack of resources to threats of punishment. Pursuit of the correct or more desirable action is often impaired by the effective lack of freedom of persons and peoples.

The opposition to apartheid provides an interesting case. The five questions of justice listed in the previous section focus on the rules of the game. Apartheid in South Africa is a social problem that took a long time to define and build consensus around. Ethical questions proved to be a catalyst as people asked:

1. What liberty or self-determination do black people have?
2. What opportunities do blacks have as compared to whites?
3. What resources to blacks have to meet their needs? Or what do they receive in proportion to their efforts?
4. Who is able to help in solving the problems of the blacks and are they helping?
5. Is there due legal process?

After determining what is the case, reflection moves to what should be. If one holds a com-munitarian ethic, the judgment on apartheid cannot be negative on every level. But it has taken forty years to arrive at consensus and that consensus is fragile indeed.

A similar process is evident in the case of pollution (a business-caused problem):

1. Are people free to choose the quality of the environment?
2. Are people who are affected by pollution able to participate in processes to do something about it?
3. How are the benefits and costs of pollution distributed?
4. Are those who are able to resolve the problem doing what they can?
5. Is the legal system fair in terms of sanctions and compensation? In the end, what are people's rights and what should be happening?

People will respond to these questions in different ways depending on their worldview. As mentioned earlier, the worldview problems must be thrashed out, for they are critical to establishing the legitimacy or illegitimacy of the rules of behavior society abides by. Rules of the game are legitimated (or delegitimated) by worldview and related cultural values. To get at apartheid the theological underpinnings of the Dutch Reformed Church had to be delegitimized. Likewise, to get at pollution the ideology of a certain type of economic progress had to be questioned. Such dynamics invite conflict which can lead to change. For example, conflict between social rules on pollution and corporate practice can create conflicts in managers and even lead to whistleblowing. In South Africa, conflict between religious rules of fellowship and social apartheid can create conflict in those who try to follow both.

Business ethics is fundamentally about social change (Buchholz 1982, Chapter 5). Social change is brought about by a number of mechanisms. First, there is technical innovation. In the case of apartheid, modern communications media play a vital role. In pollution, the technology to dispose of toxic wastes is pivotal. Second, values are a catalyst for social change. Values and ethical principles directly express worldview. The value of human dignity is the basis of anti-apartheid. Values of ecology, stewardship of the earth, and environmental protection are basic to antipollution movements. Third, social conflict (not necessarily violent) stimulates social change. This is increasingly coming to the fore in South Africa. Also, the environmental movement has made use of both demonstrations and legal conflicts to accentuate their stand.

Finally, great leaders and elite groups (whether in educational, religious, or other circles) can spark change. Black consciousness in South Africa owes its development to courageous leaders, who were almost alone in going against the tide decades ago. The rise of the environmental movement was likewise stimulated by small groups who became ecologically conscious and slowly disseminated their position.

As a complex process of social change, business ethics in the cases of pollution and apartheid involves a wide variety of multiple agents on both individual and group levels, as well as local, domestic, and international levels. In addition, each of these protagonists is involved in an innumerable variety of actions, spanning private voluntary initiatives, public policy and legislation, and measures to change not only corporate but industry-wide practices. All the actions explained here lead to a wide spectrum of outcomes on economic, political, and sociocultural levels. Efforts to end pollution create new economic enterprises, new public policy to protect the environment, and new relations between society and nature. Ending apartheid will radically change political institutions, economic opportunities, and the cultural vision of South African society.

One of the most difficult tasks of business ethics is to clarify the roles of all the individuals involved in a problem. I do not maintain that social problems are reducible to individual responsibilities (for the rules of the game and cultural legitimation are precisely shared behavioral routines and shared patterns of meaning). But individual roles and responsibilities are highly important. They are also difficult to spell out in detail. Prime Minister Botha, Bishop Tutu, and literally thousands of others have significant roles to play in apartheid. None has total control. In fact, so far the focus of their activities has principally been the rules of the game, legitimation, and due process (or the lack thereof) mentioned previously. The pollution case likewise draws in corporate engineers and consultants, managers, community leaders, ecologists, politicians, and government civil service and other interest groups.

Business ethics is not merely a quick fix for a problem. It is a long historical process of social change. Unlike individual ethics (where responsibility is primarily vested in one person and where the time-frame is relatively short), a problem in business ethics manifests many responsibilities and a life-span of ten years to generations. Apartheid problems have existed for more than forty years; the resolution process could easily last another fifteen to twenty-five years. Environmental pollution problems seem to have a minimal span of ten years. Certain toxic wastes still elude solutions although they have been a problem for many years.

Business ethics is also concerned with individual change within social change. The process is itself social. It involves many years of dialogue to establish the nobility of ultimate ends and values, the adequacy of proximate ends, the suitability of means, the development of social consciousness, the worthiness of the intentions of those who act or fail to act, the fairness of consequences, and the degree of effective freedom of various agents. As business ethics moves from initial question to consensus and political will, it aims to see (to grasp the facts of the problem as best as possible), to judge (to morally evaluate the problem) and to act (to galvanize the political will to create a better alternative). It is necessary to stimulate awareness of the issue, to develop a consensus to change it, and to figure out appropriate strategies and a fair sharing of social benefits and costs in changing the issue. None of these points is easy; the last one is especially difficult.

VII. CONCLUSION: SOME SUGGESTIONS FOR BUSINESS

The main questions for business enterprises is how to prepare themselves for and insert themselves into the social-ethical process. First, corporate leaders must clarify their worldviews and related ethical principles. As Miesing and Preble (1985) have demonstrated, business philosophies right now are in a confusing state. Both formal seminars (Jones 1982) as well as general business education should be revamped.

Second, ethical considerations should not be added on as an afterthought (Pastin 1984, 1985; McCoy 1985). Ethics is not an add-on to economic functions. It is inherent to them. It cannot be handled by the public relations part of the firm, but only by managers and others concerned about asking the right questions. How to do this not clear. Carroll and Hoy (1984) have, however, made some interesting suggestions on integrating such policy into strategic management. They combine policy formulation on the macro level with implementation devolving on the corpora-

tion's micro level. They made the same point that Pastin and McCoy made: ethics must be part of the strategy from the beginning.

The institutionalizing of new forms of management are still being tested. This should not be surprising, given the new sociological nature of the corporation. Filios (1984) has assessed the potential of social audits; Maitland (1985) brings out the difficulties of business self-regulation; Cressey and Moore (1983) discuss the relevance of codes of conduct. Two points run through these articles. Ethical action that incurs costs and weakens profits weakens the position of management. Solutions that are not industry-wide also weaken management in terms of competitiveness in the marketplace.

These observations reinforce my position that business ethics is primarily concerned with changing the rules of the game. Specifically, the conduct of the industry, not just the corporation or the individual, must be changed. The willingness of shareholders, workers, and the public to equitably share the costs in terms of lower dividends and wages and increased costs at the consumer level is part of any sensible solution. The generation of society-wide benefits calls for an equitable society-wide sharing of costs.

Business would be well-served if it would not be defensive about questions of ethics, but rather undertake ethics in the positive spirit of Socrates: the unexamined life of our structures and institutions is not worth living. In this light McCoy (1985) calls for a proactive rather than a reactive stance. Business leaders are members of many other institutions besides their own enterprises. They would be well-poised, in all of their roles, to be parts of the creative processes of business and social ethics. Some will find McCoy's proactive stance distasteful just as people found the original quest of Socrates a bothersome attack on their institutions. But others will be invigorated by the challenge to be artisans of justice and peace in a dynamic and developing society.

REFERENCES

Andrews, Kenneth R. 1984. "Difficulties in Overseeing Ethical Policy," *California Management Review*, 27 (4), 134–146.

Beauchamp, Tom L., and Norman E. Bowie. 1983. *Ethical Theory and Business, 3rd ed.* Englewood Cliffs, N.J.: Prentice-Hall.

Bellah, Robert N., Richard Madsen, William M. Sullivan, Ann Swidler, and Steven M. Tipton. 1985. *Habits of the Heart: Individualism and Commitment in American Life.* Berkeley, Calif.: University of California Press.

Blostrom, Robert L. 1975. *Business and Society: Environment and Responsibility, 3rd ed.* New York: McGraw-Hill.

Bower, Joseph C. 1983. "Managing for Efficiency, Managing for Equity," *Harvard Business Review*, 61, 83–90.

Buchholz, Rogene A. 1982. *Business Environment and Public Policy.* Englewood Cliffs, N.J.: Prentice-Hall.

Carroll, Archie B., and Frank Hoy. 1984. "Integrating Corporate Social Policy Into Strategic Management," *The Journal of Business Strategy*, 4 (3), 48–57.

Cavanagh, Gerald. 1976. *American Business Values in Transition.* Englewood Cliffs, N.J.: Prentice-Hall.

Chamberlain, Neil W. 1977. *Remaking American Values.* New York: Basic Books.

Coye, Ray. 1986. "Individual Values and Business Ethics," *Journal of Business Ethics*, 5 (1), 45–49.

Cressey, Donald R., and Charles A. Moore. 1983. "Managerial Values and Corporate Codes of Conduct," *California Management Review*, 25 (4), 53–77.

Donaldson, Thomas, and Patricia H. Werhane. 1983. *Ethical Issues in Business—A Philosophical Approach*, Englewood Cliffs, N.J.: Prentice-Hall.

Drucker, Peter. 1981. "What is Business Ethics?" *The Public Interest*, 3, 18–56.

Filios, Vasilio P. 1984. "Corporate Social Responsibility and Public Accountability," *Journal of Business Ethics*, 3 (4), 305–314.

Friedman, Milton. 1962. *Capitalism and Freedom.* Chicago: University of Chicago Press.

Goodpaster, Kenneth E. 1985. "Business Ethics, Ideology and the Naturalistic Fallacy," *Journal of Business Ethics*, 4 (4), 227–232.

Goodpaster, Kenneth E., and John B. Matthews. 1983. "Can a Corporation have Conscience?" in T.L. Beauchamp and Norman E. Bowie, eds., *Ethical Theory and Business*, pp. 68–80.

Hennessey, John W., Jr. 1985. "Ethical Aspects of the South African Investment Debate on American University Campuses," mimeograph, Dartmouth College, Hanover, N.H.

Hirschman, Albert O. 1985. "Against Parsimony: Three Easy Ways of Complicating Economic Decisions," *Economics and Philosophy*, 1 (1), 7–21.

Hood, Sydney. 1967. *Human Values and Economic Policy.* New York: New York University Press.

Hosmer, Larue T. 1984. "Managerial Ethics and Microeconomic Efficiency," *Journal of Business Ethics*, 3 (4), 315–328.

Jones, Donald G. 1982. *Doing Ethics in Business.* Cambridge, MA: Oelgeschlager, Gunn and Hain.

Kossell, Clifford. 1981. "Global Community and Subsidiarity," *Communion* 8 (2), 3.

Kegos, Phillip V. 1985. "Defining Business Ethics—Like Nailing Jello to a Wall," *Journal of Business Ethics*, 4 (5), 387–394.

Lodge, George. 1975. *The New American Ideology.* New York: Alfred Knopf.

Luthans, Fred, and Richard M. Hodgetts. 1976. *Social Issues in Business.* New York: MacMillan.

McCoy, Charles S. 1985. *Management of Values—The Ethical Difference in Corporate Policy.* Marshfield, Mass.: Pitman.

McMahon, Thomas F. 1985. "The Construction of Religious Tradition to Business Ethics," *Journal of Business Ethics*, 4 (4) 341–344.

Maitland, Ian. 1985. "The Limits of Business Self-Regulation," *California Management Review*, 27 (3), 132–146.

Miesing, Paul, and John F. Preble. 1985. "A Comparison of five Business Philosophies," *Journal of Business Ethics*, 4 (6), 465–477.

Mintzberg, Henry. 1983. "The Case for Corporate Social Responsibility," *The Journal of Business Strategy*, 4 (2), 3–15.

Moser, Martin. 1986. " A Framework for Analyzing

Corporate Social Responsibility," *Journal of Business Ethics*, 5 (1), 69–72.

Nader, Ralph. 1984. "Refining Corporate Governance," *California Management Review*, 24 (4), 126–133.

Nisbet, Robert. 1977. "Capitalism and the Intellectuals," *Wall Street Journal*, September 16.

O'Toole, James. 1979. "What's Ahead for the Business-Government Relationship?" *Harvard Business Review*, 57, 94–105.

Pastin, Mark. 1984. "Ethics as an Integrating Force in Management," *Journal of Business Ethics*, 3 (4), 295–305.

———. 1985. "Management Think," *Journal of Business Ethics*, 4 (4), 341–344.

Pemberton, Prentiss L., and Daniel Rush Finn. 1955. *Toward a Christian Economic Ethics— Stewardship and Social Power*. Minneapolis, Minn.: Winston Press.

Rawls, John. 1975. *A Theory of Justice*. Cambridge, Mass.: Harvard University Press.

Samuelson, Paul. 1977. *Economics*. New York: McGraw-Hill.

Sethi, S. Prakash. 1982. *Up Against the Corporate Wall, 2nd ed.* Englewood Cliffs, N.J.: Prentice-Hall.

Sethi, S. Prakash, and Nobuaki Namiki. 1983. "Managing Public Affairs: The Public Backlash Against PAC's," *California Management Review*, 25 (3), 133–144.

Steidlmeier, Paul. 1984. *Social Justice Ministry: Foundations and Concerns*. New York: LeJacq Publishing Co.

Stevens, Edward. 1979. *Business Ethics*. New York: Paulist Press.

Sturdivant, Frederick D. 1984. *Business and Society, A Managerial Approach, 3rd ed.* Homewood, Ill.: Richard D. Irwin.

Williams, Oliver F. 1985. "Investments in South Africa—A Christian Moral Argument," mimeograph, Notre Dame University.

2

The Political Economy of Regulation: An Analysis of Market Failures

Robert G. Harris

James M. Carman

This article is concerned with the social control of business in a predominantly market economy. Charles Lindblom (1977) has identified five major methods of social control: authority, exchange, persuasion, morality, and tradition (custom). Authority, (that is, most of what we call public policy) is difficult to establish and expensive to administer. Furthermore, in societies that value the rights and freedoms of individuals, there are strong preferences for restricting the use of authority. A central postulate of democratic theory, therefore, is that authority ought to be employed only when other methods of social control fail. Therein lies the logic of this article.

Of the five types of social control, we are concerned primarily with the interaction between authority and market exchange. It is our view that the relationship between public policy and markets (that is, between authority and exchange in Lindblom's terms) can be characterized in the following way. In a market economy, the authority of the state is employed to create and protect the property and other rights requisite to market exchange. Individuals, acting alone or in voluntary association, produce, exchange, and consume goods and services. As long as these private actions are consistent with social values and goals, there is a strong argument against public intervention. If failures occur, however, authority is employed to correct them (by modifying existing markets, creating new markets, or substituting authority for markets). But as markets sometimes fail, so too do political remedies. We must choose, then, among highly imperfect institutions; we make these choices in the belief that, in any particular set of circumstances, one method of control may produce better results than another.

Here and in the succeeding article in this book we present a conceptual scheme for identifying and classifying the effects and interactions between exchange and authority as methods of social control. Our approach in this endeavor is institutional (see Arndt 1981) and can be illustrated as follows:

| Legal Framework | → | Market Exchange | → | Market Failures | → |
| Regulatory Responses | → | Regulatory Failures | → | Public Choice | |

Although the linear representation here is simple, it represents a highly complex, interactive process, providing a general framework for analyzing the ways in which society makes trade-offs between two allocative mechanisms: market exchange and political authority. We do not mean to imply, however, that the scheme presented here actually describes that process.

Although democratic societies may have a strong value preference for relying on private exchange as a method of social control, markets do not exist in a state of nature; they must be created. Unless there is a system for creating and protecting property rights, one has nothing to exchange (or at least one is constantly threatened by involuntary loss of the potential objects of exchange).[1] Furthermore, in a developed economy, where exchange is seldom extemporaneous and often complex, the state must provide a set of contractual rights and a system for enforcing them. Even the most extreme libertarian grants these as legitimate functions of the state. What is important to our argument is that these political acts are inherently regulatory in function, if not in intent; that is, the way in which property and contract rights are (or are not) defined has enormous consequences for the actions of market agents and outcomes of market transactions.

The role of the state in creating markets is critical to our understanding of market failures. In many cases, failures result not because a market is working improperly, but because the market does not exist, is incomplete, or is presently constrained by regulation. Thus, we need to distinguish between the inherent limits of markets and the failures of existing markets. If the failures are inher-

ent in market exchange as a method of control, that suggests using a nonmarket solution. If the failure is one of existing markets, one option is to extend, or modify, existing property, contract, or liability rights.

TYPES OF MARKETS

Before proceeding to market failures, it may be helpful to present a very brief classification of types of market linkages. David Revzan was fond of defining a market as a "meeting of minds." But in advanced societies these meetings occur in an extraordinary number and complexity of ways. Although highly simplified, this myriad of market types can be categorized as follows:[2]

Auction markets: in the ideal case, the identities of the buyer and seller are unknown to each other; a disinterested auctioneer simply matches up buy and sell orders; terms of trade do not take account of past or future transactions (for example, commodities, securities markets).

Bidding markets: like auction markets in some respects, but with one crucial difference—the auction is conducted by either the buyer or the seller, who is therefore not a disinterested intermediary (for example, oil leasing, government procurement).

Relational markets: there is a personal (though not intimate) relationship between the buyer and seller, who meet by phone or by mail; furthermore, by relational, we mean that the terms and conditions of any single transaction are influenced by prior or potential transactions between the same parties (for example, retail goods and services markets).

Contractual markets: there is a contractual relationship between buyer and seller that transcends a single transaction and covers a wide range of goods and/or services, including supplies, advertising, architectural services, financing, management services (for example, retail franchises).

Obligational markets: there is a contractual relationship between buyer and seller spanning a period of time; the conditions of exchange include provisions that shift the locus of control over, but not ownership of, the object exchange to the buyer (for example, employment contracts, which give the employer authority over the employee; equity investment, in which the shareholder gives to managers control over the use of the capital).[3]

There is one other characteristic of markets that is critical to our analysis of the authority-exchange relationship, namely their interconnectedness. Each market has its own institutional characteristics, rich and complex, changing and developing over time. Markets are also connected to many other markets, some in a direct fashion, more in indirect ways. Just as the intended, beneficial consequences of market outcomes are transmitted across markets, so too are market failures. Accordingly, in analyzing and deciding public policies toward markets, we must take explicit account of these interdependencies. These intermarket effects may be classified as horizontal or vertical. For example, undue bargaining power in a labor market clearly affects the prices of the products of the producers, and thereby the sales of complementary and substitute goods and services. Thus, public policies can, and often do, attempt to remedy failures in one market by modifying outcomes in related markets. By the same measure, public policies directed at correcting a failure in one market will have side effects in other markets.

THE IDEAL MARKET

As there are strong value preferences for one method of social control over another, so there are value preferences and differences in perceptions about how each of these control methods does or ought to work. There are norms about what constitutes a fair exchange and a recognition that certain conditions must apply, more or less, in order for a control method to work the way it is supposed to. In the case of market exchange, classical political economy defines this ideal type as the perfectly competitive market, and specifies the following conditions for market success:

Perfect competition: subjects to the exchange should have relatively equal bargaining positions (that is, neither should have power over the other).

Perfect information: subjects should be fully informed about the object of exchange and about other exchange possibilities (for example, the prices and product attributes of substitutes).

Absence of externalities: all of the consequences of the exchange process (including pre-exchange production and post-exchange consumption or use) should be internalized in the exchange.

Divisibility: the object of exchange must be divisible into exchangeable units.

Excludability: the subjects of exchange can exclude nonsubjects from the benefits of the exchange.

Zero transactions costs: there are no barriers to exchange, so that the market instantaneously clears at a price the equilibrates current supply and demand conditions.

Zero entry barriers: there are no long-run supply constraints that inhibit additional production when demand exceeds supply in the short-run.

Economic rationality: subjects to the exchange act to maximize their individual self-interest, as measured in materialistic terms (that is, utility maximization by consumers, profit maximization by producers).

Fair distribution of wealth and income: distribution of economic resources available for exchange is consistent with social consensus of fairness; in a market economy, that means that each individual has wealth and income corresponding to his production of economic goods and services.

These are ideal conditions that never literally hold true in any market; there is considerable controversy regarding the extent to which these conditions typically hold true in markets. Indeed, this difference in opinion is a major component of political ideology: the libertarian believes markets to be almost always nearly perfect (at least if given sufficient time to reach equilibrium), whereas the liberal (as the term is presently employed) believes that markets are often fundamentally flawed. Hence, the libertarian favors exchange over authority as a control mechanism, while the liberal often favors authority over markets.

TYPES OF MARKET FAILURES

Although ideological differences involved in this debate often color perceptions of what is actually happening, the measurement problem of determining when a market should be considered a failure may be a more serious impediment to public choice between exchange and authority than are ideological differences. While we will expand on this point now, the typology of market failure should be free of value considerations. By market failure (the reader might prefer to substitute market imperfections), we mean to identify those possible instances in which the ideal conditions for a market success do not hold. We do not mean to suggest that in each instance a regulatory response is desirable.

In our typology, we specify the nature of the failures as they relate to the classical ideal conditions for market exchange. This is a descriptive, not normative, statement. Although we have attempted to develop a descriptive typology that is unambiguous, inclusive, and mutually exclusive, we readily acknowledge that any particular attribute or outcome of market exchange could be classified in a number of other ways.[4]

Because of their classical roots, the ideal conditions overemphasize static, structural market attributes and underemphasize dynamic and functional considerations. It is not our intent to champion that perspective; we recognize, for example, that the dynamic benefits of economic profits flowing to research and development and thence to product improvements, or products and services, are real. The question is, How imperfect can markets be before they become socially undesirable? In attempting to answer that question, scholars have attempted to define a concept of workable or effective competition in a market, then to address the measurement suggested by that definition. One definition that is useful for present purposes (but certainly not easy to make operational) is that competitive market exchange is workable when there is no regulatory response that would result in greater social gains than social losses (Markham 1950).

Such a rule could be applied in deciding whether to intervene in a given market, and in choosing among regulatory responses. In response to dangerous drugs, for example, we might prohibit their exchange, require sellers to disclose information regarding the dangers of consuming their products, or leave the market alone. The choice among these options depends on the perceived harms of the market solution, as compared to the costs of exercising authority to modify market outcomes. We address regulatory failures, and the implications of those failures for public policies toward markets, in the succeeding article. The typology of market failures is presented in table 1. The remainder of this section is a discussion of the elements of the type typology, and illustrative examples of each type.

Imperfect Competition

In order for market exchange to function well as a method of social control, subjects of exchange cannot have unequal bargaining positions (since we assume that self-interest would cause them to exploit that bargaining advantage, resulting in unfair terms of exchange). Although we might measure bar-

TABLE 1. Types of Market Failures.

Type of Failure	Nature of Failure	Examples of Failure
Imperfect competition		
Natural monopoly	Economies of scale	Electric utilities
Monopoly(sony)	Bargaining power	Standard Oil (pre-1912)
Oligopoly(sony)	Interdependent conduct	Tobacco
Monopol(son)istic competition	Transaction costs; excess capacity	Retail sale of convenience goods
Excessive competiton	Fluctuating supply/demand	Trucking
Anticompetitive conduct	Collusion; predation	OPEC cartel; AT&T; MCI
Imperfect information		
Bounded rationality	Uninformed exchange	Professional services
Information costs	Uninformed exchange	Life insurance
Asymmetric information	Unequal bargaining	"Lemons"
Misinformation	Misinformed exchange	Wonder bread
Lack of information	Uninformed exchange	New therapeutic drugs
Side effects		
Internalities	Transmittal of costs to nonsubjects	Health effects of tobacco
Negative externalities	Overconsumption; costs imposed on nonsubjects	Air pollution; communicable diseases
Positive externalities	Underconsumption; benefits accrue to nonsubjects	Innoculations against communicable diseases
Public goods	Indivisibility; nonexcludability; zero MC	Street lighting; parks; national defense
(De)merit goods	Divergence of private wants, social values	Education; (gambling)
Income maldistribution		
Factor market failures	Any of above	Employee discrimination
Economic vs. social value	Earned income not equal to social worth	Children; disabled; "superstars"
Intergenerational transfers	Inconsistency with value that income be "earned"	Inheritances; socially advantaged upbringing

Source: From *Journal of Macromarketing*, vol. 3, no. 1 (Spring 1983), p. 53.

Robert G. Harris / James M. Carman

gaining position or power directly, we can more easily infer it from the structure of the market, that is, the number and size distribution of buyers and sellers in the market, and the conditions of entry into and exit from the market. The classical definitions of industrial organization identifies those market structures in which market failures are most likely.

Natural Monopoly. Natural monopoly is due to economies of scale (or scope in a multiproduct producer) relative to total market demand, which only one (or a few) producer(s) can produce at minimum cost. When these economies are of dominating importance, markets fail because too many firms will produce at costs exceeding the minimum achievable (technical inefficiency), or too few firms will exist in the market (so each seller will market power). Examples are electric utilities, postal services, and highway systems.

Monopoly (sony). Although a monopoly is not achieved by economies of scale, one seller (buyer) has power in the exchange because it is the sole available subject to exchange. Libertarians argue that the only monopolies are created by government. Liberals argue that there are no monopolies only because the antitrust laws have prohibited them. In any event, we cannot think of any clear cases of monopoly that are not based on economies of scale.

Oligopoly (sony). Whether natural (economies of scale) or not, sellers (buyers) have power in the market because there are too few sellers (buyers). Thus, while there may be some gains from economies of scale, there will be a concomitant increase in the market power of the oligopolists. Examples of oligopoly are tobacco, cement, and paper carton markets. Examples of oligopsony are labor markets in which a few employers account for a large share of total employment.

Monopolistic (sonistic) Competition. Even though there are a large number of sellers (buyers), they have some power over buyers (sellers) because transactions costs inhibit competition. Examples are retail markets in which shopping costs are high relative to the total transaction value (for example, convenience goods).

Excessive Competition

If supply or demand fluctuates unpredictably over time, there may be excessive entry by producers during peak demand, resulting in excess capacity during off-peak demand. Furthermore, if capital is specialized, supply adjustments may take longer than the duration of the fluctuation and prices will be driven below long-run average costs. Or, if storage costs are high, producers may sell output below costs to avoid those costs. In addition to the instability in supply and loss of income by producers, excessive competition may induce producers to reduce the quality of their services, perhaps with jeopardy to consumers. Examples are agricultural markets (for example, the hog cycle) and trucking and airline (pre-regulation) companies.

Anticompetitive Conduct

Because of the potential economic gains, sellers (buyers) may commit acts in concert with (collusion) or against (predation) other sellers in order to enhance their position in the market. In the short run these acts may raise (collusion) or lower (predation) prices and correspondingly reduce or increase output relative to the competitive levels. By modifying the market structure, both collusion and predation raise prices and reduce output in the long run. There are numerous examples in both product and service markets. There is one other class of anticompetitive behavior, unfair trade practices (for example, misleading advertising), which we treat as an informational failure rather than as a competitive failure.

Imperfect Information

In order for markets to work well, subjects to exchange must be fully informed about the object of exchange and about conditions and objects in other markets; ideally, information is perfect and costless. In highly localized, premodern economies, buyers and sellers may have had something approaching perfect information. But in developed economies, with geographically dispersed markets, complex goods and services produced by very large, anonymous organizations, and many available substitutes and complements, information is highly imperfect and very costly. There are several distinct types of information failures:

Bounded Rationality. Even if information was costless, it would not be perfect, in that information has value only if the subject has the knowledge needed to use the information. Given the limits of individuals to analyze, store, and retrieve information, we can predict that many exchange transactions will not be fully informed. An example is the prescription of surgical services by the doctor (seller) when the patient (buyer) lacks knowledge (and often the emotional or physical stamina to procure it) required to assess needs for, or benefits of, those services. Closely related to bounded rationality is the problem of cognitive dissonance, which causes individuals to fail to acknowledge (or even receive) information even when it is presented to them. An example is the consumers who will not accept scientific evidence of the health effects of smoking.

Information Costs. Even when information is readily available, it is seldom costless. Because of the money and opportunity costs of obtaining information, subjects to exchange often act without full information. The problem is most serious when: (1) the product or service is purchased infrequently; (2) performance characteristics are difficult to evaluate either before or soon after purchase; (3) the rate of technological change is rapid relative to the interval between purchases; and (4) the terms of exchange change rapidly relative to the purchase interval. Examples are life insurance and automobile tires (Holton 1978, 1981).

Asymmetric Information. Because there are economies of scale in the collection, storage, retrieval, and analysis of information, subjects who engage in many exchanges involving the same object will typically have an information advantage. Thus, because a producer typically sells more of a given object than a consumer buys, there often exists an asymmetry between producers and consumers. Moreover, self-interest causes producers to exploit this information advantage in the exchange process. Note two important exceptions to this rule of asymmetry. In industrial markets, purchasing agents specialize in particular goods or services, so the buyer may have better (or at least as good as) information than the seller. In factor markets, buyers may have considerably better information about working conditions (for example, toxic fumes or hazardous machinery) than the seller of labor services, or better information about the financial condition and prospects of the company than the seller of capital.

Misinformation. Because information is costly but often essential to exchange, subjects have economic incentives to provide information to other potential subjects to exchange. Sellers advertise and promote their products by providing information about the attributes of their products, and the ways in which they satisfy buyers' needs or wants.

Sellers also provide information about the offerings of other sellers, either explicitly (as in comparative advertising) or implicitly (as in persuading consumers to buy one class of objects rather than another). Unfortunately, sellers also have economic incentives to misinform potential buyers about their products or the products of others. For the very reason that buyers lack information about the relative merits of available products, they are often unable to distinguish good information from bad information. Examples of misinformation are when sellers use advertising to create the impression of product differentiation (and a corresponding willingness to pay higher prices) for homogeneous products; when professionals advise clients to purchase services not needed by the buyer; when employers mislead workers about the health effects of workplace pollution; when managers mislead shareholders about the terms of an acquisition offer.

Lack of information. As human knowledge is limited, important information about a product does not exist. The fact that both seller and buyer are equally ignorant is of no relief in such cases. This problem is especially relevant to the negative attributes (or side effects) of objects of exchange. Examples are when long-term effects of therapeutic drugs and effects of asbestos on workers' health are not known.

Information as Object of Exchange. When information is itself the object of exchange, there are severe limits as to what information about the product can be revealed without revealing the product itself. Furthermore, once revealed, the cost of reproducing information is often so low that the producer of the information has difficulty internalizing the value of his product. We will discuss this issue further under the section entitled "Public Goods."

Side Effects

All goods have their bads, in their production, their consumption, or both. Sometimes those side effects accrue to subjects of the exchange (internalities); often they accrue to individuals who are not subjects to the exchange (externalities). In either case, market exchange is often imperfect because the terms of exchange will probably not incorporate all of the consequences of the production and consumption of the object of exchange.

Internalities. If the side effects are borne by a subject of exchange (for example, the consumer of the product or the provider of labor services), and there is no information failure (that is, the subject is aware of the side effect and incorporates that information in the exchange terms), then there is no immediate market failure. But side effects can be transmitted through other markets; if, for example, the side effect raises health care costs but insurance premiums are not sensitive to the higher risk, then the internality is externalized in the form of higher premiums to other individuals.

Another type of internality imposes negative side effects on other users (whether as producers or consumers) when too many users attempt to consume a service at the same time. This congestion effect is not really an externality, since the costs are borne by those involved in the exchange process. Examples of internalities are waiting lines at banks and highway congestion.

Negative Externalities. When negative side effects of production or consumption are borne by nonsubjects, resource allocation will be distorted by overproduction and overconsumption. Examples are pollution by manufacturing plants, automobiles, or smokers; reckless driving; transmitting contagious diseases due to improper sanitation by providers of personal care services.

Positive Externalities. When some of the positive effects of production or consumption are realized by nonsubjects, underproduction and underconsumption result. Examples are innoculation against contagious disease reduce the probability of incidence to the uninnoculated as well as the innoculated; education (presumably) benefits all members of society, in addition to the person receiving the education.

Public Goods

In order for exchange to function well, the objects of exchange must be private, in the sense that they are divisible into exchangeable units and that nonsubjects can be excluded from the benefits of exchange. By public goods, we mean economically valuable goods or services that are characterized by indivisibility and nonexcludability. When goods cannot be privatized for these reasons, exchange fails because of the free-rider problem. Although individuals would benefit from the provision of the good, none has an adequate incentive to purchase the good; no one individual can afford to purchase the entire (indivisible) good, but if enough others purchase the good, the nonpurchasers can still enjoy the benefits. Examples are street lighting, urban "green space," and national defense.

As already noted, information is a most important class of public goods. Intellectual products (for example, books), inventions, and production know-how (that is, trade secrets) are all instances of public goods that are characterized by indivisibility and nonexcludability. When information is an important attribute of an object of exchange, markets fail because free-riders can obtain the value of the product without buying from the seller. Brand names and corporate good will are instances of public goods from which markets cannot exclude other subjects (for example, competitors) from realizing the benefits.

Two additional features of public goods should be noted. First, there is seldom an absolute barrier to excludability; rather there would be a waste of economic resources in excluding on-purchasers (for example, shading, directing, or placing street lighting to privatize the benefits). Second, by definition of indivisibility, the marginal costs of providing the goods to consumers is (until a congestion point) near zero. So, although we could use pricing to limit entry to parks, it would violate one norm of competitive markets: that price reflect the marginal social cost of production.

(De)Merit Goods

The normative theory of exchange assumes that individuals are economically rational: that individuals are capable of knowing what is good for them (or bad for them) and acting accordingly. On this premise are based the principles of individual freedom and consumer sovereignty. In all societies, however, value conflicts exist between individual and social preferences about economic goods and services, often because the production or consumption of economic goods runs counter to noneconomic (for example, religious or ethical) social values.[5] Markets are not capable of providing optimal allocation of resources if social, rather than personal, values are used as the welfare criterion. So, although black markets may work exceedingly well for some products and services, they fail as a means of social control by providing too many demerit goods and too few merit goods. Examples of demerit goods are gambling, prostitution, alcohol, tobacco, and recreational drugs. An example of merit goods is education (even if there are no externalities, society believes that individuals are better off with an education, whether or not the individual is of the same opinion).

Rents

While exchange is premised on the existence of scarcity (if all goods were limitless, there would be no need for private property

Robert G. Harris / James M. Carman

and no need to exchange), the normative theory of exchange assumes that, over the long run, there are no inherent limits to the production of any particular object of exchange. Indeed, one chief attribute of markets is that prices send signals to potential producers indicating the need for additional production, inducing entry, capacity, and returning the market to equilibrium. Markets fail when there exists a long-run inelasticity of supply, preventing production from expanding sufficiently, so that existing producers realize prices exceeding the competitive level. Whereas monopoly profits result from an inelastic demand curve (which by definition indicates that the market is not perfectly competitive), rents are attributable to an inelastic supply curve. Examples are petroleum, natural gas extraction, and urban land markets.

We should note here that scarcity-induced rents are very often generated by authority, rather than by market failures. In these instances, there are no natural limits on the factors of production (or at least those limits would be reached at a higher level of output). Rather, there are regulatory constraints that prohibit or inhibit access to, or use of, the factors required to increase production and eliminate rents. Examples are housing rents due to zoning laws that restrict the density of housing units, and petroleum extraction rents due to limiting access to oil reserves.

Maldistribution of Income and Wealth

Exchange is a method of allocating and distributing resources: how much of which goods get produced and by whom are they consumed. Allocation is the domain of intermediate and final goods and services markets, whereas distribution is principally controlled in factor markets. In a market system, society believes that income—personal control of exchangeable goods and services—ought to be a function of the individual's economic contribution to society. But our ethical system also believes that each person has an inherent value, quite apart from his or her economic worth. Thus, markets fail when there is an incongruence between economic and social value, or when income does not reflect rue economic value. Aid to Dependent Children, for example, is a social program predicated on the belief that a child's value is not reflected in the low income of his or her parent(s).

Failures in Factor Markets. As already noted, all the market failures just classified exist in factor markets. When they occur, there is a misallocation of resources (too many objects will be produced if the workers are underpaid; or, fixed factors will be underutilized if workers are paid more than their production justifies). Moreover, imperfections in factor markets will affect the distribution of wealth and income among factors.

Discrimination. One particular factor market failure is discrimination, which violates the normative standards that subjects are economically rational (that is, personal attributes of subjects should have no effect on the terms of exchange). When discrimination occurs, individuals may be unable to sell their labor services, or may have to sell them at a less than fair price. Discrimination also occurs in labor-related consumer markets, such as schools and universities. When the sellers of educational services discriminate against potential consumers on noneconomic grounds, there is a misallocation of educational resources and the possibility of losses in income-earning potential by those discriminated against.

Social versus Economic Value. Even if factor markets were perfect, individuals might not possess sufficient economically valuable resources to earn an income that is consistent with social values. There are three main classes of individuals for whom this is likely to be true: children, who have yet attained economic value; disabled, who for reasons of physical or mental impairment have limited economic value; and elderly, whose economic value has declined due to age. There may also be cases where individuals earn more than what society deems the individuals are worth. An example is highly paid celebrities.

Intergenerational Transfers. One other source of distributional market failures is attributable to differences in interpersonal transfers of wealth. Here there is a conflict between the norm of individual freedom (control over the use of resources includes the right to give them to others) and the norm that individuals' income should reflect their own economic contribution to society. Hence, one rationale for inheritance taxes (quite apart from raising revenues) is to prevent individuals from receiving substantial unearned income. Note that these transfers include services (for example, a good upbringing, which enhances income-earning potential) as well as tangible assets (for example, a money inheritance).

NOTES

An earlier version of this article was published in the *Journal of Macromarketing* in Spring 1983.

1. For a more thorough discussion of the relationship between property rights and marketing systems, see Carman (1982).

2. This system of classification is consistent with the types of marketing channels identified in Carman (1982), page 206.

3. According to Williamson's view (1975), this amounts to a substitution of hierarchy for market as the means of control (as in the distinction between Mac-Donald's franchised outlets and their company-owned outlets). Because there is a market for employees to manage and staff company-owned, we view hierarchy and market as complementary means of control.

4. For the classic typology of market failures, see Bator (1958).

5. For an excellent review of sumptuary laws, see Hollander (1982).

BIBLIOGRAPHY

Arndt, Johan, "The Political Economy of Marketing Systems: Reviving the Institutional Approach," *Journal of Macromarketing,* Fall 1981.

Bator, Francis E., "Anatomy of Market Failure," *Quarterly Journal of Economics,* August 1958, pp. 351–379.

Breyer, Stephen, *Regulation and its Reform.* Harvard University Press, Cambridge, Mass., 1982.

Carman, James M., "Private Property and the Regulation of Vertical Channel Systems," *Journal of Macromarketing,* Spring 1982.

Caves, Richard E., and Marc J. Roberts, eds., *Regulating the Product: Quality and Variety.* Ballinger, Cambridge, Mass., 1975.

Coase, R.H., "The Problem of Social Cost," *Journal of Law and Economics* 3 (October 1960):1–44.

Commons, John R., *Legal Foundations of Capitalism. University of Wisconsin Press, Madison,* 1959.

Crozier, Michel, *The Bureaucratic Phenomenon.* University of Chicago Press, Chicago, 1964.

Fritschler, A. Lee, and Bernard H. Ross, *Business Regulation and Government Decision Making.* Winthrop Press, Cambridge, Mass., 1980.

Hawley, Ellis, "Three Facets of Hooverian Associationalism," in *Regulation in Perspective,* Thomas K. McCraw, ed. Harvard University Press, Cambridge, Mass., 1981.

Hemenway, David, *Industrywide Voluntary Product Standards.* Ballinger, Cambridge, Mass., 1975.

Hollander, Stanley C., "Sumptuary Legislation — Demarketing by Edict," presented to the Seventh Annual Macromarketing Seminar, Boulder, Colo., 1982.

Holton, Richard H., "Advances in the Backward Art of Spending Money," in *Regulating Business: The Search for an Optimum.* Institute for Contemporary Studies, San Francisco, 1978.

Holton, Richard H., "Public Regulation of Consumer Information: The Life Insurance Case," in *Regulation of Marketing and the Public Interest,* P.E. Balderston, J.M. Carman and F.N. Nicosia, eds. Pergamon Press, New York, 1981.

Lindblom, Charles E. *Politics and Markets.* Basic Books, New York, 1977.

Markham, J.N., "An Alternative Approach to the Concept of Workable Competition," *American Economic Review* 40 (June 1950):349–361.

Robert G. Harris / James M. Carman

McGraw, Thomas K. (ed.), *Regulation in Perspective: Historical Essay*. Harvard Business School Press, Boston, 1981.

Mueller, Dennis C., *Public Choice*. Cambridge University Press, Cambridge, 1979.

Olson, Mancur, *The Logic of Collective Action*. Harvard University Press, Cambridge, Mass., 1965.

Samuels, Warren, *The Classical Theory of Economic Policy*. World Publishing Company, New York, 1966.

Schelling, Thomas C., "On the Ecology of Micromotives," *The Public Interest*, Fall 1971, pp. 59–98.

Schmalansee, Richard, *The Control of Natural Monopolies*. Lexington Books, Lexington, Mass., 1979.

Schultze, Charles L., *The Public Use of Private Interest*. Brookings Institution, Washington, D.C., 1977.

Weldenbaum, Muarry L., *Business, Government and the Public*. Prentice-Hall, Englewood Cliffs, N.J., 1981.

Williamson, Oliver E., *Markets and Hierarchies: Analysis and Antitrust Implications*. Free Press, New York, 1975.

Wilson, James Q., ed., *The Politics of Regulation*. Basic Books, New York, 1980.

Wolf, Charles, Jr., "A Theory of Nonmarket Failure: Framework for Implementation Analysis," *The Journal of Law and Economics*, October 1978, pp. 107–139.

3

The Political Economy of Regulation:
An Analysis of Regulatory Responses

James M. Carman

Robert G. Harris

Since markets cannot function without a system of property and contract rights, there are no pure market economies.[1] What we mean by a market economy is that society has a strong value preference for using exchange as the method of resource allocation, distribution, and social control, and markets are in fact the predominant means of social control. Conversely, there is no economy without markets, but nonmarket economies are those in which there is a normative preference for using authority, tradition, or persuasion, rather than exchange, as the primary means of social control.

We have already assumed that the United States is a market society in that there is a preference for market solutions. However, that leaves an enormous range of differences over the extent to which, and the actual cases in which, authority will be used to create, modify, or substitute for markets. As markets are exceedingly varied and complex, so too are the instruments of authority. Furthermore, there are few cases in which a single type of authority is employed; regulations come in bunches. In any particular market

there is a nexus of rights and regulations that affect the subjects, objects, and medium or terms of exchange.

As background to our discussion of the types of regulation, there are several important dimensions of authority worth delineating. The first dimension is a continuum from private to public exercise of authority. Perhaps the most private of political institutions is the family, in which certain individuals have authority over other individuals, as a consequence of public policy and private economic power. Next, there are private associations, to which the members contract certain elements of authority, but only under the auspices of a more general social contract (for example, rights of religious association, labor unions, or private property associations). In some cases, however, the state can make membership in these private associations mandatory (that is, as a condition of having an exchange relationship) as in closed shops in labor markets, or membership in professional societies as a condition for selling the corresponding professional services. In some cases, private associations are assigned regulatory functions by the state, giving them a quasipublic character (professional licensing bodies). Finally, even at the public level of authority, one can distinguish regulations by the scope of the political authority (as in city, county, state, regional, and national governments). In some cases, political jurisdiction has inherent rights under the prevailing social contract (the national and state governments). Other units of government do not have sovereignty, but have been delegated their authority by some higher level of government (for example, city charters granted by states).

Along a second dimension of political authority are regulatory instruments that are more or less compatible with exchange. Although continuous, we can distinguish five discrete categories:

1. *Market creating*: public policies designed to create markets by establishing rights, incentives, and opportunities for exchange (for example, creating a market for air pollution rights).

2. *Market facilitating*: policies that promote or improve the operation of markets by reducing transactions costs, enhancing incentives, or internalizing benefits and costs (for example, public investment in transportation to expand the geographic scope of markets by reducing transport costs).

3. *Market modifying*: regulations that attempt to change the conduct of the subjects, objects, medium or terms of exchange, in order to produce outcomes different from those the market would otherwise produce (for example, agricultural marketing orders).

4. *Market substituting*: policies that create substitutes for markets; instruments of political authority are used to allocate or distribute resources or control conduct of individuals or organizations; outcomes are achieved by the exercise of authority rather than by exchange, (for example, the provision of public school education through rationing rather than through market exchange).

5. *Market proscribing*: policies that attempt to prohibit exchanges by particular subjects or of particular objects, with no attempt to use authority as a substitute method for achieving a given outcome; rather, authority is used in an effort to prevent that outcome from occurring (for example, laws prohibiting the sale of dangerous drugs).

A third dimension along which policies differ is their respective degree of coercion or compulsion. At one extreme, there are laws or policies carrying virtually no compulsion, because they are superfluous (that is, people would have acted in the legally prescribed way with or without the law); unenforced (for lack of adequate enforcement capacity, prosecutorial discretion or social consensus that it is a bad law); or though enforced, the sanctions imposed are not sufficiently severe to have much effect on conduct. At the other extreme, policies can be extremely coercive, when enforcement and sanctions are highly effective and the conduct prescribed or proscribed by the law is greatly different from individual preferences. Most laws, of course, lie in the middle ground in which individuals' conduct is modified, but with no great sense of loss of personal freedom due to a high degree of compulsion. When categorizing policies with respect to coerciveness, it should be noted that laws often require us to do what is good for us and others; we are happy to comply with the law, and happy to have the law so that others will comply as well (for example, traffic laws).[2]

These three dimensions of authority—the degree of publicness, the degree of compatibility with exchange, and the degree of compulsion—explain much of the ideological battle over the use of authority in general, or the selection of public policies in particular. Libertarians prefer instruments of authority that are more private and less public, most compatible with markets, and least coercive. Conservatives tend to prefer policies that protect prevailing property interests (whether compatible with markets or not) and that are coercive (for example, heavy penalties for socially unacceptable behavior). Liberals tend to favor public authority instruments that constrain, replace, or limit the scope of exchange. One might characterize the recent wave of neoliberalism as a shift in liberal thought toward public policies more compatible with, rather than hostile toward, market exchange and private incentives.

TYPES OF REGULATIONS

We have attempted to order our typology of regulations along these three dimensions. Thus, we have arranged policy instruments from most to least compatible with markets, from most private to most public, and from least to most cohesive. This is done for the sake of logical organization, not necessarily as a reflection of our own ideological preferences.

One is tempted to argue that a particular type of regulatory response is most appropriate to deal with a particular type of market failure; certainly there are those who offer specific responses as a panacea. If this were so, then we could map the responses onto the failures and provide a guide as to what kind of response to use on any particular problem. But political reality is quite the contrary: there is no one-to-one correspondence between each respective type of market failure and regulatory response. Although certain responses may be recognized as more appropriate, and hence more often used in response to particular market failures, public policy

makers have historically applied almost every type of response to each type of market failure. Table 1 summarizes the types and categories of regulatory responses to market failures.

Legal Rights

In a market-oriented economy, legal rights are essential to the creation and functioning of markets. The definitions of these rights sometimes determine whether exchange will even occur; more often, they affect the terms of exchange. They do so by designating property that can be exchanged (property rights) and are protected (criminal law); assigning transactions and compliance costs (contract rights); defining liability for intended or unintended consequences of exchange (liability rights); allowing, facilitating, or denying associational rights (corporate law, collective bargaining rights); delineating the range of applicability of the rights; and establishing the rules of evidence, proof, proceeding, and standing (civil and administrative procedural rights and due process rights).

In the U.S. legal system, these rights are defined and protected through a hierarchy of common, administrative, statutory, and constitutional laws. All of these evolve historically, which is to say that precedence and tradition are powerful determinants of legal policies and their interpretation by legislative, judicial, executive, and administrative agencies. The continual redefinition, expansion, or contraction of legal rights reflects prevailing social consensus, legal and political theory, and the perceived effects of current and potential definitions. Although legal instruments of authority are seldom selected solely on the basis of their effects on exchange relations, it is undeniable that they have important exchange-regulatory intent and consequences.

James M. Carman / Robert G. Harris

TABLE 1. Types of Regulations.

Type of Response	Variations	Examples
Legal rights	Property rights	Land ownership
	Contracts rights	Compliance enforcement
	Associational rights	Public utility franchises
	Procedural rights	Rule-making participation
	Due process	Corporation as "person"
Information responses		
Promoting markets	Protection from liability	Consumer reports
	Allowing cooperative action	Better Business Bureau
Disclosure	Available on request	Worker health records
	Public reporting	SEC Financial reports
	Provision in exchange	Labeling laws
Content	Specific	Sugar content of food
	Comprehensive	Therapeutic drug insert
Protection	Privacy rights	Confidential records
	Accuracy of information	Credit reporting
	Agreement of owner	Patents, trademarks
Public provision	Available on request	Consumer buying guides
	General dissemination	Auto safety records
	Mandatory consumption	Public health education
Standards		
Compliance	Voluntary	Uniform package sizes
	Mandatory	Milk processing
Object of standard	Producers	Occupational licensing
	Production process	Food processing
	Product	Auto safety standards
	Consumption process	Speed limits
	Consumer	Drivers' licensing
Source of standard	Market incentives	CP/M° operating system
	Private provision	Underwriter's laboratory
	Exchange transactions	Procurement standards
	Private collective action	FASB account principles
	Public agencies	Restaurant sanitation
Nature of standard	Performance	Allowable emissions
	Design	Catalytic converters
Taxes/subsidies		
Form of transfer	Money payments	Income tax, Soc. Security
	Stamps, coupons	Food stamps
	Discounts	Senior citizens/transit
	Services in kind	Indigent medical services
Method of transfer	Incentive for private action	Charitable deductions
	Internal cross-subsidies	Regulated prices
	Rationing	Import quotas
	Direct	Income tax, Soc. Security
Object of transfer	Exchanged objects	Sales, excise taxes
	Production process	Effluent charges/subsidies
	Factors of production	Personal income tax
	Ownership	Property taxes
		Corporate income tax

TABLE 1. *(cont)*

Type of Response	Variations	Examples
Controls on collective action		
Horizontal structure	Prohibiting mergers	Sherman Act
	Public franchise	"Regulated" industries
Vertical structure	Prohibiting mergers	Clayton Act
Horizontal conduct	Limits on investment	Joint venture restrictions
	Limits on collusion	Price fixing
	Exemptions from limits	Agricultural cooperatives
Vertical conduct	Limits on cooperation	Boycotts
	Limits on private restraints	Resale price maintenance
	Limits on differences in terms of trade	Price discrimination; exclusive dealing
Price controls		
Compliance	Voluntary	Wage, price guidelines
	Incentives	"Tax Incentive Plan"
	Mandatory	Published tariffs
Source of controls	Contractual	Uranium contract use
	Private cooperation	Food marketing coops
	Public sanction of associational control	State liquor boards
	Public agencies	Public utility commissions
Nature of controls	Price information	Posting, public provision
	Allowable price range	ICC zone of reasonableness
	Public approval of prices	Public utility commissions
	Price setting	Postal rates
Applicability	Seller-specific	Electricity rates
	Class of sellers	Truck rates; minimum wage
	General	Wage/price freeze
Allocative controls	Price subsidies	Food stampss
	Mandate exchange	Common carrier obligation
	Restricting exchange	Rationing coupons
	Proscribing exchange	Cocaine, child labor
Public provision	Quasipublic enterprise	ComSat
	Public enterprise/prices	TVA
	Public agency/user charges	Highways, universities
	Public agency/rationing	Social service agencies

Source: From *Journal of Macromarketing,* vol. 4, no. 1 (Spring 1984), pp. 50–51.

Information Responses

Authority can be used in a variety of ways to generate and disseminate information. Within this category, there is a hierarchy of responses that merely create or extend markets to those that inhibit markets in information, and to those that substitute public for private provision of information.

Information Markets. By means of property rights (or exemptions from liability), authority can be used to facilitate private markets for information, in which individuals exchange for the information needed to make rational decisions in exchange transactions (consumer reports). Policies can also facilitate the voluntary, private provision and production of information by exempting such activ-

James M. Carman / Robert G. Harris

ities from general proscriptions against cooperation among competitors (Better Business Bureau).

Disclosure. Authority can require disclosure of information by the possessor of the information. This typically means that subjects to exchange must provide information regarding the object or terms of exchange. Variants of disclosure requirements include: making information available on demand (allowing workers to inspect health and safety records), public reporting (filing 10-K financial statements), and providing specific disclosure (packaging or labeling laws). The required content of disclosure may range from very narrow (salt content of foods) to very broad (all known attributes and side effects of a therapeutic drug). Authority can also be used to prevent private associations from inhibiting the flow of information (for example, recent Federal Trade Commission rulings prevent professional societies from banning price advertising in their professional codes of ethics).

Protection of Information. Because of the public good aspects of information, authority can be used to prevent the collection or dissemination of information. These remedies include protection against unwarranted intrusions into personal affairs (rights of privacy, confidential records); proscriptions about the accuracy of information content (personal or corporate credit reports); or use of the information without the agreement of the owner of the information (patents, trademarks, copyrights, trade secrets).

Public Provision of Information. Political authority can also be used to actually provide information about the subjects, objects, or terms of exchange to the general public or to specific audiences. The public provision of information can take the form of general distribution through public media

(automobile safety records and crash test results); distribution of materials on request by individuals (agricultural market-information services); or mandatory consumption of information by individuals in government institutions (public-health information in public schools).

Production of Information. Government can regulate information by requiring private parties to produce (or government can produce) information that might not otherwise exist. Required product testing by private parties or government agencies is the most prominent instance of information production by exercise of authority.

Standards Remedies

Even if information were free, human rationality is limited, so more information is not necessarily better. In complex market economies, the frequency and complexity of exchange generates information overload. In recognition of these limits, authority is employed to reduce the need for information by creating standards applicable to exchange relations. By indicating that the object of the standard meets or exceeds some threshold level on one (or more) attribute(s), subjects of exchange need less or no information about that attribute. Unfortunately, standards are so varied and complex that they cannot be reduced to a linear hierarchy of types. Rather, we identify the several dimensions on which standards differ and discrete categories of standards.

Compliance. Standards can range from purely voluntary (uniform package sizes) to highly mandatory, meaning that products failing to meet the standard are excluded from legal markets (for example, milk standards).

Object of the Standard. Standards can be applied to the producers (professional certification or licensing), the production process (workplace safety standards), the product (auto safety standards),[3] the consumption process (highway speed limits), the consumers (driver's licensing), and the complementary goods and services (highway safety standards, lead content of gasoline). The oldest use of standards regulates the quantities, rather than qualities, of goods exchanged (standard weights and measures). In traditional regulation (the regulated industries in transportation, communications, energy distribution, and financial services), authority is used to comprehensively regulate the production and provision of goods and services, although we sometimes separate responsibility for quality regulation from quantity and price regulation between agencies (Federal Aviation Administration regulates airline safety, whereas the Civil Aeronautics Board regulates entry, exit, quantity, and price of service).

Source of Standards. We can also distinguish standards by the process by which standards are developed, promulgated, and/or enforced. Standards are regularly generated by market processes, of course, when firms have incentives to standardize product attributes even though no authority requires them to do so (as in the adoption of PC-DOS operating systems for sixteen-bit microprocessors). Authority can be used to promote private contractual standards (legally enforceable exchange terms, as in procurement contracts or collective bargaining agreements) and private associational standards (promulgated by industry trade association, privately or publicly enforced, as in SEC-encouraged standards generated by the Financial Standards Accounting Board).[4] Standards are promulgated and enforced by public agencies (usually with private participation), as in public health and sanitation standards for restaurant and personal care establishments.

Nature of Standards. We can also categorize standards as performance-oriented, design-oriented, or ingredient-oriented. Performance standards establish threshold levels for outcomes, while leaving producers or consumers discretion as to the method of achieving the specified performance (for example, specifying the units of emitants allowed from a factory). Design standards require that the object of the standard be manufactured or operate in a specific way (for example, requiring manufacturers to install catalytic converters to control emissions). Ingredient standards specify actual, minimum, and/or maximum ingredients required in order for the product to be sold, or in order to be designated by a commonly accepted name (for example, mayonnaise).

Taxes and Subsidies

There are three general purposes served by government fiscal policies and operations: allocation, distribution, and stabilization. Government collects revenues to cover the costs of government; to redistribute income among individuals; and to stabilize prices, reach full employment, and reach full economic growth. Our concern here is with the use of taxes or subsidies as the means of correcting market failures, that is, with the regulatory functions of fiscal policies. In thereby limiting the discussion, we do not mean to suggest that there are not other important functions of taxes and subsidies.

Taxes and subsidies are logically similar, although of opposite sign. The one logical difference between them as instruments of authority is that, in any given instance, there is almost always a higher degree of coercion attached to taxes than to subsidies. Someone eligible for Social Security payments can simply not request them, or refuse them if offered, with no legal sanction. One does not have the same option with respect to payment of Social Security taxes, however. Having acknowledged this distinction, it will greatly expedite the discussion to treat taxes and subsidies as roughly equivalent instruments of public policy, except that in one case the transfer of resources is negative, in the other, positive.

Form of Transfer. Taxes or subsidies can take one of several forms. The most commonly used means of transfer is money (or near-money) payments (as in Social Security). The second form of transfers is stamps or coupons, which can be spent like money, but only for the purchase of specified goods or services (food stamps, educational vouchers). The third form of transfer is through the price mechanism, that is, modifying the terms of exchange so that the subjects pay (receive) less (more) than the market-determined price (senior citizen discounts). If these exchanges are made at a zero price, we can classify them as a fourth form of transfers, namely the direct provision of goods and services (indigent medical services, urban playgrounds).

Method of Transfer. Authority can be used directly or indirectly to tax and subsidize. Indirect methods include creating incentives for private, voluntary transfers among individuals and associations (charitable giving promoted by tax deductibility). Transfers can also be achieved by regulating the prices of goods and services (long distance telephone users being taxed to subsidize local telephone users). Another indirect public method of transfer is to ration or restrict markets, so as to affect the income of factors in the market (subsidizing the domestic auto producers, shareholders, and employees by import quotas on Japanese autos). Finally, transfers can be made directly (income taxes, Social Security payments).

Object of Transfer. Transfers vary in the object and range of their applicability. One generic class of transfers is directed toward objects transferred in exchange; goods and services are taxed or subsidized, either in general (sales tax) or specific (excise tax). Taxes or subsidies can be applied to the side effects of production, consumption, or exchange (effluent taxes, emission-control subsidies). Another category of transfers is tied to the ownership (rather than transfer) of goods (property taxes). Another generic class of transfers is related to the earnings of factors of production (personal income, capital gains taxes). Finally, transfers can be directed at producing agencies (corporate income taxes, subsidies to mass transit agencies or universities).

Controls on Collective Action

Given the nature of the consumption, production, and exchange processes, collective organizations are a virtual necessity in modern economies. Collective action has three main purposes: (1) to realize economies of scale in production, (2) to internalize the benefits of productive actions, and (3) to change the balance of power between participants in the exchange process. The state allows and encourages collective action by a variety of regulatory instruments already covered, including associational rights.[5] Surely the most important of these are the rights of incorporation granted to companies and labor unions (including limited liability and equity ownership and transfer rights in the first case, collective bargaining and grievance procedural rights in the second). Authority also promotes collective action by use of taxes and subsidies: by granting subsidies to collective agents (government grants to private social service agencies or research institutes), by exempting contributions to collective from taxation (contributions to charitable agencies are tax deductible, whereas contributions made directly to needy individuals are not), and by exempting collective agencies from taxation (tax exempt status of nonprofit organizations). In addition to these regulatory instruments, authority is used to control markets and market failures by directly shaping the structure of markets and controlling the conduct of organizations in the following ways.

Horizontal Structure. In order to affect bargaining positions in the exchange process, authority shapes the structure of competitors (buyers or sellers). While property rights and the rights of incorporation create a presumption that organizations may grow and expand without further approval, authority can be used to specifically deny such expansion when it threatens the competitive process (antitrust laws on mergers and acquisitions). A more restrictive class of structural controls are entry and exit regulation, which strictly limit the opportunity of producers to enter a market, or to exit from it (public franchises in transportation, communications, and financial services).[6] Although authority primarily has been concerned with power within a given market, there are also controls that span markets, since power in one market might give an unequal bargaining position in another market (restrictions on conglomerate mergers, restrictions on the activities of bank-holding companies).

Vertical Structure. All markets exhibit a high degree of vertical interdependence, with goods moving through many successive transactions from the original source to the final consumer. Accordingly, authority can be employed to regulate the vertical structure of markets, especially those involving economic organizations on both sides of exchange. Structural controls may specify the conditions under which firms will be allowed to vertically integrate across channel levels, or actually prohibit such vertical integration (statutes on vertical mergers).

Horizontal Conduct Controls. In order to shape market structure, authority allows, encourages, and prohibits competitors from cooperating in various ways. To promote the flow of information and the establishment of standards, competitors are usually allowed to cooperate in those areas. Cooperation in research and development, investments in productive capacity, and marketing activities may be allowed or denied (joint-venture regulations). Because of its onerous effects on bargaining, cooperation on the design of the product or on the terms of exchange (especially price) is often prohibited (Sherman and Clayton proscriptions against restraints in trade). In cases where there is a perceived imbalance in bargaining positions, however, cooperation among competitors is allowed, usually by exemption from laws prohibiting such cooperation (antitrust exemptions granted to agricultural marketing cooperatives, the rationale for which is the market failure of excessive competition; buying cooperatives).

Vertical Conduct Controls. In recognition of the complexity of channels of distribution, the state regulates relations among members of the channel, by allowing acts of cooperation (cooperative advertising), denying other acts of cooperation (boycotts), prohibiting certain restrictions in the terms of trade (resale price maintenance), and setting limits on discriminatory treatment in the terms of trade (Robinson-Patman proscriptions on price discrimination, provisions in the proposed AT&T consent decree requiring local operating companies to provide equal access to competing long-distance signal carriers).

Price Controls

Because prices are so central to the allocative functioning of markets, and so critical to the distributional consequences of exchange, authority is used to influence or determine the prices at which exchanges occur. As already noted, prices may be influenced by the imposition of taxes or granting of subsidies, and by controls on the structure of markets and the conduct of subjects in markets. In addition, there are class-of-authority instruments aimed more or less directly at prices themselves, either because other forms of control have failed to produce the desired result or because price controls are preferred to alternative forms of control.

There are a number of dimensions on which price controls vary, and the number of permutations across dimensions is very large. Rather than identifying discrete types of price controls, we will discuss the dimensions that characterize any particular control instrument, and attempt to identify the variants on each dimension.

Compliance. Price controls range from purely voluntary (wage and price guidelines), to quasi-voluntary (use of economic incentives to induce particular pricing behavior, the Tax Incentive Plan for restricting wage increases in labor markets), to mandatory (published tariffs in regulated industries).

Source of Controls. As with standards, prices can be established, and compliance enforced, in a number of ways. The most private method of price control is private exchange, as enforced by contractual rights (long-term supply contracts). Prices also can be established by private agreement among competitors (producer cartels), although this form of price control is often precluded by controls on collective action. Authority can be used to establish or sanction price controls

(fee schedules established by professional societies), which means that public authority is employed to enforce compliance with the controls. Price controls can be established by private agencies or association, but submitted to public authority for approval and implementation (state liquor control boards). Finally, price controls can be generated and enforced by public agencies, although usually with procedural rights assuring private participation.

Nature of Controls. Although price controls are always directed at the price terms of exchange, they vary in the manner by which the intended results are achieved. The most marketlike forms of price control are related to price information: requiring disclosure (price posting of wholesale liquor prices to dealers or posting of gasoline prices at the pump); precluding private control on disclosure (banning professional code limits on price advertising); and public provision (comparative price studies published by government agencies). Direct intervention in the pricing process includes establishing a zone within which private parties can set prices (the zone of reasonableness recently adopted by the Interstate Commerce Commission); requiring specific approval of privately set prices (most administrative agencies only approve prices, not actually set them); and establishing the price at which goods or services will be exchanged (postal rates, minimum wages).

Applicability of Controls. Price controls can be applied very narrowly to a specific transaction, or to all transactions between a particular seller (buyer) and its buyers (local telephone rates are seller-specific). More generally, price controls can be applied to all sellers (buyers) in a broad class (motor carrier rates). The most general type of price controls applies to whole sectors of the economy, or even, hypothetically to all prices in the economy (general price freeze). While price controls are most often applied to goods and services in intermediate and final markets, they can also be used in factor markets (minimum wage laws, interest rate ceilings).

Direct Allocative Controls

Prices and rationing are alternative means of allocating or distributing resources. Although rationed goods often carry prices, the defining characteristic of rationing is that exchange is no longer a purely voluntary act by the parties to the exchange: there is some compulsion (in addition to economic incentives) at work on either or both sides of the transaction. Rationing can be implemented directly by public agency or through private exchange transaction channels (public schools versus educational vouchers for private schools). Furthermore, rationing can be positive or negative: it can be used to facilitate the transfer of resources or restrict exchange transactions. We can distinguish the following type of allocative controls.

Price Subsidies. As we indicated previously, subsidies can be granted in the form of stamps or coupons, which can be used along with money in the purchase of specified goods or services. The function of the subsidies in these cases is to increase the ration of those goods to the recipients of the coupons (that is, relative to their ration under market prices). This form of rationing is not intended to limit or restrict the allocation of goods to nonrecipients of the subsidies, although it may have that affect (by increasing the demand for, and therefore market-equilibrating price of, the subsidized goods). It should be noted that this form of rationing may actually be intended to subsidize the producers of the goods, rather than the consumers (hence the support of agricultural lobbies for the food stamp program).

Mandating Exchange. Goods and services also can be positively rationed by requiring sellers to exchange with specified buyers (either at a privately negotiated price or at a regulated price). This form of rationing is commonly employed in public utilities and common carriers, wherein franchised producers are required to provide services on demand to all potential buyers within their franchise area, and at published tariffs. As in price subsidies, the intent of this rationing is to increase, rather than decrease, the volume of exchange; it may also have the effect of restricting exchange (some classes of buyers usually pay implicit taxes in order to subsidize the provision of services to customers whose revenues do not cover the cost of service).

Restricting Exchange. In the event of excess demand for goods, allocative controls can be used to restrict production, exchange, and/or consumption of certain goods and services. Under these controls, money alone is an insufficient means of payment; stamps, coupons, or some other evidence of authority is also required (ration coupons during World War II). Allocative controls also can be applied to factor markets, as in laws regulating hours of employment, or credit allocation.

Proscribing Exchange. The most market-delimiting form of allocative controls is the prohibition of (legal) exchange of goods and services. This form of control is typically directed at those instances in which there is a substantial conflict between market outcomes (in the absence of controls) and prevailing social values (that is, demerit goods). The most emphatic application of this form of control is embodied in the Emancipation Proclamation, which forbade exchange of human beings, and in the labor laws designed to protect children from exploitation in labor markets. As applied to consumer markets, proscriptive controls apply to goods (dangerous drugs) and services (prostitution). We might add that market responses to these prohibitions is a rather striking example of the limits of enforcement and level of compliance with acts of authority.

Government Provision of Goods and Services

As has been noted in the previous sections on regulatory responses, authority can be exercised by allowing, encouraging, or requiring specified conducts or outcomes of private parties, or it can be implemented by the state itself. Depending on the actual configuration of public action, then, authority is more or less consistent with market exchange. When the government is merely providing information that facilitates and improves the operation of markets, there is no conflict between politics and markets. The government can also influence market outcomes by its own actions in the marketplace, as in the use of procurement standards to influence product design (for example, purchasing government auto fleets with air bags to help auto makers on the scale necessary to economically offer them as an option to other customers).

Beyond these market facilitating acts, though, government can be directly involved in markets by substituting for them. Through the use of public enterprise, for example, the government grants to itself the franchise necessary for transacting in that market (postal services). By holding the rights of ownership to itself, government can more or less exclude the enterprise from capital markets and substitute public authority for market control of the firm; along this dimension are quasipublic enterprises (ConRail, ComSat) and government enterprises (U.S. Postal Service). Having established agencies of government as the provider of goods and services, these agencies differ in whether their output is exchanged through markets with prices (public universities), quasiprices (user charges such as gasoline excise taxes), or rations (social services).

TYPES OF REGULATORY FAILURES

This section presents a typology of regulatory failures—that is, how and why public actions intended to correct market failures (at last purportedly) fail to achieve their goals. This section provides guidelines for deciding when regulatory action may be justified and for choosing among alternative regulatory responses.

To set the stage for this typology, we provide a summary of regulatory responses and market failures. While we would expect fundamental rights and the common law to affect virtually all types of market failures, it would seem logical that other regulatory responses would be used to solve specific types of market failures. Table 2 shows quite a different picture. It is possible to cite instances in which each type of regulation is being used in response to each type of market failure.

Thus, while we will say something about the design of regulatory responses and their likelihood of success, it is not possible to specify a single kind of remedy that should be applied to each particular type of market failure: the uses of regulatory instruments are more pervasive, and their success or failure more complicated. Key questions that should be addressed in evaluating regulatory responses are:

Are the consequences of a market failure sufficient to justify the cost of the regulation and the performance that it can reasonably be expected to achieve?

Do the apparent shortcomings of a given regulation stem from its design or implementation, or are they inherent in the nature of the original market failure?

Are there other regulatory responses that would be more likely to achieve better performance or be more cost effective?

Will a regulatory response that is success-

TABLE 2. Typology of Market Failures and Regulatory Responses.

Regulatory Responses	Types of Market Failures							
	Monopoly Power	Anticompetitive Conduct	Excessive Competition	Imperfect Information	Externalities/ Side Effects	Public Goods	(De)Merit Goods	Income Distribution
Legal rights and liabilities	Unenforceable contracts (e.g., cartels)	Criminal antitrust statutes	Bankruptcy laws	Product liability; commercial libel limits	Nonsmoking workplace rights	Anti-discrimination laws	Controlled substance criminal liabilities	Limits on right-to-fire employment-at-will
Information	Line-of-business reporting	Ban of professional advertising restrictions	Licensing boards' information services	Cigarette packaging/ advertising warnings	Toxic waste "sight right-to-know" ordinances	Public health information	Ratings of movies	State employment agencies
Standards	Electric utility service reliability	Fair trade laws	Aircraft maintenance standards	Funeral industry disclosure requirements	Automobiles catalytic converters	Federal highway design standards	State accreditation of schools	Equal opportunity employment standards
Taxes/ subsidies	Excess profits tax (WWII)	Antitrust civil fines	Local air service subsidies	FDA's "failure-to-disclose" fines	Fines for air-water effluent violations	Tax exemption of non-profit schools	National endowments for arts-humanities	A.I.D., Medicare
Controls on/rights of collective action	Antitrust/ restraint of trade (telephone)	Boycott restrictions	Legal cartels (agricultural marketing boards)	Class action product liability	Class action environmental suits	Permit control on parades/ demonstrations in public places	Antitrust exemption for newspapers	Labor union organizing, collective bargaining
Price controls	Utility rate regulation	Predatory pricing limits	Minimum rate regulation	State insurance regulation	Peacetime price/wage controls	Deposit bottle bills to combat litter	State liquor price controls	Lifeline utility rates
Allocative controls	Equal carrier access (telephone)	Antidumping provisions	Entry controls (taxi, motor carrier permits)	Prescription drugs	Offshore drilling rights	Allocation of radio and TV broadcast license	Public school attendance requirements	Import preferences to Third World countries
Public provision	Highways; municipal electric utilities	Law concerning political debates on TV	Depository insurance; crop loans	Consumer buying guides	Public schools and higher education	National parks and forests	Public schools and higher education	Social welfare services

ful in the short term prove to be a failure over the longer term?

Are there secondary or aggregate effects of a regulation on the marketing system or other social systems that outweigh the direct or immediate effects of the regulation?

Public Choice Failures

While most public-policy analyses are typically cast in terms of economic efficiency, fairness, freedom, and equity are criteria that are more basic to a democratic society. Indeed, the most fundamental basis for a market economy is that only a free-market system is consistent with political freedom and individual liberty. Moreover, democratic societies regularly use methods of organization and control that are not efficient in the narrow sense of the term. Perhaps the best example of inefficiency in a democratic society is an election. Imagine bearing the costs of having millions of people go to the polls when a small random sample of the population could produce the same result at a fraction of the cost, although with some small margin of sampling error. In democratic societies, we do use representational methods to increase efficiency over ongoing town meetings. In addition to elections, our primary institutions of public choice are legislatures, judiciaries, and executive agencies. As with markets, we can identify the ideal character of these institutions, but we use those ideals as standards against which to measure or compare realities. As markets fail, so do the institutions and instruments of authority. Some failures are inherent in the public-choice process itself.[7]

Transaction Costs. Public choice is a costly proposition, regardless of the method or object of choice. For this reason, public choices have a natural longevity, the duration of which is determined by a subsequent act of public choice that eliminates, modifies, or substitutes for prior choice. While in markets we often make frequent, periodic choices (which store to shop at, which brand of soft drink to buy), we make public choices much less frequently. By and large, prevailing policies are the accumulation of prior public choices. As circumstances change over time, we should expect that, even if the policy were once appropriate, it will become less so over time. But because of the transactions costs of public choice, we do not spontaneously change policies in accord with changing circumstances.

Electoral Failures. Elections play three different roles in public choice: (1) by referenda, voters actually decide public policy; (2) by electing legislators, voters decide who will make policy decisions; and (3) by electing executives, voters decide who will make and/or implement policy decisions. Although there are some similarities between markets and elections (enough so that modern political economists refer to the supply of and demand for political services and the marketing of candidates), there are some fundamental differences.

The most critical difference between markets and politics is that there can be no exchange; candidates for elected office can promise to support certain policies or promote certain values if elected, but they cannot offer anything specific in exchange for someone's vote. Even if such a promise were made, it would be an unenforceable contract between the parties (which is not to deny that such promises have been made, and parties have attempted to enforce such contracts, albeit in violation of the law). In short, elections lack the reciprocity essential to exchange.

Elections differ most from markets in their inherently collective nature. Whereas market exchanges are acts of private, individual choice, elections must necessarily be acts of public, collective choice (Olson 1971). Unless we impose a rule of unanimity (which would make public choice impossible in most electorates), election results will favor some individuals over others. Indeed, a central feature of the social contract in democratic societies is that individuals agree to accept the results of elections, even when they lose.

As a consequence of majority rule, the result of an election is a public good in that an individual voter can neither determine the outcome nor be excluded from incurring the benefits or costs of the outcome. As a public good, the electoral process suffers from the problem of free riders. No matter how or even whether one individual votes, the outcome will be the same. So even though elections may have very important consequences for individuals, they have little incentive to become well informed, or even participate in the process.

Even when citizens do vote, elections suffer from a number of problems not unlike market failures. There are very serious information failures: compared to most economic products and services, public choices are exceedingly more complex. In order for elections to work well, voters must understand the nature and consequences of alternative votes; such information is always costly, time-consuming to process, often unavailable, and sometimes misleading. Issues of public choice are on occasion so complex that not even the experts fully understand the alternatives, much less the electorate.

Another electoral failure relates to the bundling of issues. Although market goods are a bundle of desired attributes, we typically have considerable choice among bundles. Indeed, some tied sales are illegal. In elections, we are usually limited to two (or other small number) of choices: yes or no on referenda, Democratic or Republican representation. Because an elected official will represent his/her constituency on countless issues of public choice, it is a certainty that there will be differences between the votes or the legislator (or the acts of an executive or judge) and the preferences of any given voter. Thus, bundling forces individuals to make difficult trade-offs among issues; they may favor one candidate's stand on transportation policy, another on energy policies.

Alternatively, some voters may use a choice process that places such importance on a particular high saliency issue that the candidates' position on that single issue may determine their vote. The result may be that the winning candidate, while favoring the right position on the single issue, may have positions on other issues that are at odds with the majority of the electorate.

Legislative Failures. Once elected, legislators ideally act in the interests of a majority of their constituency, although that necessarily means action against the interests of some constituents on any given issue. Moreover, we assume that legislators are not fundamentally different from other individuals, so we expect them to behave (if sometimes opportunistically) in their own self-interest. Given the costs of conducting electoral campaigns, and the need for organized support to overcome information failures, one significant failure is the influence of resourceful, vocal, well-organized citizens in the legislative process. Legislators also suffer from information failures, in that the issues they decide are extremely complex individually, and usually bundled together in legislative acts.

Other legislative failures relate to their representation and organizational structure. These structural failures include: (1) the over-representation of rural interests in the U.S. Senate or state senates (that is, citizens in jurisdiction with small populations have far more senators per capita than those in populous jurisdictions); (2) the committee and seniority systems concentrate power in the hands of a minority of representatives, whose interests (or even whose constituents' interests) are not necessarily those of a majority of the electorate; and (3) the complexity and number of issues is such that elected representatives increasingly depend on staff whose private interests (for example, future employment with lobbying organizations) may differ from constituents' interests.

Jurisdictional Failures. Whether public choice is made directly through elections or through representation, it can create externalities not dissimilar to those found in market systems. Externalities occur because public policies of a given jurisdiction can have effects on citizens or activities in other jurisdictions. Examples of these externalities include air or water pollution moving across state lines, liberal corporate charter provisions causing companies to incorporate in a state other than the one in which they principally do business, and interstate differences in taxes or subsidies causing personal movement to lower tax or higher welfare states. At the highest level, jurisdictional failures arise among nation states, where the consequences of regulatory or market failures of one country may fall on the populace of other countries. Indeed, nationalistic self-interest might seek such results, especially when reciprocity or retaliation is improbable.

Design Failures

As we have shown in table 2, many different types of regulation are used to prevent, modify, and shift the costs/benefits of each type of market failure. Regardless of the type of the intent or method of regulation, policies fail in part because policy makers often lack the information needed to (1) correctly assess the nature and extent of the market failure, (2) evaluate the direct effects of alternative responses, (3) evaluate the side effects of al-

ternative responses, (4) correctly predict the incidence of costs and benefits of the regulation, or (5) simply design a regulatory response that will solve the market failure. In some cases, the necessary information is simply not available (that is, it lies beyond the limits of human knowledge or is prohibitively expensive to obtain). In other cases, the problem is one of information asymmetry: the parties to be regulated have, or control access to, the information needed for the policy design, but the public policy makers do not. Participants in the policy design process will exploit this asymmetry to gain strategic advantage. These information failures, combined with the legislative failures just described, lead to, ex post, poorly designed regulation.

A special kind of information failure concerns external and side effects. Efforts to regulate one market or product almost inevitably affect other goods or markets. Regulating auto emissions by requiring the installation of catalytic converters dramatically shifts the demand for converters while decreasing the demand for research and development into superior methods of emission control. There is virtually no limit to these side effects, as they are transmitted, like ripples, from one market to another. In the worst cases, negative effects are amplified in magnitude; in such cases, regulation may be successful where it was intended, but still is a failure overall because the indirect effects outweigh the direct benefits.

Even where there are discernible benefits of regulation, there are always costs as well. The self-evident costs are those incurred by the government in implementing a policy, but these are sometimes small relative to the total costs, which include the costs of complying with the regulation by private parties. Because the costs and benefits of a regulation are seldom, if ever, borne by the same parties in the same proportions, there are inevitably distributional consequences of regulation, whatever their primary purpose may be.[8]

Implementation Failures

Once policies are selected, through the democratic public-choice process (either in the present or very distant past), they must be implemented to have an effect on private conduct or market outcomes. The legislature delegates responsibility for implementation to an agency of the government, a quasi-public agency (one with legal powers granted by the state), or a voluntary association of individuals. Although legislative enactments sometimes contain specific provisions regarding delegation, more often acts are implicitly delegated on the basis of general principles (or laws) of delegation. Thus, the implementation of contract compliance provisions falls to the judicial system as a matter of constitutional principle. Sometimes legislative acts create new agencies for implementation of the policies in the act, although even then legislatures are constrained by legal separation of power, jurisdictional rights among units of government, and the organization of those units.

Although there are a large variety of institutional mechanisms for implementing public policies, we will concentrate our attention by grouping into four classes: judicial agencies, bureaucratic agencies, public boards, and private associations. While all of these suffer from more or less the same generical institutional failures (mainly, information failures, transactions costs, free riders and agent-principal problems), the manifestations of these failures differ across institutional types. It is because of these differences that we choose one agency of implementation over another in order to minimize the failures and improve performance and outcomes.

Judicial Failures. The distinguishing characteristic of judicial agencies is that they implement policies by deciding whether par-

ties have, in a given instance, complied with prevailing policies (constitutional, statutory, administrative, or common law). The parties engaged in the process can be individuals, associations, or other public agencies. Typically, these decisions are made in an adversarial process, which has a number of institutional implications.

First, principals in the dispute (plaintiff, prosecutor, or defendant) are represented by agents (lawyers) who receive income for their services. Self-interested behavior of agents often conflicts with the interests of the principals (for example, expending resources to appeal a decision that will surely be upheld).

Second, the adversaries in the dispute represent only two of the interests affected by the decision; there are externalities of judicial acts both positive and negative (for example, establishing a precedent that will be used in future cases). One of the most frequently cited failures of regulatory agencies is of this sort: the tendency of agencies to be captured by well-organized interested parties, to the exclusion of other interests.

Third, the information available to the decision maker (judge, jury, or regulatory commission) will depend in large part on the evidentiary submissions of the parties, with consequent information failures. Information needed for a good decision may not exist, or it may be concealed. The quality of the information presented is dependent on the representational abilities of the agents and the resources of the principals; if there is an imbalance in abilities or resources, the decision process may not be fair.

Finally, there are inherent limits of judicial decisions (as opposed to executive actions); courts have very limited enforcement capabilities. Though actions can be prevented (injunctions), courts are generally limited to punishing or compensating for acts that have already occurred. When those acts have irreversible, irreparable, or otherwise noncompensable consequences, courts cannot remedy them.

Bureaucratic Failures. Responsibility for interpretation and implementation of public policies are commonly assigned to agencies of government. The standard organizational form of these agencies is bureaucratic, hence the classification of the failures associated with implementation by public agencies. Because individuals in bureaucracies are self-interested, a most significant class of bureaucratic failure is the pursuit of organizational objectives contrary to the objectives of the public policies (Crozer 1963). One prominent instance of such behavior is budget-maximization, but there are many others as well: promoting policies that will further the career objectives of agency employees, acting favorably toward parties for financial gain or future employment prospects, or interpreting policies in a manner consistent with personal values, but inconsistent with the social values on which the policies are premised (Fritschler and Ross 1980; Wilson 1980).

Bureaucracies also fail due to information failures. As they often are dependent on regulated industries for data and analysis, they are subject to opportunistic behavior by those parties. In any case, the issues they must decide and the actions they must take to successfully implement policies are complex, sometimes beyond the limits of bounded rationality.[9]

The most widely noted failure of bureaucracies is their cost, which is indeed staggering (add up the combined expenditures of all levels of government). But as recent studies have shown (Weidenbaum 1981), the costs of bureaucracy are quite small compared to the costs of compliance with the regulations they impose. Even so, these costs must be measured in relative terms, since alternative institutional forms are not costless.

Finally, there are bureaucratic failures of a jurisdictional kind, due to overlapping jurisdictions across agencies or levels of government (for example, attempts by the CAB, FAA, and OSHA to regulate airline working conditions; or the myriad of environmental reports and approvals required for new factory construction). Although many of these are instances of turf protection by agencies, they also result from the inherent structure of governmental authority in a society that values separation of powers and checks and balances. Even in societies of this persuasion, however, there are organizational alternatives. In the United States, the checks are principally through a congressional committee; in the United Kingdom, the checks are principally through the Exchequer; in India, the checks are principally through purposely given overlapping authority to agencies in other ministries.

Quasipublic Agency Failures. One common technique to get around the suboptimization, information failures, and high cost of bureaucracies is the public board. In this structure, private citizens are appointed to sit on a regulatory board. In some cases they serve for only expenses; in other cases they may receive a fee. However, they are not career civil servants. These appointments should reduce costs. The citizens are appointed because, when viewed as a whole, they represent the broad interests of the society, and therefore, are unlikely to seek objectives other than those of society. They are also selected because they have some expert knowledge in the field they are appointed to regulate. Thus, they should overcome some informational failures, and if provided with some agency staff support, they should at least be able to ask the right questions.

Unfortunately, such boards can exhibit failures on all counts. First, since they are expert, active citizens, they are busy. They many not always have the motivation to prepare their positions and decisions as carefully as the society would like. Thus, the staff involvement and costs are as great or greater than if the board were not there. Second, how does an executive branch select a board that represents society, is motivated to serve, and is expert in the special field (as well as active in the right political faction)? The answer is often to pick persons from the field being regulated. Even if true public members are on such boards, they often defer to the expertness of the industry members. Thus, such boards often use their additional information to serve the special interests of the regulated rather than the interests of the society.

Private Association and Self-Regulation Failures. The problems just cited may not be serious if the regulation is concerned with efficacy, internal equity, health, and safety with regard to the practice of a particular profession. In such cases, responsibility for implementing public policies is often granted to private associations in such professions. Normally, these delegations of authority involve individuals or organizations with economic interests affected by the policy, for example, professional licensing boards and agricultural marketing boards. Here, one of the failures of public boards becomes far more serious in such attempts at self-regulation. Clearly, the association's authority can be used in the self-interest of the members of the association without regard to unrepresented interests. This problem is exacerbated by the problems of bounded rationality and asymmetric information. The costs or benefits of authority are usually distributed very unevenly, for example, the benefits of milk price-supports accrue mainly to a few thousand producers, while the costs are borne by tens of millions of consumers. In these circumstances, it is quite rational for the producer group of individuals to devote their time, energy, and resources to the formation and implementation of authority, while the rest of society ignores the situation.

Another class of failures of self-regulation relates to the appointed citizens' limited authority. When we delegate authority to private associations, we specifically limit that grant, either in the terms of the act authorizing the delegation or by more general legal principles. Thus, private remedies sometimes fail because the private association lacks the authority to obtain a sufficient degree of compliance for its policies. This is especially true when there are public goods at issue, as when the benefits or costs of labor organizing for collective bargaining accrue to all employees, whether or not they participate in the organizing and bargaining process.

Finally, policy implementation by a private association often fails due to agent-principal problems. Authority is seldom exercised directly by the members of an association. Having received a grant of authority from the state, they in turn delegate the responsibility for implementation to administrators or representatives, who may or may not be members of the class of recipients of authority (staff members of professional licensing boards or trade associations). As self-interested individuals, these agents may behave opportunistically to advance their own interests at the expense of the association members.

IMPLICATIONS FOR PUBLIC POLICY

During the mid-1960s to the mid-1980s, public policies in the United States have undergone historic changes. We have witnessed, on the one hand, an enormous increase in the degree and extent of social regulation such as equal employment, environmental and consumer protection, occupational and product safety, financial disclosure, and civil rights. On the other hand, deregulation of whole industries has occurred in trucking, airlines, telephone equipment, intercity telecommunications, and securities brokerage. What accounts for these seemingly contradictory trends, and what do they tell us about public policies toward business and business-government relations?

There seem to be four general forces at work. First, as the structure of markets changes, so does the structure of regulation. Regulations that were once well-suited for a given market failure no longer fit the situation well. This clearly happened in the deregulation of airlines, trucking, and intercity telecommunications. Airlines and trucking were, when first regulated, infant industries subject to problems of excessive competition. By the 1970s, though, both were mature industries with well-developed route systems serving every corner of the nation. The costs of price controls far exceed the benefits, as the results of deregulation have demonstrated. When telecommunications was first regulated, the basic technology was wire and poles, with substantial economies of scale, making the industry a natural monopoly. With the development of microwave communications in the 1950s, and its widespread adoption by the 1970s, the industry was no longer a natural monopoly. Again, a change in economic conditions justified a shift in public policy. The same is true of social regulation, but with a resulting increase, rather than decrease, in regulation.

A second force underlying regulatory change is changing public attitudes about what constitutes market failures. Neither environmental pollution nor racial employment discrimination were new problems in the 1960s, yet neither had occupied prominent positions on the public-policy agenda. Led perhaps by populist journalism and mass communications media, public perceptions of the social harms caused by these and other market failures increased dramatically. Legislative hearings shed the search light of political attention and public opinion on these problems, new laws were enacted, and whole new regulatory agencies created. It may well be that, as a body politic, we over-reacted to the problems, weighing the costs of market failures while discounting the costs of regulatory intervention. But the point here is that

changing public values and attitudes do cause changes in public policies toward business.

The third force affecting regulatory change is the growth of knowledge regarding the consequences of production and consumption activities. There have been many cases of externalities, for example, that simply were not known, sometimes for decades. The long-term health effects of workplace environments and consumer products have become much better understood with recent advances in medical knowledge. We did not regulate in the past because we literally did not know of, or understand the sources of, harms to public health and safety. As our knowledge improves, we can change the mix of markets and regulations to better achieve efficiency and equity objectives. Many changes in occupational safety, product safety, and related regulations exemplify the application of new knowledge in the policy-making process.

Increasing knowledge of political, social, and economic institutions, and their consequences represents a fourth major factor affecting regulatory change. As we learn more about regulation and markets and the costs and benefits of using these institutions as methods of economic organization, we use that knowledge to increase, decrease, or modify regulation to improve social performance. Many of the important regulatory changes of the past few years embody innovative techniques or institutional forms. As with all forms of innovation, the development of better ways of regulating can reduce the costs, and increase the effectiveness of regulation.

Finally, regulatory change is driven by shifts in the general conditions of the economy. While market failures can be costly in human terms, regulation can be costly in economic terms. As a society, we are continually confronted with the choice of whether to regulate, but, more fundamentally, how much can we afford to regulate. As the United States has declined from its former position of a dominant world economic power, we have had to confront the ultimate economic choice: of deciding how much public provision of goods, and how much public protection from bads, we are willing to pay for. That is a central source of the tension and the vitality of a democratic society.

NOTES

1. For this view of the legal framework of markets, we owe intellectual debts to Commons (1959) and Samuels (1966). For full bibliographic references, see the bibliography of the preceding article in this book.

2. Schelling (1971) presents an insightful analysis of the use of laws or other instruments of authority in cases involving congestion or free riders.

3. For an excellent set of essays on product quality regulation, see Caves and Roberts (1975).

4. Hemenway (1975) is a thorough analysis of voluntary product standards, with several case studies.

5. Hawley (1981) presents a very interesting discussion of associationalism: the use of public authority to promote social control by private associations.

6. Schmalansee (1979) offers a comprehensive review of the rationale for, and implementation of natural monopoly regulation, and an excellent bibliography of recent theoretical and empirical research in that field.

7. For an excellent synthesis and survey of the public choice literature, see Mueller (1979).

8. Weidenbaum (1981) has estimated compliance costs to be a large multiple of government expenditures on regulation.

9. For a discussion of the role of information and knowledge in regulation, see Hays, Samuel P., "Political Choice in Regulatory Administration," in McCraw (1981).

James M. Carman / Robert G. Harris

4

Managing Corporate Social Responsibility in a Changing Legal Environment

David Silverstein

INTRODUCTION

"Fear of litigation is shaking America's business structure," begins a recent issue of an executive advisory publication. Indeed, during the past several years, two major American businesses, Johns-Manville Sales Corporation and A.H. Robins Corporation, have been driven into bankruptcy proceedings by an avalanche of law suits. Many other firms are battling for survival amidst damages claims totaling billions of dollars. These include products liability actions by consumers, pollution and toxic waste disposal actions by individuals and local communities, and hazardous workplace and employment discrimination claims by employees.

Specific examples of the litigation crisis abound. In recent years, business journals, trade publications and newspapers have carried front page stories about each of the following diverse legal attacks on established American business:

Cigarettes American tobacco companies are besieged by lawsuits brought on behalf of cigarette smokers or their families seeking millions of dollars in damages for the illnesses and deaths which they assert were caused by smoking. So far, tobacco companies have won every case, but the number of these suits continues to mushroom.

Workplace Safety Three former managers, including the president, of a now-defunct Illinois chemical plant, were sentenced to 25-year prison terms after being convicted of homicide in connection with the death of an employee who inhaled a lethal dose of toxic fumes while working in the plant.

Outside Directors Corporations are finding it difficult to retain outside directors on their boards because directors and officers liability coverage has become either unavailable or prohibitively costly. Firms have become desperate enough to ask

Reprinted with permission from the author and the *American Business Law Journal.*

their shareholders to approve resolutions limiting directors' personal liability in future shareholders' derivative actions as an alternative to insurance.

Alcohol Bars, package goods stores, and restaurants are being sued with increasing frequency by patrons, as well as by injured third parties, when motor vehicle accidents are linked to alcohol consumption.

Handguns In a recent Maryland Court of Appeals decision that stunned even veteran observers, a handgun manufacturer was held legally liable to a shooting victim for selling a so-called "Saturday night special" that subsequently was used during a robbery attempt.

Many business and political leaders claim that our legal system has lost touch with modern commercial realities and therefore should be changed. A growing number of executives and management scholars, however, now perceive that business horizons must expand to encompass a wider array of social, moral and ethical concerns. Under the rubric of "corporate social responsibility," or "social assessment," numerous journal articles and entire business school courses are now devoted to refuting the popular gospel that "the business of business is to earn profits." Instead of too quickly making whipping boys of supposedly greedy and insensitive managers, or condemning an allegedly archaic legal system, we should consider the possibility that the real problem lies not so much on either side but rather in the center—specifically in a lack of understanding and the absence of workable channels of communication between our lawmakers and our managers. If America's managers have misunderstood the nature of the American legal system and its historical interaction with our commercial system, they have also failed to timely recognize the signposts that might otherwise have alerted them to important future legal changes.

The imperative for managers to better understand the changing legal environment of business and to anticipate the future direction of the business-government interface has never been greater. The barriers to achieving this understanding, however, are formidable. To anticipate and plan for changes in the business-government relationship requires three skills that few American managers have had the patience or the incentive to cultivate: (1) an understanding of how the business-government relationship has been altered historically in response to environmental forces; (2) a recognition of the environmental forces at work today shaping the business-government interface of tomorrow; and, (3) a strategic planning timeframe that is considerably longer than the short-term, quarterly bottom line approach to which many modern managers subscribe.

This article argues that managing corporate social responsibility in a changing legal environment requires managers to engage in enlightened, long-range strategic forecasting with respect to legal environment issues. In part one, this article presents a classic case study of short-sighted mismanagement and suggests how a common management misperception about the nature of the legal system may have contributed to the problem. In part two, this article reviews the foundations of two traditional approaches to corporate social responsibility. The potential in some situations for conflicting management strategies under these models is then described. In the third part, this article examines how management forecasting of future legal regulation could help to bridge the gap between the traditional approaches. This article argues that by viewing the dominant environmental forces at work in the marketplace today from a dynamic perspective, astute managers can make reliable predictions about the changing legal environment and thereby better position their firms to meet future legal challenges.

David Silverstein

The Asbestos Lawsuits

The Manville Bankruptcy. On August 26, 1982, Johns-Manville Sales Corporation (Manville), a multibillion dollar conglomerate, and its principal American and Canadian affiliates, voluntarily filed for reorganization under Chapter 11 of the Federal Bankruptcy Act. Manville's management cited the crushing financial burden of defending more than 15,000 lawsuits filed by former employees, or their next-of-kin, for injuries or death caused by exposure to asbestos while working for the company.

Although the company has disposed of almost 1900 such claims in 1981 at an average cost of $15,000, more recently costs had risen to almost $21,000 per claim, and approximately $40,000 if legal expenses were included. Moreover, new lawsuits were being filed at the rate of 500 a month; a study forecast further that at least 32,000 new asbestos lawsuits were likely in the future. James F. Beasley, Treasurer of Manville, predicted that the total cost of the asbestos litigation over the next 20 years could range from $2 billion upwards. The filing under Chapter 11 automatically suspended further proceedings in the pending lawsuits and temporarily halted the filing of new suits against Manville.

The Asbestos Hazard. There is still considerable medical and legal controversy over how much Manville's management knew about the dangers of exposure to asbestos prior to a 1964 report by Dr. Irving J. Selikoff at Mt. Sinai School of Medicine in New York. Selikoff's report later became accepted by most of the industry. But there is evidence that as early as 1929, and certainly during the 1930's, Manville's management was aware of a potential health hazard associated with asbestos. Indeed, there is strong evidence that Sumner Simpson, president of Manville from 1929 until 1948, took steps to keep information about the danger of asbestos from Manville employees and the general public.

At the same time, in exposing its employees to asbestos without special protective measures, Manville was *not* acting in violation of any existing federal or state laws or regulations. In fact, at the time, no special safety standards had been promulgated with respect to asbestos exposure. Only in 1970 did Congress enact the Occupational Safety and Health Act (OSHA).

The Impact of the Wilson *Case.* Manville's management may well have regarded July 30, 1982 as a critical turning point in Manville's defense of the asbestos litigations. On that date, less than a month before Manville filed for reorganization under Chapter 11, the United States Court of Appeals for the District of Columbia Circuit ruled against Manville on a key legal issue.

In the case of *Wilson v. Johns-Manville Sales Corporation*, the Federal Court of Appeals reversed an order by the District Court dismissing a survival and wrongful death action brought by Henry Wilson's widow on the grounds that the suit was not timely filed. In so doing, the Court of Appeals adopted the so-called "discovery" rule under which a "cause of action accrues when the plaintiff knows or through the exercise of due diligence should have known of the injury." Although the *Wilson* court was not the first to depart from the traditional tort doctrine that "the cause of action accrues at the time of invasion of [plaintiff's] body," this to changed conditions."

How is it possible, Manville's management might well have asked, to do business in a rational manner when, more than forty years after a situation arises, the legal rules governing that situation are abruptly altered? In this case, Henry J. Wilson, beginning in 1941, was employed by Manville as an insulation worker at various construction sites in the metropolitan Washington, D.C. area. As a regular and integral part of his employment, Wilson handled asbestos. On February 14, 1973, x-rays revealed that Wilson was suffering from a mild case of asbestosis, a noncancerous irritation of the lungs caused by inhalation of asbestos dust. Although Wilson's health rapidly deteriorated from this point on, not until February of 1978 was Wilson diagnosed a shaving mesothelioma, a rare form of cancer associated almost exclusively with exposure to particulate asbestos. Henry Wilson died on May 17, 1978.

The Myth That Law is Static.

Whether it is proper to impose liability in a case like *Johns-Manville* raises sensitive questions which go to the heart of the delicate balance between business and society in a market economy. Unfortunately, the answers to these questions are generally misunderstood by a large segment of American managers who seem to regard this case as an anomaly. They see Manville as a victim to be pitied rather than as an example to be heeded. The Manville experience, however, contains important lessons about managing corporate social responsibility.

The primary lesson of the *Manville* case is that, at least in the United States, law is both dynamic and one of the principal linkages between business and society. Unless some type of "preemptive" action is taken by business managers out of enlightened self-interest, important issues of corporate social responsibility will, sooner or later, be translated into demands by society on the legal system. Initially the legal system may reject societal demands which markedly depart from established legal doctrines; but, eventually, as the demands multiply, the system is likely to respond either through the promulgation of new legislation or by action of the courts, or both.

New legislation cannot have retroactive application. It can, however, force affected businesses to alter established patterns of conduct in the future, for example by requiring the installation of expensive pollution control equipment or by mandating complex new procedures for addressing employee grievances. In many of these cases, business might have avoided costly and burdensome legal regulation by voluntarily adopting less onerous self-regulation in time to stem the legal response.

The common law courts generally have been hesitant to assume a law-making role and deferred instead to the legislative branch the problems of handling difficult or novel issues of law. Where the legislatures have been slow to respond to new social demands, however, the courts have frequently overcome their reluctance and attempted to fashion novel judicial solutions to the problems. Under the separation of powers doctrine, American courts should not, at least in theory, "make" law. Fashioning judicial remedies to novel legal problems, therefore, typically involves redefining existing legal standards. The judicial process thus can result in law having retrospective as well as prospective effects. It is through this process of judicial interpretation and redefinition of the law that a company like Manville may suddenly find itself legally liable for millions of dollars in damages for activities that were not, at the time they occurred, in violation of any legal standards then existing.

Very few managers who lack formal legal training comprehend this important feature of our legal system. Business is accustomed to thinking of the law as relatively static and therefore predictable. But the success of our legal system is accounted for by its ability to accommodate new demands through carefully balancing the attributes of predictability and flexibility. The law is continuously changing in response to new social pressures; and, today, a successful manager must be sensitive to the myriad signs and nuances which may signal future redefinition of the legal standards applicable to a particular industry. Based on those signs and nuances, the manager must be capable of making reliable predictions about the nature and timing of legal changes and adapting his firm's policies accordingly. The *Manville* case is not an anomaly. Manville is simply one of the early victims in what is certain to be a long line of expensive lessons in corporate social responsibility during the remainder of this century.

THE LIMITATIONS OF TRADITIONAL APPROACHES TO CORPORATE SOCIAL RESPONSIBILITY.

With hindsight, it is easy to criticize Manville's management for not adopting a more proactive stance at the first hints of a potential asbestos hazard. But given the limitations to the traditional approaches to corporate social responsibility, the response by Manville to the early warning signals should not be surprising.

Under traditional social responsibility models, managers often must choose between a short-term (and possibly, short-sighted) profit-maximizatiation response or, alternatively, a more costly, long-term social welfare strategy. The outcome of the more expensive, long-term strategy, however, is often speculative and can be justified to shareholders only by reference to seemingly vague notions of ethics and community welfare. A manager who desires to act in a socially responsible manner may encounter enormous financial pressures from impatient stockholders looking for quick returns on their investments. Management scholar Peter Drucker recently observed that his long-standing problem has been exacerbated by the growing concentration of publicly held stock in the hands of a few large, and demanding, institutional investors."

This section examines how, under the constraints of modern financial markets, the dichotomy between the traditional approaches to corporate social responsibility can become a barrier to managers pursuing more enlightened social policies.

The Traditional Approaches to Corporate Social Responsibility

The "Profit Maximization" Approach. Today, the "profit maximization" approach to social responsibility in business is most commonly associated with noted University of Chicago economist Milton Friedman. Corporations, according to Friedman, possess neither the authority nor the moral right to divert shareholders' profits for the general public welfare. Managers are merely agents of the stockholders, and thus have no right to spend or give away corporate monies except in the interest of increasing shareholder wealth. Any stockholder is free to use his dividends to support any worthy causes he may choose, but the choice should *not* be made for him by a company president who may not share either his values or priorities. Friedman therefore concludes that "there is one and only one social responsibility of business—to use its resources and engage in activities designed to increase its profits...."

In part, this philosophy is related to Adam Smith's renowned "invisible hand" doctrine. One interpretation of the "invisible hand" doctrine holds that individuals and, by implication, businesses and governments, cannot be "do-gooders" even if they try because no one has access to complete and perfect knowledge about the universe. What may initially seem like a good thing can ultimately produce disastrous consequences. The history of importing new strains of plants and animals, such as the gypsy moth, provides a familiar and bitter example of this process at work.

Instead of trying to do good, the argument goes, individuals should simply seek to maximize profits. Profit-seeking frees us from having to make controversial value judgments. The "invisible hand" doctrine assures us that profit-seeking will invariably lead to the most economically efficient allocation of scarce resources which, in turn, will produce the greatest utility for the world taken as a whole. Any deviation from or interference with this utilitarian "invisible hand" process, even if well-intentioned, can only lead to market distortions which reduce the world's net welfare. Such interference with free-market operations may succeed in improving the lot of certain individuals or groups or businesses, but this form of wealth transfer is inefficient. The net gain realized by those who are made better off by these market distortions will be smaller than the net loss realized by those who, as a result, are hurt. Accordingly, social welfare is best served through the invisible hand of the market.

The Social Welfare Approach.

Advocates of the social welfare approach to corporate social responsibility pose the fundamental question of why, in modern society, should the corporate manager by "the legitimate arbiter of the competing claims of stockholders, workers, consumers, the managers themselves and generations as yet unborn." Why should the awesome responsibility for dividing up the social pie among the many competing groups of stakeholders, including those who cannot even speak for themselves, be entrusted to private enterprise managers whose principal concern is to earn profits.

Some champions of the capitalist system were "optimistic that we can rely on the growing social conscience of the industrial manager to perform this function equitably." But the general public, and even many managers experienced in the intense pressures of the modern business world to maximize short-term profits, may not share this optimism. The social welfare approach is an alternative to the specter of ever-growing government regulation of business to protect all groups of stakeholders.

The social welfare approach holds that a business should act in an ethical, responsible manner even if there is no existing law requiring such conduct and even if there is no immediate, quantifiable benefit to the business which balances out the cost of taking the action. Although advocates of this approach broadly appeal to generally accepted standards of ethics and morality, almost invariably there is also an implicit or explicit attempt to justify such behavior in terms of the long-term economic interests of the firm and the business community generally.

Justification of the social welfare approach by reference to business' long-run economic interests not only bolsters the ethical arguments but, in addition, may be necessitated by legal doctrines which hold a corporate officer accountable to the company's shareholders. To the extent that this approach relies on such economic justification, however, it differs from the profit-maximization approach more in terms of the relevant timeframe than in matters of substance. This article does not add to the large and growing literature on the ethical basis for the social welfare approach. Instead, it focuses on the key legal and economic arguments that are mustered in support of the social welfare approach.

Social responsibility proponents focus a particularly critical eye on so-called "big business"—the giant multinational conglomerates and Fortune 500 companies. "Big business," it is argued, controls a disproportionate amount of wealth and wields a degree of political power today which is unprecedented. Some of these companies have been accused of literally buying the elections of friendly political leaders and the passage of favorable legislation in certain countries. Even in the United States, we recognize the enormous impact of highly paid lobbyist, political action committees, campaign contributions, and media advertising by large corporations. Furthermore, ownership of these giant corporations is so dispersed that the shareholders, in reality, exercise little real control over management. Therefore, social responsibility proponents urge that big business owes an obligation to society to act in a socially responsive manner even if such action is not legally mandated. Furthermore, over the long term, the argument goes, social responsibility will lead to a more favorable business climate that will benefit all businesses.

Even with all of its wealth and power, observe some social responsibility advocates, big business is still critically dependent on maintaining the continued goodwill and cooperation of society. First, without the cooperation of employees, consumers, and the general public, business would have neither products to sell nor anyone to sell them to. Second, big business as we know it today exists only by virtue of its ability to organize and carry on business in the special legal form of the corporation. Corporations enjoy three unique and critical attributes: limited legal liability, perpetual life, and the ability to multiply by establishing subsidiaries. Under common law, these three attributes were unavailable to alternative forms of business organizations, such as sole proprietorships and partnerships.

It should be sobering for managers to realize, therefore, that there is no natural right endowing big business with the natural ability to organize in the corporate form. If corporations should become too heavy-handed, too uncaring, too detached from social priorities, and too selfishly wrapped up in their profit-making, society has not only the ability to further regulate these businesses but also possesses the ultimate power to cripple or destroy them. For these reasons, argue the social responsibility advocates, big business must view social responsibility in terms of long-range survival, not just short-term profit-maximization. *The problem is that, in some situations, the profit-maximization and social welfare approaches lead to different and conflicting management strategies.*

The Potential for Conflicting Management Strategies

Economist John Maynard Keynes observed the "[i]n the long run we are all dead." Indeed, Sumner Simpson, Manville's president from 1929 until 1948, and most, if not all, of Manville's stockholders during this period died well before the asbestos bubble burst in 1982. In view of the long latency period for the development of asbestosis and mesothelioma, it is conceivable, perhaps even likely, that with the benefit of fifty years' foresight Manville's management (with stockholders' blessings) would have responded no differently to the asbestos problem.

Many common social responsibility issues have long latency periods. Some might argue that it is the very characteristic that distinguishes the "social welfare" and profit-maximization viewpoints. If "long" is considered to be anything beyond current management's anticipated tenure, then a wide range of everyday management actions are long-run decisions. Certainly it will be decades, or longer, before management decisions on air and water pollution, disposal of toxic chemicals and nuclear wastes, safety of new drugs and food additives, and exposure to toxic chemicals in the workplace will be proven to be adequate or lacking.

In the meantime, the two traditional approaches to social responsibility afford neither a sufficient economic incentive nor a sound legal justification for managers to exceed existing legal standards. In the modern financial market, management's performance is judged not only annually at shareholder's meetings, not just by quarterly earnings and dividends reports, but daily by anxious investors who watch the rise or fall in the price of the company's stock. No matter how earnestly a manager embraces the concept of social welfare, the manager can never afford to lose sight of the responsibility owed to current stockholders. Partly as a result of managerial subservience to investor sentiments, there is a potential for different and conflicting management strategies under the two traditional approaches to corporate social responsibility.

Type 1 Management Responsiveness —Obeying the Law.

Management strategies as dictated by the traditional approaches, however, will not always directly clash. For example, at least in broad terms, both approaches support compliance with the existing law. For reference purposes, business behavior wherein the dominant motivation is obeying the law will be designated "Type 1" management responsiveness. Where an existing statute, administrative regulation or judicial decision squarely mandates certain business behavior—and establishes adequate legal sanctions in the form of criminal fines, civil damages, and threat of an injunction to insure compliance—there is relatively minimal conflict between the management response dictated by profit-maximization and the indicated by social welfare.

Some familiar examples of Type 1 management behavior include: business paying minimum wage even though some employees might work for less; U.S. auto companies equipping new automobiles with emission control systems even though many consumers might prefer to pay less and forego emission controls; and, cigarette manufacturers putting health warnings on packaging even though many smokers would prefer not to be constantly reminded of the hazards. In each of these cases, the dominant explanation for the management decision is fear of legal sanctions for failing to comply.

Type 2 Management Responsiveness —Enlightened Self-Interest.

In addition to responsiveness based simply on obeying the law, there is a second managerial motivation that generates relatively minimal conflict between the two traditional approaches. The second approach applies where, even in the absence of any clearly applicable legal sanctions, the net cost to a firm of taking a socially responsive action is more than offset by the resulting net gains. This type of management responsiveness can be called "enlightened self-interest": the firm acts not because it is required by law to do so but rather because the action is viewed as being in its own economic best interest. For reference purposes, socially responsible behavior wherein the dominant management motivation is enlightened self-interest will be designated "Type 2" management responsiveness. Whether a manager takes action, and the nature of an action will, in large part, be dictated by assessing the costs against the anticipated benefits to the company. A prudent manager will choose a course of action such that the anticipated stream of future benefits to the company, computed over a reasonable time horizon and discounted back to present value, outweighs current associated expenditures as well as looking attractive compared with alternative investment opportunities.

One of the most common examples of Type 2 management responsiveness is corporate charitable contributions. Because charitable contributions are not required by law, they are typically rationalized to shareholders on the basis of the favorable publicity and public relations generated by such contributions. There may also be a "pumping-priming" effect, as where a computer firm contributes hardware or software to educational institutions with the expectation of cultivating a future customer base among today's students. Moreover, the out-of-pocket cost to a business of making a charitable contribution is reduced because of the availability of an income tax deduction. Having the government pick up one-third to one-half of the cost of a firm's advertising and public relations makes the economics of corporate giving look especially attractive. Of course, the value of advertising and goodwill is difficult to quantify, especially over a period of time. Still, it is relatively easy to identify the basic elements of the cost-benefit analysis in this example.

Although the quantum of social good might be identical, it would be highly unusual for a company's chief executive to make an anonymous charitable contribution from his firm's coffers. In such a case, because the contribution was anonymous, the firm would receive none of the beneficial advertising and publicity ordinarily associated with charitable contributions by business. The firm might still benefit from the tax deduction, but there would be few if any direct benefits to the firm to offset the residual costs.

Such action by a corporate officer might also provoke a legal challenge. Corporate officers are agents of the firm. Under familiar agency doctrines and the "business judgment" rule, a corporate officer owes a fiduciary duty to the corporation, including the obligation to act within the scope of his authority. An agent who acts "ultra vires"—i.e., beyond the scope of his authority—may be held personally accountable to the firm in a "shareholders's derivative action." It is not uncommon, for instance, for disgruntled stockholders to assert that company officers are making excessive or inappropriate charitable contributions with funds that should rightfully either be paid out as dividends or else reinvested in the company to increase shareholder equity. The "ultra vires" doctrine explains at least in part, why advocates of social responsibility in business resort to long-term economic justifications in support of their ethical arguments.

Another example of Type 2 management responsiveness is where a firm (or, in many cases, an entire industry) elects to "voluntarily" take certain action in the hope of either delaying or ameliorating legal regulation which could otherwise be fare more costly and burdensome. Such "preemptive" action is widespread both inside and outside of business. Preemptive strategy typically involves

trying to co-opt a significant proportion of one's critics by adopting a moderate, middle-of-the-road position. This strategy may enable a firm to undercut the power of extremists who are advocating a more radical approach. In addition, by also launching a counteroffensive including an education and public awareness campaign, it may be possible to turn around public opinion on a particular issue if strong sentiments have not yet crystallized. In a similar fashion, pending legislation may be thwarted by a timely combination of self-regulation and public education.

In these examples of Type 2 management responsiveness, there is a greater potential for conflict between the management strategies dictated by the traditional approaches to social responsibility. For social welfare proponents, the focus would be on the anticipated social benefits; for profit-maximizers, on the other hand, the focus would be on the remote or speculative nature of the firm's benefits. The end result in cases of this type is often a compromise that goes further than some profit-maximizers might endorse, but not nearly as far as social welfare advocates would like.

Management Responsiveness in a Johns-Manville Type of Case. The greatest potential for conflicting management strategies, however, is where a firm must decide whether to exceed existing legal standards out of fear that in the future those legal standards will be changed by judicial decision, and that those modified standards will then be applied retroactively. This, of course, is exactly the dilemma posed by cases like *Johns-Manville*. Type 1 management responsiveness does not address the *Johns-Manville* type of case because Type 1 only deals with obeying existing laws. But in a *Johns-Manville* type of case, existing laws may be inadequate to protect society.

The *Johns-Manville* case might be addressed with Type 2 management responsiveness. But, in this example, the long latency period before an injury becomes manifest probably insures that the firm's managers and shareholders at the time of inaction will not be the ones ultimately held accountable. Instead, it is future generations of managers and shareholders, as in the *Manville* case, who will be required to pay for the mistakes of their predecessors. Under these circumstances enlightened self-interest seems to dictate doing no more than what is required by existing law. Managers with a static view of the legal system will assume that their obligations are satisfied by complying with existing legal standards, and that there is no adequate economic justification for exceeding of case that the limitations of the traditional approaches to corporate social responsibility become most apparent. Only when a manager factors into his enlightened self-interest calculations the likelihood of a case law-generated legal change, with its potentially devastating impact on the firm, does a plausible argument for exceeding existing legal standards begin to emerge.

Two significant issues become apparent when we contrast the static and dynamic views of the legal system in this context. First, the dynamic approach is inherently better managerial decisionmaking. That is because it incorporates a factor (the changing legal system) that is essential to high quality decisionmaking. Accordingly, managers who utilize the dynamic approach would be functioning in a more competent fashion.

Secondly, use of the prevailing static view would skew managerial decisions. Decisions grounded on the static view would systematically favor the profit-maximization outcome and slight the social welfare outcome. That is because costs to the firm associated with prospective legal changes are ignored. The costs almost always justify a decision more oriented toward social welfare. Including these costs in decisionmaking based soley on the profit-maximization orientation would cause the decisions to move closer to the social welfare

view. Perhaps in some specific cases, such as *Johns-Manville*, they would merge into common, or at least quite similar, managerial conclusions.

THE DYNAMIC LEGAL SYSTEM— BRIDGING THE GAP BETWEEN PROFIT—MAXIMIZATION AND SOCIAL WELFARE

The preceeding section argued that in certain cases, especially those involving a long latency period, the dichotomy between the traditional approaches to corporate social responsibility may create a gap in which there is neither sufficient economic incentive nor sound legal justification for managers to exceed existing legal standards. The consequences of this gap is a reactive management strategy that responds only to immediate economic and legal pressures. This section argues that a better understanding by managers of the dynamic nature of the American legal system can help to bridge this gap by providing both an incentive and a justification for a proactive management strategy, which may include going well beyond that which is required by existing laws.

The Litigation Audit

Borrowing from the terminology of the "social audit" or "social assessment system" which is commonly used in discussing corporate social responsibility, the process described in this section might be called a "litigation audit." The essential elements of this process are: first, that a manager recognize an evolving legal issue which may affect his firm long before it becomes embodied in legislation or judicial decisions; second, that he determine in which direction the issue is evolving, and how rapidly; and, third, that he decide how best to respond.

David Silverstein

Short-Term Environmental Scanning.
There are many signs in the immediate legal environment to which a manager might turn for guidance in beginning a "litigation audit." He might look, for example, at existing legislation, regulation or judicial decisions in neighboring jurisdictions; at failed legislative efforts in his own state or at the federal level; and at the amount of media attention a particular issue is attracting. Such environmental scanning is important in highlighting areas of potential legal change. By themselves, however, these signals only appear too late to be of real use because they predict only short-term changes. Beyond specific signals about evolving problem areas, a manager must also be attuned to long-range social trends and their likely impact on the legal regulation of business.

Alternative Long-Term Prediction Techniques. Assessing the impact of long-range social trends on the legal system requires that a manager engage in a certain amount of social and legal forecasting. Modern legal forecasting techniques range from the familiar application of laws and precedents to new fact situations, a traditional function of lawyers and judges, to the sophisticated, computer-based sociological analysis used, for example, in jury selection. Other legal forecasting models are based on historical analysis, on jurisprudence, on technological innovations, and still others on fundamental economic analysis. All of these techniques for forecasting legal change require that a manager understand certain aspects of the change process generally and, in particular, that the manager be aware of the key linkages between law and social change in the United States.

The Common Context of Legal Forecasting Techniques. In broad terms, "change" can be classified as either continuous/evolutionary or discontinuous/ revolutionary. Furthermore, "change" can be either spontaneous or planned. The legal process is usually one of continuous, evolutionary change because it normally operates within the existing social order. More controversial is whether, and to what extent, legal change can be planned.

There is a long-standing controversy over whether law "leads" change or "follows" change, i.e., embodies change which has already occurred. Some scholars believe in the efficacy of planned legal change through the medium of rationally-construed reforming laws. This is commonly referred to as a "top-down" or "instrumental" approach because it involves rules from the upper echelons of government being imposed on society, typically through the intermediary of a bureaucracy. Other scholars believe, however, that legal change can only be effective when it comes from the "bottom up" through the evolution of customary law. These scholars argue that courts and legislatures should act only when popular custom has evolved to embrace the new norms of conduct. Still another group of scholars has endeavored to strike a middle ground between the instrumentalist and customary law approaches by pragmatically acknowledging that, in order to effective, an instrumentalist legal strategy must systematically take into account the culture and customary law of the society in question.

If legal change occurred randomly and wholly without warning in our society (as many managers mistakenly believe) as the result of instrumentalist law-making, the only feasible strategy would be a reactive one, namely to delay any response until a new statute, administrative regulation of judicial decision became law. But this kind of arbitrariness and unpredictability in the legal system would be seriously prejudicial to the functioning of the commercial system. Indeed, some legal scholars have argued that it was the existence of a rational, autonomous and, therefore, predictable legal system which facilitated the rise of capitalism in England and Western Europe during the sixteenth and seventeenth centuries.

Irrespective of the theory of jurisprudence to which one subscribes, the reality is that we have a legal system in which the need for predictability must be carefully balanced against the need for flexibility. Neither a rigid, inflexible rule of law nor a system which readily bends to every whim can provide long-term stability. In the United States at least, legal change occurs in a continuous, orderly way through accepted processes and within certain parameters established by American society. As a result, for any situation which might arise, at a given point in time there is a limited and, to an extent, predictable constellation of possible legal outcomes. Through familiar legal doctrines such as stare decisis, equity and legal fictions, the courts can, in effect, "pour new wine into old bottles" and thereby achieve modest incremental change without undermining the fundamental predictability of the legal system. Eventually any legislation may supersede such judicial lawmaking. Understanding this incremental process of law and social change is the first step for a manager trying to cope with a changing legal environment. The second step is for a manager to select one of the forecasting techniques.

Selecting Forecasting Techniques. The long-term forecasting techniques mentioned above vary significantly in their maturity and usefulness to managers. The application of precedents to new facts and the sociological analysis of jurors are probably the most mature. Historical analysis is certainly more mature than jurisprudential, technological, or economic forecasts of legal changes.

The techniques also have differing predictive attributes. Thus, sociological analysis may accurately predict jury decisions and perhaps legislative decision. On the other hand,

the jurisprudential approach may be most effective in predicting judge-made law. Technological and economic-based forecasts of legal change might best presage changes in business law. In contrast, the historical approach may be the broadest forecaster of legal change—able to predict changes in many legal fields and from all law-making institutions.

Technological grounded forecasting might only forecast changes in narrow areas of the law—those related to a particular technology. Jurisprudential and historical-based forecasts, on the other hand, these may be able to predict broad changes, changes that are most likely to have major impact on big business. Also, the time horizons might vary significantly among these relatively long-term techniques. Historical analysis might forecast farthest into the future while a technology-based forecast probably would have the shortest range.

At this early stage in this field's development, historical-based forecasting may be both the most mature and the most useful to today's managers. The following section elaborates by example some of the strengths and weaknesses of this forecasting approach.

History as an Illustrative Guide for Predicting Legal Change

Law as a Response to Public Opinion. At the turn of the century, English legal scholar A.V. Dicey argued that, because of the nature of a modern democratic society, the law is invariably responsive to public opinion. Dicey was aghast at the wave of social welfare legislation which had swept across England during the late 1800's, disrupting cherished legal doctrines like "freedom of contract" and leading to what Dicey thought was an unhealthy degree of government involvement in the commercial system.

According to Dicey, "the law of a country

may fail, for a time, to represent public opinion owing to the lack of any legislative [or judicial] organ which adequately responds to the sentiment of the age." But, in general, he believed the legal system would eventually be responsive to genuine and persistent social demands whether or not it was in the long-run best interests of the country. "Nowhere," he observed, "have changes in popular convictions or wishes found anything like such rapid and immediate expression in alterations of the law as they have in Great Britain during the nineteenth century.... [I]t is at bottom opinion which controls legislation."

Mendelson's Stages-of-Growth Model.
Other legal scholars have noted a corresponding responsiveness of the American legal system to social needs. Wallace Mendelson, for example, has presented a development model for the United States based on three distinct periods of evolution of the business-government interface: Stage 1—the era of nationalism; Stage 2—the era of industrialization; and Stage 3—the era of the welfare state.

Stage 1—The Era of Nationalism. Mendelson's Stage 1 was post-independence America of the late 18th and early 19th centuries, a time during which the strains of different cultures and commercial interests among the thirteen original states, coupled with mutual suspicion and distrust, threatened to tear apart the new nation. According to Mendelson, the overriding need and goal of the times was to achieve political integration by sacrificing individual states' rights in the interest of federalism. All of the leading Supreme Court decisions of that era, says Mendelson, reflect "with compelling simplicity a vision of national unity and national supremacy." These early Supreme Court cases, argues Mendelson, provided "cement for the Union...."

Stage 2—The Era of Industrialization. By the middle of the 1800's Mendelson says, the United States had successfully overcome the hurdle of achieving national unity and was well on its way into Stage 2, the era of industrialization or, in the words of economist Walt Rostow, the "take-off" into economic growth. Stage 2 in Mendelson's development model was characterized by a laissez-faire legal system designed "to increase production by promoting economic freedom." He notes that these laissez-faire policies found expression in such specific legal rules as "caveat emptor" (let the buyer beware) and "privity of contract" that "protected manufacturers of defective goods from liability to third-party consumers, and in ... [the fellow servant rule] that all but freed employers from the cost of industrial accidents."

The objective of these legal rules, according to Mendelson, was to promote the accumulation of capital, without which the Industrial Revolution never could have succeeded. If the legal system had immediately placed on America's newly emerging infant industries the full burden of the social costs of industrialization, it might have squelched these businesses before they ever got off the ground. "Decisions that block the claims of labor and consumer," says Mendelson, "promote growth of investment capital. And if a 'traditional' society wants mass production, its first economic task is to accumulate capital."

But, Mendelson asks, how does a developing country accumulate capital? Some capital can be borrowed as indeed the United States did heavily during the 19th century. Mainly, however, a country must save which, Mendelson says, "means much more than putting money in a bank."

It means ... society must refrain from using all its current energies and materials to satisfy its current wants, no matter how urgent these may be. Saving is the act by which a . . . [nation] releases some portion of its labor and material resources from the task of providing for the present so that both can be applied to building for the future.

When the Supreme Court suppressed worker and consumer claims and taught us the blessings of laissez faire and the Gospel of Wealth, it fostered capital accumulation. Its decisions were part of a socialization process that glorified private enterprise and for a time at least kept the common man in his humble place. This, with the resulting stimulation of business energy and appetite, is the crux of economic modernization. To put it crudely, the court promoted the savings and managerial effort that built our mass producing factories. The common man paid dearly in his standard of living as he has in all industrialized countries including Soviet Russia.

Similar observations about the role of law and government in business during this period of time are also expressed by another legal scholar, Carl Auerbach. Auerbach says of this period:

The achievements of the 19th century American capitalism were great. But its social costs were very high. The law did little to curb the extravagant exploitation of our natural resources. Forests were despoiled. Soil was permitted to erode. Game was exterminated. Air and water supplies were polluted and fish life destroyed. Natural gas was burned to get oil, which was squandered. Unplanned railroad development left a heritage of problems with which we are still struggling today.

Human resources were also cruelly used. The public health was nobody's concern. The workday and work week were very long and earnings very low, though conditions of the American worker in the 19th century were probably better than the conditions of the worker anywhere else. Workers and their families bore the staggering costs of industrial accidents. The business cycle which recurred throughout the 19th century, victimized farmers and workers.

Stage 3 — The Era of the Welfare State. The excesses of big business began at last to provoke public reaction and calls for change. Auerbach notes that the latter part of the 19th century was a period of growing social unrest in the United States.

Social unrest grew and found expression in the protest movements of the farmers; the railroad strikes of 1877 and 1894; the Haymarket bomb throwing in 1886; the Homestead strike riot of 1892 and Coxey's army of the unemployed in 1894. This unrest found political expression in the bitter Presidential campaigns of the 1890's.

Before the close of the 19th century, the law began to do something about these unintended consequences of rapid industrialization based upon private economic decisionmaking in order to allocate, in a more just and humane fashion, the material and human costs which did not show up in the accounts of any private firm.

This marked the transition of the United States from Mendelson's Stage 2 into Stage 3, the era of the welfare state. By this time, the industrialization of America was well underway and the position of big business secure. According to Mendelson:

Having achieved mass production, the United Stated entered stage three — the era of the welfare state. Consumer goods were so potentially plentiful and so near at hand that there was less need to restrain consumption. We could afford Social Security, collective bargaining, minimum wages, the forty-hour week, Medicare, and similar measures. The common element in these programs is a redistribution of wealth. Income that earlier might have been channeled toward capital formation was now diverted to provide goods and services for the common man. His fathers' unwilling investment in American plant capacity began at last to pay him dividends.

Summarizing the achievements of Stage 3, Mendelson observes: "The weak have inherited the judicial world just as the nationalists did in stage one, and the industrialists in stage two."

Manifestations of the welfare state were by no means limited to judicial law, however. Auerbach notes that the new social priorities of the 20th century were also expressed in United States antitrust laws that prohibited monopolization and conspiracies to restrain trade; in public utility regulation; in laws designed to insure minimum standards of decent life (public school systems, factory safety legislation, laws regulating employment of women and children, minimum wage laws, workman's compensation and disability laws, and unemployment insurance laws); in laws to protect consumers (public health legislation, pure food and drug laws, laws prohibiting false labeling and advertising, laws regulating the issuance of securities and the operations of the stock exchanges, and laws requiring insurance of bank deposits); and laws for protecting the environment.

According to Auerbach, in Stage 3, the era of the welfare state, market forces continue to play an important but greatly circumscribed role in business:

Markets—the arenas of private economic decision-making—continue to play a crucial role in reflecting consumer wants, in distributing the national income, in determining the rate of economic growth and in making possible the development of private, countervailing power. But these mar-

kets are no longer self-regulating; they are regulated by law to satisfy the claims and achieve the ends I have tried to describe. A tolerable measure of social justice and individual freedom has thereby been achieved in our society as a result not of the pursuit of a vision of an ideal economic system but of the political struggle which individuals and groups have waged, according to the rules of democracy, to satisfy their claims.

Thus, as Dicey argued with respect to England, law and the legal system in the United States also play a pivotal role as a linkage between business and the public opinion. Historically, the business-government interface in this country has, with some lag time, been quite responsive to public opinion; and, there is no reason to believe that this lagged relationship will not continue to operate in the future.

The Legal Environment of the 21st Century. The preceding analysis suggests that the business-government relationship that will be characteristic of the 21st century in this country is being shaped by historical forces at work in the United States today. Many of these forces are not yet reflected in any statutes or judicial decisions. The challenge for today's managers is to recognize these issues and discern the relevant social trends in time to adapt their firms' policies and to have a meaningful impact on the final results.

Mendelson's stages-of-growth analysis of the evolution of business-government relations in the United States provides a point of departure for predicting the future legal environment of business. Mendelson's central argument was that the growing abundance of resources and the success of American business during Stage 2, the era of industrialization, paved the way and provided the public impetus for the transition into Stage 3, the era of the welfare state. He observed that "centuries of development have repealed for a time at least the iron law of scarcity." This made it both possible and desirable for the emphasis of the legal system to shift from a stance protecting business and promoting capital accumulation to stimulating a fairer and more equitable distribution of wealth.

If the economic and social forces that provided the impetus for the transition to the welfare state continue to dominate our society, we can expect the next stage of development, Stage 4 in Mendelson's model, to resemble a "super welfare state" thereby continuing the trend toward greater legal regulation of business and greater government intervention in the commercial system. If a federally-legislated minimum wage is characteristic of Stage 3, will Stage 4 include guaranteed employment and a minimum income, for example? Many other countries around the world currently have welfare states that far exceed anything now found in the United States. Is the United States heading in this direction?

Alternatively, is it possible that the pendulum has swung as far in the direction of the welfare state as it is going to, at least for the current cycle? In the face of a growing scarcity of natural resources and increasingly competitive international pressures, has the United States now entered an era of retrenchment? Is the dominant need today not for more redistribution but rather for a new round of investment and capital accumulation to revitalize American industry?

In this case, we might expect Stage 4 to look a good deal more like Stage 2 than 3. We might expect, for example, a growing trend away from government intervention in business and a return to laissez-faire. We might expect to see deregulation of regulated industries, less rigorous enforcement of the antitrust laws, pull-backs in consumer and environmental protection laws, and efforts to limit the liability of manufacturers to consumers and of employers to workers. Indeed,

these are the very trends which, it seems, have dominated many sectors of the American economy since the late 1970's. Projecting into the 21st century, the deregulatory environment of the 1980's may suggest that a new "golden age" for at least some American industries is in the offing. In either case, managers clearly must be sensitive, as well as responsive, to the broad historical trends, and the legal ramifications of those trends which affect their firms.

The "Zone of Discretion" Spectrum— A Link Between Legal Change and Business Planning

Understanding the process of legal change and forecasting its impact, however, are only two of the three steps needed for a manager to cope with a changing legal environment. The third step is to link that understanding to concrete management strategies and broad business policies.

Robert Ackerman, a scholar of management studies, has put his finger on the problem by criticizing the tendency of managers to see legal issues in black and white terms instead of as a spectrum of varying shades of gray. Such a spectrum is illustrated in Figure 1.

FIGURE 1.

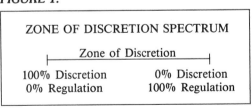

Ackerman argues that managers tend to view legal issues too simplistically as falling either at one end of this spectrum or the other. By treating a legal environment issue in this way, however, a manager may be forfeiting the opportunity to exercise influence during the most critical time period—that period when the legal issues are neither black nor white, which Ackerman calls the "Zone of Discretion." Here is the way Ackerman describes this middle period:

There is an argument that appears to justify ignoring the administrative implications of managing corporate responsiveness. It holds that social expectations for business's behavior become legitimate only when then government requires compliance, and to the extent that governmental regulations exact penalties, a social issue is converted into an economic one and so can be managed just like any other business problem. The fallacy in this reasoning lies in the premise that corporate action on social issues is either voluntary or required. In fact, during the period when responsiveness is most important, it is neither.

For every issue there is a time period before it becomes a matter of social concern, and espousing the issue may even arouse economic and social sanctions. There is also a time when its acceptance is so widespread that adherence is an unquestioned part of doing business (child labor laws create little anxiety in 1973).

Between those two points there is a period of uncertainty as to the strength and durability of public support for the issues, standards of socially acceptable behavior, timing of desired conformity, and technologies or resources available for complying. This period might be called a zone of discretion in which the signals the company receives from the environment are unclear. It cannot avoid responding in some way, but it still has discretion in the timing and strength of the response.

Some legal environment issues, according to Ackerman, "have progressed so far through the Zone of Discretion that their final dimensions are beginning to take shape. As examples, Ackerman cites the areas of equal employment opportunity and protection of the environment. These areas are now heavily regulated by legislation, administrative regulation, and judicial decisions leaving little room for the exercise of managerial discretion. But other areas, says Ackerman, "are much less well defined." For these issues, still squarely in the middle of the zone of discretion, astute and perceptive managers have considerable leeway in either heading off future legal regulation or in helping to shape its final dimensions and in preparing their firms to deal with the consequences. Clearly, forecasting legal change can enrich the benefits of Ackerman's paradigm.

Management Responses to a Changing Legal Environment

As discussed above, between the extremes of regulation and no-regulation on the scale of Figure 1 lies Ackerman's zone of discretion. We can now link this region on Ackerman's scale to Type 1 management responsiveness based on legal regulation and Type 2 management responsiveness based on enlightened self-interest.

The right end of Ackerman's zone of discretion represents the region where Type 1 management responsiveness dominates because legal regulation significantly restricts managerial discretion. Toward the middle and left of Ackerman's zone of discretion, however, the various forms of Type 2 management responsiveness become increasingly important. With Type 2 management responsiveness, there is no legal regulation which mandates any specific management action. Whether a manager takes action and, if so, the nature of that response will, in large part, be dictated by assessing the costs against the anticipated benefits to the company. Correspondingly, in the middle and left parts of the zone of discretion, management responsiveness is neither wholly voluntary nor legally mandated. Managers' hands are not completely tied; but neither do managers enjoy unlimited discretion about when and how to respond to social demands.

In view of the preceding discussion about the dynamic legal system, it should now be clear that the cost-benefit analysis implicit in the enlightened self-interest approach cannot properly assume that the law will remain static. Instead, knowledge about the dynamic legal system, including projections about the nature and timing of possible legal changes, must be factored into the equation. When the dynamic legal system is brought into this analysis, the evaluation of alternative management strategies may change dramatically.

For example, when the management assumption of static law is dropped, "preemptive" action, one form of Type 2 management responsiveness, becomes much easier to reconcile with profit-maximization. The promulgation of "voluntary" standards or codes of conduct by many industries and trade associations can be more easily justified on this basis. Through such preemptive action, a firm or an industry may be able to undercut and deflate, or at least delay, snowballing public support for legal intervention.

A specific example would be a firm that is besieged by complaints from the local community over excessive pollution. At the same time, because the local community also comprises stakeholders who benefit from the presence of the firm, e.g., employees, suppliers and consumers, any "killer" instinct is sure to be tempered. By "voluntarily" effecting modest pollution controls, the firm may be able to placate enough of the community to head off the enactment of more stringent, and costly, local regulation. Such action is readily justified when the likelihood of legal change is explicitly weighed in the policymaking process. Thus, in this example, a dynamic law

approach makes the social welfare viewpoint more compatible with profit-maximization.

In a situation where legal intervention appears inevitable and imminent, a dynamic law approach may lead to a counter-intuitive business strategy. Instead of fighting a losing battle to prevent government regulation for instance, a firm might actually decide to support legislation in the relevant area rather than risk the less-predictable outcome of a court decision. One benefit of this approach is that legislation has only prospective effect whereas a court decision may have retroactive application. Second, a firm or industry, through lobbying efforts and public education programs, can influence the final outcome of the legislative process to insure the minimum possible damage to business. Third, legislation helps to establish a level playing field by insuring that all competitors in the industry will face a comparable cost and marketing structure in which no one can compete unfairly by cutting corners. Faced with a loss of consumer confidence and added packaging costs following the contaminated "Tylenol" crises, Johnson & Johnson first actively promoted federal regulation mandating tamper-resistant packaging for over-the-counter medication, and, after the second occurrence, urged that over-the-counter capsule medication be discontinued and replaced by a new "caplet" form. The company was certainly not oblivious to the fact that such actions would compel its competitors to make product and packaging changes, including incurring expenditures, comparable to what it was planning to do anyway.

Another contemporary example of such preemptive action involves the growing legal crackdown on drunken driving. In response to increasing numbers of lawsuits, skyrocketing insurance premiums and growing public criticism, some innovative bars have initiated "designated driver" programs. Typically under such programs, a group of individuals travelling together to a bar is encouraged to designate one member as the "driver" who agrees not to consume alcoholic beverages for the evening. The designated driver may be offered free soft drinks all evening, a free admission pass for his next visit and a free drink coupon good for a future visit when someone else will be the designated driver.

How much does it cost for a bar to run such a program? Arguably, the small costs will be recouped many fold through attracting increased business, promoting return business, and encouraging greater consumption by those who are drinking. Accepting that alcohol consumption is both legal and a popular social pastime, programs like this which increase public safety must be applauded from a social welfare standpoint. But why must managers be bludgeoned by lawsuits and insurance premiums into taking measures that might have been in their best business interest from the outset? A better understanding by managers of the dynamic legal system might have led sooner to such an imaginative and compassionate response to this problem.

Johns-Manville Company is a final example of the potential impact of the dynamic legal system on managing corporate social responsibility. As discussed earlier, this is one of the toughest social responsibility problems to analyze because it involved a latency period of thirty to forty years. As observed, it is conceivable that even with the benefit of foresight Manville's management would have addressed the asbestos problem no differently. But, no one knew in advance how long it would take for injuries in these kinds of cases to manifest themselves, or how long it would then take for medical science to make the necessary linkages and for the legal system to respond. It might indeed take thirty to forty years; but, the problem might also break wide open in a matter of months, affecting current management and current shareholders. Therefore, when this kind of a problem is viewed in a dynamic law framework, at least a modestly proactive management strategy can be reconciled with profit-maximization.

In response to the first hints of a health hazard associated with asbestos, Manville's management elected to take no special preventive measures and, worse, even tried to cover up what little information about asbestos was then available. What alternatives were available to Manville and how costly would it have been to implement them? One wonders, for example, how much it would have cost Manville to install better ventilation equipment in work areas and to provide employees with simple paper face masks. If Manville had made a full disclosure to its employees of what little was then known about the dangers of asbestos, how many would have left their jobs, especially during the depression days of the 1930's? How many of these same employees, if asked, would have willingly signed contract disclaimers expressly waiving their rights to sue the company for future injuries resulting from working with asbestos? If such contract disclaimers had been coupled with full disclosure and some preventive measures by Manville, there is at least a reasonable public policy argument in favor of enforcing such provisions absent conflicting regulations.

The modest measures outline above might, in time, have proven ineffective in either protecting the employees' health or in protecting Manville from legal liability. On the other hand, at a relatively minimal cost, many employee lives and company dollars might have been spared if only management recognition of the dynamic legal system had induced them to go beyond the existing legal standards. Thus, even in this extreme type of situation, the dynamic law approach can make social welfare more compatible with profit-maximization.

CONCLUSION

Modern business managers are walking a narrow and precarious tightrope between preserving the essence of a market economy, with a broad scope of discretion for private enterprise managers, and a command economy in which managerial discretion has been forfeited to government fiat. Many of the key legal environmental issues that will impact business in the next century are today still located well within a Zone of Discretion where managers may exercise considerable leeway in shaping and responding to those social demands. If management fails to fulfill its social responsibilities at a time when action is still largely voluntary, it will almost certainly face more costly and burdensome regulation in the future.

This article argued that the dichotomy between the traditional profit-maximization and social welfare approaches to corporate responsibility is accentuated by a static view of the law. A better understanding by managers of the dynamic nature of the American legal system, along with a conscious attempt to make sophisticated predictions about the changing legal environment, can help eliminate the gap between the social welfare and profit-maximization views. In general, incorporating predictions about legal changes in managerical decisionmaking should shift many decisions in the direction of social welfare. Specifically, this article proposed a "litigation audit" for managers consisting of identifying relevant evolving legal issues, forecasting the probable direction and speed of their evolution, and crafting appropriate management responses. Early perception of potential legal environment problems combined with imaginative and compassionate responses is the dual challenge of managing corporate social responsibility in a changing legal environment.

5

A Conceptual Framework for Environmental Analysis of Social Issues and Evaluation of Business Response Patterns

S. Prakash Sethi

UNIVERSITY OF TEXAS—DALLAS

A conceptual framework is developed to analyze and evaluate business response patterns under different temporal and sociocultural conditions. Corporate responses are classified along three dimensions: corporate behavior or social obligation, social responsibility, and social responsiveness. The contextual component (external environment) is analyzed by dividing the elapsed time between the emergence of a problem and its ultimate solution into four categories: the preproblem stage, the problem identification stage, the remedy and relief stage, and the prevention stage. Examples of current application of the framework and directions for future research are indicated.

Business institutions in the United States and other industrially advanced countries have suffered a marked loss in social credibility. While business institutions justifiably take credit for tremendous strides made in living standards, they are accused of causing a host of environment-related and sociopoli-

S. Prakash Sethi is Professor of International Business and Business and Social Policy and Director of the Center for Research in Business and Social Policy, School of Management, The University of Texas at Dallas.

Reprinted with permission from the *Academy of Management Review.*

tical problems and of being insensitive to societal needs. Considerable pressure is put on business institutions to improve their management of social issues, and many institutions, especially large corporations, have taken steps to deal with a variety of social issues. The types of issues that business should tackle and the adequacy of their responses have spawned a whole new field of study, grouped under the rubric of business and society. However, a relative lack of development of a conceptual and analytical framework has hampered a systematic study of comparison and evaluation of corporate social responses and the environmental conditions that lead to the success or failure of specific responses to societal problems (12, 18).

This article attempts to develop an analytical framework to facilitate comparisons of business institutions and of the nature of business responses to social pressures under varying situational contexts and environmental conditions.

THE FRAMEWORK

The analytical framework proposed here is classificatory. The classes are broadly defined because both the types of issues covered and the environmental context within which they must be analyzed are so complex. Sociocultural and political phenomena, involving interactions among human beings and social institutions, are difficult to analyze in precise quantitative terms. Arbitrary precisions in the definition of variables is just as likely to conceal valuable information as to elucidate. A showing of causal relationships among variables so defined may be erroneous, since the underlying variables are interdependent. One should be wary of words that *simplify* when the reality they are presumed to describe is *complex*. Precision, under these circumstances, tends to force one into fixed positions which are intellectually difficult to defend and emotionally difficult to withdraw from. Thus, a framework that attempts to develop a broad classificatory scheme is the only approach both feasible and of some practical value.

The Social Context of Corporate Performance

An evaluation of corporate performance or the performance of any other social institution must be to a large extent culturally and temporally determined. A specific action is more or less socially responsible *only* within the framework of time, environment, and the nature of the parties involved. The same activity may be considered socially responsible at one time, under one set of circumstances, and in one culture, and socially irresponsible at another time. No system for evaluating corporate social performance can therefore ignore the cultural and sociopolitical environment, and the criteria used must necessarily be general and flexible (23).

Nevertheless, a classificatory scheme must have at least the following two properties if we are to make valid cross-cultural comparisons: (a) stable classifications and (b) stable meanings. The categories for classifying corporate activities should be stable so that while the nature of those activities and public expectations may change, the scheme should be able to accommodate them to make historical comparisons. The definitions of various classes should be such that they can be applied across firms, industries, and social systems.

The framework developed herein meets these criteria and suggests a rationale by which corporate activities can be analyzed in terms of social relevance so that comparisons over time and across industries and nations are possible. The framework consists of two sets of components. The *first* deals with categorization of the types of corporate responses. These are defined not in terms of specific activities, but in terms of types of underlying rationale applied in responding to social pressures. The *second* component deals with the definition of the external environment or the context within which the corporate response is being made and evaluated. The emphasis is not on the specifics of a particular social situation or problem, but on the generalized external conditions created by a multitude of acts by various social actors that are essentially similar within a given temporal and contextual frame.

This approach enables us to determine a logical and therefore acceptable external criterion against which a corporation's perfor-

S. Prakash Sethi

mance can be measured in a societal context. Thus it becomes an important complement to research and writing dealing with the issue of the measurement of corporate social performance generally treated under the somewhat misleading title of "corporate social audit" (1, 4, 6, 7, 9, 13, 14, 20).

DIMENSIONS OF CORPORATE SOCIAL PERFORMANCE

Business responds to two kinds of social forces; market and nonmarket. In the case of market forces, a firm adapts by varying its product, service, promotion, and price mix to meet changing consumer needs and expectations. Adequacy of response can be measured in terms of profitability and growth of the firm. All market actions have some nonmarket or indirect consequences for the society. These second-order effects are generally termed *externalities* (e.g., pollution) and have traditionally been borne by society as a whole.

There have been increasing societal pressures in every industrialized nation for business to minimize the second-order effects of its activities and also to take a more active part and assume greater responsibility for correcting the social ills that inevitably do occur. *It is the business response to the nonmarket forces, commonly termed social responsibility and social responsiveness of business, that is the focus of our inquiry.*

Corporations, like all other social institutions, are an integral part of a society and must depend on it for their existence, continuity and growth. They therefore constantly strive to pattern their activities so that they are in congruence with the goals of the overall social system.

It would improve our understanding of the situation if we were to analyze the logic of business actions in terms of the role of business in society. Business is a social institution and therefore must depend on society's acceptance of its role and activities if it is to survive and grow. At any given time, there is likely to be a gap between business performance and societal expectations caused by certain business actions or changing expectations. A continuously widening gap will cause business to lose its legitimacy and will threaten its survival. Business must therefore strive to narrow this "legitimacy" gap to claim its share of society's physical and human resources and to maintain maximum discretionary control over its internal decision-making and external dealings (15). The quest for legitimacy by the corporation and doubts by its critics about the legitimacy of some of its actions are at the core of the entire controversy pertaining to the concept of corporate social performance.

One way to evaluate corporate social performance is to use the yardstick of legitimacy. Given that both corporations and their critics seek to narrow the gap between corporate performance and societal expectations, the social relevance and validity of any corporate action depends on one's concept of legitimacy. Viewed in this respect, corporate behavior can be described as a three-stage phenomenon based on the changing notion of legitimacy from very narrow to very broad. Legitimization involves the types of corporate activities as well as: the process of internal decision making; the perception of the external environment; the manipulation of that environment—physical, social, and political—to make it more receptive to corporate activities; and the nature of accountability to other institutions in the system. The corporate behavior thus determined can be defined as social obligation, social responsibility, or social responsiveness (15).

Corporate Behavior as Social Obligation

First, corporate behavior in response to market forces or legal constraints is defined as *social obligation.* The criteria for legitimacy in this arena are economic and legal only. Milton Friedman (8) and Henry Manne (10) believe that a corporation is a special-purpose institution and that it leaves this arena at its own risk. The legitimacy criteria are met by the corporation through its ability to compete for resources in the marketplace and through conducting its operations within the legal constraints imposed by the social system.

This simplistic argument hides much more than it explains. Competition for resources is not an adequate criterion. Corporations constantly strive to free themselves from the discipline of the market through increase in size, diversification, and generation of consumer loyalty by advertising and other means of persuasion. But even in an ideal situation, the ethics of the marketplace provide only one kind of legitimacy, which nations have been known to reject in times of national crisis or for activities deemed vital to the nation's well-being.

TABLE 1. Business Strategies for Narrowing the Legitimacy Gap.

Business Performance	Legitimacy Gap	Societal Expectations
1. Does not change performance, but changes public perception of business performance through education and information.		
2. If changes in public perception are not possible, change the symbols used to describe business performance, thereby making it congruent with public perception. Note that no change in actual performance is called for.		
3. Attempt to change societal expectations of business performance through education and information.		
4. In case strategies 1 through 3 are unsuccessful in completely bridging the legitimacy gap, bring about changes in business performance, thereby closely matching it with society's expectations.		

Nor can the legality of an act be used as a criterion. Norms in a social system are developed from a voluntary consensus among various groups. Under these conditions, laws tend to codify socially accepted behavior and seldom lead social change. *The traditional economic and legal criteria are necessary but not sufficient conditions of corporate legitimacy.* The corporation that flouts them will not survive, even the mere satisfaction of these criteria does not ensure its continued existence.

Corporate Behavior as Social Responsibility

Second, most of the conflicts between large corporations and various social institutions during the last two decades or so in the United States and other industrialized nations of the free world fall into the category of *social responsibility.* Although relatively few corporations have been accused of violating the laws of their nations, they have been increasingly criticized for failing to meet societal expectations and to adapt their behavior to changing social norms. Thus, *social responsibility implies bringing corporate behavior up to a level where it is in congruence with currently prevailing social norms, values, and performance expectations.*

Social responsibility does not require a radical departure from normal patterns of corporate activities or behavior. It is simply a step ahead — before the new societal expectations are codified into legal requirements. *While the concept of social obligation is proscriptive in nature, the concept of social responsibility is prescriptive.*

Corporate Behavior as Social Responsiveness

The *third* stage of the adaptation of corporate behavior to social needs is in terms of *social responsiveness.* The process of adaptation is only partially served if corporations

S. Prakash Sethi

confine changes in behavior to those concerns that emanate from their actions in the marketplace—those related to their business activities. Examples of such behavior are installing devices to remove pollutants from factory smokestacks or paying immediate and fair compensation to victims of pollution or product-related injuries.

The issue in terms of social responsiveness is not how corporations should respond to social pressures, but what their long-run role in a dynamic social system should be. The corporation here is expected to anticipate the changes that may be a result of the corporation's current activities, or they may be due to the emergence of social problems in which corporations must play an important role. Again, *while social responsibility related activities are prescriptive in nature, activities related to social responsiveness are proactive, i.e., anticipatory and preventive in nature.*

Table 2 summarizes dimensions and attributes of corporate behavior under the three stages. These dimensions are not intended to be inclusive, but are indicative of the type of analysis that this framework makes possible. Additional categories can be developed relating to specific activities in which a business is engaged. Such an approach may indeed be desirable when this framework is to be applied to evaluate the behavior of specific companies and industries.

THE EXTERNAL ENVIRONMENT

We must also develop a schema to distinguish among the various external environments—physical, economic, and sociopolitical—within which a given corporate response to a set of social problems must be evaluated. This has been accomplished by dividing the elapsed time between the emergence of a problem and its solution and ultimate elimination into four categories or stages: (a) preproblem, (b) identification, (c) remedy and re-

lief, and (d) prevention. There is some overlap because social problems do not fall neatly into discrete groups, nor can they always be solved in distinct successive steps. However, the arrangement facilitates our analysis of environmental conditions and the adequacy of various corporate responses.

The Preproblem Stage

In the process of manufacturing and marketing, business firms are constantly engaged in a series of transactions with individuals and social groups. These transactions have certain direct and indirect adverse effects on the parties involved. The *first* type pertains to the normal leakages and shortfalls found in any manufacturing activity and is unavoidable. The *second* type of negative side-effect pertains to actions by individual firms to cut corners in product quality, service, or manufacturing processes either under competitive pressures or to increase short-run profits. Taken individually, each incident is not significant in terms of its impact either on the corporation or the affected party. However, when similar acts are performed by a large number of companies and continued over a long period, their cumulative effect is substantial. When that happens, a problem is born.

The elapsed time at the preproblem stage is probably the longest of all the four steps, although there is a tendency for the time span to become narrower with increasing industrialization. Most individuals and institutions respond to the problem passively. Their efforts are aimed at adaptation, and the problem is treated as given. Elevation to the problem identification stage varies with different cultures and is based on the relative sociopolitical strength of the affecting and affected groups, the availability of necessary expertise to various groups, the relative size of the affected area relative to total area and population, the existence of mass communication

TABLE 2. A Three-Stage Schema for Classifying Corporate Behavior.

Dimensions of Behavior	Stage One: Social Obligation Proscriptive	Stage Two: Social Responsibility Prescriptive	Stage Three: Social Responsiveness Anticipatory and Preventive
Search for legitimacy	Confines legitimacy to legal and economic criteria only; does not violate laws; equates profitable operations with fulfilling social expectations.	Accepts the reality of limited relevance of legal and market criteria of legitimacy in actual practice. Willing to consider and accept broader —extra legal and extra market— criteria for measuring corporate performance and social role.	Accepts its role as defined by the social system and therefore subject to change; recognizes importance of profitable operations but includes other criteria.
Ethical norms	Considers business value-managers expected to behave according to their own ethical standards.	Defines norms in community related terms, i.e., good corporate citizen. Avoids taking moral stand on issues which may harm its economic interests or go against prevailing social norms (majority views).	Takes definite stand on issues of public concern; advocates institutional ethical norms even though they may seem detrimental to its immediate economic interest or prevailing social norms.
Social accountability for corporate actions	Construes narrowly as limited to stock-holders; jealously guards its prerogatives against outsiders.	Individual managers responsible not only for their own ethical standards but also for the collectivity of corporation. Construes narrowly for legal purposes, but broadened to include groups affected by its actions; management more outward looking.	Willing to account for its actions to other groups, even those not directly affected by its actions.
Operating strategy	Exploitative and defensive adaptation. Maximum externalization of costs.	Reactive adaptation. Where identifiable, internalize previously external costs. Maintain current standards of physical and social environment. Compensate victims of pollution and other corporate-related activities even in the absence of clearly established legal grounds. Develop industry-wide standards.	Proactive adaptation. Takes lead in developing and adapting new technology for environmental protectors. Evaluates side effects of corporate actions and eliminates them prior to the action being taken. Anticipates future social changes and develops internal structures to cope with them.

TABLE 2. *(cont)*

Dimensions of Behavior	Stage One: Social Obligation Proscriptive	Stage Two: Social Responsibility Prescriptive	Stage Three: Social Responsiveness Anticipatory and Preventive
Response to social pressures	Maintains low public profile, but, if attacked, uses PR methods to upgrade its public image; denies any deficiencies; blames public dissatisfaction on ignorance or failure to understand corporate functions; discloses information only where legally required.	Accepts responsibility for solving current problems; will admit deficiencies in former practices and attempt to persuade public that its current practices meet social norms; attitude toward critics conciliatory; freer information disclosures than state one.	Willingly discusses activities with outside groups; makes information freely available to public; accepts formal and informal inputs from outside groups in decision making. Is willing to be publicly evaluated for its various activities.
Activities pertaining to governmental actions	Strongly resists any regulation of its activities except when it needs help to protect its market position; avoids contact; resists any demands for information beyond that legally required.	Preserves management discretion in corporate decisions, but cooperates with government in research to improve industrywide standards; participates in political processes and encourages employees to do likewise.	Openly communicates with government; assists in enforcing existing laws and developing evaluations of business practices; objects publicly to governmental activities that it feels are detrimental to the public good.
Legislative and political activities	Seeks to maintain status quo; actively opposes laws that would internalize any previously externalized costs; seeks to keep lobbying activities secret.	Willing to work with outside groups for good environmental laws; concedes need for change in some status quo laws; less secrecy in lobbying than state one.	Avoids meddling in politics and does not pursue special interest laws; assists legislative bodies in developing better laws where relevant; promotes honesty and openness in government and in its own lobbying activities.
Philanthropy	Contributes only when direct benefit to it clearly shown; otherwise, views contributions as responsibility of individual employees.	Contributes to noncontroversial and established causes; matches employee contributions.	Activities of state two, *plus* support and contributions to new, controversial groups whose needs it sees as unfulfilled and increasingly important.

systems in the society, and the access to media by various groups.

The Identification Stage

Once the impact of a problem has become significant enough, there is a drive among the affected groups to define it, identify its causes, and relate it to the source. This is one of the most difficult stages in the whole process. *First,* the business entity could not have known of the problem because technology for its detection did not exist. Therefore, the most responsible businesses following the best safety procedures will be found years later to have polluted the environment, exposed their workers to rare forms of cancer, or sold potentially dangerous products. In most cases, direct linkages between cause and effect are all but impossible to find. The best that can be accomplished is to show through inference and statistical weight of evidence that a given source was the major contributor to the problem.

Second, a given adverse effect can be caused by a variety of sources or factors, and direct linkages are therefore impossible to establish. An example is cigarette smoking and lung cancer. Despite overwhelming statistical evidence, tobacco companies in the United States maintain that no direct cause-and-effect relationship has been established between smoking and cancer (17). A *third* difficulty arises when no adequate definitive proof is possible because the symptoms appear years later—e.g., cancer caused in workers in manufacturing processes using asbestos fiber (5) or polyvinyl chloride (24). A *fourth* difficulty deals with situations in which irreparable damage has been done by the time proof is available, and no corrective or preventive measures are possible—e.g., the use of fluorocarbons in aerosol sprays and their impact on the ozone layer of the stratosphere (25).

The definition of the problem may also involve the vested interest or value-orientation of a particular group. Thus conservationists may bemoan the logging of virgin redwoods and call it a national calamity, whereas local communities and loggers may want to preserve their jobs and may therefore resist the establishment of a redwood national park. What is a problem to one group may appear to be an obstruction to another (16).

The Remedy and Relief Stage

Once a causal linkage has been established, the question of compensatory and/or punitive damages to the affected parties must be considered. This stage is marked by intense activity by the various parties to the conflict, with many questions involved. *One* is the determination of the injured parties and the extent of their damage. A *second* question has to do with the assumption of responsibility for payment of claims—the company and the insurance carrier. An equally important *third* issue is the role played by courts, legislatures and executive and administrative agencies of the government.

Certain interrelated issues must be considered. For example, is it socially desirable to make companies pay all the costs of a particular type of pollution not intentionally created? If a particular business or industry is forced to pay the total cost, how will this affect workers, stockholders, and lenders whose livelihood and life savings may be dependent on the profitability of that business or industry? The effect of the health of a particular industry on the total economy is also important in considering who should pay for the damages. Thus, government sometimes may be called upon to subsidize payments regardless of which party is at fault. An example is the United States government subsidies to support pension payments to coal miners who had contracted black lung disease during a particular time period.

The Prevention Stage

At this point the problem has achieved a level of maturity. The causal sources are either well established or easily identifiable. The attempt now is to develop long-range programs to prevent the recurrence of the problem. These include development of substitute materials, product redesign, restructuring organizations and decision-making processes, public education, and emergence of new special-interest groups to bring about necessary political and legislative changes. It should be noted that the prevention stage is not sequential, but generally overlaps with the problem identification and remedy and relief stages. The prevention stage, in order to be successful, calls for two changes: a qualitative change in the value sets of business and government, and a modification of the social arrangements among various groups in the social system.

This stage is marked by uncertainty and difficulty in making an accurate appraisal of potential costs and benefits. The strategies to be pursued by society would, of necessity, involve unproved technologies and unfamiliar sociopolitical arrangements. Thus, it is not uncommon to find a high degree of self-righteousness in the pronouncements of various groups, which may be long on rhetoric but short on substance. Groups tend to advocate solutions that favor their particular viewpoint while understating the potential costs to those groups having opposing viewpoints. The ideological anti-business bias of certain groups at this stage could be as harmful to the development of socially equitable and technologically feasible long-term solutions as the tendency among some business people to resist every demand for change as not technically feasible, expensive, or unnecessary.

APPLYING THE FRAMEWORK

The analytical model described above can be used both to understand better how social conflicts develop and how firms respond to predict the effectiveness of particular corporate response patterns to different stages of conflict resolution. In this section, the application of the framework is demonstrated in analyzing a major social conflict involving the operations of large corporations in less developed countries. The conflict had to do with the sale of infant formula foods, and the analysis was carried out by Sethi and Post (19). Two other studies have applied this framework in comparing the responses of the United States and Japanese business corporations to societal pressures in their respective countries (18) and in analyzing the performance of regulatory agencies in the United States (21).

The Situational Context: Evolution of the Infant Formula Controversy

The first criticism of the industry and its promotional activities can be traced to the late 1960s when Dr. Jelliffe, Director of the Caribbean Food and Nutrition Institute in Jamaica, conducted research studies. His findings and criticism culminated in an international conference of experts in Bogota, Colombia in 1970, under the auspices of the U.N.'s Protein Calories Advisory Group (PAG), and a follow-up session in Singapore in 1972. The PAG issued an official statement (PAG Statement #23) in 1973 recommending that breastfeeding be supported and promoted in LDCs and that commercial promotion be restrained, industry and/or LDC governments.

The first public identification of the issue occurred in 1973 with the appearance of several articles about the problem in *The New*

Internationalist (22). This, in turn, spurred Mike Muller to undertake a series of interviews and observations which were eventually published in 1974 as a pamphlet titled *The Baby Killer* (11) with a German translation published in Switzerland under the title, *Nestle' Totet Kinder* (Nestle Kills Babies). Nestle's lawsuit against the public action group that published the pamphlet produced a period of intense advocacy surrounding the trial in the Swiss courts. Thus, between 1974 and mid-1976 when the case was decided, the issue received considerable international media coverage.

Institutionalized pressures began in earnest in 1975 when shareholder resolutions were filed for consideration at the annual meetings of the American infant formula companies. This pressure has continued, and several institutional investors (universities, the Rockefeller and Ford Foundations) have taken positions questioning the responsiveness of the firms to the controversy. Church groups, through the Interfaith Council on Corporate Responsibility of the National Council of Churches, have led the fight to coordinate the shareholders' campaigns. Most recently, some public interest groups have launched a campaign to boycott Nestle products in the United States. At the LDC level, the government of Papua New Guinea recently passed a law declaring baby bottles, nipples, and pacifiers health hazards and their sale restricted through prescription only. The objective was to discourage indiscriminate promotion, sale, and consumption of infant food formulas (2).

The preproblem stage of the infant formula case existed prior to the 1970s. During this time, the adverse impacts on LDCs were not yet articulated. By the early 1970s, the identification stage had been reached, as professional criticism grew and articles and stories began to appear in the mass media.

The remedy and relief stage seems to have begun in 1975, primarily through the Nestle trial in Switzerland and the shareholder resolutions filed in the United States. The life cycle of the controversy has not yet reached the preventive stage.

The Nature of Corporate Response

The MNC's response during the pre-problem stage was of the social obligation type, responding only to prevailing law and market condition. The principal industry effort during the problem identification stage was participation in the conference sponsored by PAG. Abbott (Ross), AHO (Wyeth), and Nestle each sent representatives to these meetings as did a number of British, European, and Japanese companies. For most companies, this seemed to mark a decision point between the *social obligation* phase and the *social responsibility* phase. Only a few firms, notably Abbott (Ross), moved to an approach that included steps to mitigate their negative impact in the LDCs. For AHP (Wyeth), Borden, Nestle, and others, this did not occur until 1974 when first plans were occurring for the formation of an international trade organization.

In November, 1975, representatives of nine MNC manufacturers met in Zurich, Switzerland, and decided to form an international council to be known as the International Council Infant Food Industries (ICIFI). Nestle, AHP (Wyeth), and Abbott (Ross) participated in these discussions along with several European and four Japanese companies. Others, such as Borden and Bristol Myers sent representatives to the sessions, but chose not to participate actively or join the council. ICIFI urged its members to adopt a code of marketing ethics, requiring the members to recognize the primacy of breastfeeding in all of their product information and to eliminate in-hospital promotion and solicitation by personnel who were paid on a sales commission basis. For those companies that joined, it appears to have marked a passage into the *social*

TABLE 3. Socio-Political Dimensions of Infant Formula Foods Controversy: Patterns of Industry Responses (5 MNCs).

Patterns of Industry Response	Stages of Conflict Evolution			
	PreProblem Stage (Pre-1970)	Identification Stage (1970)	Remedy & Relief Stage (1976)	Prevention Stage (1977–)
Social Obligation (Do what is required by law)	Bristol-Myers (Mead Johnson Div.) Borden Nestle— American Home Products (Wyeth Lab.) Abbott (Ross Lab.)	Bristol-Myers (Mead Johnson Div.) Borden Nestle— American Home Products (Wyeth Lab.)	Bristol-Myers (Mead Johnson Div.) Borden	Bristol-Myers (Mead Johnson Div.)
Social Responsibility (Mitigate Negative impacts)		Abbott (Ross Lab.)	Nestle— American Home Products (Wyeth Lab.)	Borden Nestle— American Home Products (Wyeth Lab.)
Social Responsiveness (Promote positive change)			Abbott (Ross Lab.)	Abbott (Ross Lab.)

responsibility phase where efforts were undertaken to mitigate negative social impacts.

There was criticism of the ICIFI code from the beginning, and Abbott (Ross) withdrew from the organization, arguing that the code was too weak. The company then adopted its own more restrictive code which included a provision prohibiting consumer oriented mass advertising. Additional criticisms have led to some incremental changes which have strengthened the "professional" character of sales activity, but which have not yet proscribed all consumer oriented mass advertising; indeed, the critics continue to charge that the response at the user level has been insufficient. As a public issue matures, companies may adopt actions which operate to prevent further growth in the legitimacy gap by minimizing or eliminating the underlying sources of criticism (*prevention stage*). In 1977, Abbott (Ross) announced its intention to commit nearly $100,000 to a breast feeding campaign in developing nations, budgeted

$175,000 for independent research on breast-feeding, infant formula, and LDCs, and announced a plan for a continuing cooperative effort to review the situation with its critics. ICIFI has also begun working informally with international health agencies to prepare educational materials for use in LDCs and is supporting scientific research about breast feeding, infant formula products, and LDC environments.

Borden has also moved from the social obligation to social responsibility stage. The company did not have shareholder resolutions filed with it until 1977. The filing seems to have facilitated a management review of promotional strategies in LDCs. Abbott (Ross) Laboratories' attempt to act in ways that will create positive impacts in LDCs thereby signals a shift to a *social responsiveness stage*. Granting that there is some danger of sending "double signals" to its sales force, the company seems to have adopted a posture that will permit it to sell its products in appropriate circumstances, while assisting the LDCs to encourage breastfeeding where that is most appropriate.

Table 3 describes the patterns of responses from social obligation to social responsiveness as the evolution of the controversy moves from the preproblem to prevention stage.

CONCLUSION

The framework developed here has been shown to have wide applicability in analyzing social systems within and between nations. My current research is designed to further elaborate the framework to study the interaction between external environment on corporate structure and internal decision making. Studies are also under way that apply this framework to a comparative analysis of children's television programming and advertising in different countries (3) and social performance evaluation of specific regulatory agencies in the United States (21).

NOTES

1. Abt, Clark. *Social Audit* (New York: American Management Association, 1977).

2. "Baby Bottles Banned in New Guinea," *The Dallas Morning News,* November 3, 1977, p. 8-C.

3. Bagot, Diane. "Children's Television: Advertising and Programming, A Cross-Cultural Study," Working Paper, School of Management, The University of Texas at Dallas, 1978.

4. Bauer, Raymond A., and Dan H. Fenn, Jr., *The Corporate Social Audit* (New York: Russell Sage Foundation, 1972).

5. Brodeur, Paul. *Expendable Americans* (New York: The Viking Press, 1974).

6. Dierkes, Meinolf, and Raymond A. Bauer. *Corporate Social Accounting* (New York: Praeger, 1973).

7. Estes, Ralph W. *Corporate Social Accounting* (Los Angeles: Melville Publishing Co., 1976).

8. Friedman, Milton. *Capitalism and Freedom* (Chicago: The University of Chicago Press, 1962).

9. Linowes, David F. *Strategies for Survival* (New York: American Management Association, 1973).

10. Manne, Henry G., and Henry C. Wallich. *The Modern Corporation and Social Responsibility* (Washington, D.C.: American Enterprise Institute for Public Policy Research, 1972).

11. Muller, Mike. *The Baby Killer,* 2nd ed. (London, England: War on Want, 1975).

12. Preston, Lee E., and James E. Post. *Private Management and Public Policy: The Principle of Public Responsibility* (Englewood Cliffs, New Jersey: Prentice-Hall, Inc., 1975).

13. Seidler, Lee J., and Lynn L. Seidler. *Social Accounting: Theory Issues, and Cases* (Los Angeles: Melville Publishing Co., 1975).

14. Sethi, S. Prakash. "Corporate Social Audit: An Emerging Trend in Measuring Corporate Social Performance." In Dow Votaw and S. Prakash Sethi (Eds.), *The Corporate Dilemma: Traditional Values versus Contemporary Problems* (Englewood Cliffs, New Jersey: Prentice-Hall, Inc., 1973), pp. 214–231.

15. Sethi, S. Prakash. "Dimensions of Corporate Social Performance: An Analytical Framework for Measurement and Evaluation" *California Management Review.* (Spring, 1975), pp. 58–64.

16. Sethi, S. Prakash. *Up Against the Corporate Wall: Modern Corporations and Social Issues,* 3rd ed. (Englewood Cliffs, New Jersey: Prentice-Hall, Inc., 1977).

17. Sethi, S. Prakash. *Promises of the Good Life: Social Consequences of Private Marketing Decisions* (Homewood, Illinois: Richard D. Irwin, Inc., 1979).

18. Sethi, S. Prakash. "An Analytical Framework for Making Cross-Cultural Comparisons of Business Responses to Social Pressures: The Case of the United States and Japan," in Lee E. Preston (Ed.), *Research in Corporate Social Performance and Policy.* (Greenwich, Connecticut: Jai Press, 1978).

19. Sethi, S. Prakash, and James E. Post. "Infant Formula Marketing in Less Developed Countries: An Analysis of Secondary Effects," in Subhash C. Jain (Ed.), *Research Frontiers in Marketing: Dialogues and Directions,* 1978 Educators' Proceedings, Series #43, (Chicago, Illinois: American Marketing Association, 1978), pp. 271–275.

20. Shocker, Allan D., and S. Prakash Sethi. "An Approach to Incorporating Social Preferences to Developing Corporate Action Strategies." In S. Prakash Sethi (Ed.), *The Unstable Ground: Corporate Social Policy in a Dynamic Society* (Los Angeles, California: Melville Publishing Co., 1974), pp. 67–80.

21. Swanson, Carl L. "An Analytical Framework to Appraise the Performance of Regulatory Agencies in the Context of the Public Interest" in Jeffrey S. Susbauer (Ed.), *Academy of Management Proceedings*, 1978, pp. 260–264.

22. "The Baby Food Controversy." *The New Internationalist*, August, 1973, p. 10.

23. Votaw, Dow, and S. Prakash Sethi (Eds.). *The Corporate Dilemma: Traditional Values Versus Contemporary Social Problems* (Englewood Cliffs, New Jersey: Prentice-Hall, Inc., 1973), pp. 9–45, 167–91.

24. Weaver, Paul H. "On the Horns of the Vinyl Chloride Dilemma," *Fortune*, October, 1974, pp. 150.

25. "Why Aerosols Are Under Attack," *Business Week*, February 17, 1975, pp. 50–51.

6

Corporate Social Responsibility and Firm Financial Performance

Jean B. McGuire

CONCORDIA UNIVERSITY

Alison Sundgren
Thomas Schneeweis

UNIVERSITY OF MASSACHUSETTS

Using Fortune *magazine's ratings of corporate reputations, we analyzed the relationships between perceptions of firms' corporate social responsibility and measures of their financial performance. Results show that a firm's prior performance, assessed by both stock-market returns and accounting-based measures, is more closely related to corporate social responsibility than is subsequent performance. Results also show that measures of risk are more closely associated with social responsibility than previous studies have suggested.*

The management literature has acknowledged social responsibility as an important corporate duty (Quinn, Mintzberg, & James, 1987). Given the significance of corporate social responsibility in corporate decision making, the relationship between a firm's social and ethical policies or actions and its financial performance (Arlow & Gannon, 1982; Ullmann, 1985) is an important topic.

Various arguments have been made regarding the relationship between firms' social responsibility and their financial performance. One view is that firms face a trade-off between social responsibility and financial performance. Those holding this view propose that firms incur costs from socially responsible actions that put them at an economic disadvantage compared to other, less responsible, firms (Aupperle, Carroll, & Hatfield, 1985; Ullmann, 1985; Vance, 1975). A second, contrasting viewpoint is that the explicit costs of corporate social responsibility are minimal and that firms may actually benefit from socially responsible actions in terms of employee morale and productivity (Moskowitz, 1972; Parket & Eibert, 1975; Soloman

The cooperation of *Fortune* magazine in providing data from its annual survey is gratefully acknowledged. Bradford Knipes assisted in data analysis and commented on earlier drafts of this article. The authors gratefully acknowledge the reviewers' comments. Reprinted with permission from the *Academy of Management Review.*

& Hansen, 1985). A third perspective is that the costs of socially responsible actions are significant but are offset by a reduction in other firm costs. For instance, stakeholder theory (Cornell & Shapiro, 1987) suggests that a firm must satisfy not only stockholders and bondholders, but also those with less explicit, or implicit, claims. Stakeholder theory further suggests that implicit claims like product quality are less costly to a firm than explicit claims like wage contracts or stockholder or bondholder demands. Low social responsibility, however, may encourage some stakeholders to doubt the ability of a firm to honor implicit claims and may increase the number of a firm's more costly explicit claims.

In addition, Alexander and Bucholtz (1978) and Bowman and Haire (1975) have suggested that stakeholders and stock- and bondholders may see corporate social responsibility as indicating management skill. In short, a firm has an investment in reputation, including its reputation for being socially responsible. An increase in perceived social responsibility may improve the image of the firm's management and permit it to exchange costly explicit claims for less costly implicit charges. In contrast, a decline in the level of stakeholders' view of a firm's social responsibility may reduce its reputation and result in an increase in costly explicit claims.

In this study, we used data from the *Fortune* survey of corporate reputations to examine two aspects of the relationship between corporate social responsibility and firm financial performance that previous research has ignored. First, we not only measured performance in terms of accounting and stock-market-based measures but also in terms of risk. Second, we examined not only the extent to which social responsibility predicted financial performance but also whether prior financial performance predicted social responsibility. This study also improved on the methodology used in previous studies by using evaluations of social responsibility made by knowledgeable external sources.

THEORETICAL FRAMEWORK

Research into the relationship between corporate social responsibility and financial performance has been based on several theoretical arguments. Those who have suggested a negative relation between social responsibility and financial performance have argued that high responsibility results in additional costs that put a firm at an economic disadvantage compared to other, less socially responsible firms (Bragdon & Marlin, 1985; Vance, 1975). These added costs may result from actions like making extensive charitable contributions, promoting community development plans, maintaining plants in economically depressed locations, and establishing environmental protection procedures. In addition, concern for social responsibility may limit a firm's strategic alternatives. For example, a firm may forgo certain product lines, such as weapons or pesticides, and avoid plant relocations and investment opportunities in certain locations (e.g., South Africa).

In contrast, other scholars investigating corporate social responsibility and performance have argued for a positive association. Several authors have cited improved employee and customer goodwill as an important outcome of social responsibility (Davis, 1975; Soloman & Hansen, 1985). For example, a firm perceived as high in social responsibility may face relatively few labor problems, and customers may be favorably disposed to its products. Socially responsible activities may also improve a firm's standing with such important constituencies as bankers, investors, and government officials. Improved relationships with these constituencies may bring economic benefits (Moussavi & Evans, 1986). Indeed, banks and other institutional investors have reported social considerations to be a factor in their investment decisions (Spicer, 1978). High corporate social responsibility may therefore improve a firm's access to sources of capital.

Lastly, modern corporate stakeholder theory (Cornell & Shapiro, 1987) contends that the value of a firm depends on the cost not only of explicit claims but also of implicit claims. From this viewpoint, the set of claimants on a firm's resources goes beyond the stockholders and bondholders to include stakeholders who have explicit claims on the firm like wage contracts and others with whom the firm has made implicit contracts, involving, for instance, quality service and social responsibility. If a firm does not act in a socially responsible manner, parties to implicit contracts concerning the social responsibility of the firm may attempt to transform those implicit agreements into explicit agreements that will be more costly to it. For example, if a firm fails to meet promises to government officials in regard to actions that affect the environment (dumping, etc.), government agencies may find it necessary to pass more stringent regulations, constituting explicit contracts, to force the firm to act in a socially responsible manner. Moreover, socially, irresponsible actions may spill over to other implicit stakeholders, who may doubt whether the firm would honor their claims. Thus, firms with an image of high corporate social responsibility may find that they have more low-cost implicit claims than other firms and thus have higher financial performance (Cornell & Shapiro, 1987).

Although theory and research have focused primarily on the relationship between corporate social responsibility and measures of financial performance, an argument for a relationship between social responsibility and such measures of financial risk as variance in earnings and in stock returns can also be made (Spicer, 1978; Ullmann, 1985). First, low levels of social responsibility may increase a firm's financial risk. Investors may consider less socially responsible firms to be riskier investments because they see management skills at the firm as low (Alexander & Bucholtz, 1978; Spicer, 1978). Investors and other constituencies may also anticipate an increase in firm costs owing to lack of social responsibility. For example, the government may levy fines, and law suits, such as those recently filed against pharmaceutical, chemical, and asbestos firms, that may threaten a firm's very existence. Perceptions of low social responsibility may also decrease a firm's ability to obtain capital at consistent rates.

In contrast, a high degree of corporate social responsibility may permit a firm to have relatively low financial risk as the result of more stable relations with the government and the financial community. In addition, to the degree that a firm has high social responsibility, it may also have a low percentage of total debt to total assets. A low total debt ensures that a firm can easily continue to satisfy implicit claims. Thus, compared to other firms, firms with high social responsibility may have lower market- and accounting-based total risk because they are less sensitive to certain external events, like governmental actions, and have a lower debt. The impact of social responsibility on measures of a firm's systematic risk may, however, be minimal, since most events affecting a firm's level of social responsibility do not systematically affect all other firms in the marketplace (Cornell & Shapiro, 1987).

Most studies have related social responsibility and concurrent financial performance. We also explored the effects of prior and subsequent performance on subsequent and prior evaluations of corporate social responsibility. The theoretical arguments suggested regarding the concurrent relationship between corporate social responsibility and financial performance also apply to the relationship with subsequent financial perfor-

Jean B. McGuire / Alison Sundgren / Thomas Schneeweis

mance. The benefits of social responsibility cited earlier (e.g., employee motivation, customer goodwill) may carry over into later periods. To the degree that a firm with relatively high social responsibility can implement implicit contracts, its financial performance may improve and variability in market- and accounting-based performance measures may decline.

Corporate social responsibility may also be linked to past firm performance. Its financial performance may influence a firm's evolving social policy and actions (Ullmann, 1985). Policies and expenditures, particularly in discretionary areas such as social programs, may be especially sensitive to the existence of slack resources (Cyert & March, 1963). If corporate social responsibility is viewed as a significant cost, firms with relatively high past financial performance may be more willing to absorb these costs in the future (Parket & Eibert, 1975; Ullmann, 1985). In contrast, less profitable firms may be less willing to undertake socially responsible actions.

PREVIOUS RESEARCH

Previous research has yielded mixed results regarding the relationships between corporate social responsibility and measures of firm performance. Reviews by Aupperle and colleagues (1985), Cochran and Wood (1984), and Ullmann (1985) have all found mixed results concerning the concurrent relationship between social responsibility and firm performance. Ullmann suggested that those conflicting results may derive, in part, from differences in research methodologies and measures of financial performance.

Studies using stock-market-based measures of return have reported mixed results regarding the relationship between social responsibility and performance. Moskowitz (1972) ranked 67 selected firms in terms of his evaluation of their level of social responsibility

and reported higher than average stock returns for highly ranked firms. Vance (1975), however, found a subset of the firms rated by Moskowitz had lower stock-market performance than a comparison sample of firms listed in the New York Stock Exchange Composite Index, Dow Jones Industrials, and Standard and Poor's Industrials. The studies by Vance and Moskowitz, however, both failed to adjust for risk. Other studies that have attempted to adjust stock-return performance measures for risk have found little relationship between social responsibility and market performance. Alexander and Bucholtz (1978), using the firms listed in Moskowitz's study, found little association between social responsibility and risk-adjusted return on securities.[1]

Studies examining the relationship between social responsibility and accounting-based performance measures have generally found positive results. Bragdon and Marlin (1972), Bowman and Haire (1975), and Parket and Eibert (1975) found generally positive associations between corporate social responsibility and accounting-based measures of performance. However, those studies did not control for the possible effects of other variables. Later studies that have attempted to control for differences in risk have offered more cautious support for the relationship between social responsibility and accounting-based performance measures. Cochran and Wood (1984) found a positive correlation between social responsibility and accounting performance after controlling for the age of assets. In contrast, Aupperle and colleagues (1985) found no significant relationships between social responsibility and a firm's ROA adjusted by its ranking in the Value Line Safety Index. Since financial risk and performance vary with industry, Sturdivant and Ginter (1977) compared accounting-based measures of performance for a subsample of the firms rated by Moskowitz to industry averages. They categorized firms as best, honorably mentioned, and worst in terms of social responsibility. Firms given an honorable mention had higher accounting-based performance than the other firms.

Previous studies on the relationship between social responsibility and risk have also produced mixed results. Spicer (1978) found that firms rated high on social performance, as measured by pollution control activities, had lower total and systematic risk than less socially responsible firms. Aupperle and colleagues also (1985) found a negative association between corporate social responsibility and accounting-based risk but found that the association between market-based risk and social responsibility was insignificant.

Previous studies have also employed varying measures of corporate social responsibility. Three methods have commonly been used. The first uses expert evaluations of corporate policies. The validity of this methodology, of course, depends on the skill and qualifications of those making the assessments (Abbott & Monsen, 1979). Previous studies have used an index from the Council of Concerned Businessmen (Sturdivant & Ginter, 1977) and two rankings from *Business and Society* (Moskowitz, 1972, 1975). The validity of these indexes is subject to criticism. Moskowitz's ratings were based on his own evaluation. In the case of the ratings published in 1975, done on samples of businessmen and M.B.A. students, the expertise of the evaluators and the accuracy of the information are questionable (Bowman & Haire, 1975).

Other researchers have used content analysis of corporate annual reports or other corporate documents (Abbot & Monsen, 1979); Anderson & Frankel, 1980; Bowman & Haire, 1975; Preston, 1978). Such measures, however, confuse social orientation with corporate actions (Arlow & Gannon, 1982; Ullmann, 1985). Moreover, such documents often have more public relations value than informational value. The relationship between such public statements and actual corporate actions is uncertain. Bowman and Haire found a positive association between emphasis on corporate social responsibility in annual reports and the Moskowitz ratings. Preston, however, found no relation between these variables. Parket and Eibert (1975) used a corporation's willingness to respond to a questionnaire on social responsibility as an indicator of the firm's concern with the issue.

The third method of measuring corporate social responsibility uses performance in controlling pollution as a proxy measure. The Council of Concerned Businessmen Pollution Performance Index is frequently used (Bragdon & Marlin, 1972; Folger & Nutt, 1975; Spicer, 1978). Pollution control, however, reflects only one aspect of social responsibility and is only valid for certain industries (Bragdon & Marlin, 1972).

The types of measures previous studies have used influence results because accounting- and stock-market-based performance measures focus on different aspects of performance, and each is subject to particular biases (McGuire, Schneeweis, & Hill, 1986). Accounting-based measures tap only historical aspects of firm performance (McGuire, Schneeweis, & Hill, 1986). Moreover, they are subject to bias from managerial manipulation and differences in accounting procedures (Branch, 1983; Brilloff, 1972, 1976). Accounting performance should also be adjusted for risk, industry characteristics, and other variables (Aaker & Jacobson, 1987; Arlow & Gannon, 1982; Davidson, Worrell, & Gilberton, 1986; Michel & Shaked, 1984; Ullmann, 1985).

To avoid the problems of accounting-based measures, some authors have used stock-market-based measures of performance. Market returns have several advantages over accounting-based measures: they are (1) less susceptible to differential accounting procedures and managerial manipulation and (2) represent investors' evaluations of a firm's ability to generate future economic earnings rather than past performance.

Problems also exist, however, with the use of stock-market-based measures of performance (McGuire, Schneeweis, & Branch, 1986). Ullmann (1985) suggested that the use of market measures implies that investors' valuation of firm performance is proper performance measure. Since firms face multiple constituencies (Pfeffer & Salancik, 1978), sole concentration on investors' evaluations may not be sufficient.

Given the debate over the proper measure of financial performance, in this study we used both accounting- and stock-market-based measures to investigate the relationships between concurrently, previously, and subsequently measured firm performance and corporate social responsibility. We also improved upon the methodology used in previous studies by using evaluations of corporate social responsibility from knowledgeable external sources.

METHODS

Data

Data on corporate social responsibility were obtained from *Fortune* magazine's annual survey of corporate reputations. *Fortune* has conducted the survey each fall since 1982 and published summary results each January. The survey covers the largest firms in 20–25 industry groups (the number of industry groups varies from year to year). Over 8,000 executives, outside directors, and corporate analysts are asked to rate the ten largest companies in their industry on eight attributes: financial soundness, long-term investment value, use of corporate assets, quality of management, innovativeness, quality of products or services, use of corporate talent, and community and environmental responsibility. Ratings are on a scale of 0 (poor) to 10 (excel-

lent). The response rate of those surveyed has averaged almost 50 percent for each year of the survey (*Fortune*, 1983, 1986). Chakravarthy (1986) and Wartick (1987) have also used this data set.

The *Fortune* magazine survey was chosen for several reasons. First, it provides comparable data over an extended period. Second, the number of respondents is comparable or superior to those of other ratings. Third, respondents rate only firms in an industry with which they are familiar. They have direct access to internal firm and industry information that is particularly critical in the area of corporate social responsibility, where annual reports and other official documents provide incomplete and inconsistent information (Bowman & Haire, 1979).[2]

Evidence for the validity of the evaluations comes from empirical studies using other dimensions of the *Fortune* survey (Chakravarthy, 1986; McGuire, Schneeweis, & Branch, 1987). Those studies have found that the *Fortune* evaluations of firms' financial performance are highly correlated with accounting- and stock-market-based performance measures. Major changes in a firm's ranking often correspond to specific events, such as product changes or lawsuits, or to changes in performance (*Fortune*, 1986). The *Fortune* ratings differ from those of other evaluators of social responsibility in that the respondents are selected for their knowledge of a particular industry rather than for their specific knowledge of or interest in corporate social responsibility. Thus, their interpretation and evaluation of social responsibility may differ from those of others who are specifically interested in the issue. Wartick (1987), however, found the *Fortune* ratings to be associated with membership in the Issues Management Association, which suggests that the ratings do indicate an orientation toward corporate social responsibility.[3]

To evaluate the reliability of the ratings, we checked for consistency between the 1985 and 1986 evaluations. Although some modification of the ratings could be expected because of changing conditions and firm actions, major modifications would suggest lack of reliability. It should also be noted that the respondents *Fortune* uses change slightly each year. The correlation between the two sets of evaluations was .899.

Measures of Financial Performance

Data on accounting- and stock-market-based measures of firm performance and risk were obtained from the COMPUSTAT data base. The Appendix defines the measures of firm performance and risk we used. Market performance was measured by risk-adjusted return, or alpha, and total return. Market risk measures were beta, a measure of systematic risk, and the standard deviation of total return. Accounting-based performance measures were return on assets (ROA), total assets, sales growth, asset growth, and operating income growth. The ratio of debt to assets, operating leverage, and the standard deviation of operating income were our accounting-based measures of risk.

Periods of Analysis

Two sets of ratings of corporate social responsibility were used in this analysis. First, we computed average rankings for the period 1983–85, including the 98 firms and industries that appeared in all the yearly surveys and for which financial performance data were available. Second, to permit analysis of the relationship between corporate social responsibility and previous and subsequent firm financial performance, we used ratings of social responsibility for one year, 1983. *Fortune* produced these ratings in late 1982 and published them in January 1983. All the 131 firms rated by *Fortune* and for which financial performance data were available were included in this analysis.[4]

Financial performance variables were averaged over two periods: 1982–84 and 1977–81. Tables 1 and 2 show correlations among the financial variables for the periods studied. The financial performance variables for 1982–84 are contemporaneous with the 1983–85 social responsibility ratings and subsequent to the 1983 ratings. Thus, by comparing the 1982–84 financial performance ratings to the average *Fortune* rating for 1983–85, we could examine the concurrent relationship between corporate social responsibility and financial performance. Analysis of 1983 ratings in relation to the 1977–81 and 1982–84 financial performance variables permitted us to evaluate the relation between prior financial performance and corporate social responsibility using the 1977–81 measures and to evaluate subsequent financial performance using the 1982–84 data.

RESULTS

Correlational Analysis

Concurrent performance. Table 3 presents the correlations between contemporaneous evaluations of corporate social performance (1983–85) and accounting- and market-based performance measures (1982–84). Correlations between social responsibility and stock-market-based measures of performance are insignificant (.04 and −.07), suggesting that there is little contemporaneous association. Three of the accounting-based measures of performance, however, are significantly correlated with corporate social responsibility. ROA and total assets show positive relationships (.47 and .20, respectively), and operating income growth has a negative correlation (−.21). The positive association between ROA, an accounting-based measure of contemporaneous performance, and corporate social responsibility supports the view that, through

Jean B. McGuire / Alison Sundgren / Thomas Schneeweis

TABLE 1. *Correlations Among 1977-81 Financial Variables.*[a]

Variables	1	2	3	4	5	6	7	8	9	10	11	12
1. 1983 corporate social responsibility												
2. ROA	.51**											
3. Average assets	.15	−.05										
4. Operating income growth	.04	.16*	−.15									
5. Sales growth	.15	.17*	−.02	.81**								
6. Asset growth	.35**	.22*	.22*	−.15	−.02							
7. Alpha	.17*	−.17*	−.17*	.62**	.49**	.42**						
8. Total return	.08	.23**	−.23**	.66**	.53**	.46**	.96**					
9. Debt to assets	−.49**	−.68**	.20*	.05	.09	.01	.01	.05				
10. Operating leverage	.23**	.25**	.07	.24**	.12	.08	.21*	.17*	.11			
11. Standard deviation of operating income	.16*	.09	.84**	−.20*	−.02	.03	−.16*	−.20*	.05	.02		
12. Beta	−.32**	−.12	−.27**	.21*	.27**	.23**	.10	.35**	.15	.09	−.16*	
13. Standard deviation of total return	−.44**	−.29**	−.27**	.18*	.15	−.14	.01	.24**	.28**	−.12	−.18*	.89**

[a]$N = 131$
*$p < .05$
**$p < .01$

97

TABLE 2. Correlations Among 1982-84 Financial Variables.[a]

Variables	1	2	3	4	5	6	7	8	9	10	11	12
1. 1983 corporate social responsibility												
2. ROA	.41**											
3. Average assets	.15	.01										
4. Operating income growth	−.03	.02	.11									
5. Sales growth	.02	.16*	.10	−.68**								
6. Asset growth	.03	.11	.15	.43**	.71**							
7. Alpha	−.07	.29**	.12	.11	.42**	.14						
8. Total return	−.15	.22**	.16*	.51**	.54**	.38**	.93**					
9. Debt to assets	−.44**	−.47**	.32**	.15	.13	.14	.17*	.25**				
10. Operating leverage	−.06	−.03	.16*	−.08	−.08	−.04	−.04	−.06	.11			
11. Standard deviation of operating income	.09	.18*	.74**	.32**	.21*	.12	.22*	.24**	.13	.08		
12. Beta	−.32**	−.27**	.08	.11	.10	.13	−.53**	−.18*	.13	−.05	−.03	
13. Standard deviation of total return	−.44*	−.37**	.14	.09	−.05	−.14	−.45**	−.19*	.32**	.00	.32**	.77**

[a]$N = 131$
*$p < .05$
**$p < .01$

TABLE 3. *Correlations Between Corporate Social Responsibility and Firm Performance.*[a]

Performance Dimensions	1983–85 Social Responsibility and 1982–84 Performance	1983 Social Responsibility and 1977–81 Performance	1983 Social Responsibility and 1982–84 Performance
ROA	.47**	.52**	.41**
Total assets	.20	.15	.15
Operating income growth	−.21	.04	−.03
Sales growth	.04	.15	.02
Asset growth	.03	.35**	.03
Alpha	.04	.17*	−.07
Total return	−.07	.08	−.15
Debt/assets	−.49**	−.49**	−.44**
Operating leverage	−.05	.23**	−.06
Standard deviation of operating income	.11	.15	.09
Beta	−.27*	−.32**	−.32**
Standard deviation of total return	−.45**	−.44**	−.44**

[a]N = 98, 131, and 131 for columns 1, 2, and 3, respectively.
*$p < .05$
**$p < .01$

its effects on stakeholders, social responsibility affects financial performance (Cornell & Shapiro, 1987). The negative association with operating income growth might be due to the high social responsibility ratings of several mature firms such as IBM (*Fortune*, 1983, 1986) that may tend to have more stable earnings than other firms. The other accounting measures have little association with corporate social responsibility.

The accounting- and stock-market-based risk measures tend to be negatively associated with social responsibility. Both beta and the standard deviation of total return show negative correlations (−.27 and −.45, respectively). One accounting-based risk measure, the ratio of debt to assets, has a significant negative association with corporate social responsibility. These results are also consistent with the view (Cornell & Shapiro, 1987) that firms with many implicit contracts with stake-

holders may have lower debt than other firms.

Pre- and post-survey analysis.
Analysis of the concurrently measured relationship between social responsibility and financial performance does not address the question of whether prior high financial performance allows a firm to engage in future socially responsible activities or if significant associations between current social responsibility and performance are artifacts of previous high performance. Table 3 presents results of the correlation analysis between prior firm financial performance and corporate social responsibility. The level of correlation for two measures of market return, total return and alpha, provides little support for the relationship between prior stock-market performance and subsequent social responsibility: the correlations are positive but significant

only for alpha. Of the accounting-based performance measures, ROA, sales growth, and asset growth are associated with high perceived social responsibility (.52, .15, and .35), but correlations for the other accounting performance measures are insignificant. Corporate social responsibility is negatively associated with risk as measured by the ratio of debt to assets ($-.49$), beta ($-.32$), and the standard deviation of total return ($-.44$) and positively associated with operating leverage. These results suggest that low-risk firms and firms with a high return on assets will later have an image of high social responsibility.

Table 3 also shows the correlations between corporate social responsibility and performance measured at a later time. ROA is again highly correlated with social responsibility; measures of stock-market performance, however, show little association with

it. However, both stock-market and accounting-based risk measures are negatively correlated with previous social responsibility (debt to assets $-.44$, beta, $-.32$; standard deviation of total return, $-.44$).

Regression Analysis

To test the multivariate relationship between corporate social responsibility and firm performance, we also conducted regression analyses. Since measures of financial performance tend to be correlated (McGuire, Schneeweis, & Branch, 1986), care must be taken in interpreting individual regression coefficients. Table 4 presents the results of stepwise regression analyses using perceived corporate social responsibility in 1983 as the independent variable.

TABLE 4. Results of Regression Analysis Predicting 1983 Corporate Social Responsibility.

Variables	Beta	F	Multiple R	R^2	Adjusted R^2	F
Prior accounting performance						
ROA	.669	44.07	.514	.265		
Average assets	.141	3.55	.543	.269		
Sales growth	.641	3.71	.548	.301		
Operating income growth	$-.364$	2.92	.563	.317		
Variables as a set					.294	13.73**
Prior market performance						
Alpha	1.121	19.28	.168	.028		
Total return	$-.963$	16.11	.378	.143		
Variables as a set					.129	10.04**
Prior accounting risk						
Debt/assets	.279	39.18	.493	.242		
Standard deviation of operating income	.357	5.46	.526	.276		
Operating leverage	.398	4.68	.551	.304		
Variables as a set					.287	17.34*
Prior market risk						
Standard deviation of total return	$-.235$	16.50	.437	.191		
Beta	.537	2.92	.459	.211		
Variables as a set					.211	16.02**
Subsequent accounting performance						
ROA	.590	24.59	.413	.171		
Average assets	.973	3.31	.437	.191		

TABLE 4. (cont)

Variables	Beta	F	Multiple R	R²	Adjusted R²	F
Sales growth	−.148	0.12	.441	.195		
Operating income growth	−.496	0.63	.442	.195		
Variables as a set					.195	7.16**
Subsequent market performance						
Total return	−.346	5.85	.146	.021		
Alpha	.241	3.80	.227	.052		
Variables as a set					.052	3.26*
Subsequent account risk						
Debt/asset	−.253	30.37	.437	.191		
Standard deviation of operating income	.281	3.36	.461	.212		
Operating leverage	.494	0.49	.462	.213		
Variables as a set					.193	16.75**
Subsequent market risk						
Standard deviation of total return	−.211	22.46	.361	.131		
Beta	.572	6.46	.148	.175		
Variables as a set					.287	17.34**
Prior accounting risk/return						
ROA	.317	4.66	.514	.265		
Debt/assets	−.215	11.17	.549	.301		
Average assets	.368	6.96	.594	.353		
Sales growth	.717	3.21	.613	.376		
Operating leverage	.288	2.34	.620	.384		
Operating income growth	−.342	2.26	.626	.392		
Standard deviation of operating income	−.419	2.04	.634	.402		
Asset growth	.869	0.71	.635	.403		
Variables as a set					.361	9.61**
Prior market risk/return						
Standard deviation of total return	−.217	13.85	.438	.192		
Total return	.117	3.40	.475	.226		
Beta	.347	1.11	.482	.232		
Variables as a set					.233	12.03**
Subsequent accounting risk/return						
Debt/asset	−.259	23.40	.437	.191		
Average assets	.323	16.43	.535	.286		
ROA	.327	6.37	.564	.318		
Standard deviation of operating income	−.519	4.88	.585	.342		
Operating income growth	.796	0.17	.588	.346		
Operating leverage	−.583	0.48	.591	.349		
Sales growth	.951	0.57	.591	.349		
Variables as a set					.309	8.82*
Subsequent market risk/return						
Standard deviation of return	−.220	25.43	.361	.131		
Alpha	−.125	6.62	.448	.201		
Beta	.380	2.69	.457	.219		
Variables as a set					.199	11.09**

*p < .05
**p < .01

Prior stock-market and accounting-based performance measures were used separately to predict social responsibility. Accounting-based performance had a higher explanatory value than stock-market performance (R^2 = .294 and .129, respectively). Accounting risk variables also appeared to produce a better explanatory model than stock-market risk variables (R^2 = .287 and .211, respectively). One possible reason for these results is that two market-based measures, total return and beta, are related primarily to systematic movements among all firms. In contrast, accounting measures are more likely to capture unique, or unsystematic, firm attributes. Since actions leading to high or low perceived corporate social responsibility may be predominately unsystematic, accounting performance may better capture social responsibility.

Subsequently measured accounting-based performance appeared to be a better predictor of social responsibility than subsequent stock-market performance (R^2 = .195 and .052, respectively). In contrast, subsequent stock-market risk produced a better explanatory model than subsequent accounting risk (R^2 = .193 and .287).

A comparison of equations using performance measured before and after 1983 thus suggests that perceptions of social responsibility are more closely associated with prior financial performance than with subsequent financial performance. With only one exception, prior performance and risk were better predictors than were subsequent performance and risk. The results of regression equations in which both market- and accounting-based risk and return are used to explain social responsibility offer further support. In all cases, the equations using prior accounting- and stock-market-based measures of risk and return had a higher predictive value than those using subsequent measures.

DISCUSSION

The correlation and regression results presented in this study suggest several conclusions. First, although performance tended to predict corporate social responsibility better than risk, measures of risk also explained a significant portion of the variability in social responsibility across firms. We noted earlier that theoretical arguments can be made for a relationship between social responsibility and firm risk. Lack of social responsibility may expose a firm to significant additional risk from lawsuits and fines and may limit its strategic options. Rather than looking for increased profitability from socially responsible actions, managers and those interested in the financial impact of social responsibility might look toward reduced risk. Since high risk must be balanced by high returns, firms with low social responsibility should earn high returns to justify the increased risk. Our data, however, suggest that firms low in social responsibility also experience lower ROA and stock-market returns than do firms high in social responsibility.

Second, accounting-based measures, particularly ROA, proved to be better predictors of corporate social responsibility than market measures. There may be several reasons for this trend. If perceptions of social responsibility are firm-specific (unsystematic), accounting measures of return should be more sensitive to them than stock-market measures, which reflect systematic market trends. Moreover, indexes are subject to managerial manipulation (Branch, 1983, Briloff, 1972, 1976) and tend to be stable over time (McGuire, Schneeweis, & Hill, 1986). Stock-market returns are more variable over time since they primarily respond to unexpected changes in information.

Perhaps most interesting is that prior performance is generally a better predictor of corporate social responsibility than subsequent performance. Thus, associations found between concurrent social responsibility and performance may partially be artifacts of previous high financial performance. Firms with high performance and low risk may be better able to afford to act in a socially responsible manner. Links between responsibility and subsequent financial performance may also be artifacts of prior high performance and the stability of accounting return data. Subsequent studies should attempt to separate the effects of prior, current, and future firm performance on the relationship between financial performance and corporate social responsibility.

CONCLUSIONS

The results of this study suggest several conclusions and avenues for future research. First, rather than examining the relationship between corporate social responsibility and a firm's subsequent financial performance, future research should investigate the influence of prior firm performance. In essence, it may be more fruitful to consider financial performance as a variable influencing social responsibility than the reverse. Previous studies have emphasized management preferences, industry, and organizational characteristics as influencing social responsibility (Arlow & Gannon, 1982; Sturdivant & Ginter, 1977). Second, the results suggest reduction of firm risk as an important benefit of social responsibility, on that previous research focusing on firm profitability and stock-market return has overlooked. Investigation of these two areas would do more to move research on social responsibility into theoretically and empirically fruitful areas than does investigation of concurrent measures (Ullmann, 1985).

This study also suggests that researchers give increased attention to the measure of firm performance used in studies of corporate social responsibility. Davidson, Worrell, and Gilberton (1986) noted that researchers have viewed the choice of performance variables as relatively straightforward compared to the problems of measuring corporate social responsibility. They further suggested that social responsibility may influence various aspects of firm performance in different ways. The inconsistency of results obtained using various financial performance variables supports that suggestion. Thus, this study adds to the growing body of literature indicating that the choice of performance variable can have substantive implications for the results of research and that researchers must carefully choose performance measures that are appropriate to the particular research question they are investigating. The results reported here also support the importance of controlling for risk in studies of social responsibility because adjusting for risk affects performance measures.

Although the *Fortune* data have provided a measure of corporate social responsibility new to the literature, the validity and appropriateness of this measure require further examination. As do other measures of social responsibility, the *Fortune* ratings may reflect the biases of the evaluators, who may not have defined or evaluated corporate social responsibility as other, less financially oriented evaluators might have. In addition, the context and purposes of the *Fortune* evaluation, which differ from those of other evaluations, may have influenced results.

However, major shortcomings in current research in corporate social responsibility have been the difficulty of measuring that concept (Abbott & Monsen, 1979; Ullmann, 1985) and consequent reliance on a limited set of measures. The introduction of a new measure of social responsibility helps reduce the mono-measure bias that has plagued the current body of research.

REFERENCES

Aaker, D., & Jacobson, R. 1987. The role of risk in explaining differences in profitability. *Academy of Management Journal*, 30: 277–296.

Abbott, W.F., & Monsen, R. 1979. On the measurement of corporate social responsibility: Self-reported disclosure as a measure of corporate social involvement. *Academy of Management Journal*, 22: 501–515.

Alexander, G., & Bucholtz, R. 1978. Corporate social responsibility and stock market performance. *Academy of Management Journal*, 21: 479–486.

Anderson, J.C., & Frankel, A.W. 1980. Voluntary social reporting: An isobeta portfolio analysis. *Accounting Review*, 55: 467–479.

Arlow, P., & Gannon, M. 1982. Social responsiveness, corporate structure, and economic performance. *Academy of Management Review*, 7: 235–241.

Aupperle, K., Carroll, A., & Hatfield, J. 1985. An empirical examination of the relationship between corporate social responsibility and profitability. *Academy of Management Journal*, 28: 446–463.

Bowman, E., & Haire, M. 1975. A strategic posture towards CSR. *California Management Review*, 18(2): 49–58.

Bradgon, J.H., & Marlin, J. 1972. Is pollution profitable? *Risk Management*, 19(4): 9–18.

Branch, B. 1983. *Misleading accounting: The danger and the potential*. Working paper, University of Massachusetts, Amherst.

Briloff, R. 1972. *Unaccountable accounting*. New York: Harper & Row.

Briloff, R. 1976. *The truth about corporate accounting*. New York: Harper & Row.

Carroll, A.B. 1979. A three-dimensional conceptual model of corporate social responsibility. *Academy of Management Review*, 4: 497–505.

Chakravarthy, B. 1986. Measuring strategic performance. *Strategic Management Journal*, 7: 437–458.

Cochran, P., & Wood, R. 1984. Corporate social responsibility and financial performance. *Academy of Management Journal*, 27: 42–56.

Cornell, B., & Shapiro, A. 1987. Corporate stakeholders and corporate finance. *Financial Management*, 16: 5–14.

Council on Economic Priorities. 1987. *Rating American's corporate conscience*. Reading, Mass.: Addison-Wesley.

Cyert, R.M., & March, J.G. 1963. *A behavioral theory of the firm*. Englewood Cliffs, N.J.: Prentice-Hall.

Davidson, W.N., Worrell, D.L., & Gilbertson, D. 1986. *The appropriateness of using accounting data in studies relating corporate social responsibility to firm financial performance*. Paper presented at the Academy of Management annual meeting, Chicago.

Folger, H., & Nutt, F. 1975. A note on social responsibility and stock valuation. *Academy of Management Journal*, 18: 155–159.

Fortune. 1983. Ranking America's corporations. 107(1): 34–44.

Fortune. 1986. American's most admired corporations. 113(1); 18–27.

Lubatkin, M., & Shrieves, R. 1986. Towards a reconciliation of market performance measures to strategic management research. *Academy of Management Review*, 11: 497–512.

McGuire, J., Schneeweis, T., & Branch, B. 1986. *A comparison of alternative measures of corporate performance*. Unpublished manuscript, University of Massachusetts, Amherst.

McGuire, J., Schneeweis, T., & Branch, B. 1987. *Perceptions of management quality and firm financial performance*. Unpublished manuscript, University of Massachusetts, Amherst.

McGuire, J., Schneeweis, T., & Hill, J. 1986. An analysis of alternative measures of strategic performance. In R. Lamb & P. Stravastrava (Eds.), *Advances in strategic management*, vol. 4: 107–153. Greenwich, Conn.: JAI Press.

Michel, A., & Shaked, I. 1984. Does business diversification affect performance? *Financial Management*, 12(2): 18–25.

Moskowitz, M. 1972. Choosing socially responsible stocks. *Business and Society*, 1: 71–75.

Moskowitz, M. 1975. Profiles in corporate social responsibility. *Business and Society*, 13: 29–42.

Moussavi, F., & Evans, D. 1986. *An attributional approach to measuring corporate social performance*. Paper presented at the Academy of Management meetings, San Diego.

Parket, R., & Eibert, H. 1975. Social responsibility: The underlying factors. *Business Horizons*, 18: 5–10.

Pfeffer, J., & Salancik, G. 1978. *The external control of organizations.* New York: Harper & Row.

Preston, L.E. 1978. Analyzing corporate social performance: Methods and results. *Journal of Contemporary Business,* 7: 135–149.

Quinn, J., Mintzberg, H., & James, R. 1987. *The strategy process.* Englewood Cliffs, N.J.: Prentice-Hall.

Soloman, R., & Hansen, K. 1985. *It's a good business.* New York: Athenaeum.

Spicer, B.H. 1978. Investors, corporate social performance, and information disclosure: An empirical study. *Accounting Review,* 53: 94–111.

Sturdivant, F.D., & Ginter, J.L. 1977. Corporate social responsiveness. *California Management Review,* 19(3): 30–39.

Ullmann, A. 1985. Data in search of a theory: A critical examination of the relationships among social performance, social disclosures, and economic performance. *Academy of Management Review,* 10: 540–577.

Vance, S. 1975. Are socially responsible firms good investment risks? *Management Review,* 64: 18–24.

Wartick, S. 1987. *The contribution of issues management to corporate performance.* Paper presented at the Academy of Management meetings, New Orleans.

NOTES

1. Adjusting for beta adjusts for systematic or general market risk. Lubatkin and Shrieves (1986) and Aaker and Jacobson (1987) discuss the adjustment of market-based performance measures for risk.

2. Industry analysts follow firms in a particular industry and advise investment houses and other institutional investors. Their livelihood, and that of their employers and investors, depends on their knowledge of firms in an industry. Since corporate social responsibility is one consideration in analysts' investment decisions (Spicer, 1978), they would be knowledgeable in this aspect of firm performance.

3. To further validate the ratings, we compared the *Fortune* ratings to a rating of corporate social responsibility produced by the Council on Economic Priorities (1987). The council evaluated consumer products firms on charitable contributions, representation of women and minorities on their boards of directors and in executive positions, social disclosure, South Africa involvement, and nuclear and nonnuclear arms production. Ratings of the 58 firms by both sources were compared by summing the number of "positive" or "socially responsible" evaluations given by the Council of Economic Priorities. The correlation between the two sets of evaluations was .47. Although the correlation is not as strong as would have been hoped, it is of interest. The Council of Economic Priorities ratings covered only consumer products, thus excluding many of the industries surveyed by *Fortune.* Moreover, differing definitions of corporate social responsibility likely influenced the correlation. For example, the council considered holding contracts for arms production to indicate lack of corporate social responsibility and it is unlikely that the *Fortune* evaluators did so.

4. The mean social responsibility rating for the 1983 survey was 6.01, with a standard deviation of .774. The mean 1983–85 rating was 6.31, with a standard deviation of .688. The means and standard deviations of the other variables are available from the authors.

7

Ethical and Legal Aspects of Managing Corporate Cultures

Bruce H. Drake

Eileen Drake

In the rush to create more competitive corporate cultures, important principles based on ethics and law have been neglected. A strong part of the appeal of the literature on corporate culture is that it cites examples of companies, such as IBM and Hewlett-Packard, where employees appear to be treated in a fair and responsible fashion. But how can managers judge what is fair and responsible treatment? Reliance solely on subjective measures (e.g., "what my feelings tell me is right") can lead to vague and inconsistent management policies. Recommendations for managing corporate cultures, read alone, provide little in the way of principled guidelines for employment relationships; they focus on shaping values related to performance without adequate regard for ethical and legal consequences. This article exam-

ines some of the risks of managing corporate cultures and recommends principles from ethics literature and employment law that can help foster fairer and more responsible employment practices.

CORPORATE CULTURE

In the broadest sense, corporate culture can be defined as:

A pattern of basic assumptions—invented, discovered, or developed by a given group as it learns to cope with its problems of external adaptation and internal integration—that has worked well enough to be considered valid and, therefore, to be taught to new members as the correct way to perceive, think, and feel in relation to those problems.[1]

The culture literature presents numerous examples of companies whose high commitment to shared values contributes to corporate excellence. Virtually every writer on

The authors would like to thank Gerald Cavanagh, Terence Mitchell, Dennis Moberg, and Jim Stuart for their valuable suggestions on earlier drafts of this article.

these "strong culture" companies cites stories of how employees are valued in these organizations. Themes like "respect for the individual," "integrity," and the creation of "family feelings" permeate books such as *A Passion of Excellence*. Stories of positive treatment of employees are contrasted with "horror" stories, such as the employee who first learned of his termination when he saw his desk being burned at the curbside.

Part of the challenge in managing corporate culture involves the effort to resolve the underlying tensions between the interests of the organization and the interests of its individual employees. If organizations had only positive stories, and if the objectives and means of creating strong cultures coincided with what is considered ethical and legal conduct, then there would be no problem. However, both positive and negative stories can often be found in the same organization, reflecting dilemmas of organizational life:

The common stories seem to express tensions that arise from a conflict between organizational exigencies and the values of individual employees, which are, in turn, reflective of the values of the larger society. For example, employees may value equality, security, and control, while organizations may demand the right to threaten these values in order to survive.[2]

Tensions between organization and individual interests are recognized in the corporate culture literature, but there is considerable disagreement over which values should be stressed. Some authors suggest that humanitarian values, self-actualization, and individualism have been overemphasized.[3] Others counter that the stress on performance objectives has neglected the principles of individual rights and moral development.[4] Moreover, the recommendations are often inconsistent. For example, principles of commitment and long-term employment conflict

with recommendations for radical staffing reductions to create leaner organizations. There also is an ongoing controversy over whether strong cultures unduly limit dissent and individual freedom.

Understanding employment ethics and legal principles and their interrelationship with corporate culture theories can help managers anticipate problems in shaping company operating values. Potential conflicts with otherwise commendable values are often not apparent. For example, one major company includes the following precepts in its philosophy:

Commitments are long term: if career problems occur at some point, reassignment is a better alternative than termination.

Management must be ethical: Decisions and actions must be consistently beyond question from an ethics standpoint. Management, by telling the truth, treating all employees equitably, has established credibility that is ethical.[5]

The manager operating under stated principles like these must understand both the ethical and legal implication of these policies in order to effectively administer them.

FRAMEWORK FOR ETHICAL AND LEGAL CONCERNS

Issues of fairness in employment relationships emerge as one of the most common themes in the literature on corporate culture. This article focuses on two fairness issues which are contained in the two precepts quoted above: job security and equitable treatment of employees. Figure 1 outlines the relationships between these two issues and the ethical and legal principles discussed in this article.

FIGURE 1. *Ethical and Legal Concerns in Managing Corporate Cultures.*

	Ethical Concerns	*Legal Concerns*
Job Security	Contract flaws: lack of full knowledge of contract terms, misrepresentation, coercion.	Creation of implied contracts: gaps between "promises" and actual practice.
Equitable Treatment	Governance flaws: Overemphasis on performance outcomes vs. political rights, due process and moral development.	Limitations on management rights: emerging fairness principles.

ETHICS OF MANAGING CORPORATE CULTURE

The two cultural issues of job security and equitable treatment parallel ethical principles associated with contractual and political models of organization.[6] Security issues involve "contractual" obligations between an employer and employee within a traditional employment relationship. Equitable treatment involves rights to due process and fair dealing within organizations based on analogies of citizens' rights within democratic communities.

Job Security

In terms of job security, the linkage of ethics and culture is based on the notion that the culture that management is attempting to create essentially represents a contract indicating the appropriate values, beliefs, behavior, and practices of the organization. It states management expectations regarding the mutual obligations of the parties in the employment relationship. By accepting employment with the organization, an individual enters into a contract containing these mutual obligations.

Four requirements must be met in order for contracts to be ethical:

1. Both of the parties to a contract must have full knowledge of the nature of the agreement they are entering.

2. Neither party to a contract may intentionally misrepresent the facts of the contractual situation to the other party.

3. Neither party to the contract must be forced to enter the contract under duress or coercion.

4. The contract must not bind the parties to an immoral act.[7]

These ethical requirements apply to initial contracts as well as to any changes made in the contracts; that is, to the corporate culture at the time an employee is hired as well as to management actions taken to change the existing culture.

Full Knowledge of Nature and Terms of Agreement. Several writers discuss the gap that exists between stated objectives or aspirations and actual day-to-day practices.[8] For example, while a company might say that it values people, its record can contradict what it says. Given this gap, it can be quite difficult for an employee to obtain full knowledge about actual practices within a company.

There are three reasons for the gap between stated and operating values. First, there may be a mismatch between the aspirations for the internal culture and the external realities: internal aspirations might have been unrealistically high or external conditions might have changed and reduced resources available to support proposed personnel practices. Second, managers may have underestimated the difficulty of changing corporate cultures, particularly in the larger established companies. Both of these situations can occur despite good intentions.

A third inconsistency also results if managers become too self-reliant. Discussions of culture all too often encourage managers to trust their own judgment and vision. One writer asserts that "leaders should not apologize or be cautious about their assumptions."[9] Others, in referring to systems for career planning and performance appraisal, plans for management succession, and the like, state that "symbolic managers go a step further. More often than not they ignore the formal systems for human resource management and do what seems right culturally."[10] This reliance on a manager's intuitive sense of values may lead to actions that are neither consistent with stated policies nor equitable with regard to their impact on employees. It is extremely difficult for employees to ascertain the nuances of such practices.

Furthermore, the gap can be exacerbated if the culture is codified in written documents that exist only as a facade. Some writers suggest that all organizations at least should give the appearance of a culture founded on ethical principles, even if they do not actually practice what they profess:

If you still covet the mystical glue, consider the obvious, low-cost adhesives. A tactic fairly standard by now is to develop a statement of corporate purpose, an awesome list of what the company believes in, and then remind everyone of it constantly. To be consistent, tailor your formal systems, structures and personnel policies to reflect those declarations.[11]

Other writers are critical of approaches to managing culture through formal statements of organizational philosophy, creeds, and charters:

Such public statements may have a value for leaders as a way of emphasizing special things to be attended to in the organization, as values around which to "rally the troops," and as reminders of fundamental

assumptions not to be forgotten; but formal statements cannot be seen as a way of defining the culture of an organization. At best they cover a small, publicly relevant segment of the culture, those aspects that leaders find useful to publish as an ideology for the organization.[12]

Such comments can be misleading to managers because they treat statements of values as mere artifacts and they suggest that corporate philosophies, as "espoused theories," are less real than the underlying cultural patterns found in daily practice. However, these formal statements do, in fact, create expectations on the part of employees and therefore must be taken seriously.

Misrepresentation of Intentions. From an ethical perspective, contracts include both the terms of the agreement and the integrity of the relationship between the parties. Thus, both the intentions of the parties and their commitment to expressed values need to be evaluated.

One writer suggests four stages of commitment to values and beliefs.[13] Stage one involves people holding complete and unquestioned beliefs. In stage two, people acknowledge alternative beliefs, but remain committed to their own values. The first two types of people represent "believers." At stage three, people become "non-believers." They suspend their earlier beliefs, "choosing to stop believing the myth or to stop perceiving any value in the ritual." Personal gain becomes the basis for compliance, but these values do not become internalized. Stage four represents a reversal, where people become "seekers," actively choosing to believe in a set of values or symbols that inspire hope, identity, or inspiration. These people have a need for meaning; they are willing to suspend their disbelief in order to reestablish and share in meaningful involvements.

Due to their commitment to values, believers and seekers are not likely to misrepresent their intentions or the values they intend to uphold in a relationship. Although they may be avid shapers of corporate cultures, using many of the same symbolic methods as a non-believer manager, they do so in order to create and share in a meaningful culture. While their aspirations may be difficult to attain, they sincerely believe that the values they are shaping will benefit their employees. Their methods openly, if not energetically, exemplify the values they seek to inculcate in others.

In contrast, a non-believer manager will shape values to attract and enhance employee commitment to contracts without fully intending to uphold these values. It is this type of manager that one writer had in mind when he criticized *In Search of Excellence* for suggesting the ease of manipulating employees through culture: "They point out that the great leader 'is concerned with the tricks of the pedagogue, the mentor, the linguist, the more successfully to become the value shaper, the exemplar, the maker of meanings.' "[14] Because they do not personally adopt or fully implement these professed values, these non-believer managers violate contractual ethics prohibiting the misrepresentation of intention.

Free Consent/Absence of Coercion.
Free consent and absence of coercion are criteria for moral contracts that apply to both initial contractual relationships and to methods later used to change these relationships. Agreements should be voluntary.

Deception and manipulation are both attempts to get a person to do (or believe) something that the person would not do (or believe) if he or she knew what was going on . . . they fail to respect a person's right to be treated only as he or she has freely and knowingly consented to be

treated. Such moral disrespect is exhibited in many of these [cultural] tactics that take advantage of our emotional dependencies and vulnerabilities.[15]

Employees will vary as to their vulnerability to manipulation. Nonbelievers are probably the least vulnerable because they do not take cultural assertions at fact value.[16] However, writers on culture suggest many people could be vulnerable due to their unsatisfied needs for meaning and belonging.[17] Manipulating or creating psychological dependencies through seductive socialization methods or humility-inducing experiences (often associated with strong culture companies) would certainly fail to meet the ethical standards against entering contracts under duress or coercion.[18]

Few writers on corporate culture directly advocate coercion. However, stories abound of aggressive leadership methods being used where a radical change is needed to reorient a company that is stagnant or significantly misaligned with its strategic environment. Strong action is often recommended in these "extenuating" circumstances. One author even advocates "coercive persuasion":

- make sure people you want to retain find it hard to leave;
- consistently challenge old assumptions; and
- provide psychological safety or rewards for any movement in the direction of new assumptions.[19]

The design of such methods, based on prisoner-of-war analogies, is hardly reassuring from an ethical perspective.

Exclusion of Immoral Acts.
The corporate culture literature is relatively silent on morality. Some writers note that the corpo-

rate philosophies of companies such as Dayton-Hudson and Intel require ethical conduct on the part of employees, while other writers offer examples of companies such as ARCO and Norwest that provide opportunities for employees to challenge existing corporate practices.[20] Overall, however, the literature cites few ethical heroes and there seems to be a pervasive assumption that managers will not require employees to engage in unethical or immoral acts. This line of reasoning furthermore presumes that while immoral acts may result from pressure to perform, such acts are not officially approved.

While ethical heroes seldom appear in the corporate culture literature, they are the center of attention in the literature on whistle-blowing and principles dissent.[21] This literature is concerned with company practices that limit employee rights to freedom of expression and inhibit criticism of activities endangering the public welfare. The concern is not just that companies may pressure employees into immoral behavior, but that they also may punish employees who voice their concerns over unethical practices. Requiring improper behavior or preventing employees from criticizing such practices constitutes an unethical contract.

Maintaining Contractual Relationships.

Assuming the initial contract is established in an ethical manner, do parties have an ethical obligation to maintain the contract if the duration of the contract is not specified? From a libertarian perspective, it can be argued that the only basic right is a negative right to be free from coercion.[22] This would require contracts to be freely entered, but it also would allow them to be freely terminated at any time by either party. Kant's categorical imperative, however, requires that people should not be treated only as means, but also as ends. In other words, an employer should not terminate a contract based solely on cor-

porate convenience, but also should consider the concerns and needs of the employee. Furthermore, since employees are people, they should be treated as moral agents: "simply by hiring a person, an employer enters into a moral relationship . . . it includes treating employees with respect and dignity as rational adults."[23] For long-term employees, these expectations develop into "implied moral contracts":

> If her expectations of job security are supported by positive reviews, raises and promotions there is an implication, although admittedly not a requirement, that this employment is permanent. . . . This implies a moral expectation: the reciprocity of respect and job security in return for continued loyalty and productivity.[24]

Thus, the ethical principles underlying contract theory require that the terms of fair and mutually agreed upon employment relationships should continue to be honored.

Equitable Treatment

The management of corporate cultures can also be assessed in relation to the second theme of fairness in employment relationships, that involving equitable treatment. In addition to traditional ethical concerns governing contractual relationships, the issues of equality, justice, and responsible treatment are considered as rights by many writers who view organizations as political systems. The argument is that business organizations are analogous to communities; as such, businesses should offer employees the same rights or civil liberties that they enjoy as citizens.[25] These rights include privacy, freedom of conscience, freedom of speech and assembly, and opportunity to participate in government decisions. In order to protect these rights, many writers suggest extending to all employees due-process procedures to allow a fair hearing on grievances and to appeal sanctions or dismissals resulting from exercising these rights.[26]

Three justifications are offered for protecting these political rights within organizations: Organization performance, balance of power, and employee development. In the corporate culture literature, participation and freedom of speech are justified primarily in terms of their instrumental value in enhancing motivation, organizational innovation, and adaptation. This American emphasis on the effectiveness of participation contrasts with European concerns for participation as a means of counterbalancing the unequal power held by employers.[27] The concern for balancing power is a central argument of writers who believe that strong culture companies tend to stifle the expression of divergent values.[28] Pastin, in fact, argues that high ethic companies should have weak cultures to preserve pluralistic values.[29]

Employees also are entitled to equitable treatment by virtue of their requirements for psychological and moral development. As human beings, they deserve respect and fair treatment that encourages personal growth, fulfillment, human dignity, and emotional health.[30] The achievement of higher levels of development requires an ongoing questioning of values, identify, and commitments to one's company and community.[31] Protecting individual rights also assists in developing critical analytic skills essential to individual conscience and the heightened capacity to make moral judgments.[32] From this perspective, it is insufficient to assume that managers will act ethically. Responsible companies not only should protect employees' right to criticize current practices; they should actively encourage employees to question and clarify their own values as well as the values of the corporation.

LEGAL ASPECTS OF MANAGING CORPORATE CULTURE

Whereas ethics writers stress the optimal features of the employment relationship, employment law theories focus on the minimum restraints placed on the organization. Thus, while ethics asks the question, "What is the *best* the employer should do for its employees?" the law asks, "What is the *least* the employer must do for its employees?" Historically, the answer to the legal question was "very little." Without a written contract or collective-bargaining agreement, employment for an indefinite term traditionally was considered to be at the will of the employer, subject to termination at any time, for any reason or for no reason. In the past decade, however, courts have increasingly abandoned their reluctance to become involved in the employment relationship.

State courts have adopted two different conceptual frameworks for these issues: an implied contract theory derived from *contract law*; and a public policy theory derived from *tort law*. The contract framework focuses on traditional contract issues of whether the employer made a promise to the employee, whether the promise was breached, and what monetary damages are required to restore to the employee the value of the contract promise. The tort framework focuses on whether the employer violated a duty or obligation imposed by law or "public policy," whether the employee was harmed by the employer's conduct, and what damages are required to make the employee whole or, in some cases, to punish the employer. (Contract damages generally are limited to lost wages and fringe benefits; tort damages, in addition to lost wages and benefits, can include other monetary losses, pain and suffering, damage to reputation, or punitive damages.)

These legal constraints have serious implications for managing corporate cultures. In shaping a culture, management may very well be creating legally enforceable rights for its employees or it may be setting the standard by which its actual behavior will be evaluated by a judge or jury in court. Those policies intended to be merely statements of aspirations or goals for managers, for example, may be held to be legally enforceable contractual promises to employees. Discharge of a long-term employee without good cause or terminating a "whistle-blowing" employee may render the employer liable under public policy or "tort" theories.

The two themes of job security and equitable treatment central to ethical considerations of managing corporate culture also are fundamental to these legal developments. Many principles addressed in ethics literature now appear in court decisions, although in different conceptual frameworks.

Job Security

Courts, like ethics writers, have adopted contract theory to deal with issues of job security. Even where there is no actual written employment contract, a contract may be implied from written or oral statements of the employer or from the employer's course of conduct with its employees. This contract theory now is widely recognized in the courts.

One of the seminal and most illustrative court decisions on this theory is the Michigan Supreme Court's decision in *Toussaint v. Blue Cross & Blue Shield of Michigan*. Charles Toussaint held a middle management position with Blue Cross for five years before he was terminated. In a lawsuit challenging the termination, he alleged that Blue Cross had promised him in his pre-employment interviews that he would not be discharged "as long as I did my job." He also based the suit on statements in Blue Cross's 260-page policy manual containing such corporate culture rhetoric as promises "[to] provide for the ad-

ministration of fair, consistent and reasonable corrective discipline" and "to treat employees leaving Blue Cross in a fair and consistent manner and to release employees for just cause only."

Commenting first about the alleged promise to terminate only for cause, the court stated:

> We see no reason why an employment contract which does not have a definite term—the term is "indefinite"—cannot legally provide job security. When a prospective employee inquires about job security and the employer agrees that the employee shall be employed as long as he does the job, a fair construction is that the employer has agreed to give up his right to discharge at will without assigning cause and may discharge only for cause (good or just cause).

The court also concluded that the company's policy manual had become part of Toussaint's employment contract:

> We hold that employer statements of policy, such as the Blue Cross Supervisory Manual and Guidelines, can give rise to contractual rights in employees without evidence that the parties mutually agreed that the policy statements would create contractual rights in the employee, and, hence [sic] although the statement of policy is signed by neither party, can be unilaterally amended by the employer without notice to the employee, and contains no reference to a specific employee, his job description or compensation, and although no reference was made to the policy statement in preeemployment interviews and the employee does not learn of its existence until after his hiring.

Under contract theory statements (written or oral) and practices forming the organization's culture may become legally binding employee rights. This theory could be applied to more than just the terms under which an employer can terminate an employee. For example, if courts determine that an employer can create contract terms through the contents of an employee handbook or policy statements communicated to employees, an employer could be subject to suit for breach of contract for failure to comply with any "promise" it made (i.e., hours of work, compensation, discipline procedures, annual performance appraisals, internal review or grievance systems).

Thus, the gap that may occur between a stated corporate culture and actual practice has significant legal, as well as ethical, implications. Unless the organization's policy statements are clearly identified as only aspirations or goals, and are understood to be such by employees, the organization may be legally held to its published statements rather than its actual practice. Where there is such a gap, a court may focus on the employees' beliefs about what constitutes the terms of the employment contract, rather than on the employer's intention. As stated in the *Toussaint* decision:

> While an employer need not establish personnel policies or practices, where an employer chooses to establish such policies and practices and makes them known to its employees, the employment relationship is presumably enhanced. The employer secures an orderly, cooperative and loyal work force, and the employee the peace of mind associated with job security and the conviction that he will be treated fairly. No pre-employment negotiations need take place *and the parties' minds need not meet on the subject*; nor does it matter that the employee knows nothing of the employer's policies and practices or that the employer may change them unilaterally. *It is enough that the employer chooses, presumably in its*

interest, to create an environment in which the employee believes that, whatever the personnel policies and practices, they are established and official at any given time, purport to be fair, and are applied consistently and uniformly to each employee. The employer has then created a situation "instinct with an obligation." [emphasis added]

The legal contract theory thus parallels the ethics contract theory in emphasizing the importance of full knowledge of the nature and terms of the agreement. Full knowledge on the part of the employer is critical because of the risk of a breach of contract suit where the employer's actual practice, whether intentionally or unintentionally, is inconsistent with published policy statements. Full knowledge on the part of employees also is important to help eliminate perceived gaps between policies and practices. Perceived discrepancies can lead to lawsuits as easily as actual discrepancies, and some courts have been willing to base a decision on the employee's understanding (or misunderstanding) of the policy where there is a dispute over its meaning. The legal contract theory differs from the ethics theory, though, in the elements of intentional misrepresentation of facts, coercion, and exclusion of immoral acts. Under the law, these are tort theories and not part of contract law. As such, they arise more in the context of "equitable treatment" than "job security."

Equitable Treatment

As in ethics, there is a legal concept of "equitable treatment" that is broader than the issue of constitutional or statutory civil rights. Ethics literature phrases it in terms of fundamental fairness and due process. The term "due process' usually is not used in legal cases addressing private employment situations because historically it has meant a constitutional right to a fair and full hearing in circumstances of governmental action. However, paralleling the development of contract limitations on employment-at-will has been the development of a variety of legal approaches incorporating public policy, good faith, and fairness constraints on employer action. As previously stated, these have developed as tort theories, rather than as contract principles, and involve both different legal principles and a broader range of damages.

Among the legal approaches to equitable treatment that have been successful in state courts have been theories of wrongful discharge in violation of public policy, an implied covenant of good faith and fair dealing, and intentional infliction of emotional distress (sometimes called outrageous conduct).

Public Policy. Many courts have recognized public policy exceptions to employment-at-will. These cases generally involve employees who have pursued a statutory or constitutional right relating to their employment, those who have "blown the whistle" on an employer who was acting illegally, or those who refused to participate in the employer's illegal conduct. The Oregon Supreme Court has held employers liable for the tort of wrongful discharge for terminating an employee who insisted on serving jury duty against the employer's will (*Nees v. Hocks*); for terminating an employee who refused to sign a false statement to help the employer discharge a black employee (*Delaney v. Taco Time Int'l*); or for terminating an employee who protested unlawful sexual harassment (*Holien v. Sears, Roebuck & Co.*). In *Thompson v. St. Regis Paper Co.*, the Washington Supreme Court recognized a public policy exception where the plaintiff alleged he was terminated because he instituted accurate accounting procedures in compliance with federal law, but against his employer's will. Discharges for filing a workers' compensation claim and for refusing to violate a state statute were recognized as causes of action

for wrongful discharge by the Michigan Court of Appeals in *Sventko v. Kroger Co.* and *Trombetta v. Detroit, Toledo and Ironton R. Co.*, respectively. A California employee who alleged that he was discharged for refusing to participate in an illegal price-fixing scheme stated a cause of action for wrongful discharge in *Tameny v. Atlantic Richfield*. Similarly, the discharge of a truck driver who reported spoiled milk to the state health department led to a suit for wrongful discharge in *Garibaldi v. Lucky Food Stores, Inc.*

Good Faith and Fair Dealing. Courts in California and some other states have recognized an implied covenant of good faith and fair dealing in employment relationships, particularly in cases of long-term employees (*Cleary v. American Airlines, Inc.*). This covenant is recognized in implied employment contracts, as well as written ones, even when there is no stated or implied promise to discharge only for good cause. (Curiously, though, breach of this implied covenant is not considered to be a breach of the employment contract, but rather a tort.) The California courts, for example, define the covenant as an underlying principle requiring the employer to deal openly, fairly, and equitably with employees and to give them the benefit of the company's policies and regulations adopted for their protection (*Rulon-Miller v. International Business Machines Corp.*). Other states, such as Massachusetts, have recognized a narrower concept of good faith and fair dealing that prevents an employer from terminating or demoting an employee to avoid payment of benefits which have already accrued by virtue of the employee's past service (*McCone v. New England Tel. and Tel. Co.*).

Intentional Infliction of Emotional Distress. The common law tort of intentional infliction of emotional distress is frequently raised as a claim in conjunction with employment termination. Strip-searching an employee without reasonable basis in front of an angry customer just to satisfy the customer (*Bodewig v. K-Mart, Inc.*) or unfounded accusations of theft accompanied by a lengthy inquisition-type interrogation and threats to bring criminal charges (*Smithson v. Nordstrom, Inc.*) are among the more obvious examples of "outrageous conduct."

In *Rulon-Miller v. International Business Machines Corp.*, though, the "outrageousness" was less apparent. In that case, the California Court of Appeals affirmed a $300,000 judgment against IBM for both breach of implied covenant of good faith and fair dealing and intentional infliction of emotional distress when a low-level manager was terminated because she was having a romantic relationship with the manager of a competing business. IBM had circulated a policy memorandum to all managers affirming the company's "strict regard for [an employee's] right to personal privacy." The jury found that Rulon-Miller's termination was in bad faith because her manager did not believe she had violated any company policy and the company policy itself protected her right to date the manager of the rival firm. The jury also determined that Rulon-Miller's manager had terminated her in "an extreme and outrageous" manner by first pretending to give her a week to choose between her job and her relationship and the next day "removing any free choice on her part" when he made the decision for her and terminated her. The manager's conduct, the Court of Appeals concluded, was degrading and debilitating.

Regardless of how the legal "equitable treatment" theory is labelled, the underlying concept is that of fairness. In adopting these tort theories, courts are showing a greater willingness to test employer actions, not just against the employer's own stated policies, but against societal values and ethical norms. What is not yet clear is how far the courts will be willing to go in this area: whether the courts will continue to focus on the minimum constraints imposed by the law on employer conduct or whether they will begin to hold employers to the more optimal standards of conduct debated in the ethics literature.

CONCLUSIONS

Managers concerned with incorporating ethical and legal principles into their attempts to enhance their corporate cultures are faced with a dilemma. Focusing on one set of principles to the exclusion of the other is clearly counter-productive. Focusing only on what the law requires (the least one has to do) will generate a negative tone to the corporate culture. Statements of employee rights might be avoided altogether or appended with such clear disclaimers preserving management rights that the net effect would be greater insecurity on the part of employees. Focusing only on what ethics would advocate (the best one should do) is equally unrealistic. It would create such high expectations that attempts to achieve them almost inevitably would lead to frustration and unrest. Some compromises are required. The following are four suggestions for merging the two sets of concerns in shaping and managing a more responsible corporate culture.

Recommendation 1. *Be realistic in setting values and goals regarding employment relationships. Do not promise what the organization cannot deliver.*

In shaping a corporate culture managers should address issues of job security and equitable treatment that meet the overall needs of their organization. In doing so, they should forego popular rhetoric for realistic statements of company policies and expectations. Both ethical and legal principles consider culture statements to be binding promises or contracts. Making promises that cannot be met violates the organization's ethical and legal obligations to its employees. The same principles require that culture statements be supported by procedures and practices geared to meeting culture objectives and that these practices be periodically reviewed for consistency with stated values.

Recommendation 2. *Encourage input from throughout the organization regarding appropriate values and practices for implementing the culture. Choose values that represent the views of employees as well as managers.*

While most writers on corporate culture encourage the development of a bill of rights or other statement of corporate values, too often participation is restricted to the "vision" of leaders or the input of a top management committee. More attention should be given to practices, such as at Dana and Apple Computer, where employees contribute to the formulation and annual review of corporate values. This gives employees a greater sense of involvement and increases the opportunity for full knowledge of the culture by management and the employees.

Recommendation 3. *Do not automatically opt for ˈa "strong" culture. Explore methods to provide for diversity and dissent, such as grievance or complaint mechanisms or other internal review procedures.*

Managers should weigh the merits as well as the criticisms of "strong" cultures. Arguments for strong cultures stress that they provide stable expectations about what behavior counts in the organization. Shared values, which include fairness and integrity, should encourage ethical behavior.[33] However, strong culture companies are "tough" in enforcing values and develop extensive selection, socialization, and reward systems to ensure support of their values. Critics are particularly concerned that these methods restrict fundamental rights to hold and express personal values. Open-door policies, surveys and forums to review corporate values, ethics

committees, and ombudsmen or internal review/grievance procedures can be used both as sources of employee input and as methods to resolve employee concerns. Practices that allow for commitment to shared values while preserving individual rights to question these values may better meet the ethical rights of employees and satisfy any legal obligations of fairness.

Recommendation 4. *Provide training programs for managers and supervisors adopting and implementing the corporate values. These programs should explain the underlying ethical and legal principles and present the practical aspects of carrying out procedural guidelines.*

Training should be provided at two stages: prior to the adoption of a culture and prior to the implementation of the culture. The advice of legal staff and outside experts on employment ethics should be sought at both stages. Training should focus on the ethical and legal principles underlying corporate values and also should stress the practical aspects of carrying out procedural guidelines. This training will have ongoing benefits in guiding managers to a more reasoned and consistent application of fairness values in employment decisions. The organization will be better able to meet its ethical obligations while reducing the risk of legal challenge to its decisions.

NOTES

1. Edgar H. Schein, *Organizational Cultures and Leadership* (San Francisco, CA: Jossey-Bass, 1985), p. 9.

2. J. Martin, M. Feldman, M. Hatch, and S. Sitkin, "The Uniqueness Paradox in Organizational Stories," *Administrative Science Quarterly* (September 1983), p. 447.

3. Terrance E. Deal and Alan A. Kennedy, *Corporate Cultures* (Reading, MA: Addison-Wesley, 1982); Schein, op. cit.; Richard Pascale "The Paradox of Corporate Cultures: Reconciling Ourselves to Socialization," *California Management Review* (Winter 1985), pp. 25–41.

4. Terence R. Mitchell, *"In Search of Excellence* Versus *100 Best Companies to Work for in America:* A Question of Perspectives and Values," *Academy of Management Review* (April 1985), pp. 350–355; Stanley Deetz, "Ethical Considerations in Cultural Research in Organizations," in Peter Frost, Larry Moore, Meryl Louis, Craig Lundberg, and Joanne Martin, eds. *Organizational Culture* (Beverly Hills, CA: Sage, 1985), pp. 253–269.

5. William G. Ouchi, *Theory Z* (Reading, MA: Addison-Wesley, 1981), pp. 252–253.

6. Manuel G. Velasquez, *Business Ethics: Concepts and Cases* (Englewood Cliffs, NJ: Prentice Hall, 1982); Patricia H. Werhane, *Persons, Rights, and Corporations* (Englewood Cliffs, NJ: Prentice-Hall, 1985).

7. Velasquez, op. cit., p. 65.

8. Stanley M. Davis, *Managing Corporate Culture* (Cambridge, MA: Ballinger, 1984); Schein, op. cit.

9. Schein, op. cit., p. 139.

10. Deal and Kennedy, op. cit.

11. Bro Uttal, "The Corporate Culture Vultures," *Fortune,* October 17, 1983, p. 72.

12. Schein, op. cit., p. 147.

13. Thomas C. Dandridge, "The Life Stages of a Symbol: When Symbols Work and When They Can't," in Peter Frost, L. Moore, M. Louis, C. Lundberg, and J. Martin, eds., *Organizational Culture* (Beverly Hills, CA: Sage, 1985).

14. Mitchell, op. cit., p. 52.

15. Velasquez, op. cit., p. 332.

16. Velasquez, op. cit., p. 334.

17. Thomas A. Peters and Robert H. Waterman, *In Search of Excellence: Lessons from America's Best Run Companies* (New York, NY: Harper and Row, 1982); William G. Ouchi and Alfred M. Jaeger, "Type Z Organization: Stability in the Midst of Mobility," *Academy of Management Review* (April 1978), pp. 305–314.

18. Roy J. Lewicki, "Seduction and Commitment in the Organization," in W. Clay Hamner, ed., *Organizational Shock* (New York, NY: Wiley, 1980), pp. 80–93; Pascale, op. cit.

19. Schein, op. cit., p. 294.

20. James O'Toole, *Vanguard Management: Redesigning the Corporate Future* (Garden City, NY: Doubleday, 1985).

21. David W. Ewing, *Do it My Way or You're Fired* (New York, NY: John Wiley, 1983); Jill W. Graham, "Principled Organizational Dissent: A Theoretical Essay," in Barry M. Staw and Larry L. Cummings, eds. *Research in Organizational Behavior,* Volume 8 (Greenwich, CT: JAI Press, 1986).

22. R. Nozik, *Anarchy, State and Utopia* (New York, NY: Basic Books, 1974).

23. Werhane, op. cit., p. 145.

24. Ibid.

25. Ewing, op. cit.; John Rawls, A *Theory of Justice* (Cambridge, MA: Harvard University Press, 1971); William G. Scott, Terence R. Mitchell, and Neuman S. Peery, "Organizational Governance," in Paul C. Nystrom and William H. Starbuck, eds., *Handbook of Organizational Design* (New York, NY: Oxford University Press, 1981), pp. 135–151; Velasquez, op. cit.

26. Ewing, op. cit.; Graham, op. cit.; Scott, op. cit.

27. Ewing, op. cit.; Anthony T. Oliver, "The Disappearing Right to Terminate Employees at Will," *Personnel Journal* (December 1982), pp. 910–917; Clyde W. Summers, "Protecting all Employees against Unjust Dismissal," *Harvard Business Review* (January/February 1980), pp. 132–139.

28. Deetz, op. cit.; O'Toole, op. cit.

29. Mark Pastin, *The Hard Problems of Management: Gaining the Ethics Edge* (San Francisco, CA: Jossey-Bass, 1986).

30. Deetz, op. cit.; Ewing, op. cit.; Werhand, op. cit.

31. Robert Kegan, *The Evolving Self: Problem and Process in Human Development* (Cambridge, MA: Harvard University Press, 1982); Robert N. Bellah, Richard Madsen, William M. Sullivan, Ann Swidler, and Steven M. Tipton, *Habits of the Heart: Individualism and Commitment in American Life* (Berkeley, CA: University of California Press, 1985).

32. Graham, op. cit.; Scott, op. cit.

33. Barry Posner, James Kouzes, and Warren Schmidt, "Shared Values Make a Difference: An Empirical Test of Corporate Culture," *Human Resource Management* (Fall 1985), pp. 293–309.

LEGAL CITATIONS

Bodewig v. K-Mart, Inc., 54 Or App 480, 635 P2d 657 (1981).

Cleary v. American Airlines, Inc., 111 Cal. App 3d 443, 168 Cal Rptr 722 (1980).

Delaney v. Taco Time Int'l., 297 Or 10, 681 P2d 114 (1984).

Garibaldi v. Lucky Food Stores, Inc., 726 F2d 1367 (9th Cir. 1984).

Holien v. Sears, Roebuck & Co., 298 Or 76, 689 P2d 1291 (1984).

McCone v. New England Tel. and Tel. Co., 393 Mass 231, 471 NE 2d 47 (1984).

Bruce H. Drake / Eileen Drake

Nees v. Hocks, 272 Or 210, 536 P2d 512 (1975).

Rulon-Miller v. International Business Machines Corp., 162 Cal App 3d 241, 208 Cal Rptr 524 (1984).

Smithson v. Nordstrom, Inc., 63 Or App 423, 664 2d 1119 (1983).

Sventko v. Kroger Co., 69 Mich App 644, 245 NW 2d 151 (1976).

Tameny v. Atlantic Richfield, 27 Cal 3d 167, 164 Cal Rptr 839 (1980).

Thompson v. St. Regis Paper Co., 102 Wash 2nd 219, 685 P2d 1081 (1984).

Toussaint v. Blue Cross & Blue Shield of Michigan, 408 Mich 579, 292 NW 2d 880 (1980).

Trombetta v. Detroit, Toledo and Ironton R. Co., 81 Mich App 489, 265 NW2d 385 (1978).

8
Ethics and Competitiveness— Putting First Things First

John F. Akers

IBM CORPORATION

John Akers, Chairman of the Board of IBM, argues that business ethics are a key component of our competitiveness as a society. How can we ensure that we work in an atmosphere characterized by mutual trust and confidence? Although business schools can and should engage in some forms of ethical instruction, the work cannot begin—or end—there. Instruction must begin in childhood and encompass such practical devices as role models and codes of conduct; it must include a demanding study of history and literature; and above all it must recognize business's proper place within a greater hierarchy. Ed.

I should like to consider a subject central to international economic competitiveness: ethics. Let me urge at the outset that all of us in management look at both these words— ethics and competitiveness—with a wide angle of vision. When we think of competitiveness we should think not just as Americans, Europeans, or Japanese seeking our own selfish beggar-thy-neighbor advantage, but as managers striving to succeed in an increasingly interdependent world, with the poten-

Reprinted from *Ethics and Competitiveness—Putting First Things First* by John F. Akers, *Sloan Management Review* (Winter 1989), pp. 69–71, by permission of the publisher. Copyright © 1989 by the Sloan Management Review Association. All rights reserved.

tial for improved living standards for all. And when we think of ethics, we should think not just as managers focusing on a narrow preserve labeled business ethics, but as citizens of a larger society.

Ethics and competitiveness are inseparable. We compete as a society. No society anywhere will compete very long or successfully with people stabbing each other in the back; with people trying to steal from each other; with everything requiring notarized confirmation because you can't trust the other fellow; with every little squabble ending in litigation; and with government writing reams of regulatory legislation, tying business hand and foot to keep it honest.

That is a recipe not only for headaches in running a company; it is a recipe for a nation to become wasteful, inefficient, and noncompetitive. There is no escaping this fact: the greater the measure of mutual trust and confidence in the ethics of a society, the greater its economic strength.

I do not say the sky is falling here in the United States. I do not think we had a great ethical height in the good old days from which we've been tumbling downhill. We do face ethical and competitive problems, to be sure. We have all been reading about religious leaders who steal from their congregations, Wall Street brokers who profit from their insider status, assorted politicians and influence peddlers, law students who plagiarize, medical professors who falsify their research results, and Pentagon employees who sell classified information. But most of us can agree with Thomas Jefferson that all human beings are endowed with a moral sense—that the average farmer behind a plow can decide a moral question as well as a university professor. Like Jefferson, we can have confidence in the man in the street, whether that street is in Armonk, San Francisco, or Cambridge—or in London, Paris, or Tokyo.

That common moral sense, however, does not come out of nowhere or perpetuate itself automatically. Every generation must keep it alive and flourishing. All of us can think of means to this end. Here are three suggestions.

ETHICAL BUTTRESSES

First, we should fortify the practical ethical buttresses that help all of us—from childhood on—know and understand and do exactly what is required of us. The simplest and most powerful buttress is the role model: parents and others who by precept and example set us straight on good and evil, right and wrong. Of all the role models in my own life, I think

perhaps the most durable is my grandfather—a flinty New England headmaster whose portrait hangs in my home. To this day, whenever I go by it I check the knot in my tie and stiffen my backbone.

There are many other ethical buttresses. Some, despite condescending sophisticates, are simple credos: "A Scout is trustworthy, loyal, helpful, friendly, courteous, kind, obedient, cheerful, thrifty, brave, clean, and reverent"; or "a cadet will not lie, cheat or steal or tolerate those who do." There are institutionalized buttresses like the honor system, by which college students police themselves—no plagiarism, no cheating on examinations. I find it ludicrous that even divinity schools and law schools and departments of philosohpy—not to mention other parts of the university—have to pay proctors to pad up and down the aisles at examination time to make sure nobody is looking at crib notes or copying from a neighbor. A century and a half after Jefferson introduced the honor system at the University of Virginia, it is unfortunate that every college and university in America has not yet adopted it.

Finally there are professional standards and business codes of conduct, which spell out strict policies on such things as insider trading, gifts and entertainment, kickbacks, and conflicts of interest.

It is naive to believe these buttresses will solve all our problems. But it is equally naive to expect ethical behavior to occur in the absence of clear requirements and consequences.

CAN OUR SCHOOLS TEACH ETHICS?

The time has come to take a hard look at ethical teaching in our schools—and I don't just mean graduate schools of business. We know John Shad is giving the Harvard Business School most of a $30-million endowment to be devoted to studying and teaching ethics. And we know that MIT Sloan School dean Lester Thurow and other educators have openly disagreed with this undertaking.

Let's begin by defining what we are talking about. Many businesspeople facing student audiences have been appalled by knee-jerk assertions that it is open-and-shut immorality to do business in South Africa, to produce weapons for the military, to decide against setting up a day-care center, to run a nuclear power plant, or even to make a profit. An enormous amount of work needs to be done to help young people think clearly about complex questions like these, which defy pseudomoralistic answers. They require instead incisive definition and analysis, and a clear-headed understanding of a company's sometimes conflicting responsiblities—to its employees, its stockholders, and its country. And these responsibilities often require some agonizingly difficult choices.

I wholeheartedly favor ethical instruction—in a business school or anywhere else in the university—that strengthens such analytical capabilities. I also favor ethical examination of workplace safety, consumer protection, environmental safeguards, and the rights of the individual employee within the organization.

But recall what Samuel Johnson once said: If a person doesn't know the difference between good and evil, "when he leaves our house, let us count our spoons." If an MBA candidate doesn't know the difference between honesty and crime, between lying and telling the truth, then business school, in all probability, will not produce a born-again convert.

Elementary, grass-roots instruction on why it is bad to sneak, cheat, or steal—such instruction in a school of business administration is much too little, far too late. That's not the place to start. The place to start is kindergarten.

There are, to be sure, vexing constitutional and other problems over prayer in the classroom. But we need not wait for the debate to end—if it ever does—before we begin to reinvigorate ethical instruction in our schools. We can start now, in kindergarten through twelfth grade, and not by feeding our children some vague abstractions called "values." I mean we should start with a clear-cut study of the past. Our ethical standards come out of the past—out of our inheritance as a people: religious, philosophical, historical. And the more we know of that past, the more sure-footedly we can inculcate ethical conduct in the future.

If you want to know about Tammy Bakker, Senator Daniel Patrick Moynihan says, read Sinclair Lewis; if you want to know about insider trading, read Ida Tarbell. If you want to know what it is like to operate in a jungle where the individual predator profits as society suffers, read Thomas Hobbes and John Locke. If you want to understand the conflict between the demands of the organization and the conscience of the individual, read Thoreau on civil disobedience and Sophocles's *Antigone*. If you want to know about civility, read the words of Confucius. And if you want to know about courage, temperance, truthfulness, and justice, read Aristotle or the Bible.

When I hear reports that American high-school students know little or nothing about Chaucer or Walt Whitman or the Civil War or the Old Testament prophets, what bothers me most is not that they exhibit intellectual ignorance. What bothers me is that they have missed the humane lessons in individual ethical conduct that we find in the annals of world history, the biographies of great men and women, and the works of supreme imaginative literature.

A great classical writer once defined history as "philosophy learned from example." And a distinguished Brattle Street resident of

Cambridge, Henry Wadsworth Longfellow, gave us this eloquent summary:

> Lives of great men all remind us
> We can make our lives sublime,
> And departing, leave behind us
> Footprints on the sands of time.

FIRST THINGS FIRST

My third suggestion is this: let's keep our sense of order straight. Let's put first things first.

We have all heard shortsighted businesspeople attribute a quotation to Vince Lombardi: "Winning is not the most important thing; it's the *only* thing." That's a good quotation for firing up a team, but as a business philosophy it is sheer nonsense. There is another, much better Lombardi quotation. He once said he expected his players to have three kinds of loyalty: to God, to their families, and to the Green Bay Packers, "in that order."

He knew that some things count more than others. Businessmen and women can be unabashedly proud of their companies. But the good of an entire society transcends that of any single corporation. The moral order of the world transcends any single nation-state. And one cannot be a good business leader— or a good doctor or lawyer or engineer— without understanding the place of business in the greater scheme of things.

There is an incandescent example of a group who understood this fact: who saw life steadily, saw it whole, and saw it in a hierarchy—the delegates who drafted the U.S. Constitution in Philadelphia 200 years ago. What do we remember the oldest of them—Benjamin Franklin—for? Not for his vigorous advice on how to get up early in the morning, drive a business, make a profit, and win success in the marketplace, though he did all these things with gusto. We remember him and the others in Philadelphia—and those who signed the Declaration of Independence—because they did not see winning or self-advancement or even life itself as the *only* thing. To something greater than themselves—to a new nation "conceived in liberty and dedicated to the proposition that all men are created equal"—to that concept they pledged all subordinate things— their lives, their fortunes, and their sacred honor.

We should never forget their example.

So there are three suggestions:

- Fortify our ethical buttresses—role models, codes of conduct, the honor system.
- Reinvigorate our children's study of the past.
- Keep our priorities straight.

If we do these things, we shall go far toward discharging our responsibilities as managers and as human beings: contribute to our countries' strengths, heighten their capacity for leadership in an increasingly competitive and productive world, and keep them on the right track as we close out this century and enter the twenty-first.

9

Economic Theories of Organization

Charles Perrow

DEPARTMENT OF SOCIOLOGY, ORGANIZATION AND
MANAGEMENT, YALE UNIVERSITY

Until the last ten years or so the relationship between economics and organizational analysis has been a quite distant one. Most economic theorists treated the organization as an entrepreneur in a field of entrepreneurs, and saw little need to inquire into the nature of the organization itself. On the other hand, organizational analysts paid relatively little attention to the interaction of organizations, even less to industry characteristics, and virtually none to the role of organizations in the economy as a whole. The organization responded to an environment, and its response was the focus of interest, not the environment. This has changed. Two closely related bodies of theory in economics — agency theory and transaction-cost analysis — have taken the internal operation of the firm as problematical and have investigated it. Agency theory has focused upon the problem the "principal" has in controlling the employee ("agent"), and transaction-cost analysis has focused upon the advantages of eliminating market contracts by incorporating supplies and distributors into one's own firm — the replacement of the market by a hierarchy. Organizational analysts, on the other hand, have begun to develop the notion of the environment in a variety of ways, some of which involve networks of organizations, other take account of industry characteristics (but as yet none has studied the dynamics of the economy as a whole). These ventures by the two disciplines, if I may speak of organizational analysis as a discipline, are, of course, to be welcomed for a variety of obvious reasons. The two disciplines have much to learn from each other. A less obvious reason for welcoming the developments will concern me in this article, and it is a somewhat perverse one. I find the formulations regarding human behavior and organizations by the economists to be not only wrong but dangerous. However, I find my own field of organizational analysis, and sociology in general, to be insufficiently developed to convincingly demonstrate the full measure of error. Therein resides the danger. But it is also an opportunity.

We are forced to develop an adequate answer to the characterization of human behav-

Kluwer Academic Publishers.

ior as preeminently the self-interested maximization of utilities, and forced to make a discriminating analysis of the rise of large corporations. The first, self-interested behavior, has been a controversial view of human nature since the first marginalist doctrines two centuries ago, and our contribution to that intractable debate will be largely to try to keep alive alternative notions of human nature. The second, the rise of giant bureaucracies, is of more recent origin, and we have a chance of making a somewhat larger contribution there. I will start with agency theory, but spend most of this essay on transaction-cost analysis.

AGENCY THEORY

Agency theory refers to a contract in which one party is designated as the principal, and the other, the agent. The agent contracts to carry out certain activities for the principal, and the principal contracts to reward the agent accordingly.[1] Three assumptions are at the core of agency theory. The first is the one common to most economists: individuals maximize their own self-interest. The second is more specific to agency theory: social life is a series of contracts, or exchanges, governed by competitive self-interest. The third applies to internal organizational analysis: monitoring contracts is costly and somewhat ineffective, especially in organizations, thus encouraging self-interested behavior, shirking, and especially opportunism with guile, or to put it more simply—cheating. Contracts *will* be violated because of self-interest, and *can* be violated because of the costs and ineffectiveness of surveillance. The theory then attempts to build models, almost always without empirical data, regarding the most effective ways to write and monitor contracts to minimize their violations.

If these assumptions sound extreme, note that they are widely shared. We invoke them when we blame unpleasant results on others, rather than ourselves or the situation. We say "he was supposed to do that and didn't," or "she should have known," or "he works for me and I told him not to do that." All assume either the difficulty of controlling subordinates or agents, or the opportunism of subordinates, or both when dealing with team efforts. We all invoke agency theory. we can all point to people who did not do their share and thus got more rewards than they deserved—the "free rider" problem celebrated by mancur Oslen.[3]

for agency theorists, even if the deception that occurs is unintended, without guile, and merely due to the slippage that occurs in social life, such as in missed signals, forgetfulness, or chance serendipity, the rational individual will turn it to his or her self-interest if that is possible. There is no occasion when behavior will intendedly be other-regarding, rather than self-regarding, on any predictable basis or to any significant degree. Presumably there might be behavior that is neither self- or other-regarding, but is neutral in its consequences, but this is never discussed and would probably be regarded as unmotivated or even nonrational behavior. Agency theory, along with transaction-cost analysis, assumes that "human nature as we know it," as Oliver Williamson puts it, is prone to opportunism with guile.

This condition accounts for capitalism. Alchian and Demsetz give us the scenario.[3] Four people performing a cooperative task, say loading trucks, find that the risk of any one of them slacking is such that they hire a fifth to monitor their work. The monitor has to have the power to hire and fire, thus we have a manager. She also appropriates a part of the income of the group, in the form of a salary. In order to motivate her to do the difficult job of watching the others work, she also gets any residual income or profit left over after paying the wages and her salary.

(Measuring the work of others and watching them is universally regarded by these theorists as requiring more rewards than doing the work itself). If she or the team decide to purchase equipment to increase their performance, say a fork-lift truck, they go to the money lenders. The level of trust being what it is, the money lenders set up a monitor to monitor the manager so as to assure them that their investment is protected. *They* then appropriate the residual income or profit. We now have stockholders, a board of directors, a CEO, management, workers and capital equipment—in short, capitalism. It all started because four workers could not trust one another.

At least one heroic assumption is at work in agency theory—that human nature as we know it is ruled only or primarily by self-interest. Combined with the problems and costs of monitoring it means that people, being prone to cheating, will get the chance to do so. But human nature as I know it signifies primarily a *lack of instinctual responses*, compared to nonhuman nature, and this means humans are highly adaptive (as well as inventive and variable and so on). If so, the setting in which interactions or contracts occur is the most important thing to consider in explaining behavior. Some settings, or organizational structures, as I shall argue shortly, will promote self-interested behavior, others promote other-regarding behavior, and still others will be neutral. Furthermore, I follow Herbert Simon[4] and assume that rationality is bounded, or limited. If so, even where self-interest is encouraged by the context of behavior, humans (1) do not have clear utilities to maximize, (2) do not have much of the information needed to maximize utilities, and (3) do not know of cause-effect relations regarding maximization. Agency theorists do not model the context of behavior, nor the slippage occasioned by limited rationality, even though both of these should account for most of any observed variance in behavior.

A second problem is less with the model than its application, though I believe the model builders nearly intend a biased application. When dealing with principal-agent relationships within organizations they almost invariably assume that it is the agent that is opportunistic, even to the point of cheating, rather than the principal. This may stem from unrealistic assumptions about an unimpacted (i.e., highly fluid) market for labor: the assumption that there is no authority relationship within firms, but only a series of contracts, because if the principal cheats, the agent is free to go elsewhere. Because agents (employees) generally don't go elsewhere, theorists assume any contract violations must be on their part rather than the principal's part. Were an authority relationship admitted, (even the simple one that suggests the boss is free to fire employees, and maintain the firm by hiring others, while employees are not free to fire the boss and maintain the firm[5]) then the unequal power of the parties to the contract would have to be admitted. Once unequal power is entertained, it becomes obvious that, given self-interested behavior, the boss has more occasions for cheating on employees than the reverse. He may exploit them, either by breaking the contract, or not including in the contract matters that violate their self-interest.

This focus upon agent opportunism to the exclusion of principal opportunism extends to the agency theory work on "adverse selection"—hiring a poorly qualified agent. The principal has a problem, they say: the agent may misrepresent her "type," that is, her training, skills, and character, when seeking employment. Elaborate models deal with this form of cheating.[6] But I could find no model in the literature that considered that the principal also has a "type" and might misrepresent it to the prospective agent, e.g. in terms of hazardous working conditions, production pressures, adequacy of equipment, fairness of supervision, advancement possi-

Charles Perrow

bilities, amount of compulsory overtime, etc. Agency theorists might argue that the principal who misrepresents himself will suffer a loss of reputation and thus not get agents, but prospective agents probably cannot determine the reputation accurately beforehand, will bear the costs of seeking a new job and perhaps relocation, and may simply find that "elsewhere" also exploits. The employment relationship is an asymmetrical one; this is neglected by the theory, just as is the possibility that the principal's type may be misrepresented. Agency theory appears to be ideologically incapable of keeping an eye on both ends of the contract, and incapable of noting any permanent asymmetry of resources and power stemming from the context.

Why, then, bother with it? First, because it, along with transaction-cost economics, is experiencing an amazing growth in popularity among organizational theorists,[7] possibly because it is so simple as to promise to cut through the complexities most of us are entangled in, and because it touches upon something we all like to do—blame our fellow workers or particularly our subordinates for failures that may well be a result of the situation or even our own behavior. It is also in keeping with a recent presidential campaign theme of self-interest: are *you* better off today, not your community, city or nation, and not the less fortunate members of the community, city or nation, and not the prospects for the next generation—just you. There appears to be a basic cultural shift over the last two hundred or so years toward the celebration of self-interest.

The second reason we should bother with it is that it highlights the varying degree to which the major organizational theories recognize the asymmetry of power in organizations. Briefly, agency theory comes close to zero in this respect; in fact I suspect it may be designed to distract us from the existence of power differences. Human-relations theory does better; it recognizes the responsibility of

masters to use their power wisely and humanely.[8] As such, it recognizes, to at least a limited extent, that behavior is structurally determined and leaders are responsible for that structure. Classical bureaucratic theory pursues power and structure further, finding that power operates through such structural devices such as specialization, formalization, centralization, and hierarchy. It assumes that while shirking and deceptive representation of one's type will be problems, employment status is evidence that employees accept the necessity of unequal power relations, and can do little, other than shirk, to maximize their utilities at the expense of owners. The major problems of organization with both the human relations and bureaucratic model are not shirking by agents, but establishing routines, innovation when needed, and the coordination of the output of diverse units. Under the conditions of wage dependency and profit maximization, employee utilities are likely to be limited to continual employment, interesting work, opportunity to use and develop skills, safe work, some autonomy, and some influence in decisions that affect the efficiency of the organization.

What I have referred to as the neo-Weberian model goes even further in recognizing power differences and undercutting agency theory. It makes a central point of the fact that groups legitimately vie for power, as in the contest of sales and production; they seek to use the organization for their own ends, but these are rarely maximizing leisure or even income; because of bounded rationality one's interests are problematic at best, and the role of premise-setting and unobtrusive controls in capitalists societies overrides the simple determination of interest. Thus, agency theory, by anchoring extreme assumptions about power and preferences, gives us a scale for judging theories.

But the best reason to pay attention to agency theory is that it forces us to consider the conditions under which organizations may promote competitive self-interested behavior, and when they will promote other-regarding behavior. I will consider only short-run consequences of behavior where some immediate self-interest such as status, power, or income appears to be sacrificed in order to either not harm another, or to actually help another. In the world of organizations competitive self-regarding behavior appears to be favored by such conditions as the following:

1. *Self-interested behavior is favored when continuing interactions are minimized.* Some examples: a highly fluid ("unimpacted") labor market where job seekers are not constrained by personal or family ties to friends and the community when they seek work locations; "spot contracting" in a labor market as with migrant workers, temporary help, high turnover fast food franchises, all of which maximize free movement of labor; heavy emphasis upon individual promotions or individual, rather than group, job rotations; rewarding loyalty to the firm rather than more proximate groups such as your own group and the other groups it interacts with.

2. *Self-interested behavior is favored where storage of rewards and surpluses by individuals is encouraged.* The tax structure favors individual rather than group rewards; organizational hierarchy promotes it, steep salary structures reinforce it; a stable class system (minimal redistribution of wealth) provides the context for it.

3. *Self-interested behavior is favored where the measurement of individual effort or contribution is encouraged.* This is done through personnel evaluations, promotions, piece rates, and the celebration of leadership; it is a continuing legacy of nineteenth-century individualism, celebrating individual rather than cooperative effort.

4. *Self-interesed behavior is favored where we minimize interdependent effort through design of work flow and equipment.* Work flow and equipment can minimize cooperative effort and responsibility by breaking up tasks and favoring assembly lines; precise contractual relationships promote this; so does the presumption that shirking is potentially rampant and that installing surveillance systems thwarts it.

5. *Self-interested behavior is favored where there is a preference for leadership stability and generalized authority.* This occurs when leaders are held to be all-competent and the position held continuously. Instead, we could alternate leadership tasks according to the skills of the individuals, thus avoiding stable patterns of dependency in subordinates and self-fulfilling assumptions of expertise in leaders. This is possibly a legacy of individualism and private ownership rights.

6. *Self-interested behavior is favored where tall hierarchies are favored.* These are based upon unequal rewards and notions that coordination must be imperatively achieved.

It might be argued that I have just described capitalist organizations in the United States, and thus agency theory is appropriate. There are several responses. First, while capitalist organizations do encourage self-interested behavior, this does not mean that human nature is self-interested; it may be the situation or context, that is, the organizational structures fostered by capitalism, that encourages it. The counter argument then would be that public organizations also have these characteristics, and even most organizations in the so-called socialist states. I would still resist the agency-theory formulation on the grounds that once what I call "factory bureaucracy" (specialization, formalizations, centralization, and hierarchy) is made possible by creating a wage-dependent population, only extraordinary resistance to economic and political elites will prevent factory bureaucracy from spreading to noneconomic organizations and to other nations. Next I would note that even in factory bureaucracy the overwhelming preponderance of behavior is cooperative and "neutral-regarding," and some is even other-regarding. Many have argued that social life would be impossible without other-regarding and neutral forms of behavior.

Finally, I would argue that the task is to create structures that minimize self-regarding behavior, and there is evidence that organizations vary considerably in this respect. Indeed there are some recognized firms which appear to minimize self-interested behavior. Joyce Rothschilde-Witte describes many in her work, though they are small and unstable; Rosabeth Kanter and others argue that large ones can be designed in this way; Japanese firms, while far from ideal in many respects, do minimize some of the six characteristics that encourage self-interested behavior. It may be that some small, innovative, high-technology firms require some to be successful, and Scandinavian societies, in particular, Sweden, have successfully developed some alternative structures, and in a shorter period than it took most Western countries to develop capitalist structures.[9]

Agency, theory, then forces us to recognize the extent to which we are all agency theorists in our worse moments, blaming others when the structure or ourselves should be blamed; forces us to examine the structures that evoke different kinds of behavior; reminds us that, easy as it is to say so, human behavior is not rooted in some vague notion of "human nature as we find it," but depends upon the contexts that we create. Each generation of organizational analysts should be reminded of these key points, and be forced to continually explore them. For this, we might be grateful for agency theory, despite its very conservative political bias.

TRANSACTION-COST ECONOMICS

Transaction-cost economics (TCE), largely the creation of economist Oliver Williamson following early work of John Commons and Ronald Coase, is less politically conservative than agency theory.[10] In contrast to most agency theory it recognizes authority relations, denies that it is useful to consider the organization as nothing more than a series of contracts between parties, and recognizes some of the societal problems associated with giant corporations. It is also far more attentive to bounded rationality and sociological and structural variables. It has received much acclaim in the organizational literature, and indeed it claims to supplant most existing organizational theories. Like agency theory, however, it is based upon a self-interest model of human behavior, and is relentlessly and explicitly an efficiency argument. Its appearance should prompt organization theorists, especially left-leaning ones, into some vigorous work, and for this reason we should welcome it.

The theory raises many issues that need discussion by organizational analysts. I will make the following arguments: we need a better formulation of some of our fuzzy notions of trust, and it provides one; we need more awareness of the economic concepts regarding industries and market characteristics, and TCE provides this; we have not explored issues of mergers sufficiently, such as the effect upon complexity and tight coupling, and a critique of TCE will encourage this; discussion of market concentration, monopoly power, and the growth of huge organizations needs to include standard economic concepts more than has been the practice; TCE concepts provide a way of bridging inter- and intra-organizational analysis more than has been our practice; the issue of markets versus hierarchies is falsely posed by this theory and we can use this opportunity to reconceptualize an important area of interorganizational analysis; and, perhaps most important, Williamson does not ask simply why there are so many big firms, but asks where will big firms fail to appear, a question even left-leaning organizational theorists have failed to ask. Thus, though I think TCE is a wrong theory, it forces us to address questions we have tended to neglect or improperly pose. This part of my essay will range widely and necessarily briefly over these several issues; each could be an essay in its own right. I hope it will stimulate more searching essays by others.

THE THEORY

Transaction-costs economics is an efficiency argument for the present state of affairs, as most mainstream economic theories are, arguing that the appearance of giant organizations in some industries represents the most efficient way of producing goods for an industrial society. Distortions are acknowledged, and that the government should get out of this or that, but in general capitalism and the free market produce the most efficient economic system, apparently despite the fact that the market is supplanted by hierarchies. Williamson is explicit regarding efficiency, by which he means the efficiency of organizational forms, not the efficiency of specific practices or machines or sales techniques or transportation devices, though the efficiently run organization will seek out these other operating efficiencies. Discussing the shift from many organizations to a few large ones over the century, he says "I argue that efficiency is the main and only systematic factor responsible for the organizational changes that have occurred."[11]

There are four components in his theory: uncertainty, small-numbers bargaining, bounded rationality, and opportunism. Bounded rationality and opportunism are ever present, but will only result in large firms where there is uncertainty and small-numbers bargaining.

Uncertainty refers to changes in the environment that the owner cannot forsee or control; it provides the dynamic element that makes equilibrium of the market unstable.

Small-numbers bargaining means that once a long-term contract has been signed, with suppliers, or workers or customers, the normal market situation is disturbed. The parties to the contract have privileged positions because they have more experience with the other party, and more specialized resources to serve it, than those in the market that sought but did not get the contract.

For example, if you find that your supplier's quality is slipping, you may be reluctant to break the contract and find another because you are set up to deal with that supplier; you have made an investment in routines and have experience with that firm's supplies and procedures and idiosyncrasies, and that investment will be lost. Or, within the firm, after employees have worked for you for awhile, they gain experience and skills, and if they threaten to quit or strike you cannot simply hire others that will immediately be as productive.

A related concept is *asset specificity*. If, by working for a firm at a specialized job, one develops specific skills that job seekers outside the organization don't have, one has specific assets, and this gives one some bargaining power. The employer has to think twice about firing the person, or about refusing a demand for a raise. While I think this concept is useful, the bilateral nature of exchange renders it opaque: because these assets are specific to this firm, it gives the boss some power too—the employees specific skills will give him or her no bargaining advantage over another potential employer because the skills are specific to this one organization. This is rarely acknowledged by Williamson. A similar bilateral relationship occurs between supplier and customer, which Williamson does acknowledge.

Bounded rationality creates a problem because of *opportunism*. Lacking perfect information about suppliers or workers allows them to behave opportunistically. You cannot judge the claim of the supplier that labor problems or raw material problems delay deliveries, and you cannot costlessly turn to another supplier. Similarly, the customer may misrepresent his problems to the supplier, and fail to honor the contract. But an alternative customer is not always available. Such situations are called "market failures"; uncertainty about labor or supplies or demand, when combined with small-numbers bargaining, and the lack of adequate information and the chance of opportunism all disrupt the normal market relationships. In the normal, neoclassical market, a large number of suppliers and producers bargain daily over prices. The market assures the lowest possible prices, adjusts to changes in demand immediately, and discourages opportunism because opportunists will not find people to trade with the next day. Instead, we find uncertainty, small numbers, bounded rationality, and opportunism, that is, a failure to achieve the classical market.

Well, that's serious. (It is also the rule in our economy; the markets of neoclassical theory are few in number and small in impact). What is to be done? Williamson and capitalists have the solution: Vertical integration. One can integrate forward by buying out the person one sells to (or setting up one's own distribution services) or integrate backwards by buying out one's supplier (or building one's own source of supply). If the supplier is part of your firm you can control her. It eliminates the leverage she had as one of a handful of suppliers that you had to depend upon. She won't dare lie about labor problems or raw material problems because you can check the

books (controlling opportunism). And you will not have to write all those contracts with her, trying to specify complex future contingencies, and have your people checking to see that all the promises are fulfilled. This way you reduce the costs of transacting business, hence the term transaction-cost economics. There will be other economies, such as economies of scale though they are not stressed by Williamson, but these economies are likely to be quite small. For Williamson, minimizing transaction costs is the key to efficiency, and it explains concentration of production in large firms better than several competing theories, including Marxist and other power theories, historian Alfred Chandler's theory of coordination and throughput spped, technological arguments, and those that deal with the strategic use of finance.[12]

The development of large firms, so evident in our twentieth-century economic history, does not occur in all areas, however, and the ability to explain why markets will persist in some areas while they disappear in others would indicate the power of his theory. The question has often been asked, why, if giant firms are more efficient, do we not have just one giant firm? Here the potential pay-off of TCE becomes apparent.

Markets, argues Williamson, will continue to exist if spot contracts will do the job efficiently. The market for supplies is cleared each day, so to speak, if transactions are one-shot, so no long-term contacts need to be written. The firm that wishes to buy some furniture asks for bids and selects the lowest, just as a person shops for a television. There is no opportunity for cheating on long-term delivery contracts, no "first mover advantages" (where the first firm to get the contract has an inside track on all future contracts because of small-numbers bargaining). Markets can also survive if there is little uncertainty in price, volume, production costs, labor relations, and the like, even if the market is not a spot one. Standard supplies (toilet paper, business forms, batteries, picks and shovels) are available from many sources, have clear prices, and the quality is readily judged. Markets will also survive if the costs of entry (starting up a production facility) are low; entrepreneurs will see that existing producers are making a lot of money and so they will come in and thus bring the price down because of competition. The cost of entry will be more likely to be low if the technology is well known. Predictable high-volume demand also reduces uncertainty and favors market transactions instead of vertical integration. Thus, hierarchy replaces markets when there are long-term contracts in an uncertain environment and the barriers to entry are reasonably high, because the costs of opportunism are reduced by substituting an authority relationship ("you now work for me") for a contractual one.

THE VALUE OF THEORY

Williamson's work highlights a number of variables that organizational theorists unforntunately neglect. Take the notion of "asset specificity." We are wont to invoke vague terms such as tradition, or trust, when we encounter long-term relationships between firms and suppliers, or firms and customers, or even a supervisor and workers. A good part of that tradition or trust may lie in the bilateral dependency of each of the parties. The supplier is as dependent upon the customer as he is upon her, because of asset specificity. The assets of the supplier are highly specific in order to meet the specific demands of the customer, and the customer's products are made more specific or inflexible because of the specificity of the supplier's components. (Note, though, that using this concept with its clear bilateral implications reduces any efficiency difference between markets and hierarchies because relationships in both will

tend towards an equilibrium. Because hierarchies have replaced some markets, Williamson must explain the disappearance of bilaterality and the trust it implies on other than efficiency grounds.)

A similar argument can be made regarding the tasks the supervisor wants done, and the skills the workers have developed. Asset specificity, in a sense, demands the continuity that we call tradition, and produces the repeated interactions that we call trust. Locating the source of tradition and trust in an economic relationship need not remove the sociological concern with the social and cultural content of these transactions. One reason trust may appear in bilateral exchanges is that the parties get to know crucial non-economic aspects of each other and of their interdependency. Political, ethical, and cultural values are exchanged and modified. The economic relationship becomes "embedded" (as Granovetter terms it, in his important essays on economics and sociology)[13] in social and cultural exchanges, and the strictly economic and strictly self-interested nature of the exchange is modified and over-laid. But Williamson reminds us that it cannot be ignored, and economic concepts help us to see it.

The bilateral relationship may not be equal, we should note. Generally, the larger firm has the greatest leverage. If the larger firm is the buyer its purchasing power allows it to find another source of supply, and probably do it more readily than the supplier can develop another customer. Similarly, the employer would prefer to retain the experienced employee, but can replace her, while she will have more trouble finding another employer, unless unusual skills or an unusual labor market exists. But any analysis of the concepts of trust and tradition had best be aware of Williamson's discussion of small numbers bargaining and asset specificity.

Nor have organizational theorists paid much attention to the characteristics of market transactions. Distinguishing spot from long-term contracts, many bargainers from small numbers of them, degrees of substitutability of goods or services, and stability and instability of demand, technologies, and so on may not appear to be a signal contribution. In one form or another these ideas are used by many theorists. But Williamson links them together, makes them explicit, and demands that issues of market concentration, monopoly power, the growth of huge organizations, and the like be addressed with these considerations in mind. In particular, formalizing the argument about transactions allows us to focus on the important question of why hierarchies replace markets.

Furthermore, because the concepts can be applied both to the relations between organizations, and to relationships within organizations, we get a fruitful link between the nature of markets (interorganizational relationships) and the nature of firms (intraorganizational relationships). By allowing us to make the link Williamson also brings into organizational analysis a field that it has neglected—industrial economics, which deals with the characteristics of industries (concentration, size, rates of change, characteristics of customers, and so on), though the literature has left the firms themselves as empty shells. Williamson provides us with some of the most relevant aspects of industrial economics, packaged for organizational theory.

Finally, Williamson restates the problem "why so many big firms?" as: why do we get big firms (hierarchies) in some areas and not in others. This is a more interesting and more tractable problem. (The historian Alfred DuPont Chandler also raises it in this form and treats it as the main question a historian of business organizations should answer.[14]) Marxists have an answer of a sort for the first question: the disappearance of small firms and the growth of big ones is the product of the dynamics of capitalism—a ceaseless search for ever more profits, wherein the big fish gobble up the small. But they have no answer for the second question: when will markets (small firms) persist, despite the existence of powerful organizations nearby that seek ever more profits. These are questions that an organizational theory that has finally met the environment should be preoccupied with; we deal with them at the margins of our work, but we have not directly confronted them. Williamson has.

THE CRITICISMS

An extended example will illustrate some major criticisms one can make of TCE, and then we will review the criticisms of other scholars. My example is intended to explore a variety of issues regarding the costs of integration; I argue that the costs are born because the advantages are not efficiency, but appropriating profitable businesses and establishing market control. I do not believe that the costs of vertical integration have been systematically assessed in the literature; if not, and if my fictional example rings true, we owe this assessment to the challenge of Williamson's argument. In general, the criticisms of Williamson are likely to enrich the field more than his theory has.

TCE would have us explain why firms are not engaged in only one single function, such as grinding values, which are sent to another firm that puts them in an engine block that a third has made, and so on. But systems with that much specialization disappeared one or two centuries ago, for the most part. The real question is why does a firm that is *already* large, buy up another good sized firm? Why merge *two hierarchies*, rather than why move from a bunch of tiny firms to a few big ones?

Consider this hypothetical account of a firm called Engines, Inc. It has about a thousand employees producing engines for air conditioning systems. It then buys out a firm, Radiators, Inc., with three hundred employees, that supplies radiators for these engines. Engines, reflecting its new acquisition, renames itself the ACE Company (for air conditioning equipment). TCE would have use believe that the costs of long-term contracts between Engines and Radiators were too high, so Engines bought Radiators in 1980. ACE now controls all the people that were owners and employees of Radiators and can reduce opportunism on the part of these people and save on lawyers who write contracts and accountants that monitor them. But is there really a savings?

Prior to 1980, there were two sets of transaction costs: writing and monitoring the contracts between Radiators and Engines, and the costs that each of the firms had in dealing with other parts of its environment. The second costs are not reduced. When Engines buys Radiators out, it must continue to deal with the environment that Radiators had to deal with, for example, buying metal and other supplies, dealing with the government, with labor, the community and so on. As we shall see these costs may actually rise because the form of transactions will change somewhat under the new ownership. The transaction costs associated with the Radiators-Engines relationship will certainly change, but I will argue that they are actually likely to rise, rather than fall, as far as Engines is concerned.

If the market for air conditioning equipment declines, the new firm, ACE, cannot simply tell its supplier of radiators that it is canceling its order (with due notice, or even a penalty), or cutting the size of a new one, thus making Radiators suffer all or most of the loss. ACE itself has to absorb the loss of business (fixed capital lying idle, layoffs with unemployment insurance costs, excess managerial staff, and loss of profit-generating activity). The sum total of transaction costs remain; their location is different. (One of the problems with TCE is that the definition of a transaction cost is altogether too flexible for a convincing test of the theory; but shutting down facilities and laying off experienced employees seem to qualify as transaction costs.)

Suppose the opposite happened, and the demand for its product soared. The radiator division within ACE can build new facilities to expand its production no faster than Radiators could (though it might get capital a bit faster if ACE had some lying around); there is no saving here. In fact, there might be a loss. Radiators might have added facilities to meet the new demand, calculating that if the rise in demand by Engines turned out to be temporary, they still might be able to sell their excess to other engine companies. But ACE might find it awkward to become a supplier to its own competitors (though it happens regularly in a few industries such as electronics), and the competitors would probably prefer to buy from suppliers they can control rather than from a competitor. Thus ACE is less likely to risk an expansion of facilities. Some flexibility is lost in the acquisition.

Well, what about opportunism? Ms. Radoe, once the head of Radiators is now the General Manager of the Radiator division of ACE. According to TCE she can now be watched much more carefully (ACE has the information on her behavior) and any disputes between her and, say, the Chief Operating Officer, Mr. Enginee (the former head of Engines who now oversees the radiator and engines divisions) can be settled "by fiat," that is, a direct order. Before, there were transaction costs—contract writing, bargaining, legal actions, and so on. If Mr. Enginee needs support for disciplining Ms. Radoe if fiat is resisted, he can turn to the Chief Executive Officer of ACE, Mr. Banke. Mr. Banke was an officer of the bank that provided the loan for buying up the radiator company. As a condition of that loan, he was made CEO of the company. (He need not know anything about air conditioning, but he must know about transaction costs, according to TCE, because these efficiencies count the most. He does, as a finance man and banker.)

But what is Ms. Radoe likely to be doing in her new position? Here we will use the assumptions about opportunism and competitive self-interest that Williamson shares with agency theory. We will assume that the firm is structured, as most are, to encourage competitive self-interest. When Ms. Radoe headed up Radiators she worked extremely hard because she owned the company and got the profits from it. No motivation to shirk, or slack, on her part. But at ACE she gets a salary (and perhaps a bonus) rather than direct profits. She has less incentive to work hard, and indeed, more to shirk, or even steal. Reflecting the incentives problem, ACE may develop an elaborate bonus plan based in part on the performance of Ms. Radoe's division and in part on the performance of the firm as a whole, as other companies have done. Such plans have led to fierce controversy over internal pricing decisions within firms—a substantial transaction cost. Is the radiator division being charged more than its share of the overhead, and thus its internal profits are set lower than they would be if it were independent? Robert Eccles details the extensive transactions costs and political problems of internal pricing schemes, necessary once the market no longer exists. He concludes from extensive research that firms perceive the costs of *internal* transactions to be higher than external ones, and did not find TCE useful in understanding the transfer pricing problem.[15]

No doubt, given the emphasis upon opportunism in TCE, Ms. Radoe will also be required to monitor it in her subordinates, just as she did when she owned the firm. But if there is no bonus plan she has less incentive to do so; their slacking or stealing will have a trivial effect upon her income, though it should not become so gross as to invite an inspection from Mr. Enginee or Mr. Banke. If there is a bonus plan she will take up her superior's time by arguing about internal pricing, as Eccles documents.

Furthermore, Mr. Enginee, who used to watch her intermittently from a distance when she was his supplier, now has to watch her continually as her superior. Her division draws upon the resources of ACE and affects its accounting and personnel practices. Another set of transaction costs have increased. If she allowed rampant opportunism on the part of her employees when she headed up Radiators it was of no concern to Mr. Enginee. It just meant she got less out of them and thus less profits; perhaps if she treated them well and they worked hard she made more profits, though we could have reservations about that. But the price to Mr. Enginee was not affected, so he did not need to bother about it. He was only concerned with the contract, not her whole firm. Now he is held accountable for the whole division; if they slack, the profits to ACE are reduced. (Setting the radiator division up as a "profit center" is of little help. Contracts must still be written. If it is made maximally independent, with no more interactions than when it was a supplier of radiators to Engines, it may as well have remained a separate firm because there are no transaction cost savings—with one very important difference: as a separate firm ACE would not "appropriate its profit stream," as economists put it. That is, the profits now go to ACE, not to Ms. Radoe. We will later count this as possibly the primary motive for acquisitions.)

One can imagine Mr. Enginee going home one night to tell Mrs. Enginee, "What a mistake. I read Oliver Williamson and it looked as if Engines was ripe for savings on transactions costs. You know, he is the one that called Perrow's theory "bankrupt" in that book where Perrow criticized Williamson.[16] Well, we had this small-numbers bargaining situation with big Ms. Radoe, and long-term contracts, uncertainty about product demand, and all the rest including opportunism on her part—she claimed those leaky radiators were the result of poor handling by us and threatened to sue us if we refused to pay. So I decided to buy her out. She was working eighty hours a week and she didn't like her reputation for driving her employees, so she was willing to come to work for us."

"But I had to let Mr. Banke come in as CEO in order to get capital for the buyout. Williamson never mentioned that there are large costs in acquiring even small firms. It was profitable, so we could raise the money, and it should increase our profits—Mr. Banke and the stockholders will get them and not Ms. Radoe. But it saddled us with three hundred employees and all kinds of commitments at a time when sales were falling. We are losing money, not her." (Or, "Now that sales are booming it is we that have to pay for the increase in overtime and other special production costs, whereas before she would have had to take less profit on each item because of the contract, at no cost to us.") [TCE neglects to consider all transaction costs. Flexibility in response to changes is reduced.]

"Furthermore," he continues, turning up his custom-built air conditioner as he gets more heated, "I have had a hell of a time getting their accounting and information-management system to link up with ours. Theirs was fine for their product and volume, while ours doesn't work well for them. But we have to have an integrated financial statement by law and the bankers demand certain kinds of reports, personnel needed to standardize and so on. So I had to hire more accountants, and Ms. Radoe complains that she can't watch performances and budgets as closely now." [Internal coordinating costs rise when different operations must be combined. Accounting and surveillance systems must be standardized while variable, tailor-made systems would be more effective; there are costs to decentralizing large, complex systems that do not appear in smaller, simpler ones.]

"It's even worse. In 1979, before we bought them, I used to call up two or three other radiator firms and find out what they were charging for various models, and she knew it, so she kept her prices in line. Now I don't have a good idea of the costs of our radiators because of internal-pricing problems. The accountants say the radiator division is a profit center, but it has to contribute to the firm's overhead and advertising costs, some personnel costs, a lot of staff running back and forth to her city, and we just don't know if the prices they charge us for radiators are fair or not. It would cost us a lot to find out if they are fair." [Internal pricing and internal cost systems are unreliable and expensive; the market provides comparatively cheap and reliable information.]

"When Radoe had labor trouble before the merger we just invoked the contract and it cost her plenty to fight that union, but it was her money (and her temper). We gave a little, of course, we couldn't hang a good supplier, and buying elsewhere was expensive. But all in all it only cost us about ten percent in profits for the quarter. But now we have to bear the total cost. Our industrial relations manager doesn't know that union. The union is mad because of the strike two years ago. (It's very hard to put a price on the quality of labor relations when you buy a firm. Those agency theorists call it reputation and think that it can be priced like radiators, but it is hard to verify and easy for a firm to exaggerate with a bit of strategic public relations, classy accounting, and mimicry of leading firms in the field. The people at Radiators mislead us and I think we should have paid less because of the labor problem.) Any settlement they get will rev up our other union. And while Radoe was willing to do battle with the union and take the losses when she headed the firm, now I don't really think she sees the urgency of the labor problem as much as when she owned Radiators." [Costs of acquisitions are poorly estimated and subject to opportunism. Reputation is subject to "isomorphic pressures," that is, firms come to look alike by imitating superficial attributes of leading firms.[17] Unexpected interactions are increased in large systems.]

"We are still having problems with leaky radiators and the squabbling and charges between the radiator division and the engine division is worse than before the acquisition because personality clashes now make it more difficult. Not only are there problems with getting information about who is really responsible in the market (Williamson calls the problem "information impactedness") but it can be worse in your own firm, especially when you try to do two different things, such as making stationary engines *and* radiators; the two processes, and the organizations and the personnel are just different." [Information and control within the firm is subject to political and personality problems that may make it more expensive and less reliable than in the market. Coordination of diverse activities within a firm is expensive; such coordination is not needed in the market.]

"I would like to sell the division, but the transactions cost of selling it, after all those of buying it (which Williamson never mentioned), would just be too great. I agree with Perrow. You only should integrate forward or backward when it means you can get more market control, or get your hands on a very profitable piece of property and keep those profits for yourself."[18] Mrs. Enginee's only comment was, "Dear, you read too many books."

As lighthearted as this vignette may sound, it contains some important points. As Williamson himself notes in one chapter of his book on TCE, there are transaction costs within the firm as well as between firms, and his examples suggest that some are higher in hierarchies than in markets.[19] We should also note that markets can be efficient in establishing prices, whereas firms find "internal pricing" (the allocation of costs to various units) difficult and a highly politicized process. The incentive structure is artificial and politicized in hierarchies as compared to markets. Settling disputes by "fiat" is difficult because of the very things Williamson has made us aware of—asset specificity and small numbers bargaining *within* the firm. Not all transaction costs are counted in Williamson's argument. Uncertainty affects internalized units as severely as it affects independent firms in the market; fluctuation in demand and supplies, labor problems, problems with competitors and so on do not disappear, and their resolution may be more difficult in a large firm. Opportunism, to the extent that it is a problem, will accompany the acquired firm because it is a hierarchy itself, and persist within the acquiring firm. Costs that could be externalized, and risks that could be born by the independent firm must be internalized by the acquiring firm, and it may have less flexibility in dealing with them because of long-term commitments and the power of groups with specific assets within the firm. Finally, while my account at several points favors markets over hierarchy, it does not assume a neoclassical perfect market. These rarely exist. Markets tend to be concentrated, rigged, protected, and inefficient. However, I would still give two cheers for markets, and only one for hierarchies, if only because of the power of giant firms to shape our premises to their own ends. (Three cheers for the market socialism described by Branko Horvat.[20]) But in any case the TCE argument is markets versus hierarchies, so the comparison has to be in these terms.

Lying behind my fiction is a more general point that goes beyond the critique of TCE: there is an advantage to decoupled units in a system, and a disadvantage to tight coupling. For instances, Radiators devised accounting and information management systems that were tailored to its specific operations; integrating it with the systems that were good for Engines entailed changes that made the new systems less efficient. The labor relations of Radiators may have been bad from some points of view, but they were not entangled with those of Engines. In the combined firm, ACE, any settlement for the radiator division will have an impact upon the engine division. Engines was buffered from changes in demand by Radiators, which absorbed some of the shock; ACE had to absorb all the shock.

Furthermore, Engines had the people and offices that knew how to deal with large suppliers, and thus could move quickly if demand was up; ACE lost some of that expertise, raising its transaction costs. When demand was down, Radiators suffered, but at least it could look for other customers, lowering its price (and profits). But as a division of ACE, it will find it more difficult to sell radiators to ACE's competitors. As a division, it probably can't trim its overhead during slack times as well as it could as an independent firm; some of the overhead costs assigned to it in ACE are "lumpy," that is, not divisible; overhead is a difficult thing to cut in large firms during retrenchment because of structural problems; it impacts all divisions regardless of their individual needs.

Finally, it is possible (though hardly inevitable) that Radiators could more easily change its production methods and incorporate new technologies than the division within ACE. As an independent firm, it can do what it wants with production as long as it meets the quality standards of the customer, Engines. As a division it interfaces with the rest of the organization at many points, and changes may be resisted by people at some of those points who see disadvantages in the changes. (Were ACE to provide significant research and development services for the division, this might change, but there is evidence to suggest that smaller firms are the more innovative.)

These are arguments for loosely-linked components of a system where there are likely to be uncertainties or shocks from the environment or from within. Tightly coupled systems have advantages, certainly; resources can often be more efficiently used, there is less redundancy and waste, and the processes are faster. But these advantages only appear if there is little uncertainty in the system—few "exogenous" shocks (those coming from without the system); few endogenous shocks (those coming from within), plenty of time to recover from shocks, and many different paths to recovery. Most industries do not have these luxuries, and thus loose coupling is likely to be a more efficient system property than tight coupling. Loose coupling is associated with a large number of small units engaged in straight forward bilateral exchanges.[22]

CAUSES OF HIERARCHY

Efficiency, as realized by the reduction of transaction costs, is thus an uncertain accompaniment of vertical integration, and some flexibility and buffering may be lost in the process. Clearly, in a comparison of two firms in the same industry with the same market power, political ties, etc. the more efficient will prosper and survive, and reducing transaction costs will make some unknown contribution to efficiency. But comparing firms with efficient and inefficient internal operations is not the issue; it is the grounds for vertical and horizontal integration in parts of the economy that must be explained. I will sketch a possible explanation that relies primarily on the gross size of potential profits as realized through three factors: appropriation of "profit streams" of other companies, market control, and government tolerance or support.

A firm requires various "factors of production" such as land, labor, capital, supplies, technologies, and outlets. Advantages in any of these by one firm will lead to its growth relative to its competitors. Growth also requires at least tolerance on the part of the government, though it will benefit from a variety of state enabling factors (anti-union legislation, limits on liabilities, tax policies, tariffs) and from state resources (contracts, loans, access to minerals on public property). Many of these will favor a whole industry, allowing it to prosper and grow, and thus provide an incentive for some in the industry to take over other firms. There is little incentive for absorbing enterprises in a low-profit or low-growth industry; while the purchase price will reflect the stock market's evaluation of the industry and the firm, to the extent that future growth possibilities are good and greater market control over pricing and competitive products is possible, firms will reap advantages from attractive industries net of the existing stock price.

For the firm to grow there must be market growth, through the discovery or creation of new markets or expanding existing ones. Because firm growth will be challenged by the growth of other firms, and markets are not infinite, it must keep competitors out entirely, or failing that, limit or reduce the number of competitors. An illustration in the music recording industry provides an example of the *growth* of transaction costs with concentration, and their probable decline with competition.[2] Under oligopolistic conditions prevailing until the 1950s, transactions costs for the major firms were high, not low, because they had to maintain stables of recording stars on long-term contracts, control all outlets, and keep producers and manufacturing units on their payrolls. When intense competition set in because of technological changes that lowered entry costs and allowed numerous small firms to enter the market and expand it (by catering to untapped tastes for unconventional popular music), the transaction costs were probably greatly reduced. Companies established spot contracts with producers, stars, and manufacturers, and let them bear the risks of market uncertainty. But this also meant that the small firms could reap the profits when they were lucky, so the concentration ratio plummeted, and the profits of

the majors did not grow as fast as the industry profits. The major firms managed to get control of the market again through various devices, appropriating the industry profit streams, but incurring the increased costs of internalizing risks and market fluxuations, controlling outlets, financing "payola," and standardizing tastes once more.

Another example provides specific evidence of the irrelevancy of narrow efficiency, and a critique of both Williamson and Alfred DuPont Chandler's "visible hand" theory.[23] At the end of the nineteenth century, the iron and steel company of Andrew Carnegie grew phenomenally (and later became the basis of U.S. Steel). An associate of Carnegie, James Howard Bridges, addressed the issue of transaction costs. It is particularly relevant because Carnegie was a fanatic on cost cutting in production areas and developed sophisticated bookkeeping devices to keep his transaction and production costs low. However, Bridges stated that "it was other considerations than increased efficiency and economy that promoted the first and perfect combination of the Carnegie properties," that is, the growth of his empire. There was no plan to the acquisitions, he flatly states. Instead, as Bridges details, there was the coveting of the high profits of other corporations; maneuvering to get rid of an officer; eliminating a competitor by getting the railroad pool to cut it out of the deals to provide cheap freight, until he could buy the competitor at distress prices (Carnegie was paying dividends of 40 percent at the time), and so on. He found the profits on the ore companies to be very large, so he moved in and through a combination of financial power and threats acquired a good bit of the Mesabi range, and when the ore boat companies would not reduce their prices, set up his own. His company was immensely rich and powerful. He did not have to worry about transaction costs, and they did not motivate his actions.[24]

Because of the factors of production it is

unwise to consider strategies of market growth and competition only in terms of the firm; other organizations in the environment are crucial. Perhaps of most importance is the source of investment capital, a competitive but still concentrated system of banks, insurance companies, investment houses, and venture capital firms. Holding liquid (readily available) assets, they can provide the means for one firm to buy out competitors (with no efficiency gain), to finance price wars that force out competition, to buy up and destroy competitive goods or services (as the DuPont and General Motors interests were able to destroy much of public city transport in the United States in order to increase the demand for cars, and force the construction, through taxes, of roadways for them to run on[25]), or for firms to move to low-wage areas. Banks, insurance companies, and investment firms can make legal or illegal donations to politicians and political parties here and abroad to influence government actions that will tend to increase concentration in industries and reduce competition. They are not particularly concerned with the efficiency of a loan applicant, but with the opportunities the industry provides and the applicant's ability to exploit opportunities in it.

Firms, generally with resources from the financial community, may also use the patent system and other devices, legal and illegal, to gain control of new technologies and in some cases perhaps restrict their development in order to increase market control, and thus size. (Charges of suppressing innovations are common, but hard to prove. Industrial espionage is widespread and acknowledged, however.) Firms may conspire with suppliers or customers to undercut competitors and drive them out with illegal rebates, espionage, and defamation; concentrated industries can benefit all concerned: suppliers, producers, and distributors. Of course, fraud and force can be used to gain market control or other advantages, and our industrial history right up to the present is replete with examples. Some of our largest firms have fraud and force as active ingredients in their early history, quite possible contributing significantly to their present dominance. The age of the "robber barons" coincided with the great vertical and horizontal concentrations of industrial power.

As a few firms eliminate the competition and as they integrate vertically many opportunities for exercising power appear. Prices can be increased, and thus profits. With larger and fewer firms, the cost of entry for potential competitors goes up even though there is the attraction of large profits; new firms must start large. Market domination also slows the rate of innovation, limiting expensive changes and prolonging the returns on expensive capital investments. Fewer producers can also mean more coordinated lobbying activity regarding tariff protection, subsidized research, investment tax credits, and so on; more concentrated economic power with regard to labor, more plant location incentives from local government, and local tax abatements. These are a few of the benefits of size in our economy. Thus, even if the acquired facility is not highly profitable in itself, it may add to the power and thus the profits of the acquiring firm.

I apologize for an account that will be obvious to many readers, but the above account is necessary to raise the more difficult question: Why do we not have a few large firms dominating each industry? Why is steel concentrated but furniture not? Traditionally, factors such as size of capital investment, transportation costs, perishability of goods, and so forth have explained the differences in concentration rates. (A high concentration ratio is equivalent to the degree of hierarchy; technically hierarchy is a feature of organizational forms, not of industries, but if a decent-sized industry has over, say, 50 percent of its capacity in the hands of four firms, the firms will be very large and in almost all cases hierarchical firms). I would like to put these explanations in a somewhat different light and argue that markets persist where large profits are not available, and in some cases where government policy prevents concentration.

Until recently, when financial considerations prompted the growth of conglomerates—firms that incorporated unrelated activities—most profit-seeking acquisitions were in closely related fields, such as suppliers, competitors, or distributors. The acquiring firm simply had more information about these types of firms, and had experience with the product. There may be economies of scale and benefits from smoother coordination of the enlarged input-throughput-output cycle achieved by acquisitions of closely related firms, but I believe these were secondary motives. Firms with resources will attempt to buy firms that are making good profits; transaction-costs savings or scale economies are of little importance if the profits to be gained are small. The purchase price will reflect the profitability of the firm, of course, profitable firms will have high stock values and cost more. But future profits are to be realized by the market power and political power that comes with increased size; neither unprofitable firms nor unprofitable industries favor the realization of such power.

Of course, the target firm must have sufficient amounts of profits (regardless of the rate of profits) to offset the costs of acquisition and integration. A very large firm will not usually be very interested in a tiny one no matter how profitable, though it does happen. A moderate-sized firm, however, would be interested. Note that the increased profits of the acquiring firm do not mean that the acquisition is more profitably run, or that transaction costs have been saved, only that its profits have been appropriated, that is, assumed by the acquiring firm. (This is important in judging efficiency questions; increased profits or rates of profit after acquisi-

tion do not necessarily mean more efficiency; they can mean less competitive pricing and tax advantages.)

There are many highly profitable small firms that are not targets for acquisition. They can exist where there are small or localized markets. For example, the market for specialized luxury goods is small. The market for ethnic goods or foods is generally localized. Some items have small markets because they are unique or idiosyncratic. We speak of such markets as "niches," small crevices in the economy where a few producers can make a lot of money, but the demand is fairly inelastic (it won't grow much because it is so specialized), thus there is no possibility for increased market control (too small a market) or expanding the market. The large firm has no interest in such firms; though the rate of profit in some niches is large, its absolute amount can be small; additionally, its absolute amount must be great enough to offset the substantial costs of integrating small, diverse businesses into a large firm. Acquisitions are not costless; there are transaction costs and organizational redesign costs, as illustrated in the case of the ACE firm.

Industries need not be forever unprofitable or fragmented into niches. In the nineteenth century the modest profits of the hundreds of small flour mills hardly made them a target for acquisitions, because they sold to middlemen and grocers who dumped the flour into a bin labeled "flour." By promoting branded flour through advertising ("as pure as the drifted snow") market control was achieved and a few large milling companies soon dominated the industry and still do. Much the same thing has happened with restaurants serving limited, quickly prepared meals, though here we must admit the importance of organizational efficiencies including reduced transaction costs. Small restaurants always existed, and were mom-and-pop operations requiring long hours and generating low profits. As the demand for quick meals out increased, heavily advertised chains moved in and took over the market. By combining the advantages of centralized control with nominal local ownership, they have been able to reap the advantages of low-paid local labor with high turnover, and nominal owners who work the long hours of mom and pop. Centralized buying, heavy advertising, and rigid procedures have no doubt contributed to the profitability of these chains, so in this one case we might say that profits may stem from efficiencies, including centralized control of transactions costs.

In addition to market control and acquiring profitable investments, financial "manipulation" plays a role in mergers. In some cases the profit rate of acquired subsidiaries will actually decline after the merger, but capital accumulation by investors and officers through financial manipulations, rather than firm profit, is then the goal. This occurred when U.S. Steel was formed by buying up many steel firms. Much money was made through issues of watered stock, making it a very profitable move for the investors, even though operating efficiencies declined. The decline was offset by enormous market power by the new combine. Today, stock manipulation, appropriation of cash flows (milking the profitable acquisition without reinvestment), and buying footholds in new markets figure prominently in merger and acquisition strategies, so prominently that it has become a national scandal. Lower transaction costs presumably play no role in these manipulations; indeed, transaction costs are greatly increased, but fortunes are made anyway.[26]

Though it is somewhat less apparent today because of the weakness of unions, control of labor has also been a motivation for acquisitions, resulting in increased profits though no increase in production efficiency. Acquiring facilities in low-wage areas; acquiring non-union facilities and using this as a means of attacking the unions in the existing facilities; and absorbing a sufficient proportion of the local work force to be able to control local wage rates are some of the tactics.

The creation of large, market-dominating firms also requires the acquiescence of the federal government. Large firms flourish in the national defense industry because the government favors them for military defense reasons. In fact, such firms are occasionally "bailed out" by awarding handsome government contracts because letting them go under would remove resources the government feels we need. One does not start up a giant aircraft and missile firm easily or quickly. Their "efficiency" is of secondary importance.[27] State banking laws have restricted the centralization of banking in the United States; a change in laws could produce a movement towards "hierarchy" that would not be caused by transaction costs efficiencies, but rather, market control and the acquisition of profitable properties. Thus, the absence of federal enabling actions will help account for the persistence of markets.

A final concern that can lead to the persistence of at least some degree of market phenomena rather than very high concentration ratios in an industry is a recognition that some degree of loose coupling is efficient. This appears to be the reason why the big three automobile companies control, but do not own, their distributors.[28] Though the manufacturing of autos is highly concentrated, the distribution system appears to be a market with many small dealers. But I would count this as a "controlled market"; the manufacturers exercise great control over it. The retail dealers sign long-term contracts that govern the number and type of cars they are *allowed* to receive (a problem when a model turns out to be a "hot" seller and the contract cannot be revised), and the number and type of cars they *must* receive (a problem for disposing of the poor sellers, the "dogs"). These long-term contracts favor the seller. Contracts also cover how much of the cost of failures the dealer must bear under the warranty, how much they can charge for repairs in some cases, how much advertising they must do and so on. The dealer has discretion only on trade-in prices or preparation prices or other deals that make the final selling price somewhat flexible. Otherwise, the dealer is quite constrained; indeed, the manufacturer may unilaterally and without warning raise the wholesale price to the dealer without posting a higher retail price, thus cutting the dealer's rate of profit. The argument is sometimes made that car dealers represent flexible adaptations to local markets, and thus are more efficient than if owned and controlled outright by the manufacturers. This does not appear to be so; they cannot order just the makes and volume they wish, the prices can be changed, warranty work is tightly regulated by complex contracts written by the manufacturer, and advertising is regulated. They can be flexible and adaptive only in their used-car line.

The effect of this is to require the dealers to absorb the market declines (they have to cut their profit to get rid of the quota of cars they must buy) even though they cannot fully participate in market rises (they cannot get all the hot selling models they want). Cost of entry is not large for them, but as small businesspeople they do invest their own capital. They are forced to ride out poor times making little or no profit. A few dealerships do very well indeed, but most do not. Yet there are always small businesspeople willing to take the risk. Thus, the manufacturers are buffered from fluctuations in the market for cars and from the yearly gamble on model changes and new models. Because the profitability of dealerships overall is only modest and subject to much uncertainty, it is not worthwhile for the manufacturers to integrate forward into a business over which they already have considerable control.

While we have many dealer firms, we really have a controlled market with many small firms rather than either a hierarchy or a market. Most franchises, as in fast foods, are devices to spread risks and buffer the headquarters from uncertainties. Given the limited occasions for entrepreneurship in our economy for people without wealth or highly unique skills, there are always many who are willing to work very hard for low and risky returns. Though controlled, they have more autonomy than employees of large corporations.

Thus, we would expect to find small firms persisting in areas of the economy that show low overall industry profitability (unless the industry can be restructured to promote branded products or other forms of market control—there is always a drive to do that); where there are idiosyncratic factors despite high profits (local markets, niches); where the market cannot grow despite profitability (inelastic demand); or where government restrictions obtain. Finally, hierarchies are probably self-limiting; at some point, which varies according to technologies, capital requirements, and the shape of the market, firms probably lose control over some of their subsidiaries and the complex, internal interactions, and the ability to respond to external shocks, and lose out. The subsidiaries are sold off, or their efficiency declines to the point where they lose money despite substantial market control and other advantages of size, and someone else moves in. Some minimal efficiency *is* necessary of course, but transaction costs rarely play a significant role.

This brief sketch of some of the forces contributing to hierarchy and economic concentration in our society stands in marked contrast to economic motives of efficiency in the face of opportunism and transaction costs. It is neither original or novel, but suggests the range of structural variables that are neglected by economic interpretations of organizational behavior.[29]

BEYOND MARKETS AND HIERARCHY

The distinction between markets and hierarchies is an old one in economics, though Williamson has given it new life. It is a useful one because it frames questions we might not otherwise ask. But there is increasing evidence that this formulation hides as much as it reveals. Scholars are beginning to note that some markets are quite hierarchically organized, and that some hierarchies have many phenomena associated with markets. This suggests that we might abandon the distinction for some purposes and seek other ways to characterize interdependent behavior within and between organizations, or even to attack, once again, the recalcitrant conceptual problem of boundaries—what is the boundary between a supplier and a customer, the government and a firm, or between two industries. Rapid industrial change since the 1950s has made these questions pressing. I cannot even suggest answers to the problem of characterizing interdependencies and questioning formal definitions of boundaries here, but only conclude by mentioning some of the more interesting research that raises these questions. To a considerable degree this research and theorizing has either been stimulated by Williamson's work, or at least posed as a critique of it. It is one of the reasons we should be thankful for TCE. The general point is that large firms may be so large as to operate like markets, and markets appear to be hierarchically, diagonally and horizontally so organized as to make the notion of independent, autonomous price givers and takers questionable. These "markets" may be governed by forces that most economists would not recognize as plausible.

A striking piece by Ronald Dore, a British sociologist familiar with Japanese history and industry, argues that Japanese industry is more efficient, over all, because the contracting involves a significant degree of goodwill, give-and-take, long-term horizons, and in general, an avoidance of opportunism. The classical market of economists is only efficient in allocating goods (if that). Citing the work of renegade economist Harvey Liebenstein for support, Dore argues that there are a number of efficiencies other than allocating goods that are more important, and they are realized by trust, non-competitive relations, and mutual assistance in time of need. These other efficiencies include rapid spread of innovation; shared information on changing market situations and consumer choices; aggressive search for new uses of labor and capital if old markets decline; flexibility in task assignments; and the disaggregation of industry when desirable (for example, he cites the move from hierarchy to small firms in the textile industry in Japan). Finally, he questions whether this is necessarily a product of Japanese culture; much more cut-throat, self-interested practices prevailed *in Japan* during the 1920s and again immediately after World War II. He also finds evidence for goodwill and suspension of self-interest in the United States and England, especially in industries or in firms noted for their emphasis upon quality, rather than quantity. There is a mine of research projects in this attractive essay.[30]

Arthur Stinchcombe considers several industries such as defense contracting, large civil engineering firms, and franchise networks, noting how their relations with their customers tend to be hierarchically organized, even though these would seem to be examples of markets.[31] In defense contracting the Department of Defense is very intimate with the contractors, putting inspectors and accountants in their firms, much as a multidivisional corporation puts inspectors and accountants into each of its divisions. This is true of consumer-goods industries too. Chevrolet treats it supposedly independent suppliers almost as profit centers and risk bearers, controlling much of what they do. On the other hand, hierarchies develop profit centers and divisions that bargain with each other and the main office in a market-like arrangement, encountering the large costs of simulating a market with "shadow prices" and numerous complex accounting practices that simulate a market relationship.

Harrison White argues, in a suggestive paper that blurs the distinction between markets and hierarchy, that the principal-agent model is misleading. He describes the principal-agent relationship as a reflexive one that oscillates, dissolves, and is born again, making it difficult and arbitrary to designate who is agent and who is principal. Ranging from the ancient Roman empire to high-technology industries, it is an effective though not very explicit criticism of TCE.[32] More generally, I think the interdependencies among economic units and among principles and agents should be analyzed in terms of such contextual influences that I argued will influence the degree of self-regarding and other-regarding behavior that is encouraged—such contexts as the length and durability of relationships, the distribution or centralized storage of surpluses, calculation of group efforts, rotation of authority, and extent of surveillance.

Sociologists and other organizational theorists are positioned to explore these problems because they embrace a more system-wide viewpoint than economists, with attendant developments in network theory, evolutionary models, and attention to the environment in general. Their work is not disabled by assumptions of rational or primarily self-interested behavior, but look at the contexts that call out rational, nonrational, self-regarding, and other-regarding behavior. This broader inquiry is, in part occasioned by the challenge that economists have presented by their foray into the world of organizations, a challenge that resembles the theme of the novel and movie *The Invasion of the Body-Snatchers*, where human forms are retained but all that we value about human behavior—

its spontaneity, unpredictability, selflessness, plurality of values, reciprocal influence, and resentment of domination—has disappeared.

ACKNOWLEDGMENTS

This article draws heavily on chapter 7 of the third edition of my book *Complex Organizations: A Critical Essay* (New York: Random House, 1986), where the issues are discussed at somewhat greater length.

NOTES

1. My primary sources for agency theory are Armen A. Alchian and Harold Demsetz, "Production, Information Cost, and Economic Organization," *American Economic Review*, 1972, 777-95, 795; Eugene F. Fama, "Agency Problems and the Theory of the Firm," *Journal of Political Economy* 88, 1980, 288-305; Eugene Fama and Michael Jensen, "Separation of Ownership and Control," *Journal of Law and Economics* 26 (June 1983), 301-25, and Michael Jensen and William Meckling, "Theory of the Firm: Managerial Behavior, Agency Costs, and Ownership Structure," *Journal of Financial Economics* 3, October 1976, 305-360, 309. The best exposition of the theory I have seen is by political scientist Terry Moe, "The New Economics of Organization," *American Journal of Political Science*, 28:4, November 1984, 739-77, 741.

2. Mancur Olson Jr., *The Logic of Collective Action*, revised edition, (New York: Schocken Books, 1971).

3. Alcian and Demsetz, "Production." I have elaborated their example.

4. James March and Herbert Simon, *Organizations*, (New York: Wiley, 1958). I have discussed bounded rationality and its link to domination in Charles Perrow, *Complex Organizations: A Critical Essay*, third edition, (New York: Random House, 1986), chapter 4.

5. See the review of Terry Moe, "The New Economics."

6. Louis Putterman "On Some Recent Explanations of Why Capital Hires Labor," *Economic Inquiry* 33, April 1984, 171-87.

7. For the popularity of agency theory see Moe, "The New Economics"; for the popularity of closely related transaction-cost economics see William Ouchi, "Markets, Bureaucracies and Clans," *Administrative Science Quar-*

terly, 25, March, 1980, 129–41. Citations to both theories are mounting in the journals, such as *Administrative Science Quarterly,* and books discussing them are appearing, e.g. Arthur Francis, Jeremy Turk, and Paul Willman, eds., *Power, Efficiency and Institutions,* (London: Heinemann, 1983).

8. For a discussion of human relations, bureaucratic, and neo-Weberian theories see chapters 1, 3, and 4 of Perrow, *Complex Organizations.*

9. Rothschild-Witt, Joyce, "The Collectivist Organization: An Alternative to Rational Bureaucratic Models," *American Sociological Review,* 44, 1979, 509–27; Rosabeth Kanter, *The Change Masters,* New York: Simon and Schuster, 1983; Branko Horvat, *The Political Economy of Socialism,* 1982.

10. The basic work is Oliver Williamson, *Markets and Hierarchies: Analysis and Antitrust Implications,* (New York: The Free Press, 1975). A new volume under preparation by Williamson incorporates more organizational and sociological variables, and attacks a wide range of problems from the markets and hierarchies viewpoint.

11. Oliver Williamson, "Organizational Innovation: The Transaction-cost Approach," in J. Ronen, ed., *Entrepreneurship,* (Lexington, Mass.: Heath Lexington, 1983), 101–34. Quote from 125.

12. Ibid., 125.

13. Mark Granovetter, "Economic Action and Social Structure, and Mark Granovetter, "Labor Mobility, Internal Markets and Job Matching: A Comparison of the Sociological and Economic Approaches," both unpublished manuscripts, (Department of Sociology, State University of New York at Stony Brook, n.d.). The first was published in a shorter version that suffers from strict copyediting in *American Journal of Sociology* 91:3, November 1985, 481–510.

14. Alfred D. Chandler, *The Visible Hand: The Managerial Revolution in American Business,* (Cambridge, Mass.: Harvard University Press, 1977).

15. Robert G. Eccles, "Control with Fairness in Transfer Pricing," *Harvard Business Review,* November-December 1983, 149–61, and "Transfer Pricing as a Problem of Agency," unpublished manuscript, (Harvard Business School, February 1984), and *The Transfer Pricing Problem: A Theory for Practice,* (Boston: Lexington Books, 1984).

16. Olivier Williamson and William Ouchi, "A Rejoinder," in Andrew Van de Ven and William Joyce, eds., *Perspectives on Organization Design and Behavior,* (New York: Wiley Interscience, 1981), 390.

17. Paul J. DiMaggio and Walter W. Powell, "The Iron Cage Revisited: Institutional Isomorphism and Collective Rationality in Organizational Fields," *American Sociological Review,* 48, 1983, 147–60.

18. Charles Perrow, "Markets, Hierarchies and Hegemony: A Critique of Chandler and Williamson," in Van de Ven and Joyce, *Perspectives,* 371–86, 403–404.

19. Williamson, *Markets and Hierarchies,* chapter 7. In a new work, The Economic Institutions of Capitalism (New York: The Free Press, 1985), he emphasizes this even more. Because transactions costs have not been operationalized, which would make measurement possible, the fundamental issue of whether they are higher between firms or higher within them will probably never be settled. See my comments on this issue in "Markets, Hierarchies and Hegemony: A Critique of Chandler and Williamson," in Van de Ven and Joyce, *Perspectives,* 371–86.

20. Horvat, *Political Economy.*

21. Perrow, Charles, *Normal Accidents: Living with High Risk Technologies,* (Basic Books, 1984), chapters 3, 9.

22. Perrow, Charles, *Complex Organizations,* chapter 6.

23. See the discussion in Perrow, "Markets, Hierarchies and Hegemony" in Van de Ven and Joyce, *Perspectives.*

24. J.H. Bridges, *The Inside History of the Carnegie Steel Company,* (New York: Aldine Press, 1903), 135, 168, passim. For a survey of industries and their history of aggressive market control written by industrial economists — a breed apart from the "new institutional economists" we are dealing with and ignored by the latter — see: Adams, Walter, and Scherer, *Industrial Market Structure and Economic Performance,* second ed., 1980, especially chapter 6.

25. Yago, Glen, *The Decline of Transit,* (Cambridge, Mass.: Cambridge University Press, 1983).

26. While it is not conclusive, the evidence on the performance of acquired units should induce skepticism regarding the efficiency of acquisition policies. Birch followed 6,400 firms that were acquired during 1972–1974, and compared their before and after growth rates with the 1.3 million firms that were not acquired. He found that, in Rothschild-Witt's summary, "conglomerates tend to acquire fast-growing, profitable, well-managed businesses, contrary to the theory that they seek out poorly-managed, inefficient firms," that is, those that might have, among other things, high transaction costs internally or with the environment. However, growth is not speeded up after the acquisition; in fact, "firms that remain independent grow faster than acquired firms." A congressional study found that firms that were acquired

subsequently had lower rates of job creation, productivity, and innovation. David Birch, "The Job Creation Process," (Cambridge, Mass.: MIT Program on Neighborhood Regional Change, 1979). See also, Committee on Small Business, U.S. House Representatives, "Conglomerate Mergers—Their Effects on Small Business and Local Communities," (Washington D.C.: U.S. Government Printing Office (House Document No. 96–343), October 2, 1980). Both are discussed in Rothschild-Witt, Joyce, "Worker Ownership: Collective Response to an Elite-Generated Crisis," *Research in Social Movements, Conflict and Change*, 6, 1984, JAI Press, 67–94, a sobering, informative review of worker-ownership developments.

27. Seymour Melman, *Pentagon Capitalism: The Political Economy of War*, (New York: McGraw Hill Book Co., 1970).

28. Kenneth McNeil and Richard Miller, "The Profitability of Consumer Practices Warranty Policies in the Auto Industry," *Administrative Science Quarterly*, 25, 1980, 407–26; and J. Patrick Wright, *On A Clear Day You Can See General Motors*, (New York: Avon Books, 1979), and Harvey Farberman, "Criminogenic Market Structures: The Auto Industry," *Sociological Quarterly*, 16, 1975, 438–57.

29. There are other criticisms of Williamson's work, and the related work of Alfred Chandler. Williamson explored the early history of capitalism, arguing that hierarchies proved to be more efficient than cooperatives and inside contracting, but the economic historian S.R.H. Jones wrote a devastating critique of Williamson's evidence and interpretation. Richard DuBoff, a historian, and Edward Herman, an economist, reviewed the work of Chandler very critically, presenting evidence that the emergence of several of the hierarchies Chandler described had much more to do with market power than coordinating efficiencies (and I have made a similar criticism with more modest evidence). In a volume devoted to Williamson's work, Arthur Francis has a perceptive essay on the issue of efficiency versus market power. See S.R.H. Jones, "The Organization of Work; A Historical Dimension," *Journal of Economic Behavior and Organization*, 3:2–3, 1982, 117–37, replying to Oliver Williamson, "The Organization of Work: A Comparative Institutional Assessment," *Journal of Economic Behavior and Organization*, 1, 1980, 5–38 (with a further exchange in volume 4, 57–68). Richard B. Du Boff and Edward S. Herman, "Alfred Chandler's New Business History: A Review," *Politics and Society* 10:1, 1980, 87–110, and Perrow, "Markets, Hierarchies and Hegemony" in Van de Ven and Joyce, *Perspectives*; Arthur Francis, "Markets and Hierarchies: Efficiency or Domination?" in Arthur Francis, Jeremy Turk, and Paul Willman, eds., *Power, Efficiency and Institutions*, (London: Heineman, 1983), 105–116.

30. Ronald Dore, "Goodwill and the Spirit of Market Capitalism," *British Journal of Sociology*, 34 December, 1983, 459–82. Harvey Liebenstein, *Beyond Economic Man: A New Foundation for Microeconomics*, Cambridge Mass.: Harvard University Press, 1976.

31. Arthur Stinchcombe, "Contracts as Hierarchical Documents," Work Report 65, Institute of Industrial Economics, (Bergen, 1984).

32. Harrison White, "Agency as Control," unpub., (Cambridge, Mass.: Harvard University, 1983), and Robert G. Eccles and Harrison White, "Firm and Market Interfaces of Profit Center Control", unpub., (Cambridge, Mass.: Harvard University, February 1984). See also, for an industry study, W. Graham Astley and Charles J. Fombrun, "Technological Innovation and Industrial Structure: The Case of Tele-Communications," in *Advances in Strategic Management* 1, 205–29, 1983, JAI Press. See also the interesting discussion of industrial markets in Sweden, developing the notion of heterogenous markets, in contrast to homogenous ones found in neoclassical economic theory, and of "nets," those parts of the industrial "network" where strong complementary pervails, in Ingemund Hagg and Jan Johanson, *Firms in Networks—New Perspectives on Competitive Power*, (Stockholm, Sweden: Business and Social Research Institute, September, 1983).

II

Special Issues

10

Toward a Definition of Insider Trading

Iman Anabtawi*

The law governing insider trading is unclear and controversial. The legal confusion surrounding insider trading results from the absence of either case law or statutory specification of a clear theory on which to base insider liability. Commentators, the Securities and Exchange Commission ("SEC"), and courts have relied on inconsistent articulations of who should be barred from trading, and Congress has given only limited consideration to legislative proposals to define insider trading. The economic impact of a law against insider trading is also unsettled. Law and economics articles differ sharply over whether it is desirable to place a prohibition on insider activity and over what form any such rule should take.

This note provides a coherent theoretical framework, grounded in efficiency analysis, for administrative, legislative, and judicial decision-makers to use in developing insider trading law. Part I of the note discusses the economic relevance of the allocation of initial property rights to firm-specific information

Third year student, Stanford Law School.

and describes the placement of these rights under existing law. Part II considers alternative perspectives that might be used to choose an appropriate insider trading rule. Part III presents an efficiency rationale for prohibiting various market participants from trading on material, nonpublic information. Part IV offers guidance for fashioning a definition of insider trading consistent with the results of the note's analysis and raises questions for further study.

I. THE LAW AND ECONOMICS OF INSIDER TRADING

A. The Economic Relevance of the Law Governing Insider Trading

Traders on public securities markets have asymmetric access to firm-specific information that potentially affects share prices. At one end of the trading information spectrum are corporate insiders—directors, officers, and employees—who are the first tier of people to receive firm-specific information as it is

151

disseminated. At the opposite end are market participants who trade on the basis of factors unrelated to firm-specific information, such as where their darts strike the financial pages. At interim points along the spectrum are market analysts and the confidants and tippees of insiders.

The determination of where on the spectrum the law should draw the prohibitive insider trading line involves a choice of where the law should, in the first instance, place property rights to valuable information. Absent transaction costs associated with rearranging property rights, it does not matter where the law initially allocates property rights to valuable information because interested parties will reallocate those rights until they exhaust gains from trade available from such reallocation. If, however, transaction costs are significant, the initial allocation of rights is important because transaction costs will prevent the market from shifting the property rights to their most efficient position or, at least, make shifting costly.

If the transaction costs of moving from one allocation to another are symmetric and non-zero, then it is efficient to place the property right where the market most often would have placed it absent transaction costs. This placement automatically minimizes the sum of expected transaction costs from shifting the property right and lost gains from trade from failures to shift it where the transaction costs of shifting would have exceeded the expected benefits of the shift. If transaction costs are asymmetric, it may be efficient to place the property right to inside information where fewer parties prefer it if the costs of shifting into that placement are sufficiently high. In this case, the total costs of foregone efficient shifting into the less popular position would overwhelm the total transaction costs of shifting into the more popular position. If transaction costs are asymmetric, efficient allocation would therefore place the property right so as to minimize the sum of (i) the expected transaction costs of reallocating the property right away from its initial placement in cases where such reallocation is efficient and (ii) the expected costs of foregone shifting when transaction costs exceed the expected benefits of the shift.

Regardless of where the law places the property right to valuable information, it is reasonable to assume that there will be some shifting out of the position by right-holders who do not value their right to trade on inside information as highly as certain non-right-holders. Specifically, if the chosen legal rule on insider trading bans trading by some classes of information traders, individuals who hold rights of action against insiders may prefer to contract away those rights to insiders. For example, shareholders with limited technical knowledge about the firm may choose to give up their rights to prevent managers from insider trading in exchange for reducing managers' salaried compensation. The transaction costs of reassigning rights to information would include identifying parties with rights of action against insiders, negotiating agreements with management that would trade off, for example, salaried compensation for insider trading rights, and drawing up contractual agreements to submit to shareholder vote. Alternatively, if insider trading is not banned, individuals could contract to ban it in situations where they feel they can appropriate gains from trade from doing so. In either case, the efficient initial legal placement of the right to trade on inside information will be at the point where we anticipate that total *ex ante* transaction costs will be lower. This determination will depend on the magnitude of the costs of reallocating and the volume of expected reallocations away from the initial placement.

The costs of reallocating property rights to inside information may be significant enough to prevent parties from shifting the rights when it would otherwise be mutually beneficial for them to do so. Because reallocation in one direction or the other involves similar contractual arrangements, minimizing the costs of a misallocation in the initial placement of the property rights involves an inquiry into the position out of which parties will least often want to shift. Even if transaction costs were low, the legal system's placement of the property right to information would be economically relevant because the benefits associated with shifting the right to its most efficient position accrue to society generally through, for example, second-round effects of increases in aggregate wealth such as greater consumer spending. By permitting only parties with private rights of action against insiders to negotiate to reallocate property rights to information, the rights may be allocated inefficiently. Allowing society as a whole, however, to register its preferences by negotiating property rights would not be feasible. This difficulty provides another argument for using a legal rule to place the property right to inside information in its most efficient position.

B. The Law Governing Insider Trading

The legal framework governing insider trading is the product of federal statutory and case law. The definition of insider trading liability within this framework has, however, been developed inconsistently and without rigorous investigation of the impact on market efficiency of trading by various categories of information traders.

The first source of insider trading regulation is section 16 of the Securities Exchange Act of 1934, which imposes trading restrictions on directors, officers, and 10 percent owners of any class of equity securities. These statutory insiders must report to the SEC their registered equity holdings and their monthly positional changes. Section 16 additionally prohibits these insiders from selling short and entitles the issuer of the traded

stock to sue to recover any profit the insiders earned through a sale-purchase or purchase-sale transaction in any six-month period. These restrictions apply to section 16 insiders regardless of whether they base their trades on access to material nonpublic information.

The second source of regulation of insider trading is section 10(b) of the Securities Exchange Act of 1934. Implemented by rule 10b-5, this section is the general "catch-all" prohibition of fraudulent activity under which insider trading cases are most often brought. Under rule 10b-5, an insider must disclose material inside information or refrain from trading on the basis of it. The major challenge that courts have faced in applying rule 10b-5 has been determining who is an insider. Under current doctrine, traders do not incur insider trading liability merely because they hold an informational advantage. The Supreme Court in *Chiarella v. United States* specifically rejected such a "parity of information" doctrine, under which those in the market with superior information about a stock must disclose it or refrain from trading on it. Instead, the Court limited the application of the "disclose or refrain" provision of rule 10b-5 to situations in which the trader is someone in whom the party alleging harm placed trust and confidence or in which the trader is an agent or a fiduciary of the complaining party.

Insider liability under rule 10b-5 is therefore premised on a duty to disclose or refrain from trading arising from a relationship of trust and confidence between the trader and the shareholders of the stock in which she trades. This reading of rule 10b-5 reaches anyone under a duty to place shareholder welfare before her own, such as corporate insiders and employees. It also applies to those working for a firm, such as attorneys, accountants, or consultants, whom the company retains as its agents and in whom it places trust and confidence. Finally, in *Dirk v. SEC*, the Supreme Court held that tippees of rule 10b-5 insiders may be liable for insider trading. Such liability arises when a tippee trades on inside information provided by an insider with an improper motive and when the tippee knows or has reason to know that the insider has done so. Improper motives usually involve an insider's desire to profit through the trades of a tippee.

The SEC has promulgated an extension of rule 10b-5 liability under the "misappropriation theory." Under this theory, on which an eight-member Supreme Court has split evenly, one who misappropriates material nonpublic information in breach of a duty arising out of a relationship of trust and confidence and who uses that information in a securities transaction is liable for insider trading. In other words, the misappropriation would be considered fraud on the rightful possessor of the information and would apply whether or not the trader owed a duty to shareholders of the traded stock. *Carpenter v. United States* provides an example of such misappropriation. Winans, a *Wall Street Journal* reporter, provided stockbrokers with information that was to appear in his forthcoming "Heard on the Street" columns. Under the misappropriation theory, Winans breached a duty to his employer, the *Wall Street Journal*, by revealing information which was the property of the newspaper.

The final federal proscription of insider activity is SEC rule 14e-3. This rule makes it illegal to trade on the basis of material nonpublic information of a tender offer if knowledge of the offer comes from the offering party, the issuer of the securities, or any officer, director, partner, or employee of either the offering person or the issuer. Under this rule, it is illegal, for example, for a tippee of a bidder to trade in either the bidder's or the target's stock even if the tippee owes no fiduciary duty to the shareholders of the target company and regardless of the motive of the tipper. Rule 14e-3 is based on the Commission's view that trading by persons in possession of material nonpublic information relating to a tender offer results in unfair disparities in market information and market disruption.

II. A FRAMEWORK FOR ANALYSIS

Insider trading law affects both market efficiency and the distribution of potential profits from trading. Yet, in defining the scope of insider liability, the law has developed without solid foundations in either efficiency or equity theory. This note offers a coherent account, under plausible, specified assumptions, of the impact on market efficiency of trading by various categories of information traders. By adopting a legal rule that improves efficiency, it is possible to arrive at allocations which improve one party's welfare at no expense to the welfare of any other party. In contrast, distributional adjustments merely transfer wealth from one party to another. From a distributional standpoint, the universe of shareholders in the market suffers no direct losses from insider activity. All gains or losses that might have been made by one market player in the absence of insider trading are simply transferred to another market player in the presence of insider trading.

To illustrate the distributional impact of alternative rules for insider activity, it is useful to distinguish among four classes of traders in the market: (1) insiders; (2) uninformed outsiders, who trade randomly; (3) firm-specific analysts, who study financial data and market prospects of selected companies; and (4) analysts who watch insiders. Figures 1 and 2 represent share price paths of Company X, a publicly traded company that will be the target of a tender offer. Let t denote time; let A denote the price at which the market values each share of Company X in the absence of any knowledge of the forthcoming tender offer; and let B denote the price at which the market values each share of Company X with knowledge of the offer. Suppose that at time $t = 0$ only the insider knows of a tender offer for the shares of Company X and that the offer will be announced publicly at time $t = 1$. Then, in the interval $t[0,1]$, there would accrue to Company X shareholders a windfall of B-A. If our four types of traders trade in shares of Company X, the way in which the windfall is distributed will depend on the share price path over the interval. This path is, in turn, determined by the rule governing insider trading over the period.

Consider first the distribution of shareholder gain under an insider trading rule that adopts a pure parity of information theory, defining insider trading as any trading on the basis of any nonpublic information. A person privy to any nonpublic information would therefore be required to disclose the information or refrain from trading. In a world where this rule is perfectly enforced, analysts would fall within the class of persons required to disclose or refrain from trading, and no research would be done because analysts would be unable to earn any return from their investments in information gathering. Corporate insiders would similarly not be permitted to trade. The price path under parity with complete enforcement can therefore be drawn as in Figure 1. Random net buyers over the interval would gain exactly the foregone windfall profits of random net sellers. In a world of imperfect enforcement, insiders and analysts could earn a return from their informational advantage. These traders would, however, have to conceal themselves among traders without superior information in order to avoid detection through suspicious volumes or price effects of their transactions which might occur through signaling. Over the interval $t[0,1]$, insiders, analysts and random net buyers would capture the windfall from net sellers.

Moving from a parity of information rule to the present law changes the distribution of the windfall accruing to shareholders of Company X as a result of a tender offer for the company. Because present law does not mandate parity of information among market players, analysts may legitimately and profitably trade on the information they gather and on their analysis of that information. In comparison with a parity rule, under the present law the price path over the interval $t[0,1]$, holding constant all events other than the dissemination of knowledge of the tender offer at time $t = 1$, changes. Empirical studies of share price movements of target firms have found that the targets' daily share prices increase monotonically in the days preceding the announcement of the offer. This suggests that the price path under present law can be drawn as in Figure 2.

Under the altered price path shown in Figure 2, the distribution of the windfall changes from that of pure parity scenario. Random buyers lose because they pay H at time $t = .5$ rather then the A they pay under parity. Ran-

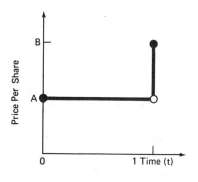

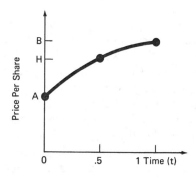

dom sellers gain because they receive H rather than A. Insider traders must now pay more to buy each share, but they can buy more while still concealing their trades because they can now conceal themselves among analysts as well. Thus, analysts and information traders might either be better or worse off under less stringent laws. The important point is that, net of efficiency effects, a change in the legal rule alters only the distribution of the windfall, not its size.

The specification of a legal rule affects not only the way in which wealth is distributed but also the aggregate amount of wealth available for distribution. An allocatively efficient legal rule is one under which no gains from trade can be obtained from any reallocation of the rights involved. This note adopts an efficiency approach to determining where the law should in the first instance place the property right to inside information because a distributional approach to the making of a legal rule will not necessarily generate a rule that maximizes the aggregate level of wealth available to society (that is, that exhausts gains available from trading rights to valuable information). Once an efficient legal rule is specified, distributional theorists may, through taxes and transfers, reallocate wealth in accordance with some normative social theory.

III. AN EFFICIENCY RATIONALE FOR PROHIBITING INSIDER TRADING

The economic argument for or against insider trading hinges on efficiently allocating property rights to information—that is, on allocating them where the transaction costs of reallocating them are minimal. Giving managers the right to trade on inside information is likely to be inefficient for three reasons: It leaves risk on risk averse individuals; it leads to perverse incentive effects on man-

agers; and it creates a problem of adverse selection in that it will attract managers who are more likely to manipulate company resources for their own, rather than for shareholder, welfare. In contrast, insider trading may move prices toward their true values faster than they could otherwise arrive there and may reduce expenditures of market participants on information gathering. This section develops and assesses the strengths of these opposing effects.

A. Principal-Agent Relationships in the Context of the Separation of Ownership and Control

In a principal-agent relationship, one party, the principal, stands to benefit from the activity of the other party, the agent. Agency problems arise whenever principals delegate to agents responsibility for taking actions that cannot be perfectly observed and which affect the utility of the two groups in different ways. If the principal could costlessly monitor the agent's actions, she could relate compensation directly to those actions. When the principal cannot costlessly observe the actions taken by the agent, the problem of moral hazard arises. The agent has a self interest in taking actions which fail to maximize the utility of the principal, and the principal cannot enforce the optimal contract because she cannot verify *ex post* the agent's actions. The consequent problem is to design a compensation contract which provides the agent with incentives that maximize the principal's utility, subject to the constraint that it is costly to monitor the agent's actions.

In a context where shareholders of a firm are viewed as principals and managers as agents, where the actions of the agents are defined in terms of the effort they invest in maximizing expected company profits, and where monitoring of effort is costly, moral hazard arises because the incentives of managers and shareholders are imperfectly aligned. The level of managerial effort affects the utility of both managers and shareholders. Shareholders' utility depends positively on expected profits, which, in turn, depend positively on managerial effort. Managers are also interested in increased profits because profits are signals to shareholders of managerial performance. Managerial utility depends, however, not only positively on company profits but also negatively on the costs of expending effort. Because shareholders cannot costlessly monitor managers in order to distinguish between profit changes that result from managerial behavior and those that result from random, firm-specific shocks, shareholders face the hazard that managers will fail to maximize shareholder wealth.

Detractors of prohibitions against insider trading have seized on the compensation issue to argue that placing the property right to inside information with managers is a solution to the principal-agent problem between managers and shareholders. Inclusion of a property right to inside information in a management compensation contract is, however, unlikely to lead to an efficient fee schedule for three reasons. First, under plausible assumptions about the relative risk preferences of shareholders and managers, insider trading by managers leaves uncaptured gains from trade which can be generated through reallocating from managers to shareholders the risk associated with the returns from insider trading. Second, allowing insider trading by managers affects managerial conduct, leading to perverse incentive effects which exacerbate the problem of moral hazard that shareholders face. Finally, the presence of insider trading rights in managerial compensation contracts creates an adverse selection problem for shareholders: The more heavily a compensation scheme depends on remuneration through insider trading, the larger will be the proportion of prospective managers in any given pool of applicants for management positions who will manipulate company re-

sources for their own, rather than for shareholder, welfare. The remainder of this section analyzes each of these effects separately and shows that they reinforce each other in demonstrating the efficiency losses that result from using insider trading as an element of a managerial compensation scheme.

1. Efficient Risk Bearing and Gains from Trade in the Presence of Costly Monitoring.
The relative risk preferences of managers and shareholders are one determinant of the efficient allocation of risk between the two groups. Harris and Raviv have shown that in the standard principal-agent model, where the agent's effort is unobservable, first best incentives for managers are achieved if the agent is risk neutral and all risk relating to compensation is allocated to the agent. If, however, the agent is risk averse, the optimal contract leaves some risk with the principal.

The proposition that there are gains from trade to be realized from withholding insider trading rights from managerial compensation packages depends on three assumptions. First, it requires that shareholders be less risk averse than managers. If this were not true, shifting risk toward shareholders would involve a devaluation of the property right relative to its former allocation. Second, it requires that shareholders be able for some time interval to assert a valuable property interest over inside information that is not retained by managers. If shareholders could not appropriate gains from possessing the information, because, say, market analysts are quicker than shareholders to exploit information when managers are prohibited from fully exhausting trading profits based on the information, then shareholders would not attach value to the property right to the information. Although the market analysts in this example would attach value to banning insider trading by managers, their potential gains from such an arrangement are likely to be too uncertain and too widely dispersed to permit them to bribe shareholders to negotiate away their rights of action against managers for insider trading. Third, the proposition requires that gains achieved from shifts in the property right not be fully offset by changes in incentive effects that result from risk reallocation. All three assumptions are plausible.

The assumption that managers are more risk averse than investors is realistic because managers cannot diversify the impact of company profits on their portfolios as easily as can shareholders. On the one hand, shareholders can eliminate much of the risk related to the performance of a particular firm by investing in a variety of corporations or other income-producing opportunities. Managers, on the other hand, have a larger proportion of their wealth in the form of human capital. Thus, managers are more sensitive to the volatility of their compensation than shareholders are to the volatility of their returns.

Defense of the assumption that shareholders can appropriate the trading profits which managers prohibited from insider trading do not capture depends on the distribution of information among the remaining potential traders. The windfall arising from disclosure of what was previously inside information accrues to anyone holding shares over the interval between the time before price begins to rise in response to the undisclosed information and the point of disclosure, at which time price responds fully to the information released. Where managers are permitted to trade on information superior to that of shareholders, shareholders will be systematically disadvantaged when trading the company's stock. On average, shareholders will be net sellers to insiders whenever insiders know of an impending share price rise because insiders will place themselves on the purchasing side of the market. When insiders are eliminated from the market for shares, shareholders no longer face the same informational disadvantage. What then matters is who, next

to corporate insiders, possesses the best knowledge of undisclosed information. Though it is true that market analysts may possess superior analytical ability or prove superior information gatherers than ordinary shareholders, this is not necessarily so. Institutions with sophisticated investment departments comprise a significant percentage of shareholders. Moreover, shareholders have firm-specific interests in the companies whose shares they hold and may follow rumors surrounding the firm as closely as analysts, who have not yet taken positions in the stock. In the absence of rules requiring parity of information, some traders will always be at a relative informational disadvantage. But as long as shareholders know that their effective access to firm-specific information is equal to that of other market players, they will value the exclusion of corporate insiders from the market.

Finally, the assumption that the net gains available from reallocation toward efficient risk bearing offset any incentive benefits from permitting trading by corporate insiders is also realistic. Some argue that it is possible that insider trading by management is so superior an incentive scheme that allocating the property right to management would create gains overwhelming any gains from trade lost because of inefficient risk assignments. This possibility is rejected below.

Under the foregoing assumptions, gains from trade will result from shifting the risk associated with insider trading returns away from managers and toward shareholders. Suppose that the right to trade on inside information is equivalent each year to the right to participate in a fifty-fifty gamble with payoff of $0 or $200. A risk neutral participant would pay up to $100 for the right to the gamble. A risk averse participant would pay less, $90, for example, representing $100 discounted by the risk premium needed to compensate her for the greater risk associated with this form of remuneration compared to a certain $100.

If the risk averse participant begins with the right to the gamble, a transaction in which the risk neutral party buys the right to the gamble for any amount between $90 and $100 will make both parties better off. Analogizing the right to trade on inside information to the gamble, both shareholders and managers can be made better off if shareholders offer managers increased salary in exchange for an agreement by managers to refrain from trading on confidential information.

The presence of costs which shareholders must pay in order to monitor managers who contract to refrain from insider trading complicates the analysis. If monitoring is costless, shareholders will be able to determine whether managers have earned profits from insider trading in breach of their compensation contracts. If, however, shareholders cannot enforce agreements requiring managers to refrain from insider trading, the value of the information to shareholders will be diminished or even eliminated as signaling by manager-insiders drives the share price toward its post-disclosure level, leaving shareholders with little or no opportunity to appropriate profits from their knowledge of a future share price adjustment.

Where monitoring is costless, shareholders will be able to determine perfectly whether managers have earned profits from insider trading. In such a world, the optimal compensation contract will prohibit managers from engaging in insider trading. Risk neutral investors would pay up to $100 for the rights to this future income stream, and risk averse managers would forego it for some amount greater than $90. The exact price at which this transfer would occur will depend on the bargaining strengths of the two groups. The important observation for our purposes is that investors and managers are both better off by $10 — the difference between the $100 that investors are willing to pay and the $90 that managers are willing to accept — because they have agreed to allocate the gains from anticipatory trading to investors rather than to managers.

Monitoring, however, is costly. In the presence of costly monitoring of managerial insider trading activity, a shift from managers to shareholders of the right to trade on inside information will generate gains from trade whose value will be diminished by the monitoring costs required to enforce the contract. This implies that there will be gains from trade that can be profitably captured up to the point at which monitoring costs equal the gains from trade arising from reallocations toward efficient risk bearing.

2. Managerial incentives.

Critics of prohibitions of insider trading recognize that giving risk averse managers a property right in a risky stream of returns involves lost gains from trade available from reallocating the risk to shareholders. They argue, however, that a compensation scheme based on insider trading is a solution to the incentive compatibility problem raised by principal-agent relationships. In defense of insider trading, Carlton and Fischel, for example, remark that insider trading increases managers' incentives to invest in firm-specific human capital because they can appropriate the results of their efforts through trading. Manne argues that alternative compensation schemes fail to provide managers with incentives as powerful as those generated by insider trading rights. According to Manne, returns to entrepreneurial activity are distributed broadly over time. Therefore, current compensation in the form of salaries or bonuses cannot be accurately linked to managerial performance. Fama has suggested a compensation scheme in which wages are revised *ex post* managerial performance. This would permit compensation to be based on realized performance over a specified period. Such a scheme, however, entails negotiation costs. Moreover, because firms can observe company profits but not the efforts of managers, they will be unable to disaggregate profit changes attributable to managerial conduct from those attributable to firm-specific shocks. They will also be unable to distinguish among contributions made by different managers within the firm.

Advocates of insider trading compensation schemes find the plans attractive because they allow managers to profit from their efforts on behalf of the firm without having to negotiate with owners. When managers believe their entrepreneurial activities will enhance the value of the firm, they can invest in the company's shares at their discretion. Having acquired an interest in the future course of the share price, managers will concentrate their efforts on behalf of the company to ensure that their programs will succeed and the resulting enhanced performance be disclosed. If it is true that insider trading compensation schemes encourage managers to operate in the interest of shareholders to a greater extent than do other schemes, then it is possible that gains in managerial efficiency will outweigh losses from inefficient risk bearing so that the insider trading scheme will enhance overall shareholder welfare.

The difficulty with this defense of insider trading is that alternative fee schedules are equally likely to align manager and shareholder interests but pose less danger to shareholders. Stock options, for example, are traditional compensation items that are used to deal with agency problems. The proportion of compensation that stock options comprise can be adjusted to allocate different risk levels to managers, depending on the degree of their risk aversion. Stock options also enhance managers' incentives to expend effort on behalf of their firm. Tying their fortunes more closely to those of the firm makes it more likely that managers will operate in the interests of shareholders whenever shareholders' and managers' incentives would otherwise have conflicted more dramatically.

Stock options are, in fact, more effective than insider trading schemes at aligning incentives of management and shareholders in two respects. First, managers are less likely to be free rider beneficiaries of stock option returns than of inside information. If managers are allotted property rights in inside information, they can profit from them either when the information is casually acquired or when it is created through deliberate entrepreneurial activity. Stock option rights also permit managers to profit through casually acquired information. Stock option rewards, however, accrue only from increases in share price. In contrast, insider trading profits are available regardless of the direction in which share prices move. Hence, under a stock option compensation scheme there will be fewer occasions on which managers will have opportunities to gain through casually acquired rather than deliberately created opportunities.

Second, an insider trading scheme presents managers with opportunities to gain on the upswing and on the downswing of share prices. Managers can therefore take deliberate actions to induce downswings that profit managers but not shareholders. It is possible that labor market reputation effects would constrain managers from deliberately reducing the share values of their firms. Insider trading, however, is an attractive compensation element precisely because shareholders cannot observe managers' behavior, and they want to provide managers with incentives to work on their behalf. If managerial actions cannot be monitored, then shareholders cannot distinguish falling share prices that result from manipulative behavior of managers from those resulting from random shocks. Consequently, labor market reputation effects will not constrain managers from profiting at the expense of shareholders.

In a world of imperfect monitoring, the benefits that insider trading proponents attribute to insider trading compensation schemes can be achieved by alternatives which do not create perverse incentives.

Rather than counteracting inefficient risk bearing arrangements by enhancing managerial incentives, permitting insider trading compounds efficiency losses by encouraging destructive managerial behavior. It follows that efficiency gains from banning insider trading can be profitably captured up to the point at which monitoring costs equal the sum of gains in managerial efficiency from abolishing insider trading based compensation schemes and gains from trade which can be achieved through reallocating risk toward the less risk averse party.

3. Adverse selection. The presence of rights to inside information in managerial compensation schemes aggravates problems of moral hazard that shareholders face by creating perverse incentive effects and by creating adverse selection problems when owners enter the market for new managers. The problem of adverse selection arises in cases of asymmetric information between parties where, for example, the principal cannot determine some characteristic of the manager which is known to the manager and which is relevant to determining future company profits.

In the manager-shareholder context, the problem of adverse selection arises because owners who hire managers cannot distinguish between managers who are hard workers and those who are shirkers. The pool of applicants for managerial positions is sensitive to the compensation package with which managers will be remunerated. In other words, the proportion of shirkers and hard workers for a given number of applicants will change with changes in the compensation scheme. Firms who offer compensation in the form of insider trading will attract a larger proportion of applicants who are shirkers than will firms who offer compensation in the form of salaries and stock options: Shirkers will be less heavily attracted by the prospect of rewards which depend on effort and entrepreneurial

contributions to the firm than by a compensation scheme which offers them potential profits based not on the direction in which share prices move but only on the magnitude of the difference between actual outcomes and those expected by the market. Owners of firms permitting insider trading will, on average, hire more shirkers than will firms with alternative compensation packages.

The same point applies to the risk preferences of managers in the firm's pool of prospective employees. Compensation packages which include risky streams of income will be more likely to attract risk seeking managers than will less risky compensation arrangements because risk seekers value risky streams more highly. Applicant pools for managerial positions which offer the right to trade on inside information will therefore contain higher proportions of risk seekers than risk avoiders. Carlton and Fischel have suggested that this effect may benefit firms because managers are generally more risk averse than shareholders would like them to be. As Leftwich and Verrecchia have pointed out, however, insider trading opportunities make managers' expected utilities depend on gains from insider trading, which increase with the variance of the underlying stream. This means that when managers are choosing projects in which to invest company resources, they may be drawn to projects which are riskier but which offer lower or equivalent expected returns than others. This suggests that less risk aversion by managers does not necessarily better align shareholder and managerial interests.

The recognition that adverse selection problems aggravate moral hazard in the context of a principal-agent model with insider trading makes it even more likely that managerial compensation schemes which involve insider trading rights will attract or generate a management corps with perverse incentives. From the perspective of the firm, it is rational to ban insider trading if the costs of monitoring managers are less than the gains from trade between shareholders and managers plus the gains available from selecting a managerial compensation scheme that best aligns management and shareholder incentives. Assuming monitoring and enforcement costs are sufficiently low, a rule against insider trading appears to be consistent with economically efficient compensation schemes. Indeed, the argument that corporations have an economic rationale for allowing insider trading is plausible only under unlikely assumptions: Managers are less risk averse than shareholders; moral hazard problems do not result from insider trading-based compensation arrangements; and rights to a risky stream of income do not induce managers to shirk or to adopt projects involving uncompensated risk.

B. Price Efficiency Effects of Insider Trading

Many commentators favor abolishing restrictions on insider trading because they believe that trading on inside information moves share prices toward their true values more quickly than if insider trading were banned. These critics make the argument in two parts. First, they argue that the speed and accuracy with which the stock market reflects the true value of shares is important because it creates conditions under which financial capital is allocated to its highest valued uses. Second, they argue that insider trading is a good mechanism for ensuring that prices quickly and accurately reflect their true values.

The price efficiency argument against prohibiting insider trading stresses the importance to the economy of directing financial capital to those places where society values it most. Stock prices are considered to be at their true values if they fluctuate randomly around the present values of the expected stream of future company returns. If stock

prices deviate systematically from their true values, then savers and investors will base resource allocation decisions on incorrect measures of company returns. One example of the way in which stock prices affect resource allocation decisions is in the market for financial capital. Firms' abilities to raise financial capital to finance expansion or research and development depends on share prices. If a firm's value is underrepresented by its share price because, for example, the firm has strategic reasons for not divulging information about a valuable discovery, a marketing strategy, or an expansion or acquisition plan, then it will be more costly than it would otherwise be for that firm to raise capital in the equity market. The firm will not, therefore, engage in the correct amount of investing, and resources will not flow to those uses which society values most highly. Share prices also affect the allocation of financial capital through their presence as observable independent variables in econometric models on which forecasts of inflation and interest rates are based. These variables, in turn, influence the timing and nature of investment decisions by firms. Finally, stock prices are a component of shareholder wealth, on which the consumption and savings decisions of households are based.

Opponents of restrictions on insider trading argue that trading by insiders moves share prices toward their true values and is therefore desirable. According to the semi-strong version of the efficient capital markets hypothesis, all publicly available information is incorporated into share prices instantaneously. Price adjustments on information not publicly available to traders are, however, incorporated into prices through signaling—the conspicuous trading of insiders that reveals superior information about the issuer. Scholes has shown that even relatively large swings in the supply or demand of particular securities have no observable effect on price. Rather, price changes occur because the identity of the buyer or seller signals information about the issuer. Thus, insider trading advocates argue that, at least to the extent that insider activity reveals the presence of valuable information in the possession of the insider, insider trading moves prices in the correct direction more rapidly than if insider trading were prohibited and information disclosed subsequent to the time that insiders would have begun trading on it.

A serious difficulty with this price efficiency rationale for insider trading is that illegal insider trading has not been shown empirically to have any significant effect on share prices. A recent study examined increases in stock prices of target firms in 172 successful tender offers over a three-week period before their announcement. The authors found that by one day prior to the announcement the average stock price had appreciated to 38.8 percent of its price one day after the tender offer announcement. The study showed, however, that a significant portion of the runup could be explained by three legally available influences on pre-bid trading—media speculation, the bidder's foothold acquisition in the target, and whether the bid was friendly or hostile. Thus a large portion of the runup could be explained by factors other than illegal insider trading.

Another criticism of the price efficiency rationale for insider trading is that permitting insider trading may delay or distort the transmission of valuable information to the market. This would occur if insiders at lower echelons of management concealed information from their superiors in order to avoid the danger of an early price runup which would diminish their gains and leave them with too little time to arrange financing for their trades. It might also occur if members of the firm deliberately released false information in order to take advantage of profits available from resulting price swings.

Finally, even if the effect of price adjustment on market efficiency were important,

permitting insider trading is likely to be an inefficient mechanism for introducing information into share prices. If it is efficient for shares to be priced correctly, then this could be achieved instantaneously by adopting a disclosure rule requiring full disclosure by the company of material nonpublic information. There will, of course, be situations in which immediate full disclosure is undesirable for reasons associated with, for example, encouraging research and development. In these cases, however, there is no reason to believe that insider trading leads to an optimal price adjustment path for the company's shares.

Insider trading may move prices toward their true values faster than they would otherwise arrive there. The effect of its doing so is, however, likely to be trivial in relation to the distortions insider trading creates by generating perverse incentives and additional transaction costs.

C. Transaction Costs Arising from Insider Trading

A number of transaction costs arise from the presence of insiders in the stock market. These costs arise because insiders present the market with an asymmetry of information which cannot be corrected by the research or analysis of other traders. The particular informational asymmetry associated with the presence of insiders is eliminated only when the insider's material nonpublic information is made public.

One transaction cost to which insider trading gives rise relates to the impact of insider activity on the operation of the securities exchanges. In practice, the securities markets are managed by market makers, or specialists, who smooth the flow of transactions in the markets by maintaining an inventory of stocks from which they trade. This is necessary to permit continuous trading opportunities for the market because buy and sell orders reach the market irregularly. Specialists provide immediate transactions at quotable prices. The "bid price" is that price at which traders may sell to specialists, and the "ask price" is that at which traders may buy from them. To serve these functions, specialists incur three costs. First, they incur the capital costs of holding inventories of cash and securities. Second, they incur the risk bearing costs of holding an unwanted inventory position. Third, specialists face the risk of trading with insiders with information superior to their own.

The presence of insiders in the market therefore creates an adverse selection problem for the specialist. In other words, specialists cannot in their dealings distinguish between insiders (information traders), who will systematically out-perform specialists by selling to them shares whose prices will fall and buying from them those whose prices will rise, and traders without superior information (liquidity traders), who will not systematically out-perform specialists. The greater the proportion of information traders to liquidity traders that the specialists perceive they face, the wider their bid-ask spreads become in order to compensate themselves for their losses to insiders.

A legal regime that permits insider activity will cause specialists to revise upward the probability that they are trading with an insider in any given trade. Permitting insider activity would therefore raise bid-ask spreads facing both information and liquidity traders. One effect of this increase would be to reduce the equilibrium volume of trading by driving marginal liquidity traders out of the market; the greater the spread facing traders, the greater their anticipation of the stock's future price rise must be to induce them to purchase it. This gives rise to another possible effect of the wider bid-ask spreads resulting from insider activity. If liquidity traders are to remain in the market, they will offer lower bid prices to specialists when purchasing shares in order to hold constant their expected profits from their purchases. Because the bid-ask spread is fixed by specialists as a precondition to their trading, the lower bid price must be generated through a lower share price net of the bid-ask spread. The result for firms is that the cost of using the market for financing rises, thereby altering the proportion of the funds they choose to derive from debt and equity.

A second social loss to which insider trading relates is the cost to society of duplicative information gathering by market players. Greater expenditures for information and research increase the accuracy of investors' expectations of future price changes. Once information is publicly disclosed, prices of securities adjust to reflect the value of the new information. This makes it valuable for traders to invest in information gathering up to the point at which their marginal profit from doing so equals their marginal cost of gathering new information. The introduction of information into share prices is valuable because it moves prices toward their true values. The lower the costs of information gathering required to move prices, the lower is the cost to society of having correctly priced shares. The presence of insiders in the market affects the incentives of outsiders to gather trading information. First, insiders obtain information about future changes in the market value of a security prior to outsiders because they have access to information about corporate decisions and events before outside shareholders or the public. Second, insiders acquire their information at low or no cost. Proponents of insider trading argue that insiders can capture gains from changes in market value associated with new information before outsiders, regardless of the information produced by outsiders. They argue that outsiders' trading provides no private return when insiders are trading because insiders trade until share prices fully adjust, leaving no return to outsiders who invest in duplicative information gathering. Insider trading, they conclude, reduces the overall amount of money that society spends to achieve an adjustment in share prices because it eliminates the cost to society of duplicative information gathering by outsiders.

In fact, the presence of insiders in the market does reduce duplicative information gathering but does not eliminate it. Only if insider trading results in immediate price adjustment would it be unwarranted for outsiders to engage in information search. This is because, as long as prices do not adjust immediately, there remains a disparity between full information prices and prices facing outsiders. This makes it rational for outsiders to spend an amount of money on search related to the expected change in prices. As noted above, insider trading does not lead to immediate full price adjustment. This can be achieved only through public disclosure. Thus, insider trading at best reduces duplicative information gathering by outsiders to an extent that depends on the speed of price adjustment in response to insiders' trades.

In short, the presence of insiders in the market affects transaction costs of trading in two ways. First, it raises the bid-ask spreads facing all traders, thereby reducing the expected return to shareholding, driving marginal outsiders from the market, and making it more costly for firms to raise funds through the capital market. Second, insider activity will somewhat reduce duplicative information gathering and hence the total cost associated with price adjustment on the market. The net effect of insider trading on transaction costs is therefore unclear. This suggests that transaction costs should not be a determining factor in formulating a rule to govern insider trading.

IV. CONCLUSION

Under the efficiency analysis conducted in this note, only insider activity that results in harm to society beyond direct wealth transfers should be prohibited. Viewing traders along an information spectrum, where corporate insiders lie at one end and where traders informed only by the public media lie at the other, only in the case of information trading by corporate insiders is the harm from information trading unambiguous. A prohibition of insider trading can be justified on efficiency grounds only where insiders are defined narrowly in a way that prevents corporate insiders from profiting from inside information. This supports a broad prohibition against trading by any director, officer, or employee in her company's stock or in the stock of any company in which her company has a present or prospective business interest. This latter condition would be satisfied, for example, in situations where the corporate insider considered trading in shares of a company which her own company was considering acquiring. In order to make this prohibition effective against circumvention, insider trading law would also have to prohibit trading by tippees who were tipped by corporate insiders for improper purposes, such as personal gain.

The pricing and transaction cost prongs of this note's efficiency analysis do not provide conclusive results that support any restrictions on information trading beyond those on corporate insiders. Price adjustments occur only imperfectly as a result of insider trading and can be better achieved through carefully developed disclosure rules. Transaction costs in the form of wider bid-ask spreads arise as a result of insider activity but are offset by the reduction in the costs of information gathering that the presence of insiders in the market implies.

An appeal to concerns falling under the rubrics of distribution, theft, or fraud may, of course, provide a broader basis for insider liability. This note has aimed only to show that an appeal to economic efficiency does not. In the process, it has raised a number of questions for further study. Specifically, once some restrictions on insider trading are plausibly defended on efficiency grounds, it becomes relevant to determine (1) the optimal level of and investment in monitoring; (2) who should monitor; and (3) the level of damages that achieves efficient deterrence.

11

Eclipse of the Public Corporation

Michael C. Jensen

The publicly held corporation, the main engine of economic progress in the United States for a century, has outlived its usefulness in many sectors of the economy and is being eclipsed.

New organizations are emerging in its place — organizations that are corporate in form but have no public shareholders and are not listed or traded on organized exchanges. These organizations use public and private debt, rather than public equity, as their major source of capital. Their primary owners are not households but large institutions and entrepreneurs that designate agents to manage and monitor on their behalf and bind those

Michael C. Jenson is the Edsel Bryant Ford Professor of Business Administration at the Harvard Business School and founding editor of the *Journal of Financial Economics*. His research and writing have figured prominently in the national debate over corporate governance and mergers and acquisitions. This article draws from Mr. Jensen's book, *Organizational Change and the Market for Corporate Control*, to be published by Basil Blackwell in 1990.

agents with large equity interests and contracts governing the use and distribution of cash.

Takeovers, corporate breakups, divisional spinoffs, leveraged buyouts, and going-private transactions, are the most visible manifestations of a massive organizational change in the economy. These transactions have inspired criticism, even outrage, among many business leaders and government officials, who have called for regulatory and legislative restrictions. The backlash is understandable. Change is threatening; in this case, the threat is aimed at the senior executives of many of our largest companies.

Despite the protests, this organizational innovation should be encourages. By resolving the central weakness of the public corporation — the conflict between owners and managers over the control and use of corporate resources — these new organizations are making remarkable gains in operating efficiency, employee productivity, and shareholder value. Over the long term, they will enhance U.S. economic performance relative to our most formidable international competitor, Japan, whose companies are moving in the opposite direction. The governance and financial structures of Japan's public companies increasingly resemble U.S. companies of the mid-1960s and early 1970s—an era of gross corporate waste management that triggered the organizational transformation now under way in the United States.

THE PRIVATIZATION OF EQUITY

The last share of publicly traded common stock owned by an individual will be sold in the year 2003, if current trends persist. This forecast may be fanciful (short-term trends never persist), but the basic direction is clear. By the turn of the century, the primacy of public stock ownership in the United States may have all but disappeared.

Households have been liquidating their direct holdings and indirect positions (through channels like mutual funds) at an unprecedented rate. Over the last five years, they have been net sellers of more than $500 billion of common stock, 38% of their holdings at the beginning of 1984.

Why have stock prices risen sharply despite this massive sell-off? Because there has been one huge buyer—corporations themselves. LBOs, MBOs, share repurchases, leveraged mergers and acquisitions, and takeovers have been contracting the supply of publicly held equity. In 1988, 5% of the market value of public equity (more than $130 billion) disappeared through these kinds of transactions, even after adding back all of the new issues brought to market during the year.

Of course, the risks and returns from the underlying corporate assets have not disappeared. To some extent they now reside in quasi-equity debt instruments like high-yield bonds, whose total market value exceeds $200 billion. But many of the risks and returns still exist as equity; they just take the form of large positions of privately held equity. The "privatization of equity" is now a central feature of corporate ownership in the United States.

Historically, public stock markets dominated by individual investors developed to a greater extent in the United States than in any other country. Broad public ownership offered managers a reasonably priced source of more or less permanent equity capital that could buffer the company against adversity in a way debt could not. Share ownership allowed individual investors to participate in equity returns and get the benefits of liquidity (because they could sell their shares) and diversification (because they could hold a small number of shares from many corporations).

The virtues of broad public ownership are not what they used to be, for managers or investors. One important factor is the emergence of an active market for corporate control. A capital structure consisting mostly of equity still offers managers protection against the risks of economic downturn. But it also carries substantial risks of inviting a hostile takeover or other threats to management control.

The role of the public market has also changed because investors themselves have changed. For decades, stock ownership has been migrating from direct holdings by millions of individuals to indirect beneficial ownership through large pools of capital—in particular, the huge corporate and governmental pension funds whose total value exceeded $1.5 trillion in 1988. These institutional funds, which now comprise more than 40% of total stock ownership, used to behave like large public investors. They kept diversified by retaining many different investment managers, each of whom traded an array of highly liquid public securities. But their investment philosophy has been evolving in recent years to include participation in a select number of private illiquid investments and private pools of equity capital. This new investment philosophy makes broad public markets less essential for institutions.

Large pools of capital such as pension funds and endowments don't really need the liquidity the public market offers. Liquidity serves two basic purposes. It allows investors to meet unexpected cash needs and to trade their stocks. Unlike individuals, the large funds can project their cash needs well into the future based on predictable factors such as employee demographics, life expectancies, and health trends. So they can take a long-term view of investment returns and keep their holdings in illiquid assets.

Fund managers are also realizing that trading is a tough discipline in which they hold little comparative advantage. Trading is a zero-sum game played in a fairly efficient market against equally talented rivals. Worse still, large funds face diseconomies of scale when executing trades. The larger a fund, the more difficult it is to trade quickly, based on transient information advantages. The very act of trading moves markets.

Still, these managers remain charged with generating returns in excess of passive benchmarks. Enter the market for private assets such as real estate, venture capital, and, more recently, the market for corporate control and restructurings. Instead of trading a large number of small, liquid positions, the funds can buy and own smaller numbers of large, illiquid positions in a form where they (or, more likely,

their agents) participate more actively with management in the control of the assets.

This alternative can be a positive-sum game; real changes in corporate policies can be a route to enhanced value. The very large funds also have a competitive advantage here. The larger their positions, the more actively they can participate in the ownership and management of the underlying assets. In the extreme, as with LBO funds, these changes can be dramatic. The LBO fund itself becomes the managing owner in partnership with company managers. In short, large institutional funds can behave more like owners and less like traders.

The same basic changes are at work in a wide variety of corporate recapitalizations where outside (or related) parties acquire large, relatively nontraded equity positions. Large pools of capital can participate in these private equity positions yet remain diversified by virtue of their own enormous size. Smaller funds and households cannot.

In the short run, this new investment philosophy has been, in the aggregate, a great success. Without the sobering influence of an economic contraction, the returns from these private investments have been very attractive. In the long run, the institutions' new philosophy is ushering in a system of equity ownership dominated by "private positions" that resembles ownership systems in Germany and Japan. Individual investors in this system will increasingly be free riders on the coattails of a small number of very large private investors rather than the central feature of the financial markets.

Jay O. Light

Jay O. Light is the George Fisher Baker, Jr. Professor of Business Administration at the Harvard Business School.

Consider these developments in the 1980s:

The capital markets are in transition. The total market value of equity in publicly held companies has tripled over the past decade—from $1 trillion in 1979 to more than $3 trillion in 1989. But newly acquired capital comes increasingly from private placements, which have expanded more than ten times since 1980, to a rate of $200 billion in 1988. Private placements of debt and equity now account for more than 40% of annual corporate financings. Meanwhile, in every year since 1983, at least 5% of the outstanding value of corporate equity has disappeared through stock repurchases, takeovers, and going-private transactions. Finally, households are sharply reducing their stock holdings.[1] (See the insert, "The Privatization of Equity.")

The most widespread going-private transaction, the leveraged buyout, is becoming larger and more frequent. In 1988, the total value of the 214 public-company and divisional buyouts exceeded $77 billion—nearly one-third of the value of all mergers and acquisitions. The total value of the 75 buyouts in 1979 was only $1.3 billion (in constant 1988 dollars), while the

175 buyouts completed in 1983 had a total value of $16.6 billion. This process is just getting started; the $77 billion of LBOs in 1988 represented only 2.5% of outstanding public-company equity. (See the table, "Rise of the LBO.")

Entire industries are being reshaped. Just five years ago, the leading U.S. truck and automobile tire manufacturers were independent and diversified public companies. Today each is a vastly different enterprise. Uniroyal went private in 1985 and later merged its tire-making operations with those of B.F. Goodrich to form a new private company called Uniroyal Goodrich. In late 1986, Goodyear borrowed $2.6 billion and repurchased nearly half its outstanding shares to fend off a hostile tender offer by Sir James Goldsmith. It retained its core tire and rubber business while moving to divest an array of unrelated operations, including its Celeron oil and gas subsidiary, California-to-Texas oil pipeline, aerospace operation, and Arizona resort hotel. In 1987, GenCorp issued $1.75 billion of debt to repurchase more than half its outstanding shares. It divested several operations, including its General Tire subsidiary, to pay down the debt and focus on

Rise of the LBO

	Public-Company Buyouts		Divisional Buyouts		Total Value of Buyouts (In billions of 1988 dollars)
Year	Number	Average Value (In millions of 1988 dollars)	Number	Average Value (In millions of 1988 dollars)	
1979	16	$ 64.9	59	$ 5.4	$ 1.4
1980	13	106.0	47	34.5	3.0
1981	17	179.1	83	21.0	4.8
1982	31	112.2	115	40.7	8.2
1983	36	235.8	139	58.2	16.6
1984	57	473.6	122	104.0	39.7
1985	76	349.4	132	110.1	41.0
1986	76	303.3	144	180.7	49.0
1987	47	488.7	90	144.2	36.0
1988	125	487.4	89	181.3	77.0

Source: George P. Baker, "Management Compensation and Divisional Leveraged Buyouts," unpublished dissertation, Harvard Business School, 1986. Updates from W.T. Grimm, *Mergerstat Review 1988,* Transactions with no public data are valued at the average price of public transaction.

Michael C. Jensen

aerospace and defense. Last year, Firestone was sold to Bridgestone, Japan's largest tire maker, for $2.6 billion, a transaction that created shareholder gains of $1.6 billion.

Developments as striking as the restructuring of our financial markets and major industries reflect underlying economic forces more fundamental and powerful than financial manipulation, management greed, reckless speculation, and the other colorful epithets used by defenders of the corporate status quo. The forces behind the decline of the public corporation differ from industry to industry. But its decline is real, enduring, and highly productive. It is not merely a function of the tax deductibility of interest. Nor does it reflect a transitory LBO phase through which companies pass before investment bankers and managers cash out by taking them public again. Nor, finally, is it premised on a systematic fleecing of shareholders and bondholders by managers and other insiders with superior information about the true value of corporate assets.

The current trends do not imply that the public corporation has no future. The conventional twentieth-century model of corporate governance—dispersed public ownership, professional managers without substantial equity holdings, a board of directors dominated by management-appointed outsiders—remain a viable option in some areas of the economy, particularly for growth companies whose profitable investment opportunities exceed the cash they generate internally. Such companies can be found in industries like computers and electronics, biotechnology, pharmaceuticals, and financial services. Companies choosing among a surplus of profitable projects are unlikely to invest systematically in unprofitable ones, especially when they must regularly turn to the capital markets to raise investment funds.

The public corporation is not suitable in industries where long-term growth is slow, where internally generated funds outstrip the opportunities to invest them profitably, or where downsizing is the most productive long-term strategy. In the tire industry, the shift to radials, which last three times longer than bias-ply tires, meant that manufacturers needed less capacity to meet world demand. Overcapacity inevitably forced a restructuring. The tenfold increase in oil prices from 1973 to 1981, which triggered worldwide conservation measures, forced oil producers into a similar retrenchment.[2]

Industries under similar pressure today include steel, chemicals, brewing, tobacco, television and radio broadcasting, wood and paper products. In these and other cash-rich, low-growth or declining sectors, the pressures on management to waste cash flow through organizational slack or investments in unsound projects is often irresistible. It is in precisely these sectors that the publicly held corporation has declined most rapidly. Barring regulatory interference, the public corporation is also likely to decline in industries such as aerospace, automobiles and auto parts, banking, electric power generation, food processing, industrial and farm implements, and transportation equipment.

The public corporation is a social invention of vast historical importance. Its genius is rooted in its capacity to spread financial risk over the diversified portfolios of millions of individuals and institutions and to allow investors to customize risk to their unique circumstances and predilections. By diversifying risks that would otherwise be borne by owner-entrepreneurs and by facilitating the creation of a liquid market for exchanging risk, the public corporation lowered the cost of capital. The tradable claims on corporate ownership (common stock) also allowed risk to be borne by investors best able to bear it, without requiring them to manage the corporations they owned.

From the beginning, though, these risk-bearing benefits came at a cost. Tradable ownership claims create fundamental conflicts of interest between those who bear risk (the shareholders) and those who manage risk (the executives). The genius of the new organizations is that they eliminate much of the loss created by conflict between owners and managers, without eliminating the vital functions of risk diversification and liquidity once performed exclusively by the public equity markets.

In theory, these new organizations should not be necessary. Three major forces are said to control management in the public corporation: the product markets, internal control systems led by the board of directors, and the capital markets. But product markets often have not played a disciplining role. For most of the last 60 years, a large and vibrant domestic market created for U.S. companies economies of scale and significant cost advantages over foreign rivals. Recent reversals at the hands of the Japanese and others have not been severe enough to sap most companies of their financial independence. The idea that outside directors with little of no equity stake in the company could effectively monitor and discipline the managers who selected them has proven hollow at best. In practice, only the capital markets have played much of a control function—and for a long time they were hampered by legal constraints.

Indeed, the fact that takeover and LBO premiums average 50% above market price illustrates how much value public-company managers can destroy before they face a serious threat of disturbance. Takeovers and buyouts both create new value and unlock value destroyed by management through misguided policies. I estimate that transactions associated with the market for corporate control unlocked shareholder gains (in target companies alone) of more than $500 billion between 1977 and 1988—more than 50% of the cash dividends paid by the entire corporate sector over this same period.

The widespread waste and inefficiency of the public corporation and its inability to adapt to changing economic circumstances have generated a wave of organizational innovation over the last 15 years—innovation driven by the rebirth of "active investors." By active investors I mean investors who hold large equity or debt positions, sit on boards of directors, monitor and sometimes dismiss management, are involved with the long-term strategic direction of the companies they invest in, and sometimes manage the companies themselves.

Active investors are creating a new model of general management. These investors include LBO partnerships such as Kohlberg Krevis Roberts and Clayton & Dubilier; entrepreneurs such has Carl Icahn, Ronald Perelman, Laurence Tisch, Robert Bass, William Simon, Irwin Jacobs, and Warren Buffett; the merchant banking arms of Wall Street houses such as Morgan Stanley, Lazard Frères, and Merrill Lynch; and family funds such as those controlled by the Pritzkers and the Bronfmans. Their model is build around highly leveraged financial structure, pay-for-performance compensation systems, substantial equity ownership by managers and directors, and contracts with owners and creditors that limit both cross-subsidization among business units and the waste of free cash flow. Consistent with modern finance theory, these organizations are not managed to maximize earnings per share but rather to maximize *value*, with a strong emphasis on cash flow.

More than any other factor, these organizations' resolution of the owner-manager conflict explains how they can motivate the same people, managing the same resources, to perform so much more effectively under private ownership than in the publicly held corporate form.

In effect, LBO partnerships and the merchant banks are rediscovering the role played by active investors prior to 1940, when Wall

Street banks such as J.P. Morgan & Company were directly involved in the strategy and governance of the public companies they helped create. At the height of his prominence, Morgan and his small group of partners served on the boards of U.S. Steel, International Harvester, First National Bank of New York, and a host of railroads, and were a powerful management force in these and other companies.

Morgan's model of investor activism disappeared largely as a result of populist laws and regulations approved in the wake of the Great Depression. These laws and regulations—including the Glass-Steagall Banking Act of 1933, the Securities Act of 1933, the Securities Exchange Act of 1934, the Chandler Bankruptcy Revision Act of 1938, and the Investment Company Act of 1940—may have once had their place. But they also created an intricate web of restrictions on company "insiders" (corporate officers, directors, or investors with more than a 10% ownership interest), restrictions on bank involvement in corporate reorganizations, court precedents, and business practices that raised the cost of being an active investor. Their long-term effect has been to insulate management from effective monitoring and to set the stage for the eclipse of the public corporation.

Indeed, the high cost of being an active investor has left financial institutions and money management firms, which control more than 40% of all corporate equity in the United States, almost completely uninvolved in the major decisions and long-term strategies of the companies their clients own. They are almost never represented on corporate boards. They use the proxy mechanism rarely and usually ineffectively, notwithstanding recent efforts by the Council of Institutional Investors and other shareholder activists to gain a larger voice in corporate affairs.

All told, institutional investors are remarkably powerless; they have few options to express dissatisfaction with management other than to sell their shares and vote with their feet. Corporate managers criticize institutional sell-offs as examples of portfolio churning and short-term investor horizons. One guesses these same managers much prefer churning to a system in which large investors on the boards of their companies have direct power to monitor and correct mistakes. Managers really want passive investors who can't sell their shares.

The absence of effective monitoring led to such large inefficiencies that the new generation of active investors arose to recapture the lost value. These investors overcome the costs of the outmoded legal constraints by purchasing entire companies—and using debt and high equity ownership to force effective self-monitoring.

A central weakness and source of waste in the public corporation is the conflict between shareholders and managers over the payout of free cash flow—that is, cash flow in excess of that required to fund all investment projects with positive net present values when discounted at the relevant cost of capital. For a company to operate efficiently and maximize value, free cash flow must be distributed to shareholders rather than retained. But this happens infrequently; senior management has few incentives to distribute the funds, and there exist few mechanisms to compel distribution.

A vivid example is the senior management of Ford Motor Company, which sits on nearly $15 billion in cash and marketable securities in an industry with excess capacity. Ford's management has been deliberating about acquiring financial service companies, aerospace companies, or making some other multibillion-dollar diversification move—rather than deliberating about effectively distributing Ford's excess cash to its owners so they can decide how to reinvest it.

Ford is not alone. Corporate managers generally don't disgorge cash unless they are forced to do so. In 1988, the 1,000 largest public companies (by sales) generated total funds of $1.6 trillion. Yet they distributed only $108 billion as dividends and another $51 billion through share repurchases.[3]

Managers have incentives to retain cash in part because cash reserves increase their autonomy vis-à-vis the capital markets. Large cash balances (and independence from the capital markets) can serve a competitive purpose, but they often lead to waste and inefficiency. Consider a hypothetical world in which companies distribute excess cash to shareholders and then must convince the capital markets to supply funds as sound economic projects arise. Shareholders are at a great advantage in this world, where management's plans are subject to enhanced monitoring by the capital markets. Wall Street's analytical, due diligence, and pricing disciplines give shareholders more power to quash wasteful projects.

Managers also resist distributing cash to shareholders because retaining cash increases the size of the companies they run—and managers have many incentives to expand company size beyond that which maximizes shareholder wealth. compensation is one of the most important incentives. Many studies document that increases in executive pay are strongly related to increases in corporate size rather then value.[4]

The tendency of companies to reward middle managers through promotions rather than annual performance bonuses also creates a cultural bias toward growth. Organizations must grow in order to generate new positions to feed their promotion-based reward systems.

Finally, corporate growth enhances the social prominence, public prestige, and political power of senior executives. Rare is the CEO who wants to be remembered as presiding over an enterprise that makes fewer products in fewer plants in fewer countries than when he or she took office—even when such a course increases productivity and adds hundreds of millions of dollars of shareholder value. The perquisites of executive suite can be substantial, and they usually increase with company size.

The struggle over free cash flow is at the heart of the role of debt in the decline of the public corporation. Bank loans, mezzanine securities, and high-yield bonds have fueled the wave of takeovers, restructurings, and going-private transactions. The combined borrowings of all nonfinancial corporations in the United States approached $2 trillion in 1988, up from $835 billion in 1979. The interest charges on these borrowings represent more than 20% of corporate cash flows, high by historical standards.[5]

This perceived "leveraging of corporate America" is perhaps the central source of anxiety among defenders of the public corporation and critics of the new organizational forms. But most critics miss three important points. First, the trebling of the market value of public-company equity over the last decade means that corporate borrowing had to increase to avoid a major *de*leveraging.

Second, debt creation *without retention of the proceeds of the issue* helps limit the waste of free cash flow by compelling managers to pay out funds they would otherwise retain. Debt is in effect a substitute for dividends—a mechanism to force managers to disgorge cash rather than spend it on empire-building projects with low or negative returns, bloated staffs, indulgent perquisites, and organizational inefficiencies.

By issuing debt in exchange for stock, companies bond their managers' promise to pay out future cash flows in a way that simple dividend increases do not. "Permanent" dividend increases or multiyear share repurchase programs (two ways public companies can distribute excess cash to shareholders) involve no contractual commitments by managers to owners. It's easy for managers to cut dividends or scale back share repurchases.

Take the case of General Motors. On March 3, 1987, several months after the departure of GM's only active investor, H. Ross Perot, the company announced a program to repurchase up to 20% of its common stock by the end of 1990. As of mid-1989, GM had purchased only 5% of its outstanding common shares, even though its $6.8 billion cash balance was more than enough to complete the program. Given the management's poor performance over the past decade, shareholders would be better off making their own investment decisions with the cash GM is retaining. From 1977 to 1987, the company made capital expenditures of $77.5 billion while its U.S. market share declined by 10 points.

Borrowing allows for no such managerial discretion. Companies whose managers fail to make promised interest and principal payments can be declared insolvent and possibly hauled into bankruptcy court. In the imagery of G. Bennett Stewart and David M. Glassman, "Equity is soft, debt hard. Equity is forgiving, debt insistent. Equity is a pillow, debt a sword."[6] Some may find it curious that a company's creditors wield far more power over managers than its public shareholders, but it is also undeniable.

Third, debt is a powerful agent for change. For all the deeply felt anxiety about excessive borrowing, "overleveraging" can be desirable and effective when it makes economic sense to break up a company, sell off parts of the business, and refocus its energies on a few core operations. Companies that assume so much debt they cannot meet the debt service payments out of operating cash flow force themselves to rethink their entire strategy and structure. Overleveraging creates the crisis atmosphere managers require to slash unsound investment programs, shrink overhead, and dispose of assets that are more valuable outside the company. The proceeds generated by these overdue restructurings can then be used to reduce debt to more sustainable levels, creating a leaner, more efficient and competitive organization.

In other circumstances, the violation of debt covenants creates a board-level crisis that brings new actors onto the scene, motivates a fresh review of top management and strategy, and accelerates response. The case of Revco D.S., Inc., one of the handful of leveraged buyouts to reach formal bankruptcy, makes the point well.

Critics cite Revco's bankruptcy petition, filed in July 1988, as an example of the financial perils associated with LBO debt. I take a different view. The $1.25 billion buyout, announced in December, 1986, did dramatically increase Revco's annual interest charges. But several other factors contributed to its troubles, including management's decision to overhaul pricing, stocking, and merchandise layout in the company's drugstore chain. This mistaken strategic redirection left customers confused and dissatisfied, and Revco's performance suffered. Before the buyout, and without the burden of interest payments, management could have pursued these policies for a long period of time, destroying much of the company's value in the process. Within six months, however, debt served as a brake on management's mistakes, motivating the board and creditors to reorganize the company before even more value was lost.[7]

Developments at Goodyear also illustrate how debt can force managers to adopt value-creating policies they would otherwise resist. Soon after his company warded off Sir James Goldsmith's tender offer, Goodyear chairman Robert Mercer offered his version of the raiders' creed: "Give my your undervalued assets, your plants, your expenditures for technology, research and development, the hopes and aspirations of your people, your stake with your customers, your pension funds, and I will enhance myself and the dealmakers."[8]

What Mr. Mercer failed to note is that Goodyear's forced restructuring dramatically increase the company's value to shareholders by compelling him to disgorge cash and shed unproductive assets. Two years after this bitter complaint, Tom Barrett, who succeeded Mercer as Goodyear's CEO, was asked whether the company's restructuring had hurt the quality of its tires or the efficiency of its plants. "No," he replied. "We've been able to invest and continue to invest and do the things we've needed to do to be competitive."[9]

Robert Mercer's harsh words are characteristic of the business establishment's response to the eclipse of the public corporation. What explains such vehement opposition to a trend that clearly benefits shareholders and the economy? One important factor, as my Harvard Business School colleague Amar Bhide suggests, is that Wall Street now competes directly with senior management as a steward of shareholder wealth. With its vast increases in data, talent, and technology, Wall Street can allocate capital among competing businesses and monitor and discipline management more effectively than the CEO and headquarters staff of the typical diversified company. KKR's New York offices and Irwin Jacobs' Minneapolis base are direct substitutes for corporate headquarters in Akron or Peoria. CEOs worry that they and their staffs will lose lucrative jobs in favor of competing organizations. Many are right to worry; the performance of active investors versus the public corporation leaves little doubt as to which is superior.

Active investors are creating new models of general management, the most widespread of which I call the LBO Association. A typical LBO Association consists of three main constituencies: an LBO partnership that sponsors going-private transactions and counsels and monitors management in an ongoing cooperative relationship; company managers who hold substantial equity stakes in an LBO division and stay on after the buyout; and the institutional investors (insurance companies, pension funds, and money management firms) that fund the limited partnerships that

purchase equity and lend money (along with banks) to finance the transactions.

Much like a traditional conglomerate, LBO Associations have many divisions or business units, companies they have taken private at different points in time. KKR, for example, controls a diverse collection of 19 businesses including all or part of Beatrice, Duracell, Motel 6, Owens-Illinois, RJR Nabisco, and Safeway. But LBO Associations differ from publicly held conglomerates in at least four important respects. (See the illustration, "Public Company vs. LBO Association.")

Management incentives are built around a strong relationship between pay and performance. Compensation systems in LBO Associations usually have higher upper bounds than do public companies (or no upper bounds at all), tie bonuses much more closely to cash flow and debt retirement than to accounting earnings, and otherwise closely link management pay to divisional performance. Unfortunately, because these companies are private, little data are available on salaries and bonuses.

Public data are available on stock ownership, however, and equity holdings are a vital part of the reward system in LBO Associations. The University of Chicago's Steven Kaplan studied all public-company buyouts from 1979 through 1985 with a purchase price of at least $50 million.[10] Business-unit chiefs hold a median equity position of 6.4% in their unit. Even without considering bonus and incentive plans, a $1,000 increase in shareholder value triggers a $64 increase in the personal wealth of business-unit chiefs. The median public-company CEO holds only .25% of the company's equity. Counting *all* sources of compensation—including salary, bonus, deferred compensation, stock options, and dismissal penalties—the personal wealth of the median public-company CEO increases by only $3.25 for a $1,000 increase in shareholder value.[11]

Thus the salary of the typical LBO

Public Company vs. LBO Association

Typical Public Company

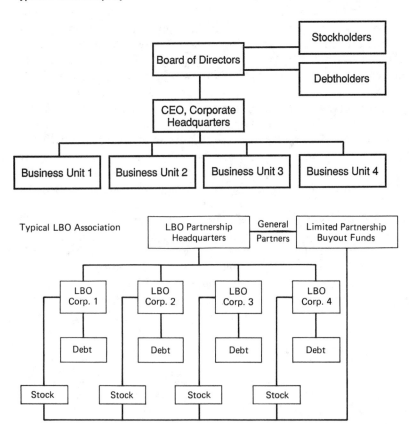

Typical LBO Association

business-unit manager is almost 20 times more sensitive to performance than that of the typical public-company manager. This comparison understates the true differences in compensation. The personal wealth of managing partners in an LBO partnership (in effect, the CEOs of the LBO Associations) is tied almost exclusively to the performance of the companies they control. The general partners in an LBO Association typically receive (through overrides and direct equity holdings) 20% or more of the gains in the value of the divisions they help manage. This implies a pay-for-performance sensitivity of $200 for every $1,000 in added shareholder value. It's not hard to understand why an executive who receives $200 for every $1,000 increase in shareholder value will unlock more value than an executive who receives $3.25.

LBO Associations are more decentralized than publicly held conglomerates. The LBO Association substitutes compensation incentives and ownership for direct monitoring by headquarters. The headquarters of KKR, the world's largest LBO partnership, has only 16 professionals and 44 additional employees. In contrast, Atlanta headquarters of RJR Nabisco employed 470 people when KKR took it private last year in a $25 billion transaction. At the time of the Goldsmith tender offer for Goodyear, the company's Akron headquarters had more than 5,000 people on its salaried payroll.

It is physically impossible for KKR and other LBO partnerships to become intimately involved in the day-to-day decisions of their operating units. They rely instead on stock ownership, incentive pay that rewards cash flow, and other compensation techniques to motivate managers to maximize value without bureaucratic oversight. My survey of 7 LBO partnerships found an average headquarters staff of 13 professional and 19 nonprofessionals that oversees almost 24 business units with total annual sales of more than $11 billion. (See the table, "LBO Partnerships Keep Staff Lean.")

LBO Associations rely heavily on leverage. The average debt ratio (long-term debt as a percentage of debt plus equity) for public companies prior to buyout is about 20%. The Kaplan study shows the average debt ratio for an LBO is 85% on completion of the buyout.

Intensive use of debt dramatically shrinks the amount of equity in a company. This allows the LBO general partners and divisional managers to control a large fraction of the total ownership without requiring huge investments they would be unable to make or large grants of free equity. For example, in a company with $1 billion in assets and a debt ratio of 20%, management would have to raise $80 million to buy 10% of the equity. If that same company had a debt ratio of 90%, management would have to raise only $10 million to control a 10% stake. By concentrating equity holdings among managers and LBO partners, debt intensifies the ownership incentives that are so important to efficiency.

High debt also allows LBO Associations and other private organizations to tap the benefits of risk diversification once provided only by the public equity market. Intensive use of debt means much of it must be in the form of public, high-yield, noninvestment-grade securities, better known as junk bonds. This debt, which was pioneered by Drexel Burnham Lambert, reflects more of the risk borne by shareholders in the typical public company. Placing this public debt in the well-

LBO Partnerships Keep Staff Lean

LBO Partnership	Year Started	Number of Professionals	Number of Nonprofessionals	Number of Business Units	Combined Annual Revenues (In billions of dollars)
Berkshire Partners	1986	14	6	15	$ 1
Butler Capital	1979	8	14	33	2.3
Clayton & Dubilier	1976	10	11	8	4.8
Gibbons Green van Amerongen	1969	6	7	12	5.3
Kohlberg Kravis Roberts	1976	16	44	19	58.7
Thomas H. Lee Co.	1974	15	12	25	8
Odyssey Partners	1950	19	39	53	N.A.

Michael C. Jensen

diversified portfolios of large financial institutions spreads equitylike risk among millions of investors, who are the ultimate beneficiaries of mutual funds and pension funds—without requiring those risks to be held as equity. Indeed, high-yield debt is probably the most important and productive capital market innovation in the last 40 years.

LBO Associations have well-defined obligations to their creditors and residual claimants. Most buyout funds are organized as limited partnerships in which the partners of the sponsoring LBO firm serve as general partners. The buyout fund purchases most of the equity and sometimes provides debt financing. The limited partnership agreement denies the general partner the right to transfer cash or other resources from one LBO division to another. That is, all returns from a business must be distributed to the limited partners and other equity holders of that business. Such binding agreements reduce the risk of unproductive reinvestment by prohibiting cross-subsidization among LBO units. In effect, the LBO sponsor must ask its institutional investors for permission to reinvest funds, a striking difference from the power of public-company managers to freely shift resources among business units.

The management, compensation, and financial structures of the LBO Association square neatly with the rebirth of active investors. Institutional investors delegate the job of being active monitors to agents best qualified to play the role. The LBO partnerships bond their performance by investing their own resources and reputations in the transaction and taking the bulk of their compensation as a share in the companies' increased value.

To be sure, this delegation is not without its tensions. The fact that LBO partnerships and divisional managers control the LBO Association's small equity base but hold little of the debt creates incentives for them to take high-risk management gambles. If their gambles succeed, they reap large rewards by in-creasing their equity value; if their gambles fail, creditors bear much of the cost. But the reputational consequences of such reckless behavior can be large. As long as creditors behave rationally, an LBO partnership that tries to profit at the expense of its creditors or walks away from a deal gone sour will not be able to raise funds for future investments.

To date, the performance of LBO Associations has been remarkable. Indeed, it is difficult of find any systematic losers in these transactions, and almost all of the gains appear to come from real increases in productivity. The best studies of LBO performance reach the following conclusions:

LBOs create large gains for shareholders. Studies estimate that the average total premium to public shareholders ranges from 40% to 56%.[12] Kaplan finds that in buyouts that go public again or are otherwise sold (which occurs on average 2.7 years after the original transaction), total shareholder value increases by an average of 235%, or nearly 100% above market-adjusted returns over the same period.[13]. These returns are distributed about equally between prebuyout shareholders and the suppliers of debt and equity to transaction. Prebuyout shareholders earn average market-adjusted premiums of 38%, while the total return to capital (debt plus equity) for buyout investors is 42%. This return to buyout investors is measured on the total purchase price of the LBO, not the buyout equity. Because equity returns are almost a pure risk premium, and therefore independent of the amount invested, they are very high. The median market-adjusted return on buyout equity is 785%, or 125% per year.

Value gains do not come at the expense of other financial constituencies. Some critics argue that buyout investors, especially managers, earn excessive returns by using inside information to exploit public shareholders. Managers do face severe conflicts of interest in these transactions; they cannot simultaneously act as buyer and agent for the seller. But equity-opening managers who are not part of post-buyout management teams systematically sell their shares into LBOs. This would be foolish if the buyout were significantly underpriced in light of inside information, assuming that these non-participating insiders have the same inside information as the continuing management team. Moreover, LBO auctions are becoming common; underpriced buyout proposals (including those initiated by management) quickly generate competing bids.

No doubt some bondholders have lost value through going-private transactions. By my estimate, RJR Nabisco's prebuyout bondholders lost almost $300 million through the downgrading of their claims on the newly leveraged company. This is a small sum in comparison to the $12 billion in total gains the transaction produced. As yet, there is no evidence that bondholders lose on average from LBOs. Evidence on LBOs completed through 1986 does show that holders of convertible bonds and preferred stock gain a statistically significant amount and that straight bondholders suffer no significant gains or losses.[14]

New data may document losses for bondholders in recent transactions. But the expropriation of wealth from bondholders should not be a continuing problem. The financial community is perfecting many techniques, including poison puts and repurchase provisions, to protect bondholders in the event of substantial restructurings. In fact, versions of these loss-prevention techniques have been available for some time. In the past, bondholders such as Metropolitan Life, which sued RJR Nabisco over the declining value of the company's bonds, chose not to pay the premium for protection.

LBOs increase operating efficiency without massive layoffs or big cuts in research and development. Kaplan finds that average operating earnings increase by 42% from the year prior to the buyout to the third year after the buyout. Cash flows increase by 96% over this same period. Other studies document significant improvements in profit margins, sales per employee, working capital, inventories, and receivables.[15] Those who doubt these findings might take a moment to scan the business press, which has chronicled the impressive postbuyout performance of companies such as Levi Strauss, A.O. Scott, Safeway, and Weirton Steel.

Importantly, employment does not fall systematically after buyouts, although is does not grow as quickly as in comparable companies. Median employment for all companies in the Kaplan study, including those engaged in substantial divestitures, increased by nearly 1%. Companies without significant divestitures increased employment by 5%.

Moreover, the great concern about the effect of buyouts on R&D and capital investment is unwarranted. The low-growth companies that make the best candidates for LBOs don't invest heavily in R&D to begin with. Of the 76 companies in the Kaplan study, only 7 spent more than 1% of sales on R&D before the buyout. Another recent study shows that R&D as a fraction of sales grows at the same rate in LBOs as in comparable public companies.[16] According to Kaplan's study, capital expenditures are 20% lower in LBOs than in comparable non-LBO companies. Because these cuts are taking place in low-growth or declining industries and are accompanied by a doubling of market-adjusted value, they appear to be coming from reductions in low-return projects rather than productive investments.

Taxpayers do not subsidize going-private transactions. Much has been made of the charge that large increases in debt virtually eliminate the tax obligations of an LBO. This argument overlooks five sources of additional tax revenues generated by buyouts: capital gains taxes paid by pre-buyout shareholders; capital gains taxes paid on postbuyout asset sales; tax payments on the large increases in operating earnings generated by efficiency gains; tax payments by creditors who receive interest payments on the LBO debt; and taxes generated by more efficient use of the company's total capital.

Overall, the U.S. Treasury collects an estimated 230% more revenues in the year after a buyout than it would have otherwise and 61% more in long-term present value. The $12 billion gain associated with the RJR Nabisco buyout will generate net tax revenues of $3.3 billion in the first year of the buyout; the company paid $370 million in federal taxes in the year before the buyout. In the long term, the transaction will generate total taxes with an estimated present value of $3.8 billion.[17]

LBO sponsors do not have to take their companies public for them to succeed. Most LBO transactions are completed with a goal of returning the reconfigured company to the public market within three to five years. But recent evidence indicates that LBO sponsors are keeping their companies under private ownership. Huge efficiency gains and high-return asset sales produce enough cash to pay down debt and allow LBOs to generate handsome returns as going concerns. The very proliferation of these transactions has helped create a more efficient infrastructure and

liquid market for buying and selling divisions and companies. Thus LBO investors can "cash out"in a secondary LBO or private sale without recourse to a public offering. One recent study finds that only 5% of the more than 1,300 LBOs between 1981 and 1986 have gone public again.[18]

Public companies can learn form LBO Associations and emulate many of their characteristics. But this requires major changes in corporate structure, philosophy, and focus. They can reduce the waste of free cash flow by borrowing to repurchase stock or pay large dividends. They can alter their charters to encourage large investors or experiment with alliances with active investors such as Lazard Frères' Corporate Partners fund. They can increase equity ownership by directors, managers, and employees. They can enhance incentives through pay-for-performance systems based on cash flow and value rather than accounting earnings. They can decentralize management by rethinking the role of corporate headquarters and shrinking their staffs.

Some corporations are experimenting with such changes—FMC, Holiday, Owens-Corning—and the results have been impressive. But only a coordinated attack on the status quo will halt the eclipse of the public company. It is unlikely such an attack will proceed fast enough or go far enough.

Who can argue with a new model of enterprise that aligns the interests of owners and managers, improves efficiency and productivity, and unlocks hundreds of billions of dollars of shareholder value? Many people, it seems, mainly because these organizations rely so heavily on debt. As I've discussed, debt is crucial to management discipline and resolving the conflict over free cash flow. But critics, even some who concede the control function of debt, argue that the costs of leverage outweigh the benefits.

Wall Street economist Henry Kaufman, a prominent critic of the going-private trend, issued a typical warning earlier this year: "Any sever shock—a sharp increase in interest rates in response to Federal Reserve credit restraint, or an outright recession that makes the whole stock market vulnerable, or some breakdown in the ability of foreign firms to bid for pieces of U.S. companies—will drive debt-burdened companies to the government's doorstep to plead for special assistance."[19]

The relationship between debt and insolvency is perhaps the least understood aspect of this entire organizational evolution. New hedging techniques mean the risk associated with a given level of corporate debt is lower today than it was five years ago. Much of the bank debt associated with LBOs (which typically represents about half of the total debt) is done through floating-rate instruments. But few LBOs accept unlimited exposure to interest rate fluctuations. They purchase caps to set a ceiling on interest charges or use swaps to convert floating-rate debt into fixed-rate debt. In fact, most banks require such risk management techniques as a condition of lending.

Critics of leverage also fail to appreciate that insolvency in and of itself is not always something to avoid—and that the costs of becoming insolvent are likely to be much smaller in the new world of high leverage than in the old world of equity-dominated balance sheets. The proliferation of takeovers, LBOs, and other going-private transactions has inspired innovations in the reorganization and workout process. I refer to these innovations as "the privatization of bankruptcy." LBOs *do* get in financial trouble more frequently than public companies do. But few LBOs ever enter formal bankruptcy. They are reorganized quickly (a few months is common), often under new management, and at much lower costs than under a court-supervised process.

How can insolvency be less costly in a world of high leverage? Consider an oversimplified example. Companies A and B are identical in every respect except for their financial structures. Each has a going-concern value of $100 million (the discounted value of its expected future cash flows) and a liquidation or salvage value of $10 million. Company A has an equity-dominated balance sheet with a debt ratio of 20%, common for large public companies. Highly leveraged Company B has a debt ratio of 85%, common for LBOs. (See the illustration, "The Privatization of Bankruptcy.")

Now both companies experience business reversals. What happens? Company B will get in trouble with its creditors much sooner than Company A. After all, Company B's going-concern value doesn't have to shrink very much for it to be unable to meet its payments on $85 million of debt. But when it does run into trouble, its going-concern value will be nowhere near its liquidation value. If the going-concern value shrinks to $80 million, there remains $70 million of value to preserve by avoiding liquidation. So Company B's creditors have strong incentives to preserve the remaining value by quickly and efficiently reorganizing their claims outside the courtroom.

No such incentives operate on Company A. Its going-concern value can fall dramatically before creditors worry about their $20 million of debt. By the time creditors do intervene, Company A's going-concern value will have plummeted. And if Company A's value falls to under $20 million, it is much more likely than Company B to be worth less than its $10 million salvage value. Liquidation in this situation is the likely and rational outcome, with all its attendant conflicts, dislocations, and costs.

The evolving U.S. system of corporate governance and finance exhibits many characteristics of the postwar Japanese system. LBO partnerships act much like the main banks

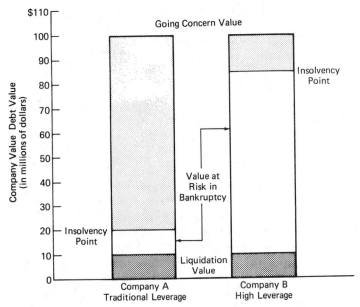

The Privatization of Bankruptcy

(the real power center) in Japan's *keiretsu* business groupings. The keiretsu make extensive use of leverage and intercorporate holdings of debt and equity. Banks commonly hold substantial equity in their client companies and have their own executives help them out of difficulty. (For years, Nissan has been run by an alumnus of the Industrial Bank of Japan, who became CEO as part of the bank's effort to keep the company out of bankruptcy.) Other personnel, including CFOs, move frequently between banks and companies as part of an ongoing relationship that involves training, consulting, and monitoring. Japanese banks allow companies to enter formal bankruptcy only when liquidation makes economic sense—that is, when a company is worth more dead than alive. Japanese corporate boards are composed almost exclusively of insiders.

Ironically, even as more U.S. companies come to resemble Japanese companies, Japan's public companies are becoming more like U.S. companies of 15 years ago. Japanese shareholders have seldom had any power. The banks' chief disciplinary tool, their power to withhold capital from high-growth, cash starved companies, has been vastly reduced as a result of several factors. Japan's victories in world product markets have left its companies awash in profits. The development of domestic and international capital markets has created ready alternatives to bank loans, while deregulation has liberalized corporate access to these funds. Finally, new legal constraints prevent banks from holding more than 5% of the equity of any company, which reduces their incentive to engage in active monitoring.

Many of Japan's public companies are flooded with free cash flow far in excess of their opportunities to invest in profitable internal growth. In 1987, more than 40% of Japan's large public companies had no net bank borrowings—that is, cash balances larger than their short- and long-term borrowings. Toyota, with a cash hoard of $10.4 billion, more than 25% of its total assets, is commonly referred to as the Toyota Bank.[20]

In short, Japanese managers are increasingly unconstrained and unmonitored. They face no effective internal controls, little control from the product markets their companies already dominate, and fewer controls from the banking system because of self-financing, direct access to capital markets, and lower debt ratios. Unless shareholders and creditors discover ways to prohibit their managers from behaving like U.S. managers, Japanese companies will make uneconomic acquisition and diversification moves, generate internal waste, and engage in other value-destroying activities. The long-term result will be the growth of bureaucracy and inefficiency and the demise of product quality and organizational responsiveness—until the waste becomes so severe it triggers a market for corporate control to remedy the excesses.

The Japanese remedy will reflect that country's unique legal system and cultural practices. But just as hostile takeovers, LBOs, and other control transactions went from unacceptable behavior in the united States to a driving force in corporate restructuring, so too will they take hold in Japan—once the potential returns outweigh the costs and risks of challenging the corporate status quo.

Meanwhile, in the United States, the organizational changes revitalizing the corporate sector will create more nimble enterprises and help reverse our losses in world product markets. As this profound innovation continues, however, people will make mistakes. To learn, we have to push new policies to the margin. It will be natural to see more failed deals.

There are already some worrisome structural issues. I look with discomfort on the dangerous tendency of LBO partnerships, bolstered by their success, to take more of their compensation in front-end fees rather than in back-end profits earned through increased equity value. As management fees and the fees for completing deals get larger, the incentives to do deals, rather than good deals, also increases. Institutional investors (and the economy as a whole) are best served when the LBO partnership is the last member of the LBO Association to get paid and when the LBO partnership gets paid as a fraction of the back-end value of the deals, including losses.

Moreover, we have yet to fully understand the limitations on the size of this new organizational form. LBO partnerships are understandably tempted to increase the reach of their talented monitors by reconfiguring divisions as acquisition vehicles. This will be difficult to accomplish successfully. It is likely to require bigger staffs, greater centralization of decision rights, and dilution of the high pay-for-performance sensitivity that is so crucial to success. As LBO Associations expand, they run the risk of recreating the bureaucratic waste of the diversified public corporation.

These and other problems should not cloud there marketable benefits associated with the eclipse of the large public corporation. What surprises me is how few mistakes have occurred thus far in an organizational change as profound as any since World War II.

NOTES

1. Equity values based on trends in the Wilshire index. Private-placement data from IDD Information Services as published in Sarah Bartlett, "Private Market's Growing Edge," *New York Times*, June 20, 1989.

2. For more analysis of the oil industry, see my article, "The Takeover Controversy: Analysis and Evidence," in *Corporate Restructuring and Executive Compensation* (Cambridge, Mass: Ballinger, 1989).

3. Calculated from Standard & Poor's Compustat file.

4. Kevin J. Murphy, "Corporate Performance and Managerial Remuneration," *Journal of Accounting and Economics*, 1985, vol. 7, no. 1–3.

5. Federal Reserve Board, Balance Sheets of U.S. Economy.

6. G. Bennett Stewart III and David M. Glassman, "The Motives and Methods of Corporate Restructuring: Part II," *Journal of Applied Corporate Finance*, Summer 1988.

7. Stephen Phillips, "Revco: Anatomy of an LBO that Failed," *Business Week*, October 3, 1988.

8. "A Hollow Victory for Bob Mercer," *Industry Week*, February 23, 1987.

9. Jonathan P. Hicks, "The Importance of Being Biggest," *New York Times*, June 20, 1989.

10. Steven Kaplan, "Sources of Value in Management Buyouts," *Journal of Financial Economics*, forthcoming.

11. Michael C. Jensen and Kevin J. Murphy, "Performance Pay and Top Management Incentives," *Journal of Political Economy*, forthcoming.

12. Yakov Amihuc, "Leveraged Management Buyouts and Shareholders' Wealth," in *Leveraged Management Buyouts: Causes and Consequences* (Homewood, Ill. Dow Jones-Irwin, 1989).

13. That is, returns net of the returns that would normally be earned on these securities, given their level of systematic risk (beta) and general market returns.

14. L. Marais, K. Schipper, and A. Smith, "Wealth Effects of Going Private for Senior Securities," *Journal of Financial Economics*, 1989, vol. 23, no.1.

15. In addition to Kaplan, see Abbie Smith, "Corporate Ownership Structure and Performance," un-published paper, University of Chicago, 1989. See also Frank R. Lichtenberg and Donald Siegel, "The Effects of Leveraged Buyouts on Productivity and Related Aspects of Firm Behavior," *National Bureau of Economic Research*, 1989.

16. Lichtenberg and Siegel, NBER, 1989.

17. Michael C. Jensen, Robert Kaplan, and Laura Stiglin, "Effects of LBOs on Tax Revenues of the U.S. Treasury," *Tax Notes*, February 6, 1989.

18. Chris Muscarella and Michael Vetsuypens, "Efficiency and Organizational Structure: A Study of Reverse LBOs," unpublished paper, Southern Methodist University, April 1989.

19. Henry Kaufman, "Bush's First Priority: Stopping the Buyout Mania," *Washington Post*, January 1, 1989.

20. Average (book value) debt ratios fell from 77% in 1976 to 68% in 1987. Given the 390% increase in stock prices over this period, market-value debt ratios fell even more dramatically. Figures calculated from the NEEDS Nikkei Financials file for all companies on the First Section of the Tokyo Stock Exchange.

12

Corporate Takeovers, Mergers and Acquisitions — Public Policy Implications *

I. STATEMENT OF MR. MICHAEL C. JENSEN **

Contrary to many assertions in the popular press, I believe there is no evidence whatsoever that takeovers in the aggregate are harming employees or shareholders. In fact, there is a very good deal of carefully collected evidence that indicates that they are creating large benefits. The Office of the Chief Economist of the SEC estimates that those benefits total over $35 billion in shareholder gains in the last 4 years alone.

The takeover market is appropriately interpreted as an agent for change, and change as we know generates great unease—here especially, in the executive suites.

*These materials have been excerpted from *Corporate Takeovers*, Hearing Before the Subcommittee on Telecommunications, Consumer Protection and Finance, 1985.

**Excerpted and condensed from the oral statement of Michael C. Jensen, Graduate School of Management, University of Rochester; Frederic M. Scherer, Department of Economics, Swarthmore College; and Warren A. Law, Harvard Business School.

Takeover activities are bringing about a large reshuffling of control of assets and the uses to which those assets are put. This also generates unease on the part of those who face those changes.

This restructuring of corporate America I believe is healthy and should not be restricted. Divestitures, split-ups, and liquidations, are an important part of this activity that is breathing new life into corporate America, shaking up the old ways of doing things and generating large benefits.

Divestitures and liquidations do not mean the assets are thrown away or dumped on the scrap heap, but rather that the assets are redeployed to more valuable and productive uses. In fact, I think the so-called bust-ups represent a strong private force to eliminate bigness for bigness' sake. It eliminates inefficient combinations of assets that have grown up for whatever reason, sometimes that means from unwise takeovers in the past.

I would like to spend a moment addressing the issue regarding where these benefits come from.

The oil industry seems to me to be a particularly good example, first because it is a major source of benefits, and second, it is one that gets so much attention.

I have predicted for well over a year now that we should find a reduction in the rate of expenditure on exploration and development in the oil industry and in fact that the takeover market was going to help bring that about. That reduction in the exploration and development expenditures in the oil industry, Mr. Chairman, is in the longrun interest of the stockholders as well as the economy. It is a longrun focus, not a shortrun focus.

Let me explain why. A number of factors that affect the industry have changed dramatically in the last decade. A tenfold increase in oil prices, substantial increases in real interest rates, a reduction in the future rate of growth of crude oil prices, reduced consumption of energy, and increased cost of exploration and development.

Now, every single one of these implies that the level of reserves, the inventory that we have, is too high, it should be reduced. The optimal level of crude oil inventory has fallen. The Japanese have taught us and the rest of corporate America that economizing on inventory is an enormously productive activity. We should not be surprised to find that this is true in the oil industry as well. The issue is not whether we are going to discover the oil but when, whether we do it now or 5 years from now when it is more valuable to us.

If you are going to reduce the level of reserves from what they are now to an optimal level, that means that exploration and development has to fall dramatically. Past practices that have grown up over a long time in the industry have resulted in rules of thumb leading managers to react to these changes very slowly.

Since holding reserves is an activity that is subject to large economies of scale, and exploration and development is one that is not subject to economies of scale, some of the firms in the oil industry simply had to go out

of business. We could let that happen through bankruptcy courts and a long, slow death or have it happen in a very efficient way through takeovers.

That desirable economic change has been signaled to top level managers by the fact that they could buy oil reserves on Wall Street "cheaply" relative to what it costs to punch new holes in the ground. That was not because Wall Street was not valuing the reserves efficiently or accurately, Wall Street was. They were also valuing accurately the tax that was imposed on those reserves by nonoptimal expenditures on exploration and development and on bloated refining and distribution facilities that are no longer needed, given the new rules of the game.

In conclusion, I see no evidence or logic that indicates Federal regulation of the takeover market is desirable. Indeed, I think this is best left to the voluntary contractual processes between shareholder and management and to corporate charters and State Law. Most proposals for new regulations that I have seen both harm the shareholder and reduce productivity, but will benefit some special interests. The problem is the benefits in each of these cases will be smaller than the overall costs to society. I urge you to resist these pressures.

II. STATEMENT OF MR. F.M. SCHERER***

The Subcommittee has asked me to address the implications of takeovers for the management and efficiency of target enterprises. In receiving such an assignment, one is well-advised to heed the counsel of James Bond: "Never say never." Especially in the world of mergers, anything can happen. The objective must be to identify *average* propen-

***Excerpted from the written testimony of F.M. Scherer.

sities, not the extremes of behavior that surely exist.

1. The CEA Report

In a chapter of its 1985 annual report, the President's Council of Economic Advisers (CEA) sets matters straight. As a whole, it concludes (p. 196), mergers and acquisitions "improve efficiency, transfer scarce resources to higher valued uses, and stimulate effective corporate management." The analysis is remarkable, strongly reminiscent of the apologetics course I took as a parochial high school senior. Unfortunately, like all apologiae, its conclusions rest upon tenets of faith that are not provable. And more importantly, it fails to examine critically either those underlying premises or substantial blocks of evidence inconsistent with its conclusions. Permit me to elaborate.

1. For one, a paradox is implied but not acknowledged. Following a theme first articulated by Adolf Berle and Gardiner Means in 1932, the CEA report asserts (p. 188) that management may operate the corporation in management's best interests rather than in the interests of shareholders. It then identifies two possible curbs on the abuse of managerial discretion: hiring and firing, and takeovers. It fails to mention the constraint emphasized by economists since the time of Adam Smith; product market competition.[1] Under strong competitive pressure, management cannot stray long and far from the profit-maximizing behavior that contributes to efficient resource allocation and use.[2] If takeovers are needed to constrain managerial discretion, product market competition must somehow be insufficient. This is a paradoxical implication for an Administration insisting on other occasions that antitrust laws regarding indus-

trial structure must be relaxed and accepting limitations on import competition in such major industries as autos, steel, and textiles.

2. Takeovers, and especially hostile takeovers, are a relatively new and growing phenomenon. The average number of successful or partly successful tender offers per year (not all of which were contested) has been estimated as follows:[3]

1956–59	2.0
1960–64	9.0
1965–69	41.2
1970–74	25.6
1975–79	70.9

If takeovers are an important disciplinary mechanism stimulating managerial efficiency, one might expect the rapid increase in takeover activity during the late 1960s and late 1970s to have been followed by improved overall economic performance — e.g., on such dimensions as productivity growth. In fact, the annual growth of output per work hour in the economy's private nonfarm business sector declined from 2.6 percent over 1947–64 to 1.7 percent over 1964–74 to 1.4 percent over 1974–84. At the least, the CEA ought to explain why industrial productivity growth in the 1950s and early 1960s was so strong *despite* the absence of appreciable takeover discipline. And if it avows a reverse chain of causation — with the rise in takeover activity spurred by declining economic performance — it should present a well-specified explanation of how the two movements are related.

3. The CEA's conclusion that takeovers increase economic efficiency is based upon evidence from numerous stock market "event" studies analyzing how the prices of acquired and acquiring company shares

change when an acquisition event is announced and/or consummated. Increases in both parties' share prices, or increases in one without a decrease in the other, are said to show efficiency gains, e.g., as a new management is installed to alter the acquired firm's operating policies. The CEA report and most event studies fail to mention that there is an alternative hypothesis consistent with the observed stock price behavior: that the market had undervalued the acquired firm's shares.[4] Under this alternative, undervaluation makes the acquired firm an attractive takeover candidate, even when a premium must be paid, and the takeover act per se sends a signal to market participants prompting them to revise their evaluations. In other words, it is the stock market, not management of the target firm, which has erred and needs disciplining. "Event" analysts dismiss this alternative hypothesis by assuming that the stock market does not make such mistakes because it is "efficient," impounding continuously all available information on each company's worth. But this assumption is taken axiomatically, i.e., on faith, rather than with compelling proof. Indeed, it is singularly difficult to prove or disprove. The efficient markets axiom is the classic stuff of theological disputes.

4. The typical stock market "event" study compares stock price behavior during periods 10 to 30 days before and after the announcement or consummation event under scrutiny. Although the text is unclear, I believe it is these decidedly short-run analyses to which the CEA refers (p. 197) in claiming that it has cited "the best available evidence." The Council fails completely to mention the findings of those relatively few studies that have taken a longer perspective (usually 12 months). As Professor Jensen's survey of the literature reports:[5]

. . . Several studies show indications of systematic reductions in the stock prices of bidding firms in the year following the event. These post-outcome negative abnormal returns are unsettling because they are inconsistent with market efficiency and suggest that changes in stock price during takeovers overestimate the future efficiency gains from mergers. . . . Explanation of these post-event negative abnormal returns is currently an unsettled issue.

None of the event studies known to me looks beyond a one-year perspective. In fact, the hyper-active conglomerate acquirers of the late 1960s, though evaluated favorably by the stock market at the time, tended to experience dramatic stock price declines over the decade following their period of peak acquisition activity. Thus, the CEA has ignored evidence of critical significance.

5. Neither the "event" studies nor the CEA report look behind the stock price movements accompanying takeovers to the actual changes in management policies and profit performance that follow merger. Thus, they leave unexplored the possibility that acquiring firms and their stockholders had expectations at the time of takeover inconsistent with the ultimate ensuing reality.

6. Even accepting the stock market "event" study findings at their advocates' face interpretation, an absolutely fundamental point is overlooked. Suppose it were true that managers have not served their stockholders well, failing to maximize profits. What profits have they failed to maximize: short-run, long-run, or what? The textbook answer is that managers should maximize profits over time, with each successive year's returns discounted more heavily according to the discount factor revealed in

the market cost of capital. But here problems intrude.

For one, even at best, discount rates in the United States are high both absolutely and relative to those encountered by our most formidable overseas competitors. It is estimated that in 1979, before the Federal Reserve Board tightened money supplies, the after-tax cost of industrial capital services in the United States was on the order of 20 percent, compared to 4.6 percent in Japan.[6] Such differences have a major impact on far-sighted investments. An R&D project costing $1 million today and yielding a one-shot payoff of $3.5 million seven years hence would pass muster at a 5% discount rate (and at any discount rate up to 18%), but not at 20%.

Operating company executives may be induced to pursue even more short-sighted policies by the role fund managers play. By my tabulation, 34 percent of 912 corporations on *Business Week's* "Investment Outlook Scoreboard: 1984" (December 26, 1983) had 50 percent or more of their stock held by institutions. Many (to be sure, not all) of those fund managers are under intense pressure to perform *this year* and will tender shares if a premium can be offered in the expectation of a takeover that biases operating policies toward short-term payoffs. To avert takeover, incumbent operators may be forced to follow suit.

One prominent species of short-run policies is the "cash cow" strategy under which a business is starved of R&D, equipment modernization, and advertising funds, and/or prices are set at high levels inviting competitor inroads, leaving in the end a depleted, non-competitive shell. One might have been blase about the pursuit of such policies when the American market was insular so that, say, U.S. Steel's market share loss was Inland's or National's gain. Yet absent artificial trade barriers, we are insulated no longer, so it is at

least as likely that the market position loss of a firm pursuing short-sighted cash cow policies will mean a gain for Kawasaki, Nissan, or BASF. And once market position is lost, business strategists agree, it is very difficult to recoup. So even though short-run profit maximization is what shareholders want, or at least what many key shareholders want, it is far from clear that such behavior is good for the nation and to be encouraged.

2. How To Learn What We Need To Know?

I have been critical of the stock market "event" studies, and the CEA's reliance upon them, because I am convinced they do not reveal the full and essential truth of what is happening on the takeover front. How then are we to learn what we must know in order to formulate well-founded public policies (or non-policies)?

One way is simply to listen to what mergermakers say about why they do what they do. If we did only this, we would learn that many mergers (not all) *are* motivated by an undervalued assets theory, i.e., by the belief that the market, not operating management, has erred. I have never been able to understand why efficient market theorists, who believe so passionately that investors are sufficiently well-informed to bring the stock market continuously to a full-information equilibrium, are unwilling to conduct in-depth studies of the behavior of a sample of professional investors and merger-makers and learn what makes them tick. If a Jesuit had the opportunity to interview God, would he demur in the fear that his beliefs might be undermined? To be sure, there is a risk of interviewee dissembling, especially when merger policies might be shaped by what the questioner learns. But this is a problem with which social scientists have long known how to cope.

A related path to understanding is to compile historical case studies of actual merger experiences. Under a National Science Foundation grant, I have done this for 15 acquisitions that were subsequently sold off.[7] Since sell-off might be a sign of failure, the sample is by design a biased one. Its justification is that the cohort of divestitures is quantitatively significant—by the CEA's reckoning (p. 195), comprising about one-third of all merger activity. It is important therefore to learn what happened to induce sell-off and what it implies for the efficiency theory of takeovers.

A third way is to find out how mergers affected the actual profitability of acquired units—those that were retained, *and* those that were sold off. Using the Federal Trade Commission's Line of Business program resources, David Ravenscraft of the FTC staff and I have nearly finished developing an unprecedentedly rich data base on the financial consequences of merger. For nearly 4,000 individual business units (e.g., company divisions), it links in 27 years of merger history and seven years of sell-off history. It is, we believe, the best such data base ever assembled in any nation.

3. Some Early Findings

My case study analysis is completed except for final follow-ups. Analysis of our financial data set began only in late November and will continue through the spring and summer.[8] Thus, our findings are preliminary and subject to revision. Some of the most important insights follow:

1. At least for our 15 sell-off case study sample, the originally acquired companies were considered by their acquirers to be preponderantly well-managed and promising, not the laggards emphasized in the management-displacement-by-takeover theory. Even for the exceptional acquired companies with pre-merger performance problems, the acquiring firm was attracted by depressed stock prices and had no resources to effect wholesale managerial displacements. Key incumbent executives were urged to remain on board.

2. In several cases, policies were changed after acquisition toward a greater emphasis on short-run profits. Eventually these new policies caused problems ranging from equipment obsolescence and inability to compete on equal terms with domestic and foreign rivals to a "They're bleeding us—why should I exert myself?" attitude on the part of operating level managers and workers.

3. The "cash cow" hypothesis is also supported by our early quantitative analyses of 2,982 business units. Although in existence longer on average, acquired lines of business had 1977 market shares no larger on average than new internal growth "start-up" units. There is preliminary evidence of a decline in acquired unit profitability, the longer it had been under the acquiring corporation's control.

4. By far the most frequent reason for sell-off was the emergence of acquired unit operating problems the parent corporation was unable to solve. In nearly half of the 15 cases, the problems were aggravated by inept parent supervision that sapped operating management morale or delayed responses to emerging business crises.

5. Five of the 15 sell-off cases were marked by a lack of direct serious problems (although in two, sell-off occurred because of managerial breakdowns in similar sister units). In at least three and perhaps four of the cases, the parent—acquiree relationship was beneficial on balance to the acquired unit. The most important benefit was an infusion of funds the acquired entity would have had trouble raising on its own. Such capital availability constraints, it should be noted, are difficult to reconcile with the efficient capital market as-

sumptions underlying takeover "event" studies.

6. All but three of the case study sell-offs entailed a transition from conglomerate organization to either free-standing operation (e.g., through leveraged buyouts) or a horizontal merger. Improved operating efficiency almost invariably followed departure from conglomerate control. However, in some cases, financing costs and cash constraints forced short-sighted investment policies.

7. From our early quantitative analysis, there is evidence that on average, acquisitions were less profitable for the acquiring firms than the maintenance of existing businesses and the internal development of new business lines. This finding is consistent with the evidence of long-term stock price declines for active conglomerate acquirers. However, it is tentative, since it does not take into account tax advantages and certain selection biases that will be analyzed in coming months.

8. Our quantitative data sample includes rather few units subjected to contested takeovers. Preliminary analysis reveals that baseline profitability following involuntary takeover was below norms for voluntarily acquired and home-grown business units, although the difference is not statistically significant.

III. STATEMENT OF M.T. BOONE PICKENS****

The key to keep in mind as you deliberate on this issue is that the companies involved in mergers and acquisitions are not owned by managements but by stockholders. It is the stockholders' interests which should be paramount. Forty-two million Americans own

****Excerpted from the oral statement of M.T. Boone Pickens.

stock in publicly traded companies, and that is one out of every six people, or more than 100,000 voters in each congressional district in the United States.

These stockholders have placed their investment in the hands of management, and they expect that management will do its best to keep the market value of their investments as close as possible to its true value. Restrictions on legitimate tender offers would deprive these investors of a basic property right, that right to sell.

Mergers are also part of the market for managerial control. The economic report of the President state on page 9 that, "Management must demonstrate that its performance is competitive with the performance of other potential managers, and the value of management's performance must be reflected in the corporation's stock price."

Do not be misled by the notion that merger activity in the threat of a takeover diverts management away from its duties. If management had been fulfilling those duties and keeping the share price up, it would not be vulnerable to takeover. Mergers do not divert management from managing. It diverts them from fishing and hunting camps.

In the three recent takeover attempts in which Mesa has been involved, 750,000 stockholders have made pre-tax profit of $14 billion in taxes. I receive hundreds of letters from Gulf and Phillips shareholders supporting Mesa's efforts.

In any takeover there is legitimate concern on the part of employees as to their future welfare. Mesa understands these fears; also how important it is to have the support of the community and employees in an acquisition. That is why we made a concerted effort to tell the employees and communities involved with Gulf and Phillips that if we were successful in our takeover attempt, we would maintain their company's headquarters in the present location and move there to manage the company.

Michael C. Jensen

The closing thought I would like to leave with you is that we must remember once again that constituency whose fate we are dealing with. Stockholders, whether they are individuals or institutions, provide the capital that runs corporate America. There are individuals represented by institutions, and that is $100 billion invested for employees at AT&T, General Electric, DuPont and USTI, and they represent hundreds of billions of dollars invested in teacher retirement funds, university endowment funds, and union pension plans.

Institutions are not faceless money-management organizations. They represent millions of individuals. Institutions have a responsibility to look out for the best interests of these people. Any restriction on institutional shareholders could cause them to reconsider their participation in our equity markets, and that would leave a vacuum that could not be filled.

In conclusion, when we talk of mergers and acquisitions, we are not talking simply of money; we are talking about the investments of millions of Americans, their life savings and their retirement funds.

IV. STATEMENT OF SIR JAMES GOLDSMITH *****

The dominant ideology of Europe has fluctuated between Socialism and State Corporatism. These have been the root causes of the European economic disease. State Corporatism is based on the conviction that the activities of a nation can best be managed through the triangular cooperation of the state, business and trade unions. For example, corporatists believe that salaries and prices in whole industries and nationwide can be settled annually by negotiations between employer as-

*****Excerpted from the oral statement of Sir James Goldsmith.

sociations and trade unions, presided over by government. They do not believe in the mechanisms of the marketplace which they feel are brutal and destabilizing.

At the base of the pyramid or triangle is big business and big unions. At the peak is government. As a result, a mutuality of interest, indeed a certain complicity, has evolved between big corporate management, trade union leaders and government bureaucrats. They need each other. Small and medium sized business has no natural place in such a system. In Great Britain, for example, an official inquiry on small firms has revealed that small businesses accounted for a smaller proportion of output and employment than in any other industrialized country.

Here in the USA, you have followed a very different route, a route which has led to a new industrial revolution. Some call it a techno-scientific revolution. Some call it an entrepreneurial revolution. Since 1965, while Europe has been losing jobs at a truly alarming rate, your revolution has created 35 million new jobs. The new jobs are coming from small and medium sized businesses usually run by innovators and entrepreneurs whereas large and mature industries are shedding employment each year. This shift is fundamental because, contrary to Europe, it reduces the role and power of the megacorporations and the trade unions. It creates a polyculture of businesses all competing one against the other. It creates a truly competitive economy and in a truly competitive economy either you do it right or you get eliminated. Mega-companies either get it right or they get taken over. Trade unions have to agree to competitive practices or unionized companies perish and trade union membership is correspondingly reduced.

During the past few months in the United States, there has been a national debate about hostile takeovers. It seems to me that this debate is really about your new entrepreneurial revolution and the freedoms that have engendered it. The question really being asked is whether or not large corporations should be treated like institutions and should be granted special protection from the marketplace.

Who would have believed a few years ago that conglomerates, created at the time by freewheeling entrepreneurs, today are described by some as sacrosanct institutions which should be protected from the marketplace by special legislation. All that has changed in many of these companies is that the flame of the founder has been replaced by the complacency of the bureaucrat. And because the members of such bureaucracies control the disposition of vast amounts of other people's money and the power and patronage that accompany it, they feel they are part of the establishment and therefore deserve special privileges.

For many years conventional wisdom has been that bigness, in itself, is somehow good. It allowed for magnificent investment projects without recourse to leverage; it allowed companies to diversify and this was supposed to protect them against cyclical swings, and as far as management was concerned, bigness put their companies beyond the threat of hostile takeovers.

That thinking has now been challenged. Big investment, in itself, is not necessarily a virtue.

Diversification can sometimes protect groups against such cyclical swings but also many companies have proved unable to handle the diversity of problems and opportunities which arise in multi-industry corporations.

Finally, the financial markets now are big enough to finance a challenge even to huge corporations. The market will put up the money if it believes that the fundamental value of a company is much greater than its market value and that the fundamental values can be liberated.

Some corporate managements react to this situation by creating a panoply of artificial devices to entrench themselves. They also appear before your committee to plead for special protection. Others take the positive steps which are needed to deploy their assets properly.

I would only like to make an obvious point. Corporations are owned by their shareholders. Management is employed by shareholders to look after shareholder interests. Devices like poison pills, paying greenmail, scorched earth, defensive acquisitions, super majority voting, staggered boards, etc..., should all be subject to prior and free vote by shareholders and should not be imposed unilaterally by management as a method of entrenchment. When management acts unilaterally, without consulting shareholders, it is seeking protection not for their shareholders but from their shareholders. Often management will have a good case to make. If so, it should make it and convince its constituents.

My only qualification to this is that the effects of such special resolutions, even if approved by shareholders, should not become permanent. Management should not be entrenched forever. Life tenure is seldom healthy.

It must be remembered that almost always, directors are not chosen and elected by shareholders. Normally, shareholders are asked to vote on a list of directors proposed by management. There are no primaries and only very rarely, and at a great cost, is an alternative list of candidates proposed to shareholders and this is within the context of proxy fights. So in effect, directors are co-opted by their future colleagues and shareholders do no more than ratify the proposals.

That is why I would strongly recommend that although management entrenchment and anti-takeover devices are legitimate when approved by shareholders, nonetheless they should be the subject of a regular vote and therefore, should be submitted annually to shareholder consideration. This would avoid life tenure of corporate management.

Shareholders on the other hand would be wise to eliminate conflicts of interest with management. Management sometimes is tempted by size, shareholders want value. Management is fearful of takeovers because of the inevitable uncertainties of change after many years of loyal service to their company. Shareholders should align the interests of management with their own by substantial incentive schemes and firm termination agreements, sometimes called "golden parachutes."

V. STATEMENT OF
MR. ANDREW C. SIGLER [******]

The Business Roundtable's position is that the whole hostile takeover phenomenon, both sides, the defensive and the offensive side, is causing serious damage to the economic system. I will explain that position in some quick detail, and we have some suggestions for corrections.

Behind the smokescreen of doing good for shareholders and punishing stupid, entrenched management, and using the magic cloak of the word "free market," a small group is systematically extracting the equity from corporations and replacing it with debt, and incidentally accumulating major wealth.

Now, anyone who believes that there is no difference between debt and equity in the guts of the economic system just doesn't understand how the system really works. The basic unit we use in this system, basic business unit, is the corporation. We generally measure the strength of that corporation, its ability to perform its normal function to grow, et cetera, by the amount of its equity.

Now, we think it is fiscal insanity to let the

***** Excerpted from the oral statement of Andrew C. Sigler, Chairman of the Business Roundtable's Corporate Responsibility Task Force.

country go on with this type of phenomenon because the country loses. When the equity moves out, it does not go into equity of another company, so the economic system in effect is losing the fuel that makes it run.

In 1984 $90 billion of equity was extracted from this economic system in a year when, under the kind of conditions we had in 1984, a pretty good year, it should have grown. We are at a time when we are doing all the talk about competitiveness internationally. This process is weakening the ability of the corporations to perform.

Now, the whole area of who buys junk bonds and that leveraging problem is outside of the scope of what I think I have any expertise to talk on, but certainly by the law of averages some of them are going to go bad, and that can create all sorts of problems in other areas, as you know.

Now, the game is played by going after a stock and putting it in play who has a situation where the value of its stock is significantly less than the market value of its assets, as Mr. LeBaron pointed out. An asset play, in other words. The way the system works today, the way stocks are valued in the marketplace, if you go through a whole business cycle, there are very few companies that wouldn't find themselves in that position at some stage there.

Now, I think we have to take a quick look at these shareholders we are all talking about protecting. The shareholders today are principally firms, professionally managed firms. Some $1.5 trillion are managed professionally. Some two-thirds of the equity in the New York Stock Exchange is owned by these funds, and in a company like Champion, over three-quarters of our stock falls into that category.

These are very sophisticated people. They value a company's stock based on its current earnings or its current prospects. They weigh that investment opportunity against their other alternatives. There are no speculative runups anymore. The end result of this kind of ownership has been reducing the P/E ratios of companies substantially in the last 4 or 5 years. Of course, that has been greatly pushed along by the high interest rates that we have had.

I think the other part of the shareholders, we have to look at our ownership. We have an ownership today of the economic system of this country that feels that its principal responsibility is to the people whose money it manages, with very little feeling about what its real ownership is. In fact, if I heard him right, I think I heard Mr. LeBaron say that it might be something to think of in terms of selling that vote—renting, I think, was the expression.

The rhetoric of the raider is that he is doing everything for the shareholder. What we are really saying is we are willing to liquidate important parts of the strength of the economy to give more money to our pension funds. The real irony of that is that the assurance that an individual will indeed receive his pension is dependent upon the long-term viability of that institution that he works for. Annual up and down performance of the pension fund has very little to do with guaranteeing the success of that.

A quick comment on free market. We don't feel that anything about the whole tender process is free. It's all covered by one segment of law or the other, from the securities acts, the Williams Act, Hart-Scott-Rodino, et cetera. So we don't think there would be a free market self-correction. We just don't think that's in the cards. Therefore, if it is deemed that reform is necessary, it will have to be federally legislated, at least to the extent that the Federal Government would have to allow the States to come back into the regulation of the raider, which is now covered by the Williams Act.

The use of the words free market in the sense of free market for corporations is novel.

It has never really been used before the last 2 years. It has no economic history. It is a clever use of words to put something that we all greatly believe in on top of a brand new and very controversial phenomenon.

Now, as far as the Roundtable is concerned, in the current situation we have suggestions. Our goal is to stop the chaos and put more order into the process and ensure better disclosure. There have been a number of good proposals in this area which we find ourselves being able to agree with. So we think a proposal should include the following features.

A trigger point in stock. A person can't buy beyond a certain point—a suggestion is from 5 to 15 percent—I don't think that makes much difference if it doesn't become so large as to be a controlling factor—He cannot buy more than that, a person, unless the board of directors says he can. If they say he can, fine. If they say he can't—and we feel very strongly the board has to be brought back into this process because if you really look at it, the definition hostile comes about because the board is against it—if the board says no, then the next step is to bid for the whole company. Again, if the board says no, he can have a shareholders' vote called for immediately to vote on his proposition.

Now, what we would propose is more a proxy form than a tender form because, no matter what has been said previously, we think that full disclosure is extremely necessary and hasn't been done as well as possible—isn't done as well as possible now—and the proxy process allows both sides to be required to lay out whether they have the financing, what are they going to do with the company when it's through, and all of those things. It requires the board and management to defend itself as to why it should not approve that kind of an offer.

We feel that if this type of process is put in place, a lot of the things that we all look at as bad in the defending situations—the green-mail and those—will fall out as being not necessary.

VI. STATEMENT OF FELIX G. ROHATYN *******

Let me start off in terms of a general recommendation which I'm making here today, which deals with the securities industry as we are looking at it. I think the problems that we're looking at in our industry, which started off with insider trading, which went on into the junk bond area, which are now expanding beyond that or looking into block trading areas or looking into relationships between arbitrage and merger and acquisition activity.

I think by the time these current investigations are finished, that you're going to want to take an overall look at the structure of the industry that is very, very difficult for you to do in this subcommittee in terms of the relationships within the industry of, say, arbitrage to investment banking, which—we gave up arbitrage fifteen years ago; that may not be right, but we thought it was right—but new entrants into the industry, block trading's relationship to merger and acquisition activity, junk bond investment levels, et cetera—and I think the time has come to set up a commission such as the Cohen Commission of the 1961-'63 period to look at the structure of the industry. It's gotten very, very complicated. You are dealing with world markets. You're dealing with new technologies, and I think the time has come for the Congress to ask for that review.

In terms of takeovers, the SIA has recently proposed some legislative changes. I support those. I've supported them for a long time. I

*******Excerpted from the oral statement of Felix G. Rohatyn, Partner, Lazard Freres and Co.; and Alan Greenspan, President, Townsend-Greenspan and Co., Inc.

don't think they go quite far enough, because they don't address really the problems in the junk bond area, and they don't address the structural issues involved in our industry.

Those seem to me to involve really three issues. One is the question of illegal activity. Second is the implication to the economy of the present level of takeover activity, with specific focus on leverage.

With respect to illegal activity, I support the increase in the enforcement capacity of the SEC, and I think people who break the law should be thrown in jail. I think they ought to go in for longer periods than they've been convicted to so far, but that is a question of judgment.

I think that the ethics of our own business have to be looked at a little more carefully by those of us who run it. I think the growth in our business has been so dramatic that it's been very difficult for those firms, especially the ones that have been growing at spectacular rates, to keep track of actually a sense of continuity and a sense of history about the organizations we are running.

I would also mention that merger and takeover activity includes not only investment bankers; it includes lawyers. It's an international activity. It includes commercial banks. It includes arbitrageurs. And last but not least, it includes very large financial institutions which buy a lot of the paper.

I think the things you have to look at are the integrity of the markets, the safety of financial institutions, and the constructive use of capital. And I think that even though over the long run, capital markets self-correct, in this case that hasn't happened.

I would like to say at the outset that I make no difference between hostile and friendly takeovers. The question of friendliness or hostility is a subjective question. I don't think the Congress or anybody else can get into that issue.

My concern is with the unequal treatment

of shareholders, with unsound financial structures, and with the destabilizing impact of large-scale trading activities, arbitrage activities, as an integral part of takeovers. Bids that are made subject to financing, for instance, in the junk bond area create the possibilities of manipulation. Arbitrageur activity does put companies in play, and whether the result is greenmail or a white knight, the result is usually a very large profit for the raider and not necessarily any great risk.

On the other side of the ledger, defensive maneuvers that have been created to protect companies against raiders are probably as damaging ultimately to the companies themselves and to the economy in terms of taking on enormous amounts of leverage and making the companies less competitive.

The tactics that are connected with defense, in my judgment, are probably as noxious as some of the tactics on offense—lockups, poison pills, selective repurchases. Those are all things that are really harmful to the shareholders.

Now as a result of this activity, financial structures have been badly eroded. I'm sure that it would surprise Cities Service and Gulf to hear that Mr. Pickens was not raiding them, but was simply taking on some kind of friendly discussion with them. But in any case, these mergers did take place. The very largest oil company mergers did take place as a result of raids or threats of raids, many of those financed or committed to be financed with junk bonds, and I do believe that what's happened to the industry is not in the interests of this country.

Now added to this question of unequal treatment of shareholders and unsound financial structures is the fact that the market speculation has become all-pervasive, that arbitrage activity and accumulation of large blocs of stock in the hands of speculative holders are putting companies in play, that we've seen arbitrageurs financed by junk bonds, when the raiders are also being financed by junk bonds, and I think that's an unhealthy relationship.

And last but not least, which is a major concern of mine, is the behavior of institutional investors who are now also behaving like casino players. You have $125, $150 billion worth of junk bonds that have been issued. Clearly, they have been bought by major institutions, institutions that are fiduciaries for retirees, for pensioners, for policy holders, et cetera.

Obviously not all of these junk bonds were issued in connection with mergers and acquisitions, but maybe $35, $40, $50 billion, which is still a great deal of money by anybody's standards. And I believe that there is a risk that in a recession these bonds could get into difficulties, and the taxpayers would be at risk.

I think this is not in the interest of either our economy or this country or what we're trying to do in this country in terms of long-term investment. I'd like to see us limit the amount of junk bonds that federally-insured institutions can carry to some percentage of their portfolio.

I'd like to see a requirement of a higher standard of care and prudence by managers of financial institutions, who are not all geniuses, despite what I've heard here earlier, and make their indemnification provisions and their legal protections subject to maybe a greater exercise of care when they're buying this kind of paper.

I know some of these issues are not the direct responsibility of this subcommittee. I'd like to look at possibly limiting the tax deductibility of high-leverage structures that have acquired significant amounts of their own or some other company's assets within a certain period of time, because essentially what we're doing is subsidizing through the tax system the use of junk bonds.

Clearly, I think that 100-percent financing commitments should be available to companies before they are allowed to make a tender offer. I would lengthen the tender offer period and require one price for the tender offer.

I would clearly close the 13(d) window and eliminate the partnership exemptions under the Hart-Scott-Rodino Act.

At the same time, I think if you do that, you should eliminate the defensive excesses, the greenmail. I think the principle of "One share, one vote" is important. I think you should eliminate poison pills, crown jewel options, and require a shareholder vote on any major restructuring proposals.

I think you might consider, in terms of financial institutions—not "you," as I said, because it's not the subject of this subcommittee—of looking at taxation of tax-free financial institutions on short-swing profits, because that's not the business they are supposed to be in.

4. Some Further Insights

Our case study sample contained two contested takeover cases—Lykes' acquisition of Youngstown Sheet & Tube and International Nickel's acquisition of ESB Inc. It is instructive to examine briefly what happened in those cases and in another on which I have been a consultant.

Youngstown's fortunes were already waning when it was acquired in 1969 at depressed stock prices by the Lykes ocean shipping enterprise. Lykes clearly did not stem the decline. To the contrary, after the merger, Youngstown's most seasoned managers bailed out with golden parachutes, and the new chief executive installed by Lykes attempted, except for a brief period, to run the business from far-off New Orleans without much understanding of steel-making's intricacies. Burdened with a heavy load of acquisition-related debt and preferred stock service obligations, Lykes was forced to bleed cash from Youngstown, leaving little for modernization. Of the capital improvements that were undertaken,

some were extraordinarily poorly planned and executed. Morale plummeted, and operating efficiency at the renovated Indiana Harbor works remained far below industry norms. With import competition increasing, Youngstown's financial results worsened, leading in September 1977 to major plant closures at Youngstown, Ohio. These directly triggered the Congressional Steel Caucus to demand government action that ultimately took the form of the ill-fated Trigger Price Mechanism. In 1978, Youngstown was acquired by the LTV Corporation in a horizontal merger that led to the correction of many previous operating problems.

Inco's 1974 contested acquisition of battery-maker ESB is considered a milestone in takeover history because it was aided for the first time by a blue-ribbon investment banking house, Morgan Stanley. Inco made its attempt because it had considerable cash, wanted to diversify, and identified the battery business as its most promising diversification avenue. It is in the nature of contested takeovers that the target firm does not disclose to the would-be acquirer its internal problems, and significant problems were slowly but invisibly gathering momentum at the time of the takeover. Direct managerial control of ESB by Inco was delayed for $3^{1}/_{2}$ years by an antitrust hold-separate agreement, although parent and subsidiary maintained close liaison and conferred regularly on strategic plans. Even so, when he took over in 1978, Inco's chosen chief executive was unprepared for operational crises resulting from poor product strategy decisions, declining automobile battery demand, and unexpected executive turnover. The crises were aggravated by financial difficulties into which the parent had fallen, making it impossible for Inco to help ESB (which previously enjoyed excellent credit lines) overcome its problems. ESB profits vanished, leading to the divestiture of fragmented and atrophied business units in 1982. The automobile battery market share of

ESB's keystone Exide Division had fallen from 16 percent in the early 1970s to 5.5 percent. Dry cell producer Ray-O-Vac was sold off with a weak strategic position in the crucial alkaline cell market. Over the acquisition's eight-year duration, Inco had lost its total initial investment in ESB.

In 1981, Mobil Oil sought to acquire an unwilling Marathon Oil Corporation. Mobil, which at first offered $85 and then $108 per share of Marathon's common stock, conducted internal analyses valuing Marathon's domestic oil reserves at approximately $180 per share. I agreed to help Marathon resist the takeover attempt because I recognized Marathon as the leading seller of gasoline to price-competitive independent retailers in the Midwest—a supply policy inconsistent with Mobil's historical business strategy. As I worked with Marathon staff to learn more about its operations, however, I discovered another virtue. Marathon appeared to be unusually lean and tightly-managed, able to make decisions and respond to market changes much more rapidly than the giant petroleum companies. I have only fragments of evidence on how it has fared under the parentage of "white knight" U.S. Steel. According to *Business Week*, "Marathon [still] hasn't been encumbered by a bureaucracy.... [The Yates and Brae Field] properties, combined with a fairly efficient marketing and refining operation, have helped keep Marathon highly profitable."[9] Yet according to the president of a gasoline retailing firm with whom I discussed post-merger developments, Marathon's decision-making has slowed perceptibly since the merger.

5. Conclusion

The CEA report says that takeovers "improve efficiency ... and stimulate effective corporate management." Perhaps. But a balanced verdict is not yet in. My case study evidence, biased toward less successful acquisitions, reveals that takeovers by firms with no managerial expertise in the acquired entity's line can be downright efficiency-impairing. It and the first results of our quantitative analyses reveal that takeovers frequently lead to short-run profit-maximizing strategies, eventually leaving wasted corporate hulks in their wake. In the long run, our nation's industrial strength will suffer from such behavior. One hopes that business leaders will learn from bad experience and studies such as ours not to make acquisitions they cannot manage and to manage better what they acquire. Yet the continuing stream of conglomerate takeovers inspires doubts. Moreover, there are persistent structural and institutional incentives for takeovers, or defensive behavior, biased toward short-run profitability.

I cannot claim to know what to do about the problem. It is far from clear that mere procedural reforms will help much. Entrepreneurs are adept at finding loopholes and circumventions. True reform is more likely to come from fundamental changes in macroeconomic policies affecting the cost of capital, in the tax laws favoring mergers, in our view of institutional shareholder obligations, and last but not least, in our understanding of how takeover behavior affects the choice between short- and long-run goals. These are questions I must defer to another day, when my research on the problem has advanced farther.

NOTES

1. See Adam Smith's discourse on the East India Company in *The Wealth of Nations*, especially Book IV, Chapter VII, Part Third.

2. See the papers by Carl Kaysen and Shorey Peterson in a Symposium on Corporate Capitalism, *Quarterly Journal of Economics*, February 1965, pp. 1–51.

3. From Douglas V. Austin, "Tender Offer Update: 1978–1979," *Mergers & Acquisitions*, Summer 1980, p. 16.

4. For recognition of this alternative by the author of a leading textbook on corporate finance, see the testimony of J. Fred Weston in the Senate Judiciary Committee, Subcommittee on Antitrust and Monopoly, hearings, *Mergers and Economic Concentration* (1979), pp. 557–565.

5. Michael C. Jensen and Richard S. Ruback, "The Market for Corporate Control: The Scientific Evidence," *Journal of Financial Economics*, vol. 11 (1983), pp. 20–22.

6. George N. Hatsopoulos, *High Cost of Capital: Handicap of American Industry* (American Business Conference: 1983), p. 118.

7. F.M. Scherer, "Mergers, Sell-Offs, and Managerial Behavior," forthcoming in the proceedings of an AT&T—Columbia Business School conference on strategic planning (September 1984).

8. The first paper, David Ravenscraft and F.M. Scherer, "Mergers and Financial Performance," was presented at the meetings of the Econometric Society in December 1984.

9. "The Toughest Job in Business," *Business Week*, Feb. 25, 1985, pp. 54, 53.

13

Corporate Crimes and Executive Liability: Analysis, Trends and Policy Guidelines

S. Prakash Sethi and
Parveen C. Chopra

The 1980s saw soaring Wall Street profits, massive take overs resulting in more than 30,000 businesses restructuring,[1] often at the expense of consumers and workers, a shake up on Wall Street and several corporations as well as executives tried for criminal negligence and sentenced behind bars with fines in the millions and millions of dollars. Will the 1990s follow the same trend?

Ever since the emergence of large corporations, nations have attempted, with varying degrees of success, to come to grips with the problem of making these institutions adapt to changing societal expectations. Although public control and regulation of corporations have taken different forms in different societies, their aims have been essentially similar:

1. to improve efficiency in the production of socially desirable goods and services;

2. to ensure that the use of human and physical resources conforms to societal expectations;

3. to ensure equitable bargaining conditions and rights for various economic and social groups that must deal with corporations, either directly or indirectly; and

4. to ensure that social priorities and public policy alternatives are freely determined without being disproportionately influenced by large corporations.

A variety of incentives and penalties have been developed to ensure compliance. Incentives have included tax concessions, preference in the allocation of scarce material and human resources, greater discretion in managing corporate internal affairs, and increased economic rewards and social recognition for executives. The penalties have included withdrawal of tax benefits, nonavailability of resources, loss of discretion in management, personal and corporate economic penalties and loss of social status, and, in serious cases lately, imprisonment for the offending executives.

In the recent past, top executives and corporate officers have only rarely faced imprisonment as a penalty for criminal violation of legal statutes, even where an executive was found to have direct complicity and/or involvement in the corporation's illegal acts. Prison sentences have been levied most often where a corporate executive was convicted of a law violation involving a company's stockholders. Otherwise, executives have almost invariably been protected by the corporate veil of secrecy. In the event the corporate veil was pierced and the executive found guilty, he was seldom imprisoned and his fines were invariably paid by the corporation. No significant social stigma ensued, and the offender received both moral and social support from his peer group, which considered such crimes to be "technical" violations of law and misfortunate for the offender who was caught.[2]

This situation has now changed rather drastically. There has been an enormous increase in the nature and extent of business activities subjected to governmental regulation or control. In addition to expansion of regulation of corporate activities in the traditional areas of securities, fraud, investment, financial abuse or misappropriation of funds, and market behavior, new activities such as product safety, environmental pollution, and hazardous working conditions or in-plant safety come about with the growing realization that corporate law violations affecting public health and safety, called social welfare more recently corporate crimes, are more pervasive than originally perceived and more difficult to control.

The findings of a recent study of illegal corporate behavior conducted under the auspices of National Institute of Law Enforcement Assistance Administration (LEAA study) are worth noting.[3] The study analyzed data for the 582 largest publicly owned corporations (477 manufacturing, 18 wholesale, 66 retail, and 21 service) for "initiation of enforcement action" for law violation by 24 federal agencies during the years 1975 and 1976.[4] The LEAA study found that 60 percent of the corporations studied had at least one action initiated against them. Actions were classified into serious, moderate, and minor violations.

In the manufacturing sector, 300 parent corporations had an average of 4.8 actions taken against them. Almost half of the parent manufacturing corporations had one or more serious or moderate violations. More than 40 percent of the manufacturing corporations engaged in repeated violations. One parent corporation had 62 actions initiated against it.

Over three-fourths of all actions were in the manufacturing, environmental, and labor areas. About one-fourth of the corporations violated these regulations at least once. Illegal corporate behavior was found least often in the financial and trade areas, but even here 5 to 10 percent of the corporations did violate. Large corporations had a greater proportion of violations than their share in the sample would indicate; over 70 percent of the actions were against them, and they had more than two-thirds of all serious or moderate violations.

The increased regulation has been accompanied by willingness of the courts to preserve human resources of our society which has expanded the scope of executive liability in corporations. In the 1980s the courts took a much stricter view of executive liability as compared to earlier decades and have held executives personally responsible for corporate violations. Executives had to face both civil and criminal charges for negligence of duty and were made to serve sentences of various lengths behind bars in addition to severe penalties running into millions and sometimes hundreds of millions[5] of dollars depending upon the nature of the corporate crime.

A summary of some of the cases that follows indicates that the trend for holding an executive criminally responsible is on the increase. In the 1970s the courts had taken a serious view of SEC violations and held the executives criminally responsible for such violations. While this trend got stronger in the

1980s, crimes of work safety and environmental pollution have started receiving the same level of seriousness from courts as financial crimes.

Mr. Ivan Boesky was sentenced to three years in prison and paid $100 million in penalties on the charge of insider trading. Mr. Barr of United American Banks is serving an 18 year sentence for illegal loans. Hundreds of savings and loan associations were found in deep financial troubles in the 1980s. The ones that took the wrong route were not only seized by the government or made insolvent but its executives were held responsible for

TABLE 1. Recent Punishments for Financial and Security Crimes by Corporations.
Corporations and Executives charged for criminal and civil violations under SEC Act[†].

Corporations	Crime	Punishment
1. Drexel Burnham Lambert Group (DBL)*	Criminal charges of mail, wire and security fraud against DBL. Mr. Michael Miliken, Head of Junk Bond Operations charged with 98 counts of insider trading, mail fraud, racketeering, etc. Decision is still awaited as of 1990. In addition, civil violations filed by SEC in Sept, 1988 have yet to be decided.	DBL pleaded guilty to criminal charges and paid $650 million in fines and restitution. DBL was also barred to pay a bonus of $200 million to Mr. Miliken. DBL was barred by FSLIC from underwriting junk bond issues from which it draws 90% of its profits. Industry experts believe that punishment by SEC is a hard hitting blow to DBL.
2. Ivan F. Boesky Co.*	Criminal charge of conspiring to file false statements.	Ivan Boesky pleaded guilty and was sentenced to 3 years in prison. He was also fined $100 million as a penalty.
3. Lincoln Savings and Loan Co., California**	Fraud and mismanagement	Lincoln Co., was seized by government management and its collapse will cost the taxpayers $2 billion. The case is still in the court.
4. Warner Lambert Co.*	Death of 6 employees due to explosion was tried as 6 counts of manslaughter and 6 counts of criminally negligent homicide.	Eventually the W.L. Co., was exonerated of criminal charges but the company was required to pay $11 million to different parties. In addition the manufacturers of machinery used in production process Hamac-Hansella, a West German machinery manufacturer; and other vendors. Petrochemicals, Texas; and Liquid Carbonics, New Jersey were fined $.5 million. Additional payments ranging from $10,000 to $200,000 were made by 12 other defendants. The Chicle factory was closed and W.L. Co., spent another $7 million to help employees due to the plant closing.

*Sethi, Prakash S. *Up Against The Corporate Wall:* Modern Corporations and Social Issues of the Nineties (NJ: Prentice Hall, 1990).

**New York Times,* "Business People: Financial Newsmakers of 1989." January 1, 1990, p. 33.

***Stedman, Michael J., "Doing Time: Advice From a Jailed Banker." *Bankers Monthly,* Volume 105, No. 11, November 1988, pp. 16–22.

****Adler, William M., and Binstein, Michael, "The Speaker and the Sleazy Banker." *Bankers Monthly, Volume 105, No. 3, March 1988, pp. 79–84.*

†Ed. Note: This article was originally published before some of these cases were completed in the courts.

fraud, mismanagement, falsification of financial statements, sham transactions to earn bogus profits, money laundering, etc. and charged for racketeering and barred from doing certain operations that were illegal. Drexel Burnham Lambert (DBL) Group pleaded guilty to criminal charges and paid $650 million in fines and restitution. DBL was also barred from underwriting junk bond issues which produced 90% of its profits in 1989. In addition Mr. Michael Miliken, Head of Junk Bond Operations is still being tried on 98 charges of insider trading, mail fraud, racketeering, etc. It's clear that in the 1990s we will see many more organizations being sued for illegality because the banking industry is still not out of the woods as yet. Federal bail out of the Savings and Loan industry will cost taxpayers more than $100 billion over the next decade and Lincoln Savings and Loan Company's collapse alone will cost $2 billion making it the costliest failure on record. Back in 1986 the total bank frauds were estimated to be only $1.1 billion.[6] This means a nine times increase in bank failures due to frauds in the 1990s as compared to the mid 1980s.

SEC in the past has emphasized that the Justice Department and FBI were too busy dealing with more violent crimes and probably did not have enough knowledge and experience in securities fraud to adequately deal with sophisticated crimes of information, in which a crucial fact was kept away from the victim investor. As a result, this has led to SEC pleading for certain police powers to regulate SEC laws effectively.[7] Whether SEC pursues this direction more emphatically remains to be seen. But meanwhile FBI has assigned the top 5 national investigative priority to white collar crimes.[8]

There is no other alternative except to be ethical and legal on the part of an executive since even close contacts and power of a high government official like the Speaker of the House could not save a banker.[9] Another

Banker who is serving 18 years in jail advises fellow bankers to avoid risky real estate and energy loans as well as loans to friends and family members.[10] Even the liability insurance policies provide no coverage to pay fines nor do they cover expenses for legal defense on account of criminal charges. An insurance company providing such a coverage would probably be viewed as encouraging criminal acts.[11]

Another area in which the judicial system seems to be trying to make punishment fit the corporate crime is serious health and safety violations under the Occupational and Safety Health Act. In the 1980s fines have increased and so have the jail sentences. Previously corporations could get away with civil fines for serious injuries or even death of a worker in the 1970s. In fact the highest fine imposed by OSHA so far was $2.6 million in the case of Iowa Beef Processors, the largest in the industry, where safety related accidents were a routine. Even there when management did not agree to the modernization plan this fine was increased to $5.6 million. The National Film Recovery Systems Inc. Illinois case is a trend setter for the 1990s. The owner and executives in this case were charged criminally with the death of a worker who died in the plant due to the use of Cyanide about which the worker was not informed. The owner and executives were jailed for 25 years each and fined for murder, involuntary manslaughter and reckless conduct. In another case of a death of two construction workers, the three executives of Sabine Consolidated have been indicted on criminal charges. Even where it was not possible to foresee the dangerous outcome of worker death or injury the fines were so heavy that the corporation ceased to function. Warner Lambert Co. decided to close its Chicle division Plant in New York and paid $11 million to various parties and spent another $7 million to help employees due to plant closings. Even manufacturers of machinery and suppliers of raw material could not escape strict penalties.

Even in the case of EPA violations twenty corporate executives were jailed for violations of toxic wastes disposal laws. Chemical accidents can probably do the most damage not only to corporate members but also to the community at large. The recent case of the Union Carbide plant at Bhopal, India in which more than 3,500 have died so far due

TABLE 2. Punishments for Recent Corporate Crimes of Health and Safety.
Corporations and executives charged for criminal and civil violations under OSHA.

Corporation	Crime	Punishment
1. Iowa Beef Processors*	Worker injuries due to safety hazards.	The initial fine of $2.6 million was increased to $5.6 million for lack of cooperation on the part of management to create safe working conditions through modernization of plant as ordered by OSHA. This is OSHA's largest fine ever.
2. National Film Recovery Systems Inc., Illinois*	Criminal charge of murder and involuntary manslaughter for the death of a worker due to use of cyanide for which worker was uniformed. In addition, management was charged on 20 counts of reckless conduct.	Owner as well as managers involved were each sentenced to 25 years in the custody of the Illinois Dept of Corrections and also fined $10,000 each on murder convictions. In addition, each defendant was fined $10,000 for involuntary manslaughter and $14,000 each for the reckless conduct conviction.
3. Sabine Consolidated Inc.**	Death of 2 construction workers on the job was tried as criminally negligent homicide.	Three executives were indicted on criminal charges.
4. United American Bank***	Illegal loans	The Chief Loan Officer Mr. Barr was sentenced twice to Federal Penitentiaries and is currently serving his 18 years. FDIC was required to pay $700 million for illegal loans.
5. Vernon Savings and Loan, Texas****	Falsification of financial statements. Sham transactions to earn bogus profits and generating two sets of minutes of board meetings.	Vernon Savings declared insolvent. Don Dixon who pushed the Bank into over $350 million of debt by sham transactions has been charged by FSLIC for racketeering. Almost all of its thrift loans were in default.

*Sethi, Prakash S. *Up Against The Corporate Wall:* Modern Corporations and Social Issues of the Nineties (NJ: Prentice Hall, 1990).

**New York Times*, "Business People; Financial Newsmakers of 1989." January 1, 1990, p. 33.

***Stedman, Michael J., "Doing Time: Advice From a Jailed Banker." *Bankers Monthly,* Volume 105, No. 11, November 1988, pp. 16–22.

****Adler, William M., and Binstein, Michael, "The Speaker and the Sleazy Banker." *Bankers Monthly,* Volume 105, No. 3, March 1988, pp. 79–84.

TABLE 3. Recent Punishments For Environmental Crimes By Corporations.
Corporations and executives charged for criminal and civil violations under EPA and Toxic Substances Control Act.

Corporations	Crime	Punishment
Companies in Los Angeles County, CA*	Violations of toxic waste disposal laws.	Los Angeles county has jailed 20 executives during the past 2 years for violations of toxic waste disposal laws. In addition, all occupational deaths are being tried as possible homicides.
Union Carbide Plant at Bhopal, India**	Methyl Isocyanate chemical (MIC) killed more than 3,500 and injured scores of thousands.	Bhopal plant in India was closed permanently. President of Union Carbide USA was arrested and ordered to leave the country. UC (USA) agreed to pay $470 million in an out of court settlement with the government of India which has been upheld once by the Supreme Court of India. Lately with a change in government in India, the new government has decided to challenge UC's agreement with the previous government on the grounds of insufficiency for over 3,500 deaths and injuries to over 20,000 people.

*Tasini, Jonathan, "The Clamor to Make Punishment Fit the Corporate Crime," *Business Week,* February 10, 1986, p. 73.

***Newsday, "The Top 10: You Pick 'Em—We Can't," December 1989, p. 5.

to the use of Methyl Isolyanate is an eye opener. The plant was closed permanently by the government and Chairman Anderson of Union Carbide was arrested and then released in Bhopal. A court approved settlement of $470 million, which was considered too meager in international circles and by the relatives of victims in India was challenged in the Supreme Court of India, bringing an end to litigation process for the time being, that has lasted for five years and consumed an enormous amount of legal costs. The newly elected government has threatened to reopen the case.

The recent trends raise questions about the new role of courts, changing relationships between business and other social institutions, social expectations of corporate executives, and the effect of expanding personal criminal liability on corporate decision making and performance and, by implication, on economic growth and social welfare. Even if one accepts the desirability of the social goals that these means are intended to achieve, there is a question as to whether imposition of absolute and vicarious personal criminal liability on corporate executives is the best way to achieve these goals.

EXPANSION OF THE SCOPE OF EXECUTIVE CRIMINAL LIABILITY

Several studies from the United States, France, Great Britain, and India provide a vivid picture of the increasing risk of exposure of a corporate executive to criminal and civil prosecution in the course of managing the day-to-day affairs of a company.

FILM RECOVERY SYSTEMS, INC.

It raises the serious question of the extent of an officer's culpability for serious harm, and even death caused to workers from unsafe working conditions.

The Film Recovery case is a landmark in the corporate crimes field because for the first time corporate officials have been found guilty in a job related death. In other cases corporate executives have been charged with manslaughter but more often than not, it is the corporation that ended up paying the fines, and the executives got off with a slap on their wrists.[12]

On June 14, 1985 Judge Ronald J.P. Banks, sitting on a non-jury trial, convicted three executives of National Film Recovery Systems, a small firm then based in Elk Grove, Illinois, of murder in the death of one employee, Mr. Stefan Golab, 61, a Polish immigrant who had been on the job for only two months.

The victim, Stefan Golab left his native Poland in November 1981 to start a new life in the United States. On December 26, 1982, he began work as a laborer for Film Recovery Systems, which operated to recover silver from used photographic film. He was on the job barely two months when on February 10, 1983 he met his death.[13]

The Defendants

In October, 1983 Grand Jury indicted the three corporations involved and five executives. The three corporations were Metallic Marketing, Inc. (MMI), Film Recovery Systems, Inc. (FRS) and B.R. McKay and Sons who were charged with involuntary manslaughter on November 21, 1983. The same Grand Jury charged the Corporate managers (Steven O'Neil, President of FRS; Gerald Pett, V.P. of FRS, Charles Kirschbaum, Plant Manager at Elk Grove; Daniel Rodriguez, Job Supervisor at Elk Grove, and Michael Mackay, a Director of FRS whose company, B.R. Mackay and Sons, owned half of FRS) with twenty violations of reckless conduct. On May 1, 1984 another Grand Jury (which was convened in April) indicted these same individuals for murder because they knowingly caused the death of Stefan Golab by exposing him to unsafe working conditions in the FRS work environment.[14] O'Neil claimed that he had previously worked at RKS full-time in various positions both inside and outside the plant and during this period he suffered no injury or illness.[15] At FRS he had modified the process by installing a vacuum system and an evacuation system making work conditions safer for the employees.[16]

Charges Against Corporate Defendants and Individual Defendants

On May 6, 1983, after receiving a toxicological laboratory report dated March 17, 1983, the Medical Examiner ruled that Golab died from acute cyanide poisoning through inhalation of cyanide fumes in the plant at FRS. In all, two medical examiners and two toxicologists were called in to discern the cause of death. They came up with a split verdict. One medical examiner and one toxicologist found that Golab died of heart failure; the others cited cyanide poisoning. Contrary to the defendant's assertions that Golab died of a heart failure, the prosecution claimed that Golab suffered a fatal cyanide blood concentration. The defendants were indicted for murder, involuntary manslaughter and reckless conduct. The charges alleged that Golab was hired as an employee without disclosing to him the use and attendant dangers of cyanide in the work place and failed to provide safety equipment to him and other employees through toxic exposure to a chemical used in the normal industrial process of a corporation.[17] The defendants on the other hand took the position that Golab died of heart problems of which management was not aware.[18] He had convulsed and foamed at the mouth when he collapsed and suffered from a condition which included an enlarged heart and fifty percent blockage in the two major arteries.

Role of Regulatory Agencies

In November, 1982, an inspector from the Occupational Safety and Health Administration came to the plant and, after reviewing company records related to work injuries, determined that no follow-up investigation was required. There were eight or more inspections by the Metropolitan Sanitary District between 1981 and 1983. Although odor was detected, the inspectors never reported any violations concerning improper waste discharge or pollution problems. Similarly, inspections by the Elk Grove Village Fire Department during 1980 and 1981 did not indicate any ventilation problems. In addition to governmental inspections, FRS's insurance company regularly inspected the plant and continued providing coverage. Recommendations made by it were followed through by FRS.

After Golab's death on March 11, 1983, OSHA fined $4,850 for unapproved respirators, gloves, lack of training programs regarding cyanide exposure, and for not providing emergency eyewash, protective eye gear or antidote for cyanide poisoning. Judge O'Brien reduced the fine to $2,425 because the FRS was in dire financial straits.[19] Defendants also criticized OSHA on the grounds that it tested the plant at full capacity to find toxicity levels in the environment whereas the plant normally ran at two thirds capacity.[20] A co-worker of Golab, Roman Guzoski testified that Golab had felt so ill in the work environment that he was seeking a job transfer.[21] Attorneys for Steven O'Neil, President of FRS, tried to distance him from day to day operations.[22] They argued his role was to procure film for processing and marketing the retrieved film. These roles were performed off site. It was Charles Kirschbaum who ran the plant and in his absence Gerald Pett stepped in but the latter was acquitted so the onus fell on Kirschbaum. Kirschbaum spent 6 to 8 hours a day in the plant and encouraged workers to use safety equipment even though he himself never wore such equipment nor suffered any adverse effects. In September 1982 he moved his office to a newly acquired building located adjacent to the plant building.[23] It was Daniel Rodriguez who performed the role of shop floor manager and frequently acted as interpreter for the Spanish workers.[24]

The Decision by the Lower Court. During the course of judgment Judge Banks stated that he never forgot the most important concept in criminal law, that being the defendants they are presumed innocent and that it is the burden of the state that they must prove guilt beyond a reasonable doubt."[25] Judge Banks acquitted Pett of all charges and acquitted the other defendants of said reckless conduct charges.

Thus, on June 14, 1985, at the close of all the evidence and after argument of counsel, Judge Banks found the remaining individual defendants guilty of murder and fourteen counts of reckless conduct. He also found the corporate defendants guilty of involuntary manslaughter and the fourteen reckless conduct charges.

On July 1, 1985 Judge Banks sentenced the individual defendants to twenty five years in the custody of the Illinois Department of Corrections and fined them $10,000 each on the murder conviction. In addition defendants were sentenced to serve 364 days in the custody of the Illinois Department of Corrections, on a concurrent basis, on account of reckless conduct convictions. The corporate defendants were fined $10,000 each on the involuntary manslaughter conviction and $14,000 each for the reckless conduct convictions.

Mackay, the majority owner, of B.R. Mackay and Sons, who did go through the motions of taking over FRS because of unpaid debts never faced trial. Both O'Neil and Mackay claimed that the other one was "in charge" at the time of death of Golab. The Governor of Utah refused the State of Illinois's request to extradite him twice due to the reason that the nature of charges and publicity in the news media had made "chances for a fair trial in Illinois" very slim.

Lower Court's Verdict Appealed by Defendants. Defendants have appealed the decision by Judge Banks on the ground, among others, that federal laws pre empt state laws.

In the interview, the attorney who represented Steven O'Neil, FRS and MMI indicated that the Pre-emption argument was the cornerstone of their defense. The Pre-emption doctrine is based on the contention that our federal system of government grants the federal government the ability to completely occupy a particular field or activity to the exclusion of all state actions. In summary the defense maintains that

1. Illinois law is not relevant; and

2. the defendants broke no federal law.

As of Spring 1989 the appeal was still pending and it seemed unlikely that it could be resolved before 1990. Possible reason for this could be that the court in the National Film Recovery case was awaiting an Illinois Supreme Court decision in a similar case that has been brought against Chicago Magnetic Wire Corp. The management in that Corporation was indicated for aggravated battery and reckless assault, in 1984, for injury to its employees.

The case against Chicago Magnetic Wire established another milestone in corporate crimes when it decided, on February 2, 1989 that OSHA does not bar states from prosecuting corporate officials.[26] This ruling has opened the way for similar actions against corporate executives by other states where, it is believed, at least eight actions were pending as of early 1990. Indeed it will come up for appeal to higher courts.

INSIDER TRADING— THE LEVINE BOESKY AND THE DREXEL BURNHAM LAMBERT CAPER

How and why do Innovative Entrepreneurs become White Collar Criminals? Since information gained in course of a duty to-

wards a corporation is insider information, any attempt to deceive or defraud or to gain unfair advantage of this information is like stealing some one else's property.

The line, between untrammeled greed for which there is plethora of legislation but inadequate enforcement and enlightened self-interest as espoused by Adam Smith for the success of a capitalistic system is indeed very thin. It is constantly blurred by those who make the water muddy by manipulating various financial instruments so that neither they can see their reflection clearly nor can others.

The decade of the eighties has gone down in history as a decade of mergers and takeovers that required huge amounts of financing. Out of several sources of financing for mergers one source that has gained most attention is through the sale of Junk Bonds to finance acquisitions. Ivan Boesky, CEO of Ivan F. Boesky & Company, who got caught and decided to put his former colleagues into play in order to get a good deal for himself, presents an intriguing case study in corporate crimes.

The fall of Ivan Boesky was as steep as was his meteoric rise on Wall Street and an enormous increase in his personal wealth and public image. He frequently lectured at leading business schools, became an ardent patron of the arts, and a donor to institutions of higher learning.[27]

His first use of inside information came about on February 1985, when he persuaded Mr. Dennis Levine, an Investment Banker and a rising star in the Wall Street firm of Drexel Burnham Lambert (DBL), to sell him confidential information concerning DBL's involvement in forthcoming similar activities which had not yet become public. Levine supplied Boesky with inside information between February 1985 and February 1986 which yielded Boesky some $50 million in profits. Levine was, however, nabbed by the Securities Exchange Commission (SEC) as a result of follow up on an anonymous tip. Boesky was arrested, and charged by SEC with securities fraud. He formally settled with the SEC by paying a $100 million penalty and pleaded guilty to a single criminal charge of conspiring to file false statements with the SEC. He was sentenced to three years in prison and on March 24, 1988, he surrendered to Federal authorities.[28]

The ripple effect of the Boesky affair was seen in other countries and other perpetrators in Europe, notably England and France were nabbed.[29]

It took another two years for SEC to bring charges against Miliken and Drexel Burnham Lambert (DBL). In a settlement with SEC DBL agreed to plead guilty to six counts of criminal fraud, pay a fine of $650 million and cooperate with the government in its ongoing investigation.[30] DBL also agreed to fire Mr. Michael R. Miliken, the genius behind the 1980s Junk Bond market, and also deny him his 1988 bonus estimated at over $200 million. Mr. Miliken has forcefully denied any wrong doing and has not yet settled with the government. He is challenging DBL settlement as partially illegal and is also fighting his dismissal and bonus forfeiture by DBL.[31]

SECURITY LAWS AND INSIDER INFORMATION

The Glass Stegall Act of 1933 was formed after the stock market crash in October 1929, to regulate the Financial Markets. It separated Commercial Banks from Investment Banks. The Securities Act of 1934 led to the creation of Securities and Exchange Commission to police all financial markets. In 1940, the Investment Admissions Act was enacted to permit the courts to prosecute any operation that led to deceit or fraud of the consumer. The 1968 enactment in the form of Williams Act requires that anyone accumulating a stock has to give notice in additions to other restrictions imposed by it. Rule 10b (17 C.F.R. 240) of the Securities and Exchange Commission Act of 1934 is most relevant to insider information.

For one to be guilty of insider trading there must have been some kind of breach of a duty to keep information confidential. In addition there must be intent to defraud or deceive or act with reckless disregard toward deception or fraud. The definition of insider trading is set by precedent and each situation must be looked on a case by case basis.

During the past few years there has been an avalanche of insider cases brought against Printers (Chiarelli and *Business Week*), reporters (Winans), brokerage house employees (Siegel, Wang), brokers (Jeffries), major executives (Thayer), lawyers and arbitrage deal makers (Boesky). Major suspicion has countered on Wall Street stalwarts such as Drexel Burnham Lambert, Kidder Peabody, Merrill Lynch and Goldman Sachs.[32]

Much of present activity goes back to a case brought by the SEC against Texas Gulf Sulphur (TGS) in 1964.[33] This landmark case gave directions as to when management can release to the public major corporate developments and the exercise of corporate stock. The "disclosure-or-refrain rule states that persons, or at least some persons, who possess material non-public information pertaining to the value of a corporation's securities cannot buy or sell the securities unless they first disclose the information." The scope of "disclosure-or-refrain rule" has further been extended under rule 10b-5 of the SEC Act of 1934 and other anti-fraud provisions such as Section 206 of The Investment Advisors Act and The Williams Act, to restrict the conduct of outsiders trading on information that affects securities prices though unrelated to corporate prospects (e.g., information that somebody is about to make a tender offer or publish a "sell" recommendation that is expected to have a sharp and immediate, if only short term, impact on stock prices).

SEC has used misappropriation theory to nail those who take advantage of information that is someone else's property. The misappropriation theory holds that it is the theft, or misappropriation, of confidential information by someone such as an investment banker or lawyer entrusted with it, that gives rise to criminal liability.[34] This theory was upheld by the Supreme Court in the R. Foster Winans case.

In 1984, The Insider Trading Sanctions Act was enacted into law. It gave the SEC authority to seek monetary penalties and fines up to three times the defendant's illegal profits.[35] The legal basis still remains ambiguous and as a result leaves too much discretionary power with SEC. In order to bring clarity to the issue of insider trading SEC proposed a new definition in the Insider Trading Act of 1987. The newly proposed definition combines elements of misappropriation theory with a portrait of the insider as an agent.[36]

Even though Supreme Court had upheld the misappropriation theory, it proved inconclusive on stock fraud since the judges were evenly split at 4–4.[37]

Despite momentum gained in the recent past, for a precise definition and all concerned parties (Congress, SEC, and financial community), showing a compromising attitude, the matter remains unresolved. Even the 1988 congressional legislation on insider trading does not offer an acceptable solution. There seems to be a debate going on over the rules of the game governing financial markets. Will financial markets be better served through new legislation or better enforcement of present rules be called for?

Many think that stiffer penalties are called for. Currently the maximum sentence is five years in America, perhaps ten years would be more of a deterrent to Levine/Boesky/Miliken—DBL scandals. In addition these penalties need to be enforced and plea-bargaining needs to be cut down drastically.

Until insider trading has a uniform definition across all borders, it will be hard to eliminate. Nonetheless, newer technology like the NYSE's Automatic Search and Match System (ASAM) that stores information on 500,000 American executives including the clubs they belong to, where they lived and used to work, and so on, legality of which has yet to be established, would be of great help in the 1990s. It can detect price jumps that are not easily explainable and contain suspicious patterns of stock dealings in less than two hours instead of the six weeks it used to take beforehand. It also shows when, at what price, and for whom the trade was executed. It is this new technology, along with precise definition of security laws, and increased powers for SEC in implementation that corporate crimes in the 1990s will be restricted in insider trading.

IOWA BEEF PROCESSORS, INC. (IBP, INC.)

Unsafe Working Conditions and Labor Practices in the Meat Industry.

Janet Henrich had worked at IBP, Inc. (formerly known as Iowa Beef Processors, Inc.) for only a week when the machine with tooth rollers and a fine blade grabbed her gloved right hand and pulled it through, skinning it very much like another piece of meat. Four of her tendons were severed in addition to damaged nerves in her hand and fingers. There was no safety switch. As Janet went to the hospital, the machine was hosed off and another person continued work on the same machine. The workers and the union claimed that such incidents were not uncommon.[38]

High Accident Rates in the Industry

The meat packing industry is one of the most dangerous in the entire economy. It has 26.3 injuries per 100 full-time workers, it ranked fourth in 1985 behind manufacturers of structural wood members (28.3) sawmill operations (27.8) and mobile home manufacturers (27.3). Such industries, with higher rates of accidents, are characterized by hard physical labor including tools that can do bodily harm if not used properly. A job in the meat packing industry does not demand great skills, but it does call for vigilance and attention.[39] A momentary lapse can result in injury. A very high proportion of 100,000 employees who work in the meat packing industry perform monotonous repetitive motion jobs at their assigned stations on the assembly line. A person may perform the same cuts a thousand times an hour. There is constant pressure to keep pace with the conveyor belt. No wonder that Charles Dickens called a worker "an appendage of the machine."[40]

Occupation Safety and Health Administration (OSHA) and IBP

OSHA, a branch of the Labor Department, proposed a $2.59 million fine against IBP, the nation's largest meat packing company, based on a complaint from the IBP Workers Union, the United Food and Commercial Workers Union (UFCW). The charges were that IBP failed to report 1,038 job-related injuries and illnesses at its plant in Dakota City, Nebraska, from January 1985 through December 1986. In announcing the action, Assistant Labor Secretary John A. Pendergrass said, "This case is the worst example of under reporting injuries and illnesses to workers ever encountered by OSHA in its sixteen year history."[41]

IBP, Inc. is a subsidiary of Occidental Petroleum and lists sales of $6.82 billion a year. Occidental acquired IBP in 1981 for $795 million. In 1980 IBP had profits of $53 million on sales of $4.8 billion. After acquisition, earnings increased to 104.8 million on sales of $5.0 billion. In 1985 the earnings further increased to $144.6 million on sales of $6.5 billion.

IBP is a giant in the industry. It employs approximately 18,000 workers (roughly 18% of the industry workforce) in 10 beef plants and 4 pork plants that are located in 8 states. In 1986 IBP processed 7.9 million cattle and 4.4 million hogs, a record for the company.

IBP and the Union.

The United Food and Commercial Workers Union filed a complaint against IBP alleging that IBP kept a fraudulent set of books regarding job safety with the intent of deceiving OSHA and forestalling plant inspections. This complaint led to the $2.46 million fine assessed against IBP by OSHA. The complaint was filed during a period when relations between the Union and the corporation were strained.

According to the Union, management is concerned only with profits—the bottom line. This goal was so important to management that it would trade workers' safety to enhance it. Union sees management as having adopted a strategy of Union busting.

The Meat Packing Industry and IBP

Based on 1985 data the Union claimed that there were 30.4 work-related injuries and illnesses for every 100 workers in meat packing; of these, 15.1 (per hundred) led to time away from work.

According to the American Meat Institute, the industry's trade and lobbying group, the injury incidence rate has declined by 23% since 1979. In human terms, the reduction in meat packing injuries translates to 16–17 thousand fewer workers hurt on the job today than in 1979. Still there is room for improvement and industry is striving to reduce the injuries.[42]

The worst safety problem at the IBP Dakota City plant, according to the Union, was due to excessive chain speeds, workforce turnover, improper training, and production receiving priority over worker safety.

The Union alleged that new workers hired by IBP were usually young mothers between the ages of 18 and 25; of Mexican and southeast Asian origin. The turnover rate was 500% and it was considered beneficial to profits.

Mr. C. Manly Molpus, President of the American Meat Institute and Mr. Robert L. Peterson, chairman and Chief Executive Officer of IBP, among others, provided testimony before the subcommittee on Employment and Housing of the U.S. House of Representatives' House Government Operations Committee, in May 1987, on safety in the meat industry. Mr. Molpus emphasized two dimensions of safety. The first aspect of safety to him was the production of safe products for the consumer that was regulated by USDA inspections who administered most intensive health-related regulatory programs in Government. As a result, the American consumer enjoys the world's safest supply of meat products. In regard to the second aspect of safety he referred to the Bureau of Labor Statistics reports that indicate meat packing plants (S1C Code 2011) have reduced their injury incidence rates by 23% during the period from 1979 to 1985.[43]

Mr. Peterson, the Chairman and CEO of IBP directly countered the testimony of UFCW witness before the subcommittee. He denied that meat processing plants were unclean or unsafe because they were frequently subject to unannounced OSHA inspections. He pointed out to the 200 inspectors from the Department of Agriculture in the plant to ensure that the plant and equipment were clean and that the meat was processed under the stringent sanitary conditions. He insisted that IBP was not indifferent to the issue of worker safety.[44]

IBP Changes Its Outlook Towards Union

Soon after the initial fine imposed by OSHA, IBP started modernization of its Da-kota plant which was found to be inadequate and thus unacceptable to OSHA. UFCW launched a major publicity campaign highlighting IBP's unsafe working conditions while showing willingness to work with IBP management. Congressional inquiry further intensified the negative public image of IBP. OSHA fined another $3.0 million making it a total of $5.6 million, the agency's largest fine ever.

IBP changed its outlook towards the UFCW and voluntarily recognized the Union at its Joslin, Illinois plant where it had resisted workers' efforts to organize themselves.[45] This was a major shift in management policy towards the Union. This has resulted in rapid growth in Union membership. Finally there is peace but how long will it last? Only time will tell.

The people of the State of New York v. Warner-Lambert Company et al.

The New York manufacturing plant owned and operated by the American Chicle Division of the Warner-Lambert Corporation was destroyed by an explosion and fire resulting in the death of six employees, with burns and injuries to 54 of 118 employees who were working at the time of the explosion. Many of the injured employees had to be hospitalized for an extended period of time. The two corporations involved, the Warner Lambert Company and the American Chicle Division, along with the four corporate officers were indicted before the Grand Jury for six counts of manslaughter in the second degree and six counts of criminally negligent homicide.[46]

According to the District Attorney, the deaths, injuries, and physical damage resulted from the explosion of a heavy concentration of ambient magnesium stearate (MS) dust that was present in the Freshen-Up department. The dust explosion was preceded by a low level detonation which was attributed to a mechanical sparking or heat induced breakup of the parts of the Uniplast equipment in one of several lines of production. Warner-Lambert's experts contended that the creation of volatile liquid oxygen from the use of stable liquid nitrogen could not reasonably have been foreseen. In addition, the New York City Department of OSHA never warned of any risk associated with the use of liquid nitrogen.

After long arduous legal battles, the court dismissed the indictments on grounds that the evidence was not legally sufficient to impose the charges of criminal liability on any of the defendants. But the W.L. Corporation, the manufacturer who supplied machinery as well as other suppliers were fined $16 million dollars and the plant was closed by the Warner-Lambert Company permanently.

United States v. Park

On June 9, 1975, the U.S. Supreme Court upheld the conviction of John R. Park, the Chief Executive Officer of Acme Products, Inc., Philadelphia, for rodent infestation in the supermarket chain's Baltimore warehouse by the Federal Food and Drug Administration (FDA). The U.S. Supreme Court decided that the Chief Executive Officer of a corporation can be found personally guilty of the criminal charges, if unsanitary conditions anywhere in his company contaminate food or otherwise endanger health and/or safety.[47] Under the Dotterweich doctrine,[48] courts have held corporate officers personally liable for violations of the Food, Drug, and Cosmetic Act of 1938, even though they had no direct involvement or actual knowledge of the violation.[49] Until the Park Co. case, only executives with immediate, close supervisory responsibilities over operations where violations occurred, were held responsible.

FDA had found extensive evidence of rodent infestation and other unsanitary conditions. The United States filed a suit against Park charging them with five criminal counts of violations under the 1938 Act. Acme pleaded guilty. John R. Park, President, moved for acquittal. The government offered no evidence that Park was guilty because he was aware of the problems in the Baltimore warehouse and was the corporate officer who bore general responsibility for all company activities that would subject him to criminal liability. Park testified that although he was responsible for all Acme's employees and the general directions that company took yet the size and complexity of Acme's operations demanded that he must delegate responsibility for different phases of operations to various line and staff subordinates.

The Jury found Park guilty. Park appealed on the grounds, among other things, that the district court erred in its instructions to the jury in defining responsible relationship by stating that the statute makes individuals, as well as corporations, liable for violations, when "the individual had a responsible relation to the situation, even though he may not have participated personally." The court indicated that the definition of the "responsible relationship was really a jury question and not even subject to being defined by the court." A divided court of appeals reversed the decision and remanded the case for a new trial on the grounds that it did not dispense with the need to prove that Park was in some way personally responsible for the act constituting the crime. The Supreme Court reversed the appeals court, saying that

1. criminal liability under the Act does not turn on awareness of some wrongdoing or conscious fraud;

2. the Act permits conviction of responsible corporate officials who have the power to prevent or correct violations;

3. viewed as a whole, the jury instruction was adequate; and

4. the evidence that Park had previously been advised of unsanitary conditions at

another warehouse was admissible since it served to rebut the official's defense that he had justifiably relied on subordinates to handle sanitation matters.

The Court took the position that failure to exercise authority and supervisory responsibility was a sufficient basis for a responsible corporate executive's liability. However, the court recognized that because the act dispenses with the need to prove consciousness of wrongdoing," it may result in hardship even as applied to those who share "responsibility in the business process resulting in" a violation. However, the act "in its criminal aspect does not require that which is objectively impossible," and a defendant is permitted to claim that he was powerless to prevent or correct the violations. The burden of proof in such cases, however, rests with the defendant.

Subsequent court decisions have further limited the use of the argument of "powerlessness on the part of corporate executives in preventing unlawful activities; at present, the powerlessness defense is inapplicable when a defendant should have anticipated a problem and should have taken corrective action. In five cases after the Park judgment, where three involved convictions of corporate executives, the court found in each of the cases that corporate officials failed to exercise the high standard of care imposed by the Act. Even the "Miranda" warnings, because of criminal penalties now involved, have not been acceptable to the court.[50]

Exact title or position in the corporate hierarchy was not relevant in determining responsibility; it was sufficient to show that by "virtue of the relationship he bore to the corporation, (the executive) had the power to prevent the act complained of." The law imposes a duty on the executive to implement measures that will ensure that violations will not occur. Thus a level of absolute liability is imposed that permits no defense when the violation occurs. The FDA and the Department of Justice now favor including at least one responsible individual in all criminal prosecutions who could prevent, detect and correct the violation.

L'Affaire Chapron

Roland Wuillaume, a temporary worker hired in an asphalt plant of Huttes-Goudron et Derives (HGD), a state owned subsidiary of Carbonnages de France—Chimie (CDF), was killed while trying to connect two railroad cars that were standing on an incline. Investigations indicated lighting in the area was defective. Wuillaume had a stiff hip and his leg was considered 67 percent incapacitated. He had been in service for only seventeen days when the accident happened. He was not qualified under the law or physically capable of performing the assigned task. After the accident, HGD improved the lighting and corrected the incline in the railroad bed. In addition it posted safety regulations and installed safety-related equipment. Wuillaume had been hired as a store worker from a temporary employment agency, BIS.

Two unions, the Confederation Generale du Cadre (CGC) and the Confederation Federale du Travail (CFDT), filed a lawsuit charging that "the unions are enraged by the worker's death, and after suffering many deaths and poor and unsafe working conditions, they have decided to make an example of this case—perhaps, to force the judicial branch of the French government to take a stand." The unions also alleged that HGD had too many temporary workers and showed too little regard for its employees' health and safety.

The Executive Director of HGD, M. Jean Chapron, was charged with cumulative negligence and involuntary homicide. Chapron was charged for putting a temporary worker on the job of a specialized one. Chapron was imprisoned for five days. Georges Tredez, the director of the temporary agency, BIS, was also indicted for involuntary homicide but was not arrested.

There were sixteen other work related accidents at the HGD plant, in which nine people were burned and three others killed. In 1974 and 1975, three accidents in the company's other operations caused a total of fifty deaths and outraged the public and created tremendous controversy.

Chapron denied any negligence or culpability. His detention led to angry protests from the CGC. The 170 members of this lower-level management union working at HGD decided to strike for forty-eight hours. The investigating magistrate Patrice De Charette was criticized for injuring Chapron in the press. The Minister of Justice M. Lecanuet, intervened and freed Chapron. The criminal court judge dismissed the charges against both Chapron and Tredez. C.G.T. and CFDT were awarded 500 francs for damages; Chapron and Tredez were fined a total of 1,000 francs. The judge found Chapron was not negligent, and that the responsible party was the victim and the suit filed by his family was rejected.

The Houghton Main Prosecutions

The three top officials of the National Coal Board's mine at Houghton Main in Yorkshire were charged for failing to enforce safety procedures resulting in the death of five workers in an explosion in June 1976. The court observed although the duty of ventilation was laid squarely on the shoulders of the manager yet the maintenance of the ventilation machinery was the responsibility of the undermanager who did not agree it was necessary. The manager was discharged because he did hire competent people to carry out safety duties required by law.

The court's reluctance to hold the manager responsible was inconsistent with its findings. Was the manager not negligent in his failure to establish a more stringent system of reporting? Was the manager not negligent in failing to see that his management team acted in a competent manner? The legislative mandate was clear but the court, however, was unwilling to go so far as hold top management criminally negligent.[51]

Union Carbide India Ltd., Bhopal

The deadliest industrial accident in the history of mankind. During the early morning hours of December 3, 1984 a cloud of methyl isocyanate chemical, a chemical commonly known as MIC, escaped from the Union Carbide plant at Bhopal, a city of more than 700,000 situated 360 miles south of New Delhi, India creating the world's deadliest industrial accident. As the yellow cloud of MIC moved over the city it wiped out entire families in their sleep during the night hours. Those who woke up by the screams took to their heals but the dangerous gas had already taken the toll. It left 2,500 dead, over 200,000 exposed for long term ailments and 17,000 permanently disabled.[52] The misery and pain caused by this accident is beyond human comprehension.

In order to meet the growing needs of world population, the use of chemicals has helped to augment production worldwide. Industrial accidents in this age are going to happen but very often they can be avoided with better plant design, regulatory controls, safety procedures, appropriate training, and safety consciousness.

Lower standards and weaker controls of multi-national corporations lead to disastrous accidents like Bhopal. This accident was caused by the escape of MIC which is twice as heavy as air which means when it escapes from the plant it would stay close to the with even smaller amounts of corrosions in ground. MIC reacts to water, acids, metals, and corrosive materials even though they may be very small in proportion. Being highly flammable, it sets a volatile chain reaction pipes or tanks. The hazardous nature of MIC is well known. One of its components, Phosgene, has been used in World War I to make nerve gas that results in senseless mass killings. It also contains chlorine which is able to attack most stainless steel alloys and thus creates difficulty in storing it.[53]

Union Carbide had built three storage tanks that could contain up to 15,000 gallons of MIC in each tank. MIC is used among other things as an intermediate in manufacturing the pesticides carboryl and aldicarb which are sold in the market under the trade names of Seren and Temik.

According to the documents on file with the Environmental Protection Agency, MIC caused respiratory damage and tumors to form in test rats in an eight day inhalation study conducted in 1981 by Union Carbide for the EPA. Another similar study in 1983 for the same duration resulted in a number of animal deaths shortly after the exposure period. The effects of the chemical exposure were not examined until the 1983 study. Earlier in 1981, EPA had included MIC as part of a list of 2,300 chemicals for which chemical manufacturers were asked to submit information on production, use, and exposure data for rule making purposes but later on reduced this list to only 250 chemicals in 1982. MIC was the chemical dropped among others from the original list for the reason that the agency would be inundated with information. In its report to the EPA, Union Carbide said it would warn users of the chemical of the findings. Union Carbide concluded that no further testing of the chemical was needed and said that OSHA's workplace exposure limit of 0.02 ppm for human exposure allowed a "substantial margin of safety." The 1983 MIC study was a follow-up to the firm's original

substantial risk notice on the chemical to EPA in 1981, under section 8(e) of the Toxic Laws. As a reaction to the accident in India, Union Carbide officials halted production at their Institute plant in West Virginia, USA.[54] The Centers for Disease Control sent a team of government health and safety experts to India to help in relief efforts.

Union Carbide has been criticized for double standards because the West Virginia plant was highly automated and computerized to control the disastrous effects of MIC escape or reaction, whereas the Bhopal plant was manually operated. According to Union Carbide Corporation with headquarters in Danbury, Connecticut, that had majority control over the Bhopal plant, it was done to satisfy the government of India's guidelines to use labor rather than technology wherever possible to industrialize the economy.

Former chairman of the Union Carbide Corporation had initially taken the position that there was no difference in the plant designs of Bhopal and West Virginia but later admitted that the plant at Bhopal had violated company standards and that certain operational conditions would not have been compromised in the West Virginia plant. When he flew to India after the accident, he was arrested and held by authorities in Bhopal and later released.

More than five years after the Bhopal tragedy, in which over 3,500 perished, a constitutional bench of the Supreme Court of India upheld a compensation settlement offer of $470 million to the victims made by the American Multinational Union Carbide Corporation under a court settlement between the Union Carbide Corporation of USA and the Government of India on behalf of the victims. On petition, the Chief Justice observed, in a five-judge bench judgment "no useful purpose would have been served by giving a post decisional hearing on the case."[55]

OTHER CASES OF EXECUTIVE CRIMINAL LIABILITY

The latest charges of insider trading in blue chip firms in the 1980s have involved executives of the prestigious Wall Street firms of Kidder Peabody & Co. and Goldman, Sachs & Co. A number of executives have been arrested that included Timothy L. Tabor, a former Kidder executive; Richard Wigton, the head of over-the-counter and arbitrage trading for Kidder; and Robert M. Freeman, a Goldman partner and Chief arbitrage trader for the firm.[56] Even in the earlier part of the 1980s, the insider criminal misconduct had a major role in about half of all commercial bank failures from 1980–1983.[57] These security scandals have created deep concern about the market place. Federal courts have responded by passing jail sentences in 65% of securities violations. An example of tougher treatment by courts in such crimes is the 20 year sentence handed out to C.H. Butcher Jr. for bank fraud and other crimes that really ruined his family's banking empire.[58]

In EPA charges of criminal violations, under the Clean Water Act, the Vice President of Hudson Farms was fined $5,000 and given two years probation for compost runoff into a nearby creek. In addition, Hudson Farms Inc. was fined $50,000 on four counts of polluting White Clay Creek. The court also ruled that EPA was not required under section 309(a) to issue an abatement order as a prerequisite to criminal sanctions.[59] In June 1977, a court in Turin imposed three to six year prison sentences on five executives of a chemical plant, IPCA, where 32 workers had died of cancer of the bladder in the last twenty years.

The owner manager of a small French construction company was convicted of negligent homicide and given a six month suspended sentence and put on three-year parole for the death of a construction worker.

He resigned saying, "I cannot live for three years with the sword of Damocles hanging over my head."

The Federal Water Pollution Control Act Amendments of 1972 stipulate personal liability for executives for organizational abuse of the environment and provide both civil and criminal penalties.[60] Occupational Safety and Health statutes do not require prior knowledge or personal involvement of responsible executive for criminal sanctions.[61] The constitutionality of administrative assessment of civil penalties that tantamount to criminal sanctions has been upheld by the U.S. Supreme Court.[62] Even corporate directors, independent auditors, lawyers, investment bankers, and brokers who exercise undue care in the discharge of their duties are being held responsible.[63]

Even in the traditional area of Antitrust violations, courts are imposing stiffer fines and jail sentences. In 1977, 161 people were convicted of antitrust violations compared with 175 in 1976. However, more violators are being sent to jail. In April 1978, in an antitrust case in which several makers of electrical wiring devices were convicted of price fixing, 11 present and former officers received fines totalling $200,000 (in addition to the companies' fines of $705,000) and prison terms of one to three months. One person's sentence was suspended. The total time actually to be served—nineteen months with no parole— exceeds the total prison time previously served in the whole history of antitrust actions in the United States.[64] Amendments to Sherman's Act in 1924 increased the maximum penalties for individuals to a three year jail term and $100,000 fine.[65] The Foreign Corrupt Practices Act of 1977, designed to curb overseas illegal payoffs, provides for maximum penalties upon conviction up to $1,000,000 for corporations and $10,000 in fines and five years in jail for officers and directors.[66]

CONSEQUENCES OF CORPORATE CRIMES AND THEIR ACCOUNTABILITY

Corporate crimes are non violent criminal acts that are committed surreptitiously with a motive to gain economically at the cost of government, other businesses, customers and innocent people in society. Various estimates have been put forward as to the loss they cause to various segments. A justice department study estimated that the U.S. businesses lose $67 billion a year to internal theft and espionage alone.[67] Another study has put the white collar crime cost from $40 to $200 billion a year.[68] Computer related crimes alone accounted for as much as $8 billion a year.[69] These studies did not make reference to the increase in costs of goods and services or loss of confidence in them, consequences of aggravation of victim's financial burdens, loss of earnings due to safety violations, damage done to the environment, precious lives lost or damaged in the process as well as damage to the quality of life. Society needs to put accountability for all the unwanted consequences specifically on those executives who have the power to control them.

GLOBAL TREATMENT OF CORPORATE CRIMES

Since corporate crimes are culturally and geographically specific, various countries have shown different levels of concern through legislation and reinforcement of such crimes. During the past few decades a trend has been emerging in several countries to apply criminal laws to corporations even though a corporation cannot be said to possess criminal intent. A dynamic change has taken place in the 1980s in laws in different states in the USA that have long protected corporations from being charged with such crimes as murder and manslaughter. U.S. has taken a very serious view of such corporate crimes. There is increasing awareness now on the part of the judicial system that the best way to curb serious corporate crimes is to hold the executives responsible. Corporate owners and executives in the United States have been sentenced to various lengths of time with a maximum of 25 years for defendants in the National Film Recovery Systems case.

Since financial crimes are done under different names and accounts across the borders, a trend seems to be emerging in European countries to treat such acts as criminal. For insider trading violations, Britain has unlimited fines and 2 years of maximum jail; France has up to $800,000 in fines and a 2 year jail sentence; the Netherlands has a maximum of a $50,000 fine and a 2 year sentence. Such laws in Canada and Japan are more indeterminate.[70]

Insider trading is still viewed differently in other countries like West Germany, Italy, Switzerland, and Hong Kong. They have no insider trading laws as yet. But Switzerland like Britain has mutually agreed with the SEC to divulge the names behind secretive accounts if the evidence is strong enough.[71]

In this age of high technology computer crimes are on the rise, particularly in developed countries. Such crimes are increasing rapidly in Australia[72] and the U.K.[73] In Belgium, partial liability for crimes rests on the natural person.[74]

In the third world where several countries are still struggling to have adequate production of goods for expanding populations, the corporate crimes are more likely to emanate from the manufacturing area. But even there the governments have been reluctant to try multinationals on criminal charges. The shining example is the Bhopal case, where an American multi-national corporation agreed to pay $487 million dollars under the court supervised settlement and no criminal charges were filed. In the developing and underdeveloped countries lack of resources force the companies to take "shortcuts" that lead to potentially dangerous situations. The plant designs may be compromised. There may be hardly any agencies that control the growth of population around dangerous plants or even adequate waste disposal facilities for such plants. There is lack of training and awareness as to how dangerous the chemical and pesticide plants are. This whole set of problems, that exist in thousands of plants all over the world, have been labelled by David Weir as the Bhopal Syndrome.[75]

WHY THE EXPANDING SCOPE OF EXECUTIVE CRIMINAL LIABILITY

Traditional means of correcting corporate abuses, both conventional and unconventional, have failed in helping the society to establish societal controls. As a result, corporate legal infractions and their control must therefore be studied in the context of the relationships among socio-economic structure, criminal law, penal sanctions, and the individual executive's role and expectations in society.

Failure in Market Institutions

Under the assumptions of a competitive market system, social control over economic organizations is exercised through the nature of a company's output. Most individual corporations are small enough that, taken individually, their actions do not significantly affect the economic, sociopolitical, and physical environment. When a corporation's products or services do not meet society's needs, they are not purchased; the corporation's ability to acquire and pay for physical and human resources is thereby restricted, and eventually it ceases to exist. Under this system, it is assumed that all needs for changes will be communicated to the corporation via the external environment's response to its output. Changes in the character of the corporation's output will be carried out by the organization and will be internally generated (Figure 1, Stage 1).

As companies become large and diversified, they become increasingly immune to market discipline. The signals for change are weak and diffuse and do not always seem relevant when viewed in the context of the dominance of positive signals whose signifi-

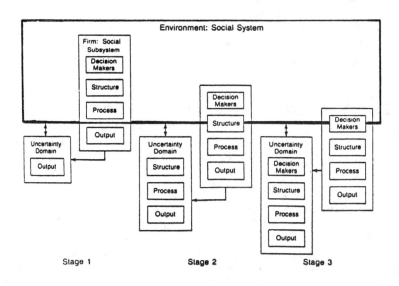

Stage 1   Stage 2   Stage 3

FIGURE 1.

cance is reinforced when the decision maker may then become subject to the tyranny of small decisions. Environmental signals for change are inadequately communicated through the market link, and members of the organization are either unwilling or unable to initiate changes within the organization that would enable it to meet societal expectations. When such changes become difficult to effect through market link, an attempt is made to control production process and decision-making structure—that is, to modify the internal environment that brings about the undesirable behavior. Thus, elements of the decision-making structure and process that were previously internal to the organization become subject to outside pressure, scrutiny, and control. A regulatory framework develops to achieve this end (Figure 1, Stage 2).

Process Controls

In the traditional areas of government regulation of economic activities, process controls have included types of marketing practices considered unfair and, therefore, illegal. New social legislation in such diverse areas as pollution controls and environmental safeguards, in-plant worker safety, and protection of employees from job discrimination based on sex, color, age, or ethnic origin have imposed new process controls—for example, installation of scrubbers on smokestacks, affirmative action programs, and justification of such corporate practices of certain jobs as suitable for males or females, and age-based mandatory retirement policies.

Experience has shown that process controls tend to produce a great deal of regulatory delay and red tape. When viewed externally, a given corporate activity—the synergistic output of all individuals within the corporation—may be considered undesirable and even illegal. When viewed from within, however, such behavior is considered normal and, in economic terms, rational. Govern-

mental institutions shift their emphasis to compliance with the letter of the law or regulations without regard to the substantive changes that necessitate these regulations. Government is always a step behind the corporation. Does the specificity of regulatory requirements become paramount in an effort to minimize the scope to failure. The regulators can never have the necessary expertise to anticipate developments in technology or to understand the organizational labyrinths through which management can work in fulfilling legal requirements without making any the carrot-and-stick approach may evoke a more reliable response in the short run, but this advantage is bought at the cost of an additional, and perhaps faster growing, need for policing. It may also retard potential technological innovation and result in greater social costs.

Controls on Persons

The failure to change corporate behavior through regulations of output results in attempts to modify behavior of decision makers through punishments that are believed to have deterrent effect. (See Figure 1, Stage 3.) The assumption here is that imposing penalties on managers will divert the same ingenuity and resourcefulness that had previously been employed to further corporate growth and subvert legal requirements toward directions considered socially more desirable. By imposing performance criteria on managers, government obviates the need to demonstrate how a given objective might be accomplished and shifts the burden of explaining why it has not been achieved.

Prison sentences come after public officials have concluded that fines alone do not work. The assumption underlying prison sentences is that the threat of punishment will lead the top-ranking executives of a corporation to exert pressure on their aides, who will in turn exert pressure on their aides—a kind of trickle-down theory of ethics.

One reported study of 275 shoe-manufacturing firms in New England tends to support this assumption. A statistical sampling of business records established that recidivism is infrequent. The experience of conviction, it appears, leads to more law-abiding behavior.[76] A government campaign to bring selected prosecutions, together with attendant publicity, the spectacle of frequent conviction, and severe punishment, may play a role in shaping community attitudes toward business conduct considered unlawful. Creating a climate of moral revulsion toward certain types of business activity by labeling the conduct criminal, and imposing prison sentences may help to decrease recidivism.[77]

Public admission of sins as an additional sanction may also aid in creating a moral climate. Tax violators in Germany are required to publish a newspaper advertisement confessing their tax fraud, stating the penalty imposed and promising not to do it again. This procedure, known as positive repentance, might be useful in inhibiting corporate offenses but might also narrow the distinction between immoral conduct and unlawful conduct.[78]

While the "law in books" pertaining to corporate crime is not dissimilar to the laws regarding other types of crimes, enforcement is characterized in the case of corporate crimes by slow, inefficient and highly differential implementation. It is no secret that corporate executives, regardless of their culpability, have not suffered the fate of common criminals in terms of incarceration for economic crimes.

There are a number of reasons for lack of enforcement of these laws in regard to corporate executives.

Status and power of executives. The law violating executives as compared to common law offenders share an affinity through schools, clubs, professional backgrounds, religious affiliations and other institutions with the groups responsible for making laws and enforcing them—legislators, judges, and prosecutors. The executives develop an ideological rationalization for the offenses they commit which are accepted by the public. Crimes involving physical violence against individuals are sternly dealt with but economic crimes are considered social aberrations and are dealt with quite differently. Corporate violators are not considered a threat to society. An executive continues to work an old job, more often than not, even after serving a criminal sentence. A corporate crime by an executive is considered as normal response to achieve organizational goals which has the higher priority than adherence to laws.

A total of 16 officers of 582 corporations were sentenced to a total of 597 days imprisonment (not suspended sentences); 360 days (60.6 percent) were accounted for by 2 officers who received 6 months each in one case. Of the remaining 234 days 1 officer received a 60-day sentence, another was sentenced to 45 days, and excluding the two 6-month sentences, the remaining 14 averaged 16.7 days; and excluding the 60-, 45-, and 30-day sentences, the remaining 11 averaged 9.0 days. The 14 executives who received 60 days or less were all involved in a price-fixing conspiracy. The other case involved tax fraud. The sentences were often suspended after some parts of them were served.[79]

The group orientation of corporate crimes depersonalizes business leadership. Thus, while the impact of corporate crime may be quite serious for the society and often more violent in its consequences than a multiplicity of individually committed street crimes, the corporate personality diffuses the individual burden of guilt. Through a battery of accountants, lawyers, scientists, and other experts, management can demonstrate the bureaucratic imperatives of shared responsibility, thereby denying or seriously weakening the notion of personal obligation.

Conflict with Social Mores

The laws against corporate crimes are not in apparent harmony with social mores. The notion of differential association is relevant here. It seems likely that a manager who is imbued with the folklore of rugged individualism is more likely to be a law violator if he associates with those who view violation of corporate laws with indifference or are themselves law violators.

Large corporations have been guilty of repeated violations.[80] A recent study by a public interest group showed that more than half the corporate members of the Business Roundtable were involved in illegal political briberies at home and payoffs abroad.[81]

The violator may identify himself as a lawbreaker but not as a criminal. Kadish calls it the problem of moral neutrality and questions the criminalization of morally neutral conduct.[82] The problem is dramatized by a study in the mid-1930s that showed prevailing opinion in Akron, Ohio, did not feel that coal miners' stealing of coal from inoperative mines was wrong. The act became wrong if the theft was for resale for profit. It was overwhelmingly recognized that the law was violated in both instances, but only one theft was considered wrong. The same population thought it was wrong for a corporation to close its plant and move to another community because of labor unrest. It was recognized, however, that the wrongful conduct by the corporation was, in fact, lawful.[83]

Post Hoc Character of Many Corporate Crimes

It would be inaccurate to assume that an increase in the highly visible types of corporate law violations indicates widespread flouting of laws by corporations. The landmark cases may indicate a prosperity to probe the laws farthest limits — quite a different practice from deliberate infractions of a known law.[84] Most corporate crimes remain non criminal for a long time because of the inability of the criminal law and enforcement agencies to keep pace with corporate practices.

The entrenched position of senior management in corporations, lack of effective means of social accountability, support for illegal actions from group norms and mores, and differential enforcement of laws against corporate crimes have all combined to provide corporate executives with an irresistible temptation to violate the law.

Inadequacy of Existing Legal Philosophy

A traditional Anglo-American concept of criminal law, namely, *mens rea,* postulates that there must be a guilty mind or wrongful purpose for a criminal offense to be punishable.[85] *Mens rea* is a societal decision, a legal principle embodied in our system of jurisprudence, that an individual is not responsible for a wrong he or she has committed and should not be punished unless, in some way, his or her mind or will can be implicated in the offense. In determining the presence or absence of *mens rea,* three elements must be considered:

1. Did the individual make a choice to commit a wrongful act?
2. Was this choice freely made?
3. Did the individual know or could he have recognized the wrongfulness of his act?

An individual who is insane is incapable of making a choice to commit a wrongful act (element 1). An individual acting under duress is not freely making a choice (element 2). An infant is not capable of knowing that a choice is wrong (element 3). *Mens rea,* in the

S. Prakash Sethi / Parveen C. Chopra

context of these three elements, recognizes the ethical need for awareness of wrongdoing to establish criminal responsibility.[86]

Large corporations employing thousands of people and making millions of decisions impose impossible burdens on society to isolate a particular decision and identify a particular individual to be held responsible where only the last link in the long decision chain is visible. For example, the black smoke billowing from a chemical plant is clearly in violation of environmental law. Who is to blame? The worker who failed to check a meter? The maintenance crew? The purchasing agent? The design engineer? Or the company president?

The problem of mens rea has been approached in any of the following three ways. Courts have adopted a posture that mens rea exists which relieves the public prosecutor from proving it by direct evidence.[87] A second more popular approach has been the establishment of strict liability by statutes.[88] It eliminates criminal intent as a large element of establishing criminal liability. The third growing approach is the concept of criminal negligence. The positive element of this vicarious liability lies in taking reasonable precautions against causing harm, and the negative elements is failure to exercise this duty.[89] Common law rather than European jurisdictions have taken a more conservative view of mens rea and have oriented toward individual rights whereas European jurisdictions have imposed sanctions on a strict liability basis because of a legislative mandate.[90]

RECENT TRENDS AND SOME POLICY OPTIONS— IMPLICATIONS FOR THE FUTURE

The opinion polls indicating that rich and poor be punished equally, increased participation in political process by the poor, women and members of minority groups, access to higher education by these groups, changes in power elites in legislative and judicial circles have eroded the support base of corporations and business leaders. Following trends in corporate criminality and executive liability have emerged and will guide the 1990s.

1. Courts have pierced through the impersonal nature of a corporation and have increasingly held executives personally responsible for criminal violations and sentenced them to as much as 20 or even 25 years of incarceration. The trend towards jail sentences, besides civil penalties, will be on the increase.

2. In the 1970s and 1980s more executives were sent behind bars for financial crimes. While this trend has established beyond uncertainty new areas of safety and environmental violations have received some serious attention and several executives have been jailed for such violations. Corporate crimes in these two areas it appears, will be viewed more seriously, while financial crimes continue to be charged criminally.

3. The U.S. Sentencing Commission that was created by Congress in 1984 to establish a new sentencing system, is likely to finalize its work by November, 1990 and would have a new criminal sentencing system with less disparity between punishments for similar crimes. One of the two alternative systems developed by the commission involves imposing of fines that would be twice or thrice the amount of loss a crime caused or the amount of gain a corporate criminal realized; while the other proposal would put crimes in categories by severity and assign each category a range of fines. In both plans, fines increase or decrease based on whether senior executives knew about the crime or participated in it and whether they tried to bribe officials. The commission would recom-

mend either of the two plans after public hearings. Guidelines would take effect on November 1, 1990 unless rejected by the U.S. Congress. Once Congress lets its review period expire, sentencing commission guidelines become mandatory for federal courts.[91]

4. The critical element in recent case laws is not the issue of personal criminal liability based on criminal intent rather it is the incidence of corporate act that is specified as illegal. Managements are self perpetuating with little control from stockholders and as a result bear the consequences for having taken the corporation in a certain direction that was illegal. The intent to do harm is being replaced by capacity to do harm. Failure to use capacity of authority carries with it a penalty for non performance.

5. The requirement that an executive must have knowledge of illegal corporate behavior is also no longer necessary. Lack of information about illegal acts does not exonerate him from his responsibility to ensure that illegal acts are not committed by the corporation.

6. A regulatory agency need not have abated the corporate crime for which it holds an executive liable. Knowledge about corporate statutory limits is expected like other substantive criminal laws.

Imposition of criminal sentence under conditions of vicarious liability could result in unintended and socially undesirable consequences. It injects a new element of uncertainty into chief executive's discretion in dealing with internal affairs and creates further strains on the interactions between corporations and other social groups including government agencies. The following issues are worth pursuing by researchers in the next decade:

1. What are the economic, social, and political implications of broad expansion of the personal liability of corporate officers for the activities of their subordinates? In particular, how would they affect the behavior of top executives and their responses to society's demand for more products, services, and employment?

2. What are the reasonable and realistic limits on the extent to which a corporate officer can be held personally liable for the acts of subordinates? How can these be ascertained, given the complexity of modern large-scale multi-national corporations?

3. In terms of corporate organizational behavior, how would increased liability affect product innovation, risk taking, market development, organizational structures, decision-making processes, and incentives and rewards systems?

4. Are certain types of activities particularly likely to expose top executives to personal liability? Given that corporations are likely to make efforts and develop procedures to minimize the impact of such activities, how would they affect the overall social goal of deterring real or alleged corporate law violations?

POLICY CONSIDERATIONS

In order to provide maximum deterrence against corporate crimes, personal criminal penalties should be made an integral part of a prevention package by the U.S. Sentencing Commission. Such penalties should be used in moderation and in conjunction with other measures, rather than as the last element in a sequential chain starting with censure and ending with imprisonment. Similar recommendations have been made earlier by Sethi[92] in a testimony on HR.4973 before the subcommittee on crime of the House Judiciary Committee.[93]

1. The frequency and incidence of prison sentences should be increased significantly so that they convey to the public a true picture of the widespread nature of corporate crimes, if that is the case. The sentences should bear a close relationship to the severity of the crime so that judges or juries would not be reluctant to impose them.

2. To create a societal consensus on the undesirability of corporate crimes, prison sentences could be accompanied by a public apology from the corporation and the executive, together with a description of their deeds. Such apologies are common in both Germany and Japan and seem to have been effective in bringing public attention—and public condemnation—to violators.

3. The prison sentence should be combined with a probationary period. An executive who is convicted of criminal wrongdoing should be barred from holding an executive level position in a publicly held company for a prescribed number of years following release from prison.

4. Corporations and individuals should be denied of all benefits—direct and indirect—accrued to them as a result of an illegal activity, following the pattern codified in 18 U.S.C. sections 1961 to 1965. This would be in addition to the usual fines or jail sentences.

5. Firms convicted of violations should be prohibited from doing business with other firms whose executives had been convicted of similar violations. Such restrictions are already imposed on Nevada's gambling industry, where firms known to have been associated with mob-tied businesses are barred from operating in the state.

6. Corporations whose operations have been in violation of criminal laws should be subjected to special reporting requirements. The company or its officers could, for example, be required to make regular periodic statements to the court stating that no violations existed. If violations were later proved, the firm or individual could be convicted of perjury as well as the violation, and the penalties naturally would be harsher.

7. Depending upon the intensity of the crime, corporations, corporate officers and its agents could be asked to pay, for their omissions and commissions of crime, in the form of common stock to a victim's compensation fund.

8. Corporations convicted of crimes could be ordered by courts to appoint financial controllers, under its supervision to regulate the behavior of convicted and guilty corporations. Such a court appointee would act as a "watch dog."

NOTES

This article is an expanded and updated version of an earlier article "The Expanding Scope of Executive Liability (Criminal and Civil) for corporate law violations by S. Prakash Sethi that appeared in the previous edition of this book.

[1] *Newsday*, "The Top 10: You Pick 'em—We Can't," December 31, 1989, p. 5.

[2] Harry V. Ball and Lawrence M. Friedman, "The Use of Criminal Sanctions in the Enforcement of Economic Legislation," 318–336; Sanford H. Kadish, "Some Observations of the Use of Criminal Sanctions in the Enforcement of Economic Legislation," 296–317, in *White Collar Crime: Offenses in Business Politics and the Professions* (Geis and Meier, eds., 1977).

[3] Marshall B. Clinard, Illegal Corporate Behavior, National Institute of Law Enforcement and Criminal Justice, Law Enforcement Assistance Administration, U.S. Department of Justice, Washington, D.C., October 1979 (hereafter referred to as LEAA study). U.S. Congress, "White Collar Crime: The Problem and the Federal Response." Subcommittee on crime of the committee on the Judiciary, U.S. Congress, 95th Congress, 2nd Session, Washington, D.C., 1978.

[4]LEAA Study, 19-20.

[5]*New York Times*, "Business People: Financial News Makers of 1989," January 1, 1990, p. 33.

[6]Pankau, Edmund J. "Beating Bank Fraud," *Security Management*, Volume 32. No. 11, November 1988, pp. 51-52.

[7]Srodes, James "Bundy Solutions," *Financial World*, Volume 158, No. 5, March 7, 1989, pp. 26, 28.

[8]Sherman, M.C. "Forging Ahead in the Battle Against Forgery and Fraud." *Bankers Monthly*, Volume 105, No. 6, June 1988, pp. 36-40.

[9]Adler, William M. and Michael Binstein, "The Speaker and the Sleazy Banker." *Bankers Monthly*, Volume 105, No. 3, March 1988, pp. 79-84.

[10]Stedman, Michael J. "Doing Time: Advice From a Jailed Banker," *Bankers Monthly*, Volume 105, No. 11, November 1988, pp. 16-22.

[11]*Best's Review*, "Underwriting Update: Corporations and Criminal Liability," Volume 85, No. 8, December 1984, pp. 74, 76.

[12]Steven Greenhouse, "3 Executives Convicted of Murder for Unsafe Workplace Conditions," *New York Times*. (June 15, 1985), pp. 1, 29.

[13]*People of the State of Illinois v. Steven O'Neil, et al.*, Appellate Court of Illinois, First Judicial District, 85-1853-1854, 1855, 1952, 1953. Consolidated, Brief of Appellants, May 10, 1986, p. xiii–xv. (All future references to this source in this text will be hereinafter referred to as Appellants' Brief followed by appropriate page number.)

[14]Appellants' Brief, p. xiii.

[15]*Ibid.*, pp. 7ff, 8–9.

[16]*Ibid.*, pp. 9–10.

[17]*Ibid.*, pp. 4–5.

[18]*Ibid.*, p. 1.

[19]Patrick Owens, "Death of Worker Puts Factory Safety on Trial." *Newsday*, (June 6, 1985). pp. 30–31.

[20]Appellants' Brief, pp. 15ff.

[21]Debbe Nelson, "Foul Haze veiled Factory Death," *The Daily Herald*, (April 16, 1985), pp. 1, 3.

[22]Appellants' Brief, pp. 16–17.

[23]*Ibid.*, pp. 17–19.

[24]*Ibid.*, pp. 19–20.

[25]Decision of Judge Banks, pp. 5–6.

[26]Susan B. Garland, "The Safety Ruling Could be Hazardous to Employers' Health." *Business Week*, February 20, 1989, p. 36.

[27]Tim Mete and Michael W. Miller, "Boesky's Rise and Fall Illustrate a Compulsion to Profit by Getting Inside Track on Market," *Wall Street Journal*, (November 17, 1986), p. 28.

[28]Chris Welles and Gary Weiss, "The Man Who Made a Career of Tempting Fate," *Business Week*, (December 1, 1986) p. 34–35. James B. Stewart and Daniel Hertzberg, "Boesky Sentence Ends Chapter in Scandal," *Wall Street Journal*, (December 21, 1987), p. 2; and Robert J. Cole, "Guilty Plea Entered By Boesky," *New York Times*, (April 24, 1987), pp. D1, D2.

[29]*U.K. News*, "Hearing Reveals More on Guiness Jigsaw" (January 23, 1989), p. 54; Steven Greenhouse, "French Report Finds Inside Trading," *New York Times*, (February 1, 1989), p. D6; Steven Greenhouse, "Modest Insider Trading Stir is a Huge Scandal in France," *New York Times*, (January 30, 1989), p. 1, D9; John Rossant and Frank J. Comes, "The Paris Bourse Calls in the Gendarmes," (March 28, 1988), p. 41.

[30]*Business Week*, "And the Next Test Will be *Giuliani v. Miliken*," (January 9, 1989), p. 37.

[31]Ann Hegedorn and Stephen J. Ader, "Miliken Challenge to Parts on Drexel Pact with U.S. Unlikely to Prevent Settlement," *Wall Street Journal*, (February 13, 1989).

[32]Brudney, V., "Insiders, Outsiders and Informational. . . ," *Harvard Law Review*, Vol. 93 (1980) pp. 322–326; Templeman, J. "The Insider Trading Dragnet is Stretching Across the Globe," *Business Week*, (March 23, 1987), pp. 50–51; Gary Weiss and A. Bianco, "Suddenly the Fish Get Bigger," *Business Week*, (March 2, 1987), pp. 28–32; and *Wall Street Journal*, "What Happened to 50 People Involved in Inside Trading Cases?", (November 18, 1987), p. 22; *Chiarella v. United States*, US, 63 L. Ed. 2nd 348, 100 Stamford, CT. (1980); Role 1065: Birth of the Concept of Market Insider and its Application in a Criminal Case—*United States v. Chiarella*," *Fordham Urban Law Journal*, 8,2 (1979-8-), p. 457.

[33]United States Court of Appeals, Second Circuit, "Securities and Exchange Commission, Plaintiff—Appellant v. Texas Gulf Sulphur Co., a Texas Corporation, et al.*, Defendants-Appellants 401 F.2d 833, (August 13, 1968), 446 F.2d 1301, (June 10, 1971); Sethi, S. Prakash, "Securities and Exchange Commission v. Texas Gulf Sulphur Company," *Up Against The Corporate Wall*, 4th ed. (Englewood Cliffs, NJ: Prentice Hall, 1982), pp. 288–316.

[34]James B. Stewart, "Death of a Theory: Supreme Court May Revamp Insider Trading Laws," *Wall Street Journal*, (September 30, 1987), p. 39; Stuart Taylor, Jr., "Justices, 8 Back Winans Conviction in Misuse of Data," *New York Times*, (November 17, 1987), pp. D1, D11.

[35]G. Robert Blakely, "Rico's Triple Damage Threat—

The Public's Secret Weapon is Boesky," *New York Times*, (December 12, 1987).

36Gregory A. Robb, "SEC Offers Legal Definition of Insider Trading in Stocks," *New York Times*, (August 8, 1987), pp. 1, 34.

37Thomas E. Ricks, "SEC Proposed Insider Trading Measure That Includes Misappropriation Theory," *Wall Street Journal*, (November 20, 1987), p. 4.

38Gene Erb, "Newspaper Finds 'Injury Epidemic' At Storm Lake," *The No Bull Sheet*, (September 1987), p. 4.

39William Glaberson, "Misery On the Meatpacking Line," *New York Times*, (June 14, 1987), pp. F1, F8,

40Dickens, Charles, *Hard Times, New National Edition*, New York: Heart's International Library Co., 1968.

41Philip Shabecoff, "OSHA Seeks $2.59 Million Fine For Meatpacker's Injury Reports," *New York Times*, (July 22, 1987), pp. A1, A20.

42"Update on Injuries," Memo from Jene Knutson to Manly Mopus, The American Meat Institute, Washington, D.C., July 28, 1987.

43C. Manly Mopus, "Testimony Regarding Safety in the Workplace" Before the House Government Operations Committee, Subcommittee on Employment and Housing, U.S. House of Representatives, American Meat Institute, Washington, D.C., (May 6, 1987).

44Robert L. Peterson, "Testimony Before the Subcommittee on Housing and Employment, House Government Operations Committee," American Meat Institute, Washington, D.C., (May 6, 1987).

45"How OSHA Helped Organize the Meatpackers," *Business Week*, (August 29, 1988), p. 82.

46Sethi, Prakash S. *Up Against the Corporate Wall: Modern Corporations and Social Issues of the Nineties*, (Englewood Cliffs, NJ: Prentice Hall, 1990). Refer to the case on *Warner-Lambert Company, et al.*

47*United States v. Park*, 421 U.S. 658, 95 S. Ct. 1903, 44 L. Ed. 2nd 789 (1975). For a detailed analysis of the case, see S. Prakash Sethi and Robert N. Katz, "The Expanding Scope of Personal Criminal Liability of Corporate Executives—Some Implications of *United States v. Park*," 32, *Food, Drug, Cosmetic Law Journal* 544–70 (1977).

48*United States v. Dotterweich*, 320 U.S. 277, 64, S. Ct. 134, 88 L. Ed. 48 (1943).

49For vicarious criminal liability of corporate executives under the Act and the Dotterweich doctrine, see Daniel O'Keefe, Jr. and Marc H. Shapiro, "Personal Criminal Liability Under the Federal Food, Drug, and Cosmetic Act: the Dotterweich Doctrine," 30, *Food, Drug, Cosmetic Law Journal*, 5 (1975).

50Daniel F. O'Keefe, "Criminal Liability: Park Up-

date," 32, *Food, Drug, Cosmetic Law Journal*, 392–404 (1977).

51Letter addressed to Dr. Keith MacMillan from F.J. Youngman, Deputy Legal Advisor, National Coal Board, dated February 8, 1978 including statement by judge of the crown court at Sheffield, dated September 2, 1977.

52Bowonder, B., Jeanne Kasperson, and Roger E. Kasperson, "Avoiding Future Bhopals," *Environment*, September 1985; Stuart Diamond, "The Bhopal Disaster: How it Happened," *New York Times*, January 28, 1985 (First in a series of articles); *Newsweek*, U.S. edition, "Bhopal: Who Was to Blame?," Mark Whitaker and Frank Gibney, Jr. in Bhopal, Sundip Mazumdar in New Delhi, Nikki Finke Greenberg in Institute, West Virginia, and Peter McKillop in New York, December 24, 1984; Alan Hall, "The Bhopal Tragedy Has Union Carbide Reeling," *Businessweek*, December 17, 1984; and David Weir, The Bhopal Syndrome: Center for Investigative Reporting, San Francisco: Sierra Club Books, 1987, p. 3. Worthy, Ward, "Methyl Isocyanate: The Chemistry of a Hazard," *Chemical and Engineering News*, February 11, 1985.

54Report No. 234, A-10.

55*Spotlight*, Chicago, "Supreme Court Upholds $470 million Settlement for Bhopal Gas Victims," Dec. 30, 1989, pp. 1, 4.

56Henriques, Diana. "Handcuffing the Street? Effects of the Inside Trading Scandal Will Be Severe," *Barron's*, Volume 67, No. 7, February 16, 1987, pp. 18–24.

57Dudine, James R., "White Collar Crime Enforcement Builds Up Muscle." ABA *Bank Compliance*, Volume 8, No. 1, Winter 1987, pp. 21–26.

58Tell, Lawrence J., "Making Punishment Fit White Collar Crime," *Business Week*, (Industrial/Technological Edition) June 15, 1987, pp. 8–85.

59*U.S. v. Hudson Farms, Inc.*, criminal indictment No. 78-222, U.S. District Court for the Eastern District of Pennsylvania, *Environmental Reporter*, November 24, 1978, 12 ERC 1944; *U.S. v. Frezzo Brothers, Inc.*, criminal No. 78-218, November 24, 1978. U.S. District Court, Eastern District of Pennsylvania, *Environmental Reporter*, 12 ERC 1481.

6033 U.S.C. 1319(b), (c), (d).

61O'Keefe and Shapiro, *supra* n.9, at 33–38.

62*Atlas Roofing Co. v. Occupational Safety Commission*, 430 U.S. 442.

63"The War on White Collar Crime," *Business Week*, June 13, 1977, at 6C; The Liability of Sitting in a Bank's Board," *Business Week*, September 26, 1966, 26; U.S. Currency Comptroller Seeks to Force Restitution to Banks for Insiders' Abuses," *Wall Street Journal*, December 7, 1977, p. 13.

[64]"Jail Terms, Fines May Be Toughest in Anti-trust History," *Dallas Times Herald*, p. 8, Feb. 6, 1978 at 8.

[65]P.L. 93-528, December 21, 1974, 88 Stat 1706.

[66]15 U.S.A. 878 dd-2; See "The Foreign Payoff Law Is a Necessity," *New York Times*, February 5, 1978.

[67]Kleinschrod, Walter A., "Thinking Like a Crook," *Administrative Management*, Volume 48, No. 1, January 1987, p. 68.

[68]Doherty, Vincent P., "Keeping White Collar Clean," *Security Management*, Volume 31, No. 4, April 1987, pp. 53-55.

[69]Bologna, Jack, "Internal Security, Issues and Answers," *Office Administration and Automation*, Volume 46, No. 7, July 1985, pp. 33-37, 81.

[70]Weld, William, "Shame and Jail Can Be Deterrents," *New York Times*, February 22, 1987, p. D1.

[71]Weld, *ibid.*, p. D1.

[72]Stanley, Philip and Pat Burgess, "Not Kid's Stuff: Invisible Eavesdroppers and Code Crackers Cost Corporations Millions," *Rydge's (Australia)*, Vol. 57, No. 8, August 1984, pp. 81-93.

[73]Ellis, Katrina and Simon Pitt, "Combating Corporate Fraud," *Management Accounting* (U.K.) Volume 66, No. 11, December 1987, p. 54.

[74]Lansing, Paul and Donald Hatfield, "Corporate Control Through the Criminal System—An Alternative Proposal," *Journal of Business Ethics (Netherlands)*, Volume 4, No. 5, October 1985, pp. 409-414.

[75]Weir, David, *The Bhopal Syndrome*, (San Francisco: Sierra Club Books, 1987), pp. 57-64.

[76]Robert E. Lane, "Why Businessmen Violate the Law," in Geis and Meir, *supra* n.1 at 102-116.

[77]Ball and Friedman, *supra* n.1, at 333-334; Kadish, *supra* n.1, at 304-308.

[78]Gilbert Egis, "Deterring Corporate Crime," in Nader and Green, *Corporate Power in America*, 1973, at 182-197.

[79]LEAA Study, xxii.

[80]Edwin H. Sutherland, "Crime of Corporations," in Geis and Meier, *supra* n.1, at 71-84; "Stiffer Sentences for Price Fixers?" *Wall Street Journal*, December 17, 1976. CF Lane, *supra* n.22, at 11-112.

[81]Judith Milleler, "Study of Questionable Payments Accents Involvement of Officers," *New York Times*, February 25, 1978, at 27.

[82]Kadish, *supra* n.1, 304-315.

[83]Ball and Friedman, *supra* n.1, at 325.

[84]Kadish, *supra* n.1, at 299-301.

[85]R.J. Urowsky, "Negligence and the General Problem of Criminal Responsibility," 81, *Yale Law Journal*, 949-979 (1972).

[86]Jerome Hall, "Negligent Behavior Should Be Excluded from Penal Liability," 63, *Columbia Law Review*, 632-644 (1963).

[87]Gerard O. Mueller, "The Devil May Care—Or Should We? A Reexamination of Criminal Negligence," 55, *Kentucky Law Journal*, 29-49 (1966).

[88]Idl; Richard A. Wasserstrum, "Strict Liability in the Criminal Law," 12, *Stanford Law Review*, 731-745 (1960).

[89]Mueller, supra n.37; Frances Bowes Sayre, "Public Welfare Offenses," *Columbia Law Journal*, 55-88 (1933); George P. Fletcher, "The Theory of Criminal Negligence; A Comparative Analysis," 119, *University of Pennsylvania Law Review*, 401-438 (1971).

[90]Fletcher, *supra* n.39, at 401-405.

[91]Wermiel, Stephen, "Sentencing Plan Likely to Upset Business Lobby," *Wall Street Journal*, January 15, 1990, pp. B1, B6.

[92]S. Prakash Sethi, "Corporate Law Violations and Executive Liability," Testimony on H.R. 4973 before the Subcommittee on Crime of the House Judiciary Committee, December 13, 1979. For additional reading on various approaches to analysis of corporate illegal behavior and proposals for regulating and deterring such behavior see: "Developments in the Laws—Corporate Crime: Regulating Corporate Behavior Through Criminal Sanctions," *Harvard Law Review*, 92, No. 6 (April 1979), 1227; "Reflections in White Collar Sentencing," *The Yale Law Journal*, 86, No. 4 (March 1977), 589; George P. Fletcher, "The Theory of Criminal Negligence; A Comparative Analysis," *University of Pennsylvania Law Review*, 119, No. 3 (January 1971), 401; "Comments: Criminal Sanctions for Corporate Illegality," *The Journal of Criminal Law and Criminology*, 69, No. 1 (Spring 1978), 40; "Toward a Rational Theory of Criminal Liability for the Corporate Executive," *The Journal of Criminal Law and Criminology*, 60, No. 1 (Spring 1978), 75.

[93]*Congressional Record*, July 27, 1979, E-3923.

14

Two Ethical Issues in Mergers and Acquisitions

Patricia H. Werhane

Abstract. With the recent rash of mergers and friendly and unfriendly takeovers, two important issues have not received sufficient attention as questionable ethical practices. One has to do with the rights of employees affected in mergers and acquisitions and the second concerns the responsibilities of shareholders during these activities. Although employees are drastically affected by a merger or an acquisition because in almost every case a number of jobs are shifted or even eliminated, employees at all levels are usually the last to find out about a merger transaction and have no part in the takeover decision. Second, if shareholders are the fiduciary beneficiaries of mergers and acquisitions, then it would appear that they have some responsibilities or obligations attached to these benefits, but little is said about such responsibilities. In this essay I shall analyze these two ethical issues, and at the end of the paper I shall suggest how they are related.

With the recent rash of mergers and friendly and unfriendly takeovers, questions have been raised concerning the ethical propriety

Patricia H. Werhane is Professor of Philosophy at Loyola University of Chicago. She is one of the founding members of the Society for Business Ethics. Her publications include Philosophical Issues in Art, Ethical Issues in Business, coedited with Tom Donaldson, Persons, Rights and Corporations, Philosophical Issues in Human Rights, edited with D. Ozar and A. R. Gini.

of these actions. Some of these have to do with the tactics companies engage in when trying to acquire a company or when trying to avoid being acquired. These include the so-called "poison-pill" tactics, greenmailing, and the institution of golden parachutes by the corporations that are threatened with acquisition, problems in good faith bargaining (as illustrated in the Texaco-Pennzoil case), the granting of lock-up options, and the usual anti-trust problems. Other issues include the rights of bondholders on both sides of a merger or acquisition, rights that are often considered secondary in light of shareholder interests, and the question of the rights of individual stockholders who are usually neglected in face of institutional shareholder power.[1]

However, two important issues have not surfaced as questionable practices deriving from mergers and takeovers, one having to do with the rights of employees in mergers and the second concerning the responsibilities of shareholders during these activities. Employees in the acquiring and in the acquired company are expected to carry out their job responsibilities both during the process of the merger or takeover and after its completion. They are supposed to carry on as if nothing had happened, despite rumors, threats of their jobs, or upheavals on all levels of management. Although employees are drastically affected by a merger or an acquisition because in almost every case a number of jobs are shifted or even eliminated after a merger, in fact except for top management, employees at all levels are usually the last to find out about a merger transaction. Yet few commentators have thought this was an issue, and almost nothing has been said about the *rights* of employees during and after the merger or acquisition. It is as if the question of how employees are affected in these sorts of transactions was unimportant or incidental to the fiduciary benefits or losses of the negotiation. Second, although a merger is said to be for the fiduciary benefit of shareholders of both parties, and indeed, this is allegedly the primary justification for a merger or an acquisition, insufficient attention has been paid to the *responsibilities* of shareholders in these activities. If shareholders are the fiduciary beneficiaries of mergers and takeovers then it would appear that they have some responsibilities or obligations attached to these benefits, but little is said about such responsibilities. In this paper I shall analyze these two issues. Although these appear to be two disparate ethical questions, at the end of the paper I shall suggest how they are related.

I

Let us turn first to the question of employee rights in a merger or acquisition. In any merger or takeover, whether or not in the end it is financially successful, there is a great deal of employee uneasiness or stress. This occurs primarily in the corporation to be acquired, but employees in the acquiring company, too, may have these worries to a lesser extent. These stresses occur because of the secrecy, ambiguity, and uncertainty surrounding the merger. No employee is sure of his or her job, of his or her status in the newly-formed company created out of the merger or acquisition, or even of the status of the division or department in which he or she is employed. Little information is disseminated to any employee. In most mergers only the top management is privy to the negotiations, and what is occurring is kept secret to prevent stock fluctuations, competing offers, and other market changes. Such secrecy seems necessary so that the merger can take place with the smallest amount of fiscal damage, but the result is the dissemination of ungrounded rumors which creates fear and thus unrest or even psychological trauma for almost every employee. In many merger situations preoccupation with the process of the takeover or the acquisition by top management is such that sometimes employee interests are neglected or even forgotten. Economic interests supersede any other concerns.

It is not that top management seeks to abrogate employee rights or injure employees. In fact it is often the converse when the merger or acquisition is seen as beneficial to the acquiring or acquired company. Indeed some mergers often preserve jobs when the

232

acquiring or acquired company is in financial or marketing difficulty. Moreover, it is often argued, and not without justification, that mergers and acquisitions protect jobs in the long run by increasing efficiently through a larger organization which can provide more capital for growth, or by expanding a market share through a merger of two similar competing enterprises. At the same time, mergers and acquisitions provide an opportunity to streamline certain divisions and to "weed out" aging, unproductive or superfluous employees. Thus increased productivity, efficiency, and profitability created by the merger or acquisition allow for expansion and provide more employment and more stable employment in the long run.

Now these arguments are all viable economic arguments based on the more general contention that a good merger serves economic interests more fully than not merging and that, from a moral point of view, in the long run the greatest economic happiness for more persons is served by this sort of transaction. What, then is at issue? The question is, do economic interests, important economic interests which affect employees as well as top management, take precedent over basic employee rights, at least under certain economic conditions?

First, what sorts of rights are entitled in these circumstances, and why is it I have called them *basic* employee rights? Employees (or at least most employees) are adults. It has been argued at length elsewhere,[2] that because employees are rational adults, they have certain rights in the workplace, those rights accorded all rational adults equally by our Constitution and Bill of Rights simply because they are persons. Included in these are the obvious ones, especially the right to freedom or the right not to be coerced which includes the right not to be forced into some situation not of one's own choice. Freedom, however, is not merely a negative right to be left alone, because free-

dom includes the right to exercise choice. Part of the exercise of freedom is illustrated in an employee's right to choose a job and to quit at any time. But another less emphasized part of the exercise of freedom is the control over one's future. For if I cannot control what happens to me at least within the limits of the kinds of choices and actions I am capable of, I am thereby coerced, because I find myself in situations not warranted by my own behavior. So employees have a second right—the right to information which affects their job, their company, and their career. Withholding that kind of information when it is available takes away self-control of one's job and future and therefore is paramount to restricting an employee's freedom of choice. Third, because the right to freedom entails its *exercise*, employees, having chosen to work and where they will work, should be allowed to participate in decisions which affect their employment.[4]

Notice that none of these rights is an absolute or unlimited right. Rather, each right is an equal right in balance with equal rights of others. That is, I have a right to control my future so long as exercising that right does not interfere with the equal rights of another person to do likewise. So an employee's right to information is both a limited and an equal right. Every employee has an equal right to employment information when that information affects her job and future, but not a right to all company information when that does not entail letting out a trade secret (e.g., the recipe for Coca Cola). It is also often contended that employees do not have rights to information when such publicity might affect adversely the market or a proposed merger or acquisition. What this view shows is that shareholder rights supersede employee rights. But if rights are equal rights, one must carefully weigh the sometimes conflicting claims of employees to information and protection of shareholder rights to their fiduciary interests. Note that this claim is different from the right of a company to protect a trade secret. In the latter case the protection of a trade secret does not interfere with employee *rights*. Not revealing the trade secrete does not hurt employees because it is not their secret, and protecting the secret usually protects the jobs and interests of employees as well. But in the former case (protecting merger secrets) not informing employees *can* affect their freedom of choice; so it is important to employee rights. While some secrecy is justified, an employee should have a right to at least as much knowledge about such activities as any other "outsiders" who often know far in advance of such affairs, since it is to the express disadvantage of an employee not to have this information. Notice, too, that in these instances shareholders, too, often do not have such information and this is unfair to them as well for the same reasons.

Similarly, the right to participate in management decisions is an equal employee right, not an unlimited one. The problem is that top management often does not include middle management or other employees in its decision-making particularly when that concerns a merger or acquisition. Yet unless one can argue conclusively that top management always represents shareholder interests, shareholders who are seldom informed or consulted about these decisions, just as employees are not consulted, then there is no justification for excluding employees from participation in these decisions just as there is no excuse for excluding shareholders until the moment before the actual merger.

Failing to honor these rights in the workplace creates two fatal problems. First, when a corporation does not respect the rights of its employees, it is threatening its own claims to those rights. It is saying that it has rights or more extensive rights than people or some people. But this implies that so-called rights are neither equal nor universal, and this implication undermines the justification for a corporate defense of *its* rights. Second, in not

upholding employee rights the corporation is in contradiction with itself. It has hired responsible adults whom it holds liable to act as morally decent persons and to perform satisfactorily in whatever jobs those persons are assigned. If employees are accountable for their performance in the workplace, if they are expected to be loyal and have other responsibilities to their employer, that employer has reciprocal responsibilities to that employee, responsibilities which are correlative to what is expected on the employer's part including respect for the employee as a person. This has to be a "good faith" employer responsibility, because although an employer can hold an employee responsible for his job performance, it is more difficult in fact for employees to hold an employer equally liable except by striking. But by not respecting the employee as a rational adult, that is, in not respecting her *equal rights*, the corporation is asking more of that employee in terms of job responsibility than it should expect, and the employee-employer accountability relationship thereby weakens or breaks down.

In the case of mergers and acquisitions the basic employee rights that are not always respected include the right to information, the right to participate in the management decision to accept or fight the merger, and job protection for long-time loyal "at will" employees. Management argues that even if such rights are accorded in the workplace under "normal" circumstances, such rights may need to be bracketed in merger situations, because economic interests outweigh respect for these rights in these economic instances.

But do economic interests supersede rights of employees in these sorts of cases? If one were starving, basic needs might supersede rights to information or participation. But the case is much less clear for mergers. Basic needs are not at stake here. In general if economic interests override rights, then one could imagine extreme situations where one could justify slave labor for example if greater economic interests are served. It is this sort of argument that white South Africans use to justify apartheid—the contention that under apartheid black South Africans are economically better off than any other blacks in Africa. Second, only 50% of all mergers are economically successful.[5] So even to make an argument that economic interests of employees will be better protected in the long run with a merger or any other major corporate reorganization which requires setting aside employee rights is not a very strong argument. Third, even when the merger is fiscally successful, there is much data to suggest that employee stress engendered by such activities translates into lowered productivity, preoccupation with self-preservation, loss of trust in top management and thereby in middle management who by implication must share blame, parochialism rather than teamwork, unwarranted power struggles, loss of efficiency and momentum, and even resignations of good people who, fearing their future unemployment, go elsewhere to better and apparently more secure jobs.[6] In non-utilitarian terms, the lack of respect for employee *rights* translates into an equal loss of commitment, loyalty, responsibility, and trust.

A defender of top management's prerogative to concentrate on fiscal interests in a merger or acquisition might counter argue as follows. A merger or acquisition is carried out only when it is in the best interests of the shareholders. Shareholders have rights, one of which is to do what they please with their shares, in this case shares of a company, so long as they do not harm others. Therefore a focus on economic interests in a merger situation merely respects these rights. However, this point is based on the premise that such shareholders' rights are equal to or more important than political rights. And that contention is unjustified for the same reason that defending the priority of economic interests is unjustified. For if shareholder rights outweigh the right to freedom which includes the right to information, a variety of abhorrent scenarios could be justified too.

Does this mean that mergers are morally wrong and should be abolished? No, that is not the argument. Mergers and acquisitions are neither right nor wrong. It is the fiduciary preoccupation of a merger which negatively affects employees and employee rights that is at issue. The latter are at least as important as the former; yet they are seldom taken into account. And by not taking employee considerations into account both the acquired company and the acquiring one threaten the viability of their own rights as well as the success of the merger.

II

Examining briefly the question of shareholder responsibility, particularly as it relates to a merger activity, in any merger, fiduciary responsibilities to shareholders are taken very seriously, for it is the shareholder who stands to benefit or lose in any stock exchange or acquisition. Shareholder pressure can force an unfriendly takeover, for example, if shareholders are thereby to gain a good price for their holdings. Shareholders, then, have rights to maximize the earnings or the price of their shares simply because they own them. Yet along with rights one also has responsibilities. For example, if one owns property on which chemical dumping is taking place, dumping for which the owner is paid, that property owner has responsibilities to contain the contamination of the chemical so that it does not damage other properties in the neighborhood. Similarly, shareholders have responsibilities connected with their right to maximize their gain as shareholders. At a minimum, they have a responsibility to be sure that management is looking after their interests. Now most of the time an individual shareholder has trouble exercising her responsibilities since she has few voting shares. But institutional shareholders such as universities and pension funds can wield a great deal of influence in corporate decision-making simply because of the number of shares they own. This has been seen to a small extent by those institutional shareholders who have withdrawn their interests in companies who do not adopt the Sullivan Principles in their South African subsidiaries. Such withdrawals have made a difference. Yet while institutions claim they are concerned, we do not always see institutional shareholders pressuring corporations who use "poison pills" or establish large "golden parachutes," questionable practices by any account, and certainly not in shareholders' best interests. What I am suggesting is that along with fiduciary rights shareholders, particularly institutional shareholders, have responsibilities, responsibilities they need to exercise particularly when mergers and acquisitions are taking place. Otherwise they cannot complain when a merger does not take place because of a poison pill tactic, when a merger is not a success, or when millions of dollars of profit are siphoned into golden parachutes.

III

Finally, what do employee rights have to do with shareholder responsibilities? There is the obvious sense that rational persons cannot be held responsible without according to them the rights which should be accorded to them just because they are persons. So if employees have responsibilities, they need to be accorded the correlative rights implied in these responsibilities. Conversely, one cannot expect to have rights of any sort without assuming the entailing responsibility. So if shareholders have fiduciary rights, by implication they also have responsibilities connected with those rights.

Secondly, using rights talk again, in addition to the relation between rights and responsibilities, rights have two other characteristics: they are universal, that is, if X is a human right, X applies to everyone, and they are equal, that is X applies to everyone equally. Shareholders who argue that they have fiduciary rights, also contend that they have the right to exercise that fiduciary claim freely and, along with that, that they have a right to enough information about the corporation to exercise that claim intelligently. This is fair enough, but if rights are universal and equal claims, and if employees are rational adults, they too have a right freely to decide on their job options and a claim to enough information to exercise that option intelligently. Those rights are often not respected by top management in merger activities. Shareholders ordinarily recognize their own rights, but they seldom consider them as equal rights of employees. If shareholders have responsibilities, perhaps one of them should be to see whether the rights they expect are being respected in the workplace of which they have a share. Most shareholders, even large institutional shareholders, of course, will argue that this is too much to expect of them. Yet not exercising their prerogatives as shareholders when such exercise might reduce both fiduciary losses and employee stress and unrest is irresponsible, because preventable harm is allowed to occur, harm which is in the shareholders' power to lessen.

Finally, shareholders might take an interest in employees for more practical reasons. If morale is bad and trust is undermined, the resulting loss of productivity and efficiency and even the loss of good managers is not in the self-interest of the shareholder. So shareholder responsibility is not only a moral obligation, it may be a smart business investment as well.

NOTES

1. See David Pauly, 'Merger Ethics Anyone?' *Newsweek*, December 9, 1985, pp. 45–47 for a litany of these issues.

2. See Patricia J. Werhane, *Persons, Rights, and Corporations* (Englewood Cliffs: Prentice-Hall, Inc., 1985), especially Part II. See also, Adina Schwartz, 'Meaningful Work', *Ethics* 92 (1982), pp. 634–46.

3. See Eric Mack, 'Natural and Contractual Rights', *Ethics* 84 (1977), pp. 153–159.

4. Schwartz, *op. cit.*

5. See Price Pritchett, *After the Merger: Managing the Shockwaves* (Homewood, Illinois: Dow-Jones-Irwin, 1985), p. 32.

6. Pritchett, *op. cit.*

Department of Philosophy,
Loyola University of Chicago,
820 North Michigan Avenue,
Chicago, IL 60611,
U.S.A.

15

The Workers' Right to Know, Participate and Refuse Hazardous Work: A Manifesto Right

Robert Sass

ABSTRACT. This paper argues that the deepening and widening of existing worker rights in work environment issues is a necessary condition to promote much needed reform in present day industry, and to reduce the frequency and severity rate of accidents and incidence of industrial disease.

I. INTRODUCTION

Worker rights in workplace health and safety is crucial in bringing about necessary

Robert Sass is Associate Professor of Industrial Relations and Organization Behaviour, and Director of the Labour Education Resource Centre, University of Saskatchewan. In 1980 he was awarded for outstanding achievement by the Canada Safety Council. His most important publications are: 'An Assessment of the Saskatchewan Trade Union Amendment Act, 1983', Saskatchewan Law Review 48, No. 1, pp. 148–169; 'Cancer in the Work Environment', Alternatives: Perspectives on Society and Environment 11, No's 3 and 4 (Summer-Fall 1983), pp. 37–43; 'The Underdevelopment of Occupational Health and Safety in Canada' in Ecology vs. Politics in Canada, ed. Dr. William Leiss, University of Toronto Press, 1979, pp. 72–96; and 'Accident Proneness: Science or Non-Science?, with Glen Crook, International Journal of Health Services 11, No. 2, 1981, pp. 175–190.

reforms in working conditions, especially their right to know about the chemicals they work with, and to participate on a daily basis regarding work environment matters—both quantitative (noise, dust, etc.) and qualitative (work organization and job design questions), and their right to refuse a job believed (not known) to be dangerous to their well-being.

It can also be argued that existing worker rights (to know, participate and refuse) should be extended and deepened to legally permit workers in industry to deal with work organization (as a social concept) and job design (individual relation to machine) matters, including pace of work, monotony, scheduling, sexual harassment, job cycle, etc., as well as those work environment matters which are important to workers (i.e. daily punishments and humiliations). The extension of the present-day legal concept of "risk" to ensure worker involvement and increased control of their working conditions can also be argued as a moral right derived from a "fundamental need" (health and safety) in the same way arguments were made on behalf of universal medical care. The extension of present-day limited or partial worker rights in occupational health and safety statutes and regulations ought to be "stretched" to deal with greater worker control over work environment matters and the work process.

While this development can be argued as a practical consideration, we must, nonetheless, classify this cluster of proposed rights as *manifesto rights* for the obvious reason that they are not generally accepted at the present time.

Presently, management and corporate *interests* go beyond what is necessary to maximize efficiency in production with equity. What is, therefore, desirable is the extension of certain civil rights into industry. And by increasing worker rights, we also increase productivity and efficiency, and, more importantly ensure greater justice in industry. This paper will specifically focus on the need to increase worker rights in regard to work environment matters. That is the right of the worker to participate in work environment issues, and to have greater control over the work process. After all, if you neglect and debase workers in order to increase efficiency, you will in the end decrease productivity and make our society poorer. Present day worker "punishments" and humiliations cannot be justified by appeals to increased productivity and economic "law." An individual worker is more than a "hand", commodity or factor of production only, but something greater, more precious and sacred than material wealth.

A. Productivity versus equity

While it is morally necessary to increase production and equitable distribution of wealth in a world where there is enormous impoverishment and widespread starvation, there is no reason why this wealth should be based upon the commodification of labour. Especially, when this form of production and organization of industry results in the de-skilling and dehumanizing of a large part of the workforce.

Current employment relations evolved during the transition from feudalism to capitalism (from simple to composite production). In jurisprudential terms, from a status to a contract society. This development by the law is based upon a "relationship of services"[1] (in contrast to commitment or obligation). According to H. Glasbeek:

> This accords with the notion that an entrepreneur in a competitive society should be free to invest and to dispose of his capital as he sees fit and to be subjected to as little external noneconomic restraint as is consonant with social needs. The upshot of legal acquiescence with this approach is the imposition of onerous duties on the employee as compared with those which burden the employer.
>
> ... even under collective bargaining regimes all the initial decisions remain an employer's to make. Thus, how much to invest, where to do so, what products shall be made, what amount, what quality, what processes are to be used, what *substances* are to be employed, and so on, are all decisions left to the employer.[2] [Emphasis mine].

In essence, employer freedom of disposition with respect to capital ownership is the supreme legitimizing principle of private ownership. This includes the right not to use, to destroy, to alienate capital ("flight of capital") and the right to buy, to organize, and to control the labour of others, as well as to make decisions concerning the goals of production and the use of surplus value.

While collective agreements and regulation may limit these rights, private ownership remains essentially undisturbed. In Canada today, it is generally accepted by arbitrators that the rights to "manage and operate the enterprise, assign work, determine work methods, procedures and equipment, schedule production, and direct the workplace" are reserved to management.[3] It is "not unusual for unions to withdraw entirely from management decisions at this level."[4]

In a recent study entitled 'The Limits of Trade Union Power in Organizational Decision Making,' the authors conclude that

Despite the popular image of powerful unions, such tangential evidence that does exist suggests that the actual power of trades unions over organizational level decisions is relatively low, irrespective of desired or actual participation in the decision making process.[5]

The prevailing residual or reserved rights theory is different from the "status quo" approach which supports the view that the *status quo* should prevail if workers or their bargaining agent oppose or disagree with a management decision until the matter is mutually resolved[6], even though the contract is silent.

Management's rights under the common law explicitly vested the employer with sole control over the business and management of its affairs, infusing the employment contract with the traditional law of "master-servant." This, in effect, divests the employer of any sense of duty, obligation and responsibility toward those he employs. The employment contract in law emphasizes the *limited* nature of the parties to each other while reserving full authority of direction and control to the employer. The result is, of course, the *limited* rights of workers.

In effect, the employment contract is in large part a legal device for guaranteeing to management the unilateral power to make rules and exercise discretion. Thus, ownership carries with it the right of "freedom of contract."[7]

This "market theory" of labour incorrectly assumes an approximate *equality* of individuals to function in the market environment, which "is an inappropriate assumption on which to base the actual right to participate."[8] The contract law of employment is partially based upon a fundamental and "empirically absurd" understanding of equality.[9]

Secondly, a major underlying assumption supporting the buying and selling of labour and management's "excessive" prerogatives under common law is our socially accepted conception of work as instrumental rather than self-fulfilling, enabling the worker to sustain status and self-respect. The acceptance of hierarchy and privilege in the organization of production reinforces the "cycle of inequality" in society.[10]

Within a prevailing class structure, the privileged view ordinary blue-collar, manual workers as 'fit' for dirty work. Harry Glasbeek states that

in as much as the argument is that the contract of employment doctrines display an assumption that a *superior-inferior relationship* is to be accepted, and that collective bargaining regimes do not share this assumption, it is also of dubious merit. This characterization of the common law is justified on the basis that employers could (and can) treat their employees as servants, as commodities, as a matter of law.[11] [Emphasis mine]

Finally, the acceptance of inequality, the instrumentality of work, and a prejudice towards ordinary workers as having "strong backs and weak minds" reinforces the present dehumanizing organization of industry and judicial and legal constructs pertaining to the employment relationship. The further acceptance of this situation is positively argued by the social value of the freedom of contract doctrine which construes the relationship between employee and employer as a *voluntary* agreement. The "lack of parity cannot be adduced as a reason for questioning this doctrine in behalf of worker rights, unless one is prepared to question it in all instances where parity is lacking."[12]

Critics of increased worker rights also argue that the establishment of such rights:

> ... will generate gross inefficiency since it will ensnarl simple employee proceedings with procedural red tape. With special rights, no employee can simply be fired or demoted; he must be given a formal hearing; and to ensure that due process is realized, complicated organizational mechanisms must be established, mechanisms that will require time and effort that might otherwise contribute to productive activities.[13]

Clearly, as Donaldson correctly observes,

> such critics envision a straightjacketed corporation management, working in an environment in which penalizing and firing workers is all but impossible. The result, presumably, will be lower working standards, lazier employees, and *widespread inefficiency*.[14] [Emphasis mine]

and so equity must be sacrificed by a supposedly greater good: efficiency.

B. Participation and productivity

To this argument one can reply that worker rights and participation might enhance efficiency. After an extensive review of the literature on this issue, Bruce Stokes states that "ample experience exists to quell most fears that employee involvement in day-to-day company decisions leads to declining economic efficiency."[15] Further, Stokes reported that:

> A 1975 National Science Foundation survey of 57 field studies of worker participation experiences in the United States found that four out of five reported productivity increases. A 1977 study by Dr. Raymond Katzell of New York University of 103 U.S. worker productivity experiments confirmed these findings. Karl Frieden, in a 1978 study for the National Center for Economic Alternatives, concluded that, "the scientific rigor of many of the studies on workers' participation is less than ideal. However, a clear pattern emerges ... supporting the proposition that increases in workers' participation result in improvements in productivity.[16]

Even The Trilateral Commission's Task Force on Industrial Relations, an important management research body, admitted that "nothing in the literature suggests that participation significantly harms productivity."[17]

There is a vast body of literature which confirms the positive correlation between worker involvement and productivity. Nonetheless, strong resistance exists against the widening of existing "partial" worker rights in industry.

During my ten year tenure as Associate Deputy Minister of Labour in the Province of Saskatchewan, I sat on a number of Boards of Directors which included union and/or worker representation. The contribution of workers and their representatives was of enormously high quality, and in regard to the bipartite Work Environment Board of the Potash Corporation of Saskatchewan, of which I was chairperson, the worker and union contribution was, in my opinion, of greater practical and intellectual merit than that of the senior management. This might be because the terms of reference of the Work Environment Board centered upon working conditions with which management was less familiar. This applies to the worker members of the mandatory joint occupational health and safety committees in Saskatchewan.[18]

Consequently, I believe that worker rights should be extended by statute in all areas of production, but full rights be accorded in matters relating to workplace health and safety. This paper will argue the necessity to "stretch" the present legal concept of risk covering dust, chemicals, lighting and other quantifiable and measurable aspects of the workplace to all work environment matters including: how the work is organized, the design of the job, pace of work, monotony, scheduling, sexual harassment, job cycle and similar work environment matters which matter to workers.

II. WORKER PARTICIPATION AND OCCUPATIONAL SAFETY

A. Introduction

Lack of worker "rights" to control work processes is a major contributor to both increased adverse stress and a worsening of accident rates. Whereas, meaningful participation and greater control has a positive effect on worker health and safety. While worker participation is viewed as a "political" goal, it is also a means to come to grips with bad working conditions.

B. Management prerogatives and the impoverishment of job content

Trade unionism represents a collective act of protecting and improving living standards by people who sell their labour power against people who buy it. This protective function is performed in various ways, but primarily through a method of determining conditions of employment by negotiations or collective bargaining between representatives of the employer and union representatives of the employees. The results of the bargaining are set forth in a written agreement covering "wages, hours and working conditions."

Historically, "working conditions" have come to mean overtime provisions, holiday pay, vacations, and other issues which generally deal with the *extrinsic* nature of work, or time away from work as opposed to the *intrinsic nature* of work, or time in work. The latter refers to the intensity of work which includes: the length of the work cycle, task variety, skills demanded, the rhythm of work, machine pacing, monotonous and repetitive work which activates only a limited part of the workers' capabilities. When these conditions are part of an authoritarian work setting and a severe structure of command, workers experience a feeling of powerlessness and alienation. They have a limited degree of self-control over their methods of work, and are even restricted in their possibilities for leaving their work station without a stand-in. The "partial" rights of labour limit workers in their involvement in decision-making at the shop-floor level. These job characteristics deny workers control over planning and work methods and are the substantive issues that define the *intrinsic nature* of work which is part of managements' rights and prerogatives. Unfortunately, neither collective agreements nor existing government statutes have pierced this impenetrable fortress. The result adversely effects both worker health and safety.

C. Worker participation and safety

In 1971 a British researcher, J.B. Cronin published an article, 'Cause and Effect Investigations into Aspects of Industrial Accidents in the United Kingdom.'[19] Studying the accident rates of 41 factories, which were essentially alike in most respects, he found that "the 'worst' factory had an accident ratio ten times that of the 'best'." Of the 41 factories, six were selected—three pairs which were very similar in plant and size and very different in accident ratio—for more careful study. Cronin found that "... there was clearly no relationship in the factories concerned between the standard of compliance with the Factories Act and the accident ratio."[20] What was the operant factor then? The results of the study "appeared to indicate some sort of direct relationship between good safety record and successful joint consultation."[21] Cronin further concluded, "Such indications as there are show the accident rate to be a function of industrial relations. What is more, of a special aspect of industrial relations: communications and participation."[22]

In the mid-1970s, as Executive Director of the Occupational Health and Safety Branch in the Saskatchewan Department of Labour I wrote a letter to Mr. Cronin seeking further empirical information in support of his thesis. On March 15, 1976, I received a response stating:

I gave up research in this field many years ago now because I found it totally impossible to get cooperation from employers once they realized the lines on which I was working. So far as they were concerned "investigation into the causes of accidents" meant bigger and better statistics and closer and closer examination of working conditions. Once they realized that I was concerned with attitudes and management methods they would have nothing of it. Revans has had much the same experience. It is much the same with publication. The editorial board of the ILR had to have a special meeting before they could pluck up courage to print that little article!

Some time ago Otto Kahn-Freund, of whom you must have heard, was anxious that Penguin Books should publish a short book on the whole of my work. But even with all the weight of Otto's reputation behind it, and that—as they say out here—

is quite something, they would not touch it. And I don't think it was the writing. Similarly with Sweet and Maxwell who actually went back on the contract.

The last meaningful thing that I was able to do was with a large local firm in Southampton which, the exception that proves the rule, was interested in what I was trying to do. I was able to do quite a complicated attitude survey of a ten per cent weighted random sample of their employees and found a quite astonishing correlation between the employees who had suffered more than one reportable accident and what might be described as "antisocial" attitudes. Indeed, the link-up was almost embarrassingly complete from a statistical point of view—made even me wonder if the computer had cooked the results![23]

In 1971 the British researchers Philip Powell, Mary Hale, Jean Martin, and Martin Simon published a study entitled, '2,000 Accidents: A Shop Floor Study of Their Causes Based on 42 Months' Continuous Observation.'[24] This exhaustive study exposed many of the myths accepted by "safety professionals" today. I will quote just one of their conclusions:

... A general social pressure to do something about risks might embarrass industrial management because it can see itself as the executive of the action required. If the management of a factory sets up a training programme which teaches people that certain of the systems in the factory involve risk of injury, it lays itself open to allegations that it is not doing enough to re-design the systems and eliminate the risks. This might be a root of the apathy we observed. In some cases, it may need strong governmental and public pressure to overcome it.[25]

Another British study, *Safety or Profit*[26] was published by researchers Theo Nichols and

Pete Armstrong in 1973. They found that there exists a fundamental conflict in conventional factories between safety and profit, and that, despite lipservice to safety rules, there is tremendous pressure on workers to place production ahead of safety:

> ... each of the accidents we have reviewed occurred in context of a process failure and whilst the men concerned were trying to maintain or restore production. In every case the dangerous situation was created in order to make it quicker and easier to do this. In every case the company's safety rules were broken. The process failures involved were not isolated events. Nor were the dangerous means used to deal with them. The men acted as they did in order to cope with the pressure from foremen and management to keep up production. This pressure was continual, process failures were fairly frequent and so the short-cutting methods used to deal with them were repeatedly employed. In each case it was only a matter of time before somebody's number came up.[27]

They further concluded:

> ... All this suggests that what is needed is some way of counteracting the *pressure for production* on the shop floor. It was just because management were not prepared to relax this pressure that men did not believe their propaganda; for in the long run such propaganda can only be effective to the extent that management *does* put safety before production.[28]

These and other studies indicate that the working conditions for every job are determined totally by the organization of work and the degree of control (or lack of control) that workers have over the means of work and the process of work. The prevailing ideology describes working conditions as a miscellaneous collection of the "physical" and "social" features of a particular job. The reality of the situation is just the opposite: the social organization of work produces both each job and its environment. What is important is the *control* over the work process.

Further it is work organization and the social relations—more particularly the power relations—within the workplace that determine the work environment with which the individual worker is faced, within which he must work—and all too often, which he must endure and suffer.

Once the power relations are seen for what they are, and once it is admitted that the preponderance of power, by far, lies with management, then it follows that "accident proneness"[29] is far more likely to lie, not with an individual worker whose power is very limited, but with a supervisor or manager, whose power is much greater.

For example, I was informed of an experiment conducted in two maintenance departments in the Vancouver Transit Company. They were five miles apart. In one department they had a high percentage of accidents while in another there was a low percentage. They switched the supervisors, and found out that the accident rates switched also. The accident rate followed the respective supervisors. Perhaps the supervisor whom the high accident rate followed should be called an "accident prone" supervisor! In all technical questions there is a social dimension.

D. The conventional wisdom of accident causation

The present widely-held management view of accident causation implies a tacit assumption that workers are primarily responsible for accidents through their "carelessness," "accident proneness," or "bad attitudes"—and that they can therefore stop accidents from happening merely by resolving to "be careful," to "obey their superiors," or to "have a positive attitude towards safety." Such an assumption is either naive or perverse. It is naive to believe that workers willingly suffer accidents and injuries, that they seek out dangerous situations just to spite management. There is no valid reason to believe that workers are any more childish, silly, or self-destructive than are accountants, bureaucrats, doctors, lawyers, scientists, managers, safety professionals—or any other group in society. On the other hand, it is perverse to avoid spending money on needed safety improvements in the plant by dogmatically adopting a victim-blaming ideology.

I want to emphasize the fact that unsafe act theories of accident causation are ideology not science. I have been at pains over a number of years to refute these ideologies. I realize, of course, that any number of articles by me will not succeed in eradicating a myth which has become so ingrained in management ideology over the better part of century. However, I would like to quote in full the abstract of an article by me published in the *International Journal of Health Services*:

The "accident proneness" thesis has been with us since the early 1900s. The early statistical studies that reputedly provided the scientific basis for this notion are examined and found to be lacking due to methodological errors and a fragmented view of industrial life. Accident proneness, as originally envisioned, has no empirical foundations. It has, however, become part of the tactical armamentarium used in "blaming the victim" for industrial accidents. It focuses on the personal characteristics of workers in relation to accident causation, while de-emphasizing the role of dangerous work environments. In this respect, it has acted as a barrier in the development of preventive occupational health and safety principles and practices. The notion has endured not only because it is tactically advantageous, but also be-

cause many members of the professions that deal with workplace accidents have accepted it without reservation and lent it credence. For the purpose of industrial accident prevention, however, it would be more appropriate to discard this notion in favor of a more integrated and broader understanding of the nature of the interaction between workers and their sociotechnical work environment.[30]

In rejecting the prevailing management ideology on safety I do not want to leave the impression that I am "tearing down" and not "building up," that I can see what is wrong but cannot offer something better. On the contrary, I believe there is a need to emphasize, in regard to accident prevention, worker rights—the right to know, the right to participate, and the right to refuse as a sound theoretical foundation.

NOTES

1. Glasbeek, Harry J., 'The Contract of Employment at Common Law,' in Anderson and Gunderson, *Union-Management relations in Canada* (Addison-Wesley, 1982), p. 73

2. *Ibid.*, pp. 73–74.

3. Swan, Kenneth P., 'Union Impact on Management of the Organization: A Legal Perspective,' in Anderson and Gunderson, *op. cit.*, p. 280.

4. *Ibid.*, p. 280.

5. Wilson, David C., Butler, Cray, Hickson and Mallory, 'The Limits of Trade Union Power in Organizational Decision Making,' *British Journal of Industrial Relations* XX, No. 3 (November 1982), p. 323.

6. A leading proponent of this approach was Bora Laskin, former Chief Justice in Canada. See: Re Peterboro Lock Mfg. Co. Ltd. (1953), 4 L.A.C. 1499, at p. 1502 (Laskin). Also, see Freedman, S., *Report of Industrial Inquiry Commission on Canadian National Railway "Run-Throughs,"* (Ottawa: Queen's Printer), 1965.

7. See Alan Fox, *Beyond Contract: Work, Power and Trust Relations*, (Faber, London) 1974, especially pp. 181–190.

8. Beatty, David M., 'Labour Is Not a Commodity' in Reiter and Swan *Studies in Contract Law*, 1980, p. 316.

9. *Ibid.*, pp. 340-1. See also R.H. Tawney, *Equality* (London: Unwin Books), 1964.

10. Fox, Alan, 'The Meaning of Work,' in *The Politics of Work and Occupations*, edited by Geoff Esland and Graheme Salaman (University of Toronto Press), 1980, pp. 172-173.

11. Glasbeek, H., *op. cit.*, p. 74.

12. Thomas Donaldson, 'Employee Rights,' Ch. 7, in *Corporations and Morality* (Prentice-Hall, Inc., Englewood Cliffs, New Jersey), 1982, p. 138.

13. *Ibid.*, p. 138.

14. *Ibid.*, p. 138.

15. Stokes, Bruce, 'Worker Participation— Productivity and the Quality of Work Life,' *Worldwatch Paper 25* (December, 1978), p. 33.

16. *Ibid.*, p. 33.

17. *Ibid.*, p. 33.

18. In 1972, the Government in Saskatchewan passed an *Occupational Health and Safety Act* which required a joint labour-management committee to be set up in places of employment with ten or more employees (Section 20). As former Executive Director of the Occupational Health and Safety Branch within the Department of Labour from 1973 to 1982, I met with many of these committees and reviewed the Occupational Health and Safety Committee *Minutes* meetings throughout my tenure in government.

19. J.B. Cronin, 'Cause and Effect? Investigations into Aspects of Industrial Accidents in the United Kingdom,' *International Labor Review 103*, 2 (Feb. 1971), pp. 99-115.

20. *Ibid.*, p. 106.

21. *Ibid.*, p. 108.

22. *Ibid.*, p. 115.

23. Letter from John B. Cronin to Robert Sass dated March 14, 1976.

24. Philip Powell, Mary Hale, Jean Martin and Martin Simon, *2,000 Accidents: A Shop Floor Study of their Causes Based on 42 Months' Continuous Observation* (London: National Institute of Industrial Psychology, 1971).

25. *Ibid.*, p. 37.

26. Theo Nichols and Pete Armstrong, *Safety or Profit: Industrial Accidents and the Conventional Wisdom.* England: Falling Wall Press, 1973).

27. *Ibid.*, p. 20.

28. *Ibid.*, p. 25.

29. Carelessness and Accident proneness are false accident causation theories which blame the victim, the worker, for accidents and deflect attention from unsafe conditions.

30. Robert Sass and Glen Crook, 'Accident Proneness: Science or Non-Science?' *International Journal of Health Services 11*, 2 (Nov. 1981), p. 175.

Faculty of Commerce,
University of Saskatchewan,
Saskatoon, Saskatchewan,
Canada

16
Societal Pressures on Business: In Whose Interest?[1]

Oliver F. Williams

Social responsibility resolutions, almost nonexistent less than twenty years ago, are now an important force in the corporate world. In 1989, 170 resolutions came to a vote, while in 1988 only 156 were presented to the shareholders. In early 1990, some 250 resolutions were being prepared, largely by religious organizations. These resolutions concern a wide array of social responsibility issues including the environment, affordable housing, family farms, smoking and health, food irradiation, transfer of technology, South Africa, Northern Ireland, infant formula, military issues, animal issues, the world debt crisis, energy issues, political action committees, and equal employment.[2]

The social responsibility resolution is only one of the tools used by citizen groups to directly affect the corporation; other direct measures include demonstrations and boycotts as well as lawsuits brought against companies. Indirectly, interest groups have an enormous influence on corporate America by actively participating in all phases of the public policy process; much of the social regulation in place today can trace its origin to the initiative, lobbying and research of one or a coalition of interest groups. The number of interest groups and lobbies in Washington, D.C. is staggering; for example, over 30 groups are lobbying for women's issues, 15 for the elderly, 50 for minorities and 30 groups focus on environmental issues. The names of many of these groups have become household words: Common Cause, the Sierra Club, the National Wildlife Federation, Ralph Nader's Congress Watch, Friends of the Earth, The Council on Economic Priorities, the National Organization for Women, and TransAfrica, to name but a few.[3]

The focus of this article will be to outline some of the reasons for the dramatic increase in citizen activism, particularly from church institutions. It will also analyze several recent cases where activists have directly confronted corporate policy in order to glean some insight that may be helpful for the future.

LIVING BETWEEN THE TIMES

Church coalitions and other activist groups that are critical of business ultimately attribute their opposition to their interest in advancing a more humane society; their protests are a tangible way of moving toward this vision. Yet it was not so long ago that there was a strong social consensus that the best way for business to advance a humane society was to compete efficiently in the market. Providing quality goods and services at the best price was taken to be business's contribution to the common good. Executives today are living between the times; that is, they are caught between the time when there was a strong social consensus that the market mechanism was the best way to control business activity, and some possible future time when society has a clear consensus about how business institutions ought to advance human welfare.

We are living in a time when this new consensus is in the making. What is clear is that economic language—the language that traditionally often provided the sole rationale for corporate decisions—is not in itself acceptable to religious activists and many other socially concerned persons. Listening to many discussions between management and corporate critics, one is struck by the fact that they are often speaking different languages: management defends decisions in the economic language of profit and loss, and critics question the same decisions in the ethical language of justice and rights. The parties of such discussions usually pass like ships in the night; in the end, these conversations generate much heat and little light.

The implications of living between the times are far-reaching and affect how managers come to think of themselves. Most people want to be decent and moral, and they would like their efforts in business to reflect these characteristics. Under the former consensus on values in the social environment, managers could have some confidence that they were meeting their obligation to human welfare by participating in the market. Today, business executives are often caught in the middle. While most would acknowledge that they must consider the social costs of economic decisions, it is seldom clear where the moral person should draw the line in assessing the social and economic values at issue. We know business corporations are not the Red Cross, but what should they be? It is here that constructive dialogue with church and other activists may be helpful.

Until relatively recently, market and legal signals were the only major social forces that caught the attention of top management. Consumer sovereignty reigned in that astute management carefully tracked consumer needs and expectations and responded with the appropriate product and price to capture the market in question. Now top management must also respond to a whole array of nonmarket forces in the form of the activities of the various interest groups referenced above. What is at stake is the very legitimacy of the business corporation, for what is going on today is a rewriting of the implicit social contract between business and society. Society has more comprehensive expectations for business and, to some extent, business had better respond. However, while it is clear that a business has a responsibility to monitor and correct the problems it has caused in society, its so-called externalities such as pollution, it is unclear how much business can tackle other social ills in a community which are unrelated to the industry. Business must develop its own vision of its role in society and some sense of what it can and cannot do for society.

Implicit in the shareholder resolutions and various political strategies of the interest groups is a new vision of the role of business in society. Business is taken to be a major actor in a dynamic social system and the activists are attempting to forge the shape of business's new role. The challenge for

Oliver F. Williams

top management is to be interactive in this process and have a hand in shaping its future destiny before public policy limits prerogatives.

WHY SO MUCH ACTIVISM?

What has given rise to this rather sudden increase in nonmarket forces or interest group activism? One of the most formative experiences that may have set the tone for activism in the United States was the civil rights movement of the 1960s. The many who participated in this event, both actively and passively, came to feel a new power to transform society. Evil did not have to be tolerated; unjust social structures could be changed with strategy and persistence. In my view, the experience of the civil rights movement, its use of the media and its creation of heroes provided the model and the power that brought the current activist movements to birth.

At the same time, several other important developments provided fertile soil for the growth of the activist movements. Traditionally the two major political parties were the vehicles that carried the concerns of the people through the public policy process, but they no longer function effectively in the eyes of many people. Interest groups today carry out many of the roles that were abdicated by the political parties. Also, during the last thirty years the media has achieved significant power to shape public opinion on social issues. Informed public opinion has led to financial and other support for a wide variety of groups championing social issues.

CHRISTIAN BELIEFS AND THE BUSINESS WORLD

While many can understand the proliferation of interest groups and the rise of shareholder activism with social responsibility reso-

lutions as a development from an environment as described above, what is not clear is why the churches have become so prominent in some of these movements. For example, in any given year the majority of social responsibility resolutions have been initiated by church groups. It may be helpful to examine the historical evolution of church involvement in the economic life of the nation.

Religion has always been considered an important force in the shaping of American life. The Frenchman Alexis de Tocqueville, writing some one hundred fifty years ago, observed that religion played an essential role in America by shaping citizens who valued just and wholesome communities; he saw religion as crucial to the fabric of the nation.[4] Max Weber, in his famous *The Protestant Ethic and the Spirit of Capitalism,* argues that capitalism would have never developed without the religious influence; some of the core virtues of religion—honesty, industry, frugality, and thrift—formed communities of men and women who were the most productive and creative in their work.

Today many mainline Protestant and Catholic churches, rather than foster "the spirit of capitalism," often appear to be its harshest critics. Through proxy resolutions, boycotts, removal of funds from banks with objectionable policies, and other strategies, church groups are increasingly applying direct pressure to business corporations. What sorts of religious convictions motivate church groups in their dealings with business? Are the churches intent on creating a culture adverse to business, or can corporate managers forge a more cooperative relationship with these powerful institutions?

Many business leaders are puzzled as to why mainline Protestant and Catholic churches are often critical of business corporations. Understanding the religious convictions of these church leaders is essential. A core conviction of Christians is that the ministry of Jesus was to proclaim the coming

Kingdom of God. While this conviction has been unchanging, the way in which the term *Kingdom of God* has been understood in the Christian community has changed radically at various periods. A new meaning of *Kingdom of God* today has resulted in a self-understanding that often prompts Christians to oppose business corporations vigorously.

The first generation of Christians understood themselves as a special community chosen by God to prepare for the sudden arrival of his kingdom. They thought that the world as they knew it was about to end, and that they would be part of a transcendent Kingdom of God, a new world somehow discontinuous with the present one. Later generations came to believe that the church was to be that community that strives for and points toward the Kingdom of God, a kingdom that would finally arrive in God's good time. The notion of a coming kingdom finds resonance in the human heart, for people have always been restless for a land of peace and happiness, of "milk and honey." In the Hebrew Scriptures the prophets speak of a time of the kingdom when the lion will lie peaceably with the lamb. Christian Scriptures record the teaching of Jesus and portray a vision of the qualities of the kingdom—peace, justice, harmony, and brotherhood. Throughout the history of Christian communities there have been a variety of ways of relating the kingdom of the times. While the notion of the kingdom provides a vision of the sort of life we ought to have, the question is whether one should try to realize the kingdom here and now, approximate it, or anticipate it?

For most of Christian history the Kingdom of God was thought to be present in the institutional church in a small way, only to be fully realized by God at the end of time. In the church communities, men and women, in the spirit of Christ, could grow in charity, compassion, generosity, and so on. They could live virtuous lives and anticipate the final coming of God's kingdom where his rule of love would finally reign. The intellectual giant who fashioned the theological synthesis that shaped the Catholic Church for over seven hundred years is Thomas Aquinas (1225–1274).[5] Aquinas, as a man of his time, was not primarily concerned with changing social structures or making the world a better place to live. For him, the whole purpose of life in this world was to become virtuous and thereby to prepare for eternal happiness in the next world. Focusing on the virtues highlighted in the Bible—faith, hope, and charity—and Aristotle's four cardinal virtues—wisdom, justice, fortitude, and temperance—Aquinas encouraged Christians to lead lives and to form societies that would accent growth in virtue.

Life as Aquinas knew it, in the thirteenth century, was based on an agricultural economy and, by contemporary standards, almost everyone was poor. Society was understood to be static, on a model ordained by God, where the ideal was for all to have sufficient goods for their particular state in life. Lords, peasants, craftsmen, and merchants were taken to be in their role according to the divine plan. Upward mobility was foreign to this world, and for one to strive to accrue wealth beyond one's level was thought to be sinful—the sin of avarice. Aquinas and other theologians of the time supplied much practical guidance on just prices, usury, and trade in order to promote and protect the virtuous character of Christians, but they would never go so far as to encourage the creation of wealth. Trade and all forms of wealth creations were suspect, for making money cultivates greed in the merchant's heart and greed corrupts the life of the community. In the Thomist perspective, honor ought to be given to virtuous persons, yet if some citizens are particularly ingenious at making money, honor will likely be bestowed on them for their riches; this will slowly erode the high moral quality of the community.

Until recent times the vision of life's purpose espoused by Aquinas was the dominant one of the churches. Today, however, there is the realization that God's plan entails that all should enjoy the good things of creation; the proclamation of the kingdom is understood to entail working for sociopolitical changes that are likely to alleviate the plight of the poor. While Christians have always been taught to be concerned for the poor, the traditional response was personal charity. Although the sixteenth-century reformers, following Martin Luther, championed structural changes in society to eliminate the causes of poverty, this emphasis was short-lived. Only in our own time do we hear the loud call from the churches for systemic changes in institutions so that wealth might be more equitably distributed.

The efforts toward systemic change and reform of business corporations are understood to be mandated by that belief that the church is the "budding and beginning of the Kingdom," and that this future kingdom, the one that God will finally bring about, lights up the visions of Christians and spurs them on to work for political forms of justice and peace here and now. The new role of the churches is to labor for the values of the Kingdom of God—justice, love, peace, brotherhood, and so on—in the sociopolitical order. To be sure, the churches never intend to de-emphasize in any way their spiritual mission, but rather seek to draw out and make explicit the implications in the social order of living the Gospel. This new perspective is fully incorporated into the teachings of the churches.

THE SOURCES OF CONFLICT

In its basic thrust, the new church's emphasis on making the world a better place is quite congruent with the ideals of many business persons and organizations. To be sure, there will always be some tension, for the

church perspective highlights God's intentions to have a world of peace and justice, and speaks in terms of ultimates that are only to be realized in eternity. The business perspective focuses on more proximate objectives and must always calculate the trade-offs involved in employing resources efficiently; freedom is a key value for corporate managers; for the wider the scope of management prerogatives, the more likely the goal in question will be achieved.

The trick is to keep the inherent tension between business and the churches on a creative track rather than a destructive one. For example, where liberation theology dominates the church discussion, there has seldom been fruitful dialogue with the business community. Some discussion of the origin and aims of liberation theology may be helpful, since this theology is often influential in the churches of developing countries.

LIBERATION VERSUS GRADUALISM: A CONTEMPORARY DEBATE

In 1970, the World Council of Churches founded the Commission for the Churches Participation in Development (CCPD); this commission has championed structural changes in society and advocated a liberation style of change in preference to the traditional gradualist approach. The World Council is presently dominated by Third World countries and its statements are sometimes militant and decidedly anticapitalist. John C. Bennett, noted Protestant social ethicist and leader in ecumenical affairs, comments that the "World Council . . . no longer reflects the older and more disciplined ethical thinking of the First World."[6] While critical, he is sympathetic to the Third World intellectuals; he goes on to say that "the First World theologians can be criticized for provincialism and complacency."

The liberation style of doing theology has its roots in the Catholic Church of Latin America, and is intended to be a direct challenge to Christians who seem all too comfortable with suffering and deprivation in this present world. The writings of these Latin American theologians are characterized by a concern to see the world from the viewpoint of poor persons, and by an all-pervasive call to realize justice and liberation from poverty, and to realize this vision soon. The dominant motif is the people's participation in overcoming their oppression. It is an emphasis on a rapid change in social structures that is characteristic of the liberation approach. Not surprisingly, liberation theology is often marked by strong anticapitalist and anti-American rhetoric; from a liberationist perspective, the United States and its economic system hold little promise for Third World development. Some church leaders, although they may not fully espouse liberation theology, often speak from its militant posture. For example, in an interview in *Forbes* magazine, Paulo Evaristo Cardinal Arns, Catholic archbishop of Sao Paulo, Brazil, when asked about the problems of inflation and unemployment in Brazil, responded: "These problems (are) consequences of the installation of the multinational corporations and of a savage capitalism that can produce these ills in order to reap greater profits later."[7] Many detailed studies by economists and scholars most sympathetic to the terrible plight of the poor in Brazil offer a much different analysis. In fact, many argue that multinationals and capitalism, with appropriate government regulation, are the only hope for the poor in Brazil.

Although there is agreement within the churches that the plight of the poor must be alleviated, there is debate over the appropriateness of liberation theology. Many are concerned with its affinity with leftist political movements. Some accuse it of too easily advocating violence as a means of social change. There are others, however, who consider it as one of the valid means of transforming society. Persons espousing this theology are sensitive people who have been deeply touched by the condition of the poor and want transformations now. There is little appetite to wait a century and a half—the time it took to fashion such wealth-producing capabilities in the West. There is scant mention of the cultivation of habits of industry and other virtues. From a liberation perspective, the key issues are not these. Rather, the focus in proclaiming the Kingdom of God is on a positive strategy to overcome "oppression of the poor by the rich" and a great optimism that together humankind can fashion a different sort of world. Gustavo Gutierrez, a pioneer in this theology, makes the point well in his A Theology of Liberation.[8]

From the point of view of today's corporate leaders, a key feature of this theology is that it has little patience in its crusade to make the world a better place. The champions of this theology are strident in their condemnation of multinationals and corporate capitalism. However, an important point here is that church leaders who espouse the more extreme forms of liberation theology are not typical, and that it would be a mistake to characterize mainline Protestant and Catholic leaders in the United States in this militant mold.

STRATEGIES OF CHURCH ACTIVISTS IN THE UNITED STATES

As two of the world's largest multinational institutions, the church and the business corporation have a pervasive influence throughout the world. While churches have always highlighted the essential connection between personal and social ethics, it is only in the last fifteen years that they have formulated strategies designed to influence the social impact of business corporations. The initial concern of churches was that their own considerable economic resources be invested with an eye toward social responsibility. Stemming from the doctrine of private property, church teaching stressed that ownership entails responsibility, and the churches tried to be models of what good economic stewardship might be.

To assist church bodies in their judgments on investments, the National Council of Churches established the Corporate Information Center (CIC) in 1971. In 1974, the CIC merged with an ad hoc group of Catholic religious orders and Protestant denominations that had formed to protest a proposed corporate mining venture in Puerto Rico. This new coalition, housed in the New York City headquarters of the National Council of Churches, is known as the Interfaith Center on Corporate Responsibility (ICCR). The staff of the center provides research on corporate social performance, and coordinates and formulates church activist strategies.

A good argument can be made that church critics are capitalism's best friend. The professional staffs of churches link the local congregations with national structures through a vast network. Activists from the church staffs and ICCR provide one channel for business leaders to keep informed of the fresh ideas of public concern. Social concern shareholder proposals, even if only representative of a minority, serve as an important safety valve. Many of the reforms enacted in business and government first surfaced in the writings and activities of church critics. Business's ability to respond to public concern is one reason it is still accepted as a vital part of our society. The continued legitimacy of the business corporation depends upon its ability to meet public expectations.

In a typical year, church proponents file over one hundred and fifty shareholder proposals but withdraw about 20 percent of these after dialogue and negotiation with the companies in question. The point here is that the church activists can be thought of as providing a service by surfacing issues of public concern such as equal employment opportunity, environmental issues, and plant closings, and that many of the apparent conflicts are settled in a spirit of mutual respect by communication and discussion.

For the most part, religious social teaching has always accepted the American economic vision of growth with equity. On balance, however, there have been many more words said about justice than growth. Often religious documents do not exhibit a clear understanding of the inevitable trade-offs necessary in any economic system. The point of most mainline religious criticism of Western capitalism has been that the virtues of entrepreneurship, productivity, creativity, and individual achievement have been stressed at the expense of concern for the fairness of the results. Most of the activities of church critics can be seen as a counterbalance, trying to ensure that the benefits and burdens of corporate activity are equitably distributed, and that the rights of the least advantaged are not neglected. From my experience with a number of business leaders, it is my impression that many see a genuine value in church activist groups. Sensitive leaders understand that the legitimacy of their institution depends on public approval and support. Insofar as activists mirror the convictions of thoughtful members of the society, their work ensures that business, with social approval, will continue to perform its vital function of providing goods and services.

Church groups have come to assume that dialogue with business groups without pressure or the threat of pressure will not be effective in resolving injustices under discussion. While there is clearly some experience on which to justify this premise, many observers, both within and outside of the churches, have cautioned activists about the unintended consequences of such a strategy. For example, consider the widely reported infant formula controversy.

THE INFANT FORMULA CONTROVERSY

The substantive issue underlying the controversy was the extremely high infant mortality rates in developing countries; corporation leaders and their critics agree on this. While no one is claiming that infant formula is the sole cause of these deaths, the critics have argued that the aggressive marketing practices have persuaded many women to shift from breastfeeding to bottlefeeding. The use of infant formula and bottlefeeding has two adverse consequences:

1. the loss of protective antibodies from breast milk; and

2. the potential to misuse the formula either by using impure water or by diluting the formula to make it last longer.

There is also the problem of illiteracy in many areas so that often the product's instructions cannot be properly understood. In addition, refrigeration was not available for most users. With this sort of analysis, in 1970, Dr. Derrick B. Jelliffe, then head of the Caribbean Food and Nutrition Institute in Jamaica, recommended that all commercial formulas be withdrawn from the market in developing countries. Needless to say, his recommendation was not without controversy. In 1975, the ICCR, along with some of its member groups, presented shareholder resolutions requesting information on marketing practices in the Third World to two of the major formula companies, Bristol-Myers and American Home Products. Abbott Laboratories, through its Ross Laboratories division, also was challenged in a shareholder resolution by church groups to examine its overseas marketing practices.

In 1977, the University of Minnesota Catholic Newman Center founded the Infant Formula Action Coalition (INFACT). This organization, along with the ICCR, organized a national boycott against the Swiss-based Nestle S.A., the largest supplier of commercial formula in the Third World. This consumer boycott continued for 6 1/2 years and was the subject of much media attention and conflict before it was suspended in late January 1984. More than seventy American organizations representing churches, doctors, nurses, teachers, and other professionals had joined the boycott.

Drawing support largely from church organizations, the Nestle boycott leaders mounted a major campaign on the premise that a serious problem could be remedied by changing objectionable marketing practices in the Third World. In 1981, the coalition's efforts to have an international code on the marketing of infant formula adopted by the World Health Organization (WHO) were successful. The voluntary code suggests that free samples, mass advertising to consumers, and a number of other sales lures should be suspended. The focus of the boycotting groups was now to pressure the industry to implement the International Code. All Nestle products and services, from Nestle Crunch candy bars to Stouffer hotels and restaurants, were under the boycott.

Throughout the conflict, charges were traded by both sides. For example, before a U.S. Senate hearing on the issue in 1978, a Nestle's spokesman argued that the protest was directed by "a worldwide church organization, with the stated purpose of undermining the free enterprise system." A June 1983 newsletter of INFACT reported a typical statement of boycott leaders: "Malnutrition, the pain of diarrhea and disease, and the constant threat of death are not the natural birthright of a child, but the result of a social system informed and directed by powerful corporations working for their own selfish interests."

Although Nestle agreed in 1982 to abide by the WHO code, it was not until 1984, after much hostility, that the church groups finally

Oliver F. Williams

suspended the boycott. Because some multi-national corporations (MNCs) have changed the way they market infant formula in the less-developed countries (LDCs), church groups may have a claim to some success. But the length of the Nestle boycott and the seeming intractability of its leaders, even in the face of Nestle's acquiescence, caused some damage both to the company and to the cohesiveness of the church groups.[9]

A senior official of Nestle said the boycott's principal cost was employee morale. When religious groups engage in protracted conflict with business, in this case to "save starving babies," it is difficult to gauge the damage to both esprit de corps and the public perception of the legitimacy of business and the economic system. Experience from this conflict between industry and religious activists would seem to indicate two sorts of serious errors. On the one hand, industry should not assume all critics are Marxist and are seeking a revolutionary socialistic system. Critics should be listened to and their remarks carefully assessed. On the other hand, critics should be straightforward with the goals they are seeking. No matter how good the end, a less than forthright means is beneath the dignity of church representatives. The church as a moral leader ought to ensure that its representatives are beyond reproach. In this light, consider the strategy on infant formula summarized by James Post in a recent article.

Societies often have difficulties in shaping "sensible" policy solutions to complex policy issues. The reason that children die in developing nations is not because infant formula is a bad product. Rather, there is an environment of poverty, illiteracy, inadequate sanitation, unhealthy water, and limited health services that create dangerous conditions for the use of formula. Marketing did not create these conditions, but marketing was a more *actionable* aspect of the problem than poverty, water, or education. . . . Because business corporations are responsive to external pressure, action targeted at them has a better chance of producing change than actions aimed at such underlying conditions as poverty and illiteracy. A marketing code will not alleviate the problems of poverty, illiteracy, and poor sanitation, but it can help to ensure that companies do not exploit such conditions to their own advantage.[10]

While this may be acceptable strategy for some consumer groups, is it the most appropriate one for the church—the model of what human community ought to be like? The church indeed must be concerned to better the lot of the poor, but are not straightforward attempts to influence public policy much more fruitful? Should not the churches' major effort be directed at securing public policy aimed at improving the underlying conditions of poverty, illiteracy, and so on? Is settling for a marketing code, settling for too little? To be sure, the churches must be involved on both levels, criticizing injustices in business as well as initiating discussion of just public policy. Too much energy spent on the former, however, may leave little for the latter. The prospect of collaborative efforts with corporations to solve poverty problems will be unlikely if churches are alienated from business. To view this point from another angle, it may be helpful to consider another current controversy, the dispute over investments in South Africa.

THE CASE OF THE ETHICS OF INVESTMENTS IN SOUTH AFRICA

As business corporations begin to assume the task of integrating ethical concerns into their economic decisions, it is becoming increasingly clear that this task is fraught with difficulties. "Business leaders must be accountable for their exercise of power, not only to stockholders but to stakeholders—all those major constituencies affected by a business: employees, suppliers, local communities, area hospitals, schools, and so on."[11] Once this dictum from the scholars in ethics and management has been accepted and actually employed in the policy process by managers, often new and unintended consequences loom on the horizon. In the pages that follow, a brief summary of the attempt by business to follow an ethical course with investments in South Africa will be discussed. The case illustrates the difficulty of trying to please the major constituencies of a business corporation and may yield much insight for managers as they struggle to integrate ethics into policy decisions in the decades ahead.

APARTHEID: AN EVIL

During the summer of 1985 I was in South Africa researching the ethics of U.S. investments there. After nearly four weeks of traveling throughout the country and interviewing almost one hundred persons—religious leaders, labor leaders, business executives, members of Parliament, black workers, and so on—I had little hope that South Africa would soon be a peaceful land. About that time I had an interview with Bishop Desmond Tutu. As I walked into his office in Johannesburg, I was greeted by an exuberant Bishop Tutu. My first question was to ask him how he kept so hopeful in the midst of such oppression and violence. He said, "Let's pray before we talk." We prayed together for several minutes. His prayer called to mind that Jesus Christ came face to face with evil, suffered death at its hands, and finally rose again, overcoming evil once and for all, and

that as followers of Christ we believe that that same pattern can be repeated in each of our lives. Bishop Tutu's challenge is not unlike the challenge that we all face: each of us, in our own way, and in our own circumstances, is challenged to overcome evil with good.

All of us know evil from personal experience, but seldom do we encounter evil structured in society so firmly and resolutely as it is in the apartheid laws of South Africa. While there are more oppressive systems in the world, apartheid is the only one based on skin color. Over 300 racial laws in South Africa deny blacks many of the rights we take for granted—the right to vote, to move about freely in their own country, to attend the better white schools and to have the opportunity for decent housing.

I met any number of blacks who had important executive positions in business firms in South Africa and yet they still had to live in a ghetto—not because they could not afford better but because, according to the Group Areas Act, land is zoned by race. South Africa's white towns and cities are generally surrounded by black townships, often bleak, dusty and despair-ridden places. Estimates are that 25 percent of the 12 million urban blacks are unemployed. The situation of over 12 million blacks living in the so-called "homelands" is much worse. South Africa appears, for the most part, to be a beautiful and wealthy country. But not for the great majority of its inhabitants. It is dominated by the 5 million whites who control 80 percent of the land.

Is it reasonable to expect a quick and peaceful solution to the racial injustices of South Africa? Almost everyone says "No." The problem is in the numbers: whites are outnumbered by blacks almost by a factor of six. The whites have tried all kinds of schemes to maintain all the power—the homelands, white job reservation, restrictions of black businesses, and so on—and for a while these policies had worked. The strategy of the white ruling class seems to have been to do anything that would hinder the emergence of a unified black political group. The name of the game was survival, and the Afrikaners (the white ruling class) played it well. Now, however, the nation is at a crossroads. The blacks are, with good cause, increasingly agitating for political and economic rights, to the point of disrupting the white economy. Can the whites broaden the democratic processes to include blacks without losing all they had ever worked for? Although the new government under State President F.W. de Klerk has spoken of a number of changes, as of yet none have been enacted which touch the core of apartheid and open the way toward a fullscale multiracial society. Many are hopeful that this transition can and will take place in the not too distant future, and that a bloodbath can be avoided. Others argue that only violence will achieve the desired result, a society that guarantees political and civil rights for all.

On February 2, 1990, South African President Frederik W. de Klerk announced some major steps that signaled an opening to a negotiated settlement. President de Klerk legalized the African National Congress and many other opposition groups, promised to free political prisoners, declared a moratorium on executions, released press restrictions, and most significantly, he called upon all parties in contention to meet at the negotiating table to form a new constitution for South Africa. While hopeful, most south Africans realized that there would be no easy path to a new political order. Only time will tell whether the white minority will freely redistribute power in the political and economic realms.

APARTHEID AND U.S. BUSINESSES IN SOUTH AFRICA

Today there is a recognition that business is part of a dynamic social system. Because business is perceived as being powerful and effective, people have come to expect that business will help solve social and political problems of a society. This expectation can be a heavy burden for business. In the South African context, the problem is even more complex, for many argue that capitalism thrives from the cheap labor afforded by apartheid and hence business interests have been apartheid's ally. For a small group of black intellectuals in South Africa, capitalism is the enemy. For the millions who earn their livelihood in the businesses of South Africa, the record is more ambiguous. There is no question that almost all blacks in South Africa are "very unhappy" with apartheid; on the other hand, one of the most reliable surveys indicates that only 24% of urban blacks support total disinvestment. If companies will use their influence and dramatically oppose apartheid, 75% of the blacks will support their presence, according to this research study.[12] In principle, most blacks do not equate capitalism with apartheid.[13]

Multinational businesses from the U.S. have had operations in South Africa for over fifty years. It is a country that has vast potential for new markets, and major companies from all over the globe sought to get a position there. At its height, the U.S. corporate presence included over 280 companies with direct investments totaling some $2 billion. What is often overlooked, however, is that South Africa is a relatively wealthy country, and that only about 4 percent of all direct investment is from foreign multinational companies; only one-fifth or .8 percent of all direct investments in South Africa were from U.S. firms in 1976, although some strategic areas, such as the major share of the computer and petroleum industries, were serviced by U.S. multinationals.

OVERCOMING APARTHEID: INITIATIVES IN THE U.S.

Concern about racist policies in South Africa on the part of U.S. groups dates back to 1912 when the NAACP provided assistance to what later became the African National Congress of South Africa. It was not until the mid-sixties, however, that college students, civil rights leaders, and church groups began to devise strategies in response to the evil of apartheid. In 1973 a major offensive was launched by church groups against bank loans to the Republic of South Africa (R.S.A.). Forty-seven banks, including some of the major U.S. banking institutions, were threatened with a mass withdrawal of deposits unless loans to R.S.A. ceased. Although the campaign did not have a significant effect on the loan policy of the banks, it did give much visibility to the apartheid problem. In 1971 the first shareholder resolution on South Africa calling for the termination of General Motors operations in R.S.A. was presented by the Episcopal Church. At the time, church officials candidly stated that their goal was *not* to have GM leave South Africa, but rather to pressure the company to use its power to help change R.S.A. government policy on the races and to better the lot of blacks at home and the workplace.[14] Until recently, this was the strategy of most U.S. church groups, even though their official positions advocated total withdrawal of U.S. firms. Since 1971 there have been over five hundred shareholder resolutions on South Africa targeted at dozens of U.S. corporations.

For the most part, until quite recently, U.S. businesses with operations in South Africa responded to the churches' call to help solve the racial problem in South Africa by adopting the code of conduct developed by the Reverend Leon H. Sullivan. Sullivan, for many years a leading black pastor in Philadelphia and a member of the Board of Directors of the General Motors Corporation, called 12 major U.S. companies together in 1977 and drew up a code of conduct that has come to be known as the Statement of Principles. If U.S. companies were in South Africa, they must pursue the following policies:

1. Non-segregation of the races in all eating, comfort and work facilities;

2. Equal and fair employment practices for all employees;

3. Equal pay for all employees doing equal or comparable work for the same period of time;

4. Initiation and development of training programs that will prepare blacks, coloreds, and Asians in substantial numbers for supervisory, administrative, clerical, and technical jobs;

5. Increasing the number of blacks, coloreds, and Asians in management and supervisory positions;

6. Improving the quality of employees' lives outside the work environment in such areas as housing, transportation, schooling, recreation and health facilities; and

7. Working to eliminate laws and customs that impede social and political justice.

(Point 7 was added in 1985 and was not in the original code). Even though U.S. corporations employed only about 90 thousand of the 9 million workers in South Africa, the efforts to dismantle apartheid by American firms have served as a beacon and a catalyst in generating reform throughout business and industry. If the non-U.S. companies who have recently adopted a code similar to the Statement of Principles are counted, almost one million blacks in South Africa enjoy the protection of the code.

Within the workplace, the code and similar measures by non-U.S. firms have long been standard policy, and many blacks report that their lives are much more humane because of them. Outside the workplace, land is still zoned by skin color and there are over 300 laws designed to enforce apartheid, the Afrikaans word for separate development (literally "Separate-hood"). In 1985, in a bold new development, the Rev. Sullivan and the signature companies added a new requirement to the code: All U.S. companies operating in South Africa would "support the ending of all apartheid laws."[15] This is now point number seven in the Statement of Principles listed above.

U.S. companies following the Statement of Principles are now actively lobbying the South African government to end apartheid laws. The lobbying, for the most part, is done through the Signatory Association, an industry association of all the U.S. firms in South Africa which have subscribed to the Principles. While at this time, in 1989, the lobbying is done quietly behind the scenes, initially it was quite public. AMCHAM wrote a hard-hitting document that placed industry squarely in opposition to the apartheid laws. Their position paper covered urbanization and influx control, housing removals, migrant labor, black business rights, and citizenship. It also argued for channels for democratic participation at all levels of government, the means of which were to be arrived at by negotiation and consultation with all leaders of the various constituencies. The final document was officially presented to a special R.S.A. Cabinet Committee and it was widely publicized. In a dramatic move, the major business groups of South Africa gave the then President, P.W. Botha, an ultimatum: He must begin to negotiate with key black leaders to abolish apartheid. To stress the urgency, some of the most prominent leaders of industry flew to Zambia and met with the leaders of the outlawed African National Congress. All this was in 1985; still, there is no significant reform, although there is some hope that the new President, F.W. de Klerk, will meet the challenge of dismantling apartheid.

Will the South African government respond to the growing demands for change, demands both from within the country and from the international community? In all fairness, most analysts candidly admit agnosticism on this point. The Reverend Leon Sullivan, in June 1987, carrying out a promise he made two years earlier, called for all U.S. companies to withdraw from South Africa by March 1988. He also asked that the U.S. initiate a total economic embargo "until statutory apartheid is ended and blacks have a clear commitment for equal political rights." While he acknowledged that the Principles had been "a tremendous force for change," he stated that much remains to be done and that more pressure is needed to force the R.S.A. government to negotiate with blacks.

U.S. COMPANIES: AN UPDATE

U.S. companies with operations in South Africa have found themselves in the midst of a major domestic controversy; determining the "right" thing to do has been exceedingly difficult. In 1986, 50 U.S. corporations left South Africa. Between 1986 and 1989, over 90 more companies withdrew. These companies include some of the giants, such as IBM, GM, Kodak, and Xerox. The reasons for the departures were well summarized in a *Wall Street Journal* story on the Xerox disinvestment in 1987. Quoting Xerox chairman, David T. Kearns, the *Journal* wrote:

Mr. Kearns said he still feels staying put is best for South Africa's 23 million blacks. But he now says leaving is what is best for Xerox. "It was clear things were continuing to deteriorate on all fronts," he said. The nation's economy and social climate were worsening; pro-disinvestment groups' criticism was rising; and Xerox was beginning to lose sales in the U.S. to local governments that were banning contracts with companies doing business there.[16]

What is the goal of the pro-disinvestment groups? My research on the South Africa question has focused on the types of arguments being made by the various leaders and groups in the struggle for black rights in the R.S.A. It may be helpful to outline this work.

THE LOGIC OF THE ARGUMENTS CONCERNING DISINVESTMENT[17]

After surveying the many ethical arguments made for and against investments in South Africa today, three main approaches emerge:

1. the "clean hands" approach;
2. the "solidarity with victims" or prophetic approach; and
3. the "stewardship" approach.

Each style has a unique dominant concern. Advocates of the clean hands approach are mainly concerned to avoid complicity in the evil of apartheid. Followers of the prophetic style emphasize the crucial need to identify with the oppressed of South Africa in a clear and dramatic manner, while followers of the stewardship approach seek to determine the best way to use corporate and government power to advance the welfare of black South Africans. Most often those arguing in the "clean hands" and prophetic modes are strong advocates of disinvestment, while the followers of the stewardship ethic often argue the case for continuing investment. Those in the debate from religious groups will find that there is not one position which is *the* Chris-

tian or Jewish answer; all three approaches can be appropriate expressions of Christian faith, for example. One's unique vocation as a Christian often determines one's ethical stance, whether it be a prophet, a steward, or pacifist. Secular humanists, analogously, may well gravitate to one of the three logics in analyzing moral issues.

THE "CLEAN HANDS" APPROACH

Apartheid, as a statutory system that bestows rights on the basis of color and race, is a denial of the fundamental value of human dignity, a value which for Christians and Jews follows from the conviction that all people are created in the image of God, and which for all humankind is enshrined in the United Nations Declaration of Human Rights. Apartheid is, without a doubt, an evil system, and many would argue that as such it should not enjoy the cooperation of people of good will in any shape or form. In this view, then, the claim on conscience to avoid evil may take precedence over the claim to fashion political and economic strategies to promote justice where these strategies entail cooperation with institutions involved with evil. Until apartheid is dismantled, economic and political cooperation is censored, according to some. Disinvestment is *the* answer. The problems many have noted with this solution however, is that it fails to help those most in need, those suffering under apartheid.

To be sure, there are very thoughtful responses to apartheid employing the "clean hands" sort of logic. Consider the position of Clifton R. Wharton, Jr., currently the top officer of TIAA-CREF and an advocate of removing all U.S. investments from South Africa:

Finally there comes a point so incompatible with one's respect for humanity itself that compromises with conscience can no longer be tolerated or rationalized. When a human situation so fundamentally affronts every tenet of human values, a public expression of personal opposition is a moral obligation.[18]

Wharton is not claiming that his stand will make things turn out right in South Africa; rather, he refuses to be an accomplice in the evil of apartheid. (It should be noted that the official stance of TIAA-CREF is not totally congruent with Wharton's personal position quoted here.) To participate in the apartheid system is to be morally culpable and the proper response, in this view, is to disassociate oneself.

THE PROPHETIC APPROACH

People who espouse the second model primarily want to make a prophetic statement so that men and women of compassion will join ranks and show solidarity with the oppressed of South Africa. This ethic generally calls for disinvestment and strong economic and trade sanctions. It draws on the biblical witness that we are all one people and are called to express our solidarity with those in special need.

Walter Fauntroy, representative of the District of Columbia in the U.S. House of Representatives and pastor of New Bethel Baptist Church in Washington, D.C., follows the prophetic logic. Fauntroy, as one of the original founders of the Free South Africa Movement, advocates a total withdrawal of U.S. investment. For Fauntroy, joining the movement and pressing for disinvestment is a moral requirement. However, he is not primarily concerned for a "clean hands," as in the model just discussed. Rather, he is making a prophetic statement, hoping that his stance will evoke similar sentiments from others who will join the resistance. The strength of this position is that it unambiguously challenges evil and wrong-doing.

The weakness of this approach is that it assumes that this is the unique moment of crisis in South Africa, when an overwhelming show of solidarity will mobilize widespread support. Yet should the broad coalition of resistance not materialize, the oppressed blacks may be even more demoralized.

THE STEWARDSHIP APPROACH

In the quest for justice in personal and communal life, the stewardship ethic acknowledges that often one is faced with choices, all of which have a regrettable aspect. Although U.S. corporate presence in South Africa may indirectly support an apartheid regime by paying taxes, that presence may at the same time be a constructive force to dismantle apartheid, and the lack of that presence may have dire consequences for many who depend on it for their livelihood. In this account the U.S. corporate presence is moral, even though it may involve cooperation with evil, for that presence is actually creating the conditions to end apartheid. In technical language, the "directly voluntary" consequence, achieving the good, occurs while reluctantly allowing an "indirectly voluntary" consequence, an evil. The judgment is made that there is a proportionately grave reason for permitting the evil affect to occur.[19]

A stewardship ethic is exemplified in the writings of Gatsha Buthelezi, Chief Minister of Kwazulu and President of Inkatha and the Black Alliance, major groups in South Africa. Buthelezi has little use for arguments from moral purity or prophetic witness but rather focuses on how corporate power can most effectively advance the welfare of blacks:

To stand on American indignant principles by withdrawing diplomatically and economically from South Africa is a luxury that the vastness of American wealth could afford. But indulgence in that luxury for the sake of purity of conscience, whatever genuine motives produce that conscience, would do no more than demonstrate the moral ineptitude of a great nation in the face of challenges from a remote area of the globe.[20]

To be sure, Buthelezi is not uncritical of U.S. corporations in South Africa; he is always prodding them to be "good stewards" and use their influence more aggressively to dismantle apartheid. Yet he is fighting to keep U.S. corporations and investments in South Africa because he needs their leverage in his struggle to overcome apartheid and he needs jobs for his people.

It has become fashionable in some quarters to consider Buthelezi as having sold out since he is the Chief Minister of Kwazulu. Such a position is a serious mistake. A *New York Times* editorial put it well:

Chief Buthelezi is unfairly caricatured by black militants as an Uncle Tom. The truth is more interesting. He has repeatedly called for the unconditional release of Nelson Mandela, jailed leader of the African National Congress. Though the chief preaches moderation, he has scorned attempts to draw him away from Mr. Mandela into talks with Pretoria on a "new dispensation" meant to prolong minority rule.[21]

Many institutional shareholders who continue to hold stock in U.S. corporations with operations in South Africa, and a number of others argue for the morality of investments in R.S.A. with the stewardship ethic. The reasoning here is that since the business community has lent its active support to the black cause, the dismantling of apartheid has begun, however slowly. In five years more changes had been consummated than in the fifty before: the repeal of the Immorality and Mixed Marriages Act, the recognition of black trade unions to the point that over one million blacks now are union members, the ending of "whites only" job reservations, the repeal of the law forbidding nonracial political parties, the establishment of a franchise for mixed-race and Indians (unsatisfactory as it is), and the granting to blacks the right to hold the deed to their land in black townships. The repeal of the pass laws and the toleration of the erosion of the Group Areas Act hold much promise. More important, U.S. business has been on the forefront of initiatives to abolish existing legislation that continues apartheid. Such matters as urbanization and influx control, housing, removals, migrant labor, black business rights, and citizenship are major items aggressively lobbied for and promoted by the business community in South Africa. The centerpiece of this business initiative is that all these matters ought to be negotiated with the acknowledged black leaders of R.S.A. While advocates of continuing U.S. investment in South Africa understand that the internal pressure of blacks themselves is crucial for dismantling apartheid, they also consider the pressure from the business community as an important aid in the struggle.

The stewardship ethic also argues that an important consequence of U.S. investments in South Africa is the attention that R.S.A. receives by the U.S. media and other institutions of U.S. society. For example, higher education in the United States has been involved in a number of programs to contribute to black advancement in South Africa. The New England Board of Higher Education has been involved in a program to raise funds to support scholarships for blacks in universities in R.S.A. The Carnegie Corporation, with the presidents of major U.S. universities, is funding and planning a number of cooperative ventures with higher education in South Africa. The U.S. South Africa Education Program (SAEP) has brought over 300 black

South African students to the United States since 1979 for graduate and undergraduate study. Someday, probably in the near future, the blacks will be governing South Africa, no matter what the Afrikaners say or do; a crucial need now is to provide numbers of blacks the education and training that they will require to have the infrastructure of black managers to administer such a nation. The U.S. corporate presence is presently a major source and catalyst for that education.

It is interesting to note that Clifton R. Wharton, Jr. originally argued from a stewardship ethic that the consequences of the U.S. corporate presence in South Africa— "practicing nondiscrimination" and "providing a progressive example"—morally justified the investments. As stated earlier, however, six years later in 1985, Wharton is an advocate of complete disinvestment. Acknowledging that the new initiatives from the business community might offer a glimmer of hope, Wharton feels compelled to champion economic withdrawal:

For the small minority of blacks employed by progressive U.S. corporations, there have been some changes for the better. But these gains are overwhelmed by the clear evidence that for the vast majority, things have gotten steadily worse, not better, during the last decade.[22]

To be sure, a serious recession has depressed South Africa, there has been an increased loss of freedom under the state of emergency, and press coverage is censored. Yet many, on the basis of gains in the past five years, are still hopeful that U.S. investments can help. For example, the former Episcopal Bishop of Washington, D.C., the late John T. Walker, an important black clergyman until his death in 1989, argued for the continued presence of U.S. companies in South Africa as long as they aggressively opposed apartheid and empowered blacks with

jobs and skills. "I don't see why liberals think there's only one way of going about accomplishing what you want to accomplish. . . . My views are not far removed from Desmond Tutu's in a practical sense."[23]

In order to understand why people like Wharton and the Rev. Leon Sullivan finally called for disinvestment, it is well to recall that most people seem to have a point beyond which they will not go in the use of the stewardship ethic; deciding when the pace of change is too slow is a very personal judgment. Some continue to ask, "Slow, compared to what?" Others reach the breaking point and say, "Here I stand; I can do no other."[24]

SANCTIONS AND DISINVESTMENT: THE APPROPRIATE RESPONSE?

The American public increasingly has become aware of apartheid for the evil that it is, and new public policy reflects this concern. In October 1986, overriding President Reagan's veto, Congress passed the Comprehensive Anti-Apartheid Act of 1986. The bill includes a ban on new U.S. loans and investments in South Africa, a curtailing of direct air links between United States and South Africa, and a prohibition on certain imports from R.S.A. including coal, steel, uranium, agricultural products, iron and textiles. While no one was under the illusion that the economic sanctions of the bill would cripple or even moderately harm the South African economy, for the items prohibited are not the major imports, the bill did send a strong signal that the U.S. supports the black cause. Further sanctions, hitting at the key imports in the annual U.S. $2.6 billion package— diamonds, ferrochrome and platinum group metals—could conceivably harm the R.S.A. economy. On the other hand, ferrochrome and the platinum group metals are considered strategic materials, and the R.S.A. is one of the few non-Soviet suppliers to the United States. Thus, it is unlikely that Congress will ban these imports without great pressure from the American people.

To be sure, sending a signal indicating which side the U.S. is on is an important move, but can U.S. economic sanctions ever be reasonably expected to yield enough pressure to move the R.S.A. government to dismantle apartheid? That is, can the departure of U.S. corporations and the cessation of U.S. bank loans and trade bring the South African economy to its knees and, therefore, its leaders to the negotiating table? In terms of the conceptual framework presented above, can economic sanctions be the primary tool of a stewardship ethic, or are they more properly the means of a prophetic or clean hands ethic. We know U.S. economic pressures can symbolically demonstrate where our loyalties are; it is a point of dispute whether such sanctions can actually hasten the dismantling of apartheid.

In an insightful study for the Institute for International Economics of 78 cases of economic sanctions, Clyde Hufbauer and Jeffrey Schott concluded that the success of sanctions depends on a number of factors. Successful uses of sanctions were generally cases marked by the following characteristics:

1. A narrowly defined objective;
2. an economically large sender country imposing the sanction on small target;
3. sanctions had an immediate effect with little chance for the target country to adjust;
4. minimal economic costs to sender;
5. economic sanctions could be imposed unilaterally without need of cooperation from other countries to be effective.[25]

Unfortunately, items 3 and 5 will almost be impossible to implement in the South Africa case. So far, sanctions have had minimal ef-

fect in R.S.A. because the nation has been able to adjust. To be sure, a number of workers have lost their jobs—mostly black workers—but this small increase in the already large unemployment ranks holds little promise for marshalling significant pressure. More importantly, the U.S. has had little success in convincing other major trading partners to join the sanctions campaign. A March 12, 1987, UPI story discussed a report from the Secretary-General of the United Nations, Javier Perez de Cuellar, where he noted that as U.S. firms were pulling out of South Africa, West Germany's Daimler-Benz and Bayerische Motorenwerke (BMW) were expanding, and Italy's Olivetti Co. was building a plant. Assuming that the U.S. could persuade the major trading partners—Japan, U.K. and the Federal Republic of Germany— this only accounts for about 50% of South Africa's trade. At this time it is difficult to see that the economic sanctions will provide the crucial pressures to cause the dismantling of apartheid, at least in the near term.

The basic premise of the sanctions advocates needs much more scrutiny, that is, the premise that the white minority regime will respond positively to blacks in the political arena under the pressure of withdrawal of foreign trade and capital. To some extent this withdrawal has already occurred, and the evidence indicates that the system of racial supremacy is relatively unaffected.[26] Past changes in the apartheid laws were all in situations of *internal* pressure when P.W. Botha had his right flank in check. There is no question that some of the pillars of apartheid are slowly crumbling; for example, the Group Areas Act which zones land by race is more and more difficult to enforce and its restrictive laws are often violated. Blacks are finally getting a taste of solidarity and the power that comes with acting together. For many, the experience of trade unions was the first opportunity to come together and speak with a common voice and focus on common aspirations. Through participation in trade unions, the blacks are getting a taste of solidarity which is uniting them in the face of the evil of apartheid. The experience of solidarity will increasingly unite blacks in consumer boycotts and other activities designed to win their civil and political rights; this, of course, assumes the blacks continue to have jobs and consumer power.

Often the call for disinvestment from South Africa is meant to be a form of economic pressure but not actually a call for all foreign investment to depart. In this scenario, disinvestment threats play a role somewhat analogous to the concept of deterrence in nuclear ethics. According to this doctrine, a threat to use nuclear weapons against an adversary deters that adversary from using military force. Of course, if the policy is effective, the nuclear weapons will never be used. Similarly, if the policy of threatening disinvestment is effective, that is, if the South African government dismantles apartheid and starts a negotiating process with acknowledged black leaders, actual disinvestment need never occur. The May 2, 1986, "Statement of the Southern African Catholic Bishops' Conference" seems to employ this logic.

We, ourselves, believe that economic pressure has been justifiably imposed to end apartheid. Moreover, we believe that such pressure should continue and, if necessary, be intensified should the developments just referred to show little hope of fundamental change. However, we do not need to point out that, in our view, intensified pressure can only be justified if applied in such a way as not to destroy the country's economy and to reduce, as far as possible, any additional suffering to the oppressed through job loss (Paragraph 10).

In recent years, however, the "hassle factor" has caused major foreign employers to leave or consider departing from South Af-

rica. It may be that this disinvestment strategy will not yield the desired objective. The call for increasing economic sanctions is often assumed to be coming from the great majority of South African blacks. Although black leaders of the African National Congress (ANC) and the United Democratic Front (UDF) have consistently called for sanctions, leaders of Inkatha, the large, predominantly Zulu group, have regularly opposed all sanctions and encouraged foreign investment. As indicated above, reliable surveys do not confirm any widespread support for disinvestment by South African blacks. To be sure, the findings of these surveys are disputed by some analysts who point to the fact that it is against the law to advocate sanctions in R.S.A. Yet the fact remains that all reputable surveys indicate that if disinvestment means loss of jobs, then blacks are not in favor of it.

THE NEED "TO DO SOMETHING": SHAREHOLDER DEMOCRACY

Shareholder resolutions continue to call for withdrawal of firms from South Africa; in 1989 over one hundred such resolutions were presented, some winning over 20% of the vote, which is a high percentage in social responsibility shareholder resolutions. There is no doubt that as managers continue to receive such resolutions, and as local governments continue to ban or restrict contracts with companies with an R.S.A. operation, more and more U.S. companies will withdraw from South Africa. For the most part, the managers believe that their operations in South Africa are helping to dismantle apartheid. As blacks become more prosperous, they become better customers; as they become free of travel restrictions, transport and recruitment costs go down. Thus, for moral as well as for self interest reasons, business is interested in ending apartheid. The dilemma for firms with operations in South Africa is that in the U.S. the idea has caught on that sanctions and disinvestment will bring about the downfall of apartheid. Stakeholder democracy insures that the firms, given a strong message, will finally all leave. The companies will depart even though the managers who know the South African scene have serious reservations that disinvestment will be a tool to dismantle apartheid. Many anti-apartheid activists in South Africa fear that even if sanctions yield lower living standards for whites they will adjust to the slower economy rather than yield black political rights with their backs to the wall. The managers must listen to their many constituencies in South Africa as well as in the United States, but finally they must listen to their shareholders and other stakeholders.

Most often, the stakeholders do not speak forcefully on social responsibility issues; most do not vote the proxies or initiate boycott legislation, however, the South Africa issue is an exception. With the South African apartheid question, there is a growing impatience and a feeling that we must do something now. Calls for sanctions and disinvestment are a very appealing response to the need "to do something." Such moves may be a dramatic statement of where we stand ("Clean Hands" or "Prophetic" stance), but they have yet to demonstrate that they can achieve the objective of dismantling apartheid ("Stewardship" ethic). One thing is certain: the departure of American business from South Africa because of pressures exerted in the U.S. has usually resulted in new non U.S. owners who are much less interested in solving social problems. The Investor Responsibility Research Center, a Washington, D.C. research group respected for its objectivity, concluded a 1988 study with the following observation: "The most notable changes in corporate conduct following disinvestment have been the cutbacks in funding for community development programs and organizations that challenge apartheid policies, as well as some

rechanneling of funds from the more progressive organizations to those deemed politically acceptable in South African terms."[27] Those arguing for withdrawal of all foreign businesses have rendered an important service in the fight against apartheid in that they have raised the general level of awareness in the U.S. of the evil of that system. The media attention given to a university endowment selling the stock of firms with operations in South Africa or to a city, county or state passing an ordinance forbidding purchases from such companies have enabled many Americans to have a fairly good idea of the injustice that permeates the daily life of the non-whites—80% of the population of South Africa. How much these moves aid in the removal of apartheid laws—the ultimate goal—remains to be seen.

Like most difficult problems, it may be that a plurality of strategies offers the best hope for the dismantling of apartheid. The disinvestment lobby has placed all of its chips on the hope that the continued withdrawal of foreign investment will so weaken the economy that the South African white leadership will come to see the wisdom of negotiating a new constitution for a multiracial society. Yet many sympathetic South Africans, both black and white, have counseled against such a "scorched earth" policy. The untold human suffering and long time frame that such a strategy is likely to entail is revolting and unacceptable to many. Some important anti-apartheid activists, such as the South African political leader, Helen Suzman, see no chance of success, in any event, with such a strategy.

There is no doubt, in my view, that external pressure is required to eliminate statutory racism in South Africa. One weapon providing pressure to eliminate apartheid that I believe gets far too little credit is the whole effort of the U.S. companies still remaining in South Africa that falls under the Statement of Principles Program, the endeavor that was founded and guided by the Reverend Leon Sullivan and continues today under a National Advisory Council. As a member of the National Advisory Council, I am not naive about the clout of the U.S. companies remaining in South Africa—only 58 of the companies still in R.S.A. are signatories with over 180 having sold their holdings. The U.S. companies' role today in the fight against apartheid is what it has always been, to be a role model, a catalyst, spurring on the vastly more numerous domestic and non-U.S. foreign companies to some significant involvement in activities to overcome apartheid. Some would say the U.S. companies are lighting a candle rather than cursing the darkness, but I am more hopeful.

A recent report on the activities of the U.S. companies in South Africa, compiled by Arthur D. Little, Inc., as a part of the requirements of the Statement of Principles for South Africa Program, notes that some 60 U.S. companies provided more than 30 million dollars this past year to programs designed to eliminate apartheid.[28] Some of these dollars went to assist in black educational endeavors but many went to activities that most South Africans consider too risky because they directly challenge the status quo and advance social change. For example, a number of the companies provided the funds and personnel to organize a black consumer boycott of the stores in Boksburg after the local city council tried to restore segregation in the down town city park. Other companies directly challenged white merchants in Johannesburg by assisting blacks in exercising their newly legislated freedom to do business in the downtown areas; this assistance was not only start-up funding, but also training in business skills and entrepreneurship.

Several companies used their influence and resources to secure the freedom of union leaders who were being detained by the police. Companies are also spending money to encourage non-racial education and medical care, a direct confrontation to the current structures based on a racial hierarchy. Many companies are buying homes in white areas and making it possible for blacks to assume ownership, thus challenging and eroding the Group Areas Act that zones land by race.

The obvious objection to all of these examples of incremental change is that the major apartheid laws are still in place. Yet it just might be that there is no quick fix for this evil. At least we ought to allow for this possibility and encourage a plurality of strategies. Companies that are willing to take up the challenge and oppose the system deserve the support of the public—or at least its toleration.

A MANAGERIAL PERSPECTIVE

History may well show that the terms of the discussion about South Africa needed a fresh review. What is the objective in calling for disinvestment and sanctions? It is clear that in the early stages of the campaign church activists, while calling for disinvestment, were primarily seeking to enlist the support of business in anti-apartheid projects. Their efforts were largely successful, through the Statement of Principles founded by Leon Sullivan and other similar codes business identified with the black cause; to be sure, for some this identification came late, but better late than never. Because of a growing impatience that the evil system of apartheid has continued to perdure, in 1985 a broad coalition of black activists, church groups and political leaders in the U.S. have rallied around the call for disinvestment and sanctions. It would appear that their call will be successful, judging from the present climate. However, it is unclear that the black cause will be advanced. The focus of the debate ought to be turned to a discussion of what is in the best interests of R.S.A. blacks, and those blacks must themselves be the decisive voice. South

African blacks have long argued for black empowerment. Only several U.S. companies have tried directly to respond to that cry; for example, the Coca Cola Company arranged for over 10,000 South Africans to be shareholders of Coke as part of the terms of the company's disinvestment. Strategies to empower blacks must be a part of our discussions and tactics. Otherwise, all those hoping to see the abolition of apartheid may witness the total withdrawal of all U.S. investments and little change in that system of racial hierarchy, a pyrrhic victory in South Africa.

Reviewing the role of business in society in the last fifty years, it is surprising how the responsibilities of business have dramatically increased. Clearly, capitalism is not static but is what some have called a moving target. Business is part of a dynamic social system, and as new social and political problems have been identified, society has repeatedly turned to business for solution. Business is perceived as being powerful and effective. However, business is also mistrusted. Bigness has always been suspect in America. Corporations often have appeared insensitive to human values; some clearly have been. Many still think that profit maximization is the sole motive of business, even though a careful analysis of many corporations would yield a much more complex pattern.

The Nestle case as well as the South Africa case are instances where multinationals assumed additional responsibilities for the complex sociocultural and environmental systems within which it was operating. However, the assumption of this responsibility was initiated and accompanied by protests, largely from religious organizations that applied pressure directly to the corporations. More prompt action may have avoided such coalitions. In the case of Nestle, there is still a protest organization with complaints to this day, even though many of the original supporters have judged the founding problem to have been solved with the formation of the Nestle Infant Formula Audit Commission. The most effective business response may be to have managers who are adept at responding promptly to those societal expectations that are feasible and judged appropriate.

Church leaders too must scrutinize their "prophets." Moral language, especially when used by church personnel, is powerful. It has a remarkable ability to arouse passions and motivate persons of religious conviction. However, moral language can be abused when it is used without careful analysis. The churches could dilute an essential part of their heritage, should they fail to exercise diligence in the use of moral language. Business leaders who are church members could perform a great service for the religious community by offering their perspective to the church. As a matter of course, top management of the future would do well to know moral language and ethical analysis, not only to protect themselves but, more importantly, to consciously expand the horizon for decision making.

NOTES

1. Part of this article appeared in an earlier version in Oliver F. Williams, "Business and Church Activism in America" in *Business and Society*, eds. S. Prakash Sethi and Cecilia M. Falbe (Lexington, MA: Lexington Books, 1987), pp. 378–390.

2. See "Preliminary Preview of 1990 Social Responsibility Resolutions" published by the Investor Responsibility Research Center, Inc., Suite 600, 1755 Massachusetts Avenue, N.W., Washington, D.C. 20036.

3. For a survey of the various interest groups, see John M. Holcomb, "Citizen Activism and Corporate Political Strategies: Evolution from 1970–1985" in *Business and Society*, eds. S. Prakash Sethi and Cecilia M. Falbe (Lexington, MA: Lexington Books, 1987), pp. 353–378.

4. Alexis de Tocqueville, *Democracy in America*, ed. Phillips Bradley (New York: Vintage Books, 1945), vol. I, p. 316. Part of this section appeared in earlier articles: "Religion: The Spirit or the Enemy of Capitalism," *Business Horizons* 26(6):6–13 (1983); and "Catholic Bishops Take on Economics," *Business and Society Review* S4(3):21–26 (1985).

5. For further elaboration of this discussion on Aquinas, see *The Judeo-Christian Vision and the Modern Corporation*, eds. Oliver F. Williams and John W. Houck (Notre Dame, IN: University of Notre Dame Press, 1982).

6. John C. Bennett, "Protestantism and Corporations," in *The Judeo-Christian Vision and the Modern Corporation*, p. 88.

7. Norman Gall, "When Capitalism and Christianity Clash," *Forbes*, September 1, 1980, pp. 100–101.

8. Gustavo Gutierrez, *A Theology of Liberation*, trans. Sister Caridad Inda and John Eagleston (Maryknoll, N.Y.: Orbis Books, 1973).

9. The Nestle case is discussed in more detail in my article, "Who Cast the First Stone," *Harvard Business Review* 62(5):151–160 (1984).

10. James E. Post, "Assessing the Nestle Boycott: Corporate Accountability and Human Rights," *California Management Review* 27(2):127 (1985).

11. For a discussion of "stakeholders" by a top manager, see Catherine B. Cleary, "Women in the Corporation: A Case Study About Justice," in *The Judeo-Christian Vision and the Modern Corporation*, eds. O.F. Williams, C.S.C., and J.W. Houck (Notre Dame, IN: University of Notre Dame Press, 1982), pp. 292–305. Also see R. Edward Freeman, *Strategic Management: A Stakeholder Approach* (Boston: Pitman, 1984).

12. M. Orkin, *Divestment: The Struggle and the Future* (Johannesburg, South Africa: Raven Press, 1986).

13. For an insightful analysis of capitalism and apartheid, see Mere Lipton, *Capitalism and Apartheid* (Totowa, New Jersey: Littlefield, Adams & Company, 1985).

14. See David Vogel, *Lobbying the Corporation: Citizen Challenges to Business Authority* (New York: Basic Books, 1978), pp. 169–200.

15. For a full discussion of the Statement of Principles, see my *The Apartheid Crisis* (San Francisco: Harper & Row, 1986).

16. Dennis Kneale, "*Xerox, Finally Succumbs to Pressure, Says It Will Sell South African Unit*," *The Wall Street Journal*, 20 March, 1987, p. 42.

17. This section has been previously published in Chapter Four of my *The Apartheid Crisis*.

18. Clifton R. Wharton, Jr., "*Economic Sanctions and Their Potential Impact on U.S. Corporate Involvement in South Africa*," House of Representatives Committee on Foreign Affairs, Subcommittee on Africa; 99th Congress, 1st Session, January 31, 1985, p. 105.

19. For an elaboration of my position on proportionality, see Oliver F. Williams, "*Business Ethics: A Trojan Horse?*" *California Management Review* 24, 1982, 14–24.

20. Mangosuthu Gatsha Buthelezi, "*Disinvestment Is Anti-Black*," *The Wall Street Journal*, 20 February, 1985, p. 32.

21. "*The Gods Are Crazy in Pretoria*," *The New York Times*, 2 December, 1986, p. 34.

22. Wharton, p. 50.

23. Michael Isikoff, "*Cleric Questions Firms' Pullout From S. Africa*," *The Washington Post*, 20 October, 1986, pp. 19–20.

24. For an insightful discussion of these two ethics, see Max Weber, "*Politics as a Vocation*," *From Max Weber: Essays in Sociology*, eds. and trans., H.H. Gerth and C. Wright Mills (New York: Oxford University Press, 1946), pp. 77–128.

25. See Clyde Hufbauer and Jeffrey Schott, *Economic Sanctions in Support of Foreign Policy Goals* (Washington, D.C.: Institute for International Economics, 1983). The summary of the characteristics is quoted from William H. Cooper, "*South African-U.S. Economic Ties: Emerging Issues, Congressional Research Service Issue Brief*, 23 October, 1986, pp. 9–10.

26. See, for example, Peter Brimelow, "*Why South Africa Shrugs at Sanctions*," *Forbes*, 9 March, 1987, pp. 101–104.

27. Jennifer Kibbe and David Hauck. *Leaving South Africa: The Impact of U.S. Corporate Disinvestment* (Washington, D.C.: Investor Responsibility Research Center, 1988), p. 34.

28. See the *Thirteenth Report on the Signatory Companies to the Statement of Principles for South Africa* available from the Industry Support Unit, Inc., Room 7E #1601, 150 East 42nd Street, New York, New York 10017-5666.

17

New Wrinkles in the Theory of Age: Demography, Norms, and Performance Ratings

Barbara S. Lawrence

UNIVERSITY OF CALIFORNIA, LOS ANGELES

Age seems to play an important role in a wide range of employee behaviors. One interpretation of this role is that it depends more on people's beliefs about age than on the ages themselves. Despite the significance of this distinction for human resource planning, it has received little attention in the organizational literature. This article proposes an explanation for socially generated age effects and presents an exploratory study that used data from an electric utility.

Looking around the basement, some of the team's brand-new members would sometimes wonder what would happen to them when they turned thirty. Being young, they could make light of the questions, and say, as one did, "When a computer engineer gets old, he gets turned out to pasture or else made into dog food."

Kidder (1981: 104)

I would like to thank Jim Rosenbaum, Bill McKelvey, Connie Gersick, Dennis Hogan, Gordon Walker, and Lynne Zucker for their helpful comments. Thanks are also due to Richard Rumelt for the off-hand remark that led to the title of this article and to the reviewers for their careful comments on the manuscript. I gratefully acknowledge those at the company studied whose participation made this work possible. This research was supported by a grant (#1 R01 AG04615) to the author from the National Institute on Aging.

Barbara S. Lawrence earned her Ph.D. degree at the Massachusetts Institute of Technology. She is an assistant professor in the Anderson Graduate School of Management at the University of California, Los Angeles. Her current research interests include age effects in organizations, the science of social science, career theory, and human resource management.

Evaluating and comparing employee ages is an everyday pastime in organizations, insignificant in its appearance, yet significant in its results. In Kidder's (1981) account of the Data General Corporation, computer engineers observe the ages of co-workers, use their observations to assess their own career prospects, and note the absence of older engineers with discomfort. These reactions are generated not from the inherent characteristics of, but from people's responses to, chronological age. To the extent that such responses mold employee behavior, they play an important role in organizations. Indeed, people's beliefs, judgments, and notions about age appear involved in a wide range of employment issues, including hiring decisions, promotion opportunities, and employee performance (Dalton & Thompson, 1971; Kanter, 1977; Rosen & Jerdee, 1976a, 1976b, 1977; Sofer, 1970). Yet despite the significance of these employment issues, the organizational literature has given little attention to such age effects.

This article proposes that socially generated age effects result from age norms that evolve, in part, from actual age distributions within organizations. Age norms are defined here as widely shared judgments of the standard or typical ages of individuals holding a role or status.[1] Despite widespread belief that age distributions, age norms, and behavior are related (Riley, Johnson, & Foner, 1972), the relationships are not well understood. Previous research has provided some support for the existence of age norms in organizations (Martin & Strauss, 1956; Sofer, 1970), but the relationship between age norms and behavior remains essentially unknown (Abeles, Steel, & Wise, 1980; Elder, 1975; Marini, 1984). More extensive evidence exists for the relationship between age distributions and behavior (Elder & Rockwell, 1976; Hogan, 1981), but unfortunately, studies of age distributions have not measured age norms. And, although the literature provides theoretical support for a relationship between age distributions and age norms (Mannheim, 1928/1952; Simmel, 1950), to my knowledge this relationship has never been evaluated. The exploratory study of the socially generated effects of age presented here thus builds on earlier work by offering a more precise statement of the relationships between age distributions, age norms, and employee behavior.

THEORETICAL BACKGROUND

Normative and Demographic Approaches

There is a long tradition of investigation of the effects of age in the sociological and anthropological literatures (Atchley, 1975; Cain, 1964; Eisenstadt, 1956; Elder, 1975; Riley, 1987; Riley et al., 1972). Linton (1940, 1942) and Parsons (1942) proposed the following explanation for why such effects take place. Chronological age is one of the few universal human experiences and as a result provides a basic structural link between individuals and social systems. People use age to classify the members of a social system into categories and to match them with roles and statuses. The matching process between age categories and roles and statuses produces widely shared beliefs about the standard or typical ages of members holding each social position. Linton suggested that the shared beliefs resulting from that process are age norms that exert considerable influence on behavior. Thus, age norms produce age effects.

Studies of such age effects have typically used one of two approaches. The *normative* approach measures the relationship between age norms and behavior. In contrast, the *demographic* approach uses age distributions as a proxy for age norms. As a result, the second approach examines the relationship between age distributions and behavior rather than that between age norms and behavior. Nevertheless, both approaches divide the human life span into groups by age. In addition, both suggest that age-group membership influences behavior: people apply positive and negative social pressures on those who deviate from behaviors considered typical for an age group. In organizations, such social pressures frequently evolve around typical ages within careers that define success and identify failures. For instance, orchestra members believe their chances for moving into top-ranked orchestras decrease after they reach their early 30s (Faulkner, 1974).

The major distinction between the normative and demographic approaches lies in their measures of age-group membership. The normative approach defines age groups, also known as age grades (Radcliffe-Brown, 1929: 21), by members' shared age judgments or age estimates of others within their social system. Several studies have supported the existence of such normative age groups within organizations. Sofer's (1970) examination of two British firms uncovered shared beliefs among mid-career managers about the typical ages for career achievement. Similarly, Martin and Strauss (1956) discussed managers' shared judgments of age-related career timetables, and Kanter (1977) observed shared age-related norms that employees use in defining fast-track and plateaued workers. In a study within an occupation, Faulkner suggested that American and Canadian hockey players exhibited a clear awareness of the "short and fateful" (1974: 142) age-related testing period for major league success.

In contrast, the demographic approach defines age groups, also known as age cohorts or age strata (Riley et al., 1972), by actual age distributions. Those who take such an approach examine an actual age distribution for some role or status and use the central tendency of that distribution to define age groups. Several studies imply a relationship between such demographic age groups and socially generated age effects. Rosenbaum's (1984) longitudinal study of mobility within a large corporation showed that employees who get behind in age-based career patterns are less likely to receive future promotions. Rosenbaum (1984: 94) suggested that the high degree of ambition, anxiety, and achievement motivation evidenced by many young employees may be explained, not by their individual personalities (Maccoby, 1977) or by the characteristics of their jobs (Whyte, 1956), but by their response to the consequences of get-ting behind schedule. Hogan (1981) identified the typical ages for the education, first jobs, and marriages of a large sample of American men and found that men who deviated in any direction from the typical ordering of those events experienced lower total earnings and higher rates of marital disruption. Hogan speculated that age norms for the ordering of the three roles, represented in his study by demographically typical ages, produced the study's results.

Although both the normative and demographic approaches have contributed to our understanding of socially generated age effects, each has limitations. First, although a number of researchers have drawn inferences about the effects of age norms on organizational careers (cf. Faulkner, 1974; Kanter, 1977; Martin & Strauss, 1956; Sofer, 1970), they have not provided a systematic examination of normative age groups. Thus, many questions remain unanswered. For instance, what are the age boundaries of normative age groups and where do those boundaries come from? How are normative age groups matched with roles and statuses within careers? If an individual deviates from the normative age group for a role or status, then how does that deviation influence the behavior of other individuals toward him or her?

Second, although demographic measures simplify studies of age effects, the rationale underlying the approach that uses such measures is that demographic age groups represent age norms. Investigators have assumed a one-to-one correspondence between the central tendencies of an age distribution and the age norms created by employees' shared age judgments. The plausibility of that assumption depends on the accuracy of employees' judgments: when age judgments are accurate, normative and demographic age groups are identical. However, research has indicated that employees frequently misperceive organizational reality (Lawrence, 1984; Rosenbaum, 1988).

The result of this potential disparity is that demographic research may not properly account for socially generated age effects. Consider, for instance, an organization in which age distributions favor promotions for young managers. For each career level, the age distribution defines a demographic age group that identifies managers as ahead of schedule, on schedule, and behind schedule in their organizational careers. If managers perceive these demographic age groups accurately, the age norms that develop for a managerial career may encourage aspiring young managers to respond with high work involvement because they accurately perceive favorable opportunities for promotion. However, when managers perceive demographic age groups inaccurately, age effects such as work involvement may bear little relationship to the actual opportunity structure. For instance, if, despite the organizational reality, managers believe that promotions favor middle-aged managers, the norms that develop might produce the M.B.A. syndrome — young employees frustrated by the perceived slowness of promotion possibilities. In such a situation, demographic research could not easily explain the observed effects of age.

Several researchers have pointed out the limitations of the two approaches. Hogan (1981), for one, suggested that demographic age transitions for roles and statuses are not the entire picture. Age norms for transitions are important explanatory variables, but little is known about such norms. He quotes from Elder (1975): "No large sample study has provided evidence on normative expectations and sanctions regarding the timing and synchronization of social roles and transitions over the life span. . . . The process by which age norms or timetables are constructed, transmitted, and learned remains largely unexplored territory" (Hogan, 1981: 13).

Thus, the connections between demographic age patterns, age norms, and behavior are still largely unexplored. Since results from both the normative and demographic approaches have suggested that those connections are significant for human resource issues, an organizational explanation for the effects of age merits further attention.

A Proposed Explanation for Socially Generated Age Effects

The following explanation is proposed: age distributions drive the development of age norms, and age norms produce age effects. The rationale for these relationships are statements by members of a social system on standards for behavior (Newcomb et al., 1965: 229; Sherif, 1936). Age-specific social norms are age norms. Members agree on the age boundaries for typical incumbents of a role or status and perceive any individual whose age violates those boundaries as deviant. Thus, age norms are widely shared judgments of the standard or typical ages of individuals holding each role or status. Homans (1950) suggested that norms evolve because people in groups develop behavioral patterns, observe them, and then agree, either explicitly or implicitly, that the patterns represent behavioral standards.

Scholars have maintained that all social systems develop age-related behavioral standards (Linton, 1936: 116–118; Murdock, 1945: 124), and the limited existing empirical evidence supports that view (Eisenstadt, 1956; Neugarten & Datan, 1973; Neugarten, Moore, & Lowe, 1965; Neugarten & Petersen, 1957; Passuth, Maines, & Neugarten, 1984). If so, it seems likely that employees observe age distributions, develop shared judgments of those distributions, and see the behavioral patterns that evolve around age as standards of behavior. Commonplace organizational gossip such as "isn't he a bit young for that job?" and "I never thought they would hire someone my age!" provide examples of how employees apply such standards in their evaluations of roles and statuses.

Explanations for why such patterns acquire meaning as behavioral standards focus on the development of normative age groups and the processes by which people distinguish "us" from "them." Work by Mannheim (1928/1952) and Ryder (1965) has suggested that normative age groups develop because individuals of similar age share comparable experiences and therefore develop like attitudes and beliefs. Within an occupational status, the central tendency of the age distribution defines a group of employees of similar age. Such employees share the experience of their life stage (cf. Gould, 1978; Levinson, 1978; Vaillant, 1977), and frequently have families at comparable stages of development. Moreover, their economic attainments afford them similar leisure activities, and, in organizations with high average tenure, they share organizational memories of "what things were like in the old days." As a result of shared experiences, employees of similar ages recognize themselves and are perceived by others as distinct groups. Thus, shared experiences define normative age groups, specify the boundaries of group membership and nonmembership, and thereby become standards of behavior.

Although the preceding discussion suggests a primary causal order for the relationships between age distributions, age norms, and employee behavior,[2] it does not imply that reciprocal relationships do not occur. In fact, age norms may influence age distributions, and employee behavior may alter age norms. For instance, over time, an age effect such as managers' ratings of employees' performance may influence the positions employees hold, thus affecting the age distribution of those positions and the norms that develop. However, the suggested causal order does mean that it would be difficult for an organization to support a change in age norms without a concomitant change in the age distribution. Reciprocal relationships are ultimately of interest to the specification of

an organizational theory of age effects but are secondary and not examined here in detail.

The aerospace industry provides an example of how the primary relationships between age distributions, age norms, and employee behavior may occur and what effect they may have on organizations. During the late 1960s and early 1970s, an economic downturn resulted in fewer entry-level engineering hires within aerospace companies. This produced organizations characterized in the mid-1980s by bimodal age distributions. The TRW Corporation, for instance, has a small number of middle-aged managers relative to the numbers of young and old managers it employs.[3] Assume for the moment that companies with such age distributions promote from within and that their growth remains fairly stable. If, as was proposed, age distributions drive the development of age norms and age norms produce age effects, the following scenario may pose a potentially serious personnel problem for such firms over the next 20 years.

For many years, demographic career patterns in aerospace companies have favored promotions for middle-aged managers. However, when the current group of older managers retires, there will not be enough top-notch middle-aged managers to fill the vacancies. That fact will create a promotional demand for younger managers and dramatically decrease the average age of middle management. It seems likely that the youngest employees will observe the promotions, note the altered age distributions, and develop age-based promotional expectations that fit their observations. Thus, age norms for middle management positions will shift suddenly from the typical middle-aged manager to the typical younger manager.

Unfortunately, only the leading edge of the younger group will experience this favorable promotion environment. As soon as all the older employees retire and the positions are filled, the availability of new vacancies will slow considerably. The younger managers who received promotions will be around for quite a while; thus, actual promotion patterns will shift again in favor of middle-aged managers. It seems unlikely that the younger age norms for middle management positions will return to middle-aged norms quite as rapidly as the actual average age for the positions increases. Until employee perceptions readjust, the discrepancy will produce a situation in which promotion expectations are regularly violated. Thus, the age effect is likely to be the creation of an unusually large, disaffected group of younger employees who may respond by decreased motivation or by seeking opportunities elsewhere.

Hypotheses

The study described in the next section examined whether the proposed relationships between age distributions, age norms, and employee behavior provide a plausible explanation for socially generated age effects. Data from an electric utility were used to examine those relationships within a managerial career. The following three hypotheses guided the empirical examination.

Managerial careers supply several advantages for studies of socially generated age effects. First, managerial careers are defined by formal status hierarchies. Position on such a hierarchy provides an explicit, unambiguous anchor for age judgments. Thus, the status of any particular career level in relation to other career levels has strong convergent and nomological validity (cf. Bagozzi, 1980) for organizational members. Second, since an individual can occupy only one level at a time, formal advancement is inevitably associated with the age of the individual. That association makes it likely that employees use age to differentiate between career levels and therefore that age norms develop.

The first question to be answered was whether managerial careers within a work organization are age graded; that is, have em-

ployees developed shared perceptions of typical ages that differ across career levels? An organizational career is age graded only when normative age groups, defined by employees' shared judgments of typical ages, distinguish between levels. In an age-graded organization, employees agree that the age groups associated with each career level are distinct. In an organization undifferentiated by age, employees agree that a manager's age is unrelated to career level.

Hypothesis 1: Normative age groups differ across career levels. If age grading exists, the second question is whether employees perceive demographic age groups accurately. As discussed in the theoretical section, the assumption supporting the use of demographic age groups to predict behavior is that employees' age judgments are accurate and that age norms therefore map directly onto actual age distributions. If that is true, employees' shared judgments of what is typical for each career level should cluster randomly around the actual typical age. Thus,

Hypothesis 2: Normative and demographic age groups for each career level are identical. Although Hypothesis 2 addresses whether misperceptions occur, it does not address why they occur. This study was not designed to test various explanations for misperceptions; however, I explored the pattern of judgment errors to assess whether they appeared random or systematic. Differences that appeared random would offer little justification for the proposed relationship between age distributions and age judgments. Differences that appeared systematic might indicate what direction future studies should take in examining the association between age distributions and age judgments.[4]

The final question was whether managers' membership in or deviation from the age groups associated with their career level influences the behavior of other employees toward them. This study examined the association between age groups and managers' performance ratings of managerial subordinates. Individuals whom managers perceive as young for their position, the "fast-trackers" or "water walkers" are generally viewed with higher regard than those who are seen as old (Kanter, 1977). Thus,

Hypothesis 3: There is a significant relationship between normative age group deviation and performance ratings. Specifically, when compared with the number of high performance ratings managers give to randomly selected managerial subordinates:

a) Managers' performance ratings of managerial subordinates are more likely to be high when managerial subordinates are younger than the normative ages for their career level.

b) Managers' performance ratings of managerial subordinates are less likely to be high when managerial subordinates are older than the normative ages for their career level.

c) Managers' performance ratings of managerial subordinates are equally likely to be high when managerial subordinates are members of the normative age group for their career level.

The explanation underlying this study suggests that a relationship between demographic age groups and performance ratings should be observed only to the extent that demographic and normative age groups are similar. If demographic and normative age groups are identical (Hypothesis 2), each should exhibit the same association with performance ratings. However, if demographic and normative age groups differ, the association between normative age groups and performance ratings should be greater than the

association between demographic age groups and performance ratings. This pattern should occur because, as I proposed, shared beliefs about standard or typical ages rather than actual standard or typical ages influence managers' performance ratings. However, if demographic age groups appear systematically related to normative age groups, the associations of demographic and normative age groups with performance ratings should exhibit a similar direction, even if the magnitude of the association differs.

METHODS

Data

Demographic and questionnaire data on managerial careers were collected from an electric utility. The Bennix Power Company (not its real name) is an old, established firm. Traditionally, people come to work in the company after finishing their schooling and remain until retirement. The average age of managerial employees is 48 years (range = 25–66), the average tenure is 24 years (range = 0–44), and the correlation between age and tenure is .78. The company's formal management hierarchy includes eight career levels: level 1 is a first-level supervisory position and level 8 includes the chief executive officer and the president. Managerial vacancies are filled internally, and advancement is a slow process. Employees have ample opportunity, therefore, to develop shared and accurate judgments of the age distribution.

The questionnaire was developed in several stages. After preliminary development, ten individuals from an executive education class who were selected for their diverse backgrounds were interviewed about specific questionnaire items and their experiences with age-related work issues. Each interview lasted one and a half to three hours. A revised version of the questionnaire was then pre-tested with the entire class (N = 36), and further revisions were made on the basis of this feedback. After the company's management agreed to participate in the project, I spent three months in the organization. My purpose was to tailor the questionnaire to the organization and to solicit additional questions of interest to its management. Discussions that included several half-day meetings were held with members of the human resources staff. In addition, I conducted four formal interviews of one and a half to three hours each with employees of varying ages, career levels, genders, and functional areas. Each of these employees completed a copy of the questionnaire before being interviewed.

After these discussions and subsequent questionnaire revisions had occurred, the company approved the questionnaire for distribution. Questionnaires were distributed through company mail, and the company permitted one follow-up memorandum. Sixty-six percent (N = 390) of all managers returned the questionnaire. Questionnaire data were checked carefully for coding errors. An independent comparison of the final data set against the original questionnaires by two coders indicated that the error rate was negligible ($<$ 0.07%). Demographic data and the company's employee performance ratings were obtained for all managers (N = 593).

Sampling bias was examined by comparing demographic characteristics of the managers who completed the questionnaire and of the population of managers. Respondents were representative of the population in career level, functional area, and gender. Response levels fluctuated by age and tenure, with the distribution of responses biased towards younger managers who had been in the company fewer years. Other comparisons were not possible because the questionnaires were answered anonymously; however, further examination of the data suggested that the age and tenure biases should not affect the results. First, neither age nor tenure is related strongly to age judgments (Lawrence, 1985). Second, tenure appears to exert no effect on age judgments independent of age. The high correlation between age and tenure prohibited a linear decomposition of age and tenure effects, so a Wilcoxon signed-ranks test was used to see whether newcomers and old-timers viewed the organization any differently. I matched 13 employee pairs (N = 26) on age, gender, functional area, and career level. One group comprised individuals who had been with the company for 2 years or less, and the other, individuals who had been with the company for 15 years or more. The results showed no significant difference between the two groups on any of the 24 age judgments assessed in this study. Thus, although it remains possible that sampling bias affected the results, it seems unlikely.

Measures

Age judgments. Respondents' judgments of the ages of managers in each career level were used to assess normative age groups. Age norms do not exist without such judgments because standards for age-typical behavior cannot be enforced without wide agreement on the typical ages. For each career level in the organization, the questionnaire asked managers' judgments of (1) the typical age of individuals in that level and (2) the age range of individuals in that level. Actual company titles for each career level were used. In the example shown in Figure 1, the

FIGURE 1. *Questionnaire Item Requesting Respondents' Age Judgments.*

1. At Bennix Power Company, my perception is that supervisors are:

respondent indicates that he believes the typical age of supervisors is 37 and that supervisors range in age from 25 to 38 years old.[5]

This study follows Homans' (1950) description of normative inference, in which standards of behavior are inferred from what people say is typical (cf. Labovitz & Hagedorn, 1973). The disadvantage of normative inference is that it does not assess directly whether subjects perceive their judgments of typical behaviors to be standards. However, direct questions concerning behavioral standards assume that people are equally aware of what behaviors are typical and what behaviors are atypical. On the basis of the preliminary interviews and questionnaire pretesting, that assumption appeared unwarranted for age. People are much better at describing the actual typical age for an activity than they are at discussing what is atypical. The social norms around age seem deeply embedded within everyday life: when asked about atypical ages, people often treat the question as absurd.[6] For that reason, respondents' age judgments of typical managers were used to define normative age groups.

Normative age groups. Age norms were defined earlier as widely shared beliefs about the standard or typical ages of individuals holding roles or statuses. The set of ages that defines the standard or typical ages for any role or status is its normative age group. There are two issues in defining normative age groups from a distribution of age judgments. One is deciding how to select the age boundaries. The other is deciding how much agreement there must be before judgments are said to be shared. This study followed Kluckhohn, who suggested that "the best conceptual model of the culture can only state correctly the central tendencies and ranges of variation" in a distribution (1951: 76).

The normative age group for each career level was defined as the age range circumscribing the central tendency in the distribution of typical age judgments. I selected age-group boundaries using the youngest and oldest ages that received at least 10 percent (N = 39) of the responses. Those age-group boundaries seem likely to be multiples of five because census reports in many countries show that people characteristically report ages that end in 0 and 5 (Shyrock, Siegel, & associates, 1980: 204). It that occurred for respondents' judgments, using means and standard deviations to define age-group boundaries might have failed to capture an important component of what managers judged to be typical.

Following Jacobsen and Van Der Voordt (1980), I considered managers' age judgments to be widely shared when the level of agreement delineated a *representative norm,* "the relative frequency of the modal category being so great that it represents the population's response for most intents and purposes" (1980: 473). For the Bennix Power Company, that level of agreement was reached when 66.6 percent of the respondents agreed on the normative age group for a career level.[7]

Demographic age groups. Demographic age groups were defined by the age range one standard deviation around the mean age of the population for each career level. I used the standard deviation to define demographic age group boundaries because it provides a generally accepted measure of central tendency.

Performance ratings. Managers' performance ratings for all managerial subordinates were obtained for the population of the company's managers who had received performance ratings the year the questionnaire was distributed (N = 542). All managers in levels 2 through 8 rate subordinate managers. Bennix's performance ratings range from unacceptable (0) to excellent (5). Most managers receive good (3) ratings (N = 305, 56.3%), suggesting this category can be interpreted as including competent but not outstanding individuals. I considered the managers whose ratings were above ($N = 161, 29.7\%$) or below ($N = 76, 14.0\%$) those of that group as the high and low performers at the company.

RESULTS

The top part of Table 1 shows the means, standard deviations, and ranges of age judgments for the eight career levels. All eight levels exhibited considerable variation in age judgments. An analysis reported elsewhere (Lawrence, 1985) has indicated that only a small portion of the variation in age judgments can be attributed to a respondent's age, organizational tenure, career level, or education.

Figure 2 shows the frequency distribution for level 1. The remaining seven distributions exhibit a similar pattern.[8] Two interesting characteristics of the frequency distributions should be noted. First, as expected, respon-

dents tended to specify ages that are multiples of five. On the average, 55 percent of the typical age judgments for each career level fell in that category. Thus, the managers studied tended to treat the interval age scale as an 11-step ordinal item and did not distinguish between ages less than five years apart. This results in peaks in the frequency distributions that have more to do with how people interpret questions about age than with the essential characteristics of the distribution.

When the distinction between ordinal and interval interpretations of the age scale are taken into account, the second salient characteristic of the distributions that emerged is that they are basically unimodal. For every career level, all ages that received more than 10 percent of the responses occurred at adjacent five-year intervals. Moreover, with few exceptions, the fraction of responses between those ages is higher than the fraction of responses between other five-year age intervals. Thus, the distributions are unimodal, both

TABLE 1. Perceived and Actual Ages for the Managerial Career at the Company Studied.

(a) Age Judgments[a]	Typical Age			Youngest Age			Oldest Age		
Career Level	Means	s.d.	Ranges	Means	s.d.	Ranges	Means	s.d.	Ranges
1. Supervisor	40.4	6.1	28–57	32.4	5.9	20–52	51.7	9.2	34–68
2. Senior supervisor	44.8	6.1	30–60	37.6	6.2	20–55	54.3	7.9	35–68
3. Division head	47.9	5.7	33–60	40.4	6.5	25–55	57.1	7.1	35–68
4. Assistant department head	49.5	5.4	35–61	42.1	5.8	28–56	57.6	6.2	39–68
5. Department head	50.7	4.8	35–62	43.2	6.1	30–61	59.0	5.3	42–69
6. Vice president	53.9	3.6	44–63	47.5	4.3	35–61	61.1	3.7	49–70
7. Senior vice president	56.4	3.2	45–65	51.0	3.7	40–61	62.2	3.0	49–70
8. President and CEO	60.5	2.5	50–75	56.9	3.8	45–64	63.9	2.2	55–74

(b) Actual Ages[b]						
Career Level	Medians	Modes	μ	σ	Ranges	N
1. Supervisor	48.0	47	47.2	8.9	25–66	287
2. Senior supervisor	49.0	48	48.1	8.1	30–64	139
3. Division head	50.0	57	49.6	9.3	28–65	96
4. Assistant department head	52.5	57	49.8	9.4	31–62	24
5. Department head	49.0	54	49.2	8.5	33–65	31
6. Vice president	52.0	53	51.1	6.1	40–61	10
7. Senior vice president	53.5	52	54.3	2.9	52–58	4
8. President and CEO	61.5	61	61.5	0.7	61–62	2

[a]Results are for a group of 390 respondents.

[b]Results are for a population of 593 managers.

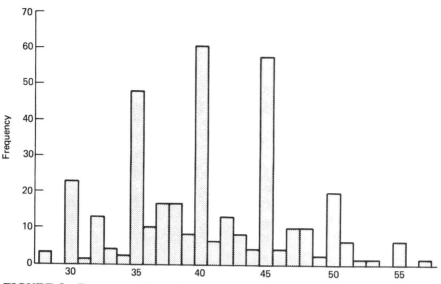

FIGURE 2. Frequency Distribution for Typical Age Judgments, Career Level 1.

for the ages that are multiples of five and for those that are not. This pattern suggests that respondents agreed that a single age group represented what is typical for each level. An alternate finding might have been a bimodal or multimodal distribution, indicating that some people believed one age group was typical and others believed a different age group was typical. This result is important because it permits the specification of a single normative age group for each career level.

The lower part of Table 1 summarizes the actual age distributions for all career levels. The youngest manager in the company was 25 and the oldest manager was 66. The age range of managers was large in each of the first five levels but decreased dramatically in levels 6 through 8. The decrease reflected the increasing ages of the youngest managers in the higher career levels. Although the ages of managers in levels 1 through 3 were somewhat normally distributed, the age distributions of levels 4 through 8 were fairly flat.

Figure 3 shows the normative and demographic age groups defined for each of the eight career levels. The specification of age groups for level 1 provides an example of the

definition process. The normative age group for level 1 is the age range defined by the youngest and oldest ages that received 10 percent of the responses. Figure 2 shows that responses on the ages 35, 40, and 45 exceeded 10 percent of the total responses (13%, 17%, and 16%). The ages between 35 and 40 accounted for 15 percent of the total responses, and the ages between 40 and 45 accounted for 9 percent. The next closest candidate for inclusion as a normative age group boundary is age 30. However, responses on this age and the ages between 30 and 35 occurred much less frequently. The fraction of responses on age 30 was 6 percent, and the fraction of responses between 30 and 35 was also 6 percent. Seventy percent of all respondents believed the typical age of level 1 managers to be between 35 and 45. Thus, I selected 35 and 45 as the normative age group boundaries for this career level.

On the average, 73 percent of all respondents agreed on the normative age groups for each career level (range = 66–81%). Thus, with the exception of level 2, which just misses the suggested 66.6 percent cutoff, the level of managers' agreement on age judg-

FIGURE 3. *Comparison of Normative and Demographic Age Groups*[a].

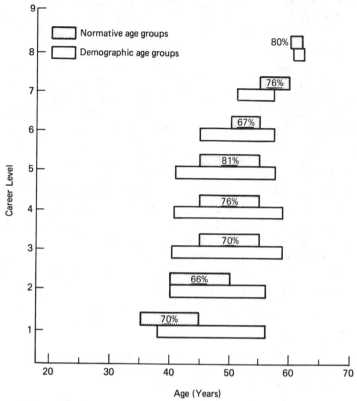

[a]The numbers within the bars defining normative age groups indicate the fraction of total responses falling within the given age range.

ments suggests these normative age groups delineate representative norms (Jacobsen & Van Der Voordt, 1980).

The demographic age group for level 1 is defined by the age range one standard deviation around the mean age. The mean age for level 1 is 47.2, and the standard deviation is 8.9. Thus, 38.3 and 56.1 are the demographic age group boundaries for this career level.

The Existence of Age Grading

Hypothesis 1 states that normative age groups differ across career levels. Figure 3 shows the comparison of normative age groups across the eight career levels. Although several normative age groups overlap, there are four mutually disjoint age categories: 35–45, 45–55, 55–60, and 60–62. Typical managers in level 1, levels 3–5, level 7, and level 8 are seen as different in age from one another; thus, the managerial career appears to be age graded.

This aggregate analysis of judgments obscures individual response patterns; it is possible, given the large variation in responses for each level, that most individual respondents did not see age differences between career levels. To take an extreme example, suppose that the typical age judgments for level 1 are uniformly distributed between the ages of 20 and 25 and that those for level 2 are uniformly distributed between 21 and 26. It may be that all respondents saw a one-year difference between the typical ages in levels 1 and 2. But it could also be that 80 percent of the respondents saw no difference and 20 percent saw a six-year difference between the typical ages in those levels. To test this possibility, I used a multivariate repeated measures test (Morrison, 1976; 141–150). The null hypothesis was that, on the average, each respondent saw no age differences between the eight career levels.

The results did not support the null hypothesis ($F_{7,332} = 984.50$; $p < .001$). Individual respondents did not think the typical age for managers was the same in all eight levels. Given that result, I computed simultaneous confidence intervals for the differences between adjacent levels to determine which career levels differed. The results showed that respondents saw managers in all adjacent career levels as differing in age. Thus, the aggregated judgments defining normative age groups do not obscure individual judgments of no age differences between career levels. If anything, aggregated judgments obscure the extent to which individuals do age grade the managerial career.

Comparison of Normative and Demographic Age Groups

Hypothesis 2 states that normative and demographic age groups for each career level are identical. Figure 3 shows the comparison of normative and demographic age groups for each career level. The groups overlap but are not identical. A comparison of the distributions underlying the two age groups corroborated the significance of their differences. If normative and demographic age groups are similar, typical age judgments should be randomly distributed around the median age for each level. Results of a binominal test (Snedecor & Cochran, 1980: 96–97) failed to support the similarity hypothesis at the .05 level for all eight levels. Respondents' judgments of age groups do not match demo-

graphic age categories; thus, managers appear to misperceive the actual distribution of age in their organization.

Although these results disconfirmed the equality assumption, normative and demographic age groups may still have been related. Thus, it was important to explore whether their differences were random or systematic. A comparison of the two sets of age groups suggested a systematic relationship. Normative and demographic age groups for each level overlap. In addition, with the exception of level 8, normative age groups constrain the range of typical ages further than the actual distribution indicates. Although normative age groups are defined by aggregated judgments, the results are consistent with the regression phenomenon observed in individual decision making. As discussed earlier, people tend to tighten boundaries when making judgments of uncertain distributions (Lichtenstein et al., 1982).

To confirm whether the regression observed at the aggregate level reflects a similar phenomenon at the individual level, average judgments for the typical as well as the youngest and oldest managers were compared with the actual ages for each level. Figure 4 shows this comparison. One set of points represents the actual youngest age compared to the average youngest age judgment, another set represents the actual oldest age compared to the average oldest age judgment, and a third set represents the actual average age compared to the average typical age judgment. When the average age judgment is accurate, points fall on the identity line. Because there is variation in judgments, a second measure of accuracy is whether the actual age is within the range of most age judgments. Career levels for which the actual age is within one standard deviation of the average judgment are indicated by an asterisk underneath the symbol.

The results of the comparison support the existence of a systematic regression in respon-

FIGURE 4. *Comparison of Actual Ages with Age Judgments[a].*

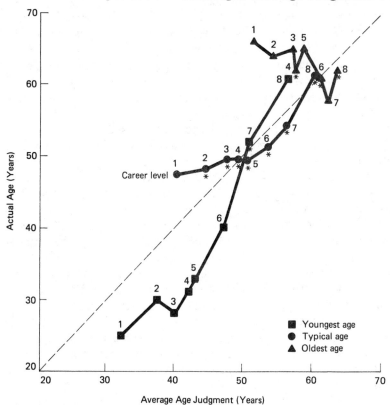

[a]For those levels marked underneath by an asterisk, the actual age falls within one standard deviation of the average age judgment.

dents' judgments at the individual level. As expected, on the average, respondents consistently overestimated the youngest age and underestimated the oldest age for each level. Judgments of average typical ages were reasonably accurate compared with judgments of the youngest and oldest ages. However, the regression observed for the extreme ages suggests that this phenomenon may explain the tightness of typical age judgment distributions that define normative age group boundaries.

The availability of information on which judgments are made may explain the relative accuracy of judgments about typical ages. People recall frequent events more easily

than infrequent events (Tversky & Kahneman, 1973, 1974). In this organizational context, managers may make judgments on the basis of whom they see, and they see the typical manager more often than they see the youngest or the oldest manager. That explanation does not account for the increasing accuracy of the youngest and oldest age judgments for the upper career levels. The actual age distributions of the upper career levels are almost flat, suggesting that there is no typical age for these high-level managers. People may make better judgments concerning them because they are highly visible and few in number.

The results presented here suggest that

managers may employ decision heuristics when making judgments about a company's age distribution. Given that shared judgments define normative age groups, such an interpretation is not inconsistent with the explanation that age norms evolve from actual distributions. Although normative and demographic age groups are not identical in this organization, they appear related systematically through judgment processes.

The Relationship Between Age Groups and Performance Ratings

Since the results did not support Hypothesis 2, Hypotheses 3a–3c were examined for both normative and demographic age groups. Those hypotheses specify the expected relationships between age-group membership and performance ratings. Figure 3 shows the normative and demographic age groups defined for each career level in the organization. These age-group definitions were used to divide the population of the firm's managers who received performance ratings ($N = 542$) into *ahead-of-schedule, on-schedule,* and *behind-schedule* categories. For example, applying normative age groups, I assigned all level 1 managers younger than 35 years of age to the ahead-of-schedule category, as well as level 2 managers younger than 40, level 3 managers younger than 45, and so forth through the eight levels. The same procedure was used to divide the population using demographic age groups.[9]

The test of Hypothesis 3 is whether the proportion of managers receiving high performance ratings in each of the ahead-of-schedule, behind-schedule, and on-schedule categories differs from what is expected for the population. The proportion of managers receiving high performance ratings in the population is 29.7 percent, so the expected frequency for each category is 29.7 percent of the frequency of respondents in that category. Observed and expected frequencies

were compared using a chi-square goodness-of-fit test.

Table 2 summarizes the results of those tests. For normative age groups, the results support Hypotheses 3a–3c. The numbers of managers receiving high performance ratings in both the ahead-of-schedule and behind-schedule categories are significantly different from what would be expected. The number of high performance ratings in the ahead-of-schedule category is significantly higher than expected and the number of high performance ratings in the behind-schedule category is significantly lower than expected. The number of managers receiving high performance ratings in the on-schedule category does not differ significantly from the number in the population.

The results for the demographic age groups are quite different. Although the results support Hypothesis 3c, they support neither Hypothesis 3a nor 3b. None of the on- or off-schedule categories discriminate the number of managers receiving high performance ratings from what is expected within the population at the .05 level.

Both normative and demographic age groups appear similarly related to managers' performance ratings. However, the relationship between age-group deviation and performance ratings is significant for normative age groups, whereas this relationship is not significant for demographic age groups. If researchers taking the demographic approach had examined age groupings in the Bennix Power Company using only these demographic specifications, they would have observed no significant relationship between managerial subordinates' age-group membership and performance ratings by supervisory managers. This finding supports the importance of studying both employees' judgments and actual age distributions in studies of socially generated age effects.

An important alternate explanation for these findings is that the probability of receiv-

TABLE 2. Frequencies of Managers Receiving Various Performance Ratings.

Schedule Categories[a]	Observed	Expected[b]	X^{2c}
(a) Normative Age Groups			
Ahead-of-schedule			
High performance ratings	34	24.35	
Low-to-average performance ratings	48	57.65	
Total	82	82.00	5.44*
On-schedule			
High performance ratings	65	55.24	
Low-to-average performance ratings	121	130.76	
Total	186	186.00	2.45
Behind-schedule			
High performance ratings	62	81.38	
Low-to-average performance ratings	212	192.62	
Total	274	274.00	6.57*
(b) Demographic Age Groups			
Ahead-of-schedule			
High performance ratings	31	23.46	
Low-to-average performance ratings	48	55.54	
Total	79	79.00	3.44
On-schedule			
High performance ratings	113	114.05	
Low-to-average performance ratings	271	269.95	
Total	384	384.00	0.01
Behind-schedule			
High performance ratings	17	23.46	
Low-to-average performance ratings	62	55.54	
Total	79	79.00	3.44

[a]The age-group definitions were used to divide the populations of managers who received performance ratings into the categories indicated.

[b]The expected frequency equals .297(N), where .297 is the proportion of managers receiving high performance ratings in the population and N is the number of respondents in the category.

[c]df = 1.

*p < .05.

ing a high performance rating is positively related with youth (Rosen & Jerdee, 1976a, 1977). Managers in the ahead-of-schedule category may receive higher performance ratings because they are younger than other managers, and younger managers receive higher ratings, regardless of age-group membership.

To examine this possibility, the relationship between age and performance was studied. Although the correlation between these two variables is not significant ($r = -.04, p =$ .35), further examination revealed they have a curvilinear relationship. The proportion of managers receiving high performance ratings is lowest among young (20–30) and old (63+) managers. It is highest among managers between the ages of 31 and 40. After 40, the proportion of managers receiving high performance ratings declines somewhat but remains relatively stable through age 62. I used these characteristics of the performance distribution to divide managers into four age cohorts: 20–30, 31–40, 41–62, and over 62. If age explains performance ratings independently of age-group membership, there should be no difference between the proportion of high performance ratings in each on- and off-schedule category. The findings summarized in Table 3 show that is not the case.

In all instances where there is a comparison age cohort, ahead-of-schedule managers are more likely to receive high performance ratings than on-schedule managers, and on-schedule managers are more likely to receive high performance ratings than behind-schedule managers. For the normatively defined categories, 48 percent of the ahead-of-schedule managers in the top-performance 31–40 year-old age cohort received high performance ratings, whereas only 33 percent of the on-schedule managers in this cohort received high performance ratings. Similarly, 42 percent of the ahead-of-schedule managers in the moderate-performance 41–62 year-old age cohort received high performance ratings, whereas only 35 percent of the on-schedule managers and 24 percent of the behind-schedule managers in this age cohort did so. The same pattern of results emerged for the demographically defined categories. Age-group membership appears related to man-agers' performance ratings, regardless of the subordinate's age.

DISCUSSION AND IMPLICATIONS

The goal of this exploratory study was to examine an explanation for socially generated age effects. The results support the plausibility of that explanation—age distributions appear distinct from, but related to, age norms, and deviation from age norms is associated with performance ratings. Further, the relationship between managers' deviations from the typical ages of the age distribution for their positions and the performance ratings they receive is not significant, whereas the comparable relationship for age norms is. The direction of the two relationships, however, is similar. These findings are not inconsistent with the interpretation that age distributions and age norms are related systematically. Moreover, these findings are consistent with the interpretation that managers respond to shared beliefs about age rather than to actual ages.

Several limitations should be noted in interpreting the results. Bennix Power Com-

TABLE 3. Proportions of Managers Receiving High Performance Ratings in Schedule Categories[a] by Age Cohort.

| | Age Cohorts[b] | | | | | | | | | |
| | 20–30 | | 31–40 | | 41–62 | | <63 | | Total | |
Schedule Categories	%	N	%	N	%	N	%	N	%	N
(a) Normative Age Groups										
Ahead-of-schedule	14	14	48	56	42	12			41	82
On-schedule			33	24	35	162			35	186
Behind-schedule					24	257	6	17	23	274
(b) Demographic Age Groups										
Ahead-of-schedule	14	14	45	65					39	79
On-schedule			40	15	29	369			29	384
Behind-schedule					26	62	6	17	22	79

[a]The age-group definitions were used to divide the population of managers into the categories indicated.

[b]The column headed % gives the proportion of managers receiving high performance ratings. The column headed N gives the total number of managers receiving performance ratings.

Barbara S. Lawrence

pany is only one organization, and we do not know how these age-related phenomena will generalize to other organizations. Preliminary interviews conducted before this research took place suggest that age judgments of career progress depend on organizational characteristics such as industry, size, age, and rate of growth. That dependence is not surprising, given that age distributions differ by occupation (Kaufman & Spilerman, 1982; Miles, 1935: 658–664; Smith, 1973). It seems likely that age grading differs in other organizations, even if the processes linking age and employee behavior remain the same. Moreover, if widely shared judgments depend on a stable organizational context such as the one studied here, it is possible that employees in organizations with high turnover or fluctuating career hierarchies do not develop such widely shared judgments and thus that age norms are either weak or nonexistent.

In addition, the data are cross-sectional. Although the explanation suggests the direction of the relationships between age distributions, age norms, and individual behavior, this research did not provide evidence on their causal order. It is not possible with cross-sectional data to state whether age-group deviation causes differences in managers' performance ratings or whether managers' performance ratings lead to changes in perceptions of typical ages and hence, age-group deviation. It is possible that both occur. The observed relationships may result from managerial decisions that become institutionalized over time and thus serve to create and reinforce the meaning of age norms. For instance, it a manger is promoted when he or she is young in terms of the current age norms for a career level, other managers in the organization may see the promotion as a signal of the promoted individual's ability (Forbes, 1987; Rosenbaum, 1988). Once defined as a high-performance employee, the manager may have an increased probability of future promotions at an early age. This process rein-

forces existing age norms and increases the likelihood of observing performance differences for ahead-of-schedule employees.

Further, although the exploratory findings showing a systematic relationship between age distributions and age judgments suggest decision heuristics at work, other explanations for the association between age distributions and age judgments should be examined. For instance, it is well known that majority opinion influences the judgments of individuals, even when majority opinion is inaccurate (Asch, 1951). As a result, if a young employee associates with older managers who still think of the organization as it was in "the good old days," the young manager's age judgments may be influenced by the groups' perceptions. It is also possible that misperceptions occur because employees' age judgments do not adjust rapidly when an organization's age distribution changes. Related work on social comparison processes (e.g., Singer, E., 1981; Singer, J.E., 1980) suggests that misperceptions may occur because of the salience of career success to employees. For instance, an employee who cares a great deal about promotion may watch fast-track managers carefully: thus, the ages of fast-trackers may influence the employee's judgments.

Finally, the meaning of the relationship between age groups and performance remains in question. Managers appear to use their subordinates' age-group membership as an implicit evaluation criterion. Yet being off schedule may have little to do with performance. Highly respected managers may choose a slower performance route even when given the opportunity to move ahead (Bailyn, 1979). As a result, it is unknown whether the differences in performance ratings observed in this study indicate perceived or actual differences in performance. However, it seems likely that such evaluations, even if originally inaccurate, become accurate over time through a social form of self-fulfilling prophecy. The process through which age norms influence behavior remains an area for further investigation.

The findings do suggest that the "unexplored territory" (Elder, 1975: 176; Hogan, 1981: 13) connecting age distributions, age norms, and employee behavior is fertile ground, not only for elaborating an explanation for age effects, but also for understanding career systems within organizations. First, shared perceptions of typical ages may indicate employees' perceptions of potential mobility. For instance, respondents believed that only level 1 managers were typically younger than 40 and that only level 7 and 8 managers were typically older than 55. Those boundaries suggest that respondents believed almost all upward movement occurred between the two ages. Forty is the age at which people begin to move to level 2, and 55 is the make-or-break age for promotion to the highest levels, a move most managers never make. Thus, in an organization where employees often remain their entire working lives, about 45 years, managers see themselves as upwardly mobile during only 15 years. Longitudinal data are not available from this company, but these perceptions are consistent with findings from Rosenbaum's (1979a, 1979b, 1984) study of a large corporation, in which the period of high career mobility was limited to a rather short timespan.

Second, age grading may play a role in demographic theories of promotion probabilities. If managers base evaluation and promotion decisions on what they currently believe is typical for a particular level, such shared age judgments may provide the link between structural and individual explanations of mobility. Stewman and Konda (1983), for example, examined demographically determined promotion probabilities in organizations. Their focus was structural, but they stated that promotions are conditional on managerial preferences. The results presented in this study suggest that such preferences may

be guided by age-graded judgments of whether subordinates are ahead of, on, or behind schedule for their career level, because managers may use such judgments as signals of a subordinate's future potential.

Third, in addition to constructing a picture of what is typical in each level, employees may also use age to project the promotion pattern between levels, thus creating a cognitive representation of an entire career. The age judgments in this study suggest several characteristics of such a shared cognitive representation. Although it remains possible that managers selectively ignore deviants, managers at the company studied appear not to realize how early promotions are occurring and seem not to recognize the number of managers who remain in one position until retirement. These inaccuracies are particularly curious because it is no secret that most managers do not leave the company until they retire. That employees overlook the existence of long-plateaued older managers may explain or reflect an American fantasy that promotion opportunity continues forever (Rosenbaum, 1984).

Another characteristic is that the managers studied created larger differences between organizational statuses than exist in reality. Compared with actuality, typical age judgments systematically exaggerated the differences between the first five career levels. In typical age judgments, levels 1 and 5 are, on the average, 10 years apart. In actuality, levels 1 and 5 are, on the average, only two years apart. Managers appear to believe they are on an age-based career ladder when, in fact, it is unclear that such a ladder exists.

Certainly, research suggests that people appear aware of age-graded timetables (Bailyn & Lynch, 1983; Kanter, 1977; Lawrence, 1980; Martin & Strauss, 1956; Sofer, 1970). The unarticulated and probably unconscious use of such timetables in evaluation, in conjunction with the appearance of age-graded norms in virtually all social systems (Lawrence, 1987: 51), suggests that age norms may be basic assumptions (Schein, 1985) within organizational cultures. If age grading occurs and differs in other organizations, career plateaus and technological obsolescence may be organizationally specific manifestations of such norms. A 35-year-old middle manager may be plateaued in one company and on a fast track in another. Mergers may be complicated when firms have top management teams of widely differing ages. And employees who choose lateral transfers or career slowdowns at the wrong age may unknowingly risk their future chances for promotion. Such organizational issues have frequently been attributed to chronological aging, but position on an age-graded timetable may better explain them.

Finally, the results suggest that age distributions may play an important role in career systems. If, as suggested by this study, age norms evolve from actual age distributions, the changing age distribution in this country may signal subsequent changes in age norms. This raises the important question of how responsive age norms are to changes in age distributions. Do employees tend to hang on to old judgments, or do they quickly perceive a changing social order? Predicting a socially generated age effect such as managerial promotion preferences thus requires knowledge of the stability of age judgments under conditions of a stable age distribution and of the dynamics that determine the time lag between a changing age distribution and subsequent changes in judgments. Moreover, if age norms do influence employee motivation and performance, understanding how such norms evolve will help promote the design of better organizational structures. Work groups selected for age diversity, for instance, may increase the range of ages considered acceptable by employees and thus increase the potential high-performance period.

Results from this study are consistent with the explanation that age distributions drive the development of age norms that in turn influence employee behavior. However, the lack of consensus on age norms suggests an addition to the theory. Some respondents thought that age norms differed from those agreed upon by most other respondents in the company, and it is interesting to speculate whether these deviant individuals experience age norms differently. Some managers may perceive but disagree with and ignore the norms, whereas others may be unaware of the norms in the first place. Assuming that some relationship exists between performance ratings and actual performance, such individual perceptions may be useful for explaining how behind-schedule managers maintain high performance in spite of the social pressures that define them as "over the hill." Thus, the effect of age norms on individuals may depend on individual differences as well as on normative and demographic age groupings. Understanding the separate effects of and the joint interaction between these three methods of matching age categories with roles and statuses helps in elaborating how people create, recreate, and maintain continuity at work by using age to index their expectations.

REFERENCES

Abeles, R.P., Steel, L., & Wise, L.L. 1980. Patterns and implications of life-course organization: Studies from Project TALENT. In P. Baltes & O.G. Brim (Eds.), *Life-span development and behavior*, vol. 3: 307–337. New York: Academic Press.

Asch, S.E. 1951. Effects of group pressure upon the modification and distortion of judgments. In H. Guetzkow (Ed.), *Groups, leadership, and men*: 177–190, Pittsburgh: Carnegie Press.

Atchley, R.C. 1975. The life course, age grading, and age-linked demands for decision making. In N. Datan & L.H. Ginsberg (Eds.), *Life-span developmental psychology: Normative life crises*: 261–278. New York: Academic Press.

Bagozzi, R.P. 1980. *Causal models in marketing*. New York: Wiley.

Bailyn, L. 1979. Taking off for the top: How much acceleration for career success? *Management Review*, 68: 18–23.

Bailyn, L., & Lynch, J.T. 1983. Engineering as a life-long career: Its meaning, its satisfactions, its difficulties. *Journal of Occupational Behaviour*, 4: 263–283.

Cain, L.D., Jr. 1964. Life course and social structure. In R.E. Faris (Ed.), *Handbook of modern sociology*: 272–309. Chicago: Rand McNally & Co.

Dalton, G.W., & Thompson, P.H. 1971. Accelerating obsolescence of older engineers. *Harvard Business Review*, 49(5): 57–67.

Eisenstadt, S.N. 1956. *From generation to generation: Age groups and social structure*. London: Free Press of Glencoe.

Elder, G.H., Jr. 1975. Age differentiation and the life course. *Annual Review of Sociology*, 1: 165–190.

Elder, G.H., Jr., & Rockwell, R.C. 1976. Marital timing in women's life patterns. *Journal of Family History*, 1: 34–53.

Faulkner, R.R. 1974. Coming of age in organizations: A comparative study of career contingencies and adult socialization. *Sociology of Work and Occupations*, 1: 131–173.

Forbes, J.B. 1987. Early intraorganizational mobility: Patterns and influences. *Academy of Management Journal*, 30: 110–125.

Gould, R.L. 1978. *Transformations: Growth and change in adult life*. New York: Simon & Schuster.

Hogan, D.P. 1981. *Transitions and social change: The early lives of American men*. New York: Academic Press.

Homans, G.C. 1950. *The human group*. New York: Harcourt, Brace & World.

Jacobsen, C., & Van Der Voordt, T.J.M. 1980. Interpreting modal frequencies to measure social norms. *Sociological Methods and Research*, 8: 470–486.

Kanter, R.M. 1977. *Men and women of the corporation*. New York: Basic Books.

Kaufman, R.L., & Spilerman, S. 1982. The age structures of occupations and jobs. *American Journal of Sociology*, 87: 827–851.

Kidder, T. 1981. *The soul of a new machine*. Boston: Little, Brown & Co.

Kluckhohn, C. 1951. The concept of culture. In D.

Lerner & H.D. Lasswell (Eds.), *The policy sciences*: 86–101. Palo Alto, Calif.: Stanford University.

Labovitz, S., & Hagedorn, R. 1973. Measuring social norms. *Pacific Sociological Review*, 16: 283–303.

Lawrence, B.S. 1980. The myth of the midlife crisis. *Sloan Management Review*, 21(3): 35–49.

Lawrence, B.S. 1984. Age grading: The implicit organizational timetable. *Journal of Occupational Behaviour*, 5: 23–35.

Lawrence, B.S. 1985. *Uncovering elements in organizational culture*. Working paper, Graduate School of Management, University of California, Los Angeles.

Lawrence, B.S. 1987. An organizational theory of age effects. In S. Bacharach & N. DiTomaso (Eds.), *Research in the sociology of organizations*, vol. 5: 37–71. Greenwich, Conn.: JAI Press.

Levinson, D.J. 1978. *The seasons of a man's life*. New York: Alfred A. Knopf.

Lichenstein, S., Fischoff, B., & Phillips, L.D. 1982. Calibration of probabilities: The state of the art to 1980. In D. Kahneman, P. Slovic, & A. Tversky (Eds.), *Judgment under uncertainty: Heuristics and biases*: 306–334. Cambridge, U.K.: Cambridge University Press.

Linton, R. 1936. *The study of man*. New York: D. Appleton-Century.

Linton, R. 1940. A neglected aspect of social organization. *American Journal of Sociology*, 45: 870–886.

Linton, R. 1942. Age and sex categories. *American Sociological Review*, 7: 589–603.

Maccoby, M. 1977. *The gamesman*. New York: Simon & Schuster.

Mannheim, K. 1928. The problem of generations. Reprinted 1952 in P. Kecskemeti (Ed. and Translator), *Essays on the sociology of knowledge*: 276–322. London: Routledge and Kegan Paul.

Marini, M.M. 1984. Age and sequencing norms in the transition to adulthood. *Social Forces*, 63: 229–244.

Martin, N.H., & Strauss, A.L. 1956. Patterns of mobility within industrial organizations. *Journal of Business*, 19: 101–110.

Miles, W.R. 1935. Age and human society. In C. Murchison (Ed.), *A handbook of social psychology*: 596–682. New York: Russell & Russell.

Morrison, D.F. 1976. *Multivariate statistical methods* (2nd ed.). New York: McGraw-Hill Book Co.

Murdock, G. 1945. The common denominator of cultures. In R. Linton (Ed.), *The science of man in the world crisis:* 123–142. New York: Columbia University Press.

Neugarten, G.L., & Datan, N. 1973. Sociological perspectives on the life cycle. In P.W. Baltes & K.W. Schaie (Eds.), *Life-span developmental psychology: Personality and socialization:* 53–69. New York: Academic Press.

Neugarten, B.L., Moore, J.W., & Lowe, J.C. 1965. Age norms, age constraints, and adult socialization. *American Journal of Sociology,* 70: 710–717.

Neugarten, B.L., & Petersen, W.A. 1957. A study of the American age-grade system. *Proceedings of the International Association of Gerontology, Fourth Congress,* 3: 497–502.

Newcomb, T.M., Turner, R., & Converse, P.E. 1965. *Social psychology: The study of human interaction.* New York: Holt, Rinehart & Winston.

Parsons, T. 1942. Age and sex in the social structure of the United States. *American Sociological Review,* 7: 604–616.

Passuth, P.M., Maines, D.R., & Neugarten, B.L. 1984. *Age norms and age constraints 20 years later.* Unpublished manuscript, Andrus Gerontology Center, University of Southern California.

Radcliffe-Brown, A.R. 1929. Age organization terminology. *Man,* 13: 21.

Riley, M.W. 1987. On the significance of age in sociology. *American Sociological Review,* 52: 1–14.

Riley, M.W., Johnson, J., & Foner, A. (Eds.) 1972. *Aging and society,* (vol. 3): *A sociology of age stratification.* New York: Russell Sage Foundation.

Rosen, B., & Jerdee, T.H. 1976a. The influence of age stereotypes on managerial decisions. *Journal of Applied Psychology,* 61: 428–432.

Rosen, B., & Jerdee, T.H. 1976b. The nature of job-related age stereotypes. *Journal of Applied Psychology,* 62: 180–183.

Rosen, B., & Jerdee, T.H. 1977. Too old or not too old. *Harvard Business Review,* 55(6): 97–107.

Rosenbaum, J.E. 1979a. Organizational career mobility: Promotion chances in a corporation during periods of growth and contraction. *American Journal of Sociology,* 85: 21–48.

Rosenbaum, J.E. 1979b. Tournament mobility: Career patterns in a corporation. *Administrative Science Quarterly,* 24: 220–240.

Rosenbaum, J.E. 1984. *Career mobility in a corporate hierarchy.* San Francisco: Academic Press.

Rosenbaum, J.E. 1988. Organizational career systems and employee misperceptions. In M.B. Arthur, D.T. Hall, & B.S. Lawrence (Eds.), *The handbook of career theory:* forthcoming. Cambridge, U.K.: Cambridge University Press.

Rosenberg, M. 1968. *The logic of survey analysis.* New York: Basic Books.

Ryder, N.B. 1965. The cohort as a concept in the study of social change. *American Sociological Review,* 30: 843–861.

Schein, E.H. 1985. *Organizational culture and leadership.* San Francisco: Jossey-Bass.

Sherif, M. 1936. *The psychology of social norms.* New York: Harper & Brothers.

Shyrock, H.S., Siegel, J.S., & associates. 1980. *The methods and materials of demography.* Washington, D.C.: U.S. Department of Commerce, Bureau of the Census.

Simmel, G. 1950. *The sociology of Georg Simmel.* Translated by K.H. Wolff. Glencoe, Ill.: Free Press.

Singer, E. 1981. Reference groups and social evaluations. In M. Rosenberg & R. Turner (Eds.), *Social psychology: Sociology perspectives:* 66–93. New York: Basic Books.

Singer, J.E. (1980). Social comparison: The process of self-evaluation. In L. Festinger (Ed.), *Retrospections on social psychology:* 158–179. New York: Oxford University Press.

Smith, J.M. 1973. Age and occupation: The determinants of male occupational age structures — hypothesis H and hypothesis A. *Journal of Gerontology,* 28: 484–490.

Snedecor, G.W., & Cochran, W.G. 1980. *Statistical methods* (7th ed.). Ames, Iowa: Iowa State University Press.

Sofer, C. 1970. *Men in mid-career: A study of British managers and technical specialists.* Cambridge, U.K.: Cambridge University Press.

Stewman, S., & Konda, S.L. 1983). Careers and organizational labor markets: Demographic models of organizational behavior. *American Journal of Sociology,* 88: 637–685.

Tversky, A., & Kahneman, D. 1973. Availability: A heuristic for judging frequency and probability. *Cognitive Psychology*, 5: 207–232.

Tversky, A., & Kahneman, D. 1974. Judgment under uncertainty: Heuristics and biases. *Science*, 185: 1124–1131.

Vaillant, G.E. 1977. *Adaptation to life*. Boston: Little, Brown & Co.

Whyte, W.H., Jr. 1956. *The organization man*. New York: Simon & Schuster.

NOTES

1. Although this approach to defining age norms differs from many in that it does not include expectations, it is consistent with approaches that define norms as "frames of reference" or standardized ways of perceiving the world (Newcomb, Turner, & Converse, 1965: 229; Sherif, 1936).

2. The order is informed by the work of Rosenberg, who suggested that "research must allow for *the dominant direction of influence of variables*" (1968: 11–13). Rosenberg also suggested two factors that indicate the dominant direction: the time order and the fixity or alterability of variables. Variables that are more fixed and less malleable than others come first within a causal sequence. The time order of variables in the explanation proposed here is suggested by the rationale underlying their relationships and supported by their relative fixity.

3. Personal communications with engineering managers and human resource staff members at the TRW Corporation provided this information.

4. For instance, decision theory suggests that, when faced with an uncertain distribution, people tend to overestimate its lower boundary and underestimate its upper boundary, thus producing a systematic regression towards the mean (Lichtenstein, Fischoff, & Phillips, 1982). Observing such a systematic pattern raises additional questions. Does the pattern occur in all organizations, or does it only occur in organizations in which employees perceive the distribution as uncertain? Under what conditions does an organization's age distribution appear uncertain to employees? If scholars can understand how employees make judgments, perhaps we can anticipate what organizational characteristics are likely to produce what patterns of age norms.

5. The visual age scale allowed people to be flexible in answering questions. Pretesting indicated that people will come up with a numerical age if forced to do so; however, they find it easier to respond to a visual picture of an entire age range. Whether the two methods would have elicited different responses is unknown. Additional study on the reliability and validity of different methods of obtaining age judgments is necessary.

6. I once asked a 45-year-old defense industry manager whether there were any standard ages within his company for middle-level managers. His reply was "Of course not. We promote the best people available." I then asked whether he would hire a 25-year-old individual in his middle-level job. This time he said, "Let's not be ridiculous." Although his response appeared reasonable to him, in some companies, for instance, start-up electronics firms, a 25-year-old middle manager would not be at all out of place. The point is that this manager was so unaware of his own age standards that he could not discuss a question concerning standard ages unless confronted with ages that grossly violated his expectations.

7. The 66.6 percent level of agreement was computed using Jacobsen and Van Der Voordt's guidelines for assessing widely shared social norms using modal frequencies. The following equation specifies the requisite level of agreement for a given study: $pk_{1rep} = \frac{1}{2}(1 + 1/k)$, where pk_{1rep} is the level of agreement required for a representative norm and K equals the number of response categories. In the firm studied, there are three response categories for each career level because an employee's age judgment can fall either within, ahead, or behind the range of normative ages. Thus, $pk_{1rep} = \frac{1}{2}(1 + \frac{1}{3}) = 66.6\%$.

8. Age judgment and actual age distributions for each level are available from the author.

9. Only managers in levels 2 through 8 gave performance ratings of managerial subordinates; therefore, before I examined the relationship between age groups and performance it was important to confirm that those managers' view of normative age groups was similar to that of the aggregate group of managers. The data show that it is. Normative age groups for managers in levels 2 through 8 are identical to the normative age groups for the aggregate group of managers. Further, the level of agreement on each career level for managers in levels 2 through 8 lies within four percentage points of the aggregate levels shown in Figure 3 (average difference = 1.8, range = 0–4). In all cases, the proportion of managers in levels 2 through 8 who agree on the normative age group exceeds the 66.6 percent cutoff.

18

The U.S. Supreme Court's "Consensus" on Affirmative Action

John Nalbandian

UNIVERSITY OF KANSAS

Eighteen years have passed since the U.S. Supreme Court's landmark decision in Griggs v. Duke Power Company. *Since that time the Court has reviewed numerous cases, and it is now possible to describe the "consensus" that the Court has reached in the way it approaches affirmative action cases. Following a review of the Court's two-part analytical approach to affirmative action, this article analyzes the Court's deliberations with respect to the competing values of individual rights, social equity, and efficiency. The future of affirmative action is examined in terms of the influence of the Court's configuration, its respect for precedent, and the way in which the value of social equity has penetrated public personnel policy and practices.*

Twenty-five years ago Congress passed the Civil Rights Act of 1964, and 18 years ago the U.S. Supreme Court provided its first signifi-

Reprinted with permission from Public Administration © Review by the American Society for Public Administration (ASPA) 1120 G Street NW 500, Washington, D.C. 20005.

John Nalbandian is an Associate Professor in the Department of Public Administration at the University of Kansas. He is working on *City Management at a Crossroads: A Crisis in Professionalism* (Jossey-Bass), and he and Donald E. Klingner are preparing a third edition of *Public Personnel Management: Contexts and Strategies* (Prentice-Hall).

cant review in *Griggs* v. *Duke Power Company*.[1] Since *Griggs*, the Court has considered several employment discrimination cases, and it finally appears possible to identify the conditions under which a public employer can consider race in personnel actions.

This article delineates those conditions by examining the analytical approach employed by the Court in deliberating employment discrimination cases. It then discusses the conflicting values debated in these cases, and in the last part it speculates on the future of affirmative action.

FACTORS IMPEDING CONSENSUS

For a number of years, the Court has confronted different issues which complicated an early answer to the question, "Under what conditions can a public employer take race into consideration in employment decisions?" On the statutory side, unanticipated issues and ambiguities resulting from legislative compromise dictated evolutionary development of the law.[2] These complicating factors are outlined before describing the Court's approach to employment discrimination cases.

First, varied statutory and constitutional issues suggest different standards of judicial review. The analysis in this article focuses on Title VII of the Civil Rights Act of 1964 as amended by the Equal Employment Act of 1972 and the Equal Protection Clause of the 14th Amendment to the United States Constitution. Cases involving claims against *private employers* have been litigated under Title VII which prohibits discrimination in employment based on race, color, religion, gender, or national origin. A case may be filed against a *public employer* under Title VII and/or as a constitutional claim under the Equal Protection Clause of the 14th Amendment. That clause says that no state shall "deny to any person within its jurisdiction the equal protection of the laws." Over the years, the Court has narrowed the differences in its approach to statutory versus constitutional issues.

Second, while administrators commonly use the term "affirmative action," the Court has struggled to sort out the legal distinctions between "color blind" personnel practices, consideration of race as one among several factors in personnel decisions, and focus on race as the major factor in employment decisions. Further confounding these distinctions are the legal differences between the vehicles of affirmative action: voluntary plans, provisions included in consent decrees, and court orders.

A third factor obscuring clear cut conclusions about the use of race consciousness in personnel actions arises from differences between the assumptions about discrimination contained in Title VII and litigation subsequently confronted. When amending Title VII in 1972, Congress acknowledged its prior naivete: "In 1964, employment discrimination tended to be viewed as a series of isolated and distinguishable events, for the most part due to ill-will on the part of some identifiable individual or organization. . . . Experience has shown this view to be false."[3] Unfortunately, the Court has had to confront cases involving systemic, yet, in some cases, unintentional discrimination where individual victims are not easily identifiable.

Growing out of these assumptions about discrimination is a fourth factor—the essentially remedial nature of Title VII and the challenge of voluntary affirmative action. The law was designed to compensate individuals who had suffered discrimination. The letter of the law did not envision the possibility of employers taking voluntary steps to overcome racial imbalances in their work force without formally having been found guilty of discrimination. Yet, starting with *Steelworkers* v. *Weber*[4] the Court observed that precluding voluntary affirmative action would run contrary to the spirit of the law.

Finally, an appeal to legislative intent to answer questions of law frequently justifies conflicting positions. This is notably true with regard to Section 706(g) of Title VII, which some justices argue was intended to permit court ordered relief only for identifiable victims of discrimination. While Chief Justice Rehnquist, a strong supporter of this interpretation, claims that the language itself is clear in 706(g), he acknowledges that the legislative history "may be fairly apportioned among both sides."[5]

Each of these factors has challenged the Court's ability definitively to interpret employment discrimination law. Further, legal debate will continue over unresolved points of law like the difference in the meaning of "strict scrutiny," standards of review in Title VII versus 14th Amendment cases, and constitutional standards of review in gender versus race-based affirmative action. Nevertheless, case law has developed since 1971, and it is possible now to generalize at least about the *reasoning* employed by the Court when analyzing employment discrimination cases.

THE COURT'S TWO-PART ANALYTICAL APPROACH

Something like a working consensus appears present within the Court that review of race-conscious affirmative action requires a two-part analysis. The first part examines the justification for taking race into consideration. The second focuses on the content of the affirmative action with particular attention to the consequences for nonminority employees.

Justification for Race-Consciousness

Justification for taking affirmative action ranges from overcoming imbalances in "traditionally segregated job categories"[6] to remediating the effects of intentional discrimination.[7] While the Court has not yet agreed fully on what constitutes sufficient justification, *the more impact the affirmative action has on nonminorities, the more justification is required.* For example, the Court determined that "societal discrimination" did not constitute justification for a race-conscious layoff provision—even though contained in a collective bargaining agreement. According to the Court, an inference of *employer* discrimination would have been required.[8]

The most stringent requirement for a public employer is demonstrating a "compelling government purpose" for the use of racial classifications in employment decisions. A lesser standard would be an "important government purpose." But in many ways the Court's argument over standards of justification are rendered moot with Justice O'Connor's observation that "The Court is in agreement that, whatever the formulation [of a level of scrutiny like 'compelling' versus 'important'] employed, remedying past or present racial discrimination by a state actor is a sufficiently weighty state interest to warrant the remedial use of a carefully constructed affirmative action program."[9]

Many administrators do not realize that an inference of employer discrimination may be drawn from a conspicuous racial imbalance in segments of the employer's work force compared to segments of a relevant labor market.[10] Wherever a strong *inference* of employment discrimination can be found, at least a "firm" basis exists for affirmative action.[11]

Means-Ends Analysis

The second half of the Court's reasoning concentrates on the substance of the race-conscious plan or relief. The Court is concerned with limiting affirmative action tightly within the scope of the problem that it is supposed to solve. Regardless of whether a Title VII or 14th Amendment claim, the Court's primary concern in evaluating the scope of affirmative action is with the burden placed on innocent nonminorities.[12]

While the Court has approved benefits to nonvictim minorities,[13] it prefers remedies which provide "make-whole relief" to identifiable victims. With make-whole relief, victims receive what they would have gotten had they not been discriminated against, and nonvictim minorities do not benefit from a racial preference. But even in cases involving make-whole relief, the Court is inclined to review the impact on nonminorities. For example, in *Teamsters* the Court granted make-whole relief but remanded the case to the District Court to determine the actual victims of discrimination. The Supreme Court said: "The District Court will again be faced with the delicate task of adjusting the remedial interests of the discriminatees and the legitimate expectations of other employees innocent of any wrongdoing."[14]

While the Court has acknowledged that innocent third parties may have to bear some of the burden in race-conscious relief,[15] it is more likely to approve where the burden is diffuse and not borne by particular individuals. In *United States* v. *Paradise*, Justice Powell expressed his standard for judging the impact on third parties. He wrote: "Unlike layoff requirements, the promotion requirement at issue in this case does not 'impose the entire burden of achieving racial equality on particular individuals,' and it does not disrupt seriously the lives of innocent individuals."[16]

In addition to this guidance, in *Paradise* Justice Powell succinctly summarized four additional criteria used by the Court to assess whether or not race-conscious relief is narrowly tailored to the problem it is supposed to solve. They are: "(i) the efficacy of alternative remedies; (ii) the planned duration of the remedy; (iii) the relationship between the percentage of minority workers to be employed and the percentage of minority group members in the relevant population or work force; and (iv) the availability of waiver provisions if the hiring plan could not be met."[17]

Paradise illustrates the applicability of Justice Powell's five criteria. The District Court had found the Alabama Department of Public Safety guilty of intentional discrimination and recalcitrant in complying with the terms of subsequent decrees, including development of a valid promotion testing procedure. Frustrated with the delays, the District Court ordered a one-for-one promotion quota which the United States, supporting the Department of Public Safety, claimed violated the Equal Protection Clause of the 14th Amendment.

With the exception of Justice Stevens, who concurred in the judgment supporting the quota but who would have granted broader discretion to the District Court because the case involved intentional discrimination by a governmental body, the Court utilized its two-pronged analysis. The Court unanimously agreed that the District Court had rightly based its enforcement order on a compelling interest in eradicating the Department of Public Safety's "pervasive, systematic, and obstinate discriminatory" exclusion of blacks.[18] The Court's disagreement centered on the nature of the remedy, with Justices Brennan, Blackmun, Marshall, and Powell concluding that it was narrowly tailored and Justices O'Connor, Scalia, and White and Chief Justice Rehnquist finding the opposite.

Justice Brennan writing for a plurality reasoned that (1) no alternatives to the quota were brought to the District Court; (2) the one-for-one requirement was flexible in several ways including: a waiver provision if no qualified minorities were available; promotion only when the Department determined the need for additional supervisory personnel; duration contingent upon the Department's development of a valid promotion procedure; and anticipation of the quota as a one-time occurrence by the District Court; (3) while the one-for-one rate failed to correspond to the 1 to 3 ratio of blacks to whites in the relevant work force, it was appropriate considering the Department's past discrimination and delays in implementing the necessary promotion procedure; and (4) the requirements did not impose an unacceptable burden on innocent nonminorities.

Justice O'Connor's dissenting opinion, joined by Chief Justice Rehnquist and Justices Scalia and White, reiterated the view she expressed in *Sheet Metal Workers* where she argued strongly against quotas—and reluctantly endorsed goals—in court-ordered remedies because of their impact on innocent nonminorities.[19] In *Paradise* she reiterated that conclusion, focusing on what she called the Court's "standardless" view of a "narrowly tailored" remedy for the discrimination which had occurred. She fundamentally objected to the District Court's failure to entertain alternative remedies more specifically targeted at the goal of inducing the Department of Public Safety to develop a valid promotion procedure. She argued that consideration of alternatives is the least action required by the "narrowly tailored" standard.[20] Second, she objected to the one-for-one ratio arguing that it far exceeded the 25 percent minority trooper force eligible for promotion and, therefore, was arbitrary.

The two-part analysis is illustrated as well in *Johnson* v. *Transportation Agency*,[21] the other case coming before the Court in 1987. The parallel analyses in contrasting cases like *Paradise* and *Johnson* underscore the Court's growing consensus on its analytical approach to employment discrimination cases. *Paradise* came to the Court involving constitutional issues stemming from a court order in response to intentional racial discrimination. The Court reviewed *Johnson* as a Title VII case involving voluntary affirmative action to overcome gender imbalances in "traditionally segregated job categories."

Paul Johnson applied for promotion to the position of road dispatcher with the Transportation Agency in Santa Clara County, California. Diane Joyce also applied for the job in which women were obviously underrepresented. The hiring authority determined both applicants to be qualified and eligible for the promotion. Under the county's affirmative action plan, Joyce was hired over Johnson who had received two more points than Joyce on the basis of an interview. Thus, the Court was faced with determining if an affirmative action plan which led to the hiring of a woman over a male violated Title VII.[22]

In a 6-3 judgment, the Court upheld the plan. Justice Brennan delivered the Court's opinion. The majority found the County's actions consistent with the provisions that the Court established in *Weber*. The County's plan was designed to break down traditionally segregated job categories. The plan established short-term goals which did not unnecessarily trammel the interests of nonminorities (males), did not require discharge of nonminorities (males) in favor of minorities (females), did not create an absolute bar to advancement of nonminorities (males), and were temporary in nature and not designed to maintain a racial (gender) balance but to eliminate an imbalance.[23]

In sum, while it is not always possible to predict the Court's decision, one can be increasingly confident that both majority and minority opinions will follow the same points of reasoning. In other words, the framework of analysis has become increasingly clear with the development of case law. The framework focuses on the justification for affirmative action and an examination to determine whether the means narrowly fit the scope of the problem. In assessing the consequences of affirmative action, the Court pays significant attention to the impact on nonminorities.

THE VALUE DEBATE WITHIN THE COURT

So far, this article has attempted to summarize the legal reasoning which underpins the Court's analysis in employment discrimination cases. But to understand more clearly the Court's direction, one must identify and examine the values debated within this analytical framework.

For 18 years the Court has debated the appropriate balance in employment discrimination cases between the competing values of individual rights, social equity, and efficiency in its effort to clarify the meaning of the law.

This section views the Court's affirmative action decisions in terms of these values.

As a value, *individual rights* includes the expectations that employees and job applicants have of fair treatment and protection from arbitrary decisions, particularly in actions affecting job security and seniority. The Court's emphasis on "make-whole relief" to identifiable victims of discrimination reflects the value of individual rights. Similarly, its emphasis on protecting the interests of nonminorities grows out of its respect for individual rights. Thus, the key task of balancing the interests of minority victims and innocent nonminorities fundamentally revolves around questions of individual rights.

While the Court does not use the term *social equity*, its opinions nevertheless reflect this value which cannot be ignored in understanding human resources policy and administration. Another term for social equity might be "distributive justice." Adherence to the value of social equity results in fair treatment of people as members of a class rather than as individuals. Preference on the basis of race, gender, age, religion, or national origin reflects the value of social equity. Social equity is frequently expressed in compensatory terms where an action is taken to overcome some classwide past injustice or hardship. Social equity results in race-conscious affirmative action to nonvictim minorities as opposed to make-whole relief to identifiable victims of discrimination. One of the most common expressions of social equity, predating affirmative action by a century, is veterans preference awarded to individuals who have served in the armed forces and who may have lost a competitive position in the labor market.

Because the Court analyzes percentages of minorities to nonminorities in a work force to make inferences about underutilization and to assess progress in overcoming the effects of past discrimination, the value of social equity frequently is confused with a similar value, "representation." Clearly, moving towards a work force that is representative of the racial balance in a relevant labor pool demonstrates affirmative action progress. However, representativeness is used as a measure or instrument of this progress, not as an end value. The goal of eradicating past discrimination expresses the end value of social equity.[24]

Frequently people look upon social equity with suspicion. Among the reasons are: a preference in this culture to make awards based on variation in individual merit rather than either/or distinctions which erase individual differences. The value of social equity necessarily highlights differences due to race, gender, and national origin in a culture which largely seeks to downplay these differences.

Efficiency in the provision of public services is commonly measured with various input/output ratios. In personnel administration efficiency is advanced generally when personnel actions are taken on the basis of merit. Thus, efficiency is reflected in affirmative action with the concern for the qualifications (knowledge, skills, and abilities) of applicants.

The history of employment discrimination cases first focused on the values of individual rights and efficiency consistent with the assumption that violations of anti-discrimination law would consist of discreet incidents involving a victim and a person who had committed a discriminatory act. Victims would receive make-whole relief which would be balanced against the rights and interests of other victims and innocent nonminorities. The Court's unanimous opinion in *Griggs* emphasized that *individuals* should be subject to color blind criteria in employment decisions. Individual rights are expressed in the view that race-conscious relief should be confined to the identifiable victims of discrimination. This view is seen clearly in *Albemarle Paper Company* v. *Moody*,[25] where the Court went to great lengths to specify how an employee could create the inference that he or she was a victim of discrimination, and in *Firefighters* v. *Stotts*,[26] where the Court implied a general policy limiting relief only to identifiable victims of discrimination.

Finally, a major expression of individual rights is the Court's concern that the burden that innocent nonminorities are called upon to bear in race-conscious relief will not cause them undue harm. This concern is expressed in all Court opinions where minority nonvictims benefit from race-conscious relief. It is even expressed where make-whole relief is involved, particularly when the job security of nonminorities might be affected. According to Justice Stewart, writing for the Court in *Teamsters*, "Especially when immediate implementation of an equitable remedy threatens to impinge upon the expectations of innocent parties, the courts must 'look to the practical realities and necessities inescapably involved in reconciling competing interests,' in order to determine the 'special blend of what is necessary, what is fair, and what is workable.'"[27]

In Justice Rehnquist's minority opinion in *Weber*, he expressed the unequivocal viewpoint that employment discrimination boils down to questions of individual rights: "I find a prohibition on all preferential treatment based on race as elementary and fundamental as the principle that "two wrongs do not make a right."[28]

The problem with approaching employment discrimination from the perspective of individual rights alone is found in situations where systemic discrimination has created insidious barriers to fair treatment. For example, where blacks know it is a waste of time to apply for a job or a promotion, make-whole relief is very difficult to assign.[29] Further, to the extent that the Court has endorsed affirmative action to overcome race and gender imbalances in traditionally segregated job categories, as it did in *Weber* and *Johnson*, trying to limit relief to identifiable victims of discrimination is impractical.

Thus, in addition to individual rights, social equity has influenced the Court's decisions. These decisions invoke preferential treatment to minorities who may not have been victims of discrimination, with preference to them stemming from their minority status as opposed to characteristics which differentiate minority members one from the other or from nonminority employees or applicants. *Weber, Sheet Metal Workers, Firefighters, Paradise,* and *Johnson* (gender) all provide some kind of goal or quota with preference to minorities. Of course, in each of these cases, the Court makes a special effort to assess the impact of the goal or quota on the rights of nonminorities, recognizing that social equity can impinge upon individual rights and that the values require some balancing.

The strongest expressions of social equity go beyond establishment of goals and quotas to remedy employer discrimination. Justice Stevens has led the argument. In *Wygant*, he wrote in a dissenting opinion that the Court "should consider whether the public interest, and the manner in which it is pursued, justifies any adverse effects on the disadvantaged groups."[30] This "public interest" standard is distinguished from the stricter standards of "compelling" or even "important" government purposes, and it would open the door to broader justification for race-conscious personnel actions. More recently, in a concurring opinion in *Johnson*, where the Court supported the use of gender classification, Justice Stevens emphasized that "the opinion does not establish the permissible outer limits of voluntary programs undertaken by employers to benefit disadvantaged groups."[31] Further, he wrote: "Instead of retroactively scrutinizing his own or society's possible exclusions of minorities in the past to determine the outer limits of a valid affirmative-action program— or indeed, any particular affirmative-action decision—in many cases the employer will find it more appropriate to consider *other le-*

gitimate reasons to give preferences to members of under-represented groups" [emphasis added].[32] These other reasons might include, "simply to eliminate from their operations all de facto embodiment of a system of racial caste."[33]

The sharper the emphasis on any particular value in a Justice's opinion, the more likely it is to be isolated and countered. Efficiency is one such counter concern, especially to social equity arguments. But the efficiency argument itself has become muted over the years; in reality it moved to the background as social equity advanced. As an example, in 1971 in *Griggs,* Chief Justice Burger delivered the Court's unanimous opinion endorsing a color blind interpretation of the law where job qualifications are the controlling factor in personnel decisions: "Congress has not commanded that the less qualified be preferred over the better qualified simply because of minority origins. Far from disparaging job qualifications as such, Congress has made such qualifications the controlling factor, so that race, religion, nationality, and sex become irrelevant."[34]

Sixteen years later in *Paradise,* the Court drew no distinction between "more or less qualified." The emphasis was solely on the "qualified," implying a dichotomy between "qualified" and "not qualified." In addition, instead of qualifications being the centerpiece as in *Griggs,* in *Paradise* they were used merely as one of several factors ameliorating the impact of a promotion quota—an expression of social equity. Delivering a plurality opinion for a 5-4 Court, Justice Brennan wrote that the promotion quota "may be waived if no qualified black candidates are available."[35]

Presently, the Court is attempting to balance the three values. This can be seen in the two most recent cases, *Paradise* and *Johnson.* In *Paradise,* a 5-4 Court supported an order for a promotion quota. But in justifying the remedy, which emphasized social equity, the Court acknowledged several qualifying conditions. Among those, in deference to the efficiency value it waived the quota in the absence of qualified minorities. In addition, the Court held that the quota would not trammel the individual rights of particular non-minorities because its impact was diffuse.

One finds similar compromises in *Johnson.* The hiring authority considered gender as a factor in the promotion decision, suggesting sensitivity to the social equity value. With respect to Johnson's individual rights, the Court argued that he was not due a promotion, and denial in this particular case would not preclude a promotion in the future. As to the efficiency value, with both candidates being certified as well-qualified in an initial assessment, both the hiring authority and the Court—with a lively dissent—found negligible the two-point difference separating Johnson from Joyce on the basis of a subsequent interview.

In sum, it is clear that those who favor class-conscious affirmative action place higher priority on social equity than those who favor individual rights. Practically speaking, while acknowledging the Court's rhetoric on efficiency, one may question the influence of this value in the Court's calculations. But regardless of the relative priorities, no decision of the Court in an employment discrimination case involving nonvictim beneficiaries is likely to occur in the near future without reflecting all three of these values.

THE FUTURE OF AFFIRMATIVE ACTION

As one speculates about the future of affirmative action and the relative priority of the values, one might consider three factors: the configuration of the U.S. Supreme Court, its respect for precedent, and the technical nature of personnel administration.[36]

Configuration of the Court

Justice Powell's retirement and Justice O'Connor's position seem critical in assessing the Court's future decisions on affirmative action. Justice Powell played a significant role in employment discrimination cases when he joined the Blackmun, Brennan, Marshall, and Stevens plurality to form a majority in *Sheet Metal Workers* and *Firefighters*. Justice O'Connor joined this new majority in *Johnson* and in *Firefighters*. Powell's move accompanied the plurality's adoption of his stricter standard of judicial review in *Sheet Metal Workers*. This is the present standard employed by the Court.

In similar fashion, it is not unreasonable to expect the plurality of Justices Blackmun, Brennan, Marshall, and Stevens to move closer to Justice O'Connor's more conservative position in order to maintain a majority. If so, despite Justice O'Connor's support in *Johnson*, the Court will place less emphasis on the value of social equity and more on individual rights. Justice O'Connor has shown no tolerance whatsoever for quotas or for quotas which purport to be goals.[37] Nonetheless, her support in *Johnson* separates her from Justices Scalia and White and from Chief Justice Rehnquist, who adhere to the view that affirmative action should focus on make-whole relief only.

Because *Johnson* involved affirmative action for women, some might argue that Justice O'Connor is more sympathetic to gender issues than to racial issues. Justice O'Connor has written opinions in several employment discrimination cases, however, and her arguments in *Johnson* appear entirely consistent with those she expressed in cases involving racial discrimination. Nothing exists in the Court's record to suggest that Justice O'Connor will show more sympathy towards affirmative action for women than for racial minorities.

If the plurality of Justices Blackmun, Bren-nan, Marshall, and Stevens are unable consistently to find areas of agreement with Justice O'Connor, Justice Kennedy's role in employment discrimination cases could become pivotal. Unfortunately, Justice Kennedy has not assembled a record comprehensive enough to permit an analysis.[38] However, it is anticipated generally that his support for affirmative action based on social equity will be modest.

Precedent

The future of affirmative action depends significantly on the respect that the newly configured Court shows for precedent, especially *University of California Regents* v. *Bakke*[39] and *Weber*. In those cases, the Court clearly ventured beyond the earlier statutory letter of the law, permitting use of race as one factor in admissions/selection decisions (*Bakke*)[40] and permitting voluntary affirmative action (*Weber*). It was apparent at the time that with *Weber* the Court had expanded its interpretation of congressional intent in Title VII. Acknowledging the Court's new and broad interpretation of Title VII in *Weber*, Justice Blackmun invited Congress to act if it took issue with the Court's interpretation which permitted voluntary affirmative action.[41]

In *Johnson*, Justice Stevens acknowledged that the Court had gone beyond the letter of the statute in its interpretation of Title VII. He agreed with the dissent's position that if the Court adhered to Congress' "color blind" rhetoric and the Court's initial interpretation of Title VII, Paul Johnson would have prevailed in his claim. However, Justice Stevens reminded the Court that, "*Bakke* and *Weber* have been decided and are now an important part of the fabric of the law. This consideration is sufficiently compelling for me to adhere to the basic construction of this legislation that the Court adopted in *Bakke* and *Weber*."[42]

In Justice O'Connor's concurring opinion in *Johnson* she picked up Justice Stevens' theme that the Court had established a precedent in *Weber* warranting respect. Thus, with Justices Stevens and O'Connor joining Justices Blackmun, Brennan, and Marshall, it is highly unlikely that the present Court will undo *Bakke*—where the Court established that race could be used as one factor in affirmative action—and *Weber*—where the Court upheld voluntary affirmative action by private sector employers and set the stage for public employers as well.

Organizational and Technical Rationality

Speculation about the future of affirmative action must go beyond prognosis of the Court's configuration and estimation of its respect for precedent. Over an 18-year period, administrators have become sensitized to Court decisions expressing the value of social equity. It is unreasonable to anticipate sudden administrative reversal of these impacts now, regardless of Court action.

In the abstract, public organizations are value systems requiring legitimacy for survival. Currently, it is hard to conceive of a public organization claiming legitimacy if it does not recognize the value of social equity in its employment practices.

But tension remains in personnel practices largely because the Court has relegated the efficiency value to a backstage role while organizations cannot. The Court has demonstrated its legal predilection to view affirmative action originally and fundamentally as an individual rights issue regardless of whether Title VII or the Constitution is involved. The impact of social equity on the efficiency value is understated because of the judicial system's fundamental orientation which features individual rights. In addition, efficiency lost relevance in the debate once the Court adopted the "qualified/not qualified" notion of efficiency over a continuum of "more/less qualified."

While casting the debate as one juxtaposing social equity and individual rights serves a juridical perspective, the Court fails to acknowledge the organizational contexts within which affirmative action actually takes place, specifically within the context of "merit." In the day-to-day routine of personnel management based on merit, the debate over affirmative action is more likely to involve social equity and efficiency rather than social equity and individual rights—although clearly, in highly visible allocational decisions, this is not the case.

The values framework summarized in this article implies that any complex public personnel policy issue must involve debates of all salient values.[43] Failure in that regard results in the neglected value expressing itself in unintended ways. This very well may be the case with affirmative action. The common employee perception—whether accurate or not—that some minority employees have received unfair preferential treatment may be attributable to the relative neglect of efficiency as a value in the Court's deliberations when contrasted to its importance as an organizational value.[44]

The debate focusing on social equity and individual rights may prevail in the foreseeable future of affirmative action. But failure to pay more attention to the value of efficiency may erode its legitimacy further in organizational settings where affirmative action must be implemented.

Given the organizational—as opposed to judicial—emphasis on efficiency, one might confidently observe that those personnel practices reflecting social equity which coincide with rather than oppose practices consistent with individual rights and efficiency will endure. This means that, even without a hint of employment discrimination, at the minimum practices like targeted recruitment; job related tests, interviews, and performance appraisals; and merit pay based on job related factors are here to stay. They are now anchored in the core of public personnel practices. One would anticipate continuing organizational emphasis on social equity where inferences of discrimination can be drawn.

In summary, the U.S. Supreme Court assesses each case based on unique points of law and patterns of fact. On that basis, one might be reluctant to predict the Court's direction. However, drawing upon knowledge of the value base of personnel policy, one gains a broad interpretive tool. Putting together the present configuration of the Court, its respect for precedent, and the value patterns implied in past decisions, one could hardly conclude that affirmative action is dead, as some might believe. However, the emphasis on social equity is likely to shift somewhat in favor of a new balance—perhaps tempered by a renewed concern for organizational efficiency—based on complementary rather than opposing expressions of social equity and individual rights. Moreover, the legitimacy of affirmative action over the longer haul depends on incorporating the value of efficiency more consistently into formal channels of judicial review as well as public policy forums and organizational practices.

NOTES

1. *Griggs v. Duke Power Company*, 401 U.S. 424 (1971).

2. In their dissent in *Teamsters v. United States*, 431 U.S. 324, p. 392 (1977), Justices Brennan and Marshall quoted the Congressional Record on this point, "in any areas where a specific contrary intention is not indicated, it was assumed that the present case law would continue to govern the applicability and construction of Title VII."

3. *Ibid.*, p. 383, fn 7.

4. *Steelworkers v. Weber*, 443 U.S. 193 (1979).

5. *Firefighters v. Cleveland*, 92 L Ed 2d 405, 437 (1986).

6. *Johnson v. Transportation Agency*, 94 L Ed 615 (1987).

7. *United States v. Paradise*, 94 L Ed 203 (1987).

8. *Wygant v. Jackson Board of Education*, 90 L Ed 2d 260, p. 269 (1986).

9. *Ibid.*, p. 276.

10. *Teamsters, supra.*, pp. 339, 358.

11. Consistent with *Teamsters*, a Title VII case, the various opinions in *Wygant, supra.*, pp. 270, 278, and 289, support this assertion with regard to constitutional review.

More specifically, whenever a person or group can demonstrate an inference of employer discrimination—usually through a labor market demographic analysis—the burden shifts to the employer to show that the underutilization of minorities results from job related personnel practices or bona fide occupational qualifications.

12. See *Sheet Metal Workers v. EEOC*, 92 L Ed 2d 344 (1986) for the Court's parallel analysis of Title VII and Equal Protection Clause claims.

13. A variety of cases have reinforced this point since *Weber, supra.* Included most recently are: *Johnson, supra.*; *Paradise, supra.*; *Sheet Metal Workers, supra.*; and *Firefighters, supra.*

14. *Teamsters, supra.*, p. 372.

15. *Wygant, supra.*, pp. 272–275.

16. *Paradise, supra.*

17. *Ibid.*, p. 233.

18. *Ibid.*, p. 221.

19. *Sheet Metal Workers, supra.*

20. *Paradise, supra.*, p. 242.

21. *Johnson, supra.*

22. The hiring authority did not regard the difference in the interview scores between Joyce and Johnson as significant (*Ibid.*, p. 626). In their dissent, pp. 650–651, Justices Scalia and White and Chief Justice Rehnquist took issue with this claim.

23. *Ibid.*, p. 629.

24. Correspondence (June 1988) with David Rosenbloom assisted my exploration of the relationship between social equity and representativeness.

25. *Albemarle Paper Company v. Moody*, 422 U.S. 405 (1975).

26. *Firefighters v. Stotts*, 467 U.S. 561, pp. 579–580, 582–583 (1984).

27. *Teamsters, supra.*, p. 375.

28. *Weber, supra.*, p. 228, fn 10.

29. See *Teamsters, supra.*, pp. 365–368, and Justices Brennan, Blackmun, and Marshall's dissenting opinion in *Stotts, supra.*, pp. 612–613.

30. *Wygant, supra.*, pp. 293–294.

31. *Johnson, supra.*, p. 637.

32. *Ibid.*, p. 640.

33. *Idem.* Justice Stevens' advocacy of race consciousness extended to the value of effectiveness as well as social equity. In *Johnson, supra.*, p. 640, and in *Wygant, supra.*, pp. 294–295, Stevens cited examples where taking race into account in personnel actions can increase the effectiveness of a work force. One example was where a police force sought to integrate itself to enhance community relations. Thus, racially balancing a work force—that is, making it representative of a relevant labor pool or community—can impact effectiveness as well as social equity. However, the two goals may be pursued independently, and, in my observation, when the Court endorses racial preference, it does so primarily in pursuit of social equity—to eradicate the effects of past discrimination—not effectiveness.

34. *Griggs, supra.*

35. *Paradise, supra.*, p. 227.

36. Omitted in this general discussion are factors like the emphasis on civil rights enforcement of the President elected in 1988 and assignment power of the Chief Justice.

37. See her dissenting opinion in *Sheet Metal Workers, supra.*, and her concurring opinion in *Johnson, supra.*

38. I acknowledge Jan G. Levine's (People for the American Way) assistance in identifying related cases. In addition to case material, U.S. Senate, Committee on the Judiciary, *Nomination of Anthony M. Kennedy To Be An Associate Justice of the United States Supreme Court,* Executive Report 100-13 (February 1, 1988), similarly yielded little relevant information.

39. *University of California Regents* v. *Bakke,* 438 U.S. 265 (1978).

40. *Bakke* produced a split court with numerous opinions. However, it is clear that by joining Justice Powell's opinion with that of Justices Brennan, White, Marshall, and Blackmun, *ibid.*, pp. 320, 326, the Court did sanction the use of race as one factor in university admissions decisions where diversity within the student body is a stated goal. Further, in *Johnson, supra.*, pp. 634–635, the Court extended *Bakke* from the context of higher education to employment discrimination.

41. *Weber, supra.*, p. 216.

42. *Johnson, supra.*, p. 639.

43. For an elaboration of the framework, see Donald E. Klingner and John Nalbandian, *Public Personnel Management: Contexts and Strategies,* 2d ed. (Englewood Cliffs, NJ: Prentice Hall, 1985) and John Nalbandian and Donald E. Klingner, "Conflict and Values in Public Personnel Administration," *Public Administration Quarterly,* vol. 11 (Spring 1987), pp. 17–33.

44. For example, according to the United States Office of Personnel Management, *Federal Employee Attitudes,* 1980, some 30 percent of the senior level federal employees surveyed in 1980–1981 indicated that they felt that minority employees were treated "better or much better" than nonminorities.

19

Price Waterhouse, Petitioner v. Ann B. Hopkins[1]

Decision: The court decided that in making employment decisions in here sex has been held to be an issue, in federal civil right law suit, must prove by preponderance of evidence that his/her decision would have been the same absent such consideration.

I. SUMMARY

A woman who was employed as a senior manager by a nationwide professional accounting firm was proposed for partnership in the firm by the partners in the office where she worked, and the firm, following its usual practice, solicited evaluations of the woman from all of its partners, nearly all of whom were men. In those evaluations, which split sharply on the question whether the woman should be granted or denied partnership, her supporters strongly praised her ability and her record of securing major contracts for the firm, but a number of evaluations sharply criticized her interpersonal skills and specifically accused her of being abrasive. Several of the evaluations on both sides made comments implying that the woman was or had been acting masculine, and one partner, in

explaining to the woman the firm's decision to hold her candidacy for reconsideration the following year, suggested that she could improve her chances for partnership by walking, talking, and dressing more femininely. After the partners in her office refused to repropose her for partnership the next year, the woman resigned and brought an action against the firm in the United States District Court for the District of Columbia, which action alleged that the firm had discriminated against her on the basis of sex in violation of Title VII of the Civil Rights Act of 1964 (42 U.S.C.S. §§ 2000e *et seq.*), party on the theory that the evaluations of the woman had been based on sexual stereotyping. The District Court (1) held the firm liable under that theory, as it found that (a) the firm and its partners had not intentionally discriminated on the basis of gender, but (b) the firm had consciously maintained a system which, in this and other partner-candidacy decisions, had given weight to biased criticisms without discouraging sexism or investigating comments to determine whether they were influenced by sexual stereotypes; and (2) ruled that, while the firm could avoid equitable relief such as an order for backpay by proving by clear and convincing evidence that it would have placed the woman's candidacy on hold even absent the discrimination, it had not met that burden of proof; but (3) concluded on other grounds that the woman was not entitled to any relief except (a) attorneys' fees and (b) the difference between her pay and that of a partner from the date she would have been elected partner until her resignation. The United States Court of Appeals for the District of Columbia Circuit (1) affirmed the District Court's judgment with regard to liability, although it held that an employer may avoid liability, and not merely equitable relief, if it proves by clear and convincing evidence that it would have made the same employment decision even if discrimination had not played a role; (2) reversed the District Court's judgment with respect to remedies; and (3) remanded the case for the determination of appropriate damages and relief.

The United States Supreme Court reversed the judgment of the Court of Appeals with respect to the firm's liability and remanded the case for further proceedings. Although unable to agree on an opinion, six members of the court agreed that (1) on some showing by the plaintiff in a Title VII action that an illegitimate factor such as gender entered into an employment decision—which showing had been sufficiently made by the woman in the case at hand—the employer may be required to prove, by a preponderance of the evidence, that it would have made the same decision absent consideration of the illegitimate factor; but (2) the courts below had erred in requiring the defendant

firm to prove this point by clear and convincing evidence.

Brennan, J., announced the judgment of the court and, in an opinion joined by *Marshall, Blackmun, and Stevens*, J. J., expressed the view that (1) when a plaintiff in a Title VII case proves that her gender played a motivating part in an employment decision, the defendant may avoid a finding of liability only by proving by a preponderance of the evidence that it would have made the same decision, for a legitimate reason, even if it had not taken the plaintiff's gender into account; (2) gender need not be a "but-for" cause of an employment decision in order for the decision to have been made "because of" sex within the prohibition of Title VII, and the burden placed on the employer under the above rule is most appropriately deemed an affirmative defense rather than a shift in the burden of proof; (3) the District Court's finding that sexual stereotyping was permitted to play a part in the evaluation of the plaintiff in this case was not clearly erroneous, given that the firm relied heavily on partner evaluations and had not disclaimed reliance on the sexual-stereotype comments, and regardless of the fact that many of those comments were made by the plaintiff's supporters; (4) in most cases the employer should be able to present some objective evidence as to its probable decision in the absence of an impermissible motive; and (5) the principles announced in this opinion apply with equal force to discrimination based on race, religion, or natural origin.

White, J., concurred in the judgment, expressing the view that (1) the plaintiff's burden was to show not that the illegitimate factor was the only, principal, or true reason for the firm's action, but that the unlawful motive was a substantial factor in the adverse employment action; (2) the burden of persuasion then should have shifted to the defendant firm to prove by a preponderance of the evidence that it would have reached the same decision in the absence of the unlawful motive; (3) if that burden of proof is carried, there is no violation of Title VII; and (4) there is no special requirement in such cases that the employer carry its burden by objective evidence, and ample proof is provided if the legitimate motive found would have been ample ground for the action taken and the employer credibly testifies that the action would have been taken for the legitimate reasons alone.

O'Connor, J., concurred in the judgment, expressing the view that (1) if a plaintiff alleging individual disparate treatment under Title VII offers direct evidence that an illegitimate criterion was a substantial factor in the employment decision in question, and proves this point by a preponderance of the evidence, then the burden shifts to the defendant employer to demonstrate by a preponderance of the evidence that, with the illegitimate factor removed, sufficient business reasons would have led to the same decision; (2) a substantive violation of Title VII occurs only when consideration of an illegitimate criterion is the "but-for" cause of an adverse employment action, but when a plaintiff makes the above showing, a reasonable factfinder could conclude, absent further explanation, that the employer's discriminatory motive "caused" its decision, and nothing in the language, history, or purpose of Title VII prohibits adoption of an evidentiary rule shifting the burden of persuasion to the employer; and (3) this burden-shift rule is part of the liability phase of the case.

Kennedy, J., joined by Rehnquist, Ch. J., and Scalia, J., dissented, expressing the view that (1) regardless of who bears the burden of proof, Title VII liability requires a finding that impermissible motives are a "but-for" cause of employment decisions; (2) while an inference of discrimination arises once a Title VII plaintiff presents a prima facie case, and

the defendant must then rebut that inference by articulating a legitimate nondiscriminatory reason for its action, the ultimate burden of persuading the trier of fact that the defendant intentionally discriminated against the plaintiff remains at all times with the plaintiff; (3) the burden-shift rule adopted by the court will benefit plaintiffs in only a limited number of cases, and will burden the courts with the difficult and confusing task of developing standards for determining when to apply that rule; and (4) since the District Court found that sex discrimination was not a "but-for" cause of the defendant's decision to put the plaintiff's partnership candidacy on hold, the case should be remanded for entry of a judgment in favor of the defendant.

A. The Majority Opinion

Ann Hopkins was a senior manager in an office of Price Waterhouse when she was proposed for partnership in 1982. She was neither offered nor denied admission to the partnership; instead, her candidacy was held for reconsideration the following year. When the partners in her office later refused to repropose her for partnership, she sued Price Waterhouse under Title VII of the Civil Rights Act of 1964, 78 Stat 258, as amended, 42 U.S.C. §§ 2000e *et seq.* [42 U.S.C.S. §§ 2000e *et seq.*], charging that the firm had discriminated against her on the basis of sex in its decisions regarding partnership. Judge Gesell in the District Court for the District of Columbia ruled in her favor on the question of liability, and the Courts of Appeals for the District of Columbia Circuit affirmed. We granted certiorari to resolve a conflict among the Court of Appeals concerning the respective burdens of proof of a defendant and plaintiff in a suit under Title VII when it has been shown that an employment decision resulted from a mixture of legitimate and illegitimate motives.

At Price Waterhouse, a nationwide professional accounting partnership, a senior manager becomes a candidate for partnership when the partners in her local office submit her name as a candidate. All of the other partners in the firm are then invited to submit written comments on each candidate—either on a "long" or a "short" form, depending on the partner's degree of exposure to the candidate. Not every partner in the firm submits comments on every candidate. After reviewing the comments and interviewing the partners who submitted them, the firm's Admissions Committee makes a recommendation to the Policy Board. This recommendation will be either that the firm accept the candidate for partnership, put her application on "hold", or deny her the promotion outright. The Policy Board then decides whether to submit the candidate's name to the entire partnership for a vote, to "hold" her candidacy, or to reject her. The recommendation of the Admissions Committee, and the decision of the Policy Board, are not controlled by fixed guidelines: a certain number of positive comments from partners will not guarantee a candidate's admission to the partnership, nor will a specific quantity of negative comments necessarily defeat her application. Price Waterhouse places no limit on the number of persons whom it will admit to the partnership in any given year.

Ann Hopkins had worked at Price Waterhouse's Office of Government Services in Washington, D.C., for five years when the partners in that office proposed her as a candidate for partnership. Of the 662 partners at the firm at that time, 7 were women. Of the 88 persons proposed for partnership that year, only 1—Hopkins—was a woman. Forty-seven of these candidates were admitted to the partnership, 21 were rejected, and 20—including Hopkins—were "held" for reconsideration the following year.[2]

Thirteen of the 32 partners who had submitted comments on Hopkins supported her

bid for partnership. Three partners recommended that her candidacy be placed on hold, eight stated that they did not have an informed opinion about her, and eight recommended that she be denied partnership.

In a jointly prepared statement supporting her candidacy, the partners in Hopkins' office showcased her successful 2-year effort to secure a $25 million contract with the Department of State, labeling it "an outstanding performance" and one that Hopkins carried out "virtually at the partner level." Despite Price Waterhouse's attempt at trial to minimize her contribution to this project, Judge Gesell specifically found that Hopkins had "played a key role in Price Waterhouse's successful effort to win a multi-million dollar contract with the Department of State. Indeed, he went on, "[n]one of the other partnership candidates at Price Waterhouse that year had a comparable record in terms of successfully securing major contracts for the partnership."

The partners in Hopkins' office praised her character as well as her accomplishments, describing her in their joint statement as "an outstanding professional" who had a "deft tough", a "strong character, independence and integrity." Clients appear to have agreed with these assessments. At trial, one official from the State Department described her as "extremely competent, intelligent," "strong and forthright, very productive, energetic and creative." Another high-ranking official praised Hopkins' decisiveness, broadmindedness, and "intellectual clarity"; she was, in his words, "a stimulating conversationalist." Evaluations such as these led Judge Gesell to conclude that Hopkins "had no difficulty dealing with clients and her clients appear to have been very pleased with her work" and that she "was generally viewed as a highly competent project leader who worked long hours, pushed vigorously to meet deadlines and demanded much from the multidisciplinary staffs with which she worked."

On too many occasions, however, Hopkins'

aggressiveness apparently spilled over into abrasiveness. Staff members seem to have borne the brunt of Hopkins' brusqueness. Long before her bid for partnership, partners evaluating her work had counseled her to improve her relations with staff members. Although later evaluations indicated an improvement, Hopkins' perceived shortcomings in this important area eventually doomed her bid for partnership. Virtually all of the partners' negative remarks about Hopkins—even those of partners supporting her—had to do with her "interpersonal skills." Both "[s]upporters and opponents of her candidacy," stressed Judge Gesell, "indicated that she was sometimes overly aggressive, unduly harsh, difficult to work with and impatient with staff."

There were clear signs, though, that some of the partners reacted negatively to Hopkins' personality because she was a woman. One partner described her as "macho"; another suggested that she "overcompensated for being a woman"; a third advised her to take "a course at charm school." Several partners criticized her use of profanity; in response, one partner suggested that those partners objected to her swearing only "because it[']s a lady using foul language." Another supporter explained that Hopkins "ha[d] matured from a tough-talking somewhat masculine hard-nosed mgr to an authoritative, formidable, but much more appealing lady ptr candidate." But it was the man who, as Judge Gesell found, bore responsibility for explaining to Hopkins the reasons for the Policy Board's decision to place her candidacy on hold who delivered the coup de grace: in order to improve her chances for partnership, Thomas Beyer advised, Hopkins should "walk more femininely, talk more femininely, dress more femininely, wear make-up, have her hair styled, and wear jewelry."

Dr. Susan Fiske, a social psychologist and Associate Professor of Psychology at Carnegie-Mellon University, testified at trial that the partnership selection process at Price Waterhouse was likely to be influenced by sex stereotyping. Her testimony focused not only on the overtly sex-based comments of partners but also on gender-neutral remarks, made by partners who knew Hopkins only slightly, that were intensely critical of her. One partner, for example, baldly stated that Hopkins was "universally disliked" by staff and another described her as "consistently annoying and irritating"; yet these were people who had had very little contact with Hopkins. According to Fiske, Hopkins' uniqueness (as the only woman in the pool of candidates) and the subjectivity of the evaluations made it likely that sharply critical remarks such as these were the product of sex stereotyping—although Fiske admitted that she could not say with certainty whether any particular comment was the result of stereotyping. Fiske based her opinion on a review of the submitted comments, explaining that it was commonly accepted practice for social psychologists to reach this kind of conclusion without having met any of the people involved in the decisionmaking process.

In previous years, other female candidates for partnership also had been evaluated in sex-based terms. As a general matter, Judge Gesell concluded, "[c]andidates were viewed favorably if partners believed they maintained their femin[in]ity while becoming effective professional mangers"; in this environment, "[t]o be identified as a 'women's lib[b]er' was regarded as [a] negative comment." In fact, the judge found that in previous years "[o]ne partner repeatedly commented that he could not consider any woman seriously as a partnership candidate and believed that women were not even capable of functioning as senior manager—yet the firm took no action to discourage his comments and recorded his vote in the overall summary of the evaluations.

Judge Gesell found that Price Waterhouse legitimately emphasized interpersonal skills in its partnership decisions, and also found that the firm had not fabricated its complaints about Hopkins' interpersonal skills as a pretext for discrimination. Moreover, he concluded, the firm did not give decisive emphasis to such traits only because Hopkins was a woman; although there were male candidates who lacked these skills but who were admitted to partnership, the judge found that these candidates possessed other, positive traits that Hopkins lacked.

The judge went on to decide, however, that some of the partners' remarks about Hopkins stemmed from an impermissibly cabined view of the proper behavior of women, and that Price Waterhouse had done nothing to disavow reliance on such comments. He held that Price Waterhouse had unlawfully discriminated against Hopkins on the basis of sex by consciously giving credence and effect to partners' comments that resulted from sex stereotyping. Noting that Price Waterhouse could avoid equitable relief by proving by clear and convincing evidence that it would have placed Hopkins' candidacy on hold even absent this discrimination, the judge decided that the firm had not carried this heavy burden.

The Court of Appeals affirmed the District Court's ultimate conclusion, but departed from its analysis in one particular; it held that even if a plaintiff proves by clear and convincing evidence, that it would have made the same decision in the absence of discrimination. Under this approach, an employer is not deemed to have violated Title VII if it proves that it would have made the same decision in the absence of an impermissible motive, whereas under the District Court's approach, the employer's proof in that respect only avoids equitable relief. We decide today that the Court of Appeals had the better approach, but that both courts erred in requiring the employer to make its proof by clear and convincing evidence.

II.

The specification of the statement of causation under Title VII is a decision about the kind of conduct that violates that statute. According to Price Waterhouse, an employer violates Title VII only if it gives decisive consideration to an employee's gender, race, national origin, or religion in making a decision that affects that employee. On Price Waterhouse's theory, even if a plaintiff shows that her gender played a part in an employment decision, it is still her burden to show that the decision would have been different if the employer had not discriminated. In Hopkins' view, on the other hand, an employer violates the statute whenever it allows one of these attributes to play any part in an employment decision. Once a plaintiff shows that this occurred, according to Hopkins, the employer's proof that it would have made the same decision in the absence of discrimination can serve to limit equitable relief but not to avoid a finding of liability. We conclude, that, as often happens, the truth lies somewhere in-between.

A.

In passing Title VII, Congress made the simple but momentous announcement that sex, race, religion, and national origin are not relevant to the selection, evaluation, or compensation of employees. Yet, the statute does not purport to limit the other qualities and characteristics that employers *may* take into account in making employment decision. The converse, therefore, of "for cause" legislation, Title VII eliminates certain bases for distinguishing among employees while otherwise preserving employers' freedom of choice. This balance between employee rights and employer prerogatives turns out to be decisive in the case before us.

Congress' intent to forbid employers to

take gender into account in making employment decisions appears on the face of the statute. In now-familiar language, the statute forbids an employer to "fail or refuse to hire or to discharge any individual, or otherwise to discriminate with respect to this compensation, terms, conditions, or privileges of employment," or to "limit, segregate, or classify his employees or applicants for employment in any way which would deprive or tend to deprive any individual of employment opportunities or otherwise adversely affect his status as an employee, *because* of such individual's . . . sex." We take these words to mean that gender must be irrelevant to employment decisions. To construe the words "because of" as colloquial shorthand for "but-for causation," as does Price Waterhouse, is to misunderstand them.

We need not leave our commonsense at the doorstep when we interpret a statute. It is difficult for us to imagine that, in the simple words "because of," Congress meant to obligate a plaintiff to identify the precise causal role played by legitimate and illegitimate motivations in the employment decision she challenges. We conclude, instead, that Congress meant to obligate her to prove that the employer relied upon sex-based considerations in coming to its decision.

Our interpretation of the words "because of" also is supported by the fact that Title VII does identify one circumstance in which an employer may take gender into account in making an employment decision, namely, when gender is a "bona fide occupational qualification [(BFOQ)] reasonably necessary to the normal operation of th[e] particular business or enterprise." The only plausible inference to draw from this provision is that, in all other circumstances, a person's gender may not be considered in making decisions that affect her. Indeed, Title VII even forbids employers to make gender an indirect stumbling block to employment opportunities. An employer may not, we have held, condition employment opportunities on the satisfaction of facially neutral tests or qualifications that have a disproportionate, adverse impact on members of protected groups when those tests or qualifications are not required for performance of the job.

To say that an employer may not take gender into account is not, however, the end of the matter, for that describes only one aspect of Title VII. The other important aspect of the statute is its preservation of an employer's remaining freedom of choice. We conclude that the preservation of this freedom means that an employer shall not be liable if it can prove that, even if it had not taken gender into account, it would have come to the same decision regarding a particular person. The statute's maintenance of employer prerogatives is evident from the statute itself and from its history, both in Congress and in this Court.

To begin with, the existence of the BFOQ exception shows Congress' unwillingness to require employers to change the very nature of their operations in response to the statute. And our emphasis on "business necessity" in disparate-impact cases, see Watson and Griggs, and on "legitimate, nondiscriminatory reason[s]" in disparate-treatment cases, see *McDonnell Douglas Corp. v. Green*, 411 U.S. 792, 802, 36 L.Ed 2d 668, 93 S. Ct 1817 (1973); *Texas Dept. of Community Affairs v. Burdine*, 450 U.S. 248, 67 L.Ed 2d 207, 101 S. Ct 1089 (1981), results from our awareness of Title VII's balance between employee rights and employer prerogatives. The broad, overriding interest, shared by employer, employee, and consumer, is efficient and trustworthy workmanship assured through fair and racially neutral employment and personnel decision. In the implementation of such decision, it is abundantly clear that Title VII tolerates no racial discrimination, subtle or otherwise.

When an employer ignored the attributes

enumerated in the statute, Congress hoped, it naturally would focus on the qualifications of the applicant or employee. The intent to drive employers to focus on qualifications rather than on race, religion, sex, or national origin is the theme of a good deal of the statute's legislative history.

Any other legislators made statements to a similar effect, we see no need to set out each remark in full here. The central point is this: while an employer may not take gender into account in making an employment decision (except in those very narrow circumstances in which gender is a BFOQ), it is free to decide against a woman for other reasons. We think these principles require that, once a plaintiff in a Title VII case shows that gender played a motivating part in an employment decision, the defendant may avoid a finding of liability only by proving that it would have made the same decision even if it had not allowed gender to play such a role. This balance of burdens is the direct result of Title VII's balance of rights.

Price Waterhouse's claim that the employer does not bear any burden of proof (if it bears one at all) until the plaintiff has shown "substantial evidence that Price Waterhouse's explanation for failing to promote Hopkins was not the 'true reason' for its action" merely restates its argument that the plaintiff in a mixed-motives case must squeeze her proof into Burdine's framework. Where a decision was the product of a mixture of legitimate and illegitimate motives, however, it simply makes no sense to ask whether the legitimate reason was *the 'true reason.'*

Oblivious to this last point, the dissent would insist that Burdine's framework (450 U.S., 67 L.Ed 2d, 101 S. Ct.) perform work that it was never intended to perform. It would require a plaintiff who challenges an adverse employment decision in which both legitimate and illegitimate considerations played a part to pretend that the decision, in fact, stemmed from a single source-for the

premise of Burdine is that *either* a legitimate *or* an illegitimate set of considerations led to the challenged decision. To say that Burdine's evidentiary scheme will not help us decide a case admittedly involving both kinds of considerations is not to cast aspersions on the utility of that scheme in the circumstances for which it was designed.

B.

In deciding as we do today, we do not traverse new ground. We have in the past confronted Title VII cases in which an employer has used an illegitimate criterion to distinguish among employees, and have held that it is the employer's burden to justify decisions resulting from that practice. When an employer has asserted that gender is a bona fide occupational qualification within the meaning of §703(e), for example, we have assumed that it is the employer who must show why it must use gender as a criterion in employment. In a related context, although the Equal Pay Act expressly permits employers to pay different wages to women where disparate pay is the result of a "factor other than sex," we have decided that it is the employer, not the employee, who must prove that the actual disparity is not sex-linked. Finally, some courts have held that under Title VII as amended by the Pregnancy Discrimination Act, it is the employer who has the burden of showing that its limitations on the work that it allows a pregnant woman to perform are necessary in light of her pregnancy. As these examples demonstrate, our assumption always has been that if an employer allows gender to affect its decisionmaking process, then it must carry the burden of justifying its ultimate decision. We have not in the past required women whose gender has proved relevant to an employment decision to establish the negative proposition that they would not have been subject to that decision had they been men, and we do not do so today.

We have reached a similar conclusion in other contexts where the law announces that a certain characteristic is irrelevant to the allocation of burdens and benefits. The plaintiff claimed that he had been discharged as a public school teacher for exercising his free-speech rights under the First Amendment. Because we did not wish to "place an employee in a better position as a result of the exercise of constitutionally protected conduct than he would have occupied had he done nothing," we concluded that such an employee "ought not to be able, by engaging in such conduct, to prevent his employer from assessing his performance record and reaching a decision not to rehire on the basis of that record." We therefore held that once the plaintiff had shown that his constitutionally protected speech was a "substantial" or "motivating factor" in the adverse treatment of him by his employer, the employer was obligated to prove "by a preponderance of the evidence that it would have reached the same decision as to [the plaintiff] even in the absence of the protected conduct."

We have, in short, been here before. Each time, we have concluded that the plaintiff who shows that an impermissible motive played a motivating part in an adverse employment decision has thereby placed upon the defendant the burden to show that it would have made the same decision in the absence of the unlawful motive. Our decision today treads this well-worn path.

C.

In saying that gender played a motivating part in an employment decision, we mean that, if we asked the employer at the moment of the decision what its reasons were and if we received a truthful response, one of those reasons would be that the applicant or employee was a woman. In the specific context of sex stereotyping, an employer who acts on the basis of a belief that a woman cannot be

aggressive, or that she must not be, has acted on the basis of gender.

Although the parties do not overtly dispute this last proposition, the placement by Price Waterhouse of "sex stereotyping" in quotation marks throughout its brief seems to us an insinuation either that such stereotyping was not present in this case or that it lacks legal relevance. We reject both possibilities. As to the existence of sex stereotyping in this case, we are not included to quarrel with the District Court's conclusion that a number of the partners' comments showed sex stereotyping at work. As for the legal relevance of sex stereotyping, we are beyond the day when an employer could evaluate employees by assuming or insisting that they matched the stereotype associated with their group, for "[i]n forbidding employers to discriminate against individuals because of their sex, Congress intended to strike at the entire spectrum of disparate treatment of men and women resulting from sex stereotypes." An employer who objects to aggressiveness in women but whose positions require this trait places women in an intolerable and impermissible Catch 22: out of a job if they behave aggressively and out of a job if they don't. Title VII lifts women out of this bind.

Remarks at work that are based on sex stereotypes do not inevitably prove that gender played a part in a particular employment decision. The plaintiff must show that the employer actually relied on her gender in making its decision. In making this showing, stereotyped remarks can certainly be evidence that gender played a part. In any event, the stereotyping in this case did not simply consist of stray remarks. On the contrary, Hopkins proved that Price Waterhouse invited partners to submit comments; that some of the comments stemmed from sex stereotypes; that an important part of the Policy Board's decision on Hopkins was an assessment of the submitted comments; and that Price Waterhouse in no way disclaimed reliance on the sex-linked evaluations. This is not, as Price Waterhouse suggests, "discrimination in the air," rather, it is, as Hopkins puts it, "discrimination brought to ground and visited upon" an employee. By focusing on Hopkins' specific proof, however, we do not suggest a limitation on the possible ways of proving that stereotyping played a motivating role in an employment decision, and we refrain from deciding here which specific facts, "standing alone," would or would not establish a plaintiff's case, since such a decision is unnecessary in this case.

As to the employer's proof, in most cases, the employer should be able to present some objective evidence as to its probable decision in the absence of an impermissible motive. Moreover, proving "that the same decision would have been justified . . . is not the same as proving that the same decision would have been made." An employer may not, in other words, prevail in a mixed-motives case by offering a legitimate and sufficient reason for its decision if that reason did not motivate it at the time of the decision. Finally, an employer may not meet its burden in such a case by merely showing that at the time of the decision it was motivated only in part by a legitimate reason. The very premise of a mixed-motives case is that a legitimate reason was present, and indeed, in this case, Price Waterhouse already has made this showing by convincing Judge Gesell that Hopkins' interpersonal problems were a legitimate concern. The employer instead must show that its legitimate reason, standing alone, would have induced it to make the same decision.

III.

The courts below held that an employer who has allowed a discriminatory impulse to play a motivating part in an employment decision must prove by clear and convincing evidence that it would have made the same decision in the absence of discrimination. We are persuaded that the better rule is that the employer must make this showing by a preponderance of the evidence.

Conventional rules of civil litigation generally apply in Title VII cases, and one of these rules is that parties to civil litigation need only prove their case by a preponderance of the evidence. Exceptions to this standard are uncommon, and in fact are ordinarily recognized only when the government seeks to take unusual coercive action—action more dramatic than entering an award of money damages or other conventional relief—against an individual.

It is true, as Hopkins emphasized, that we have noted the "clear distinction between the measure of proof necessary to establish the fact that petitioner had sustained some damage and the measure of proof necessary to enable the jury to fix the amount." Likewise, an EEOC regulation does require federal agencies proved to have violated Title VII to show by clear and convincing evidence that an individual employee is not entitled to relief. And finally, it is true that we have emphasized the importance of make-whole relief for victims of discrimination. Yet each of these sources deals with the proper determination of relief rather than with the initial finding of liability. This is seen most easily in the EEOC's regulation, which operated only after an agency or the EEOC has found that "an employee of the agency was discriminated against." Because we have held that, by proving that it would have made the same decision in the absence of discrimination, the employer may avoid a finding of liability altogether and not simply avoid certain equitable relief, these authorities do not help Hopkins to show why we should elevate the standard of proof for an employer in this position.

Although Price Waterhouse does not concretely tell us how its proof was preponderant even if it was not clear and convincing, this general claim is implicit in its request for the less stringent standard. Since the lower courts required Price Waterhouse to make its proof by clear and convincing evidence, they did not determine whether Price Waterhouse had proved by a preponderance of the evidence that it would have placed Hopkins' candidacy on hold even if it had not permitted sex-linked evaluations to play a part in the decision-making process. Thus, we shall remand this case so that that determination can be made.

IV.

The District Court found that sex stereotyping "was permitted to play a part" in the evaluation of Hopkins as a candidate for partnership. Price Waterhouse disputes both that stereotyping occurred and that it played any part in the decision to place Hopkins' candidacy on hold. In the firm's view, in other words, the District Court's factual conclusions are clearly erroneous. We do not agree.

In finding that some of the partners' comments reflected sex stereotyping, the District Court relied in part on Dr. Fiske's expert testimony. Without directly impugning Dr. Fiske's credentials or qualifications, Price Waterhouse insinuates that a social psychologist is unable to identify sex stereotyping in evaluations without investigating whether those evaluations have a basis in reality. This argument comes too late. At trial, counsel for Price Waterhouse twice assured the court that he did not question Dr. Fiske's expertise and failed to challenge the legitimacy of their discipline. Without contradiction from Price Waterhouse, Fiske testified that she discerned sex stereotyping in the partners' evaluations of Hopkins and she further explained that it was part of her business to identify stereotyping in written documents. We are not inclined to accept petitioner's belated and unsubstantiated characterization of Dr. Fiske's testimony as "gossamer evidence" based only on "intuitive hunches" and of her detection of sex stereotyping as "intuitively divined."

Indeed, we are tempted to say that Dr. Fiske's expert testimony was merely icing on Hopkins' cake. It takes no special training to discern sex stereotyping in a description of an aggressive female employee as requiring "a course at charm school." Nor, turning to Thomas Beyer's memorable advice to Hopkins, does it require expertise in psychology to know that, if an employee's flawed "interpersonal skills" can be corrected by a soft-hued suit or new shade of lipstick, perhaps it is the employee's sex and not her interpersonal skills that has drawn the criticism.

Price Waterhouse also charges that Hopkins produced no evidence that sex stereotyping played a role in the decision to place her candidacy on hold. As we have stressed, however, Hopkins showed that the partnership solicited evaluations from all of the firm's partners; that it generally relied very heavily on such evaluations in making its decision; that some of the partners' comments were the product of stereotyping; and that the firm in no way disclaimed reliance on those particular comments, either in Hopkins' case or in the past. Certainly a plausible—and, one might say, inevitable—conclusion to draw from this set of circumstances is that the Policy Board in making its decision did in fact take into account all of the partners' comments, including the comments that were motivated by stereotypical notions about women's proper deportment.

Nor is the finding that sex stereotyping played a part in the Policy Board's decision undermined by the fact that many of the suspect comments were made by supporters rather than detractors of Hopkins. A negative comment, even when made in the context of a generally favorable review, nevertheless may influence the decisionmaker to think less highly of a candidate; the Policy Board, in fact, did not simply tally the "yes's" and "no's" regarding the candidate, but carefully reviewed the content of the submitted comments. The additional suggestion that the comments were made by "persons outside the decisionmaking chain"—and therefore could not have harmed Hopkins—simply ignore the critical role that partners' comments played in the Policy Board's partnership decisions.

Price Waterhouse appears to think that we cannot affirm the factual findings of the trial court without deciding that, instead of being overbearing and aggressive and curt, Hopkins is in fact kind and considerate and patient. If this is indeed its impression, petitioner misunderstands the theory on which Hopkins prevailed. The District Judge acknowledged that Hopkins' conduct justified complaints about her behavior as a senior manager. But he also concluded that the reactions of at least some of the partners were reactions to her as a woman manager. Where an evaluation is based on a subjective assessment of a person's strengths and weaknesses, it is simply not true that each evaluator will focus on, or even mention, the same weaknesses. Thus, even if we knew that Hopkins had "personality problems," this would not tell us that the partners who cast their evaluations of Hopkins in sex-based terms would have criticized her as sharply (or criticized her at all) if she had been a man. It is not our job to review the evidence and decide that the negative reactions to Hopkins were based on reality; our perception of Hopkins' character is irrelevant. We sit not to determine whether Ms. Hopkins is nice, but to decide whether the partners reacted negatively to her personality because she is a woman.

V.

We hold that when a plaintiff in a Title VII case proves that her gender played a motivating part in an employment decision, the de-

fendant may avoid a finding of liability only by proving by a preponderance of the evidence that it would have made the same decision even if it had not taken the plaintiff's gender into account. Because the courts below erred by deciding that the defendant must make this proof by clear and convincing evidence, we reverse the Court of Appeals' judgment against Price Waterhouse on liability and remand the case to that court for further proceedings.

It is so ordered.

OPINION OF JUSTICE WHITE

Justice White, concurring in the judgment.

In my view, to determine the proper approach to causation in this case, we need look only to the Court's opinion in *Mt. Healthy City School District Bd. of Ed. v. Doyle*, 429 U.S. 274, 50 L.Ed 2d 471, 97 S. Ct 568 (1977). In Mt. Healthy, a public employee was not rehired, in part because of his exercise of First Amendment rights and in part because of permissible considerations. The Court rejected a rule of causation that focused "solely on whether protected conduct played a part, 'substantial' or otherwise, in a decision not to rehire," on the grounds that such a rule could make the employee better off by exercising his constitutional rights than by doing nothing at all. Instead, the Court outlined the following approach:

> Initially, in this case, the burden was properly placed upon respondent to show that his conduct was constitutionally protected, and that his conduct was a "substantial factor" in the Board's decision not to rehire him. Respondent having carried that burden, however, the District Court should have gone on to determine whether the Board had shown by a preponderance of the evidence that it would have reached

the same decision as to respondent's reemployment even in the absence of the protected conduct.

It is not necessary to get into semantic discussion whether the Mt. Healthy approach is "but for" causation in another guise or creates an affirmative defense on the part of the employer to see its clear application to the issues before us in this case. As in Mt. Healthy, the District Court found that the employer was motivated by both legitimate and illegitimate factors. And here, as in Mt. Healthy, and as the Court now holds, Hopkins was not required to prove that the illegitimate factor was the only, principal, or true reasons for the petitioner's action. Rather, as Justice O'Connor states, her burden was to show that the unlawful motive was a substantial factor in the adverse employment action. The burden of persuasion then should have shifted to Price Waterhouse to prove "by a preponderance of the evidence that it would have reached the same decision . . . in the absence of" the unlawful motive.

The Court has made clear that "mixed motive" cases, such as the present one, are different from pretext cases such as McDonnell Douglas and Burdine. In pretext cases, "the issue is whether either illegal or legal motives, but not both, were the 'true' motives behind the decision." *NLRB v. Transportation Management Corp.*, 462 U.S. 393, 400 n. 5, 76 L.Ed 2d 667, 103 S. Ct 2469 (1983). In mixed motive cases, however, there is no one "true" motive behind the decision. Instead, the decision is a result of multiple factors, at least one of which is legitimate. It can hardly be said that our decision in this case is a departure from cases that are "inapposite."

Because the Court of Appeals required Price Waterhouse to prove by clear and convincing evidence that it would have reached the same employment decision in the absence of the improper motive, rather than

merely requiring proof by a preponderance of the evidence as in Mt. Healthy, I concur with the judgment reversing this case in part and remanding. With respect to the employer's burden, however, the plurality seems to require, at least in most cases, that the employer submit objective evidence that the same result would have occurred absent the unlawful motivation. In my view, however, there is no special requirement that the employer carry its burden by objective evidence. In a mixed motive case, where the legitimate motive found would have been ample grounds for the action taken, and the employer credibly testifies that the action would have been taken for the legitimate reasons alone, this should be ample proof. This would even more plainly be the case where the employer denies any illegitimate motive in the first place but the court finds that illegitimate, as well as legitimate, factors motivated the adverse action.

OPINION OF JUSTICE O'CONNOR

Justice O'Connor, concurring in the judgment.

I agree with the plurality that on the facts presented in this case, the burden of persuasion should shift to the employer to demonstrate by a preponderance of the evidence that it would have reached the same decision concerning Ann Hopkins' candidacy absent consideration of her gender. I further agree that this burden shift is properly part of the liability phase of the litigation. I thus concur in the judgment of the Court. My disagreement stems from the plurality's conclusions concerning the substantive requirement of causation under the statute and its broad statements regarding the applicability of the allocation of the burden of proof applied in this case. The evidentiary rule the Court adopts today should be viewed as a supplement to the careful framework established by our unanimous decision in *McDonnell Douglas Corp. v. Green*, 411 U.S. 792, 36 L.Ed 2d 668, 93 S. Ct 1817 (1973), and *Texas Dept. of Community Affairs v. Burdine*, 450 U.S. 248, 67 L.Ed 2d 207, 101 S. Ct 1089 (1981), for use in cases such as this one where the employer has created uncertainty as to causation by knowingly giving substantial weight to an impermissible criterion. I write separately to explain why I believe such a departure from the *McDonnell Douglas* standard is justified in the circumstances presented by this and like cases, and to express my views as to when and how the strong medicine of requiring the employer to bear the burden of persuasion on the issue of causation should be administered.

I.

Title VII provides in pertinent part: "It shall be an unlawful employment practice for an employer . . . to fail or refuse to hire or to discharge any individual, or otherwise to discriminate against any individual with respect to his compensation, terms, conditions, or privileges of employment, because of such individual's race, color, religion, sex, or national origin." 42 U.S.C. §2000e-2(a) [42 U.S.C.S. §2000e-2(a)] (emphasis added). The legislative history of Title VII bears out what its plain language suggests: a substantive violation of the statute only occurs when consideration of an illegitimate criterion is the "but-for" cause of an adverse employment action. The legislative history makes it clear that Congress was attempting to eradicate discriminatory actions in the employment setting, not mere discriminatory thoughts. Critics of the bill that became Title VII labeled it a "thought control bill," and argued that it created a "punishable crime that does not require an illegal external act as a basis for judgment." 100 CONG REC 7254 (1964).

The evidence of congressional intent as to which party should bear the burden of proof on the issue of causation is considerably less clear. No doubt, as a general matter, Congress assumed that the plaintiff in a Title VII action would bear the burden of proof on the elements critical to his or her case. But in the area of tort liability, from whence the dissent's "but-for" standard of causation is derived, the law has long recognized that in certain "civil cases" leaving the burden of persuasion on the plaintiff to prove "but-for" causation would be both unfair and destructive of the deterrent purposes embodied in the concept of duty of care. Thus, in multiple causation cases, where a breach of duty has been established, the common law of torts has long shifted the burden of proof to multiple defendants to prove that their negligent actions were not the "but-for" cause of the plaintiffs injury. The same rule has been applied where the effect of a defendant's tortious conduct combines with a force of unknown or innocent origin to produce the harm to the plaintiff.

Like common law of torts, the statutory employment "tort" created by Title VII has two basic purposes. The first is to deter conduct which has been identified as contrary to public policy and harmful to society as a whole. As we have noted in the past, the award of backpay to a Title VII plaintiff provides "the spur or catalyst which causes employers and unions to self-examine and to self-evaluate their employment practices and to endeavor to eliminate, so far as possible, the last vestiges" of discrimination in employment.

Both these goals are reflected in the elements of a disparate treatment action. There is no doubt that Congress considered reliance on gender or race in making employment decisions an evil in itself. Reliance on such factors is exactly what the threat of Title VII liability was meant to deter. While the main concern of the statute was with employment opportunity, Congress was certainly not blind to the stigmatic harm which comes from being evaluated by a process which treats one as an inferior by reason of one's race or sex. Where an individual disparate treatment plaintiff has shown by a preponderance of the evidence that an illegitimate criterion was a substantial factor in an adverse employment decision, the deterrent purpose of the statute has clearly been triggered. More importantly, as an evidentiary matter, a reasonable factfinder could conclude that absent further explanation, the employer's discriminatory motivation "caused" the employment decision. The employer has not yet been shown to be a violator, but neither is it entitled to the same presumption of good faith concerning its employment decisions which is accorded employers facing only circumstantial evidence of discrimination. Both the policies behind the statute, and the evidentiary principles developed in the analogous area of causation in the law of torts, suggest that at this point the employer may be required to convince the factfinder that, despite the smoke, there is no fire.

We have given recognition to these principles in our cases which have discussed the "remedial phase" of class action disparate treatment cases. Once the class has established that discrimination against a protected group was essentially the employer's "standard practice," there has been harm to the group and injunctive relief is appropriate. But as to the individual members of the class, the liability phase of the litigation is not complete. Because the class has already demonstrated that, as a rule, illegitimate factors were considered in the employer's decisions, the burden shifts to the employer "to demonstrate that the individual applicant was denied an employment opportunity for legitimate reasons."

The individual members of a class action treatment case stand in much the same position as Ann Hopkins here. There has been a strong showing that the employer has done exactly what Title VII forbids, but the connection between the employer's illegitimate motivation and any injury to the individual plaintiff is unclear. At this point it is proper to call upon the employer to show that despite consideration of illegitimate factors the individual plaintiff would not have been hired or promoted in any event hardly seems "unfair" or contrary to the substantive command of the statute. In fact, an individual plaintiff who has shown that an illegitimate factor played a substantial role in the decision in her case has probed *more* than the class member in a Teamsters type action. The latter receives the benefit of a burden shift to the defendant based on the *likelihood* that an illegitimate criterion was a factor in the individual employment decision.

Moreover, placing the burden on the defendant in this case to prove that the same decision would have been justified by legitimate reasons is consistent with our interpretation of the constitutional guarantee of equal protection. Like a disparate treatment plaintiff, one who asserts that governmental action violates the Equal Protection Clause must show that he or she is, "the victim of intentional discrimination."

We adhered to similar principles in *Arlington Heights v. Metropolitan Housing Corp.*, 429 U.S. 252, 50 L.Ed 2d 450, 97 S. Ct 555 (1977), a case which, like this one, presented the problems of motivation and causation in the context of a multimember decisionmaking body authorized to consider a wide range of factors in arriving at its decisions. In *Arlington Heights* a group of minority plaintiffs claimed that a municipal governing body's refusal to rezone a plot of land to allow for the construction of low-income integrated housing was racially motivated. On the issue of causation, we indicated that the plaintiff was not required.

To prove that the challenged action rested solely on racially discriminatory purposes. Rarely can it be said that a legislature of administrative body operating under a broad mandate made a decision motivated solely by a single concern, or even that a particular purpose was the "dominant" or "primary" one. In fact, it is because legislators and administrators are properly concerned with balancing numerous competing considerations that courts refrain from reviewing the merits of their decisions, absent a showing of arbitrariness of irrationality. But racial discrimination is not just another competing consideration. When there is a proof that a discriminatory purpose has been a motivating factor in the decision, this judicial deference is no longer justified.

If the strong presumption of regularity and rationality of legislative decisionmaking must give way in the face of evidence that race has played a significant part in a legislative decision, I simply cannot believe that Congress intended Title VII to accord *more* deference to a private employer in the face of evidence that its decisional process has been substantially infected by discrimination. Indeed, where a public employee brings a "disparate treatment" claim under 42 U.S.C. § 1983 [42 U.S.C.S. § 1983] and the Equal Protection Clause the employee is entitled to the favorable evidentiary framework of Arlington Heights.

II.

The dissent's summary of our individual disparate treatment cases to date is fair and accurate, and amply demonstrates that the rule we adopt today is at least a change in direction from some of our prior precedents. We have indeed emphasized in the past that in an individual disparate treatment action the plaintiff bears the burden of persuasion throughout the litigation. Nor have we confined the word "protect" to the narrow definition which the plurality attempts to pin on it today. McDonnell Douglas and Burdine

clearly contemplated that a disparate treatment plaintiff could show that the employer's proffered explanation for an event was not "the true reason" either because it *never* motivated the employer in its employment decisions or because it did not do so in a particular case. *McDonnell Douglas* and *Burdine* assumed that the plaintiff would bear the burden of persuasion as to both these attacks, and we clearly depart from that framework today. Such a departure requires justification, and its outlines should be carefully drawn.

First, *McDonnell Douglas* itself dealt with a situation where the plaintiff presented no direct evidence that the employer had relied on a forbidden factor under Title VII in making an employment decision. The prima facie case established there was not difficult to prove, and was based only on the statistical probability that when a number of potential causes for an employment decision are eliminated an inference arises that an illegitimate factor was in fact the motivation behind the decision. ("[T]he *McDonnell Douglas* formula does not require direct proof of discrimination.") In the face of this inferential proof, the employer's burden was deemed to be only one of production; the employer must articulate a legitimate reason for the adverse employment action. The plaintiff must then be given an "opportunity to demonstrate by competent evidence that the presumptively valid reasons for his rejection were in fact a coverup for a racially discriminatory decision."

Second, the facts of this case, and a growing number like it decided by the Courts of Appeals, convince me that the evidentiary standard I proposed is necessary to make real the promise of *McDonnell Douglas* that "[i]n the implementation of [employment] decisions, it is abundantly clear that Title VII tolerates no . . . discrimination, subtle or otherwise." In this case, the District Court found that a number of the evaluations of Ann Hopkins submitted by partners in the firm overtly referred to her failure to conform to certain gender stereotypes as a factor militating against her election to the partnership. The District Court further found that these evaluations were given "great weight" by the decision makers at Price Waterhouse. In addition, the District Court found that the partner responsible for informing Hopkins of the factors which caused her candidacy to be placed on hold, indicated that her "professional" problems would be solved if she would "walk more femininely, talk more femininely, wear make-up, have her hair styled, and wear jewelry." As the Court of Appeals characterized it, Ann Hopkins proved that Price Waterhouse "permitt[ed] stereotypical attitudes towards women to play a significant, though unquantifiable, role in its decision not to invite her to become a partner."

At this point Ann Hopkins had taken her proof as far as it could go. She had proved discriminatory input into the decisional process, and had proved that participants in the process considered her failure to conform to the stereotypes credited by a number of the decision makers had been a substantial factor in the decision. It is as if Ann Hopkins were sitting in the hall outside the room where partnership decisions being made. As the partners filed in to consider her candidacy, she heard several of them make sexist remarks in discussing her suitability for partnership. As the decision makers exited the room, she was told by one of those privy to the decision-making process that her gender was a major reason for the rejection of her partnership bid. One would be hard pressed to think of a situation where it would be more appropriate to require the defendant to show that its decision would have been justified by wholly legitimate concerns.

Moreover, there is mounting evidence in the decisions of the lower courts that respondent here is not alone in her inability to pinpoint discrimination as the precise cause of her injury, despite having shown that it played a significant role in the decisional process. Many of these courts, which deal with the evidentiary issues in Title VII cases on a regular basis, have concluded that placing the risk of nonpersuasion on the defendant in a situation where uncertainty as to causation has been created by its consideration of an illegitimate criterion makes sense as a rule of evidence and furthers the substantive command of Title VII. Particularly in the context of the professional world, where decisions are often made by collegial bodies on the basis of largely subjective criteria, requiring the plaintiff to prove that any one factor was the definitive cause of the decision makers' action may be tantamount to declaring Title VII inapplicable to such decisions.

Finally, I am convinced that a rule shifting the burden to the defendant where the plaintiff has shown that an illegitimate criterion was a "substantial factor" in the employment decision will not conflict with other congressional policies embodied in Title VII. Title VII expressly provides that an employer need not give preferential treatment to employees of applicants of any race, color, religion, sex, or national origin in order to maintain a work force in balance with the general population. "There is no requirement in Title VII that an employer maintain a racial balance in his work force. On the contrary, any deliberate attempt to maintain a racial balance, whatever such a balance may be, would involve a violation to Title VII because maintaining such a balance would require an employer to hire or refuse to hire on the basis of race." 110 CONG REC 7213 (1964).

I believe there are significant differences between shifting the burden or persuasion to the employer in a case resting purely on statistical proof as in the disparate impact setting and shifting the burden of persuasion in a case like this one, where an employer has demonstrated by direct evidence that an illegitimate factor played a substantial role in a particular employment decision.

In my view, in order to justify shifting the burden on the issue of causation to the defendant, a disparate treatment plaintiff must show by direct evidence that an illegitimate criterion was a substantial factor in the decision. As the Court of Appeals noted below, "[w]hile most circuits have not confronted the question squarely, the consensus among those that have is that once a Title VII plaintiff has demonstrated by direct evidence that discriminatory animus played a significant or substantial role in the employment decision, the burden shifts to the employer to show that the decision would have been the same absent discrimination." Requiring that the plaintiff demonstrate that an illegitimate factor played a substantial role in the employment decision identifies those employment situations where the deterrent purpose of Title VII is most clearly implicated. As an evidentiary matter, where a plaintiff has made this type of strong showing of illicit motivation, the factfinder is entitled to presume that the employer's discriminatory animus made a difference to the outcome, absent proof to the contrary from the employer. Where a disparate treatment plaintiff has made such a showing, the burden then rests with the employer to convince the trier of fact that it is more likely than not that the decision would have been the same absent consideration of the illegitimate factor. The employer need not isolate the sole cause for the decision, rather it must demonstrate that with the illegitimate factor removed from the calculus, sufficient business reasons would have induced it to take the same employment action. This evidentiary scheme essentially requires the employer to place the employee in the same position he or she would have occupied absent discrimination. If the employer fails to carry this burden, the factfinder is justified in concluding that the decision was made "because of" consideration of the illegitimate factor and the substantive standard for liability under the statute is satisfied.

In sum, because of the concerns outlined above, and because I believe that the deterrent purpose of Title VII is disserved by a rule which places the burden of proof on plaintiffs on the issue of causation in all circumstances, I would retain but supplement the framework we established in *McDonnell Douglas* and subsequent cases. First, the plaintiff must establish the *McDonnell Douglas prima facie* case by showing membership in a protected group, qualification for the job, rejection for the position, and that after rejection the employer continued to seek applicants of complainant's general qualification. The plaintiff should also present any direct evidence of discriminatory animus in the decisional process. The defendant should then present its case, including its evidence as to legitimate, nondiscriminatory reasons for the employment decision. As the dissent notes, under this framework, the employer "has every incentive to convince the trier of fact that the decision was lawful." Once all the evidence has been received, the court should determine whether the McDonnell Douglas or Price Waterhouse framework properly applies to the evidence before it. If the plaintiff has failed to satisfy the Price Waterhouse threshold, the case should be decided under the principles enunciated in *McDonnell Douglas* and *Burdine*, with the plaintiff bearing the burden of persuasion on the ultimate issue whether the employment action was taken because of discrimination. In my view, such a system is both fair and workable and it calibrates the evidentiary requirements demanded of the parties to the goals behind the statute itself.

In this case, I agree with the plurality that petitioner should be called upon to show that the outcome would have been the same if respondent's professional merit had been its only concern. On remand, the District Court should determine whether Price Waterhouse has shown by a preponderance of the evidence that if gender had not been part of the process, its employment decision concerning Ann Hopkins would nonetheless have been the same.

THE DISSENTING OPINION

Justice Kennedy, with whom The Chief Justice and Justice Scalia join, dissenting.

Today the Court manipulates existing and complex rules for employment discrimination cases in a way certain to result in confusion. Continued adherence to the evidentiary scheme established in McDonnell Douglas and Burdine is a wiser course than creation of more disarray in an area of the law already difficult for the bench and bar, and so I must dissent.

Before turning to my reasons for disagreement with the Court's disposition of the case, it is important to review the actual holding to today's decision. I read the opinions as establishing that in a limited number of cases Title VII plaintiffs, by presenting direct and substantial evidence of discriminatory animus, may shift the burden of persuasion to the defendant to show that an adverse employment decision would have been supported by legitimate reasons. The shift in the burden of persuasion occurs only where a plaintiff proves by direct evidence that an unlawful motive was substantial factor actually relied upon in making the decision.

Where the plaintiff makes the requisite showing, the burden that shifts to the employer is to show that legitimate employment considerations would have justified the decision without reference to any impermissible motive. The employer's proof on the point is to be presented and reviewed just as with any other evidentiary question: the Court does not accept the plurality's suggestion that an employer's evidence need be "objective" or otherwise out of the ordinary.

In sum, the Court alters the evidentiary framework of *McDonnell Douglas* and *Bur-*

dine for a closely defined set of cases. Although Justice O'Connor advances some thoughtful arguments for this change, I remain convinced that it is unnecessary and unwise. More troubling is the plurality's rationale for today's decision, which includes a number of unfortunate pronouncements on both causation and methods of proof in employment discrimination cases. To demonstrate the defects in the plurality's reasoning, it is necessary to discuss first, the standard of causation in Title VII cases, and second, the burden of proof.

I.

The plurality describes this as a case about the standard of *causation* under Title VII, but I respectfully suggest that the description is misleading. Much of the plurality's rhetoric is spent denouncing a "but-for" standard of causation. The theory of Title VII liability the plurality adopts, however, essentially incorporates the but-for standard. The importance of today's decision is not the standard of causation it employs, but its shift to the defendant of the burden of proof. The plurality's causation analysis is misdirected, for it is clear that, whoever bears the burden of proof on the issue, Title VII liability requires a finding of but-for causation.

The words of Title VII are not obscure. The part of the statute relevant to this case provides that:

It shall be an unlawful employment practice for an employer
"(1) to ante, at _____, 104 L.Ed 2d 279, fail or refuse to hire or to discharge any individual, or to discriminate against any individual with respect to his compensation, terms, conditions, or privileges of employment, because of such individual's race, color, religion, sex, or national origin." 42 U.S.C. § 2000e-2(a)(1) [42 U.S.C.S. § 2000e-2(a)(1)] (emphasis added).

By any normal understanding, the phrase "because of" conveys the idea that the motive in question made a difference to the outcome. We use the words this way in everyday speech. And assuming, as the plurality does, that we ought to consider the interpretive memorandum prepared by the statute's drafters, we find that this is what the words meant to them as well.

Our decisions confirm that Title VII is not concerned with the mere presence of impermissible motives; it is directed to employment decisions that result from those motives. The verbal formulae we have used in our precedents are synonymous with but-for causation. Thus we have said that providing different insurance coverage to male and female employees violates the statute by treating the employee "in a manner which but-for that person's sex would be different."

What we tern "but-for" cause is the least rigorous standard that is consistent with the approach to causation our precedents describe. If a motive is not a but-for cause of an event, then by definition it did not make a difference to the outcome. The event would have occurred just the same without it. Common law approaches to causation often require proof of but-for cause as a starting point toward proof of legal cause. The law may require more than but-for cause, for instance proximate cause, before imposing liability. Any standard less than but-for, however, simply represents a decision to impose liability without causation.

One of the principal reasons the plurality decision may sow confusion is that it claims Title VII liability is unrelated to but-for causation, yet it adopts a but-for standard once it has placed the burden of proof as to causation upon the employer. This approach conflates the question whether causation must be shown with the question of how it is to be shown. Because the plurality's theory of Title VII causation is ultimately consistent with a but-for standard, it might be said that my disagreement with the plurality's comments on but-for cause is simply academic. But since those comments seem to influence the decision, I turn now to that part of the plurality's analysis.

The plurality begins by noting the quite unremarkable fact that Title VII is written in the present tense. It is unlawful "to fail" or "to refuse" to provide employment benefits on the basis of sex, not "to have failed" or "to have refused" to have done so. The plurality claims that the present tense excludes a but-for inquiry as the relevant standard because but-for causation is necessarily concerned with a hypothetical inquiry into how a past event would have occurred absent the contested motivation. This observation, however, tells us nothing of particular relevance to Title VII or the cause of action it creates. I am unaware of any federal prohibitory statute that is written in the past tense. Every liability determination, including the novel one constructed by the plurality, necessarily is concerned with the examination of a past event. The plurality's analysis of verb tense serves only to divert attention from the causation requirement that is made part of the statute by the "because of" phrase. That phrase, I respectfully submit, embodies a rather simple concept that the plurality labors to ignore.

We are told next that but-for cause is not required, since the words "because of" do not mean "*solely* because of." No one contends, however, that sex must be the sole cause of a decision before there is a Title VII violation. This is a separate question from whether consideration of sex must be a cause of the decision. Under the accepted approach to causation that I have discussed, sex is a cause for the employment decision whenever, either by itself or in combination with other factors, it made a difference to the decision. Discrimination need not be the sole cause in order for liability to arise, but merely a necessary element of the set of factors that caused the decision, i.e., a but-for cause. The plurality seems to say that since we know the words "because of" do not mean "solely because of," they must not mean "because of" at all. This does not follow, as a matter of either semantics or logic.

The plurality's reliance on the "bona fide occupational qualification" (BFOQ) provisions of Title VII, 42 U.S.C. §2000e-2(e) [42 U.S.C.S. §2000e-2(e)], is particularly inapt. The BFOQ provisions allow an employer, in certain cases, to make an employment decision of which it is conceded that sex is the cause. That sex may be the legitimate cause of an employment decision where gender is a BFOQ is consistent with the opposite command that a decision caused by sex in any other case justifies the imposition of Title VII liability. This principle does not support, however, the novel assertion that a violation has occurred where sex made no difference to the outcome.

The most confusing aspect of the plurality's analysis of causation and liability is its internal inconsistency. The plurality begins by saying: "When . . . an employer considers both gender and legitimate factors at the time of making a decision, that decision was 'because of' sex and the other, legitimate considerations—even if we may say later, in the context of litigation, that the decision would have been the same if gender had not been taken into account." Yet it goes on to state that "an employer shall not be liable if it can prove that, even if it had not taken gender into account, it would have come to the same decision."

Given the language of the statute, these statements cannot both be true. Title VII unambiguously states that an employer who makes decisions "because of" sex has violated the statute. The plurality's first statement therefore appears to indicate that an employer who considers illegitimate reasons when making a decision is a violator. But the opinion then tells us that the employer who shows that the same decision would have been made absent consideration of sex is not a violator. If the second statement is to be reconciled with the language of Title VII, it must be that a decision that would have been the same absent consideration of sex was not made "because of" sex. In other words, there is no violation of the statute absent but-for causation. The plurality's description of the "same decision" test it adopts supports this view. The opinion state that "[a] court that finds for a plaintiff under this standard has effectively concluded that an illegitimate motive was a 'but-for' cause of the employment decision," and that this "is not an imposition of liability 'where sex made no difference to the outcome.'"

The plurality attempts to reconcile its internal inconsistency on the causation issue by describing the employer's showing as an "affirmative defense." This is nothing more than a label, and one not found in the language or legislative history of Title VII. Section 703(a)(1) is the statutory basis of the cause of action, and the Court is obligated to explain how its disparate treatment decisions are consistent with the terms of §703(a)(1), not with general themes of legislative history or with other parts of the statute that are plainly inapposite. While the test ultimately adopted by the plurality may not be inconsistent with the terms of §703(a)(1), the same cannot be said of the plurality's reasoning with respect to causation. As Justice O'Connor describes it, the plurality "reads the causation requirement out of the statute, and then replaces it with an 'affirmative defense.'" Labels aside, the import of today's decision is not that Title VII liability can arise without but-for causation, but that in certain cases it is not the plaintiff who must prove the presence of causation, but the defendant who must prove its absence.

II.

Once the plaintiff presents a prima facie case, an inference of discrimination arises. The employer must rebut the inference by articulating a legitimate nondiscriminatory reason for its action. The final burden of persuasion, however, belongs to the plaintiff. Burdine makes clear that the "ultimate burden of persuading the trier of fact that the defendant intentionally discriminated against the plaintiff remains at all times with the plaintiff." I would adhere to this established evidentiary framework, which provides the appropriate standard for this and other individual disparate treatment cases. Today's creation of a new set of rules for "mixed-motive" cases is not mandated by the statute itself. The Court's attempt at refinement provides limited practical benefits at the cost of confusion and complexity, with the attendant risk that the trier of fact will misapprehend the controlling legal principles and reach an incorrect decision.

The plurality is mistaken in suggesting that the plaintiff in a so-called "mixed motives" case will be disadvantaged by having to "squeeze her proof into Burdine's framework." As we acknowledged in *McDonnell Douglas*, "[t]he facts necessarily will vary in Title VII cases," and the specification of the prima facie case set forth there "is not necessarily applicable in every respect to differing factual situations." The framework was "never intended to be rigid, mechanized, or ritualistic." Burdine compels the employer to come forward with its explanation of the decision and permits the plaintiff to offer evidence under either of the logical methods for proof of discrimination. This is hardly a framework that confines the plaintiff; still less is it a justification for saying that the ultimate burden of proof must be on the employer in a mixed motives case. Burdine provides an orderly and adequate way to place both inferential and direct proof before the factfinder for a determination whether intentional discrimination has caused the employment decision. Regardless of the character of the evidence presented, we have consistently held that the ultimate burden "remains at all times with the plaintiff."

In contrast to the plurality, Justice O'Connor acknowledges that the approach adopted today is a "departure from the *McDonnell Douglas* standard." Although her reasons for supporting this departure are not without force, they are not dispositive. As Justice O'Connor states, the most that can be said with respect to the Title VII itself is that "nothing in the language, history, or purpose of Title VII prohibits adoption" of the new approach. Justice O'Connor also relies on analogies from the common law of torts, other types of Title VII litigation, and our equal protection cases. These analogies demonstrate that shifts in the burden of proof are not unprecedented in the law of torts or employment discrimination. Nonetheless, I believe continued adherence to the Burdine framework is more consistent with the statutory mandate.

The potential benefits of the new approach, in my view, are overstated. First, the Court makes clear that the Price Waterhouse scheme is applicable only in those cases where the plaintiff has produced direct and substantial proof that an impermissible motive was relied upon in making the decision at issue. The burden shift properly will be found to apply in only a limited number of employment discrimination cases. The application of the new scheme, furthermore, will make a difference only in a smaller subset of cases. The practical importance of the burden of proof is the "risk of nonpersuasion," and the new system will make a difference only where the evidence is so evenly balanced that the factfinder cannot say that either side's explanation of the case is "more likely" true.

Confusion in the application of dual burden-shifting mechanisms will be most acute in cases brought under §1981 or the Age Discrimination in Employment Act (ADEA), where courts borrow the Title VII order of proof for the conduct of jury trials. Perhaps such cases in the future will require a bifurcated trial, with the jury retiring first to make the credibility findings necessary to determine whether the plaintiff has proved that an impermissible factor played a substantial part in the decision, and later hearing evidence on the "same decision" or "pretext" issues. Alternatively, perhaps the trial judge will have the unenviable task of formulating a single instruction for the jury on all of the various burdens potentially involved in the case.

I do not believe the minor refinement in Title VII procedures accomplished by today's holding can justify the difficulties that will accompany it. Rather, I "remain confident that the *McDonnell Douglas* framework permits the plaintiff meriting relief to demonstrate intentional discrimination." Although the employer does not bear the burden of persuasion under *Burdine*, it must offer clear and reasonably specific reasons for the contested decision, and has every incentive to persuade the trier of fact that the decision was lawful. Further, the suggestion that the employer should bear the burden of persuasion due to superior access to evidence has little force in the Title VII context, where the liberal discovery rules available to all litigants are supplemented by EEOC investigatory files. In sum, the *Burdine* framework provides a "sensible, orderly way to evaluate the evidence in light of common experience as it bears on the critical question of discrimina-tion," and it should continue to govern the order of proof in Title VII disparate treatment cases.

The language of Title VII and our well-considered precedents require this plaintiff [Hopkins] to establish that the decision to place her candidacy on hold was made "because of" sex. Here the District Court found that the "comments of the individual partners and the expert evidence of Dr. Fiske do not prove an intentional discriminatory motive or purpose," and that "[b]ecause plaintiff has considerable problems dealing with staff and peers, the Court cannot say that she would have been elected to partnership if the Policy Board's decision had not been tainted by sexually based evaluations." Hopkins thus failed to meet the requisite standard of proof after a full trial. I would remand the case for entry of judgment in favor of Price Waterhouse.

NOTES

1. 409 U.S. _____, 104 L.Ed 2d 268, 109 S. Ct. [No. 87-1167]. Argued October 31, 1988. Decided May 1, 1989. Editors' Note: The text contained herein is a condensed and abbreviated summary of the aforecited Supreme Court decision to demonstrate and reflect on the latest thinking of the judicial system as to the definition of various discriminatory practices and various corrective approaches that are legally required to remedy those situations.

2. Before the time for reconsideration came, two of the partners in Hopkins' office withdrew their support for her, and the office informed her that she would not be reconsidered for partnership. Hopkins then resigned. Price Waterhouse does not challenge the Court of Appeals' conclusion that the refusal to repropose her for partnership amounted to a constructive discharge.

20

Multinational Corporate Ethics: Rights and Norms

Tom Donaldson[a]

Ethical issues stemming from multinational corporate activities frequently derive from a clash between the cultural attitudes in home and host countries. When standards for pollution, discrimination, and salary schedules appear lower in a multinational's host country than in the home country, should multinational managers always insist on home country standards? Or does using home standards imply a failure to respect cultural diversity and national integrity? Is a factory worker in Mexico justified in complaining about being paid three dollars an hour for the same work a U.S. factory worker, employed by the same company, is paid ten dollars? Is an asbestos worker in India justified in criticizing the lower standards of in-plant asbestos pollution maintained by a British multinational relative to standards in Britain, when the standards in question fall within Indian government guidelines and, indeed, are stricter than the standards maintained by other Indian asbestos manufacturers? Furthermore, what obligations, if any, do multinational is have to the people they affect indirectly? If a company buys land from wealthy land owners and turns it to the production of a cash crop, should it ensure that displaced farmers will avoid malnutrition?

This article proposes two concepts for the purpose of helping answering such questions: the notion of a fundamental international right, and that of an ethical algorithm for home country managers to use in arbitrating clashes between home and host country norms.

[a]This article has been excerpted by Thomas Donaldson from his book, *The Ethics of International Business* (Oxford University Press, 1989). Copyright, Oxford University Press, 1989. Excerpts reprinted by permission. For a more complete account of the arguments offered here, see especially chapters 5 and 6 of *The Ethics of International Business*.

328

RIGHTS

Cases such as the above would be easier to solve if we could specify minimal levels of conduct for multinational corporations. One concept helpful for doing so is that of a "right," for rights specify moral minimums. Hence, we will begin by conceiving the problem of assigning minimal duties to multinational corporations through the question, "What specific rights ought multinationals to respect?"

The flip side of a right typically is a duty.[1] This, in part, is what gives aptness to Joel Feinberg's well-known definition of a right as a "justified entitlement *to* something *from* someone.[2] It is the "from someone" part of the definition which reflects the assumption of a duty, for without a correlative obligation that attaches to some moral agent or group of agents, a right is weakened—if not beyond the status of a right entirely, then significantly. If we cannot say that a multinational corporation has a duty to keep the levels of arsenic low in the work place, then the worker's right not to be poisoned means little.

One list of rights receiving significant international attention is the "Universal Declaration of Human Rights.[3] However, it and the subsequent "International Covenant on Social, Economic and Cultural Rights" have spawned enormous controversy despite the fact that the Declaration was endorsed by virtually all of the important post World War II nations in 1948 as part of the affirmation of the U.N. Charter. This should prod us to construct a shorter, and less controversial list of rights to use in interpreting the obligations of multinationals.

Let us identify some of the items that should appear on a list of fundamental international rights, and lay the groundwork for interpreting their application to multinational corporations. We earlier defined a fundamental international right as satisfying three conditions and as a right which must be respected by all international actors, including nation-states, individuals, and corporations.[b] (We may abbreviate the expression "fundamental international right" to "fundamental right.") The first and second of these conditions concern the need for the right to protect something of great importance, and to be subject to substantial and recurrent threats. The third condition establishes limitations upon the duties associated with the prospective right. We have interpreted this third, "fairness-affordability" condition to mean that for a proposed right to qualify as a genuine right, all moral agents must be able under ordinary circumstances, and after having received any charitable aid due them, to assume the various burdens and duties that fairly fall upon them in honoring the right, and, further, that some "fair" arrangement exists for sharing the duties and costs among the various agents who must honor the right. This arrangement, moreover, must allow the possibility (although not necessarily the probability) that the right will be enjoyed by most people in most instances.

Though probably not complete, the following list contains items that appear to satisfy the three conditions and hence to qualify as fundamental international rights:

1. The right to freedom of physical movement

2. The right to ownership of property

3. The right to freedom from torture

4. The right to a fair trial

5. The right to nondiscriminatory treatment (freedom from discrimination on

[b]This sentence refers to material appearing in pp. 65–80 of *The Ethics of International Business* which was omitted from this article for reasons of space. Also omitted is a discussion of a "compatibility proviso" (pp. 77–81) which serves to eliminate the need for a rights pecking order.

the basis of such characteristics as race or sex.)

6. The right to physical security
7. The right to freedom of speech and association
8. The right to minimal education
9. The right to political participation
10. The right to subsistence

This is a minimal list. Some will wish to add entries such as the right to employment, to social security, or to a certain standard of living (say, as might be prescribed by Rawls' well-known "difference" principle). Disputes also may arise about the wording or overlapping features of some rights: for example, is not the right to freedom from torture included in the right to physical security, at least when the latter is properly interpreted? We shall not attempt to resolve such controversies here. Rather, the list as presented aims to suggest, albeit incompletely, a description of a *minimal* set of rights and to serve as a beginning consensus for evaluating international conduct. If I am correct, many would wish to add entries, but few would wish to subtract them.

The list has been generated by application of the three conditions. Each reader may decide whether the ten entries fulfill these conditions; in doing so, however, remember that in constructing the list one looks for *only* those rights that can be honored in some form by *all* international moral agents, including nation-states, corporations, and individuals. Hence, to consider only the issue of affordability, each candidate for a right must be tested for "affordability" by way of the lowest common denominator—by way, for example, of the poorest nation-state. If, even after receiving its fair share of charitable aid from wealthier nations, the state cannot "afford" kidney dialysis for all citizens who need it, then the right to receive dialysis from one's nation-state will not be a fundamental inter-

national right, although dialysis may constitute a bona fide right for those living within a specific nation-state, such as Japan.

Even though the hope for a definitive interpretation of the list of rights is an illusion, we can add specificity by clarifying the correlative duties entailed for different kinds of international actors. Because by definition the list contains items that all three major classes of international actors must respect, the next task is to spell out the correlative duties that fall upon our targeted group of international actors, namely, multinational corporations.

This task requires putting the "fairness-affordability" condition to a second, and different, use. This condition was first used as one of the three criteria generating the original list of fundamental rights. There it demanded satisfaction of a fairness-affordability threshold for each potential respecter of a right. For example, if the burdens imposed by a given right are not fair (in relation to other bona fide obligations and burdens) or affordable for nation-states, individuals, and corporations, then presumably the prospective right would not qualify as a fundamental international right.[c]

In its second use, the "fairness-affordability" condition goes beyond the judgment *that* a certain fairness-affordability threshold has been crossed to the determination of *what* the proper duties are for multina-

[c]It is worth noting that fundamental international rights are not the only type of rights. In addition there are legal rights and nation-specific moral rights. For example, the right to sue for damages under the doctrine of strict liability (where compensation can be demanded even without demonstrating negligence) is a legal right in the United States, although it would not qualify as a fundamental international right and is not a legal right in some other nation-states. Similarly, the right to certain forms of technologically advanced medical care such as CAT scanning for cancerous tumors may be a nation-specific moral right in highly industrialized countries (even when it is not guaranteed as a legal right) but could not qualify at this point in history as a fundamental international right.

tional corporations in relation to a given right. In its second use, in other words, the condition's notions of fairness and affordability are invoked to help determine *which* obligations properly fall upon corporations, in contrast to individuals and nation-states. The condition can help determine the correlative duties that attach to multinational corporations in their honoring of fundamental international rights.

As we look over the list of fundamental rights, it is noteworthy that except for a few isolated instances multinational corporations have probably succeeded in fulfilling their duty not to *actively deprive* persons of their enjoyment of the rights at issue. But correlative duties involve more than failing to actively deprive people of the enjoyment of their rights. Shue, for example, notes that three types of correlative duties are possible for any right: (1) to avoid depriving; (2) to help protect from deprivation; and (3) to aid the deprived.[4]

While it is obvious that the honoring of rights clearly imposes duties of the first kind, to avoid depriving directly, it is less obvious, but frequently true, that honoring them involves acts or omissions that help prevent the deprivation of rights. If I receive a note from Murder, Incorporated, and it looks like it means business, my right to security is clearly threatened. If a third party has relevant information which if revealed to the police would help protect my right, it is not a valid excuse for the third party to say that it is Murder, Incorporated, and not the third party, who wishes to kill me. Hence, honoring rights sometimes involves not only duties to *avoid depriving*, but to *help protect from deprivation* as well. Many critics of multinationals, interestingly enough, have faulted them not for the failure to avoid depriving, but for the failure to take reasonable protective steps.

The duties associated with rights often include ones from the third category, that of *aiding the deprived*, as when a government is bound to honor the right of its citizens to adequate nutrition by distributing food in the wake of a famine or natural disaster, or when the same government in the defense of political liberty is required to demand that an employer reinstate or compensate an employee fired for voting for a particular candidate in a government election.

Nonetheless, the honoring of at least some of the ten fundamental rights by multinational corporations requires only the adoption of the first class of correlative duties, that is, only the duty to avoid depriving. The correlative duties for corporations associated with some rights do not extend to protecting from deprivation or to aiding the deprived, because of the "fairness-affordability" condition discussed earlier.

It would be unfair, not to mention unreasonable, to hold corporations to the same standards of charity and love as human individuals. Nor can they be held to the same standards to which we hold civil governments for enhancing social welfare—since many governments are formally dedicated to enhancing the welfare of, and actively preserving the liberties of, their citizens. The profit-making corporation, in contrast, is designed to achieve an economic mission and as a moral actor possesses an exceedingly narrow personality. It is an undemocratic institution, furthermore, which is ill-suited to the broader task of distributing society's goods in accordance with a conception of general welfare. The corporation is an economic animal; and although its responsibilities extend beyond maximizing return on investment for shareholders, they are informed directly by its economic mission.

The "minimal/maximal" distinction mirrors the application of the "fairness-affordability" criterion; both imply that duties of the third class, to aid the deprived, do not fall upon for-profit corporations except, of course, in instances in which a corporation itself has done the depriving. Barring highly unusual circumstances[d], both distinctions imply that whatever duties corporations may have to aid the deprived are "maximal," not "minimal," duties. They are duties whose performance is not required as a condition of honoring fundamental rights or of preserving the corporation's moral right to exist.

The same considerations are relevant when sorting out the specific correlative duties of for-profit corporations according to the fariness-affordability criterion as when distinguishing between minimal and maximal duties. For example, it would be strikingly generous for multinationals to sacrifice some of their profits to buy milk, grain, and shelter for people in poor countries, yet it seems difficult to view this as one of their minimal moral requirements, since if anyone has such minimal obligations, it is the peoples' respective governments or, perhaps, better-off individuals. This is another way of saying that it is an unfair arrangement—and hence would conflict with the fairness-affordability criterion— to demand that multinational corporations, rather than national governments, shoulder such burdens. These are maximal, not minimal, duties, and a given corporation's failure

---

[d]Extraordinary conditions are capable of creating exceptions to the principle. For example, suppose that an earthquake devastates a host country and that thousands of local residents are dying for want of blood. Suppose further that the branch of a multinational corporation happens to possess the means to provide blood on a short-term basis and hence save thousands of lives, while the local government does not. In such an instance, the company may have a minimal duty to aid in the rescue: that is, it may have a correlative duty (correlative to the right of persons to physical security) to aid the deprived. Such exceptions have analogues in the realm of individual action. For example, normally we do not consider helping a particular person in distress a "perfect" duty—a duty that one must perform. Although we may regard helping people in distress a duty, we allow considerable discretion as to when and how the helping occurs. But if one happens to be walking on a lonely mountain trail and discovers a hiker who has slipped and clings precariously to a ledge, it becomes a perfect duty to help short of risking one's own personal security.

to observe maximal duties does not deprive that corporation of its moral right to exist. Furthermore, from our analysis of rights—in which we noted that rights impose demands of minimal conduct—it follows that when a corporation fails to discharge a maximal duty to aid the deprived, the failure does not necessarily constitute a violation of someone's *rights*. A corporation's failure to help provide housing for the urban poor of a host country is not a *rights* violation.

The same, however, is not true of the second class of duties, to protect from deprivation. these duties, like those in the third class, are also usually the province of government, but it sometimes happens that the rights to which they correlate are ones whose protection is a direct outcome of ordinary corporate activities. For example, the duties associated with protecting a worker from the physical threats of other workers may fall not only upon the local police, but also to some extent upon the employer. These duties, in turn, are properly viewed as correlative duties of the right—in this instance, the worker's right—to personal security. This will become clearer in a moment when we discuss the correlative duties of specific rights.

Table 20.1 lists correlative duties that reflect the second-stage application of the "fairness-affordability" condition to the earlier list of fundamental international rights. It indicates which rights do, and which do not, impose correlative duties of the three various kinds upon multinational corporations.

A word of caution should be issued for interpreting the table: the first type of correlative obligation, not depriving directly, is broader than might be supposed at first. It includes *cooperative* as well as individual actions. Thus, if a company has personnel policies that inhibit freedom of movement, or if a multinational corporation operating in South Africa cooperates with the government's restrictions on pass laws, then those companies may be said to actively deprive persons of

TABLE 20.1. Correlative Corporate Duties.

Fundamental Rights	Minimal Correlative Duties of Multinational Corporations		
	To avoid depriving	To help protect from deprivation	To aid the deprived
Freedom of physical movement	X		
Ownership of property	X		
Freedom from torture	X		
Fair trial	X		
Nondiscriminatory treatment	X	X	
Physical security	X	X	
Freedom of speech and association	X	X	
Minimal education	X	X	
Political participation	X	X	
Subsistence	X	X	

their right to freedom of movement, despite the fact that actions of other agents (in this example, the South African government) may be essential in effecting the deprivation.[5]

Still, the list asserts that at least six of the ten fundamental rights impose correlative duties upon corporations of the second kind, that is, to protect from deprivation.[e] What follows is a brief set of commentaries discussing sample applications of each of those six rights from the perspective of such correlative duties.

SAMPLE APPLICATIONS

Discrimination

The obligation to protect a person from deprivation of the right to freedom from discrimination properly falls upon corporations as well as governments insofar as everyday corporate activities directly affect compliance with that right. Because employees and pro-

spective employees possess the moral right not to be discriminated against on the basis of race, sex, caste, class, or family affiliation, it follows that multinational corporations have an obligation not only to refrain from discrimination, but in some instances to protect the right to nondiscriminatory treatment by establishing appropriate procedures. This may require, for example, offering notice to prospective employees about the company's policy of nondiscriminatory hiring, or educating lower-level managers about the need to reward or penalize on the basis of performance rather than irrelevant criteria.

Physical Security

The right to physical security similarly entails duties of protection. If a Japanese multinational corporation operating in Nigeria hires shop workers to run metal lathes in an assembly factory, but fails to provide them with protective goggles, then the corporation has failed to honor the workers' moral right to

---

[e]It is possible to understand even the remaining four rights as imposing correlative duties to protect from deprivation by imagining unusual or hypothetical scenarios. For example, if it happened that the secret police of a host country dictatorship regularly used corporate personnel files in their efforts to kidnap and torture suspected political opponents, then the corporation would be morally obligated to object to the practice and to

refuse to make their files available. Here the corporation would have a correlative duty to protect from deprivation the right not to be tortured. The list of rights identified as imposing correlative duties of protection was limited to six, however, on the basis of the fact that their protection is directly related to activities frequently undertaken by corporations in the real world.

physical security (no matter what the local law might decree). Injuries from such a failure would be the moral responsibility of the Japanese multinational despite the fact that the company could not be said to have inflicted the injuries directly.

Free Speech and Association

In the same vein, the duty to protect from deprivation the right of free speech and association finds application in the ongoing corporate obligation not to bar the creation of labor unions. Corporations are not obliged on the basis of human rights to encourage or welcome labor unions; indeed they may oppose them using all morally acceptable means at their disposal. But neither are they morally permitted to destroy them or prevent their emergence through coercive tactics; for to do so would violate their workers' international right to association. The corporation's duty to protect from deprivation the right to association, in turn, includes refraining from lobbying host governments for restrictions that would violate the right in question, and perhaps even to protesting host government measures that do violate it. The twin phenomena of commercial concentration and the globalization of business, both associated with the rise of the multinational, have tended to weaken the bargaining power of labor. Some doubt that labor is sharing as fully as it once did from the cyclical gains of industrial productivity. This gives special significance to the right of free speech and association.

Minimal Education

The correlative duty to protect the right of education may be illustrated through the prevalence of child labor in developing countries. A multinational in Central America is not entitled to hire an eight-year-old for full-time, permanent work because, among other reasons, doing so blocks the child's ability to receive a minimally sufficient education. What counts as a "minimally sufficient" education may be debated, and it seems likely, moreover, that the specification of the right to a certain level of education depends at least in part upon the level of economic resources available in a given country; nevertheless, it is reasonable to assume that any action by a corporation which has the effect of obstructing the development of a child's ability to read or write would be proscribed on the basis of rights.

Political Participation

Clearly in some instances corporations have failed to honor the correlative duty of protecting from deprivation the right to political participation. Fortunately, the most blatant examples of direct deprivation are becoming so rare as to be nonexistent. I am referring to cases in which companies directly aid in overthrowing democratic regimes, as when United Fruit Company allegedly contributed to overthrowing a democratically elected regime in Guatemala during the 1950s.

A few corporations continue indirectly to threaten this right by failing to protect it from deprivation, however. Some persist, for example, in supporting military dictatorships in countries in which democratic sentiment is growing, and others have blatantly bribed publicly elected officials with large sums of money. Perhaps the most famous example of the latter occurred in 1972 when the prime minister of Japan was bribed with 7 million dollars by the Lockheed Corporation to secure a lucrative Tri-Star Jet contract. Here, the complaint from the perspective of this right is not against bribes or "sensitive payments" in general, but to bribes in contexts where they serve to undermine a democratic system in which publicly elected officials hold a position of public trust.

Even the buying and owning of major segments of a foreign country's land and industry has been criticized in this regard. As Brian Barry has remarked, "The paranoia created in Britain and the United States by land purchases by foreigners (especially Arabs, it seems) should serve to make it understandable that the citizenry of a country might be unhappy with a state of affairs in which the most important natural resources are in foreign ownership." At what point would Americans regard their democratic control threatened by foreign ownership of U.S. industry and resources? At 20 percent ownership? At 40 percent? At 60 percent? At 80 percent? The answer is debatable, yet there seems to be some point beyond which the right to national self-determination, and national democratic control, is violated by foreign ownership of property.[6]

Subsistence

Corporations also have duties to protect from deprivation the right to subsistence. Consider the following scenario: a number of square miles of land in an underdeveloped country has been used for many years to grow beans. Further, the bulk of the land is owned, as it has been for centuries, by two wealthy landowners. Poorer members of the community work the land and receive a portion of the crop, a portion barely sufficient to satisfy nutritional needs. Next, imagine that a multinational corporation offers the two wealthy owners a handsome sum for the land, because it plans to grow coffee for export. Now *if* — and this, admittedly, is a crucial "if" — the corporation has reason to *know* that a significant number of people in the community will suffer malnutrition as a result, that is, if it has convincing reasons to believe that either those people will not be hired by the company or will not be paid sufficiently if they are hired, or that if forced to migrate to the city they will receive less than subsistence wages (wages inadequate to provide food and shel-

ter), then the multinational may be said to have failed in its correlative duty to protect individuals from the deprivation of the right to subsistence. This is true despite the fact that the corporation would never have stooped to take food from workers' mouths, and despite the fact that the malnourished will, in Samuel Coleridge's words, "die so slowly that none call it murder."

It may be that some of the fundamental rights on our list would not be embraced, at least as formulated here, by cultures different from ours. Would, for example, the Fulanis, a nomadic cattle culture in Nigeria, subscribe to this list with the same eagerness as the citizens of Brooklyn, New York? What list would they draw up if given the chance? And could we, or should we, try to convince them that our list is preferable? Would such a dialogue even make sense?[7]

I want to acknowledge that rights may vary in priority and style of expression from one cultural group to another. Yet I maintain a that the list itself is applicable to peoples even when those peoples would fail to compose an identical list. Clearly the Fulanis do not have to *accept* the ten rights in question for it to constitute a valid means of judging their culture. If the Fulanis treat women unfairly and unequally, then at least one fundamental international right remains unfulfilled in their culture, and their culture is so much the worse as a result.

Three specific rights are especially prone to varying cultural interpretation. These are the right to nondiscriminatory treatment (with special reference to the treatment of women), to political participation, and to the ownership of property. The latter two raise tendentious political issues for cultures with traditions of communal property and nondemocratic institutions. I wish simply to grant that the list has no pretensions to solve these age-old political problems. Though I happen to subscribe to a modified Lockean notion of property in which certain political systems incorporating social ownership violate individual rights, the right to property advanced in our list need not be so narrowly interpreted. It need not, in other words, rule out any instance of public ownership. For example, even primitive societies with communal property practices might be said to recognize a modified version of the right to property if those practices entail mutually agreed-upon, and fairly applied, rules of use, benefit, and liability. The account of rights in this chapter does not presume that each and every instance of public ownership violates the right to own property.

Even so, a point exists beyond which the public ownership of property violates the individual's right to own property. The point is passed when all land and movable property is owned by the state. Is it passed when a country nationalizes its phone system? Its oil industry? Is that point passed when a primitive culture refuses to subordinate family to individual property? Although it is clear that such questions are of decisive significance, it is equally clear that establishing such a point is a task that cannot be undertaken satisfactorily here.

The same holds for interpreting the right to political participation. I happen to affirm the merits of a democratic electoral system in which representatives are chosen on the basis of one person one vote; yet the list of rights should not be interpreted to demand a photocopy of U.S.-style democracy. For example, one might imagine a small, primitive culture utilizing other fair means for reflecting participation in the political process—other than a representative electoral system—and thereby satisfying the right to political participation.

RESOLVING CULTURAL CONFLICTS

Having specified a set of fundamental international rights and correlative duties for multinational corporations, let us turn to the task of arbitrating between host and home country norms. In particular let us investigate cases of the following form:

A multinational company adopts a corporate practice which is morally and/or legally permitted in the company's *host* country, but not in its *home* country.

We shall see that although an appeal to international rights (as specified above) frequently helps to interpret such conflicts, nonetheless, in certain key instances the strategy is ineffective. In turn, we shall design a conceptual test, or ethical algorithm, for multinationals to use in distinguishing justified from unjustified applications of standards. We shall see that the presence of lower standards in the host country does sometimes justify the multinational company's adopting the lower standards, but only in certain well-defined contexts. Consider two actual instances of the problem at issue.

Case A: A new American bank in Italy was advised by its Italian attorneys to file a tax return that misstated income and expenses and consequently grossly underestimated actual taxes due. The bank learned, however, that most other Italian companies regarded the practice as standard operating procedure and merely the first move in a complex negotiating process with the Italian internal revenue service. The bank initially refused to file a fallacious return on moral grounds and submitted an "American-style" return instead. But because the resulting tax bill was many times higher than what comparable Italian companies were asked to pay, the bank changed policy in later years to agree with "Italian style."[8]

Case B: In 1966 Charles Pettis, employee of an American multinational, became resident engineer for one of the company's projects in Peru: a 146 mile, $46 million project to build a highway across the Andes. Pettis soon discovered that Peruvian safety standards were far below those in the United States. The highway design called for cutting through mountains in areas where rock formations were unstable. Unless special precautions were taken, slides could occur. Pettis blew the whistle, complaining first to Peruvian government officials and later to U.S. officials. No special precautions were taken, with the result that thirty-one men were killed by landslides during the construction of the road. Pettis was fired for his trouble and had difficulty finding a job with another company.[9]

One may well decide that home country standards were mandatory in one of the cases just described, but not in the other. One may believe that despite conforming to Peruvian standards, host country precautions in Peru were unacceptable, and, in the former case, one may acknowledge that however inequitable and inefficient Italian tax mores may be, a decision to file "Italian-style" is permissible.

Thus, despite claims to the contrary, one must reject the simple dictum that whenever the practice violates a moral standard of the home country, it is impermissible for the multinational company. Arnold Berleant has argued that the principle of equal treatment endorsed by most U.S. citizens requires that U.S. corporations pay workers in less developed countries exactly the same wages paid to U.S. workers in comparable jobs (after appropriate adjustments are made for cost of living levels in the relevant areas). But most observers, including those from the less developed countries, believe this stretches the doctrine of equality too far in a way detrimental to host countries. By arbitrarily establishing U.S. wage levels as the bench mark for fairness one eliminates the role of the international market in establishing salary levels, and this in turn eliminates the incentive U.S. corporations have to hire foreign workers. If U.S. companies felt morally bound to pay Korean workers exactly the same wages U.S. workers receive for comparable work, they would not locate in Korea. Perhaps U.S. firms should exceed market rate for foreign labor as a matter of moral principle, but to pay strictly equal rates would freeze less developed countries out of the international labor market.[10] Lacking, then, a simple formula that says "the practice is wrong when it violates the home country's norms," one seems driven to undertake a more complex analysis of the types and degrees of responsibilities multinationals possess.

A rights-based approach recommends itself as one means for interpreting conflicts in international norms. For such a purpose, it is irrelevant whether the standards of the host country comply or fail with home country standards; what is relevant is whether they meet a universal, objective minimum. In the present context, the principal advantage of a rights-based approach is to establish a firm limit to appeals made in the name of host country laws and morals—at least when the issue is a clear threat to workers' safety. Clear threats such as in-plant asbestos pollution that exceeds levels recommended by independent scientific bodies are incompatible with employees' rights, especially their right not to be harmed. It is no excuse to cite lenient host country regulations or ill-informed host country public opinion.

But even as a rights-oriented approach clarifies a moral bottom line for extreme threats to workers' safety, it leaves obscure not only the issue of less extreme threats, but of harms other than physical injury. The language of rights and harm is sufficiently vague so as to leave shrouded in uncertainty a formidable list of issues crucial to multinationals. When refined by the traditions of a national legal system, the language of rights achieves a great precision. But left to wander among the concepts of general moral theory, the language proves less exact. Granted, the well-known dangers of asbestos call for recognizing the right to workers' safety no matter how broadly the language of rights is framed. But what are we to say of a less toxic pollutant? Is the level of sulphur-dioxide air pollution we should demand in a struggling nation, say one with only a few fertilizer plants working overtime to help feed its malnourished population, the same as the level we should demand in Portland, Oregon? Or, taking a more obvious case, should the maximal level of thermal pollution generated by a poor nation's electric power plants be the same as that in West Germany? Since thermal pollution raises the temperature of a given body of water, it lowers the capacity of the water to hold oxygen and depletes the number of "higher" fish species, such as salmon and trout. But whereas the trade-off between more trout and higher output is rationally made by the West German in favor of the trout, the situation is reversed for the citizen of Chad, Africa. This should not surprise us. It has long been recognized that many rights, such as the right to medical care, are dependent for their specification on the level of economic development of the country in question.

Nor is it clear how a general appeal to rights will resolve issues that turn on the interpretation of broad social practices. For example, in the Italian tax case mentioned earlier, the propriety of submitting an "Italian" versus "American-style" tax return hinges more on the appraisal of the value of honesty in a complex economic and social system, than it does on an appeal to inalienable rights.

What is needed, then, is a test for evaluating a given practice which is more comprehensive than a simple appeal to rights. In the end nothing short of a general moral theory working in tandem with an analysis of the foundations of corporate existence is needed.

For the multinational executive there is ultimately no escape from merging the ordinary canons of economic decision making, of profit maximization and market share, with the principles of basic moral theory. Yet even the existence of a comprehensive theory of corporate morality does not preclude the possibility of discovering lower-order moral concepts to clarify the moral intuitions already in use by multinational decision makers. Apart from the need for general theories of multinational conduct we need pragmatic aids to help managers bring into focus the ethical implications of views already held. This suggests the possibility of generating an interpretive mechanism, or algorithm, which multinational managers could use in determining the implications of their own moral views about cases stated in the following form: "Is the practice permissible for the multinational company when it is morally and/or legally permitted in the host country, but not in the home country?"

The first step in creating such an ethical algorithm is to isolate the distinct sense in which the norms of the home and host country conflict. If the practice is morally and/or legally permitted in the host country, but not in the home country, then the problem falls into one of two types of conflict:

1. The moral reasons underlying the host country's view that the practice is permissible refer to the host country's relative level of economic development.

2. The moral reasons underlying the host country's view that the practice is permissible are independent of the host country's relative level of economic development.

Let us call the conflict of norms described in number 1 a type 1 conflict. In such a conflict, an African country that permits slightly higher levels of thermal pollution from electric power generation plants, or a lower minimum wage than that prescribed in European countries, would do so not because higher standards are undesirable per se, but because its level of economic development requires an ordering or priorities. In the future, when it succeeds in matching European economic achievements, it may well implement the higher standards.

Let us call the conflict of norms described in number 2 a type 2 conflict. In such cases levels of economic development play no role. For example, low-level institutional nepotism, common in many developing countries, is justified not on economic grounds but on the basis of clan and family loyalty. Presumably the same loyalties will be operative even after the country has risen to economic success—as the nepotism prevalent in Saudi Arabia indicates. The Italian tax case also reflects an Italian cultural style, a penchant for personal negotiation and an unwillingness to formalize transactions, more than a strategy based on level of economic development.

The most important reason for distinguishing between the two types of conflict is that our powers of empathy are considerably greater in instances where merely economic welfare is at stake, than in one dominated by embedded cultural values. We are simply better able to imagine ourselves in the position of citizens making trade-offs between more trout and more fertilizer than the same citizens making deep-seated, Moslem- or Hindu-influenced judgments about the importance of clan and family loyalty. This, in turn, suggests the need to utilize a different method when clarifying ethical parameters of one type of case in contrast to the other.

The status of the conflict of norms between the home and host country, whether it is type 1 or 2, does not fix the truth value of the host country's claim that the practice is permissible. The practice may or may not be permissible whether the conflict is of type 1 or 2. This, however, is not to say that the truth value of the host country's claim is independent of the conflict's type status, for a different test is required to determine whether the practice is permissible when the conflict is of type 1 rather than type 2. In a type 1 dispute, the following formula is appropriate:

The practice is permissible if and only if the members of the home country would, under conditions of economic development relevantly similar to those of the host country, regard the practice as permissible.

Under this type 1 test, excessive levels of asbestos pollution would almost certainly not be tolerated by the members of the home country under relevantly similar economic conditions, whereas higher levels of thermal pollution would be. The test, happily, explains and confirms our initial moral intuitions.

Yet, when as in type 2 conflicts the dispute between the home and host country depends upon a fundamental difference of perspective, the step to equalize hypothetically the levels of economic development is useless. A different test is needed. In type 2 conflicts the opposing evils of ethnocentricism and ethical relativism must be avoided. A multinational must forgo the temptation to remake all societies in the image of its home society, while at the same time it must reject a relativism that conveniently forgets ethics when the payoff is sufficient. Thus, the task is to tolerate cultural diversity while drawing the line at moral recklessness.

Since in type 2 cases the practice is in conflict with an embedded norm of the home country, one should first ask whether the practice is necessary to do business in the host country, for if not, the solution clearly is to adopt some other practice that is permissible from the standpoint of the home country. If petty bribery of public officials is unnecessary for the business of the Cummins Engine Company in India, then the company is obliged to abandon such bribery. If, on the other hand, the practice proves necessary for business, one must next ask whether the practice constitutes a direct violation of a basic human right. Here the notion of a fundamental international right outlined earlier specifying a minimum below which corporate conduct should not fall, has special application. If Toyota, a Japanese company, confronts South African laws that mandate systematic discrimination against nonwhites, then Toyota must refuse to comply with the laws. Thus, in type 2 cases, the practice would be permissible if and only if the answer to both of the following questions is "no."

Is it possible to conduct business successfully in the host country without undertaking the practice?

Is the practice a clear violation of a fundamental international right?

What sorts of practice might satisfy both criteria of the type 2 test? Consider the practice of low-level bribery of public officials in some developing nations. In some South American countries, for example, it is impossible for any company, foreign or national, to move goods through customs without paying low-level officials a few dollars. Indeed, the salaries of such officials are sufficiently low that one suspects that they are set with the prevalence of the practice in mind. the payments are relatively small, uniformly assessed, and accepted as standard practice by the surrounding culture. Here, the practice of petty bribery would pass the type 2 test and, barring other moral factors, would be permissible.

A further condition, however, should be placed on multinationals that undertake the practice in type 2 contexts. The companies should be willing to speak out against the practice. Even if petty bribery or low-level nepotism passes the preceding tests, it may conflict with an embedded norm of the home country, and as a representative of the home country's culture, the company is obliged to take a stand. This would be true even for issues related exclusively to financial practice, such as the Italian tax case. If the practice of underestimating taxes is (1) accepted in the host country, (2) necessary for successful business, and (3) does not violate any fundamental rights, then it satisfies the necessary conditions of permissibility. Yet insofar as it violates a norm accepted by the home country, the multinational company should make its disapproval of the practice known.

To sum up, then, two complementary tests have been proposed for determining the ultimate permissibility of the practice in question. If the practice occurs in a type 1 context, then the practice is not permissible if:

The members of the home country would not, under conditions of economic development relevantly similar to those of the host country, regard the practice as permissible.

If the practice occurs in a type 2 context, then the practice is not permissible if either one of the following criteria is true:

It is possible to conduct business successfully in the host country without undertaking the practice.

The practice is a direct violation of a fundamental international right.

Notice that the type 1 test or criterion is not reducible to the type 2 test. In order for the two tests to have equivalent outcomes, four propositions would need to be true: first, if the practice passes criterion 1, it passes criterion 2; second, if it fails criterion 1, it fails criterion 2; third, if it passes criterion 2, it passes criterion 1; and fourth, if it fails criterion 2, if fails criterion 1. But none of these propositions is true. The possibility matrix in Table 20.2 shows in rows A and B the only combinations of outcomes that are possible

TABLE 20.2. Possible Outcomes of the Ethical Algorithm.

	Criterion 1	Criterion 2
A	Fail	Fail
		equivalent outcomes
B	Pass	Pass
C	Fail	Pass
		nonequivalent outcomes
D	Pass	Fail

on the assumption that the two tests are equivalent. But they are not equivalent because the combinations of outcomes in C and D are also possible.

To illustrate, the practice may pass criterion 2 and fail criterion 1; for example, the practice of petty bribery may be necessary for business, may not violate fundamental rights, but may nonetheless be unacceptable in the home country under hypothetical lowered levels of economic development. Similarly, the practice of allowing a significant amount of sulphur-dioxide pollution (sufficient, say, to erode historic artifacts) may be necessary for business, may not violate fundamental rights, yet may be hypothetically unacceptable in the home country. Or, the practice may fail test 2 and pass test 1; for example, the practice of serving alcohol at executive dinners in a strongly Moslem country may not be necessary for business in the host country and thus impermissible by criterion 2 while being thoroughly acceptable to the members of the home country under hypothetically lowered economic conditions.

It follows, then, that the two tests are not mutually reducible. This underscores the importance of the preliminary step of classifying a given case as either type 1 or type 2. The prior act of classification explains, moreover, why all cases in row C or in row D do not have the same moral outcome. Consider, for example, the Fail-Pass case from row C concerning artifact-damaging, sulphur-dioxide pollution, mentioned earlier. It could happen that if properly classified under type 2, the

practice would be permissible, but if under type 1, it would be impermissible.

The algorithm does not obviate the need for multinational managers to appeal to moral concepts both more general and specific than the algorithm itself. It is not intended as a substitute for a general theory of morality or even an interpretation of the basic responsibilities of multinationals. Its power lies in its ability to tease out implications of the moral presuppositions of a manager's acceptance of "home" morality and in this sense to serve as a clarifying device for multinational decision making. But insofar as the context of a given conflict of norms categorizes it as type 1 rather than type 2 conflict, the algorithm makes no appeal to a universal concept of morality (as the appeal to fundamental rights does in type 2 cases) save for the purported universality of the ethics endorsed by the home country culture. This means that the force of the algorithm is relativized slightly in the direction of a single society. When the home country's morality is wrong or confused, the algorithm can reflect this ethnocentricity, leading either to a mild paternalism or to the imposition of parochial standards. For example, the home country's oversensitivity to aesthetic features of the environment may lead it to reject a given level of thermal pollution even under hypothetically lowered economic circumstances, thus yielding a paternalistic refusal to allow such levels in the host country, despite the host country's acceptance of the higher levels and its belief that tolerating such levels is necessary for stimulating economic development. Or, the home country's mistaken belief that the practice of hiring twelve-year-olds for full-time, permanent work, although happily unnecessary at its relative by high level of economic development, would be acceptable and economically necessary at a level of economic development relevantly similar to the host country's, and might lead it both to tolerate and to undertake the practice in the host country. It would be a mistake, however, to exaggerate this weakness of the algorithm; coming up with actual cases in which the force of the algorithm would be relativized is extremely difficult. Indeed, I have been unable to discover a single, nonhypothetical set of facts fitting this description.

The algorithm is not intended as a substitute for more specific guides to conduct such as the numerous codes of ethics not appearing on the international scene. A need exists for topic-specific and industry-specific codes that embody detailed safeguards against self-serving interpretations.

Despite these limitations, the algorithm has important application in countering the well-documented tendency of multinationals to mask immoral practices in the rhetoric of "tolerance" and "cultural relativity." According to this algorithm, no multinational manager can naively suggest that asbestos standards in Chile are permissible because they are accepted there. Nor can a manager infer that the standards are acceptable on the grounds that the Chilean economy is, relative to the multinational's home country, underdeveloped. A surprising amount of moral blindness occurs not because people's fundamental moral views are confused, but because their cognitive application of those views to novel situations is misguided.

NOTES

1. H.J. McCloskey, for example, understands a right as a positive entitlement that need not specify who bears the responsibility for satisfying that entitlement. H.J. Mc-Closkey, "Rights—Some Conceptual Issues," *Australasian Journal of Philosophy* 54 (1976): 99.

2. Joel Feinberg, "Duties, rights and Claims," *American Philosophical Quarterly*, 3 (1966), 137–44. See also Feinberg, "The Nature and Value of Rights," *Journal of Value Inquiry* 4 (1970): 243–57.

3. See Ian Brownlie, *Basic Documents on Human Rights* (Oxford: Oxford University Press, 1975).

4. Henry Shue, *Basic Rights* (Princeton University Press, 1980) p. 57.

5. I am indebted to Edwin Hartman for establishing this point. Hartman has suggested that this warrants establishing a fourth significant kind of duty, i.e., "avoiding helping to deprive." For a more detailed account of this interesting suggestion, see Edwin Hartman, "Comment of Donaldson's 'Rights in the Global Market,' " in Edward Freeman, ed., *The 1988 Ruffin Lectures* (New York: Oxford University Press, forthcoming).

6. Brian Barry, "Humanity and Justice in Global Perspective," in J. Koland Pennock and John W. Chapman, eds., *Ethics, Economics, and the Law: Nomos Vol. XXIV* (New York: New York University Press, 1982), pp. 219–52.

7. Both for raising these questions and in helping me formulate answers, I am indebted to William Frederick.

8. Arthur Kelly, "Case Study: Italian Bank Mores," in Thomas Donaldson, ed., *Case Studies in Business Ethics* (Englewood Cliffs, N.J.: Prentice-Hall, 1984), 37–39.

9. Charles Peters and Taylor Branch, *Blowing the Whistle: Dissent in the Public Interest* (New York: Praeger, 1974), pp. 182–85.

10. Arnold Berleant, "Multinationals and the Problem of Ethical Consistency," *Journal of Business Ethics* 3 (August 1982): 185–95. Some have argued that insulating the economies of the less developed countries would be advantageous to the less developed countries in the long run. But whether correct or not, such an argument is independent of the present issue, for it is independent of the claim that if a practice violates the norms of the home country, then it is impermissible.

21

Sovereignty at Bay:
Ten Years After

Raymond Vernon

Raymond Vernon reexamines the major assumptions underlying the analysis in Sovereignty at Bay *in the light of developments of the last decade.*

The idea of sovereignty at bay emerged in a period when the spread of multinational corporations seemed to surpass the domain of the nation-state. Such a situation, according to Vernon's seminal work, could not persist. The attempts of sovereigns to capture the benefits, avoid the costs, and harness the operations of multinationals, documented in this book, represent the reaction.

In attempting to predict the behavior of U.S.-based multinationals in the coming decade, Vernon suggests that the product-cycle hypothesis has stood up well in numerous tests but may have to be modified substantially for the future as the innovational lead of U.S. firms declines in relation to the Europeans and Japanese. Despite multiple challenges, international corporations have proved to be flexible and resilient in their ability to operate in developed and developing countries. While the evidence of whether they are maintaining centralized or more decentralized control is mixed, the prognosis for the future is a continued reliance on adhering to a common global corporate strategy.

For the future, Vernon warns that problems of multiple jurisdiction will likely intensify as diverse governments try to use multinationals as instruments for the projection of their own sovereign will.

Reprinted from *International Organization, summer 1981,* Raymond Vernon, "Sovereignty at Bay: Ten Years After," by permission of The MIT Press, Cambridge, Massachusetts. © 1981 by the Board of Regents of the University of Wisconsin System.

The author of *Sovereignty at Bay*, musing in public about his opus after ten long years, faces one very special difficulty. Practically every reader remembers the title of the book; but scarcely anyone will accurately recall its contents. For after its publication, like Aspirin and Frigidaire, the label (but not the contents) became generic. Robert Gilpin identified a "Sovereignty at Bay model," subscribed to by visionaries devoted to the proposition that the nation-state was done for, finished off by the multinational enterprise.[1] Seymour J. Rubin lustily attacked the visionaries; Lincoln Gordon ably provided supporting fire; C. Fred Bergsten was only a step behind. Even Walter B. Wriston turned briefly from his labors at building one of the world's biggest banks to cast a few stones in the same general direction.

Meanwhile, the themes of *Sovereignty at Bay*, if they were ever learned, were half-forgotten in the heady pursuit of more vulnerable quarry. Only the author and a few of his more attentive students would remember the argument of his final chapter, which concluded somewhat lugubriously:

> The basic asymmetry between multinational enterprises and national governments [that is, the capacity of the enterprises to shift some of their activities from one location to another, as compared with the commitment of the government to a fixed piece of national turf] may be tolerable up to a point, but beyond that point there is a need to reestablish balance.... If this does not happen, some of the apocalyptic projections of the future of multinational enterprise will grow more plausible.

ROOTS OF THE MULTINATIONALS

Because *Sovereignty at Bay* was one of the earlier works in a stream that would soon become a torrent, much of the book was devoted to chronicling and describing the phenomenal growth and spread of multinational enterprises. Interwoven in the history and the description, however, were inevitably some hypotheses about causes. Some of these, although still bearing a touch of novelty in 1971, seem hackneyed today—suggestive, I suppose, of their validity and durability. The increased efficiencies of communication and transportation, which had been reducing the costs of learning and the costs of control, were given appropriate credit as expediters of the multinationalizing process. Oligopoly was recognized as a near-necessary condition for breeding multinational enterprises, a conclusion that simply reaffirmed a point made ten years earlier by Stephen Hymer.[2]

Two kinds of oligopoly that seemed particularly relevant in explaining the spectacular growth of U.S.-based multinational enterprises in the postwar period were explored with special attention. (The subtitle of the book, after all, was "The Multinational Spread of U.S. Enterprise"). One was the oligopoly based upon the special technological capabilities of the participating firms, while the other was the oligopoly based on the sheer size and geographical spread of the operating firms concerned, as in the oil and metals industries. In that context, a number of hypotheses were elaborated, which later would be tested and retested in various contexts. The most widely known of these, particularly applicable to the technology-based oligopolies, came to be called the product-cycle hypothesis. I shall have more to say about that concept in a moment. But there were other propositions, which also were exposed to considerable testing in subsequent years, such as the follow-the-leader hypothesis.

These various concepts purporting to explain the growth and spread of multinational enterprises have stood up about as well as one could have hoped. The follow-the-leader hypothesis has been adequately confirmed in one or two solid studies.[3] As for the product-cycle hypothesis, there have been numerous confirming and elaborating studies,[4] as well as a few important qualifications, reservations, and demurrers.[5] On the whole, the concept seems to have had considerable utility in explaining past developments and predicting future ones.

However, what has changed—indeed, changed quite dramatically—is the applicability of the product-cycle hypothesis in explaining the present behavior and the likely future behavior of multinational enterprises based in the United States. As an explicator and predictor of U.S. performance, the product-cycle hypothesis had particular applicability to the conditions of, say, 1900 to 1970; this was a period in which the income levels of U.S. residents were higher than those in any other major market in the world, in which U.S. hourly labor costs were the highest in the world, and in which U.S. capital and raw materials were comparatively cheap. That set of unique conditions, it was posited, had been generating a stream of innovations on the part of U.S. firms responsive to their special environment. And as the income levels and relative labor costs in other countries tracked over the terrain previously traversed by the U.S. economy, U.S. innovations found a ready market in those other countries. These innovations were thought to provide an oligopolistic handhold that gave U.S. firms their dominant position in many markets of other countries.

But even as I went to press with *Sovereignty at Bay*, there were a few signs that the pattern might be losing its explanatory force for the United States. A section captioned "Toward Another Model" presented speculations about the consequences that might ensue as U.S. incomes and labor costs became more closely aligned with those of Europe and Japan. In that case, U.S.-based enterprises would no longer have the advantage of doing business in home markets under condi-

tions that were precursors of those which eventually would appear in Europe and Japan. Accordingly, the innovational lead that the Americans had enjoyed in earlier decades could be expected to shrink.

I cannot say, however, that I had the prescience to realize how rapidly the factor cost configurations of the various national markets would be brought into alignment, speeded by the rise in raw material prices, by the increasing nominal cost of capital, and by the weakness of the U.S. dollar. In my speculation about the growth of European and Japanese investment in the United States, therefore, the tone was hypothetical; there was no sense of conviction that the trend would soon develop. Intellectually, readers were put on notice; glandularly, they were not forewarned.

It was only in the latter 1970s that the convergence in the factor costs of the principal exporting countries had developed sufficiently to prompt me to reappraise the relevance of the product-cycle concept as an explicator of U.S. behavior.[6] As a result of that reappraisal, I concluded that the product-cycle concept continued to have some utility, explaining some of the trade and investment patterns visible in various countries of the world; but its utility in explaining the behavior of the U.S. economy had measurably declined.

EFFECTS OF THE MULTINATIONALS

When *Sovereignty at Bay* was published in 1971, the advocates and the opponents of multinational enterprises were already locked in furious combat. Several dozen propositions about the consequences of the operations of these enterprises had been advanced by both sides. One of the objectives of *Sovereignty at Bay* was to test the leading propositions of the opponents with such data as could be mustered for the purpose.

The issues involved were too numerous and too diverse to be effectively reviewed here. At the time when *Sovereignty at Bay* was published, however, it seemed clear that both sides were grossly overreaching in their arguments; some cases were consistent with their sweeping hypotheses, some were not. Even more often, the asserted effects of the operations of these enterprises, whether benign or destructive, could not be supported by the evidence. The classic Scotch verdict—not proven—seemed more justified than any.[7]

By 1977, however, numerous researchers all over the globe had published a great many additional studies of the multinational enterprise. Some of these studies cast new light on the issues that had been dealt with tentatively in *Sovereignty at Bay*: typical of such issues, for instance, were those relating to the technological transfer activities of the multinationals. The piling up of such evidence moved me to publish a second book on multinational enterprises, which appeared under the title of *Storm over the Multinationals*.

The added evidence reviewed in that book went some way to confirm the fact that simpleminded propositions about the effects of multinational enterprises were as a rule highly vulnerable. On the basis of the new work, it was possible to speak with somewhat greater assurance about some of the economic and political effects of multinational enterprises; but those effects were not simple. The caution with which I had approached such questions as the balance-of-payment effects, income-distribution effects, and employment effects of multinational enterprises in *Sovereignty at Bay* seemed justified by the conclusions of *Storm over the Multinationals*. Generalizations on some points are possible; but they must be framed with due regard for the vast differences in the activities of multinational enterprises. Numerous variables determine the economic effects of the operations of individual firms, including for instance, their innovative propensities and their marketing strategies. Both the uninhibited broadsides of writers such as Barnet and Müller and the more restrained generalizations of scholars such as Robert Gilpin suffer from this lack of differentiation.

THREATS TO THE MULTINATIONALS

With the acuity that goes with hindsight, I might better have entitled my 1971 volume *Everyone at Bay*, in the spirit of its closing lines. But there would be some overreaching in such a title; I could hardly claim to have foreseen the spate of expropriations and nationalizations of the foreign properties of the multinational enterprises that occurred during the first half of the 1970s. My chapter on the raw materials industries, in fact, was written in a tone of complacency that must have been insufferable at the time to some of the worried managers of the international oil companies. The mood of that portion of *Sovereignty at Bay* is captured in the final paragraph of the raw materials chapter:

Strong initiatives on the part of the governments of less developed countries to control the key factors in the exploitation of their raw materials are likely to continue. And as they do, the capacity of host governments to participate in management will increase. It is another question, however, whether the host countries will feel that their 'dependence' on the outside world has declined simply because their management role has increased. As long as the product requires marketing in foreign countries, dependence will presumably continue in some form.

Yet, as one reads the raw materials chapter with the hindsight of 1981, the argument for the increasing vulnerability of the oil companies is all there, carefully laid out under a heading dubbed "The Obsolescing Bargain." The oil-exporting countries, it was pointed out, no longer needed the oil companies as a source of capital; their taxes on the sale of crude oil were already providing a sense of independence on that score. Nor did the oil-exporting countries any longer feel shut away from access to the technology of oil exploration and exploitation; too many independent companies were bidding to provide that information and expertise. In the latter 1960s, the principal remaining source of vulnerability of the oil-exporting countries and the principal source of strength of the international oil companies was the companies' control over the channels of distribution.

What prevented me (and practically every other scholar at the time) from fully applying the lesson of the obsolescing bargain to the situation of the oil companies was our inability to appreciate that a profound shift in the supply-demand balance was taking place, which might reduce the need of the oil-exporting countries to rely on the marketing channels of the multinationals. Most of us took the chronic weakness of oil prices during most of the 1960s to mean that supplies were more than adequate. Accordingly, it was hard to contemplate that demand would soon grow so rapidly that the oil-exporting countries would feel free to cut their umbilical cord to the international oil marketers. Nor do I think that many analysts in the oil industry itself were aware of the dangers of an oil shortage at the time.

To be sure, by the latter 1960s, some thoughtful executives in the industry were deeply worried. Some were expressing alarm over the deterioration in their negotiating position, as Libya and other countries gleefully used the independent oil companies to leapfrog over one another in a continuous escalation of their terms. But so far as I know, nobody in the 1960s foresaw the great bulge in the demand for Middle East oil that would soon undermine the majors' position.

Looking back at the text of *Sovereignty at Bay* after ten years, I am frustrated by the fact that the analysis comes so close, while not quite drawing the key conclusion. The weakening of the international oil oligopoly during the 1960s is accurately enough portrayed; the appearance of the state-owned oil companies and the emergence of OPEC are appropriately chronicled. But is was not until a year or two later that I fully appreciated the key role played by the independent oil companies in weakening the position of the majors and in strengthening the negotiating hand of the oil-exporting countries. And it was a few years after that before it became evident that the period of weakening prices in the 1960s had been masking a shift in the supply-demand balance.[8]

No two persons will draw quite the same lessons from the experiences of the oil market during the 1960s and 1970s. The lessons that I draw, I suspect, will not be widely shared.

One of these is that any five-year projection of the supply-demand balance for world oil is inherently subject to gross margins of error, margins so large as to encompass both the possibilities of painful shortage and the possibilities of disconcerning glut. The importers of oil, of course, are justified in acting as if they expected an acute shortage, simply because the consequences of a shortage are so much more painful than those of a glut; prudence, therefore, demands that we act as if a shortage were inevitable. But whenever I review the various projections of supply and demand in the world oil market that are being circulated today, I am persuaded that today's projections are just as vulnerable as those of fifteen years ago.

A second conclusion, based as much on other raw materials as on oil, is that the concept of the obsolescing bargain does have a certain utility in analyzing the changing position of the multinational enterprises engaged in any given product line. Accordingly, wherever the conventional wisdom of any market turns from an expectation of shortage to an expectation of glut, I anticipate in accordance with the obsolescing bargain concept that the position of the multinationals will be somewhat strengthened.

And a third conclusion is that, for phenomena as complex as the role of multinational enterprises, scholars may be as vulnerable as laymen in speculating about the shape of future events. If scholars do their work well, their predictive models may be better crafted than those of the layman—more fully articulated, internally more consistent, more firmly based on earlier events. But scholars, perhaps more than laymen, must live with the risk of neglecting or overlooking what may prove to be the controlling factor that determines those future events.

The Problem of Multiple Jurisdiction

As the title *Sovereignty at Bay* suggests, the book was much more concerned with the interests and attitudes of government than with the aspirations and fears of the multinational enterprises themselves. Insofar as the title was justified, the justification rested on the validity of three propositions: that most governments, reluctant to give up the advantages they perceive in inviting multinational enterprises into their jurisdictions, will continue to permit a significant part of their national output to be accounted for by the affiliates of such enterprises; that the policies of any affiliate of a multinational enterprise are bound to reflect in some degree the global interests of the multinational network as a whole, and hence can never respond single-mindedly to the requirements of any one national jurisdiction; and that the network of any multinational enterprise cannot escape serving as a conduit through which sovereign states exert an influence on the economies of other sovereign states.

After ten years, I see no strong reason to modify any of these propositions. During those ten years, some foreign affiliates of multinational enterprises were nationalized, while other foreign affiliates were liquidated or sold on the initiative of their parents. But, all told, these withdrawals were only a minor fraction of the new advances that multinational enterprises were making all over the globe. In 1979 alone, for instance, U.S.-based multinationals increased their foreign investment stake by $25 billion, of which $18 billion was in developed nations and $7 billion in developing countries. Indicative of the resilience of such enterprises to the buffeting they had received only a few years earlier was the fact that nearly $4 billion of the $7 billion build-up in developing countries was in the form of fresh money remitted by the U.S. parent, while the remainder consisted of the reinvestment of past earnings.

To be sure, there have been some changes during these ten years in the identity of the world's multinational enterprises. Those based in Europe and Japan have gained a little in importance relative to those based in the United States. Moreover, the world is beginning to see enterprises of this sort that have their home bases in Spain, Brazil, Mexico, India, Hong Kong, and other such locations.[9] But these changes simply add to the sense of vitality and durability of the multinational structures.

At the same time as there have been some marginal shifts in the identity of the multinational enterprises, there have also been some marginal alterations in their business practices. U.S.-based enterprises as a class have grown somewhat less reluctant to enter into joint ventures with foreign partners than had been the case in earlier decades. Multinational enterprises from all countries have proved increasingly flexible in taking on management contracts, acceding to so-called fadeout clauses, entering into partnerships with state-owned enterprises, and involving themselves in other ambiguous arrangements.

The proliferation of such arrangements raises the question whether the various affiliates of multinational enterprises continue to respond to a common global strategy and to draw on a common pool of resources to the same degree as in the past. The available signs point in many directions. Some observers insist, for instance, that when the subsidiaries of multinational enterprises enter into partnerships with state-owned enterprises, they often manage to increase the degree of their control in the local market rather than to diminish it.[10] The increased prevalence of joint ventures and other ambiguous arrangements suggests that the authority of the parents of the multinational networks over their affiliates is being diluted. But other developments seem to be pushing in the opposite direction. For instance, there has been a constant improvement of software and communication systems for the command and control of distant subsidiaries, a trend that places new tools in the hands of headquarters staffs. In addition, the multinational enterprises in some industries, including automobiles and machinery, have been pushing toward the development of world models for their products, a trend that requires increasing integration among the production units of the multinational enterprises concerned.

I anticipate that, in the end, the generalizations will be exceedingly complex. We may well find, for instance, that in many firms control over the finance and production functions has increased, even though the physical location of these activities has been dispersed. We may find, too, that in the selection of business strategies some multinational enterprises have opted to develop maximum flexibility and adaptation toward local conditions while others in the same general product line have opted for the maximum exploitation of global economies of scale.[11]

Still, I would be surprised if on balance multinational enterprises had greatly reduced the degree of central control over their global operations. For insofar as multinational enterprises have any inherent advantages over national enterprises, those advantages must rest on the multinational character of their operations, that is to say, on their multinational strategies and their common resources. Multinational enterprises, therefore, may have no real option; by giving up their multinational advantages, they may be destroying the basis for their competitive survival.

If multinational enterprises continue to pursue some elements of a global strategy and to draw on a common pool of financial and human resources, then the problems of multiple jurisdiction will continue to play a considerable role in their operations. At times, affiliates of such enterprises will be marching to the tunes of a distant trumpet being played from the ministries of another government or from the offices of another affiliate. Some cases of this sort are well enough known; the occasional forays of the U.S. government's antitrust division in attempting to break up international restrictive business practices that affect the U.S. economy have received particular attention. But these well-publicized cases are on the whole less important than those that are less transparent. Multinational enterprises with an affiliate in Germany, for instance, will have to entertain the demand of German unions for more output and more jobs, expressed through the hard-won rights of *Mitbestimmungsrecht*; responding to such pressures, the parent enterprise may be obliged to reduce the output of its Brazilian subsidiary, thereby exporting Germany's unemployment to Brazil. For multinational enterprises with an affiliate in Mexico, the insistence of the Mexican government that the local affiliates must import less and export more may lower the output of these networks in Barcelona and Detroit. And India's insistence that foreign parents should charge their Indian subsidiaries nothing for their technology could lower the income taxes and export earnings of the parents of those subsidiaries operating from their bases in other countries.

Since 1971, the problems of multiple jurisdiction generated by the existence of multinational enterprises have grown. More than ever before, governments are telling the affiliates of multinational enterprises what they must do or not do as the price for their right to continue in business. As the world's overt trade barriers have diminished, these commands have become a principal weapon of many governments for pursuing a beggar-my-neighbor economic policy. Accordingly, when I published *Storm over the Multinationals* in 1977, I developed the jurisdictional issue in considerably greater depth than in *Sovereignty at Bay*. But the second book was launched under the shadow of the first; whatever the second book had to say, it was commonly assumed, had already been said in *Sovereignty at Bay*.[12] The heightened emphasis on the jurisdictional issue in the second book, however, seems appropriate to current circumstances.

So far, jurisdictional conflicts have been contained by the fact that not all governments are systematically playing the beggar-my-neighbor game, and by the added fact that multinational enterprises have a strong incentive for muffling the effects of the game within their respective networks. My assumption has been, however, that the number of players and the intensity of the game will gradually increase. In that case, if multinationals are to avoid being the instruments through which national jurisdictions are brought into repeated conflict, the sovereign states must be willing to agree on some international regime that can reconcile their interests. Any such agreed regime would presumably do two things: it would specify the rights of multinational enterprises in and their obligations to the international community; and it would delineate and restrain the jurisdictional reach of the governments involved,

wherever an important clash in national jurisdictions might be involved.

Since 1971, there have been dozens of projects for achieving international agreement with respect to the multinational enterprises. Most of them have included proposals to restrain the multinational enterprises in various ways; a few have proposed some guarantees for the multinational enterprises as well; but until very recently, most have neglected or avoided the pervasive problem of conflicting jurisdictions.

Indeed, some of the international actions and international proposals that have been launched since 1971 have seemed carefully designed to preserve the contradictions rather than to resolve them. The member countries of the OECD, for instance, have adopted a set of declarations proposing that each government should grant national treatment to foreign-owned subsidiaries in its jurisdictions, thus acknowledging the national character of such subsidiaries; at the same time, these governments have paid obeisance to the applicability of international law in the treatment of foreign-owned subsidiaries, whether or not such treatment conformed with national law, thus acknowledging the foreign element in the subsidiaries' identity. In a similar obfuscating mood, the developing countries, as a rule, have simultaneously insisted upon two propositions: that foreign-owned subsidiaries, being nationals of the host country, were subject to all the obligations of any other national; but that such subsidiaries, as the property of foreigners, could rightly be denied the privileges of other nationals.

I can find only one functional area in which governments have made a serious effort to reduce the conflicts or resolve the ambiguities that go with the operations of multinational enterprises.[13] The industrialized countries have managed to develop a rather extraordinary web of bilateral agreements among themselves that deal with conflicts in the application of national tax laws. Where such laws seemed to be biting twice into the same morsel of profit, governments have agreed on a division of the fare. Why governments have moved to solve the jurisdictional conflict in this field but not in others is an interesting question. Perhaps it was because, in the case of taxation, the multinational enterprises themselves had a major stake in seeing to the consummation of the necessary agreements.

So far, the world has managed to stagger on without effectively addressing the many facets of jurisdictional conflict and without directly acknowledging the inescapable fact that the behavior of any affiliate is unavoidably influenced by external forces. The various sovereigns direct their commands at a unit in the multinational network; the unit responds as it can, giving ground to the sovereign if it must; the other units in the network adjust their operations to the new situation, spreading the adjustment cost through the global system. As long as there is no overt acknowledgment of what is going on all the parties can pretend that the jurisdiction of each sovereign is unimpaired.

THE FUTURE OF THE MULTINATIONALS

Lincoln Gordon would agree, I think, that his one-time proposal for a tract entitled "Multinationals at Bay" would not arouse much interest today. The tumult of the 1970s over the multinational issue has lost some of its stridence. The incidence of nationalizations in developing countries has declined dramatically. Kolko, Williams, Barnet, and Müller seem somehow out of date, while the various scholars of *dependista* theory seem a bit jaded. The U.N. Centre on Transnational Corporations has developed a businesslike air, more akin to the professionalism of the Securities and Exchange Commission than to the prosecuting fervor of the Church Committee.

In retrospect, it appears that the numerous threats to the multinationals that were launched in the 1970s—the spate of nationalizations, the codes of conduct, the U.S. legislation against bribery, the demands and resolutions of the General Assembly—were fueled by a number of different elements. One of these was a manifestation of much larger phenomenon, namely a pervasive revulsion in much of the world against the effects of industrialization, against the symbols of entrenched authority, against the impersonal tyranny of big bureaucracies. Embodying all of these unfortunate attributes and burdened besides by the sin of being foreign, multinationals were inevitably a prime target of the period. A second factor that explained the attack on the multinationals, however, was the inexorable operation of the obsolescing bargain; as shortages appeared in various raw materials, multinationals lost the bargaining power that their marketing capabilities normally afforded.

The revulsion against bigness and bureaucracy that exploded in the late 1960s and early 1970s may have been ephemeral; but the process of the obsolescing bargain is not. From time to time, in the future as in the past, one foreign-owned industry or another will lose its defensive capabilities; and when that happens, some of those enterprises will be nationalized, joining the plantations, the power plants, and the oil wells that have been taken over by governments in years past.

But the future is no simple extrapolation of the past. Some forces seem to be speeding up the process by which the bargain between governments and foreign investors becomes obsolescent. At the same time, other forces seem to be diffusing and defusing the underlying hostility that gives the process of the obsolescing bargain some of its motive force.

The expectation that agreements between governments and investors will be breached even more quickly in the future than in the past is based on various factors. In reappraising their bargaining positions, governments are better informed and better equipped than they have ever been. Perhaps more to the point, opposition forces that are bent on embarrassing their governments have more information and more expertise. Besides, according to evidence presented in *Storm over the Multinationals*, governments are finding that in many lines of industry they have an increasing number of options for securing the capital, technology, or access to markets they require. Accordingly, although multinational enterprises taken as a class continue to account for a considerable share—even an increasing share—of the economies of most countries, individual multinationals have nothing like the bargaining position they sometimes held in the past.

Yet governments seem constrained to use their increased bargaining power in more ambiguous ways. Instead of outright nationalization, they seem disposed to settle for other arrangements, such as arrangements that make a gift of some of the equity to favored members of the local private sector or to an expanding state-owned enterprise, or contracts that allow the multinationals to manage their properties without formal ownership. Perhaps the increase in ambiguous arrangements is due to the decline in the power of the individual multinational enterprises; being less threatening, they are less to be feared. Perhaps, too, the ambiguity is due to the increasing power of the private industrialists in some countries who prefer to squeeze the foreign goose rather than to strangle it;[14] or to the unceasing struggle of the managers of some state-owned enterprises to weaken the control of their national ministries.[15] It may even be that the hostility of some countries to the multinational enterprises of others is being blunted by the growth of their own homegrown brand of multinationals.

Whatever the precise causes may be, I anticipate that business organizations with the attributes of multinational enterprises will not decline and may well grow in their relative importance in the world economy. Anticipating that development, I am brought back to what I regard as the central questions. How do the sovereign states propose to deal with the fact that so many of their enterprises are conduits through which other sovereigns exert their influence?

Perhaps they will not deal with the problem at all. There is plenty of evidence for the proposition that nations are capable of tolerating ambiguity on a massive scale for long periods of time. And there are numerous cases in which scholars, peering into the future, have mistaken bogey men for monsters. But I am betting that the problem is real and its emergence as a political issue close at hand. In any event, it is this problem that invests the title *Sovereignty at Bay* with its real meaning.

NOTES

1. Robert Gilpin, *U.S. Power and the Multinational Corporation* (New York: Basic Books, 1975), p. 220. Be it said to Gilpin's credit that although he ascribes the phrase to me, he does not list me as one who subscribes to the model. Others, however, have been less careful in their attributions.

2. S.H. Hymer, *The International Operations of National Firms: A Study of Direct Foreign Investment* (Cambridge: M.I.T. Press, 1976), based on his 1960 thesis.

3. See F.T. Knickerbocker, *Oligopolistic Reaction and Multinational Enterprise* (Boston: Harvard Business School, 1973). His subsequent work on the hypothesis, unfortunately never fully published, went even further in confirming its utility.

4. The number of such studies by now is very large. Illustrations are: L.T. Wells Jr., ed., *The Product Life Cycle and International Trade* (Boston: Harvard Business School, 1972); J.M. Finger, "A New View of the Product Cycle Theory," *Weltwirtschaftliches Archiv* 3, 1, 1975; M.P. Claudon, *International Trade and Technology: Models of Dynamic Comparative Advantage* (Washington, D.C.: University Press of America, 1977); Seev Hirsch, "The Product Cycle Model of International Trade," *Ox-*

ford *Bulletin of Economics and Statistics* 37, 4 (November 1975), pp. 305–17; Hiroki and Yoshi Tsumuri, "A Bayesian Test of the Product Life Cycle Hypothesis as Applied to the U.S. Demand for Color-TV Sets," *International Economic Review*, October 1980, pp. 581–95.

5. For instance: W.B. Walker, *Industrial Innovation and International Trading Performance* (Brighton, England: Sussex University, 1976); and Kiyoshi Kojima, "A Macroeconomic Theory of Foreign Direct Investment," *Hitotsubashi Journal of Economics* 14, 1 (June 1973).

6. Raymond Vernon, "The Product Cycle Hypothesis in a New International Environment," *Oxford Bulletin of Economics and Statistics* 41, 4 (November 1979), pp. 255–67; and Raymond Vernon, "Gone are the Cash Cows of Yesteryear," *Harvard Business Review*, November 1980, pp. 150–55.

7. For a review of many of these issues and a well-balanced critical appraisal of my views, see T.J. Biersteker, *Distortion or Development? Contending Perspectives on the Multinational Corporation* (Cambridge: M.I.T. Press, 1979).

8. Those points are developed at some length in two later publications. See Edith Penrose, "The Development of Crisis" in Raymond Vernon, ed., *The Oil Crisis* (New York: W.W. Norton, 1976), pp. 39–57; and Raymond Vernon, *Storm over the Multinationals* (Cambridge: Harvard University Press, 1977), pp. 83–87.

9. A book on this subject will shortly appear under the authorship of Louis T. Wells, Jr.

10. This is a subject that is just beginning to be researched. For an analysis covering Brazil, see Peter Evans, *Dependent Development: The Alliance of Multinational, State, and Local Capital in Brazil* (Princeton: Princeton University Press, 1979).

11. Patterns of this sort are being researched by Yves Doz at INSEAD, Fontainebleau.

12. See for instance, C.P. Kindleberger's review of *Storm over the Multinationals* in *Business History Review* 51, 4 (Winter 1979), pp. 95–97.

13. Nevertheless, there are glimmerings of some additional action eventually on the subject. Reference to the problem appears in a composite working draft of a code of conduct for multinational enterprises, prepared for consideration of an intergovernmental working group under the sponsorship of the U.N. Centre on Transnational Corporations; see Working Paper no. 7, November 1979, paragraph 56. But the prospects for action are not very great.

14. See for instance Evans, *Dependent Development*.

15. Yair Aharoni, "Managerial Discretion," in Aharoni and Vernon, eds., *State-Owned Enterprises in the Western Economies* (London: Croom Helm, 1980).

22

The New Ideology of Tort Law * **

Peter H. Schuck

The recent transformation of American tort law has attracted much attention, and with good reason. On almost all fronts and in almost all jurisdictions, liability has dramatically expanded. It does not seem to matter what kind of party is being sued. Doctor or public official, landlord or social host, government agency or product manufacturer—all are more likely to be held liable today.

Numerous legal doctrines reflect and reinforce this change. Courts have enlarged the concept of "action," a traditional prerequisite for liability, to encompass inaction. In this way, they have placed individuals under a legal duty to help strangers in many situations, thereby hauling new kinds of relationships (and nonrelationships) into the net of tort liability. They have accorded legal protec-

tion to new categories of interests, including emotional well-being, freedom from fear of cancer, and avoidance of unwanted children. They have extended the domain in time and space over which defendants' duties apply by imposing responsibility for risks that eventuate long after dependents acted and, in some toxic-tort cases, for risks that were scientifically unknowable at that time. They have accepted relatively weak claims of causation, especially in drug, toxic-tort, and medical-malpractice cases, where proving cause and effect is often difficult. They have routinely ignored or overridden express contractual limitations on tort liability, as well as implicit agreements by parties to allocate risk between themselves. They have abandoned or severely curtailed long-standing charitable, governmental, and familial immunities from tort liability.

Presumably, this expansion of liability will not continue indefinitely and without limit. Like other tides in human affairs, it will ebb as well as flow. Even so, one is struck by its duration. Tort scholars appear to agree that

*A similar version of this article appears in Walter Olson, ed., *New Directions in Liability Law*, forthcoming from the Academy of Political Science and the Manhattan Institute for Policy Research.

**Reprinted with permission of the author from: *The Public Interest*, No. 92 (Summer, 1988), pp. 93–109. © 1988 by National Affairs, Inc.

liability has expanded steadily since at least the late nineteenth century, when employers' traditional defenses against industrial-accident liability began to erode (even before the enactment of workers' compensation schemes). Some scholars argue that the trend toward wider liability may have begun earlier. Decisions like *Brown v. Kendall* (1850), which declared that, in general, liability could not be found without "fault," are an apparent exception to the trend. But Gary Schwartz and some other commentators have suggested that these decisions did not so much put new limits on liability as codify existing limits that had been concealed by earlier doctrines and practices.

Legislatures have occasionally sought to arrest this growth in certain areas; product liability and medical malpractice are obvious recent examples. But as the periodic crises in these insurance lines suggest, legislative intervention has seldom been effective in curbing the growth of liability. And at the same time, these legislatures have been busy expanding liability in other areas (as in the 1986 federal vaccine law) and in other ways (as in new laws authorizing courts to make defendants pay the attorney's fees of plaintiffs). In tort law, however, courts almost always have the last word, and that word has usually been *compensate*.

What accounts for this long period of liability growth? The answer is not at all obvious. In many other areas of the law, after all, the courts oscillate between traditionalism and innovation, self-restraint and self-assertion, and other familiar antinomies. The emphasis in constitutional law, to take one example, has cycled between governmental interests and individual liberties, federal power and states' rights, broad and strict construction. In administrative law, one observes shifts from close judicial scrutiny of agency decisions to greater deference to administrative expertise, and then back to "hard looks."

Even in private-law fields, such as domestic relations, legal evolution often seems to come full circle. Why has tort liability followed so straight a path?

Institutional developments have surely played an important role. The growth of private liability insurance, for example, has meant that more "deep pockets" are now available to satisfy judgments. But this explanation is plainly incomplete, for expanded insurance has also undercut the argument for compensation through the tort system. Prospective accident victims now purchase more of their own direct ("first-party") insurance against accident losses, and the government has established massive income-maintenance, disability, and health-insurance programs. Coverage is still far from complete, of course, but it is much more comprehensive today than ever before, even when compared with the far larger accident costs—wages, medical costs, pain and suffering, emotional harm, and third-party consortium claims—that the expansive tort law now makes compensable. In short, most accident victims would now be compensated for most of their economic losses even without having recourse to the extremely costly, protracted lottery known as the tort system.

Other explanations of a more sociological kind are equally unsatisfying. Community life in the United States is indeed fragmented, and strangers increasingly demand that tort law protect them from risks posed by people with whom they lack a relationship of trust or shared experience. But this development is not a new one. The anomie and individualism of American culture, deeply imprinted upon our law, impressed Tocqueville more than a century before David Riesman dissected it in *The Lonely Crowd*. And even Riesman's lament antedated the dramatic liability expansion of recent years.

This essay will emphasize a different cause for the expansion of liability: a change in the ideology that courts bring to tort cases. The term *ideology* is not meant pejoratively here. It simply denotes a set of assumptions by contemporary judges that organize and render coherent their perceptions of legal reality. To furnish a fully satisfying account of this ideology, it would be necessary to trace the history of its principal ideas, the social forces that have shaped it, the functions it has served, and the personalities of the individual judges who have implemented it. Such a comprehensive account is well beyond the scope of this essay. For now, it is enough to identify the nature of this ideology, to examine how it leads to expanded liability, and to consider whether the tort law that is has spawned can satisfy its own normative criteria of legitimacy and effectiveness.

Although the new ideology of tort law is complex and multifaceted, four elements stand out: (1) a profound skepticism about the role of markets in allocating risk; (2) a shift in the dominant paradigm of causation; (3) a tendency to broaden jury discretion; and (4) a preoccupation with achieving broad social goals instead of the narrower, more traditional purpose of corrective justice between the litigants. This last element entails a change in the conception of the judges' role that serves to link, legitimate, and effectuate the first three elements. Needless to say, some of these elements are further developed than others, and few courts have yet taken them as far as have the supreme courts of New Jersey and California (at least until the electoral defeat of several liberal justices in California in 1986). But anyone who has read a large sample of contemporary tort cases will recognize the importance of these elements.

DISTRUST OF MARKETS

Judges' rulings, and occasionally their supporting rhetoric, bespeak increasing skepticism about both the efficiency and the justice of permitting the market to allocate risk. This is most apparent in cases arising from disputes over liability-insurance coverage. One might expect courts to defer to bargains explicitly concluded between insurers and their customers concerning the risks a policy will cover. Yet, as Kenneth Abraham has demonstrated, courts have devised numerous techniques to reshape or interpret insurance contracts so as to provide coverage of risks that the parties never agreed to shift.[1] Although this development has affected all areas of tort law, its implications are especially profound in mass toxic-tort cases. A dramatic example occurred recently in the massive asbestos litigation pending in San Francisco. In that case, Judge Ira Brown ruled that in order to maximize the pool of funds available to compensate victims, all insurers who wrote policies over several decades would be liable for all injuries, regardless of whether any given risk came into being during any given policy period.[2]

In tort law proper, decisions concerning the allocation of risks are seldom as explicit as they are in insurance contracts, and judicial respect for them is correspondingly lower. The courts' skepticism is entirely warranted in many tort disputes in which it would have been prohibitively costly for the two sides to reach some agreement about risk, the classic example being the collision between total strangers on the highway. Such skepticism may even make sense in those cases, also common in tort law, in which the parties could in principle have bargained at low cost about risk but in which one of the parties is a "low-attention" decision maker, to use Howard Latin's phrase.

Courts' disregard for risk markets, however, now extends well beyond these kinds of situations. Increasingly, judges override market risk allocations even in those cases in which both parties are plainly "high-attention" decision makers who have already

Peter H. Schuck

engaged in actual bargaining over the very sorts of risks that are at issue. Yet many of these decisions serve no evident purpose; they do not even promote a more progressive distribution of wealth.

The traditional approach to such cases is represented by a 1927 Supreme Court decision, *Robins Dry Dock and Repair Co. v. Flint*. The defendant, a dry dock, had negligently damaged a ship and rendered it unusable for a time. The plaintiff was not the owner of the ship but a third party who had chartered the vessel and was deprived of its use. The terms of the chartering agreement relieved the plaintiff of any hiring charges in case of such mishap but did not indemnify him for his lost profits, for which he proceeded to sue the dry dock in tort. Justice Oliver Wendell Holmes, Jr. rejected the claim, holding that even if the plaintiff might recover against the owner of the vessel, who might in turn recover against the dry dock, the dry dock owed no direct obligation to its customer's customer. Such an obligation, the Court reasoned, could arise only through contract.

Contrast this decision with the 1979 case of *J'Aire Corp. v. Gregory*, in which the California Supreme Court, confronted with roughly analogous facts, had no trouble imposing tort liability. A commercial tenant sued its landlord's contractor in tort for the profits it lost when the contractor negligently delayed completing repairs to the tenant's premises. Both parties had negotiated commercial contracts with the landlord; these contracts presumably took into account the risk to all sides of an interruption of business. The tenant was hardly without remedy, since he could have sued the landlord under the lease and may even have had a direct contract remedy against the defendant as a third-party beneficiary of its promise to repair. For aught that appears, the parties were equally wealthy and equally insured. Moreover, shifting the tenant's loss to the contractor in this situation may well be economically inefficient, for two reasons. It may fail to establish incentives that minimize the costs of repair errors, since the landlord and tenant are best situated to allocate that risk between them; and it may require needless administrative outlays in the course of establishing tort liability.

The examples could easily be multiplied. In *Sprecher v. Adamson Cos.*, another California case, the court upheld a tort claim by the owner of an oceanfront home in Malibu against his uphill neighbor for failing to install a fence that might have prevented damage from a naturally occurring mud slide. The defendant did not cause the mud slide, the plaintiff could as readily and perhaps more cheaply have erected the fence, the prices of Malibu lots reflect such a common, notorious risk, and Malibu neighbors are remarkably well situated to allocate it among themselves justly and efficiently. Still, the court—rushing to the rescue of downhill members of the upper class—imposed liability. In yet another revealing group of cases, courts have overruled or seriously qualified the long-standing doctrine that prevented third-party investors from suing accountants for neglectfully preparing financial statements for client companies on which the investors relied to their detriment.

Decisions like these reflect what Grant Gilmore called "the death of contract."[3] Gilmore was referring to the courts' growing tendency to resolve contract disputes through principles drawn from tort law, with its relatively fluid legal obligations grounded in social goals, rather than from contract law, with its more structured rules grounded in the mutual consent of the parties. Gilmore's insight must now be extended to tort cases proper, where the courts are increasingly rejecting market risk allocations that would limit legal responsibility for accidental injuries.

NEW CAUSAL PARADIGMS

A plaintiff cannot establish tort liability without proving two analytically distinct propositions. He must show that a particular act or omission is what caused his injury (the "determinate plaintiff" issue), and also that a particular defendant is the one responsible for that conduct (the "determinate defendant" issue). This two-step paradigm of causation, which has governed tort law from its inception, was traditionally grounded in turn on two interrelated ideas: a moral conception of how people are responsible for actions, and a phenomenological conception of how harmful consequences come about.

The moral conception, closely linked to the norm of corrective justice, emphasized the personal responsibility of each autonomous individual for his actions. A defendant, in this conception, was liable to a plaintiff only if that particular defendant was the agent of harm to that particular plaintiff, and the extent of responsibility determined the extent of liability. The phenomenological conception was based on an essentially Newtonian understanding of how events occur: it posited a set of mechanical relationships between things and events governed by general scientific laws, so that once the defendant's action was set in motion the plaintiff's harm followed in the same way that one moving billiard ball strikes another.

These linked conceptions, of course, did not always furnish satisfactory answers to causal questions in real-world cases; indeed, perhaps no issue has bedeviled tort scholars more than that of causation. But together, the conceptions set important normative and practical limits on tort liability. Recently, however, this traditional view of causation has been challenged by a competing paradigm premised on the contingent character of all phenomena and the inevitably probabilistic nature of all causal statements. This prob-abilistic view of causation is most salient in cases of mass exposure to toxic hazards, in which it has eroded both the determinate-defendant and the determinate-plaintiff requirements.

The effect on the determinate-defendant rule is illustrated by the well-known 1980 case of *Sindell v. Abbott Laboratories*. Women whose mothers had taken diethylstilbestrol (DES) during pregnancy brought a class-action suit against eleven DES manufacturers alleging that the drug caused their vaginal cancers. The plaintiffs could not identify which particular firms had manufactured the DES that each of their mothers had taken. But the California Supreme Court nonetheless permitted their claims to go forward. Liability, the court held, could be found if the defendants' products were interchangeable and companies with a "substantial share" of the DES market were before the court as defendants. Under the court's "market share" approach, each defendant's share of liability for the plaintiff's injuries would be determined by its original share of total industry production of the drug; hence its liability would be based on the probability that its product injured a particular plaintiff, even though it might not actually have done so. This approach plainly attenuates the determinate-defendant requirement. Indeed, it may even eliminate the requirement in some cases, for it means that a manufacturer can be liable to a plaintiff who never even used its product.

In mass-exposure cases, probabilistic causation also threatens to overthrow the traditional determinate-plaintiff limit on liability. The *Agent Orange* case, a class action on behalf of 2.2 million veterans exposed to dioxin in Vietnam, demonstrates this development.[4] The causal issue in *Agent Orange* was muddied by the presence not only of indeterminate defendants (because various manufacturers' products had been mixed before being used) but also of indeterminate plaintiffs (because the veterans' symptoms could have had many causes other than exposure to the defendants' products). In approving a class-action settlement, Judge Jack Weinstein endorsed an ensemble of innovations that could vastly enlarge tort liability in indeterminate-plaintiff cases: these include the use of class actions in mass-exposure cases, the use of epidemiological and other statistical evidence rather than "particularistic" evidence to establish causation, and proportional liability for defendants that create any "excess risk" above background levels, however small. (The traditional threshold for liability is creation of a risk that is more probable than not—that is, greater than 50 percent.)

These innovations fit comfortably into what a leading proponent, David Rosenberg, has called a "public law vision of the tort system."[5] It is far too early, of course, for Rosenberg to declare victory. The recent appellate court decision in *Agent Orange*, while essentially affirming Weinstein's rulings, casts serious doubt on future use of this kind of class-action device in most cases, although that device would seem essential if epidemiological evidence and the concept of probabilistic causation are to be made use of in mass tort cases.

Still, these developments, along with some parallel changes in the legislative arena, such as the federal government's passage of the National Childhood Vaccination Act of 1986, place enormous pressure on the traditional view of causation. They may prefigure a fundamental shift in the ruling paradigms, not only of causation but also of tort law itself. Tort law is abandoning its individualistic grounding and groping toward a more collective one. Increasingly, it treats the parties less as idiosyncratic actors than as relatively interchangeable units within large, impersonal aggregations, and their actions or injuries less as discrete occurrences than as statistical events within broadly defined classes and populations.

THE EMPOWERMENT OF JURIES

The American jury evokes the mythic symbols of democracy and the living law. It is viewed, especially in tort cases, as the repository of yeoman virtues, community norms, intuitive justice, and common sense. But juries are prone to certain dangers. Their natural sympathies for the unfortunates who come before them can offend the principle of a justice blind to contingencies of wealth or status. Juries, moreover, are neither learned in the law nor elected to legislate. Their proper role is to find facts and apply existing norms, not to discern or make law in a quest for a more just society.

In principle, at least, judges control juries by making procedural and evidentiary rulings and formulating the substantive law that juries are to apply. Rising judicial caseloads, along with recent concerns about the threat that juries can pose to constitutional values, have intensified pressures to fortify these controls. In the *Agent Orange* case, Judge Weinstein granted summary judgment despite conflicts in expert medical testimony on the all-important issue of causation. In three different 1986 cases—*Celotex Corp. v. Catrett, Anderson v. Liberty Lobby, Inc.,* and *Matsushita Electric Industrial Co., Ltd. v. Zenith Radio Corp.*—the Supreme Court urged lower courts to grant summary judgment more liberally on matters ranging from defamation to antitrust.

But in tort cases, at least, this restraint on juries is blunted, neutralized, and sometimes overborne by powerful forces working to broaden their role. Perhaps the most important of these countervailing forces is the relative ambiguity of most of the substantive rules of tort law. Standards based on "reasonableness" are common in many areas of modern law, of course, but tort law's "featureless generality" (as Holmes once described it)[6]—especially its "reasonable person" negligence standard—probably surpasses that in any other field.

This generality, moreover, is unlikely to diminish in the future. Statutes are seldom used to define standards of care, and even then they are rarely binding on juries. Dogged efforts by judges and legal scholars to make tort norms more specific and outcomes more determinate will always be confounded by the factual richness and diversity of the circumstances under which tort disputes arise. In practice, then, tort juries not only find the facts but also supply the normative standards for interpreting and applying them. The latitude of juries has always been great in the United States, but is has steadily grown, as judges have increasingly employed it for broad social purposes. As tort law seeks to regulate relationships and interactions whose value conflicts are harder to resolve, with consequences that are harder to predict, even the most elaborate and refined doctrinal tools are useless unless the jury can answer the kinds of questions that courts now put to it. Those questions, however, often turn out to be intractable.

We can glimpse this dynamic at work in the case of *Barker v. Lull Engineering Co.* (1978), in which the California Supreme Court tried to define the concept of "design defect" in product-liability cases through a two-part test. One part of that test requires the jury to decide whether "the risk of danger inherent in the challenged design outweighs the benefits of such design." In applying that standard, the jury is to "consider, among other relevant factors, the gravity of the danger posed by the challenged design, the likelihood that such danger would occur, the mechanical feasibility of a safer alternative design, the financial cost of an improved design, and the adverse consequences to the product and to the consumer that would result from an alternative design."

For present purposes, it is irrelevant whether these are the "right" questions for the law to ask, or whether a jury could ever undertake the kind of analysis that would be necessary to address them responsibly and answer them competently. The point is that beneath most of today's innovative legal doctrines lies a broad set of ultimate, policy-laden factual issues that a jury must resolve if the doctrine is to be applied at all. *Barker* is not an isolated example; throughout contemporary tort law, especially (but not only) in toxic-tort cases, courts are busy elaborating new doctrines that pose questions of similar complexity and policy significance for the jury. By multiplying the occasions that call for jury discretion, these doctrines further empower the jury.

In *Rowland v. Christian* (1968), another California Supreme Court case, in which a precedent was set that has been followed in other states, the court abandoned the traditional method of evaluating the claims of people injured while on another person's land. Over the course of centuries, judges had used this method to clarify the rights and obligations of landowners and their visitors through rules that limited jury discretion and produced relatively predictable outcomes. In *Rowland*, the court jettisoned this familiar structure, substituting a new legal regime of broad jury discretion. Under this approach, landowners' obligations to persons injured on their property are now decided by juries on a case-by-case basis under a "reasonableness" standard without any meaningful guidance from the courts.

But the relation between expansive new tort doctrines and jury empowerment may run both ways. It may be that jury discretion not only follows but also *generates* the judicial innovations that expand liability. Today's judges often seem to use the jury as a kind of *deus ex machina* to relieve themselves of troublesome responsibilities, doubts, and anxieties. Judges themselves can feel freer to innovate, secure in the knowledge that it will be up to anonymous jurors to determine the concrete meaning and consequences of new doctrines.

Jurors thus serve as a buffer that insulates judges from full responsibility for what happens when their doctrinal creations are implemented. By tradition, the jury is expected to be a "black box": explanation of how it reached its decision is not even permitted (except informally, after the case is over). This lack of accountability encourages judicial irresponsibility (in this special sense). Consider an analogy: if it were somehow made easier for men to conceal their paternity, they would presumably father more children—at least until the children's mothers took a stand. Similarly, when the cost to judges of innovating goes down, it is not surprising that they engage in more of it—at least until legislatures catch on.

If this is so, then an interesting paradox follows. Courts often invoke the principle of cost internalization to justify expanding enterprise liability. But the very same courts fail to apply that principle to the judicial enterprise itself. By relying upon the opacity of jury verdicts, judges can externalize the error and administrative costs of innovative, liability-expanding doctrines onto the parties and the social system as a whole. Any remaining inhibitions about innovation are further reduced by judges' near-absolute immunity from liability for their errors.[7] The paternity analogy suggests that many of the judicial progeny spawned by this incentive structure will be illegitimate.

CHANGING LEGAL PURPOSES

From the earliest days of the common law, judges have considered how their decisions will affect the larger society outside the courtroom. Sometimes their decisions have invoked explicit social purposes, especially the deterrence of risky behavior. Nor is an emphasis on compensating injured persons anything new; it is central to any justification of tort law. Still, tort law was traditionally and preeminently the domain of corrective justice, which required a wrongdoer to return to a victim what he had "taken." This conception encouraged courts to view tort cases as essentially isolated disputes in which the law's role was simply to allocate losses between two (or among a few) injurers and victims. The court could readily adjudicate such disputes by eliciting from the parties relatively simple, comprehensible accounts of past events. And because the ultimate decision owed much to the specific facts and was not explained by the jury, it rarely constituted much of a precedent for other cases.

Today, in contrast, the law books abound with tort cases that affect not a few individuals but great aggregations of people and vast economic and social interests. The decisions in these cases are preoccupied not with meting out corrective justice between individuals based on their past interactions, but with advancing public control of large-scale activities and altering both the distribution of power and the nature of social values. In such cases, the parties are often little more than quaint anachronisms, mere placeholders for these larger social interests. Even in conventional tort cases, judges and juries increasingly act (and view themselves) as risk regulators, cost-benefit analysts, and social-problem solvers, rather than as adjudicators of isolated, morally self-contained disputes.

This shift toward a more functional view of tort law derives in part from a heightened concern for the goal of compensating victims in an era of soaring medical costs, high litigation fees, and extended life expectancies, and in part from institutional changes, such as the spread of liability insurance, that appear to make compensation more feasible. But the shift goes further. As George Priest has shown, many other functional concepts — enterprise liability, risk-spreading, deterrence through cost internalization, and incentives to produce information — have moved to the center of discussions of private tort law by contemporary judges, scholars, and litigants.[8] Administrative efficiency, another functional goal, dominates analysis of the mass-exposure cases involving asbestos, dioxin, and DES. The same goals animate most of the proposals for legislative tort reform.

The new functionalism, in supplanting the old corrective-justice ideology, has not simply changed how parties litigate tort cases and judges and juries rationalize their decisions. It has also altered the outcome of cases, systematically enlarging the scope of tort liability. Indeed, courts (and most tort scholars) cite each policy goal as a reason to expand liability; ironically, even administrative efficiency, certainly tort law's weakest suit, has been invoked — to justify abandoning negligence rules in favor of strict liability.

The courts have striven to integrate these discrete elements of the new ideology — skepticism about markets, a stochastic view of causal responsibility, broad jury discretion, and a shift to functionalism — into an intelligible, morally compelling world view, in which judges play a central policy role. Most of the courts' justificatory techniques are familiar and not particularly noteworthy. In tort cases, as in others, judges continue to reshape legal doctrine through the repertoire of methods sanctioned by a millennium of the common law. They reclassify legal categories and issues, invoke "changed conditions," choose among competing analogies, select the level of generality at which to characterize facts, carve out and widen some exceptions to rules while narrowing or abolishing others, shift burdens of proof, alter procedural settings, devise new remedies, and regulate juries. Although the case names may have changed,

the techniques with which judges make laws and apply them remain the same.

What *has* changed dramatically is the courts' conception of their own place in the ongoing business of government. Traditionally, judges tended to view themselves as adjudicators who effected legal change incrementally through the slow accretion of precedents, moving in directions that were often discernible only in hindsight. Of course, there were always exceptions: judges like Blackburn, Shaw, and Cardozo, who did not shrink from using individual tort cases to propel the law toward one policy goal or another. But even these exceptional judges felt constrained to conceal their instrumentalism by paying conspicuous obeisance to the normative premises of the common law: the rule of stare decisis, the discipline of particularized facts, the obligation to defer to the legislature, and the strong presumption in favor of private ordering. They invoked these pieties even as they flagrantly and creatively violated them.

Today both the pretense and the underlying reality have changed. Not only legal innovators like Roger Traynor and Jack Weinstein but ordinary, standard-issue judges as well increasingly regard themselves not simply as logicians and case analysts but as policymakers and systems analysts. They have become less principle-oriented and more goal-oriented.

The signs of this change can be found in almost any sample of modern tort decisions. The court's opinion usually begins with a perfunctory bow to traditional legal categories and distinctions, followed by a critique of these distinctions as "wooden" or "formalistic." The court then explains why the precedents do not ordain any particular decision in this case, leaving it free to choose the "best" rule. From that point on, instrumental rationality is the mode of analysis: the court identifies the relevant social goals (the current favorites are compensation, deterrence through cost internalization, and loss spreading), then assesses how well these goals would fare under alternative legal rules, and ends by selecting the optimal one.

In these opinions, certain rhetorical features often recur. Plausible arguments, general assertions, and profuse footnoting take the place of hard empirical evidence. The court couples facile conclusions about the perversity of the existing rule with heroic predictions about the excellent effects of the rule being adopted. It characterizes the facts of the case abstractly enough to support broad, rule-like decisions. It further enlarges its discretion by assuming that unless the legislature has spoken to an issue with unmistakable clarity, the court is on its own. It proceeds as if private behavior were infinitely plastic, easily molded by legal rules into new, more functional forms.

Contemporary tort decisions are almost wholly benefit-oriented. Although they often read like a government agency's policy memoranda, they seldom address the kinds of questions about the costs of legal change that would preoccupy any self-respecting policy analyst. It is the rare tort decision, for example, that takes seriously matters like these: the opportunity cost of adopting a particular rule; the institutional barriers to its implementation; the rule's secondary and tertiary consequences; the strategies people will use to evade it; the costs of administering it; the competence of juries to comprehend and apply it; the effects it will have on insurance markets; and its implications for more elusive, difficult-to-measure values like innovation, diversity of choice, and political accountability.

In ignoring or only casually touching on these questions, judges are no worse than most of the professors who train their law clerks — not to speak of the legislators who write the statutes they interpret. Judges are often like architects who are instructed to design a splendid, state-of-the-art edifice but are also told not to worry too much about costs because the money will be found somehow. When that is the case, it is perhaps not surprising that they come up with the juridical equivalent of Washington's Rayburn Office Building.

The problem with all this is not that the new functionalism fails to advance some of its goals all of the time or all of them some of the time. It does both. Thus, it succeeds in compensating victims — at least that tiny subset who are fortunate enough to be injured by negligent, fully insured defendants and can gain access to the tort system. And it deters some risk — at least that small subset of activities that tort law's incentives affect. In many cases, the functional approach may well be superior to what preceded it. This is true if today's judges get the rule "righter" than their predecessors, or if the rule that "defendant is almost always liable" is so much clearer than the "reasonable person" standard that people can more easily plan and bargain around it. But any gains of this kind have been purchased at an enormous price in sheer administrative cost. And the real question remains: Do functionalist courts achieve anything approaching the right mix of social goals under the present system?

BEYOND THE NEW IDEOLOGY

Policymaking in this complex world is problematic, regardless of how it is organized institutionally. The real choice is between better and worse ways of structuring it. But however wise or efficacious the courts' central role in accident-cost allocation may be, its *legitimacy* cannot really be doubted. Tort law has always been preeminently a field in which judges initially devise common-law principles to which politicians then react. All that legislators need in order to have their way is a willingness to take political responsibility for the change. They may control judicial rulings by substituting different principles or by establishing administrative regimes to supplant or supplement the common law. But if the past is prologue, they will usually acquiesce in the judicial innovation; future legislative interventions will be confined to a few areas and will not much disturb the central corpus of judicially created tort law.

Even if "liability-insurance crises" did not periodically erupt, there would be ample reason to doubt that tort litigation is a good vehicle for deciding how to distribute risks in society. These doubts remain even (or especially) when one asks the essential question: "Compared to what?" The defects of legislatures and administrative agencies have been demonstrated in great detail. But even a brief comparison of the courts' policy-making capacities with those of legislatures and agencies indicates the severe limitations on courts' competence to perform the kind of policymaking to which their new ideology of tort law commits them. The most important comparisons can be grouped under three headings: organizational expertise and rationality, success in implementation, and political responsiveness.

Judges are trained as generalist lawyers (usually as litigators), not as policy specialists. They are unlikely to acquire, or know how to exploit, the kinds of information that competent policy analysis requires. Few litigants possess the resources needed to adduce this information, and most lack adequate motivation to do so as well, such information being in the nature of a public good—one that is often marginal (or even harmful) to their cause. Only a fraction of the many social interests affected by a legal rule are represented by the parties before the court, and the relatively few tort cases that reach trial are likely to be unrepresentative of the social reality that a policy must address.

Finally, courts lack a reliable way to obtain feedback on their policies' real-world effects. They must depend for fresh information on the particular litigants and disputes that happen to come to their courtrooms, and one case is a vehicle for policy change only if it raises the same policy issues as an earlier one, but manages to provide better data for making a decision. Even if the precedent can simply be distinguished, disregarded, or overruled, a court that realizes it has made a mistake may still have to wait for a properly framed new case to come along before changing course.

Perhaps most inimical to a sound policy-making framework are the deep structures of tort law—its vestigial moralism, its adversarial, party-centered control of litigation, its radical decentralization and nonaccountability, its glacial accumulation of precedents, its factual diversity and particularity, and its view of problems only in hindsight, transfixed by palpable human suffering. The new functionalism's rejection of most of these features amounts to the deformation of tort law, and its transformation into something very different.

Even if courts could readily determine the correct social policy for distributing risk, they would be hard put to implement it. The relatively few policy instruments they possess tend to be weak, inflexible, or both. In tort cases, their principal tools are general prohibitions enforced by money damages. With the exception of nuisance cases, all they can do is order A to pay B a prescribed sum of money for breaking a rule. Leaving aside certain cases in which government is the defendant, they cannot impose fines or taxes, subsidize, educate, reorganize, inform, hire, fire, insure, establish bureaucracies, build political coalitions, or coerce third parties. The damage remedy they can deploy is undeniably important in shaping some kinds of behavior, but it affects quite a narrow band on the broad spectrum of human motivation.

The need to decide cases on principled

grounds also limits courts' ability to implement even sound intuitions about policy. When courts abandon the traditional regime of contributory negligence, for example, they nearly always feel constrained to adopt the alternative approach of "pure" comparative fault, which can be derived from general tort principles, rather than adopting any of a number of "modified" approaches that might make better policy but would require the court to select arbitrary cutoff points. Legislatures that enact reforms in this area, by contrast, virtually always choose "modified" systems.[9]

Courts have one significant advantage: they can ordinarily count on strong political support from the public. As institutions, they enjoy greater respect than markets, legislatures, or most bureaucracies inside or outside government. But adherents of the new tort ideology should not take too much comfort from this public support, which is probably more a product of what courts have traditionally done than a tribute to what they now attempt to do. In fact, the tasks of legislatures and agencies are generally more intellectually demanding, more politically sensitive, and harder to implement than the traditional functions of courts in resolving tort claims. It should come as no surprise, then, that other governing institutions have seemed to fail while courts remain popular, for they are playing very different games by altogether different rules. As courts increasingly assume the more comprehensive and problematic tasks that their new ideology thrusts upon them, and as the public learns more about how effectively they perform them, one may expect their failure rate—and the general level of public disappointment in them—to rise as well.

NOTES

1. Kenneth Abraham, *Distributing Risk: Insurance, Legal Theory, and Public Policy* (New Haven: Yale University Press, 1986).

2. Asbestos Insurance Coverage Cases, Judicial Council Coordinating Proceeding No. 1072, Superior Court, San Francisco Court, May 29, 1987.

3. Grant Gilmore, *The Death of Contract* (Columbus: Ohio State University Press, 1974).

4. Peter H. Schuck, *Agent Orange on Trial: Mass Toxic Disasters in the Courts*, enlarged ed. (Cambridge: Belknap/Harvard University Press, 1987).

5. David Rosenberg, "The Causal Connection in Mass Exposure Cases: 'A Public Law' View of the Tort System," *Harvard Law Review* 97 (1984) 849–929.

6. Oliver Wendell Holmes, Jr., *The Common Law* (Boston: Little, Brown * Co., 1881), p. 111.

7. Peter H. Schuck, *Suing Government: Citizen Remedies for Official Wrongs* (New Haven: Yale University Press, 1983), pp. 90–91.

8. George Priest, "The Invention of Enterprise Liability: A Cultural History of the Intellectual Foundations of Modern Tort Law," 14 *Journal of Legal Studies* 461–527 (1985); and "The Current Insurance Crisis and Modern Tort Law," 96 *Yale Law Journal* 1521–1590 (1987).

9. Marc Franklin and Robert Rabin, *Tort Law and Alternatives: Cases and Materials*, 4th ed. (Mineola, NY: Foundation Press, 1987), pp. 381–82.

23

The Affirmative Action Stalemate*

Nathan Glazer

Ten years ago the Supreme Court handed down its first decision on affirmative action. It dealt with the case of an applicant who had been denied admission to a medical school, while minority applicants with lesser academic qualifications had been admitted to fill a quota the medical school had set. The Supreme Court ruled, five to four, that quotas were illegal and that the applicant should be admitted. A different five-man majority (only Justice Powell was included in both majorities) also ruled that it was legitimate to take race into account in making admissions decisions. The Court seemed to have come down on both sides of the issue.

While the case was raised over admission to an educational institution, the Court's schizophrenia shaped the many decisions over employment that have come down year after year. Those affected by affirmative action—employers and employees, enforce-

*Reprinted by permission of the publishers from Affirmative Discrimination: Ethnic Inequality and Public Policy by Nathan Blazer, Cambridge, Mass.: Harvard University Press, © 1975, 1987 by Nathan Glazer.

ment agencies and lawyers, applicants to selective programs and good jobs, jobholders threatened with termination—have waited for that final, clear decision that tells us just how to separate the constitutional and the legal in preference for minorities from the unconstitutional and illegal. But the Court has shown a remarkable skillfulness in chopping up the issue into finer and finer pieces—still without drawing that clear line that settles the controversy over affirmative action. Nor, in an eight-justice court, can we expect a conclusion to this Perils-of-Pauline routine in the present session.

This situation conforms neatly with the conditions usually associated with trench warfare: neither side seems able to advance, though attacks are mounted by both, and neither is weak enough to surrender. Even more remarkable, this stasis has characterized the issue for a dozen years despite a series of kaleidoscopic political changes that many expected to lead either to a rapid reduction in the scope of affirmative action or to its unchallenged institutionalization as the way in which Americans make decisions on employment, promotion, and admission to selective institutions of higher education. Thus we have moved from a Nixon presidency, which might have been expected to oppose affirmative action, but under which its procedures were formalized and extended; to a Ford administration, which tried to take some action to limit affirmative action, but retreated in the face of effective opposition from civil rights organizations; to a Carter administration, which was comfortable with it and in some ways extended it (as in appointments to the federal judiciary); to a Reagan administration, which is hostile to it—and which, as of this writing, seven years after it came into office, and after two electoral victories, presides over affirmative action requirements that are just about identical to those first formulated in the late 1960s and early 1970s.

COURT BATTLES

The battles of politics—in presidential elections, in Congress, in the regulatory and administrative agencies—have left the overall structure of affirmative action unchanged through more than four presidential terms, and three transitions of power. Nor, surprisingly, have matters changed much in the federal courts, despite extended and endless battles. Almost every year since the mid-1970s, we have, it seems, awaited with hope or anxiety the determination of some major case by the Supreme Court that would tell us whether affirmative action transgressed the "equal protection of the laws" guaranteed by the Fourteenth Amendment and the apparent commitment to colorblindness of the Civil Rights Act of 1964, or whether, on the contrary, it was a legitimate approach to overcoming the heritage of discrimination and segregation by improving the condition of American blacks. But from the first major affirmative action decision to the most recent decisions of 1986, the Supreme

Court has been split, with five-to-four or six-to-three decisions encompassing a range of conflicting positions in both majority and minority. We will, it seems, be living with the issues raised by affirmative action for a long time.

Policies we may legitimately call "affirmative action" have been undertaken in three crucial areas: jobs and employment, desegregation of public schools, and housing. In each American blacks have suffered from severe deprivation, rooted in racist prejudice, expresses in formal or informal discrimination and segregation. This is the basic underlying ground for affirmative action: it is because the heritage of prejudice and discrimination still weighs heavily on black Americans that the question of affirmative action cannot be expected to find easy resolution.

The term "affirmative action" appears in two places in American law. We find in it the Civil Rights Act of 1964, Title VII, dealing with discrimination in employment: "If the court finds that the respondent has intentionally engaged in or is intentionally engaging in an unlawful employment practice . . . , the court may . . . order such affirmative action as may be appropriate, which may include, but is not limited to, reinstatement or hiring of employees, with or without back pay . . . , or any other equitable relief as the court deems appropriate." This applies to all employers of over fifteen persons. And it appears again in Executive Order 11246, applying to federal contractors, and imposing "affirmative action" on employment and promotion as a condition for receiving federal contracts. There is no similar requirement, either in the Civil Rights Act or in its 1972 revision or elsewhere, for "affirmative action" in admission to institutions of higher learning.[1] Yet the term has been widely applied to the practices of colleges, universities, and professional schools attempting to voluntarily increase minority enrollment. The first major case decided by the Supreme Court dealing with affirmative action arose in the context of higher education, but was widely interpreted as having some application to employment practices. This was the case of Allen Bakke, who sued the University of California because he was denied admission to the Medical School of the University of California at Davis, despite having higher grades than successful minority applicants, and received relief in the complex four-to-five decision in 1978, which simultaneously legitimated practices that could have denied him that admission.

Affirmative action in employment originally meant going beyond nondiscrimination: an employer who discriminated could not only be ordered to desist from his discriminatory practices, but could be required to compensate those against whom he had discriminated, as the references to back pay and reinstatement in the Civil Rights Act make clear. The federal contractor providing goods and services to the federal government was not only bound by the civil rights Act, like all other employers, but also, regardless of whether he had ever discriminated, had to go beyond its requirements, by engaging in "affirmative action" to make his employment and promotion opportunities available and accessible to minority applicants.

CONTROVERSY AND THE WRITTEN LAW

Affirmative action in employment became controversial only when it went beyond the written language of the Civil Rights Act and the Executive Order, and began to require employers to hire or promote specific numbers of minority applicants or employees. Federal courts and the Equal Employment Opportunity Commission effected this radical extension of the law by interpreting Title VII of the Civil Rights Act of 1964 and 1972, and by the Office of Federal Contract Compliance Programs' enforcement of the Executive Order. "Quotas" or "goals and timetables" became the buzzwords of choice in disputes over the appropriate degree of "affirmative action." Back pay to those who proved discrimination, or requirements for advertising, recruiting, or training by federal contractors, which seem to be what the Civil Rights Act and the Executive Order call for, are not what we have in mind when we speak about the controversy over affirmative action, though they have a better claim to be called affirmative action than court-ordered quotas or agency-required goals and timetables. But under expanded federal regulations and judicial decisions, affirmative action has become a matter of setting statistical goals or quotas by race for employment or promotion. The expectation of color blindness that was paramount in the mid-1960s has been replaced by policies mandating numerical requirements. That is what we mean today by affirmative action.

The critic of quotas or goals and timetables is regularly attacked for opposing affirmative action, even though he may well support the clear intention of the "affirmative action" of Title VII as understood in 1964, as well as the "affirmative action" mandated by the Executive Order of 1965. But there is no point arguing with changes in the meaning of words: whatever the term meant in the 1960s, since the 1970s affirmative action has come to mean quotas and goals and timetables.

In the same way, whatever desegregation of schools meant when the Supreme Court declared the unconstitutionality of segregation in 1954, or when Congress defined it in the Civil Rights Act of 1964, desegregation today has come to mean busing. The supporter of busing is thus said to support "desegregation," the opponent of busing is attacked for defending "segregation," even though the latter term originally meant state-ordered or city-ordered segregation of the races. But it has come to mean black concentration in schools, regardless of cause, even if that cause is residential concentration or parental choice.

In the early 1970s, the setting of statistical goals was becoming the favored means of advancing minority representation in employment and desegregating the schools; even the geographical redistribution of minority populations was being proposed. The 1954 decision of the Supreme Court declaring segregation in public schools unconstitutional, endorsed by Congress in the Civil Rights Act of 1964, had been reshaped, through court interpretations, into racial numerical requirements in schools, so that each had to attain such and such a proportion of minority and majority. The facts of residential distribution made it inevitable that such a requirement could be implemented only by transporting students to schools out of their neighborhoods: "busing" thus became the issue in public education that paralleled "affirmative action" in employment. And we also saw efforts in the early 1970s to redistribute the black population through government action, so that it would not be so highly concentrated in the central cities. Concentration led inevitably to black-majority schools, and, many believed, to reduced opportunities for employment. Here, too, the ambition was some numerical goal spelling the end of residential segregation and discrimination, but the policies with which the federal government tried to implement these aims were weak and without effect. The struggle to redistribute the black population through the construction of subsidized housing in white suburbs continues; the impact of such policies has been quite moderate, however, so (unlike affirmative action and busing) they have not become crucial national issues.

AN OLD PATTERN: IMMIGRATION AND ADVANCEMENT

The mere fact that a kind of stasis prevails, in which affirmative action is neither eliminated nor expanded, is surprising. In 1975, when I published *Affirmative Discrimination*, expansion seemed to be in the cards. If fixed numbers of blacks and other minorities had to be employed or promoted, why would such a requirement not be extended to other groups, since so many could claim to have met prejudice and discrimination? As these measures were implemented, what hope was there, since they gave advantage to some groups, that they would ever be abandoned? If busing was implemented in some cities under the lax standards set by the Supreme Court for finding state-sanctioned segregation, why would it not spread to all major cities? Once instituted, how could the assignment of students by race ever end? If these policies became a permanent part of America's policy and society, how could we ever attain the ideal of a colorblind society based on individual rights, at which American liberals had long aimed?

Undergirding these concerns was a conception of American society and the role of race and ethnicity in it. We had seen many groups become part of the United States through immigration, and we had seen each in turn overcoming some degree of discrimination to become integrated into American society. This process did not seem to need the active involvement of government, determining the proper degree of participation of each group in employment and education. It had not happened that way in the past, and there was no reason to think it had to happen that way in the future. What was needed was that barriers to economic activity and education not be imposed, and that they be lifted where they existed. These barriers had been overwhelming for blacks, the one major group in American society (aside from American Indians) that does not own its origins to free immigration. They had been lifted through the success of the civil rights struggle, and one could expect the economic and education advancement of blacks that had been evident in the 1960s to continue. If progress could be expected to continue, why were quotas and goals, busing, and numerical targets for enrollment necessary?

I did not expect—nor should anyone have expected—that each group would reflect some national average in occupation and education, because the effects of history, past experiences, and yes, discrimination and segregation would continue to be felt. But the laws against discrimination were powerful and powerfully enforced. Blacks had made great progress in the 1960s without affirmative action. They were becoming prominent in public employment—in which they had more than "their share" of jobs (though not of the best jobs). In other areas, blacks had less than "their share." But how different was this from Irish domination of police forces in the past, or Jewish concentration is small business? If this was the way things had worked in the past, I believed they would work that way in the future; the introduction of affirmative action and busing threatened only to increase racial and ethnic conflict, without achieving much for the advancement of blacks. Further, as with many government policies, affirmative action was poorly adapted even to its central objectives, because along with blacks it had targeted American Indians, Asians, and Hispanics; the latter two were mixtures of very different groups, some of which could make no claims to special governmental solicitude and "fair shares" in view of their economic and educational progress.

One fear and one hope were not realized in the dozen years since the publication of *Affirmative Discrimination*. The fear was that affirmative action would spread beyond the initial groups targeted for government concern to include others; that the opportunity

of individual Americans would come to depend on their racial and ethnic group; that ethnic and social conflict would escalate as rigid boundaries determined opportunity. This has not happened. The unrealized hope was that the progress of blacks would continue, making it evident that such measures were unnecessary.

Affirmative action has not spread markedly beyond the initial groups defined as its beneficiaries. In some areas (that of set-asides for minorities for government contracts) there has been some moderate expansion—for example, Asian Indians are now classified as minority contractors and may get the benefits of minority set-asides—but on the whole the original line dividing the benefited from all others has held. Within the initial boundaries, affirmative action, particularly as it affects blacks and women, has been institutionalized and has become an accepted part of the American economic scene. It will be very hard to uproot. There is now a serious question whether one should try.

STALEMATE

The stability we see is not only one of exhaustion and equally-matched political forces; it is also one of institutionalization—the acceptance of affirmative action as a legitimate norm by employers, even grudgingly by employees. When the Reagan administration began, after some years of quiescence that disappointed those who thought it would move against affirmative action, to finally bestir itself on this issue, it found, to its surprise, that business wanted no change in affirmative action requirements. Cities and counties did not want to be released from the consent decrees requiring goals or quotas in employment and promotion. "Businessmen like to hire by the numbers," announced a September 16, 1985 article in *Fortune*. It points out, accurately, that "so far, in spite of the Administration's rumblings, nothing much has happened that affects the way companies run their affirmative action programs. The Labor Department's Office of Federal Contract Compliance Programs, which enforces equal opportunity in companies that do business with the federal government, has gone right on enforcing the rules." (A proposal by the Department of Justice in August 1985 to modify affirmative action requirements for federal contractors ran into opposition within the Administration itself, as the Department of Justice was challenged by the Labor Department. After two years, matters now stand where they have always stood: the rules remain unaltered.) The *New York Times* reported a similar finding on March 3, 1986: big business had no argument with affirmative action requirements, even though small businesses found the rules and the paperwork they required frustrating, excessive, and unrealistic.

Affirmative action had become a norm of employer behavior. As the economic columnist Robert J. Samuelson wrote in the *Washington Post* of July 11, 1984:

These pressures [the aggressive use of antidiscrimination laws, including affirmative action] have changed the ways labor markets work. Many firms have overhauled personnel policies. Recruitment has been broadened. Tests unrelated to qualifications have been abandoned. Promotions are less informal. When positions become open, they are posted publicly so anyone (not just the boss's favorite) can apply. Formal evaluations have been strengthened so that, when a manager selects one candidate over another (say, a white man over a woman), there are objective criteria.

Equally important, women and blacks increasingly are plugged into the informal information and lobbying networks that remain critical in hiring and promotion decisions.

Even more revealing than commentary and analysis is the sort of pragmatic advice that is handed out to business. Consider for example the warnings given in the "Small Business" column of the *Wall Street Journal* on February 4, 1985:

What's wrong with asking a woman job applicant these questions: Who takes care of your children when you're at work? What if they get sick? How does your husband feel about your taking business trips? What would he say if a male employee went too?

They may seem like reasonable questions. But in fact they could be construed as biased against women and could embroil the employer in charges of discriminating against female job applicants in violation of federal or state laws because male applicants aren't asked such questions.

Employment laws contain many traps for the unwary. More are being created in court decisions . . .

Don't ask if someone has ever been arrested. (Because blacks are arrested more than whites, a federal court has held, such a question can be discriminatory against blacks.) However, asking about criminal convictions is usually safe. And not hiring a convicted felon can be justified as a business necessity for such reasons as not being able to bond the person.

Restrictive job requirements can get a company in trouble, too. It may be discriminatory to have an educational barrier to a position (only high school grads need apply) if it can't be justified as necessary to doing the job.

ENTRENCHMENT AND LEGITIMATION

Affirmative action has been institutionalize not only in business but also in government, which does not want to upset the applecart either. Thus, when the Justice Department requested that fifty-one cities, counties, and states operating under court orders and consent decrees requiring quotas or goals consider revising them, the governments involved were not eater to be released from these requirements. They may have fought them initially (ironically, almost all were the result of Justice Department suits under previous administrations), but once the quotas had been set, the state and local governments were willing to live with them.

Affirmative action is so well entrenched that the very government agencies of an administration that opposes quotas and goals report to the Equal Employment Opportunity Commission on their progress toward meeting affirmative action numerical goals! Only three agencies have resisted this requirement: the Department of Justice, the National Endowment for the Humanities, and the Federal Trade Commission. But a hundred others have not.

The institutionalization of affirmative action suggests that even with changes in its composition the Supreme Court will pause before considering the uprooting of processes so well established, involving thousands of employees, affecting the expectations of millions. And the Court is the only potential threat to continuing affirmative action. If the administrative of Ronald Reagan has done so little in seven years through administrative action, it is hardly likely it will do more in its remaining time. The "stroke of the pen" that could have radically modified or eliminated the requirement to set hiring and promotion goals by race and sex for tens of thousands of government contractors has not been delivered. To those who find affirmative action an abomination, this is a tragedy. To whose who feared its demise, it is a relief. In Congress, a point of view that may well reflect the opinions of a minority always holds sway. The protection of affirmative action is in the hands of the Congressmen who care, reflecting the views of civil rights organizations; most others stay away from the issue. "Civil Rights Lobby Plays Defense But Wins," ran a *Washington Post* headline on June 7, 1986. The *Post's* summary is correct: the civil rights lobby had blocked the nomination of William Bradford Reynolds, a critic of quotas and goals who was in charge of civil rights for the Justice Department, as Associate Attorney General; by leaking a Justice Department plan to change affirmative action requirements it had started an uproar that led the Administration to retreat into silence; it had blocked an Administration nomination to the general counsel of the EEOC; it had blocked a number of lesser judicial appointments. And it has since defeated Robert Bork's nomination to the Supreme Court.

This strength must give one pause; it seems to make nonsense of polls showing that three-quarters of Americans oppose quotas. The success of the civil rights lobby suggests that the actual structure of decision making cannot be deduced from public opinion polls, party platforms, or Congressional opinion. Many players are involved; of these, the Court remains the strongest. But I believe the underlying force that keep the system of numerical quotas and goals intact is the actual condition of blacks. It is the unrealized hope for blacks improvement, a hope that could have with reason been entertained in the early 1970s, that sustains affirmative action in employment and promotion, minority preference in admission to institutions of higher education, and busing in a number of major cities.

It is thus the condition of the black population of the United States, not the state of their rights, or the practices that affect them, that lends the strongest support to affirmative action. Other racial and minority groups are covered by affirmative action, but it is not *their* fate or *their* power or *their* claim on the American conscience that motivates this massive machinery. Japanese and Chinese moved ahead despite discrimination. Newer Asian immigrants—Filipinos, Koreans, Vietnamese, Asian Indians—can for the most part expect to do well. The Hispanic Americans are a mixed collection indeed, from the upwardly mobile Cubans to the depressed Puerto Ricans, but they would hardly have had the power to institute affirmative action or to sustain it. (Women are a separate story; their numbers ensure their protection by affirmative action.) It is the blacks who quite rightly affect the conscience of America: they were enslaved and rigidly kept down after emancipation by massive public and private discrimination and prejudice. If they had made rapid progress despite their grim history, we would undoubtedly never have felt the pressures to institute race-conscious policies in employment and discrimination. In some respects, they have made great progress. But the mass of misery characterizing their poor stands as the great argument for affirmative action.

We have seen a substantial reduction of the gap in earnings between blacks and whites, but we have seen other key measures of black well-being decline; the most important are the great increase in black female-headed families and children born out of wedlock, and the decline in the percentage of black males in the labor force. Many factors have been at work, and some measures of long-term well-being have been matched by other measures of decline. Would matters have been worse in the absence of affirmative action? That case can be made. Would they have been better in its absence? Even that case can be made. Thus Thomas Sowell and others argue that the employer who knows he must be careful in dealing with blacks in regard to promotions, pay, and terminations (because of the threat of charges of discrimination) will more cautiously select his black employees, so that the opportunities of less-skilled blacks will decline. However, this argument is decided, it seems clear that the problems that now concern black leaders—teen-age pregnancies, family breakup, drugs, female-headed families, declining participation in the work force—will hardly be solved by affirmative action.

AFFIRMATIVE ACTION AND THE BLACK CONDITION

If it is the condition of blacks, imposing itself on the American conscience, that sustains affirmative action, the obvious question is what affirmative action does for that condition.

Although we know much more about this now than we did a dozen years ago, there is still room for argument as to the effect of affirmative action on the black condition. All firms with over fifteen employees are covered by the antidiscrimination provisions of Title VII; all firms with more than one hundred employees must provide EEO-1 forms to the Equal Employment Opportunity Commission listing the numbers of each group they employ at each occupational level. Federal contractors with more than $50,000 in contracts and fifty employees must maintain affirmative action plans and report to the EEOC on how their employees break down by ethnic and racial group and occupation. It should be easy to compare firms covered by affirmative action with those not so covered. That has been done. The results are generally positive but surprisingly varied. Certainly black employment has increased in or shifted to the firms that report to EEOC and are covered by affirmative action. James P. Smith and Finis Welch, authors of *Closing the Gap: Forty Years of Economic Progress for Blacks*, report:

Black men were 10 percent less likely to work in covered firms in 1966. By 1980, however, they were 20 percent more likely to work in EEOC reporting firms. To put these changes in another way, less than half (48 percent) of black male workers were employed in EEOC covered firms in 1966; the figure rose to 60 percent by 1980.

The largest employment changes occurred between 1966 and 1970 (the first four years of reporting). Between those years, there was a 20 percent increase in the number of blacks working in covered firms. The trend continued at a diminished pace until 1974, and then apparently stabilized.

The rapid increase of the period 1966–1970 came *after* the adoption of the Civil Rights Act banning discrimination, but *before* the regulations for affirmative action were firmed up and began to be widely enforced. Nevertheless, affirmative action *per se* has had its effect: within the covered sector, black jobs shifted toward firms with contracts with the federal government. Between 1970 and 1980, black employment in non-federal contractor firms that report to the EEOC grew by 5 percent. Among federal contractors, total black employment expanded by more than 15 percent.

As large as those increases in total employment seem, they pale next to changes within the managerial and professional jobs. Black managers and professionals were half as likely as white managers and professionals to work in covered firms in 1966. By 1980, black managers and professionals were equally likely to be found in covered firms.

Jonathan Leonard's analyses also show a great increase in black employment among federal contractors.

But to concentrate only on the firms covered by affirmative action is to miss something. Smith and Welch add:

Affirmative action resulted in a radical reshuffling of black jobs in the labor force. It shifted black male employment towards EEOC covered firms and industries, and particularly into firms with federal contracts. Reshuffling is the right term, because the mirror image is that black employment in the non-covered sector plummeted.

Despite the increases in the number of blacks employed by EEOC-covered firms and federal contractors, Smith and Welch, looking at the overall gap between black and white earnings for the entire period between 1940 and 1980, find that affirmative action must have had only a slight effect. Blacks improved their position both before affirmative action and after it. Improved education, the migration of blacks from south to north, the narrowing of the difference in earnings between north and south, and the collapse of discrimination in earnings against blacks in the south after the Civil Rights Act of 1966 seem to have played the greatest role in reducing the gap between black and white earnings in recent decades. "The slowly evolving historical forces we have emphasized in this report—education and migration—were the primary determinant of the long-term black economic improvement." At best, write Smith and Welch, "affirmative action has marginally altered black wage gains during this long-term period."

Whatever the truth as to the impact of affirmative action (in terms of generating improvements for blacks in some areas, while causing decline in others), it seems clear that uprooting affirmative action would be very difficult. The Reagan administration is as determined an opponent as we are ever likely to see. But after about fifteen years of affirmative action, we have created expectations among blacks and practices in business and government that sustain it. Whatever black doubts about affirmative action there may be (and they do exist), moving against it would appear to black leaders, and to other blacks, as an attack on their interests and their well-being. A dozen years ago affirmative action was newly established, and the recollection of the intention of color blindness was strongly fixed in the minds of liberals and blacks. Today affirmative action looks back on a long history, and the memory of what was intended in 1964 recedes further and further into the distance.

HOW MUCH AFFIRMATIVE ACTION?

I believe opposition to affirmative action is often founded on a liberal vision as devoted to equality as that of its proponents. But principle often must give way to practicality and prudence: rather than an all-out assault, which it seems must fail, the issue now is to define, as some Supreme Court decisions do, where, when, for whom, and what kind of affirmative action is legitimate. Thus we should consider (though one is aware of the enormous political difficulties involved) eliminating Asians and Hispanics from the affirmative action categories. They would of course retain the protection all Americans have against discrimination on grounds of race, ethnicity, or national background. If such a limitation were possible — it could easily be done administratively — it would begin to send the message that we view affirmative action as a temporary expedient, to be increasingly dispensed with, in various areas, for various groups, over time. We should make clear, even if it is politically impossible to change the affirmative action regulations affecting blacks, that these are to be reviewed at regular intervals to determine their necessity or efficacy. Ideally, we should aim at a society in which individuals are treated without regard to race and ethnicity for purposes of employment, promotion, or admission into selective institutions: this is the kind of society, it is clear, that the majority of blacks would like to live in.

No other issue of statistical goal-setting for minority improvement remains as controversial as that of affirmative action in employment. Busing is maintained in many communities, but it is hard to believe that a new, major busing program can be instituted in any large city. Whites have always opposed it, and blacks by now are disillusioned with its promise, even when it is instituted under the best of circumstances. One has the impression the civil rights leadership continues to demand busing without any conviction that it will get more, or that if it does it will do much for the education of blacks. Just as the theme of self-help becomes the dominant one in discussions of the social problems of blacks, so it becomes increasingly important in discussions of education. It is almost inevitable that this should be so, as the educational systems of our largest cities come increasingly under black leadership.

THE HOUSING ISSUE

The campaign for residential integration has been even less successful than that for busing. The *Gautreaux* litigation in Chicago was originally designed to get subsidized housing built in white areas there. It failed in that; and it has had very little success in its later emanation, as an effort to get blacks into subsidized suburban housing. The *Mt. Laurel* litigation in New Jersey also aimed at residential integration by overcoming restraints on subsidized housing in white suburbs. Subsidized housing would make it possible for low-income people to move into higher-income towns, and would also increase the number of blacks in those towns. It has had almost as tortuous a course as the *Gartreaux* litigation, with as modest results. Residential integration does proceed, but on the basis of the economic progress of blacks, not on the basis of the governmentally-required insertion of subsidized housing for low-income and black families into middle-class areas that resist it.

The issue of housing for blacks—like the issue of education—has always been complicated, because two objectives, not necessarily consistent or in harmony, are aimed at: in education, better *and* integrated education; in housing, better *and* integrated housing. In education, the attempt to produce a higher measure of integration in the schools through busing leads to "white flight," increased disorder, disruptions of education, and, in short run at least, no major improvement. (Admittedly, one may ask whether improvement would be greater if the integration objective was abandoned; but one could answer, why not? Many school systems, after all, are led by blacks, administered by blacks, and strongly committed to improving the education of blacks.) In housing, we have a similar conflict. The policy of creating or maintaining a measure of integration is generally implemented by restricting the number of units in a development made available to blacks, in order to reduce white fears of a black majority that would lead them to move out, thus creating a segregated community. Ironically, this issue has recently pitted the Administration's chief opponent of any policy discriminating on the basis of race against a chief critic of goals and quotas in employment, who was appointed by the Administration to the United States Commission on Civil Rights. Assistant Attorney General William Bradford Reynolds has argued in federal court against an arrangement limiting the number of apartments available to blacks in Starrett City in Brooklyn, New York (a plan that was instituted to maintain Starrett City as an integrated development). Morris Abram, a lawyer who first achieved prominence fighting for civil rights in the South, defends Starrett City.

My own position is pragmatic: where integration can be maintained, as it has been in Starrett City, such policies should be allowed to continue. One would be distressed to see a policy of color blindness adhered to so absolutely that examples of residential integration, valuable—and few—as they are, and dependent on color-conscious policies, could not be maintained. But such a policy differs from a quota or goal in employment in a number of key respects: it does not undermine the rights or expectations of the previous tenants—indeed, it maintains them, for they expected and were provided with an integrated community when they moved in; it does not lower the standards for admission, by including, for example, families that would be disruptive or would be unable to pay the rent. Racial quotas in housing thus do not threaten the living environment; indeed, they protect against its deterioration. In employment, on the other hand, goals and quotas are inseparable from attacks on testing and standards.

LESSONS

The most important lesson from the study of public policies designed to improve the condition of blacks is that people will resist what government does to improve it directly more than they will any individual's effort to improve his own position. The black in a job finds no problem with his colleagues; but a problem may arise when that job is gained through quotas and goals in a particularly egregious manner. The black family sending its children to a white majority school will find no problem, if it is a neighborhood school, a private school, or a Catholic school; it may have a problem when the assignment to a school is made by government against prevalent expectations of how children are assigned to or select schools. The black family in a white majority neighborhood rarely runs into trouble; but a policy designed to spread low-income black families into middle-income areas, black or white, through subsidized housing does mean trouble. No Americans can be satisfied with the overall condition of black Americans, despite progress in recent decades; but government actions that aim at statistical goals for minorities are not likely to do better in improving that condition than the work and efforts of blacks in an open and, it is to be hoped, more prosperous society. That government should prevent and punish discrimination is universally accepted by Americans. When government tries to determine how many members of a particular ethnic group should get certain jobs or promotions, attend particular schools, or live in designated areas, however, it runs into widespread opposition.

NOTES

1. The one exception to this rule are the universities covered by the *Adams v. Richardson* litigation: public institutions (primarily in the south), formerly restricted to whites or blacks, that are now required to fulfill affirmative action goals in the recruitment of students.

24
*Corporate Political Activism**

S. Prakash Sethi

Political involvement can be broadly defined as participation in the formulation and execution of public policy at various levels of government. It has been and must always be a necessary and important activity for any private interest group in our pluralistic society. To the extent that the locus of the public policy agenda—the decisions about the future shape of society and the role of the private sector in that future—shifts from the marketplace to the political arena, it is imperative that corporations increase their political involvement. They can thus insure that public policy choices are influenced by the views of the private sector in general and by the corporate sector in particular.

Political involvement and political power are inextricably linked. Therefore, where political participation might be viewed by one group as a positive act in a democratic system, another group might construe such participation as abuse of power and an attempt to subvert democratic processes. A survey of business people might show a greater desire for political activism, whereas public opinion polls show a desire on the part of the public for business to be politically less active. The issue is not whether business should or should not be politically involved but what the nature and objective of such involvement should be. The paramount issue is that of legitimacy or societal acceptance of corporate political actions and their underlying motives.

CHALLENGE OF THE EIGHTIES

The sociopolitical environment in the United States and the Western world is poised for a significant change in the 1980s. There is a precipitous shift in public sentiment toward conservatism in political philosophy, an aversion to reliance on government to solve every real and imagined social problem, and a growing willingness to accept the discipline of the marketplace in developing social choices and in allocating the nation's

*© [1982] by the Regents of the University of California. Reprinted/condensed from the *California Management Review* Vol. 24, No. 34. By permission of The Regents.

physical and human resources. The 1980s offer the corporate community a tremendous opportunity to take public positions on current social, political, and economic issues and to play and active role in the formulation and implementation of the national agenda and public choices.

This opportunity carries with it an equally enormous responsibility. The current anti-government public sentiment is not necessarily pro business or pro big business. The public distrust of big business and business leaders is not any less than its distrust of government bureaucracies and political leaders. The style and substance of corporate political involvement and the contributions of business to the public interest will largely determine the degree of public acceptance of the corporation as a political participant and whether or not the corporation becomes a positive influence for social change. Failure to accept this challenge will leave the corporation a beleaguered giant constantly fighting elusive enemies to protect its "natural turf" but gradually giving way before changing social tides.

The purpose of this article is to describe briefly a conceptual approach by which corporations may engage in political activities and some of the consequences that might ensue. My goal is to demonstrate that political involvement should ideally be developed in terms of strategic choices to meet carefully defined policy objectives. Positive political activism carries with it certain risks that must be evaluated before selecting among the various strategies. Certain strategies of political intervention may yield short-run gains but may have serious, adverse, long-term conequences.

ENVIRONMENTAL FACTORS

Development of meaningful corporate political strategies must take into account three environmental factors.

Past Corporate Activities

Historical antecedents provide a set of criteria against which current business practices, both political and nonpolitical, are likely to be evaluated by the body politic. Past corporate abuses color the public's judgment of current corporate motives and create a perceptual stranglehold on the public's acceptance of a legitimate corporate role in the public policy process. Corporate efforts to change these perceptions will require an enormous expenditure of resources in terms of positive reinforcement and public education. Any inconsistencies in current corporate behavior and rhetoric, or the perception that the corporation is not acting in the public interest, will have a disproportionate impact on the future political role of the corporation and reinforce the negative perceptions created in the past.

Current Corporate Environment

Today's problems create pressures for devoting corporate resources to short-term business and political objectives. However, an astute, timely political strategy is typified by a "good fit" between a corporation's business objectives, its political objectives, its internal skills and capabilities to operate effectively in the political arena, and its leadership role and management style in recognizing and responding to societal issues and to the external political environment it confronts. A careful analysis of current societal needs and responses can provide a learning curve in which the potential impact of various long-term business and political strategies can be simulated and evaluated.

Future Environment

The greatest challenge facing corporations is an understanding of the societal needs of the future in developing political as well as business strategies. It would be a grievous error to extrapolate the future as if it were simply an extension of current conditions and the recent past. In a constantly changing society, such an approach will leave the corporation in an untenable position. To an extent, this future environment is influenced by current corporate activities and those of other private sector groups (economic and non-economic). Accordingly, the synergistic effect of the confluence of the political activities of these groups is hard to predict. Thus, a strategy that is implemented by a defensive or reactive response is not likely to be effective as one enforced by a set of normative goals of what should be the nature of our society in the future and how we might achieve it.

The essence of corporate political activism is for the corporation to develop a cogent view of the public interest and, then, political positions and strategies that embody this notion. The rationale for business's developing a positive notion of the public interest is best described by Paul Weaver.[1] He states that what business needs is to develop the ability to take positions that embody a clear notion of the public interest and to employ language in stating a public position that is perceived by the public as embodying such a notion. Weaver contends that what business lacks is not only a position but the habits of thinking and talking about the ways in which companies and products contribute to our way of life and help people to realize their personal objectives.

Business people cannot participate effectively in the political process until they can articulate who and what they are socially, what role their products and services play culturally, and what difference it really all makes. This demands positive political strategies, not ad hoc responses to immediate crises. Then the public interest will not be in conflict with the corporate interest. But the corporate interest must emanate from the public interest and cannot be inconsistent with it. The public interest must not be perceived, prescribed, or acted upon by the corporate community as if it were the secondary effect of corporate actions whose degree and magnitude depend on the extent to which corporate self-interest can conveniently accommodate the general interests of society.

A SCHEMATIC FRAMEWORK

Public policy is formulated through elected representatives who pass laws and through regulatory and administrative agencies that promulgate rules and regulations to interpret and enforce those laws. Private groups influence the public policy process through their electoral activities and intervention and pleadings before the regulatory bodies. Corporate political activism could be analyzed within the context of three stages. Contained within each stage are proposed or hypothesized external environmental and internal corporate conditions and anticipated political risks.

Stage 1: The Defensive Mode

The corporation perceives its objectives to be totally legitimate, considers anyone opposing those objectives to be an adversary, and generally operates by itself in the political arena. The primary corporate goal is to maintain the status quo in terms of political climate, legislative makeup, and regulatory environment. The strategies of implementation are essentially ad hoc, contextual, proscriptive, and reactive.

The external or environmental conditions conducive to the defensive mode include:

an apathetic and relatively uninformed voting populace;

a hierarchical leadership in legislative bodies with leaders exercising great power and in which incumbency is very important;

voting based on party lines and loyalty to individual candidates;

a regulatory process subservient to the elected political leadership, highly legalistic in deliberations and rule-making processes, and susceptible to high-powered lobbying;

succession to elective positions primarily through the political party hierarchy; and

nontraditional political challengers who are relatively unknown and who have no broad-based public support and little prior media exposure.

Working hypotheses suggest that the internal corporate conditions that provide the impetus for a defensive political posture are these:

The corporation is part of an industry that is old and relatively noncompetitive. It has a long and proud tradition and has set ways of doing things.

The corporation has a large asset base and a dominant market position in a given industry or geographical region.

Corporate leadership has a significant amount of discretionary funds—from political action committees or individuals—that can be used for political campaign funding.

he corporation has an autocratic or strong-willed executive officer with long tenure in office. Succession to top management is primarily from within the corporate hierarchy.

Corporate products and services are sensitive to economic cycles or adversely affect the physical environment. The company may have a monopoly or near monopoly in the marketplace.

There is a lack of emphasis on long-range or strategic planning. Growth is more dependent on market size (geographical expansion or acquisition) than on new products and research and development.

Unforeseen and unpredictable emergencies require strong, immediate action. A crisis, such as the accident at the Three Mile Island nuclear facility or the phenomenal increase in the number of imported cars, so threaten corporate survival that all long-run considerations or ideological beliefs must be suspended to achieve short-run goals and avert an immediate crisis.

The conceptual model further suggests that the political risks for the corporation for staying in the defensive mode are these:

Different corporate political activities may be mutually inconsistent, may give contradictory signals to other groups, and may have little or no long-term payoffs.

Exclusive dependence on key elected officials for achieving corporate goals may leave the corporation exposed to future risks should there be a change in the political fortunes of these officials.

Excessive direct lobbying of legislative committees and regulatory bodies may make the corporation appear as a manipulator and a power broker in the public's eye.

Other groups will be less willing to give in to corporate interests when their influence increases in political organizations.

Too many crises indicate lack of planning.

The general public has little awareness and understanding of a corporation's position and rationale on various political issues. This leads to low public credibility and denies the corporation a broad base of public support regardless of the legitimacy of its position on a given issue.

STAGE II: THE ACCOMMODATIVE MODE

The corporation perceives the achievement of its political objectives as dependent on its ability to co-opt other groups to its viewpoint and is thus willing to notify, to a limited extent, its corporate objectives in furtherance of coalition or industry-wide goals. Temporary compromises and coalitions are the norm rather than the exception. They involve bringing corporate behavior into congruence with currently prevailing societal norms, values, and performance expectations, particularly those of sympathetic groups or institutions. The accommodative mode does not require a radical departure from traditional political goals and strategies. It is simply more responsive and adaptive to a changing political structure that would bring constraints if the corporation did not alter its traditional response. Thus, this response mode is prescriptive and conciliatory.

The external or environmental conditions conducive to the accommodative mode generally include the following characteristics:

There is a constantly growing number of voters, diluting the potential impact of each individual vote. (There is increasing voter apathy toward electoral particiation.)

There is a phenomenal increase in the cost of reaching potential voters and persuading them to vote.

A situation arises in which issues become more complex, explanations more obtuse, and decisions more difficult. When confronted with difficult choices and the declining influence of the individual vote, voters are more likely to remain "rationally ignorant," to refuse to weigh issues carefully and instead to rely on superficial impressions received through the media. Voter sentiment records constant changes in opinion polls based on contrived political events, and the election of candidates depends more on advertising campaigns than on the quality of the programs offered.

Elections are decided by a minority of voters (a 40 percent turnout would mean that 21 percent of all eligible voters could determine the outcome of an issue). Those who vote are generally organized around a single or a few selected issues and are not concerned with the broad social agenda. Voter sentiment differs from general public sentiment on a given issue, such as gun control. Group coalitions and accommodations are important.

There is a fragmented political party structure with weak leadership control. Reelection is more dependent on serving a narrow constituency than on loyalty to the party's agenda.

Legislative and regulatory processes are more open and subject to public scrutiny.

There is a mass media, especially the electronic media, with a voracious appetite for news and events. Minor incidents, human errors, or instances of poor judgment escalate into national scandals with high emotional content.

A large number of special interest groups and social activists exploit the mass media for their own purposes and influence public opinion.

Positions of power in legislative bodies and regulatory agencies are acquired by social activists, who make these bodies into adversaries of business rather than impartial regulators working in the public interest.

There is growth in the number of single-issue public interest groups that maintain excellent surveillance of corporate activities and thereby reduce a corporation's flexibility to undertake programs and activities without undue external pressure.

The internal corporate conditions that provide an impetus for an accommodative political posture are these:

The corporation is of more recent origin and has not yet settled into a relatively stable, noncompetitive market environment. It is still in the process of establishing its managerial systems and organizational structure and is thus prepared to make minor modifications in its way of doing business.

The corporation has not yet established a large asset base and dominant market position in a given industry, geographic location, or product market.

While the corporation may have a strong leader at the helm, professional management is being recruited from outside the organization and tenure within the organization is no longer a guarantee of promotion to the top ranks of the organization.

Management is more sensitive to social issues and public interest groups. It has been the target of such groups or public concern about the gap between corporate and public interests and found that adversarial confrontation is not always the most effective and successful way of responding to society's needs.

The corporation has become sensitive to the need for strategic planning. It has begun to plan on the functional or business level but has not yet engaged in long-range corporate planning at top management levels. There is a growing management concern about crisis management of social issues and demand for greater use of planning concepts in responding to social needs.

The political risks for the corporation for staying in the accommodative mode are less severe than those in the defensive mode. In many cases, it is more a question of degree than substance. For example:

Different corporate political activities and positions may be mutually inconsistent, leading to a loss in long-run payoff in terms of building a loyal constituency for the corporate position.

The corporation may form coalitions with groups who enjoy short-term, but not long-term, public acceptance as acting in the public interest and thereby risk being labeled as opportunistic and losing its public credibility.

The connection between support for various political positions and immediate corporate interests may be less direct and obvious, making such programs difficult to sell to senior management and operating managers.

Corporations may exploit the "rationally ignorant" voter by launching mass media campaigns where issues are peddled like bars of soap in jingles and slogans in thirty-second commercials. While this technique may win an immediate campaign, in the long run in increases voter alienation and thus the power of single-purpose groups.

Stage III: Positive Activism

The process of adaptation is only partially served if corporations develop their political strategies in response to external factors and other groups. While this mode improves the congruence between corporate strategies and societal expectations, much more is called for. The issue in terms of the positive activism mode is not how corporations respond to external pressures but what role they play in the initiation and development of a national agenda and in the public policy process. In this mode, corporations become active in leading political change rather than responding to it. Political activism calls for the exercise of power in a manner that is in congruence with a normative and publicly defensible notion of public power. This mode is proactive in character; that is, corporate political programs anticipate the shape of things to come and develop strategies to increase the probability of the occurrence of socially desirable outcomes and prevent undesirable outcomes. The external or environmental conditions conducive to the positive activism mode are these:

a growing public acceptance of the legitimacy of corporate political activism based on responsible exercise of corporate power in the accommodative phase;

increased trust in corporations and their leaders, thereby allowing corporations greater discretion in undertaking programs and activities, and more activities under the scope of self-regulation;

an increasingly informed public less swayed by demagoguery of either the left or the right;

an open environment of public debate and communication where corporate leaders are willing to disagree publicly with each other as to what is best for society and are willing to speak out against positions advocated by other groups;

other external conditions which are the same as those in the accommodative mode;

The internal corporate conditions that provide impetus for a positive activism mode are these:

The corporation is part of an industry that is growing, has a high technology base, and is competitive in the marketplace.

The corporation is quite profitable, innovative, and aggressive, with global markets and international orientation.

Management is professional and seasoned, not young and impetuous. The top executive is decisive, has control of the organization, is respected by other managers for ability and competence rather than feared for an authoritarian management style.

Management views the corporate role in the broader sense of serving society's needs and recognizes the political interests and power of other groups in a democratic society.

Long-range planning and environmental analysis are an integral part of the corporate decision-making process.

Top management seeks to build a broader public constituency for its activities, is interested in projecting the corporation as a responsible citizen, and is willing to carry its share of responsibility in solving society's problems.

Management encourages internal dialogue and discussion before settling upon political choices and strategies.

The political risks for the corporation in the positive activism mode are these:

A corporation may become too wedded to a given public agenda, particularly one which it initiated and helped to develop, and may be reluctant to change its position when such a change is called for. This risk is not different from the one a corporation faces when it stays tied to a particular product line or market strategy with which it is associated long after it has outlived its usefulness.

Cost and benefits are more widely separated, thereby making rational analysis of alternative strategies difficult. Such a situation sometimes provides a strong executive with an opportunity to commit the corporation to his or her vision of the public interest, which may not stand rigorous analysis and debate.

All other risks are similar to those in the accommodative mode.

The political activities a corporation can undertake are classified in four categories: campaign financing, direct lobbying, coalition building, and indirect lobbying and advocacy advertising. Table 1 briefly summarizes the form such activities are likely to take under the three behavioral modes.

GUIDES FOR CORPORATE ACTION

In today's pluralistic society, political participation is not a luxury but a necessity and must receive top management attention and corporate resources to do it right and do it well. The cost of being wrong can be very high. However, political participation simply to defend a corporate position on a given social issue, to support a candidate considered friendly to the firm, or to sell the free enterprise system is not sufficient. Effective political participation demands the advancement of a coherent political position, something most business people do not have today. What they offer are positions in support of immediate, short-term commercial interests. Take the case of the automotive industry. On one hand, there is a call for less government intervention in the name of highway safety and environmental protection. On the other hand, there are requests for government loans to shore up a failing corporation and for protectionist import quotas to isolate the American automotive industry from foreign competition. It adds up to a giant contradiction that destroys public credibility in the allegiance of the business community to free enterprise concepts.

A good example of business advocating its position in terms of the public interest is the policy positions taken by the drug industry on the so-called thalidomide amendments to the Food, Drug, and Cosmetic Act. Manufacturers are required to prove the efficacy of new drugs and to evaluate adverse side effects through exhaustive, time-consuming, and costly tests before marketing them. The industry contends that overzealous implementation of the law discourages drug development and prevents the use of some drugs by patients who would benefit from them. While the amendments have been costly to the industry, a growing body of studies indicates that the amendments have caused more deaths than saved lives by preventing or delaying the approval of a number of drugs now in use in other countries. The drug industry has drawn upon these findings to define its public policy position and done so in terms of the public's interest in improving health care rather than in terms of its private interest in avoiding government regulation. Presumably, it is at least as strongly motivated by the latter as by the former, but the industry has been successful in stating its position in terms of the public interest and as a bone fide effort to address public needs.

This is not to suggest that the defensive mode of political participation may not be advisable in specific circumstances in which the firm is faced with an immediate legislative proposal that may have adverse effects upon the firm with little, it any, long-term benefits to the firm or to the public. Nor does it mean that accommodation with opposing interest groups may not be politically desirable, as illustrated by the current joint efforts of business and consumer activists to prevent further legislative curtailment of their lobbying activities at the federal level. What it does mean is that there is a need to develop a series of step-by-step strategies designed to let corporations participate in the political arena in a positive active mode.

A corporation desiring a successful political action program must take a number of

TABLE 1. *A Three-Stage Schema for Classifying Corporate Political Activities.*

Type of Political Activity	Modes of Corporate Behavior		
	Defensive Mode	*Accomodative Mode*	*Positive Activism Mode*
Campaign Financing	Incumbent legislators in key decision-making positions with direct impact on corporate interests; little consideration to political party, philosophy, principles, long-term legislative goals	Support of candidates and challengers with compatible political philosophy and legislative programs; short-run or direct corporate interests important but not dominant considerations	Support or active opposition of candidates, even at the cost of short-run corporate interests, on the basis of a normative concept of "public interest" and "policy agenda" supported by the corporation
Lobbying	Informal and secretive lobbying of key legislators to support legislation considered beneficial to the corporation; use of professional lobbyists, generally former legislators or bureaucrats; locus of activity primarily in Washington and state capitals; senior management with low visibility	Emphasis on participatory approach and industrywide solutions; emphasis on professional management with public affairs/public relations background; strong support staff in corporate headquarters; greather public visibility of senior management; public posture as reponsible corporate citizen and corporate statesman; use of social issues management concepts to identify with and respond to groups and issues that might adversely affect business interests	Direct lobbying aimed at broad programs and policies based on a cogent notion of the public agenda; issues transcending immediate corporate and even business interests; where compatible with normative and positive notions of public interest, support of legislative programs opposed by other business and industry groups; highly visible senior management, speaking out on public issues and offering advice and assistance to executivew and legislative branches
Coalition Building	Resistance to any accommodation to other groups viewpoints or interests; community affairs activities and corporate contributions that are primarily for conventional, noncontroversial programs, highly diffused but centered in re-	Support of business-oriented interest groups; where necessary and imperative, temporary coalitions set up with erstwhile opponents to develop broader support for specific programs; community affairs and contributions activities with a discretionary element; new programs and groups supported on the basis of perceived need an corporate expertise	Development of new groups and support of existing groups to develop broad coalitions in support of a national policy agenda; when necessary, taking stands that may not be of short-term benefit to the organization but which have future long-term advantages; community affairs and contributions activities forming an integral part of th eoverall corporate approach to social issues management; emphasis on the development of third sector as bulwark against increasing government encroachment in the

S. Prakash Sethi

TABLE 1. *Continued*

Type of Political Activity	Modes of Corporate Behavior		
	Defensive Mode	*Accomodative Mode*	*Positive Activism Mode*
Coalition Building (continued)	gions or locations with corporate plants or significant activities		social arena; programs with a future orientation, with emphasis on identifying special areas of need and making maximum impact through early start and research and development
Indirect Lobbying (grassroots lobbying through mass media aimed at large segments of population or members of specific groups)	Little use of indirect lobbying; advocacy advertising, when used, projects sponsor as self-righteous, defends corporation's position, or attacks not only opponent's positions but also its motives	Grassroots lobbying to specific groups sympathetic to corporate interests (stockholders, employees, pensioners); stockholder management and environmental scanning integral parts of public affairs management; extensive use of mass media to advocate public acceptance of corporate positions by projecting them to be in the public interest	Active use of mass media and special corporate publications; external communications to improve the quality and quantity of information available to the general public on complex social issues; public educaiton in addition to advocacy of specific policies and programs

preliminary steps and develop some essential mechanisms before it can determine the appropriate mode of behavior or the political activities that would be most appropriate.

Step one: corporations need an effective environmental scanning process designed to identify the scope and magnitude of the social problems as well as the nature, extent and source of the societal pressures confronting the corporation—an early warning system, using both inside and outside experts, to identify and monitor trends and emerging issues and to alert the corporation to present and potential problems in the social area.

Step two: corporations need a communications network programmed to disseminate the data developed by the early warning system to appropriate individuals and orga-

nizational units within the corporation who have the authority to respond in a meaningful manner consistent with corporate and public interests.

Step three: corporations need an internal organizational structure and decision-making processes that will develop relevant and effective responses to these external societal pressures and problems. Such responses must be proactive rather than reactive and designed to present the corporate position in a manner that embodies the notion of the public interest.

The suggestions for strategies presented below are organized into the four classifications of corporate political activities: campaign financing, direct lobbying, coalition building, and indirect lobbying (grassroots lobbying and advocacy advertising).

CAMPAIGN FINANCING

Financing of candidates for public office is the form of political participation most familiar to corporations. It is a time-honored method of influencing the formulation and implementation of public policy. It is also a mechanism for political participation that has been grossly abused in the past and that has destroyed public acceptance of the corporation as a political participant and resulted in extensive federal control of campaign financing. Political Action Committees (PACs) are now the mechanism by which corporations can channel monies to candidates for public office. Shortly after the passage of the Federal Campaign Act of 1971, corporate PACs followed their traditional patterns of campaign contributions by largely financing incumbents holding key legislative positions regardless or party affiliation or political philosophy—the defensive mode. More recently, some PACs have adopted the accommodation mode and have shown a willingness to give support to challengers who are perceived as more supportive of the values associated with the free enterprise system and to take the risk of offending an incumbent legislator who, if reelected, might act in a manner contrary to the best interests of the corporation.

Of greater significance is the movement toward positive political activism by using the legislative distinction between "contributions" and "expenditures," a distinction that received constitutional blessing from the U.S. Supreme Court in *Valeo Rom v. Buckley*. There is a growing trend for PACs to advertise their stand on public policy issues or for candidates through the expenditure route rather than make a contribution to a candidate or party without further thought as to how that money is spent, what message is publicized, or whether the policy position as advertised is consistent with that of the corporation.

There is a danger, however, that PAC ex-penditures will be used primarily to avoid the legal constraints imposed upon the amounts of money a PAC can contribute to a given candidate or party rather than to enhance the public debate on issues and candidates. If PAC expenditures are utilized to support the corporate position on issues and candidates that embody a notion of public interest, then the public policy process can be enhanced and the vitality of the nation's social, political, and economic systems can be safeguarded. If expenditures by PACs are viewed as a means of selling a corporate viewpoint and not of improving the quality of public information through an intelligent discussion of issues, public acceptance of a corporate role in the political arena will be limited and largely adversarial in nature.

The PAC mechanism can also be used as a device for developing a corporate public policy position. There is a strong indication that many PACs are run by and for the benefit of a few top officers. Yet evidence is developing that many lower-echelon personnel, frustrated with the current political process, have renewed their interest in the political system through participation in PAC activities. By broadening PAC membership to include all individuals eligible to join, including the biannual solicitation of employees permitted by law, rather than limiting PAC membership to a few top officers, the PAC can become a means of developing a public policy position on social issues that will embody a notion of public interest as viewed by the corporate constituency as a whole rather than by a few key corporate officers who may or may not be speaking for their employees or the shareholders.

LOBBYING

Business people have historically concentrated their political activities on lobbying and have achieved their most notable successes with this form of political action. But until recently, lobbying was in the defensive mode, limited to informal and secretive lobbying of key legislators using professional lobbyists who were former legislators or government officials. The democratization of the political parties, the growing independence of legislators, and the constant turnover in government officials has made this lobbying mode somewhat obsolete. Corporations are increasingly turning to an industry approach. The Business Roundtable is an excellent example of the accommodative mode. Senior management, working together, have been successful in defeating the establishment of another government agency, the proposed Consumer Protection Agency, and in turning aside legislation that might strengthen the union movement. The growth of public affairs professionals is illustrative of the greater involvement of corporations in public policy issues in the prescriptive and conciliatory mode.

The current trend is toward direct lobbying, supported by grassroots lobbying, utilizing corporate personnel who can put forward an intelligent case on a complex issue, are comfortable shirt-sleeve sessions with senatorial staffs, are prepared to answer rapid-fire questions from Capitol Hill and corporate headquarters, and can ensure that important information gets to the right people at the right time. As one long-time Washington lobbyist has observed, "My job used to be booze, broads, and golf and Burning Tree. Now it is organizing coalitions and keeping information flowing."[2]

COALITION BUILDING

In the past, corporations resisted the accommodation of any views in opposition to those held by a few key officials. Support of external organizations and groups tended to be for noncontroversial activities and centered largely in geographical areas where the corporation was doing business. But as the Washington lobbyist observed, organizing coalitions has now become a new political way of life. The success of such a coalition building can be seen in recent business campaigns against measures to authorize common-situs picketing, establish a consumer protection agency, and expand union power through labor law reform. Such success has not been without its costs. Persuaded that corporate efforts to rouse public opinion helped tilt the voting on these and other issues, some legislators are trying to stifle corporate efforts to influence public policy. Their success may depend, in large part, on whether corporate coalition building is viewed as a prescriptive response to a societal problem. Moreover, it should be undertaken as a constructive approach toward accomplishing a goal rather than a naked power play to deprive other groups of the possibility of developing reasonable compromises.

The corporation should be viewed as ready and willing to develop broad coalitions in support of a national policy agenda, including working with interest groups that may not be business oriented.

INDIRECT LOBBYING

This is one area where the corporations can have a maximum impact but so far have not done so. Unions early recognized the value of being directly involved in the electoral process and pioneered many of the grassroots lobbying techniques now used by corporations. This is changing, however. Businesses are making greater use of the Government Key Contact program and the Congressional District Identification System. The former utilizes selected individuals within the company to serve as a communication link with public officials with whom the company needs or chooses to communicate. This individual not only has a grasp of company operations and a sense of the political process, but works or lives in the district of the legislator who is to be contacted. The Congressional District Identification System is a computerized approach to organizing and targeting constituents and legislators according to defined political units. Indirect lobbying is done in political units where the corporation has its greatest constituency, statistical strength, or presence. Both techniques are a practical response to the growing sensitivity of legislators to their constituencies. As one lobbyist noted, he increasingly hears members of Congress say, "Yes, I hear you, professional lobbyist, but what do the folks back home say?"[3] Grassroots lobbying is a response to the realization by interest groups that public opinion has a greater influence over most policymakers in the post-Watergate era. More important, members of congress appear to be more responsive to the demands of their constituencies than to the wishes of party or congressional leaders.

In establishing grassroots lobbying programs, the literature emphasizes techniques—how to reach as many people as possible in the most cost-effective manner. There is little concern about the message content or whether the utilization of external communications will further the public policy position adopted by the corporation. One can anticipate public rejection of grassroots lobbying and further efforts by corporate critics to silence the business community if grassroots lobbying is viewed from the narrow perspective of means rather than as an end that will further public debate on issues and candidates.

Advocacy advertising is another facet of indirect lobbying, and it has raised important questions of public policy and corporate strategy that have generated controversy and debate.[4] Advocacy advertising is a double-edged instrument. When properly employed, it can contribute to a greater understanding on the part of the public of what can be reasonably expected of corporations in meeting societal expectations. When employed as a substitute for positive corporate action, it can lead to greater public hostility and a demand for further governmental control of management processes.

Advocacy advertising should be an integral part of the total corporate communication program and designed to communicate the firm's public policy positions. This communication must bear a close relationship to the activities of the corporation, the vision of society and its role that the corporation wishes to project, and societal expectations regarding corporate performance. Too often, advocacy advertising is confined to what the corporation wants the world to hear rather than what the world wants the corporation to talk about.

As presently constituted, the public relations department is the window of the corporation that shows the world an image the corporation has of itself. The typical public relations officer is not an expert in the company's primary activities and does not have any line responsibility or experience. More often than not, the public relations officer is reduced to the role of corporate apologist. The first change should be in the area of information dissemination. The public relations window should both project an image and take one in. The public relations officer should communicate to corporate management what the rest of the world thinks of the company and why. The public relations officer can use his or her knowledge to sensitize management to changes in the external environment and what they mean for the corporation, can become part of the environment scanning process.

It is imperative that all external communications be credible to their intended audience, given the adversary character of advocacy advertising and the low public acceptance of corporate communications.

One element of credibility would be the clear identification of the sponsoring corporation and willingness to state the nature and purpose of such advertising. Many companies have been hiding their advertising under such innocuous sounding sponsorships as "Citizens for Better Economic Environment" or "Group for Clean Nuclear Energy." There is a further need to ensure the truthfulness, accuracy, and completeness of the communication. The use of outside experts to comment on the communication would go a long way toward improving the credibility of corporate public communications and the viewpoint they support.

The cause of business is poorly served when corporate spokespeople concentrate their fire on corporate critics but refuse to speak out against business people and business practices that are illegal or socially irresponsible. By refusing to take a public position against wrong-doing, they invite criticism against all business and convey the image of business as unresponsive to the public interest. Finally, no amount of advocacy advertising is likely to yield results if there is a large gap between the image business is trying to promote and what business is actually doing. Effective advocacy advertising demands the development of public policy positions and a meaningful commitment by the corporation at all levels of management to conduct the affairs of the corporation in the public interest.

REFERENCES

Paul Weaver, "Corporations Are Defending Themselves with the Wrong Weapon," *Fortune* (June 1977), pp. 186–196.

"New Ways to Lobby a Recalcitrant Congress." *Business Week* (September 1979), pp. 140–149.

Ibid.

S. Prakash Sethi. *Advocacy Advertising and Large Corporations* (Lexington, Massachusetts: D.C. Heath & Co., 1977).